Like every good investigator, Ken Wharton is relentless in his pursuit of the facts and remains true to the evidence. Through his crisp, direct crisp storytelling he makes the past accessible for the rest of us and adds a special dimension to the study of conflict.

Martin Dillon, bestselling author of
The Dirty War, *The Trigger Men*, *The Shankill Butchers*

A former squaddie who himself patrolled the dangerous streets and lanes of Northern Ireland, Ken Wharton once again succeeds brilliantly in recreating what it was like for a soldier to be there in the darkest days of the Troubles. A must-read for anyone interested in knowing what really happened.

Toby Harnden, author of *Bandit Country: The IRA & South Armagh*
and *Dead Men Risen: The Welsh Guards & the Defining Story*
of Britain's War in Afghanistan

A crucial reminder of the sacrifices of our armed forces in Northern Ireland - even more timely with prosecutions being mooted over Bloody Sunday.

Damien Lewis, bestselling author of
Zero Six Bravo, *Operation Certain Death*, *Apache Dawn*

Without Ken's voice many of these tales would be lost to the sands of time and the courageous sacrifice of these men would be forgotten; but thanks to him they won't and their stories will live on. All of us who have ever worn green owe Ken and the men he writes of a debt; because lest we forget it could have been us.

Steven McLaughlin, bestselling author of *Squaddie*

Another compelling insight into the British Army's long war in Northern Ireland. Deeply moving, often tragic, sometimes darkly funny, it gives a startling insight into a normally unseen side of the Troubles. Students of Irish history owe the author a huge debt of gratitude for assembling such a unique and indispensable narrative.

Kevin Myers, author of *Watching the Door; Cheating Death in Belfast in the 1970s*

WASTED YEARS, WASTED LIVES

Volume 2

The British Army in Northern Ireland 1978-79

Ken M. Wharton

Helion & Company Ltd

Helion & Company Limited
26 Willow Road
Solihull
West Midlands B91 1UE
England
Tel. 0121 705 3393
Fax 0121 711 4075
Email: info@helion.co.uk
Website: www.helion.co.uk
Twitter @helionbooks
Blog http://blog.helion.co.uk/

Published by Helion & Company 2014

Designed and typeset by Farr Out Publications, Wokingham, Berkshire
Cover designed by Paul Hewitt, Battlefield Design (www.battlefield-design.co.uk)
Printed by Gutenberg Press Limited, Tarxien, Malta

The opinions expressed in this book are those of the individuals quoted and do not necessarily
accord with views held by the author or publisher.

The author would be delighted to receive comments about his writing or for future publications
at ken_wharton@hotmail.co.uk

ISBN 978-1-909982-17-8

British Library Cataloguing-in-Publication Data.
A catalogue record for this book is available from the British Library.

For details of other military history titles published by Helion & Company Limited please
contact the above address, or visit our website www.helion.co.uk.

We always welcome receiving book proposals from prospective authors.

Dedicated to the memory of Colour Sergeant Ken Ambrose

On 9 January, 2013, one of the finest soldiers in the finest Regiment in the British Army – the Royal Green Jackets – passed away. His passing was sudden and shocked all of us who were fortunate to have known him. There will be many who have worn that coveted Rifle Green beret who, like all who met him will share the shock and grief. He has enriched the lives of the soldiers he took into battle and his loved ones and family.

He was an inspiration to me; he encouraged me and he helped me. His was the first name on the dedications page of all my books and he had a pivotal role in my 2009 documentary for the History Channel, 'Soldiers' Stories.' I am proud to have known him and honoured that he chose to do so much for me. We share the loss with his lovely wife, Penny and his family.

Celer et Audux; Swift and Bold. Until the final RV.

Dedications

To every young, fresh-faced British soldier who headed to Northern Ireland with the optimistic hope of making a difference; to the eternal memory of every lad and lass who fell in Belfast, Londonderry and countless other places of the northern part of that 'Emerald Isle'

To the late Ken 'B', who did so much to help me.

To the 1,300 who never returned to their loved ones.

To Darren Ware, Dave Hallam, Ken Pettengale, Gren Wilson, Dave Judge, Tim Marsh; to the Royal Green Jackets, *Celer et Audux*

To Mike Sangster, John & Bernie Swaine, Mick Potter, Royal Artillery, *Ubique*

To Paddy Lenaghan, George Prosser, King's Regiment

To Mick 'Benny Hill' Steve 'Foxy' Norman, Andy Thomas, Royal Anglians

To Mark 'C', James Henderson, B.R., Haydn Williams, Glen Espie and the men and Greenfinches of the Ulster Defence Regiment

To Dave Parkinson, RTR

To Jay Bell, ATO

To Kenneth Anderson, Kev Wright, Tommy Clarke, Royal Corps of Transport

To Dave 'Slops' Langston, Army Catering Corps

To Eddie Atkinson & Mick Brooks, Green Howards

To Tam Hutton and the Royal Highland Fusiliers

My cousin John Leighton, a Royal Artillery TA soldier

To Helen, my partner, for all her support and energy and patience and her guidance.

To my children: Anne-Marie, Anna-Martina, Jonathan, Jenny,
Robbie, Alex and Nathan; love you all and always will.

To my grandchildren: Sherriden, Kelsy, William, Sammy
and Layla-Mae; also to Morgan Addy.

To my Aussie friends Rachel Barnard and Sophie Sheldon –
thank you for understanding what we went through.

To Donna Johnston, a very special lady.

༜

Anyone else remember being on mobiles and coming to a red light in the early
morning hours, running to take up all round defence, until the light changed to
green and returning with a bottle of milk from some poor sod's door step?
Erich Modrowics

I have long wondered what the Yanks would have done or said if, say, the
Mormons had set up a military wing that killed policeman and soldiers, and
we took collection tins around pubs so they could buy more guns.
Martin Wells

Thank you, Ken, for pursuing the publication of another book that I am
sure will tell many truths, collate a wide range of stories that might have
got lost on their own, and will serve as a record for posterity.
Andrew MacDonald, King's Royal Border Regiment

You run across gaps, hide in doorways, move all the time, even when stopped, use the locals
as human shields, kids are even better, stand at a house window, a gunman won't fire if you
have a living room window behind you. Use every trick in the book, even the dirty ones
to stay alive; it is cat and mouse out there on every patrol. On each patrol you feel like a
walking 'Figure 11' (a full sized 'running enemy' target used on the rifle ranges)
Steve Hale, Scottish soldier

It was such a terrible time for so many young men / women. Do not think any amount of pre-deployment training could prepare one for what we saw and did. Through the pain, fear and uncertainty, it was one's comrades that never came home that will never be forgotten.

Robert McGregor, Royal Artillery

We all went through the same shit, so we know what it is all about. I was 1 Scots Guards. The Regiment was formed in 1642 to pacify Ireland; 340 years later, we were still at it.

Tom Mitchell, Scots Guards

I remember in Belfast this tiny kid threw a stone at us around 9pm, one night; he must have been about six or seven, so I asked him why he threw it. He said because you are British bastards. If I had asked him why, he probably wouldn't have known.

Tony Bramley

Your books on the Troubles have grown into a wonderful volume on our war and I for one think that they have pride of place on many bookcases. Once again, well done mucker, and I look forward to the next one for two reasons – one, because of the tribute to Paul Sheppard, and the other is to add to the collection of a wonderful set of books on OP Banner.

Mark Shaw

I still feel you around me; still hear you come beside me; feel you panting in the dark. Still see your tail wagging; still hear you when you bark; can see you stand right next to me, alert and full of pride, willing to do your duty; from that you never did hide. You will always be with me until the day I die. We went through so many things, good and bad; together you and I. I was proud to serve with you, my special pal and friend; we did our job together, right until the end.

Mark Shaw, Army Dog Handlers' Unit

In special memory of my service dog, 7C55 ALI Groundhog, Northern Ireland

Contents

List of Maps and Illustrations

Maps

Illustrations

Foreword

Having reported the Northern Ireland Troubles for well over a quarter of a century, I've often been struck by the quality and standard of work of those who started out with little or no personal connection to this most complex of conflicts. Former British soldier turned Troubles chronicler Ken Wharton fits easily into this category – and *Wasted Years, Wasted Lives Volume 2: The British Army in Northern Ireland 1978-79*, his latest contribution, may yet prove to be the best example of his work so far.

Of course, it is not entirely accurate to state as I did earlier that Ken has no connection to the tribal battlefield that was – and still is – Northern Ireland. Because as a serving soldier with two NI tours under his belt he is a man who, as they say here in Ulster: "Walked the walk and talked the talk." The iconic place names of the Troubles – Creggan, Bogside, South Armagh 'Bandit Country', Falls and Shankill Roads – which were so well-known to TV audiences around the world in the recent past, fall easily from Ken's lips. In other words, he knows the territory well and that's not a bad starting point for any writer of historical fact.

As a writer, Ken Wharton's stock in trade is the quality of his first-hand accounts. Not only is the reader able to tap into the memory of the eyewitnesses Wharton interviewed for his book, they will also delight in his own personal recall of his days as a squaddie patrolling the villages, towns and cities of Northern Ireland. I remember wondering a few years ago when Ken Wharton first burst on to the Troubles book scene with his initial contribution *A Long Long War* if this was just another ex-member of the Security Services recording for posterity the fact that he had once risked life and limb serving in Northern Ireland. How misplaced my scepticism was because here we are, seven books later, and Ken Wharton shows no signs of quitting.

Wasted Years, Wasted Lives Volume 2 is the natural follow-on from Ken Wharton's last book *Wasted Years, Wasted Lives Volume 1: The British Army in Northern Ireland 1975-77*. As with all Wharton's previous books, his latest contribution has the same attention to detail. Detail has become the hallmark of a Ken Wharton book. In fact, for someone who wasn't trained in the testing world of busy newsrooms or TV studios he would put many a hard-nosed news reporter to shame. It is his commitment to delivering the very best information available which affords the reader a better understanding of very complex – and at times mystifying – situations.

As the Troubles dragged on year after year, the interest of the British public (and to a lesser extent the Northern Ireland public too) waned considerably. A 'Richter Scale' of atrocity emerged and many murders never even made the News at Ten on TV. And yet Ken Wharton – a battle-hardened soldier who had witnessed death up close – was still possessed of enough humanity to treat the passing of each victim full respect and sensitivity. His account of the shooting of 69-year-old grandmother Martha McAlpine is very moving indeed. The pensioner was standing on Belfast's Shore Road alongside three of her grandchildren – all under the age of 10. From nowhere a van containing an IRA hit-squad pulled up intent on shooting a police officer who was standing nearby. Most of the shots fired missed the officer completely, although one struck him on the leg. But another struck

Mrs McAlpine in the stomach and she died in hospital a short time later. And Wharton's account of the shooting of an infant child – who miraculously survived the ordeal – a few days before, brings the full horror of the Troubles home to the reader.

Ken Wharton's books also cover the culmination of one of the most evil episodes in the entire history of the Troubles: the conviction and sentencing of a psychopathic Loyalist killer gang known as the Shankill Butchers. Its leader, Lenny Murphy, was never convicted for many of the heinous crimes for which he was responsible. But in handing down 42 life sentences to 11 of his cohorts for their part in 19 murders of mainly innocent Catholics, the trial judge did civil society a great favour.

The army in which Ken Wharton served is no longer a feature of day-to-day life in Northern Ireland. Although the Troubles haven't completely disappeared, most of the disagreements which were previously played out violently on the streets are now dealt with in the debating chamber of the Devolved Assembly at Stormont. The Royal Ulster Constabulary has been replaced by the Police Service of Northern Ireland. The cities of Belfast, Londonderry and Armagh resemble their UK or Irish counterparts in that visitors are spoilt for choice when it comes to entertainment or dining out. Tourists abound and despite the odd blip we see on our TV screens, normality has by and large returned to this most beautiful Province.

However, we should never forget that only a few decades ago – as a result of the potent mixture of history, bad law and tribal entrenchment – civil society actually broke down in this remote corner of the United Kingdom. And it took many years to put it back on an even keel. Ken Wharton's latest book gives us some understanding of just how bad life was for everyone during those dreadful days. For students of Northern Ireland history or even just for ordinary people with a genuine interest in the place, *Wasted Years, Wasted Lives Volume 2* is essential reading. I'm convinced it will occupy pride of place on the shelves of many libraries and book collections.

Hugh Jordan, Belfast, 9 September 2013

Hugh Jordan is a senior reporter on the *Sunday World*. He has reported on Northern Ireland for many years and regularly broadcasts on TV and radio. He is also the author of two acclaimed books relating to the Northern Irish conflict.

Preface

The name Ken Wharton first came to my attention in 2008 when his first book *A Long Long War* was published. I read that he was asking for further stories and photos from former soldiers with the intention of writing a second book on the subject. This became *Bullets, Bombs and Cups of Tea*. As a soldier who had completed a tour with the gunners in 1979 – then nearly eight further years in the full-time UDR – I thought I could contribute and phoned the number. Our firm friendship started and I have had the pleasure do research for all the subsequent books – and Ken has been over to Northern Ireland twice. Whilst here, myself and my mate and former comrade BR escorted Ken and his cousin John around all the former (and some still very) hotspots to take photos for the books.

So when Ken asked me to write a Preface for this book – Volume 2 of *Wasted Years, Wasted Lives* – I was very, very honoured to be involved with what I class as must-reads for anybody interested in studying that very, to say the least, very turbulent period in the history of my country.

This volume covers the years 1978-1979 and indeed it was September 1979 that I undertook my first tour of duty in Belfast with 25th Field Regiment RA; back to the city I was born and raised in and had left three years previously to join the army. These years were very challenging for the British Army; the Ulsterisation Policy, which was implemented so the RUC could take the lead in the security battle, was gaining momentum and in my opinion 1979 was really the last year where the army could act in any way on their own initiative. When I came back in spring 1981 – just in time for the Hunger Strikes to kick off – after transferring into the UDR you could see the difference ... with the RUC far more involved at all levels.

Of course this did not happen without death or casualties; in this two-year period 70 soldiers died at the hands of the Republican Terrorists, PIRA and INLA (including 18 in one incident at Warrenpoint) with a further 70 dying of other causes such as RTAs. The RUC lost 24 over the same period.

As Ken takes the reader through to December 1979 and the dawn of a new decade which would herald in even bigger changes, once again it is the ordinary soldier who is at the heart of everything; their stories, including my own, written by their own hand in our own language – all interwoven with a daily list of bombing, shooting, death and destruction. This was, in essence, a war fought on British soil – half an hour's flight from Liverpool. Share the fear, the drama and the funny squaddie humour which got all of us who served in NI through the hard times.

Mark C, RA, UDR and Friend.
Belfast 2013

Note to the Reader

This is the companion volume to *Wasted Years, Wasted Lives Volume 1*, which covered the period 1975-77. This volume covers the following two years of 1978 and 1979. For continuity of information, it needs to be read in conjunction with the first volume. Chapter numbering follows the course set by the earlier volume and will continue from Chapter 37. There is a full Roll of Honour for the full period of the Troubles at the end, as well as an ROH for the Northern Ireland Police, the RUC.

N.B. In Volume 1 the author erroneously refers to Robert Craven as Robert Conway on page 216 and apologises for this error.

The Author: a Personal Statement

I am often asked by members of both what my son-in-law calls my 'tribe' and also by members of the general public if Ireland will ever be – indeed, should ever be – reunited. One does not intend to indulge in the semantics of a debate which can only be described as polarising, as there is – by definition – no 'middle ground'. My personal feeling is that the country will never be reunited, nor should it be just so long as the vast majority of those who live in the part of the island most likely to be disadvantaged – the Loyalists/Protestants – wish to remain British. Partition may not be ideal and it was right that the Ulster Ruling Classes had to be dragged kicking and screaming into a belated democracy. Equality had, in many ways, to be foisted upon then.

I foresee only one set of circumstances where the border might be removed and direct rule from Dublin put into effect. That is if some future British Government decides that enough is enough and pulls out – politically and economically – from Ulster. Should that day come, it will be a betrayal of those who wish to remain British and those of my comrades and others who gave life and limb to safeguard that wish.

Further to this I will not disguise my utter contempt for the Irish-American community who either overtly or tacitly supported the Republican terrorists in Ireland, North or South. I will always detest the staff and the officers of NORAID and those hateful or naïve enough to support this loathsome organisation. Remember the words of the Stiff Little Fingers' song: *'Each dollar a bullet'*. This stance will remain constant throughout all of my writings.

Abbreviations

2IC	Second in Command
3LI	Third Battalion Light Infantry
AAC	Army Air Corps
ADU	Army Dog Handling Unit
APC	Armoured Personnel Carrier
APNI	Alliance Party of Northern Ireland
ASU	Active Service Unit
ATO	Ammunition Technical Officer
AWOL	Absent Without Leave
BFBS	British Forces Broadcasting Service
Bn HQ	Battalion Headquarters
BOI	Board of Inquiry
CESA	Catholic Ex-serviceman's Association
CO	Commanding Officer
CS	Tear Gas
CVO	Casualty Visiting Officers
DC	Detective Constable
DERR	Duke of Edinburgh's Royal Regiment
DOE	Department of the Environment
DoW	Died of Wounds
DOWR	Duke of Wellington's Regiment
DUP	Democratic Unionist Party
DWR	Duke of Wellington's Regiment
EOD	Explosive Ordnance Disposal
ETA	*Euskadi Ta Askatasuna* (Basque Separatist Terrorist group)
FOI	Freedom of Information
FRG	Federal Riot Guns
GAA	Gaelic Athletic Association (Irish: *Cumann Lúthchleas Gael*)
GC	George Cross
GHQ	General Head Quarters
GPMG	General Purpose Machine Gun
GPO	General Post Office
HET	Historical Enquiries Team
HQNI	Head Quarters Northern Ireland
IJLB	Infantry Junior Leaders Battalion
INLA	Irish National Liberation Army
Int	Intelligence
IRA	Irish Republican Army
IRSP	Irish Republican Socialist Party
KIA	Killed in Action
KOSB	King's Own Scottish Borderers

LSL	Landing Ship Logistics
MO	Medical Officer
MoD	Ministry of Defence
NAAFI	Navy, Army and Air Force Institute
NCND	neither confirm nor deny
NCO	Non-Commissioned Officer
NG	Negligent Discharge
NI	Northern Ireland
NIVA	Northern Ireland Veteran's Association
NMA	National Memorial Arboretum
NORAID	Northern Aid Committee
NTH	Newtownhamilton
ODC	Ordinary decent criminals
OP	Observation Post
OTR	On the Run
Pig	Armoured Vehicle (named as such due to its pig-like appearance)
PIRA	Provisional Irish Republican Army
PLA	People's Liberation Army
POA	Prison Officers' Association
POW	Prisoner of War
PRO	Public Relations Officer
PSNI	Police Service Northern Ireland
QLR	Queen's Lancashire Regiment
QOH	Queen's Own Highlander's
QRF	Quick Reaction Force
RAF	Royal Air Force
RSF	Republican Sinn Féin
RCT	Royal Corps of Transport
RE	Royal Engineers
REHQ	Royal Engineers Headquarters
REME	Royal Electrical and Mechanical Engineers
RGJ	Royal Green Jackets
RIRA	Real Irish Republican Army
RMP	Royal Military Police
RAOC	Royal Army Ordnance Corps
ROE	Rules of Engagement
RPG-7	Rocket Propelled Grenade
RRF	Royal Regiment of Fusiliers
RRW	Royal Regiment of Wales
RSM	Regimental Sergeant Major
RTA	Road Traffic Accident
RUC	Royal Ulster Constabulary
RUCR	Royal Ulster Constabulary Reserve
RVH	Royal Victoria Hospital
SB	Special Branch
SDLP	Social Democratic and Labour Party

SF	Security Forces
SIB	Special Investigation Branch
SLR	Self Loading Rifle
SOP	Standard Operating Procedure
SUIT	Sight Unit Infantry Trilux
TA	Territorial Army
TD	*Teachta Dála* (Member of the Irish Parliament)
TAOR	Tactical Area of Responsibility
UDA	Ulster Defence Association
UDR	Ulster Defence Regiment
UFF	Ulster Freedom Fighters
USC	Ulster Special Constabulary
UTV	Ulster Television
UUP	Ulster Unionist Party
UVBT	Under vehicle booby trap
UWC	Ulster Worker's Council
VCP	Vehicle Check Point
WOII	Warrant Officer Second Class
WRAC	Women's Royal Army Corps

My Dad, the Soldier

Anita Bailkoski, Daughter of Sergeant John Haughey

My dad was my personal hero. He loved army life and enjoyed every opportunity that went with it. We had a wonderful life as a family stationed in Celle, Germany. We travelled over the Continent during the summer holidays camping and discovering new places. Dad was very loving, patient and great fun. He always had time for us kids and I still miss him. 21 January 1974 was the day my life changed. I was seven years old and the ripples in the pond that were created by my father's death still continue to this day. I will never forget it. I don't remember the first call – maybe we were still at school – but I knew my mother was preparing to visit my father in Londonderry as he had been injured in a bomb blast, but was expected to survive.

There was a knock at the door as nobody had a home phone in married quarters in those days. I remember standing with my two brothers, Martin and Andrew, to see an officer in his no 1 uniform – his polished Sam Browne belt shining in the light from the hallway. He was accompanied by another person whom I don't remember. I think somehow I had expected to see my dad magically returned from Northern Ireland as he had recently done at the Christmas just passed. It wasn't to be.

The officer was invited in and we were ushered into my bedroom to amuse ourselves. My mother already had a friend with her, Sheila Jackson, who I think was going to be looking after us while my mother was away. Sheila was a very supportive and close friend and was a person we could trust and knew well amongst the army personnel. Myself and my two brothers had no idea about what was happening; we already knew our dad had been injured and that our mother would be travelling to Northern Ireland to visit him, but we had no clue his life had been in danger.

We were called in to the living room after the officers had left. I looked at my mum. Her face looked strange – swollen and puffy from the tears. I did not understand why my mother looked so different. Mum falteringly told us: "I've got something to tell you.... Your daddy's dead, kids"... and then collapsed into tears. I was scooped into the arms of Sheila Jackson whilst my mother hugged the boys. I didn't want to cry, but felt I should. I felt numb and very strange as I had not witnessed this kind of emotion in adults before. I remember also feeling angry that nobody had warned me that my daddy might lose his life in Northern Ireland. Within 24 hours we were on a plane heading back to the UK. We had lost everything. Along with my father we lost our home, schools, friends, a support network within the regiment and a wonderful life. It was all changed.

I learnt from later reports that my father had, in a semi-conscious state, tried to enquire about the other men in his troop whilst been driven to hospital in the ambulance. Fortunately there were no other fatalities on that occasion. The irony for our family was that my dad's own family were Irish Catholics and my grandfather was born in Londonderry, but as a young child he had been burnt out of his house by the black and tans. The family then fled to the relative safety of Donegal, which is where he had grown up. I still find it so hard to fathom how my dad had been killed on the streets and by the hands of the people that his own father had been born amongst in that bloody civil war.

My dad's body was flown back to Manchester, where he had been born, and he was given a military funeral at St Catherine's RC Church where my parents had married 10 years earlier. Eight members of 94 Locating Regiment – including Major Tom Hughes – also came over. The coffin was carried through the streets of Didsbury on a 25-pound gun carriage draped with the union flag. The sudden death of my beloved grandparents 15 months later can be attributed to the stress they endured during the previous year. They were still young and vital, but died within 10 days of each other. We also lost my younger brother Andrew at the age of 18 in a car accident. I know things would have been different had my Father lived.

I try not to entertain any bitterness as it destroys people's lives even more than loss, but sometimes it is difficult. I often think about the many thousands of human beings whose lives have been blighted by the senseless murders in Northern Ireland and it helps to realise I am not alone – and I live in hope that one day I can get some kind of acceptance and peace.

Sergeant John Haughey was killed in action on 21 January 1974 on Lonemoor Road, Londonderry by an IED. His death is covered in *Sir, They're Taking the Kids Indoors: The British Army in Northern Ireland 1973-74* by Ken Wharton.

During the last seven or eight years, several authors have made some extremely flattering comments about my works. These writers include Martin Dillon, Damien Lewis, Toby Harnden, Kevin Myers, Patrick Bishop, Steven McLaughlin and Tony Clarke to name a few. To have my name mentioned in the same context as theirs is a truly humbling experience and I will be forever grateful. The following praise from the niece of one of our fallen in Northern Ireland is also truly humbling.

I had originated contact with you as I was looking for information on my uncle Lance Corporal David Card 24191193, 1RGJ; he was shot and killed by an IRA sniper in 1972 in Andersonstown, Belfast. I was aware after speaking to Philip Pickford (1RGJ) that he might be in one of your books so I managed to find your email address and wrote to you; within a day you emailed back; within 2 days we had spoken on the phone. You rang me all the way from Australia!! We had a lovely chat and you confirmed he was in 'The Bloodiest Year 1972'. I ordered my copy straight away.

In June 2013 I was very honoured to attend your book launch in Davies Street London, for your new book 'Wasted Years, Wasted Lives Volume 1'. This would be the first time of actually meeting you. Nervous and excited I got off the tube; I didn't have a clue where I was supposed to be going, so taking a look at the crowds around me, I picked on 2 people to ask for directions and they both had their backs to me. Those 2 people were you and Paddy Lenaghan; of all the people I could have picked, YOU were the first person I spoke to in London. It was just meant to be!! To cut a long story short, your book launch was a huge success; you signed my copy of 'The Bloodiest Year 1972' with a personal message that makes me emotional every time I read it. Thanks to you I met some wonderful soldiers that day: Michael 'Benny' Hill, John Hill, John Corr, Ian Flynn, Mark Campbell, Paddy Lenaghan to name just a few and of course your good self Ken. Everyone made me feel so very welcome, like part of the 'family.'

I have stayed in contact and will continue to do so, although my quest for information about Uncle David continues and the web of information is spreading but I have learnt so much more thanks to your books, and to the brave soldiers themselves for reliving their humour, sadness and fear in these books. Like I have said so many times, without you guys I would have nothing to remember my uncle by. Since meeting you I have also found him in another of your books 'Bullets, Bombs and Cups of Tea'.

Ken thank you so very much for your compelling writing in this series of books and to be frank, for having the balls to write the British soldiers' side of the story. 'The War That Never Was' will never be forgotten, nor will the tragic waste of thousands of lives.

Tammy Card, niece of David Card, KIA in Andersonstown.

Maps

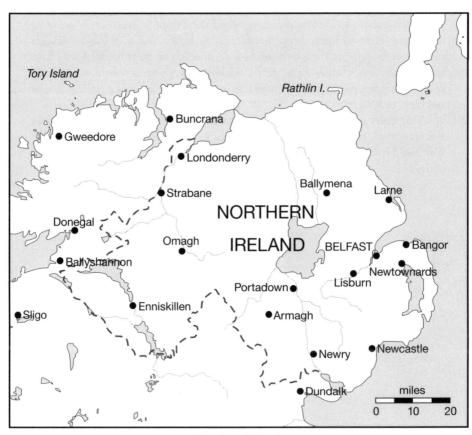

Tory Island

Rathlin I.

Buncrana

Gweedore

Londonderry

Ballymena

Larne

Strabane

NORTHERN

Donegal

IRELAND

BELFAST

Bangor

Omagh

Ballyshannon

Newtownards

Portadown

Lisburn

Sligo

Enniskillen

Armagh

Newry

Newcastle

Dundalk

miles

0   10   20

Northern Ireland

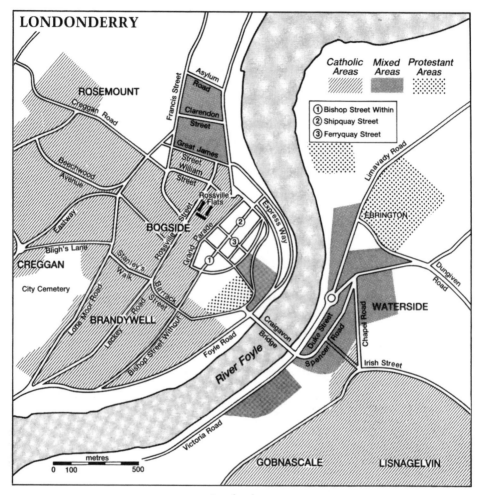

LONDONDERRY

Catholic Areas • Mixed Areas • Protestant Areas

① Bishop Street Within
② Shipquay Street
③ Ferryquay Street

ROSEMOUNT

Asylum Road
Francis Street
Cleggan Road
Clarendon Street
Great James Street
William Street
Beechwood Avenue
Eastway
Rossville Flats
Express Way
BOGSIDE
Bligh's Lane
CREGGAN
Stanley's Walk
Rossville Street
Grand Parade
Limavady Road
EBRINGTON
City Cemetery
Lone Moor Road
Leckey Road
Barrack Street
BRANDYWELL
Bishop Street Without
Foyle Road
Craigavon Bridge
Dungiven Road
Duke Street
Spencer Road
Chapel Road
WATERSIDE
Irish Street
River Foyle
Victoria Road
GOBNASCALE
LISNAGELVIN

metres
0 100   500

Londonderry

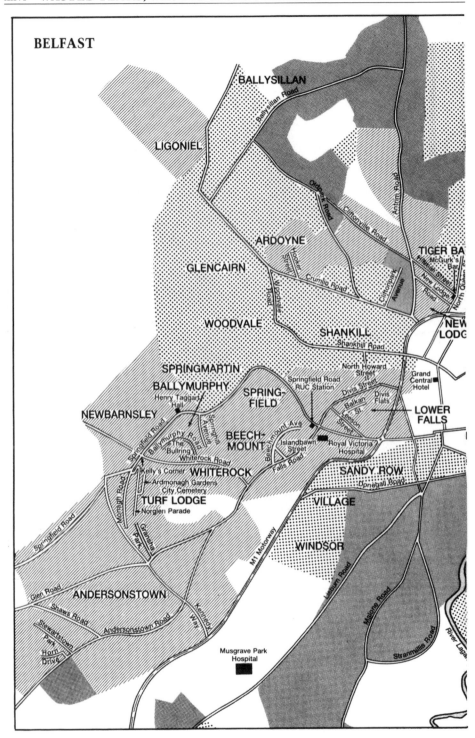

Belfast

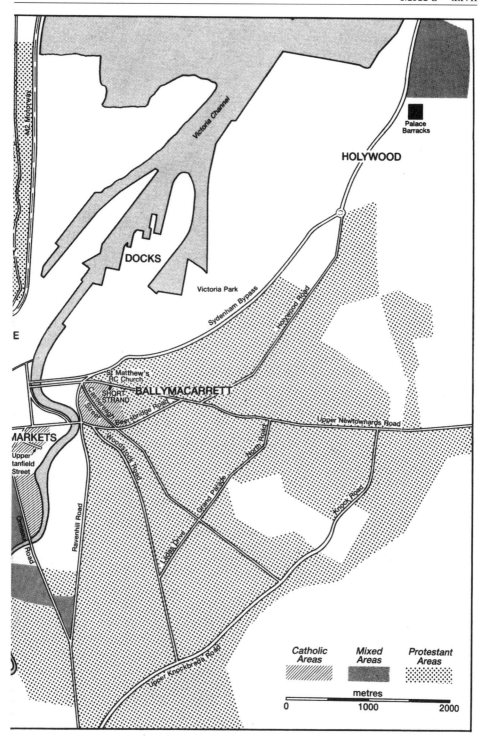

HOLYWOOD

Palace
Barracks

M2 Motorway

Victoria Channel

DOCKS

Victoria Park

Sydenham Bypass

Holywood Road

St Matthew's
RC Church

SHORT
STRAND

BALLYMACARRETT

Bridge End

Beersbridge Road

Upper Newtownards Road

E

MARKETS

Upper
Stanfield
Street

Woodstock Road

North Road

Knock Road

Ormeau Road

Ravenhill Road

Loops Drive

Grand Parade

Upper Knockbreda Road

Catholic
Areas

Mixed
Areas

Protestant
Areas

metres

0   1000   2000

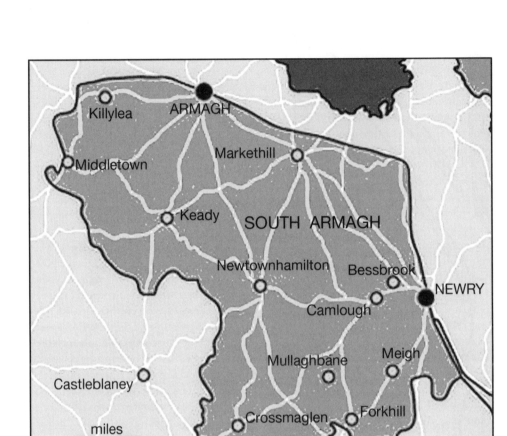

South Armagh ('bandit country')

Introduction

This book looks at the two years which witnessed the end of what was effectively the second decade of the Troubles. For those who thought that the latest tranche of violence in Ireland's troubled history would be short-lived, the opening days of 1980 which took the period into a third decade must have been most disheartening. That it did move into a fresh decade was down to several main reasons: it was down to the men of evil on both sides of the sectarian divide; it was down to the willingness of mad dogs such as the Libyan leader Gaddafi and also the USSR and the naïve Irish-Americans who funded the violence – and it was down to the determination of the British Government to support the vast majority of the population who wished to remain British.

The two years under review, whilst not as violent as the years 1972 and to a lesser extent 1975, nonetheless produced slaughter on an almost comparable scale. It was a 24 months which witnessed the PIRA atrocity with a napalm-like attack on the La Mon Restaurant in February 1978, which killed 12 people at a dog-breeders' function and terribly injured 42 more. It was a 24 months which saw the killing of 18 soldiers at Warrenpoint, Co Down on the same day as the murder of the Queen's cousin Lord Mountbatten and members of his family in August 1979. It also included the end for 11 members of the UVF known as the Shankill Butchers who were sentenced to life in prison for 19 murders. The infamous group was named for their practice of torturing and mutilating their victims with butcher's knives.

In short, for the terror groups who frequented the bars of both the Nationalist areas and the Loyalist parts of Northern Ireland, it was 'business as usual'. For the Provisional IRA – as well as the Irish National Liberation Army – it was a further period in which they attempted to push the British into the sea and sicken the British people into pressurising their Government to withdraw from the Province. For the Loyalists, it was more of the same from their 'foot soldiers' – the Ulster Freedom Fighters, the Ulster Volunteer Force and the Red Hand Commando – as they targeted Republican members, although for the most part their energy was devoted to the senseless sectarian slaughter of the Catholic population. For Loyalist murder groups such as Lenny Murphy's Shankill Butchers, it was very much 'carry on as before'. For the soldiers of the British Army – the stereotype 'piggy in the middle' – it was very much more of the same.

Ken Wharton, Gold Coast, Queensland, July 2013

Part Four

1978

This was a year in which 49 more soldiers would lose their lives and more UDR would be murdered off duty. The Republicans would continue to target and kill policemen – and sectarian deaths began after a short lull. In total 110 people would die, or 13 more in an entire year than were killed in one month in 1972. It was the year of an appalling 'napalm-like' PIRA bomb attack at La Mon which killed 12 people as they ate and drank at a quiet restaurant in Co Down.

January

J anuary was a quiet month by the murderous standards of the Troubles with only two deaths – both of UDR soldiers. There were, however, numerous near-misses and the utter tragedy of La Mon was just a few weeks away.

The first serious attacks of the New Year of 1978 took place in Castlederg, Co Tyrone and there was some confusion as to the architects of this mini blitz. The attacks bore the usual PIRA hallmarks: close to the border and a quick and easy bolthole. On the other hand the area was predominantly Nationalist and ended with a robbery which was more the trademark of the Loyalist paramilitaries. The devices were all placed by a gang of four masked men at various sites all within a mile of each other. An electrical shop in William Street, a garage in Upper Strabane Road and a grocer's in the same street were all hit by large devices which caused major damage – as well as major panic. A fourth device was planted at a large furniture store in the town. When Baskin's Grocers was robbed, the two bombers rifled the till and stole the day's takings, which led to speculation that it was Loyalists. Both the Provisionals and INLA often carried out bank and post office robberies in order to finance arms purchases, but the Loyalists were more likely to carry out the petty thefts. Whilst trying to evacuate the area, one of the bombs – at Lyon's Brothers Garage – exploded and caused some shock injuries to the RUC officers involved.

The remainder of the day saw devices planted in Londonderry, Belfast and Altnagelvin, Co Londonderry. Some were defused and others caused some damage. The following day saw a PIRA attack on a PO in Saintfield Road, South Belfast and an extremely lucky escape. The officer, aged 33 and a six-year veteran, had parked his car in his garage overnight but a bombing team had managed to get inside and planted a deadly UVBT. The officer started his car and had just started to move when the device detonated – causing him a severe wound to the leg (although he was able to limp back to the house). His wife and two young children were in the house at the time and his 12-year-old was greeted by the sight of his bloodied father with a gaping hole in his leg. The PO later recovered, but the Provisionals would ensure that many would be attending their own funerals in the troubled years to come. Later that day there was another lucky escape for a family sleeping above their shop in Winetavern Street in Belfast (close to Smithfield Market) when an incendiary device planted by the IRA exploded beneath their living quarters. The firebomb – inside a tea chest – was dragged out of the building and the family managed to escape. A spokesman for the RUC later revealed that had the family all been asleep at the time, they would have been trapped with no possibility of escape. Over the course of the Troubles, the Republicans – mainly PIRA – were responsible for the deaths of 67 children so it is highly unlikely that they would have shed tears over two more innocents.

On the 4th, the Provisionals planted another bomb at another section of the tourist economy: the Four Winds Restaurant at Knockbracken in Belfast. This was slightly different and was possibly a dress rehearsal for the La Mon. The device was attached to a safety grill over the window – a tactic which they would repeat with absolutely devastating effect the following month. The device exploded – destroying the bar, but there were no injuries. It would be repeated at the Manhattan Restaurant in Lurgan and then at the La Mon. On that same day, five young male joyriders came very close to death when they crashed through an army VCP in a stolen car. The checkpoint at the junction of the Glen Road and the Falls Road in Andersonstown was manned by soldiers based at Fort Monagh. The stolen car made no attempt to stop and under ROE it was fired upon. It crashed and four of the five occupants were wounded. All were taken to the Musgrave Park Hospital for treatment.

The following day saw more blast and incendiary devices in Belfast City Centre as the IRA attacked three major shops with devastating effect. Shortly afterwards, a PIRA bombing team planted a UVBT on a car which they wrongly assumed belonged to a PO who lived in Glengormley, North Belfast. In actual fact the car belonged to the PO's brother and as he was driving on Whitewell Road (in the direction of Antrim Road) it exploded – severely damaging the car, but miraculously leaving the man uninjured.

Two days later, acting upon information from an informer inside the Provisionals, the army raided a Catholic school in the Lower Falls area. Inside the roof space at St Louise's Girls' Secondary on St James Street, soldiers found explosives, weapons and ammunition. The ammunition could have exploded at any time and the Republican 'defenders' of the Nationalist community clearly gave no thought to the safety of the pupils. The Provisionals then planted a large device in the Capstan Lounge in Main Street, Newcastle, Co Down. Armed masked men had planted the device and then run off. The RUC were quickly on the scene, but staff were able to evacuate drinkers and surrounding premises before the resulting explosion wrecked the pub. The device was a mortar-type and caused a major fire. Further south-west, an armed gang of PIRA volunteers hijacked several lorries in Cullaville – close to Crossmaglen – and held the drivers in a derelict cottage. Army helicopters were quickly on the scene, and aided in a joint operation by RUC and Gardaí, were able to rescue the hostages. No arrests were made on either side of the border.

FORKHILL, 1978.
Ken Pettengale, Royal Green Jackets

We had settled in pretty well to our tour. Everything was going along quite nicely; out for four-day patrols in the cuds, in for sangar duties and town patrols. It was all ticking along very nicely – just as we thought it would do.

In early January of that year, we had been sent out on foot patrol and were dropped off by helicopter – Puma or Wessex, can't remember which. What I do remember is that the pilot couldn't land because the ground was too soft so we had to do a heli jump onto the boggy ground. The ground was a bit more than boggy though, and with our bergens and weapons (I was a GPMG Gunner) we sank up to our waists. I reckon we didn't go completely under purely because our packs kept us up. Anyway, we were completely soaked. It was mid-winter and it was totally freezing. We had to face four days' patrol in that condition, living under bashas and bushes … not funny!

The following morning, Sergeant 'Baz' Rimmer briefed the NCOs: due to the conditions we would go back to Forkhill, have a kit change and get back out on the ground. When I heard that, I was happy. Any time away from this shit was a bonus!

We hadn't been back in Forkhill very long – not long enough to get sorted anyway – when all of a sudden the walls of our portacabin accommodation collapsed! Stuff was flying everywhere: plates, kit, clothing, glass, loads of stuff. Then there was a huge, but muffled bang! At this point it just started to dawn on me that something wasn't right. A couple of our corporals – Dave Judge and Derek Randall – then got in among us. They calmly, but forcefully shouted: "Weapons, ammo, boots … Everybody out! Now!" Then the siren started wailing, activated by the ops room. The reaction told us what we already knew: we were under attack! There we were, stuck in a big hole in the ground and trapped by twisted metal, wood and the remnants of an SF base.

Bang, the second round went off! My training kicked in and I realised that it was a Provie mortar attack! All I wanted to do was get the hell out! I remember passing one of the Riflemen, Tom Cutbush. He was standing there holding an aluminium plate and bleeding from his head into it. He didn't look too bad and was moving along with us. I passed by him with Ian 'Blacky' Blackmore and we both made our way out to the heli-pad. I don't know why now, but I did know then that we were being covered by GPMGs in the two rear sangars.

Me and Blacky were deployed to the flank overlooking the road. I was so twitchy and had a full belt of 200 link slapped on my gun – and a couple of times I took aim on bobbing heads, but they were just civvies who were also taking cover. If I had thought about it, I would have realised the boyos were long gone.

Luckily we never lost anyone on that attack – surprisingly as the camp was full at that time. That was my baptism of fire: a harsh one, a quick one and one on which I was unable to return fire. But it wasn't over yet … the bastards still had another card to play.

The Jackets had three deaths on that tour, which will be dealt with in date order. Lieutenant-Colonel Ian Corden-Loyd (17 February); Rifleman Nicholas Smith (4 March) and Major Thomas Fowley (24 April).

On the 8th, Jack Lynch – Taoiseach (Irish Prime Minister) of the Irish Republic – called for a British declaration of intent to withdraw from Northern Ireland. The statement was supported by many in the Nationalist community in Northern Ireland. Three days later, a damning report by the Fair Employment Agency (FEA) indicated that the Catholic community experienced a higher level of unemployment than the Protestant community. In particular it pointed to the fact that Catholic men were two-and-a-half times more likely to be unemployed than Protestant men. Lynch's comments were followed up a week later when Tomás Ó Fiaich, then Catholic Primate of Ireland, was quoted in the Irish Press as saying: "I believe the British should withdraw from Ireland. I think that it is the only thing that will get things moving." The comments drew a lot of criticism from Loyalists, including Ian Paisley, then leader of the Democratic Unionist Party (DUP), who called Ó Fiaich: "... the IRA's bishop from Crossmaglen … "

A BOOZED-UP DWARF AND A SUSPECT CAR BOMB OFF SANDY ROW
Mick Kelly, Royal Artillery
On this one particular night, the Battery Commander (BC) asked me to ride 'shotgun' for him – something I enjoyed doing. It was a Saturday and the weather

ATO detonating a small bomb in a van, Hightown Road, Belfast, 1979. (© Mark 'C')

was quite warm. Most of the bars we went past looked filled to capacity. The BC would invariably stop the wagon and talk to the 'working girls' in Cecil Street and they were pleased to see him, but one took an instant dislike to me. I think the reason was that I was very much the professional when out with the BC and scarcely looked at the girls as I scanned the street whilst protecting arguably one of the most important men in the battery – if not the regiment!

A tall blonde one, who in truth wasn't a beauty and her 40th birthday was I suspect a distant memory, said to me: "You think I'm shit, didn't ye?" I knew she was from the Shankill. I told her no, but as we spoke I was still looking up the street in case the IRA sent a battalion in to ruin our evening. "Yes you do, so you do, you can't even fucking look at me." she continued. Just then, we received word of a car bomb rammed up against a pub in a street just off Sandy Row. We arrived before ATO got there and went into a side street. I was surprised to see most of the elderly residents sitting outside their terrace houses on dining room chairs chatting to each other across the street.

ATO turned up in a Saracen along with a Pig and a warrant officer got out and assessed the situation. One of the locals asked if we were going to make a bang and when we nodded, he walked into the various houses unasked and uninvited and proceeded to take out the sash windows in the upstairs rooms and lay them on the beds. He saw me looking and recognised the puzzled look of a foreigner and said: "It'll save the glass from breaking when yer man makes a bang!" One of the ATO lads told us that they were going to blow the rear windows out, but clearly felt that it wasn't a PIRA bomb as it had been hijacked locally. The

RUC told us that it was a joyriding incident which had ended in a crash. I followed the corporal, who was going at some pace. He was armed with a Browning A5 automatic shotgun and carrying a drum of don 10 wire and a package which was wrapped in what looked to be brown greaseproof paper; the drum was discarding a trail of wire behind us. The Browning shotgun is usually found fixed on the top of the wheelbarrow that ATO uses, but for some reason the wheelbarrow seemed inoperative and stayed in the Pig this night.

We turned into Sandy Row where there was a pub on the other side of the road and most of the occupants had spilled out to watch the action. A child started running from the pub crowd towards the corporal, who was armed with the shotgun. I went towards the child only to realise it was a male dwarf aged in his late twenties to early thirties. This threw me somewhat as I had no idea what this little person wanted. My wonderment ceased when he started to make a grab for the A5 Browning the corporal was holding. I was there as escort and immediately put myself between the dwarf and the corporal. The dwarf then started to try and grab my SLR. In truth I had never grappled with a little person before so was unsure what I could grab and what I couldn't. In the end I put my left hand on his head and pushed the little fella as far away as I could whilst holding my SLR in my right hand and held that as far away in the opposite direction as my arms would stretch. He was swing-punching the air between the pair of us. I was aware of laughter coming from the pub and then realised the dwarf and I had become the main attraction of the evening.

Two lads of similar age to the dwarf stepped out from the crowd. Both of them were wearing multi-patterned short-sleeve jumpers and holding straight-walled pint beer glasses. They both looked quite tall until I noticed they were wearing platform-soled shoes. They took the dwarf away – guiding him towards the crowd outside the pub who give him a big cheer with the enthusiasm that only alcohol makes possible. As I looked back the dwarf was now throwing punches at the two lads. The crowd cheered some more. I now felt a little sorry for the two who had rescued me from looking a complete twat in front of the corporal.

The corporal turned to me and said: "What I'm going to do is blow the rear window out and put an incendiary in the back to torch it." Bang! The shotgun goes off and the rear window collapses into the back seat of the stolen car – and then he tossed an incendiary device in and we raced back to the vehicles. The RUC have taken up a position at our end of the street now and as we ran past the pub – still with a healthy throng of onlookers outside … all with a glass in their hands – I look and see one of my rescuers. We grin at each other; the dwarf is nowhere to be seen. I imagine him locked in a suitcase inside the pub.

Once in a safe position, ATO screamed: "Firing now!" I had advised the residents that there would be a loud bang, but in the event we are treated to a whooshing noise as the car goes up in flames. After this the local starts to retrieve the sash windows he left on the beds and puts them back into the window frames.

ATO were waiting for the car to finish burning and declare it free from other ordnance when two low-velocity rounds are heard over our heads. As we stand and look at each other, we see two petrol bombs thrown into what looks like a builders' yard about two streets away. We run like the clappers to the end of the street – my heart and breathing are going 10 to the dozen. Looking deep into the shadows I start to notice movement; was there something or am I being a complete dick? I look again, nothing. I'm scared the sound of my breathing can be heard back at GCH.

Then I saw him – looking round a street corner about 50 yards away. He pulled his head in, but I have seen him! He starts to look round the corner again and this time I am ready for him – my right-hand thumb pushed down on the safety catch of my SLR. I try and do it as slowly as I can as I don't want to alert him to my intention of ending his life once I have confirmed that he is fully armed. His chest was visible, but I couldn't see the rifle and I assumed that he only wanted to bring the rifle to his shoulder at the last minute and shoot at us. Should I shout a warning? I couldn't remember what I was supposed to say or do when I'm about to end somebody's life. I couldn't ask the other lads because it would alert the gunman to my presence. No! No! He's moving from behind cover of the corner and his arms are moving from behind him to a firing position. I knew that I must properly identify the weapon before firing. The centre of mass is where I will place my shot. The blade of the foresight is now nicely centered on the middle of his chest. My lack of fitness and rapid breathing does not alter my point of aim.

Here it comes ... his arms are slowly sweeping round. I was sure that it was an American M1 Carbine, but why is he pointing it at the ground? The movement at his feet makes me realise he is not alone; is there another gunman in the prone position also about to fire? Who do I shoot first? But just before I shot, the 'gunmen' transformed themselves into a local resident taking a rough-coated, long-legged Jack Russell out for his evening constitution!

Soldier from 25 Field Regiment, Royal Artillery on patrol, Sandy Row, Belfast, 1979. (©Mark 'C')

Not for the first time in the Province do I feel a complete twat. I looked at the other two who were looking in the other direction: "Nah, nothing here," I said, "although I nearly had the geezer with the dog!"

The 9th saw the death of UDR NCO Robert Galloway (41), whose cause of death is listed as 'unknown'. He is laid to rest at Carnmoney Cemetery in Newtownabbey – the same resting place of the psychopathic Shankill Butcher Lenny Murphy. On the 10th, the 'economic' war continued as the Provisionals made every effort to use their explosives in order to turn the centre of Belfast into something resembling the surface of the moon. This campaign continued without let-up for the month of January – and Belfast, Londonderry, Newry and Strabane in particular all suffered as the Republican terrorists attempted to cause a commercial meltdown and ruin the Province's economy. The IRA were now trying to carry out a sustained campaign which Gerry Adams characterised as the 'Long War', with the eventual aim of weakening the British Government's resolve to remain in Ireland. In burning down the commercial heart of Northern Ireland they hoped to sicken a war-weary public into putting pressure on the British Government to expel Ulster from the United Kingdom and withdraw troops. One wonders however, what the Republican terror group expected would happen to the country's one million Protestants. The late Edward Kennedy, doyen of the IRA and the Irish-Americans, had talked of 'assisting the Scottish Protestants' into evacuating the North and, presumably, returning to Scotland whence they had come some 300 years earlier.

TURF LODGE MEMORIES
Corporal Jonathan 'Swede' Tomkinson, 2nd Battalion Queen's Regiment

I joined 'C' Company 2nd Battalion, Queen's Regiment in early August 1977 after completing basic training in Bassingbourne Barracks. The basic training was a revelation to me as I was brought up in Sweden and never experienced any particular discipline, so joining the army was something very new. Once in my platoon I was always the 'NIG' which was no surprise to me. On hearing that the battalion was being posted to Ulster early the following year, I was filled with foreboding. However, it really hit home to me in January 1978 whilst disembarking from the LSL and the RSM shouted: "Don't use all the rounds before getting to camp!" Bloody hell, this is it I thought, as I scanned every chimney and rooftop – sitting in the Bedford four-tonner en route to our company location at Fort Monagh. This was to become our base until late June. The days ceased to be weekdays or weekends; now it was patrol/standby/guard, patrol/standby/guard (apart from the R&R, which was only a drunken blur at the Union Jack club).

The posting proved to be one long bad dream and sometimes worse for me – such hatred from the locals and the tension on every patrol around Turf Lodge. Hard targeting for hours; the lift operations; mortar runs through the night and the hours spent on stag in the different sangars left me depressed and wondering what the hell I had signed up for. Never being able to sleep in proper sheets for the whole tour; always cold showers and never a full night's sleep made me feel even more depressed. I was always the 'tail-end Charlie' and the feeling of being in the sights of a potential sniper preyed on my mind. I was, of course, getting my share of abuse – bottles, urine and whatever thrown at me. I was a fresh-faced soldier raised in Uppsala, Sweden who had previously never had a bad word said to me. It was hard to cope with. The constant banging of dustbin lids, whistling and other noises kept me on my toes just waiting for the next 'contact' – of which we had many. The rioting was nearly a daily occurrence and if we were not involved, we always helped out the other platoons when things got really nasty. During the tour we had 118 searches of houses, 122 hot pursuits and 176 arrests – and this in a relatively small housing estate.

One defining moment in the tour was on 7 June around 3-3.30pm when we were patrolling out of Turf Lodge and on Norglen Parade. There was the usual mob of about 80-100 youths following our patrol, led by Sergeant 'B'. They were throwing stones, bottles and keeping me occupied as the last man. As we turned down Norglen Drive, I passed a concrete wall on my right when an enormous explosion threw me across the road. When I came to, lying in the middle of the road on my back, I looked up and thought: "Fuck, is that it?" and wondering what my parents were going to say. I seemed to just lie there for what felt like ages and then looked down the road – and through thick white smoke, two dark figures appeared. To my delight it was Martin and Phil, who grabbed me by the arms and pulled me into an empty garage. I sorted myself out and continued the patrol – although I felt sick and very dizzy. Corporal 'K' was later taken to MPH with a perforated eardrum and minor cuts.

On returning to camp I noticed that the top cover on my SLR had received a big dent so I went to the stores for a new one. I then received a bollocking for damaging army property! After this I went back to my room, hopped into my bunk and thought that there is no sympathy for you in the army. I later found out from SOCO that they had found 15 six-inch nails in the blast area. For some reason or other I wrote a few lines each day in Swedish in a little notebook and for that day, I wrote: 'Search early in the morning. Then T.L (Turf Lodge patrol) in the morning, little aggro. Cop shot in Andytown, snipe at Fort Monagh, then patrol in T.L. Nailbomb thrown at our patrol, nearly killed. Then lazed around. Mortar runs all night'.

The rest of the tour I felt surprisingly elated and grew in confidence. However, standing on the railing on the LSL taking us back to England – having handed over to 42 Commando – I did have tears in my eyes of relief; a nightmare was over. I went back to Ulster in 1980 as brick commander in a COP unit (had another incident – a 'blue on blue', which shook me up badly – and worked Co Armagh). That tour was exciting, hard and very demanding but no similar feelings as I had in 1977.

In 1998 when I was diagnosed with PTSD, I was asked by the psychologist to name 10 incidents which affected/defined my life. Ulster was mentioned four or five times. We talked at length about Ulster and my army time and as a result I was treated with EMDR and the treatment worked very well for me. Despite having a couple of relapses since, I look back on my whole army time with great pride and satisfaction of serving with such bloody good mates who were always at hand. I rarely talk about Ulster in Sweden. Nobody understands and really cares. My brother, after the first tour, asked: "How was Ulster?" I replied: "Being shot at is very dangerous." He replied: "What! You were shot at with live bullets?"

The incredulity of civvies was something which many soldiers found difficult to take. The author himself was asked ridiculous questions such as: "Does it hurt when you're shot?" "Don't know; never been shot, but I will tell you if I ever am!" "What's it like to kill someone?" "Don't know; never done it!" "It can't be dangerous over there because it is never on the news." Exasperated silence from the author. Many soldiers going back to the mainland withdrew from their civvie friends and just counted the days until they could get back to their platoons and their 'real' friends. One Green Jacket told the author – on condition that it was anonymous:

GOING HOME
Rifleman 'L', Royal Green Jackets

"When I went back to 'the Smoke' on leave, I wanted to go to all of my old muckers and tell them what had happened. I wanted to tell them about the lad from my platoon who loved playing football, but lost his lower leg in an explosion; I wanted to tell them about what it was like when a high-velocity round whips over your head; I wanted to tell them about the bricks and the ball bearings which were fired at us and the shit and the filth and the way even the women spat in our faces; I wanted to tell them about the little old lady who smiled at me and said: 'God bless you, son' and then had all her windows bricked by the scum; I wanted to tell them that, but they weren't interested. I used to go down the 'Bridge with them to watch Chelsea play, but after a while even football didn't cheer me up. My old man had served and he knew what it was like, and in the end this geezer who had fathered me but who I never liked, became my best mate in Civvie Street. He was a diamond geezer and I will never forget that. When I came out of the mob, I never bothered with the same friends again. Even today, I prefer ex-military mates."

As previously stated, there was only one Troubles-related death this month and that took place on the 12th when the IRA killed a part-time UDR soldier in Newry. Corporal Cecil Grills (56) also worked as a manager for a company in Merchant's Quay in Newry. He had finished work for the day and was en route for home when gunmen who had hidden behind a wall in Arthur Street opened fire on his car. He was struck several times in the head and chest and mortally wounded. The gunmen ran off in the direction of the Nationalist Derrybeg Estate and the part-time soldier died shortly after reaching hospital. An apologist for the Republican terror group claimed responsibility for the killing, with the sickeningly pathetic justification that Cecil Grills was a part of ' ... the British war machine'. One wonders if these people actually believed their own propaganda. At his funeral, a churchman said: "One wonders whether those who so coldly and callously took life on Thursday evening could really have known Cecil Grills and what he was really like. We feel a deep, but we believe a righteous and moral, anger over this immoral deed" ('Lost Lives', p743). The soldier had two young children under 10 and the IRA left them fatherless.

On Friday 13th, the IRA carried out a bomb attack on the Guildhall in Londonderry – causing serious damage. The building had only reopened seven months earlier following severe damage caused by an IRA firebomb attack in July 1972. The bombers had deliberately waited until the SF had been lulled into a false sense of security in the hope that 'lightning never strikes twice' before striking again at the symbol of British rule. The IRA had cleverly engineered a riot outside the building – during which mobs of youths battled with the army and police. Rocks and petrol bombs were hurled and 12 people were injured as the SF attempted to evacuate the area after a telephoned bomb warning. During a statement admitting responsibility, a spokesman for the Provisionals also admitted that they had carried out 18 major bombings in the first 12 days of the year and would continue in the same vein until ' ... a British withdrawal ... '

On that same day, an IRA volunteer threw a blast bomb over a security fence at the former RAF base at Shackleton, Ballykelly in northern Co Londonderry. It exploded – injuring one soldier slightly – but it was an alarming breach of security and prompted calls of 'what if?' An attempt was then made to cause a massive fireball when an incendiary device was left next to petrol pumps at a petrol station in Dungannon. It was defused by the army.

On the following day, the IRA started a fire in a derelict house in William Street, Londonderry on the fringes of the Nationalist Bogside. There was a possibility that this had been started as a 'come on' but as there was a clear danger that the fire could spread to neighbouring houses, an army 'Green Goddess' fire engine was called in. As the troops were fighting the blaze, IRA snipers began firing from residential homes and a total of 10 shots were fired at the soldiers. Fortunately none were injured, but because of the proximity of innocent civilians – deliberately chosen as cover by the gunmen – soldiers were unable to return fire. On the 16th, PIRA bombing teams caused the destruction of two shops and a garage on the Ormeau Road in South Belfast. Shots were fired at soldiers fighting the resultant blazes.

The 17th witnessed a blatantly obvious sectarian attack by Republican gunmen, thought to be INLA, on two Protestant men who were working on roof repairs at the Co-op store in Springfield Road, Belfast. The store had been earlier damaged in a PIRA bomb attack and the company was trying to get it back into service. Two masked gunmen climbed a ladder onto an opposite rooftop and opened fire on the rooftop workers. One man was hit in the groin, legs and face and slumped – badly wounded – but was able to maintain his finger hold on the roof. The second, in desperation, threw himself off and fell around 30 feet to the ground – breaking both wrists. A passing RUC patrol chanced upon the scene as the gunmen attempted to escape in a stolen car. A pursuit began through the Flush and then through the Beechmounts with shots being fired by both police and terrorists, which resulted in both windscreens being shattered, but the IRA gunmen escaped towards the Falls Road area. A revolver was later recovered which was linked to other shootings by the Provisionals. The Londonderry brigade was active on the same day when they deliberately targeted one company – the Irish Bonding Company – on the Pennyburn Industrial Estate. Masked gunmen raided the premises at around 17:30 hours and planted a total of five bombs – warning that they were timed to go off at intervals. Much of the bonded alcohol, wines and spirits etc was destroyed and caused the loss of several million pounds' worth of untaxed booze. Cynics suggested, not unreasonably, that this would benefit the illegal shebeens owned by the Provisionals and stocked with hijacked supplies of all manner of alcohol. A shebeen is an illicit bar or club where excisable alcoholic beverages were sold without a licence. Often the breweries would, in return for their delivery vehicles being left alone, supply the IRA with the odd lorry loaded with pub supplies. Other than that, the IRA would simply hijack a vehicle and use the goods to keep their shebeens stocked up.

On the 18th, the European Court of Human Rights made its ruling on the case of alleged ill-treatment of internees during 1971. The case had been initially referred to the European Commission by the Irish Government on 10 March 1976. On 2 September 1976 the European Commission on Human Rights decided that Britain had to answer a case of ill-treatment of internees and referred the matter to the European Court of Human Rights. The Commission found that the interrogation techniques did involve a breach of the Convention on Human Rights because they not only involved inhuman and degrading treatment, but also torture. The European Court of Human Rights however decided that the Commission was wrong to use the word 'torture' but did agree that the internees had been subjected to 'inhuman and degrading treatment'. This was a major embarrassment for the Callaghan Government, although the alleged ill-treatment had occurred under the previous Conservative administration of Edward Heath.

The following day, the 'economic war' took a new step as an additional dimension was added by the Provisionals. The newly returned Belfast fire brigade was fighting a blaze when an explosive device was discovered – strapped to a pillar – and was clearly designed to kill or maim the fire fighters. On this occasion, the device failed to explode. More bombings took place throughout Belfast and Londonderry where PIRA bombed a shopping centre – causing mass panic in Great William James as well as a nearby Protestant-owned pub. Loyalist paramilitaries who had been relatively quiet of late then attacked a minibus carrying Catholic workmen to their place of work. Gunmen, thought to be UFF, were hiding behind a wall at the junction of the Falls Road and Broadway in West Belfast and opened fire as the vehicle drove past. There were no injuries.

On the 20th, there was a major fire fight between troops based at Crossmaglen when the Provisionals opened fire on an army patrol. The battle lasted for around 30 minutes – during which over 200 rounds were fired by the terrorists, although there were no injuries. Two helicopters were called in and their searchlights were used to help capture the gunmen, who were chased in the direction of Cullaville where they melted into the border landscape. On the same day, car bombs in both Cookstown and Dungannon caused havoc and led to some minor injuries, but major damage to property. An ambush by armed PIRA volunteers in Londonderry saw three policemen wounded – one of them badly. Using a derelict house for cover, gunmen waited until their Land Rovers had just reached Lone Moor Road and Letterkenny Road on the Creggan Estate before opening fire. Using a machine gun, the gunmen registered at least 20 hits on both vehicles. Shortly after this incident, the IRA set off a car bomb whilst a large patrol of police in Cookstown were clearing the area. A total of five RUC officers and three civilians were caught in the blast. Some were badly injured by the blast, which occurred between the town post office and a large hardware shop.

On the 23rd, a major mortar attack on the SF base at Forkhill, South Armagh saw six soldiers injured; parts of the base badly damaged and a casualty evacuation by helicopters. Several explosive devices were fired into the base from the back of a lorry parked some 100 yards from the base and crashed into the sleeping quarters and toilet areas of the joint RUC/ army base. The soldiers involved were the 2nd Battalion Royal Green Jackets – motto *Celer et Audux* (*Swift and Bold*) – and whose battle honours include the incredible storming of the heights of Québec with General Wolfe in 1759. Formed as the Royal Americans, elements of this famous regiment have served their country from the American War of

Independence through two World Wars and countless colonial conflicts until it was amalgamated into the Rifles in 2007. It suffered 49 fatalities – the third highest of any unit – during the Troubles and were lucky not to lose more at Forkhill on 23 January.

THE JACKETS AT FORKHILL: VARIOUS CONTRIBUTORS
Ken Pettengale
We had settled in pretty well to our tour. Everything was going along quite nicely; out for four-day patrols in the cuds, in for sangar duties and town patrols. It was all ticking along very nicely – just as we thought it would do.

In early January of that year, we had been sent out on foot patrol and were dropped off by helicopter – Puma or Wessex, can't remember which. What I do remember is that the pilot couldn't land because the ground was too soft so we had to do a heli jump onto the boggy ground. The ground was a bit more than boggy though, and with our bergens and weapons (I was a GPMG Gunner) we sank up to our waists. I reckon we didn't go completely under purely because our packs kept us up. Anyway, we were completely soaked. It was mid-winter and it was totally freezing. We had to face four days' patrol in that condition, living under bashas and bushes … not funny!...

Alan Symons
We were soaked to the skin, freezing cold and very pissed off. Our wonderful Sergeant, Derek 'Baz' Rimmer, made the only sensible tactical decision: we lit a fucking great fire!

Ken Pettengale
The following morning, 'Baz' Rimmer – our Platoon Sergeant – briefed the NCOs: due to the conditions we would go back to Forkhill, have a kit change and get back out on the ground. When I heard that, I was happy – any time away from that shit was a bonus!

Dave Pomfrett
We were just walking down to the briefing room – probably the smallest room in the whole place – in the Forkhill Police Station. As usual, cup of tea in one hand, we had just got into the briefing room and were settling down for our Int guys to come in to brief us on any extras when BOOM! The whole place shook and like any comedy film, straight away we all did nothing … just stood still and looked around the room just to make sure we had heard correctly, then again: BOOM!

Gren Wilson
I was in the briefing room being briefed for a two-day patrol, when two large explosions violently interrupted us.

Ken Pettengale
All of a sudden the walls of our portacabin collapsed and stuff was flying everywhere: plates, kit, clothing, glass, loads of stuff. Then there was a huge, but muffled BANG!

Alan Symons
KER-FUCKING-BOOM! Pitch-black, smoke everywhere, shouting, confusion. I.A. Get under the bed and cower in the dark. KER-FUCKING-BOOM. Two more, but further away this time. Waiting for No.3; Order starts to return. "Grab your weapons, let's go!"

Gren Wilson

The room quickly emptied and the sight that came into view was one of devastation. There was people wandering around in shock with small splinter wounds. I recall a guy called Alan 'Scouse' Cole walking past me with his arms a little distance away from his side saying: "The bastards have got me."

Ken Pettengale

That was it; we all took immediate action and stood up. I think it was 'Teasy' Teasdale who drank his tea down in one as if just in case the next one spilt it. I looked to my left and Neal 'Claude' Jeeves was crouched on his knees and for protection, held above his head, was a small tin 'Tartan Bitter' ashtray. Then the door from the ops room opened and in came our OC Major Myers in his hunter wellies, wide-eyed but calm, and said: "WHAT THE BLOODY HELL WAS THAT?"

Ken Pettengale

At this point it just started to dawn on me that something wasn't right. A couple of our Cpls – one of whom was Derek 'Randy' Randall – then got in among us. They calmly, but forcefully, shouted: "Weapons, ammo, boots. Everybody OUT. NOW!" Then the siren started wailing – activated by the ops room. It dawned on me that we were under attack and here we were, stuck in a big hole in the ground and trapped by twisted metal, wood and the trappings of an SF base. Bang! The second round went off! MORTAR attack! All I wanted to do was get the hell out! I remember passing Tom Cutbush. He was standing there holding an aluminium plate and bleeding from his head into it. He didn't look too bad and was moving along with us.

Canteen at Forkhill after mortar attack. (©Alan Simons)

Riflemen Ian Blackmore and Ken Pettengale, Royal Green Jackets,
after the mortar attack at Forkhill. (©Alan Simons)

Mortar baseplate lorry before booby-trap. (©Alan Simons)

9 Platoon Royal Greenjackets accommodation after the mortar
attack at Forkhill, 23 January 1978. (©Alan Simons)

9 Platoon Royal Greenjackets accommodation after the mortar attack at Forkhill. (©Alan Simons)

Alan Symons

We were waiting for number 3. Order starts to return. "Grab your weapons, let's go!"

Dave Moloney

Not much to say about the attack itself mate as I was out on patrol near Jonesborough with John Dowling's multiple (30A). We heard the explosions and listened to the contact rep on the radio. We knew there were casualties and John made the decision to head in on foot.

Dave Judge

I had just arrived at Bessbrook Mill and was transiting through the mill on my way to join the Northern Ireland Reinforcement Training Team (NIRTT). The CO, Lieutenant-Colonel Ian Corden-Lloyd, had arranged this posting for me! I had not been at the mill for very long when there was a great deal of hurry up and hurry up some more going on! Things had gotten quite mental with H.Q. wallahs running around and shouting orders left right and centre! The RSM was close to me and I heard him asking for anyone who knew the Forkhill area? Well I had just left it and knew it like the back of my hand. It became clear that there had been a major incident there at my old company base. I piped up and told the RSM that I knew the place very well. He replied: "Of course you do! There has been a mortar attack on the base and I need to fill a chopper and get there ASAP." I didn't need any more info. I scarpered to the heli-pad and threw on what was basically my whole 1157 (everything I owned) and waited for the chopper to fill.

Ken Pettengale

Me and Blacky were deployed to the flank overlooking the road. I was so twitchy and had a full belt of 200 link slapped on my gun. A couple of times I took aim on bobbing heads, but they were just civvies who were taking cover. If I had thought about it, I would have realised the boyos were long gone. Then our real leader came in – Lieutenant-Colonel Ian Corden-Lloyd, MC – armed to the teeth and beret perfectly placed on his head and said: "Anyone hurt?" Then he and Major Myers left and they went straight out with their Rifle group – consisting of Rifleman Steve Wyatt – onto the streets of Forkhill.

We left the briefing room by the back door and as soon as we were outside we could smell burning. Nothing was on fire, but what we could smell was the after burn of the explosion and dust thick in the air. There were men shouting – not just shouting rubbish or swearing, but good, ordered shouting of instructions and names and drills; things to do; things not to do. As we reached the area of our accommodation it was: "where is our shed?" It was complete devastation and I saw our Lance Jack, Willy Wareham, in his vest calling names and getting replies. He was heading for the top of the accommodation towards the heli-pad. Willy was heading up there because his brother Graham slept in the sheds there and they had had a direct hit by mortar number two. I could hear Randy in the background telling someone to go to each sangar and check it. Soon we could hear the unmistakable sound of rotor blades circling around and I saw squaddies, riflemen, my company's fellow Jackets being pulled out of the devastation; then I went cold and thought this is serious … this is the real thing … and I will tell you I was very scared then. Someone was picking up rifles and boxes of rounds and the

Royal Engineers were already making safe the structures and probably planning a rebuild of the accommodation blocks.

Gren Wilson

Our group loaded our weapons and ran out of the camp to find the base plate, which was a flatbed lorry. We put a cordon around the area while ATO cleared the lorry to make sure it was safe to go near.

Alan Symons

Out of the gate and run up the road. Some fat bitch on her doorstep, screaming at me, something like: "I hope they got some of yer!" Cock my LMG, point it at the cow. Door closes pretty quick! Up the road and run past the flatbed with the tubes on its back. We form a cordon; adrenaline wears off, cold sets in.

Dave Judge

We took off sharpish and flew low and as fast as the bird could go. I can't remember the scene from the air at all, but on the ground it was a bomb site! The buildings were disrupted – some parts were flat-packed! Glass and splinters of wood littered the scene. It strangely looked like it had been snowing. In just local parts of the rubble there was the contents of sleeping bags – feathers sticking to all sorts of jagged edges, walls, windows, wooden steps and the like. We de-planed and I dumped all of my kit by a wall for later on as I had no intention of boarding that chopper when it left Forkhill for the mill on the return journey. The rest of the company was there. They looked like Fred Carno's army – some fully dressed and some with no shirts, but vests and flak jackets. There were some with army shirts not fastened! Not one had a helmet on! Some had no head gear at all on! They had simply swarmed out of the base like termites and took up defensive positions. I found Derek Randall and he told me what had occurred.

Dave Moloney

The rest of my team – Taffy Reinthal, Chris Brown and Alan Cole – were in our room, which was near to the seat of one of the explosions and was absolutely devastated. Luckily Taffy was uninjured whilst Chris (bed end into his thigh) and Alan (shrapnel wounds to the face) both were back on the road within 48 hrs.

Ken Pettengale

I remember the RCT drivers were starting up the sari cans (Saracens). The chefs were out in their whites – digging and moving things. Even Albert Wall was outside during daylight hours!

Dave Judge

The press had arrived. So had C.A.T.O. (Chief Ammunition Technical Officer) along with his weapons inspection team. The mortars had been transported to their firing point in a flatbed lorry – under cover in a large plywood box as a method of concealment – and the mortars fired from a timer switch, which gave the boyos time to escape. The CO gave a conference to the press in front of the now 'safe' lorry (having been cleared by CATO and his team). The press and photographers began to disperse from the scene. Two police officers decided to remove the lorry – possibly the police station – for forensic exam later. A police Sergeant named Alex Pedlar climbed into the cab to drive it away.

Gren Wilson

Boom! The cab of lorry was totally destroyed and two plain-clothed RUC officers were lying on the ground motionless. Lieutenant-Colonel Corden-Lloyd shouted to everyone to stay back as he ran to the men.

Ken Pettengale

Luckily we never lost anyone on that attack – and the camp was full at that time; that was my baptism of fire. A harsh one, a quick one and one on which I was helpless to return fire on. But the day was not over. There was another muffled bang and, I believe, a minor shock wave. The ASU who had mortared us had also booby-trapped the cab of the lorry used as the baseplate. This had gone off when two RUC detectives were moving the vehicle. I could hear more shouting and see blokes running everywhere.

One of the RUC men was seriously injured with a bad wound to the neck. I think it was Rifleman Steve Wyatt, who had shoved his beret into his neck wound to stem the loss of blood, but I don't remember any medics or ambulances at the scene at all that day – just squaddies and RUC doing their best. The RUC detective and his colleague who was also injured in the lorry blast were both back at work in just a matter of weeks. Now that was the commitment from the courageous RUC.

Gren Wilson

Someone moaned and we were ordered to get doors to use as stretchers. Within minutes the guys were being choppered to hospital. We went back into camp and started to help tidy up the place while other members of the company dug one of our guys out from under rubble. We were very lucky that day as no-one was killed or seriously injured. The only inconvenience I had was that I had to sleep in a room with part of its roof missing.

Dave Judge

Me and Derek Randall were stood to the rear of the lorry, about 10m behind it, when one of the RUC men turned the ignition key! There was a huge bang and the front left of the vehicle disintegrated. Pedlar was talking to the second officer through the open window of the passenger door. We now had two seriously injured police officers that needed immediate medical intervention and evacuation! The CO took immediate control. I think Derek 'Baz' Rimmer dealt with one of the cops; I can't remember who dealt with the other. Only first field dressings were available and it was obvious that a lot more medical attention was going to be required. We commandeered doors from houses and used them as makeshift stretchers for the casualties. I ended up looking after one cop on the door/stretcher – the cop who was stood next to the cab when it blew. Suddenly a doctor, a civvie doctor, turned up! I know not from where, but I was glad he did and he took over from me and I think he got on the chopper as it left the scene.

Dave Moloney

What really sticks in my mind – and is as clear today as it was then – is on my return some three hours later the shock of what happened and how lucky we all had been quickly sank in. There was an air of focus and underlying anger that seemed to be affecting everyone who had been involved in that day's mayhem. I had not experienced it before that day; I have, unfortunately, experienced it too many times since. It's hard to put into exact words, but I'm sure you and everyone else who have been there will understand that feeling.

Over the next 12-24 hours I came across many an old sweat (those who considered themselves hard men) in tears or wandering aimlessly around in the dark. I found one NCO in particular in tears trying to get out of the back gate. He was very distressed – almost uncontrollable. I managed to eventually calm him down and we sat by that gate for hours just talking. In the end we shook hands and promised that what had been said would remain between us and us alone. He turned out to be one of my closest mates in years to come who earned my utmost respect and covered my back on more than one occasion.

Alan Symons

We returned to base and what was left of our accommodation, which was very little. We recovered what we could of our possessions – another day in Paradise?

On the 24th, an RUC officer escaped serious injury when a well-concealed IRA sniper fired a shot at him as he locked security gates at the police station where he worked. The unnamed policeman was locking up for the night at Cloughmills RUC Station in Co Antrim when a single shot crashed into the brickwork just above his head. The month ended with more bombs in both Belfast and Londonderry and a major fire fight between the Provisionals and the army following a landmine blast at Kinawley, Co Fermanagh, which wrecked an army vehicle but only slightly wounded the occupants. The soldiers fired over 200 rounds at the bomber as he ran across fields towards the sanctuary of the Irish Republic. Sadly, no hits were recorded. On the 28th, an IRA gang staged a robbery at McCrearey's Supermarket in Co Donegal in the Irish Republic. Bernard Brown, who was in the shop at the time, attempted to prevent the robbery and was shot down in cold blood and mortally wounded; he died the following week.

The month ended with only two deaths – both were part-time UDR soldiers. The next month however would see a restaurant – known only in the East Belfast area – suddenly become, for the wrong reasons, a name on the lips of the world press.

February

January's relatively low number of deaths had proven to be a false dawn and thanks to the murderous, unjustified and inexcusable actions of the Provisional IRA, February's death toll would outdo the previous four months put together. It was a month when the Provisionals killed a part-time UDR soldier and his 10 year old daughter; it was also the month of La Mon.

The first day of the month witnessed not one, but two suicidal attempts for joyriders in a stolen car to charge through army VCPs. The first attempt succeeded as they mowed their way through a VCP on the Falls Road and shots were fired at their vehicle. Minutes later, they attempted the same trick at another VCP on the Andersonstown Road, but this time several shots hit the vehicle and it was later recovered at Milltown with bloodstains on the front passenger seat – indicating that at least one of the car thieves had been wounded. Over the next two days, PIRA exploded five more bombs in and around Belfast City Centre – causing much damage and some injuries. They were alternating genuine warnings with hoax alerts and thus attempting to throw the emergency services into total confusion. With money pouring in from the USA, Australia and other countries in order to purchase arms and explosives, they had no shortage of materiel. The UVF tried to get in on the act – although on a smaller scale and certainly in a more sectarian manner. A UVF murder gang threw two grenades at properties in Hillman Street, Belfast on the Nationalist New Lodge area. A later attack by the UVF in the area only succeeded in injuring a soldier.

On the 2nd, a Loyalist murder gang burst into a Catholic house on the Falls Road and despite their intended victim sitting down, cradling a small baby, callously opened fire and shot him five times. He was injured, but the tiny tot was hit in the jaw, thigh and arms and was rushed to the nearby RVH for emergency treatment. The child survived, but with disfiguring injuries.

On the 3rd, Bernard Brown (50), who was mortally wounded in an IRA shop robbery, died of his wounds (see previous chapter). He was shot and wounded inside the Irish Republic at Killygordon, Co Donegal. Two MPs (Military Police) were shot and wounded when IRA gunmen who had been hiding behind a wall in Crumlin Road Health Centre opened fire on the two soldiers as they waited outside the Jail on the opposite side of the Crumlin Road. Both men were badly wounded and the gunmen ran off in the direction of the nearby Nationalist Oldpark area.

On the following day, an apologist for the Provisionals was forced to make a grovelling – in this author's opinion, meaningless – apology for the killing of Martha McAlpine (69), whom they shot in North Belfast. The *heroic freedom fighters* – author's own italics – had decided to shoot a policeman who was on crowd control duties outside Crusaders AFC's ground on the Shore Road. A hijacked van pulled up to a vantage point and firing from a van with the rear windows removed, six shots were aimed at the RUC officer. Four of the shots missed, but one struck Mrs McAlpine in the stomach. She was standing with three of her grandchildren – all aged under 10 – when she was hit. She died in hospital. The policeman was wounded in the groin and collapsed in agony. An apologist for the Provisionals later spoke of a *'tragedy'* and offered their ' *... sincere condolences ...* ' The spokesman partially blamed the dead woman when he added: " *... we again warn the public to stay clear of British troops, UDR and RUC personnel ...*." Clearly the fault was not the Republican terrorists who turned an innocent pastime such as watching football into part of an urban battleground; it was the fault of the dead lady for standing too close to a policeman!

Later on the 4th, two restaurants in Belfast and the courthouse in Omagh were bombed by the IRA. There was extensive damage to all three places, but no serious injuries. The Loyalists then terrorised a group of Catholic schoolchildren when they raided a Primary School on the Springfield Road and planted a hoax bomb. The children were not to know that it was a dummy and most of them were later treated for shock.

PIG VERSUS TRANSIT VAN
Doug Hook, Royal Artillery

Whilst out on a foot patrol sometime in the early part of 1978 in North Belfast, contact (i.e. shots fired) was made with a patrol some three or four streets away. A cordon was set up to trap a vehicle seen at the shooting – a white Ford Transit van – and my patrol took up static positions at the top of Duncairn Gardens with a grand old Pig in support. We took up positions and waited and after what seemed like hours, the aforementioned transit van came into sight at the bottom of the road.

All weapons were now trained on the vehicle as it accelerated up towards us at considerable speed. Crouched in a doorway about 75 metres down from the top of the road, I heard the distinctive roar of the Pig as

its engine fired up. By this time the van had built up its speed and the Pig started to move slowly but steadily down the road – ominously in the direction of the van. The driver of the transit increased his speed to what seemed like 80 mph. Then, as if in slow motion, right in front of me the van hit the armoured vehicle head-on! Contrary to what you might imagine, the sound was not an almighty crash as I was expecting, but just a thud as the front of the van crumpled inwards to the position of the seats.

At this point I quickly assessed the possible threat – if any – from the van; no chance there. At this point I opened the Pig's passenger door to check on its driver, and fortunately the brave lad was ok. He had clearly suffered just a little whiplash and minor shock, but this was overridden by the adrenaline rush from what he had just done. Needless to say, all occupants in the Ford Transit van did not exactly jump out, and they were barely alive from the impact. I didn't see an ambulance arrive, but we found a nice little cache of weapons and ammo in the van.

The moral of this story is: never attempt to take on a Pig head-on and expect to walk away unscathed. When the army tells you to stop, you stop!

John Hume, then Deputy Leader of the Social Democratic and Labour Party (SDLP), said that the British Government should consider a third option in its search for a political solution to the conflict in Northern Ireland. The first option – of maintaining the status quo or further integration with Britain – was one which Nationalists believed the

Government had been following, and the second option was withdrawal from Northern Ireland, which was being advocated by many Nationalists. The third option was an 'agreed Ireland' where the British Government would declare that its objective was to bring the two main traditions in Ireland together in reconciliation and agreement.

On the 5th, a dramatic chase saw the arrest of three terrorists; the seizure of unprimed bombs; and probably the prevention of loss of life and damage to property. Armed men had seized a car in the Nationalist Short Strand, loaded it with explosives and then set off for an unknown destination. However, they were spotted by an RUC mobile patrol and chased. When cornered, they were arrested.

On the 7th, an inexcusable lack of security at Draperstown RUC Station in Co Londonderry almost led to the deaths of two policemen and what would have been a major coup for the Provisionals. The station in Main Street had an attached car park for police vehicles and this was penetrated overnight by a bombing team who planted a UVBT on a police car. Two officers got into the car and started the ignition and triggered the device. The car was blasted into pieces and surrounding property was badly damaged – and both officers were badly injured. Just a few hours later, PIRA was busy again – this time lying in wait for a postman in the hamlet of Rock close to Cookstown in Co Tyrone. Sergeant Jock B. Eaglesham (58), father of four, was also the local postman who gave his spare time to the UDR. He was delivering mail to a remote farmhouse when masked gunmen opened fire on his car with automatic weapons. He was hit twice in the chest and died almost immediately. He was one of two part-time UDR soldiers to be killed by the IRA in a 24-hour period.

On the following day the Provisionals stooped to another low when they killed UDR Corporal William J Gordon (41) and his daughter Lesley (10). Mr Gordon had just placed Lesley and her brother into the car and was preparing to drive them from his home in Maghera, Co Londonderry to their nearby school. As per SOP, he had checked underneath the car but must have missed the device. As he set off – watched from only a few feet away by his wife and their baby – the vehicle exploded. William and Lesley were killed instantly and his other son, Richard, was badly injured having been thrown clear of the car. Francis Hughes, a leading Provisional, was said to be behind the double murder. Some three years later, Hughes died whilst on hunger strike. His death was certainly unmourned by the Gordon family and their loved ones. He was shot and wounded the following month and imprisoned for 10 years.

On the 10th, eight schoolchildren and their driver had a most fortunate escape when, despite the certainty of the presence of children, the Provisionals planted a UVBT under a school bus driven by a UDR soldier. The bus had eight children on board and was driving between Ballymoney and Rasharkin in North Antrim. As the bus struck a ramp on the road, the device – weighing 10lbs – fell off and exploded. No-one was injured, but experts say that had the device exploded underneath the bus all on board were likely to have been killed or maimed. Could the Provisionals stoop any lower? The answer to that question was only days away. Another UDR part-timer came close to death just a few miles away from this incident. The soldier, who also worked as a farmer in Rasharkin, was in the process of opening a farm gate in order to drive his tractor through when an explosive device attached to the gate detonated. He was thrown to the ground by the blast but suffered only cuts and bruises.

In the bloody game of murderous tit-for-tat that was sectarianism, reprisals were not far behind and on the 12th, a UVF firebomb attack on the home of a Catholic family in the Oldpark Road area of North Belfast cost the lives of a grandmother and her young grandson. A Loyalist murder gang planted the device in a gas cylinder outside the home of Mary Smyth (70) in Oldpark Avenue and the blaze trapped them in the downstairs lounge. One of her sons – an ex-Internee for whom the bomb may have been intended – managed to jump from a bedroom window but his mother and his nephew, young Michael Scott (10), were burned to death. A photograph in the *Belfast Telegraph* shows an angelic-looking Michael in his school uniform; sacrificed on the un-Godly altar of sectarianism. The blaze spread to adjoining properties and a family of eight next door were pulled to safety by neighbours.

Over the course of the next two days, two more UDR soldiers died in circumstances which this author can only refer to as 'unknown causes'. On the 13th, Corporal John Hillis (38) died and the following day, Private Robert Reid (55) also died. He is buried at Christchurch Cemetery in Derriaghy near Lisburn.

Over the next several days, a series of PIRA bombs destroyed both commercial and industrial premises in Belfast and Londonderry as the seemingly endless economic warfare continued at a deadly pace. On the 16th, The *Belfast Newsletter* revealed a sensational PIRA plot to smuggle 100 expert snipers over the border in order to orchestrate a savage onslaught against troops and policemen. Intelligence experts had revealed an influx of American sniper rifles had been brought into the country – financed largely by the Irish-American NORAID – and that men were being honed in sniper skills in remote areas of Co Donegal in the Irish Republic.

On the evening of the 17th the Provisional IRA plumbed new depths of depravity that a few observers had predicted, but even fewer had dared to fear would happen. In a cowardly, murderous action for which even their most holier-than-thou apologist would struggle to find an excuse, they cold-bloodedly murdered 12 innocent people at a restaurant between Gransha and Castlereagh, Co Down. The vast majority of the dead were consumed by a napalm-like fireball which literally burned them to death where they stood or sat. An IRA unit planted an incendiary bomb attached to petrol-filled canisters on security grills outside the window of the Peacock Room of the La Mon House Hotel – located at Gransha, Co Down – about six miles southeast of central Belfast. The restaurant was packed with members of a Junior Motor Cycle Club and the Irish Collie Breeders Club. After planting the bomb, the bombers tried to send a warning from the nearest public telephone, but found that it had been vandalised. En route to find another, they were delayed again when forced to stop at a UDR VCP. By the time they were able to send the warning, only nine minutes remained before the bomb exploded at 21:00. The RUC base at Newtownards had received two further telephone warnings at 20:57 and 21:04, but by the time the latter call came in it was too late. When an officer telephoned the restaurant to issue the warning, he was told by a shocked and distraught member of staff: "For God's sake, get out here. A bomb has exploded!"

The device used was a small blast bomb attached to four large petrol canisters – each filled with a homemade napalm-like substance of petrol and sugar. The sugar would turn molten by the blast and was designed to stick to whatever it hit – a combination which caused severe burn injuries. The victims were found beneath a pile of hot ash and charred beyond recognition – making identity extremely difficult as all their individual human features had been completely burned away. Some of the bodies had shrunk so much in the intense heat that it was first believed that there were children among the victims. One doctor who saw the remains described them as being like ' ... .charred logs of wood ... .'

The following morning, the Saturday edition of the *Daily Express* cried: 'Disco Bomb Horror'. Positioned above the smiling face of the new *Doctor Who* companion, Derek Ogilvie wrote: "At least 14 (sic) people died as Ulster terrorist bombers struck at a packed teenage disco on the outskirts of Belfast. Shouting and screaming teenagers fled with their clothes on fire and others jumped from upstairs windows. Scores were rushed to hospital from the blazing building. The bomb exploded at the La Mon House country restaurant near Castlereagh where the Northern Ireland Junior Motor Cycle Club was holding its annual dance. The well-known nightspot was packed with 200 youngsters as well as people attending another function. Members' children were holding a fancy dress party in another part of the building. They were among some of the victims. One witness to last night's bomb attack said: 'The band had just struck up when there was an explosion at the back of the hall. A ball of flame spread across the room. Dozens of people, their clothes blazing, struggled to get clear.' Another said: 'I saw bodies being carried out. They looked like lumps of a log.' Another man said: 'When I arrived it didn't look too bad, but then people began being brought (out) without legs and arms. I saw some charred bodies; it was a terrible sight. There was nothing I could do.' Freelance photographer Bill Hammond said: 'There was terrible panic. At the main door, a number of people had been trampled in the rush to escape. I could hear screams from another part of the hotel where a number of people were thought to be trapped."

The first doctor to see the victims at the Ulster Hospital – Doctor Ronnie Armstrong – said he initially thought they were charred logs of wood. He had to stick his finger in two inches deep to realise they were human beings.

Hugh McGucken, Vice-Chairman of the Irish Collie Club, visited the survivors in hospital: "I walked into the ward and I'd never seen such faces, like big black footballs." His wife Irene said: "These were my friends, but I didn't recognise them. I knew Billy McDowell only by his voice. I started crying. I kept thinking how could human beings do this to other human beings? It was like being inside an incinerator plant. People said nothing or very little; they were in utter shock."

(Source: http://www.nuzhound.com/articles/Sunday_Tribune/arts2008/jan27_ thirty_years_on_La-Mon__SBreen.php)

As part of the Police investigation, 25 people were arrested in Belfast – including the man known to many squaddies as 'Teflon Man', Gerry Adams. However, he was released from custody in July 1978 and became President of Sinn Féin two months later. In September 1981 another Belfast man, Robert Murphy, was given 12 life sentences for the manslaughter of those who died. Murphy was freed on licence in 1995. As part of their bid to catch the bombers, the RUC passed out leaflets which displayed a graphic photograph of a victim's charred remains. Secretary of State for Northern Ireland, Roy Mason, described it as ' ... an act of criminal irresponsibility ... '

As a consequence of the botched attack, the PIRA Army Council gave strict instructions to all units not to bomb buses, trains or hotels – too little too late. One wonders how much celebration went on in Irish bars throughout the USA as it suddenly dawned on the naïve drinkers just exactly what their donated dollars for the 'folks back home' were actually purchasing. One suspects not much! Did the rattle of the donation tins in various Eastern seaboard Paddy's bars sound a little more like a death knoll as the news filtered through to the insular Irish-Americans? One wonders. This author wrote down these words through a veil of tears of anger – even allowing for the passage of 36 years since the atrocity.

Those who died – all Protestants – in the La Mon atrocity were: Thomas Neeson (52), father of three; Sandra Morris (27), mother of two; Christine Lockhart (32); Ian McCracken (25) and his wife Elizabeth (25); Sarah Wilson Cooper (62); Gordon Crothers (30), RUCR and his wife Joan (26), mother of one; Daniel Maghill (37); Carol Mills (27); Paul Nelson (37) and his wife Dorothy (35), mother of two. Twelve people – seven of them women – had died in the second worst atrocity of the Troubles involving civilians.

One of the survivors, Lily McDowell, told the *Sunday Tribune* on the 30th anniversary of the bombing: "It was about 9pm and we'd just finished our starter in the Peacock Room. There was a loud bang and then a huge fireball swept across the floor." She described how she and her husband headed for the exit and then: " … .beside us, a girl's hair caught fire and Billy took off his jacket to try and put it out. I lost my grip on him. I tried to escape by myself. I got down on my hands and knees – crawling along the floor. But then my way was blocked. I didn't know what by at first, but then I felt them – the dead bodies. I tried to climb over them but I couldn't. So I turned and went the other way. I'd inhaled so much smoke, I could hardly breathe. The lights went out. The room was black except for the flames. People started running and screaming – their clothes and hair ablaze. The smoke choked us. It was like a scene from hell. My hair was on fire and I was badly burned. I thought I was dying. 'Please God, let Billy live so there's somebody to take care of our sons', I whispered. I tried to say the 'Our Father'. I'd been saying it since I was a wee girl, but I couldn't remember the words. Then a voice in my head told me to be calm and try again. It all came back to me. I said the last 'Amen' and passed out."

Suzanne Breen in the *Sunday Tribune* continued: "Lily McDowell was the most seriously injured survivor. She suffered third-degree burns to half her body and spent three months in hospital – mostly on a water bed. She has had six operations, numerous skin grafts and two nervous breakdowns. The top of one arm was fused to her back and had to be surgically separated." Another survivor, Rita Morrison, described her experience: "It was like the sun exploding in front of my eyes. My husband Ernie and I were glued to the spot, but people pushed us towards the exit. When I got out, I couldn't find my daughter. I was screaming 'Elizabeth! Elizabeth! Where's my Elizabeth?'" Her daughter, Elizabeth McCracken, was amongst those killed.

The utter tragedy of La Mon had far wider-reaching consequences and Michael Stone, who I have condemned as a mad dog Loyalist killer in previous books, was apparently so overcome by the outrage that it set him on the path to joining the UDA/UFF and the Red Hand Commandos. It was a path which would culminate in the Milltown Cemetery massacre and the public lynching of two Signals' Corporals in Andersonstown in March 1988. In his self-serving autobiography *None Shall Divide Us* (John Blake Books, 2003), Stone writes of La Mon: "I was coming up to 23 when the IRA bombed the La Mon House Hotel in February 1978. I was horrified at the slaughter of innocent people caused by the blast, which came without warning. The La Mon bombing was an important step in a journey which would eventually lead me to the Republican Plot at Milltown Cemetery, almost 10 years later, with grenades around my waist and a browning in my hand.

'Twelve people were killed. Seven of the dead were women and there were three married couples amongst the toll. All the victims were attending the annual dinner dance of the Irish Collie Club. The hotel was packed with 400 people enjoying a Friday night out when the place was turned into a fireball after the IRA attached cans of petrol to the window grilles. The device ... .was designed to sweep the room like a flamethrower. As it went off, it blew out the window and sprayed the room with blazing petrol, which had been mixed with sugar to make sure it stuck to whatever it touched. The people inside didn't stand a chance. Some stumbled out of the hotel or jumped out of the windows with their hair, skin and clothes on fire." Stone managed to bluff his way into the grounds of the hotel and walked past RUC officers and firefighters and came across an object covered by a sheet of tarpaulin. He continues: "I gently pulled back one cover and quickly replaced it. It was an horrific sight. What I saw in those five seconds has stayed with me for the rest of my life. I can only describe it as looking like a lump of charred wood. I couldn't tell what gender the person was; there were no limbs and what was left of the face was a mouth wide open in a silent scream ... . I could feel anger rising in the pit of my stomach. I wanted revenge. I wanted retribution of a similar kind. I was burning with rage and hatred for the people who had done this. I wanted the Republican community to pay dearly for this atrocity." (page 54/5)

The Royal Green Jackets – still getting over the shock of the IRA mortar attack at Forkhill the previous month – were dealt another body blow by the loss of their popular commanding officer, Lieutenant-Colonel Ian Corden-Lloyd (39) and father of three, in what was thought to have been a helicopter accident. Another officer was seriously injured in the 'crash' but later recovered from his injuries. It was a widely held view that the Provisionals had long had the technology to bring down an aircraft, but it was thought on this occasion that it had been mechanical failure. Naturally a delighted spokesman for the IRA claimed that they had shot it down, but it was denied by both the MOD and HQNI. For many years the British Army denied the claim before finally acknowledging that the IRA had indeed caused the crash some years later. The helicopter came down near Jonesborough, Co Armagh having taken off shortly before from Bessbrook Mill. The official version was that the crew were taking evasive action after coming under fire and crashed when it lost control. The popular officer had been awarded the MC six years earlier for his bravery in the Province. He received a funeral with full military honours at Magdalene Hill Cemetery, close to the Jackets' spiritual home in Winchester.

SUNRAY DOWN!
Dave Pomfrett, 2nd Battalion, Royal Green Jackets
Early morning on 17 February 1978, 11 Platoon, 2nd Royal Green Jackets were laid up in an ambush on a hill overlooking a country lane somewhere in South Armagh. INT had suggested that this was to be the site of a PIRA IVCP. We were there all day, bored to hell, but nobody spoke or took the piss, which was difficult for the 'Chosen Men'. We knew that we had players nearby but no-one saw them, but we knew they would be there.

I am not sure of the timings, but at some stage a radio message was received and almost simultaneously we saw two helicopters fly past very low and very fast. The radio operator, who I think was 'Hubby' Hubbard, signalled to our Full Screw – Dave Judge – and, following further radio transmissions, cover was broken and Dave spoke two words which made us go cold; two words that I will never forget: 'Sunray Down' – and I think I could see a tear in his eye. We looked around for someone to make sense of it. However, we all knew what it meant, but we were hoping it was wrong or a drill. In silence we moved off in our bricks and I'm not sure what came next, but what I do know is there was mostly silence and no idle chat.

It was a very sad day and one of my clearest memories was of a British scout helicopter facing down a helicopter from the Irish Army – bearing in mind we were just a field away, one dry stone wall away, from the country of Eire. Like a little bulldog, the Scout was pushing forward – pushing back the bigger Sud Aviation 'Aérospatiale Alouette' helicopter as we were trying to look after our colonel – our boss – the great man that Colonel Ian was. The Irish Alouette finally gave up and flew away, although I think that the colonel's body had been taken away before our arrival.

We bashered up and brewed up later and I think stayed the night to babysit the wreckage. I think that soon after sunrise the wreckage was airlifted from the site and flown away, although my memory is not that clear on this. I do have a vision of a Wessex lifting the wrecked Gazelle. I saw Mr Schofield, who was injured in the crash, last year at the Cenotaph – marching with the Green Jackets ... still bearing his scars of that day. It was sad to hear that Sergeant Ives, the pilot that day in South Armagh, lost his own life in another helicopter crash just a few years later. This is just MY memory of this day – the day a great man lost his life; a man who is still to this day spoken of in reverence by those who knew him and by those who wish they had.

The author endorses fully the eloquent words of Dave Pomfrett; RIP, Ian Douglas Corden-Lloyd, MC – *Celer et Audux.*

One of the soldiers in the helicopter when it crashed, as stated earlier, was Captain (later Lieutenant-Colonel) Philip Schofield. Despite the anguish of his personal memories, I am most grateful to him for the following comments:

THE DEATH OF THE CO
Philip Schofield, MBE, Royal Green Jackets

It was 4.30pm on 17 February 1978. "41 Echo, Contact, wait, out." The voice of Fred Ramsden came over 'C' Company and COP nets. Sergeant Ramsden and four men – Corporal Ian 'Oscar' Ward, Riflemen Phil Vaughan, Gower and Rod Babbins – were hidden deep in the thick undergrowth of the walled garden of a Vicarage at the southern end of Jonesborough. The border with the Irish Republic ran a few hundred yards to the east of the Vicarage along the March Wall, which a mile or so further south turned west. The local Green Jacket rifle company was 'C' Company in Forkhill, commanded by Major Christopher Myers. The purpose of the OP was to monitor and observe the Edenappa Road running out of Jonesborough which the IRA used to mount illegal VCPs. IVCPs were normally done in the short, early evenings and from behind the Vicarage wall the riflemen could observe the road whilst being hidden by day. The OP would be within rifle and LMG range and able to deal with any IRA incident.

2 RGJ's CO, Colonel Corden-Lloyd, was going home on his four-day R&R the next day (Saturday, 18 February) and myself – Captain Schofield, the Close Observation Platoon (COP) commander – was due to go on leave on Monday, 21

February before being posted to a NI surveillance organisation (name deleted) for two years. The ops room immediately re-called a helicopter that had just taken off from Bessbrook and Colonel Ian and myself ran down to the helicopter pad to meet it as it returned. Off stepped Captain Tom Hamilton-Baillie, who was about to take the COP over from me. He had been on his way to 'I' Company in Newtonhamilton to be briefed.   Having been listening to the net, he was aware of what was going on and that it was a COP contact. Tom asked if he could accompany us, but the pilot had only enough fuel for two passengers and Colonel Ian refused the request.

It took us just over six minutes to get to the contact site. I was carrying my rifle (an Armalite) in case the helicopter put down and I joined the patrol on the ground. Colonel Ian only had his lap strap done up. I knew exactly where the OP was and the Gazelle flew slowly along the March Wall – about 300 yards east of it at about 50 feet – trying to identify the IRA firing positions. Sergeant Brian Ives, the pilot, was young and inexperienced but did as he was ordered. About half a mile away, the ARF (Airborne Reaction Force) scout helicopter was laying off watching what was going on. It contained the regimental medical officer, Captain Chris Box, and the three-man ARF patrol provided by 13 Platoon, 'D' Company, from 2LI comprised of Corporal John Speight, Lance-Corporal Paddy Moran and Private Josh Lay – the GPMG Gunner. At the same time a covert, plain-clothes RUC police patrol from Forkhill was driving up the Edenappa Road towards Jonesborough. At this point, the official report takes over:

"The Gazelle got to the point where it had to turn back. According to the ARF Scout, a burst of tracer came up from across the border and the Gazelle rose to 150 feet. The helicopter, avoiding the tracer fire, carried out a fast evasive manoeuvre – during which the pilot may have made an error. It appeared to stall before falling and hitting the ground. It bounced, was seen to cartwheel, hit a stone wall and landed in another field on its right side. The IRA confirmed to the press the next day that they had been firing at the helicopter, but there was no evidence that the helicopter had been hit.

The first men on the scene were the two men in plain clothes running up from the road. One was a RUC policeman (name deleted) and the other was Sergeant Welling from 'C' Company, 2RGJ. The area round it was covered in aviation fuel, debris and live rounds of ammunition that had spilled from the weapon carried on board. The pilot was underneath trapped by the battery pack but protected by his helmet. Lieutenant-Colonel Corden-Lloyd was still strapped in his seat with his head lying to the right. Captain Schofield had been catapulted from the rear seat where he had been sitting on the floor and had a deep wound to the centre of his forehead. The two men were in civilian clothes and neither the terrorists nor Close Observation Platoon team members knew who they were; consequently both sides were firing at them. Although the team was under heavy and continuous fire at the time, Captain Schofield was quickly removed to the cover of a ditch a few feet from the crash site.

The ARF scout arrived and the ARF patrol and the two men in plain clothes helped to remove the colonel from his seat and carried him to the ditch where the RMO and the medical staff made an initial assessment of the injuries. The

4

colonel was already dead. The ARF had to take cover a couple of times as the fire from PIRA was still intense and they couldn't fire back due to the amount of spilled AVGAS around the crash site. The remainder of the 2LI ARF Platoon arrived in a Wessex helicopter. The platoon had been ordered to stop carrying knives on their webbing a few days before and so had difficulty cutting the pilot out of the webbing straps on the aircraft. They lifted the main wreckage of the helicopter whilst one policeman went underneath to unstrap the pilot's helmet. The pilot was then pulled free from the wreckage. Following the crash, firing continued along the border as the terrorists extricated themselves.

The Close Observation Platoon OP provided covering fire until they were able to join the others on the crash site. By the time they got there, Captain Schofield and Sergeant Ives and the body of Colonel Corden-Lloyd had been evacuated to the Military Wing, Musgrave Park Hospital, Belfast in the Wessex helicopter – arriving there 30 minutes later. Lieutenant-Colonel Ian Corden-Lloyd was confirmed dead on arrival."

Philip Schofield

Lieutenant-Colonel McDermott FRCS, the consultant surgeon at the Musgrave Park Hospital, summarised my injuries in his report which was dated the same day: Depressed skull fracture with cerebral contusion; fracture of right elbow; fracture of spine; contusion of kidneys; multiple contusions and minor abrasions and fracture of three teeth. He wrote: "Permanent disability is likely. The prognosis of this severe combination is not good in terms of future military service. The head injury may result in some permanent intellectual deficit and problems with double vision. The spine and elbow fractures may be the cause of future disability." The injuries to Sergeant Ives are not recorded here.

An incident occurred after I had been evacuated. I wasn't there, but George Coney refers to an OP near H24 close to 'Slab' Murphy's farm. He was with Riflemen Danny Bosworth, Colin Harris and Richard 'Polly' Parrott. I think 2RGJ Close Observation Platoon had been set up and it involved a 28-minute contact with at least 12 enemy gunmen who were dressed in combat uniform.

'THAT DAY'
George Coney, Royal Green Jackets
Myself, Riflemen 'Polly' Parrot, Colonel Harris and Danny Bosworth – members of 2 RGJ's Close Observation Platoon – had been tasked to carry out an OP on 'Slab' Murphy's farm, which was located on the border crossing. I should point out that Murphy was known to have participated in several attacks on the SF, which resulted in the deaths of British soldiers. The objective of the OP was to gather information on the man so that his routine could be established and also to try and ascertain the number of men in his location. We were dropped off 2km from the objective and moved in and set up the OP on the top floor of an abandoned farmhouse about 500 metres from the objective. By 1800 hours the OP was up and running so I sent Danny and Col out to carry out a perimeter check prior to night falling. At approx. 1800 hours I received a radio call from Danny saying that there were armed men in the corner of the field he was in; they were wearing

black berets. I recalled them both to the farmhouse, but before they could get back it came under heavy and sustained gunfire from several firing points. 'Polly' was giving covering fire from the north-facing window, while at the same time getting him to call in a contact report. Whilst he attempted to radio this in, I was on the floor firing my Bren gun towards the south from the open doorway. By now, Danny and Col had got back to the farmhouse and were taking up positions on the ground floor covering the open farmyard. At this time, there was incoming small arms from multiple firing points, which lasted for approximately 28 minutes, until it slowed and stopped. I believe that this was because the Quick Reaction Force (QRF) were advancing clearing hedge lines with M79 rounds. During the firefight, we could hear the PIRA men shouting instructions to one another as our positions were very close.

Following our extraction back to base we were debriefed and in the days that followed, members of an undercover unit went back to the contact area and confirmed that there had been 24 IRA firing positions – and from the empty cases it showed that they were using 45, 9mm rounds and belt-fed 7.62. We did not claim any kills, although blood trails were found leading south; it was just another day in South Armagh.

Gerry Adams, then Vice-President of Sinn Féin, was charged with membership of the Provisional IRA. On 6 September 1978 Adams was freed when the judge hearing the case ruled that there was insufficient evidence to prove that he was a member of the IRA. This decision left many soldiers and policemen shaking their heads in disbelief. It is not recorded if later, men in white coats took the learned judge away for treatment. This author recommends that the reader peruses the words of Adams' closest comrade, Brendan 'The Dark' Hughes (1948-2008), in Ed Maloney's *Voices from The Grave*.

On the 20th, the IRA firebombed the Ulsterbus depot in Londonderry City after a gang of masked gunmen forced staff out and planted bombs. Over 30 buses were either damaged or severely damaged by the blaze, which cost over £1 million worth of damage. On Wednesday 22nd, a massive outbreak of public grief and sympathy greeted the funerals of some of the victims of the La Mon House atrocity. Belfast Airport closed for an hour and many factories – including the giant GEC – saw their workforce down tools in protest against the IRA's grotesque actions. There was a very well-observed five-minute silence throughout the Province – even in some Nationalist areas.

Four days later, an RUC officer came close to death as he drove past Creggan Bridge near Crossmaglen when a concealed landmine was detonated by remote control. An IRA bombing team – watching from concealed hillside positions close to the Irish border – detonated the device which, when it exploded, blew the RUC vehicle over and into a ditch. The officer escaped with cuts and bruises.

FACE TO FACE WITH THE IRISH ARMY
Gary Weeks, Royal Engineers
We were on what was termed 'Border Crossing-Denial' detail with my troop. We were putting in ancient Braithwaite tanks and filling them with concrete on the Irish border in Co Londonderry. We were right on the line – between north and

south – and were just fucking about, jumping into the south and back again, when all of a sudden this 'bush' in the south spoke to us!

He was telling us to watch out because the Gardai were close by and they would arrest us! Upon a closer examination, the 'bush' was a lad about the same age as us in green fatigues with an SLR rifle and belt order. We were just, what the Irish call, 'yarning' with him when the food wagons with the hay boxes for dinner turned up. It was fish and chips. We told the lad in the bush that we were off for scran and asked him what he was doing for something to eat.

He shrugged his shoulders resignedly and told us that sometime later a van would turn up on their side and they could go and buy some sarnies. Buy? We said 'fuck that' and went and got him a pack of fish and chips, which we threw to him. Suddenly all these other bushes started asking for some, so off we go and got more and throw them over, so they came out of cover to grab the food. So there we were, all young lads, different uniforms on each side of the border, eating fish and chips; surreal because we were just the same.

Just then, one called out that the guards were coming so back into the bushes – rifles pointing at us and our infantry guys pointing theirs at them. Makes you think, because the locals used to come and dig these tanks out before the concrete even dried. So a section of infantry would man an OP to stop them fucking with it; talk about being a 'goat staked out for the tiger'. I will never forget the look of those lads coming out of the OP – their eyes on stalks and edgy as fuck. It later turned out that all the Irish Army boys knocked off at 7 and went home!

As the month drew to a close, the army was accused once more of a shoot to kill policy when undercover soldiers shot two IRA men in a farm shed at Ardboe, Co Tyrone as they removed weapons from an arms cache. One of the PIRA men, Paul Duffy (21), was the nephew of a prominent SDLP politician and was a member of the East Tyrone Brigade of the IRA. He was shot dead and his comrade badly wounded. The wounded IRA man was taken under heavy guard to the Mid Ulster Hospital in Magherafelt. When this author first picked up an empty SLR 7.62mm, he was given some sound advice by his Weapons Instructor and that was to aim at the biggest body mass; don't point it unless you intend to fire; and shoot before your enemy does. Under ROE in Northern Ireland and in all combat zones involving the British Army, an individual soldier may fire if he feels that his life or the lives of his comrades are under threat. The Provisional IRA, the INLA and the Official IRA all shot to kill without hesitation and the concept of disarming a man and taking him a prisoner is both alien to them and certainly not in their 'Green Book'. The Republican and Loyalist terrorists shot to kill; so too did the men who were defending the public safety, but to protect life – not take it.

SHOOT TO KILL
Corporal 'A', Royal Green Jackets

You asked me to comment on the so-called shoot to kill policy. Well how else does one shoot? We didn't shoot to wound and we certainly were never trained to shoot the weapons out of the terrorists' hands; you want that, then go watch a cowboy film! What I will say is that we arrested scumbags like Adams, Meehan – both Martin and Seanie – Steenson, McGlinchey, Dessie O'Hare, Brendan Hughes and that other bleeder, Patrick Hughes, and we took them into custody and they went to court. Ok, so the courts let them go, but tell me this: if we had a shoot to kill policy, why didn't we slot those bastards?

On the 25th, the Vanguard Unionist Progressive Party (VUPP) was dissolved as a political party and most of the party's members joined the Ulster Unionist Party (UUP). According to the Standing Committee of Irish Catholic Bishops Conference the vast majority of Irish people wanted the conflict in Northern Ireland to end.

On the 27th, the Mountainview Tavern was again attacked by the Provisionals. The bar, which stands on the Shankill Road, is close to the Shankill Somme Association Memorial and was the scene of an earlier bomb and gun attack in April 1975 (see Chapter 4). On a visit in 2012, the author was taken into the bar for a quick drink and was later surprised to be informed that a member of the notorious Shankill Butchers was standing, watching me intently, just a few feet away. On this occasion, masked gunmen burst into the pub carting a bomb, which they placed on the floor of the bar and ordered staff and customers into the back. They grabbed the takings and ran out – and the resulting explosion wrecked the bar again. There were no injuries this time.

The final incident of this depressing month cost the life of another policeman: Constable Charles Simpson (26), father of three. An RUC mobile patrol, consisting of two Land Rovers, was on Francis Street and had just started to make the turn into Clarendon Street on the periphery of the Creggan Estate in Londonderry. As they did so, PIRA gunmen opened fire from behind a wall – hitting the RUC officer in the head and wounding one of his comrades. He was rushed to Altnagelvin Hospital but died shortly after admission. He was the second policeman to die this month after a lull of several fatality-free months.

The Constable had only been a full-time officer for a year – following three years in the RUCR – and had three sons aged five and under. When the gunmen had opened fire there were a number of children almost in the line of fire – and they had been forced to throw themselves to the ground in order to escape the hail of bullets. The mother of the children said: "It was the most callous thing to shoot when children were about. Some of my children knew to lie down, but my two girls just ran screaming as the bullets were flying …. It lasted several minutes and the noise was terrible. I could only lie flat on the floor of my hallway and scream with fear."

February had been a bloody month, but for the near-misses and narrow escapes it could have been the worst month since 1975. In all, 25 people died; the army lost six soldiers and two policemen were killed – including one in the La Mon House atrocity. A total of 16 civilians were killed – comprising 14 Protestants and two Catholics – amongst whom, taking the religion of the dead in the La Mon into consideration, 11 of the deaths were overtly sectarian. One Republican terrorist died. Republicans killed 19 people this month and Loyalists killed two.

March

S even people would die this month – including four soldiers – and it would witness the shameful sight of an IRA gunman chasing after an unarmed civilian helper and shooting her dead in a shop doorway in Belfast City Centre.

A photograph in early March on the front of the *Belfast Newsletter* showed wrecked buildings which resembled street scenes in Berlin in the April of 1945. Just as Soviet shells and Katyusha rockets and RAF bombs had pounded the city to dust, so too had the Provisional IRA attempted to bomb Belfast back to the Stone Age. The month began with the death of a soldier from the Royal Artillery and as the Troubles continued unabated and entered its 100th month, he became the 48th soldier from this regiment to die in or as a consequence of the problems which were besetting Northern Ireland.

Gunner Paul Sheppard (20) was a married soldier and lived on the Isle of Wight. He was part of a Royal Artillery foot patrol on Cliftonpark Avenue – en route for Girdwood Barracks. As the patrol left Manor Street and neared the junction with Cliftonpark Avenue, an IRA gun team – who had taken an elderly woman hostage – opened fire with an American M60 heavy machine gun. The M60 is a member of the 'family' of American general-purpose machine guns and fired 7.62mm rounds from a disintegrating belt of M13 links. There are several types of live ammunition approved for use in the M60 including ball, tracer and armour-piercing rounds. It is capable of firing 40+ rounds in a three-second burst. Gunner Sheppard was hit several times in the chest and died very quickly at the scene. A shocked eye witness said: "I had just passed some soldiers in Manor Street. Suddenly there was a burst of gunfire and bullets were just bouncing off the walls." The IRA unit – with the willing complicity of their supporters – escaped from the vicinity and spirited the weapon away. It was a heavy weapon – weighing almost 2 stone (12.7 kgs) – and a wheelbarrow was used to ferry it away. Eighteen months later, the same weapon which killed Gunner Sheppard and several other soldiers was captured by the army on the Antrim Road. One soldier told the author that for months afterwards, there were a lot of bullet strike marks across the road where the heavy-calibre rounds had landed. When, in 2012 I stood on almost the same spot as the young Artillery man was shot, the passage of almost 34 years and numerous resurfacings had eroded the marks; all visible evidence of his passing had been removed.

THE DEATH OF A GUNNER
Keith Page, Royal Artillery

'Jock', our brick commander, was a bit of a character and so were the other two blokes. He had already done a couple of tours and told us that once whilst out in the 'Cuds' (rural locations), when they got to the location it wasn't a nice sight; a body was lying in some undergrowth with a gaping wound in it. He didn't need to explain to anyone what an exit wound from a 7.62 high-velocity round looked like. He was a bit of a character and there wasn't anything that he wasn't into!

Looking out from a sangar at Kinnard Street, with the Antrim
Road visible, Belfast, 1979. (Mark 'C')

He even got us into drinking at this Loyalist shebeen – a drinking den. Only one pint per visit, but we all clambered down some dark steps – uniformed and with our SLRs slung over our shoulders. It was old and smoky and you couldn't swing a dead cat in there! It was alright at first but soon, after about four visits, we were told to sling our hooks and not come back.

There were a few other things happened on the tour which I won't go into – other people can if they wish – but you would have the MOD down on you like a ton of bricks! There were the endless cordons for car bombs and house searches and bumping into the sneaky beakies – the undercover soldiers who were covertly watching known players.

We spent some time in the Ardoyne – a real shithole of a place. Street after street of terraced houses and savagely Republican and pro-IRA. I would like to say something in memory of Gunner Paul Sheppard, who was killed in a gun battle on 1 March 1978. He was out on a mobile patrol when they came under heavy machine gun fire attack from PIRA gunmen. Myself, 'B.R.', 'Johno' and another lad called 'Jed' were doing a 48-hour stint in an OP. Johno incidentally, was to die tragically a couple of years later. You needed a breather every now and then and this time in the OP – doing 'P' checks on the radio etc – gave us that respite.

Then, out of the blue one morning, a call came through from our ops room in Flax Street Mill – crashing us out of the OP to cut the road off outside, There had been a contact and we had to stop and search the cars coming through. Rumours fly thick and fast and we knew that we had lost one of our mates; we just didn't know whom at that stage. It was only when we got back to Flax Street that we found out that it was a mate of Jed's – in fact, his best mate, Paul Sheppard.

Jed was very close to both Paul and his wife and he was devastated at the loss. My Troop Commander (TC) instructed me to watch out for Jed whenever we were out on patrol and make sure that he was careful and didn't get provoked by the locals. We were both 'tail-end Charlies' and naturally we did watch each other's backs. Back then, you were given a 72-hour R&R pass so that you could fly home and just recharge your batteries. I was due for a pass, but my TC called me over again and asked me if I would let Jed take my R&R. It didn't always end up as a rest, and on my previous one I got up to all sorts of mischief and might have been better staying in Belfast! Anyway I agreed without hesitation and Jed flew home to spend some time with Paul's wife. When he came back, he was a pitiful sight and my heart went out to the pair of them at their loss.

Just a few weeks before that contact, our brick was out on a foot patrol in the Ardoyne when of the local hard men – the top player in the area – shouted over the road to us: "Keep your heads down, boys!" If he'd have come out with a comment like that after Paul's death, I wouldn't like to even speculate on what Jed would have done to him – and he wouldn't have cared about the consequences. Even though Jed would have been in big trouble, I couldn't and wouldn't have done a thing to try and stop him. I might even have been tempted myself. It seemed to me that it was just one-way traffic all the time, and I was getting a bit fed up with it to be honest. I can only say that for the rest of the tour Jed was professional and stayed strong.

Looking out over the Ardoyne. (©Brian Sheridan)

North of Jamaica Street, Belfast. (©Brian Sheridan)

I have neglected to mention something: In the incident when Paul was killed, during the ensuing gun battle one of the blokes in the patrol saved the day by very aggressively returning fire. We heard at the time that there was a chance he was going to get mentioned in dispatches, but I've looked at the date at the time and he is not there. I think the bravery of a lot of soldiers in Northern Ireland went officially unrecorded.

I was almost in trouble one night when we were crashed out to some shops on the outskirts of the Ardoyne. I was about 10 metres away from this shop window when I heard a sort of 'vooming' noise. When I looked around, there were two incendiary devices going up. I was lucky they weren't explosive devices. There were two other deaths on the tour when the UVF made bomb attacks on two houses – killing a young boy and an elderly woman.

The last thing I remember was as we were leaving Lurgan in the four-tonner on the way to Aldergrove Airport to fly back to Germany. I was hanging out the back of the lorry waving a big flag of the Red Hand of Ulster. I was still young and caught up in it all.

GUNNER PAUL SHEPPARD
Mark Shaw, Royal Artillery
It's been so long since that fateful day when the sniper's bullets took your young life away. I have spent so many days asking why and so many nights I just sit and cry. I feel the guilt of coming back and in passing, my mind still remembers that fateful day. I will never forget you – my brother and comrade – nor will I forget the price that you paid forever in passing. Until we meet once again, I will always have the memory of your passing; the tears and the pain.

On 3 March, Norma Spence – a civilian searcher employed by the RUC – and Trooper James Nowasad of the Royal Tank Regiment were both shot dead by IRA gunmen in Lower Donegall Street, Belfast. Norma Spence (25) and Trooper Nowasad (21) were working in the city centre during a Rag Day event from Queen's University. The soldier, a married man from Fifeshire, was shot dead by gunmen in masks masquerading as students. The same men then chased Miss Spence, who was unarmed, and shot her down in cowardly fashion. Eyewitnesses stated that one of the gunmen, dressed as an Arab, walked up to the young Tankie and the soldier smiled at him. Seconds later the cowardly assassin pulled out a pistol and shot him dead at almost point-blank range. Ms Spence, who had no way of protecting herself, ran towards Church Street and she was hit three times and collapsed into a shop doorway. Her heroic killer, a man Republican apologists would call a 'soldier', stood over her to finish her off. The killers then ran off to their stolen car, which they later abandoned in Baltic Avenue in the Newington area of North Belfast. The following day, the *Glasgow Herald* under the headline: 'Fancy Dress Gunmen Kill Girl and Scots Soldier', ran the following: "The area – near the city's Cathedral – was sealed off and traffic diverted away from the main thoroughfare. Carnival atmosphere changed to shock and horror. A Students' Union spokesman said: 'I think it is terrible that the gunmen should use Rag Day as a front to kill those people.' Trooper Nowasad had been married for 18 months. His wife stayed at his unit's base in Münster, West Germany when he was sent to Northern Ireland three weeks ago for a four-month tour of duty. His father, Mr George Nowasad, who served in the army during the Second World War said: 'James joined the army as a boy soldier when he was only 15. He served in Northern Ireland last year for four months. He didn't want to go there, but he was a soldier and it was his duty. The trouble now is soldiers don't know what they are fighting for or who is the enemy. I don't know how people can kill without a reason. You need a reason."

Norma Spence's brother was due to marry the following day and following a shortened ceremony, the wedding reception and honeymoon were cancelled as the groom left to attend his sister's funeral. At her funeral, 2,000 students from Queen's University marched behind her coffin in silent protest.

'RAG DAY' SHOOTING IN BELFAST
Sergeant Murdo Macleod, Sergeant 4th Royal Tank Regiment

James 'Nifty' Nowasad was a friend of mine and I was also a good friend of the soldier who was on the sangar duties with James that day. His name was Trooper Ralph Anderson and he is the soldier in the picture which the Daily Record printed the following day – showing him sitting on the pavement with his head bowed in shock! Ralph recounted the day's event to us. He told us that the centre was busy with the Rag Day event and that he was located at the front of the public sangar when the terrorists arrived dressed as Arabs. James Nowasad was at the rear of the sangar providing protection for the civvie search staff, which included Norma. They passed by Ralph and started throwing flour, which was their 'good-natured' way of showing their annoyance to those who did not donate. This distraction was used for one of the terrorists to pull out a revolver and he shot James through the head. Panic immediately took place with everyone trying to get out of the shelter. Ralph recalled hearing the shot and reacted, but had difficulty raising his weapon. At this stage the terrorist was firing his second shot, which caught Norma in the wrist as she ran outside, but the bullet went through her wrist into her neck. She collapsed approximately 20 yards from the sangar on the street and very quickly died of her wound.

The gunmen then ran back out the way they had entered – with the crowd in absolute panic. Ralph recalls getting one round off, which missed one of the assailants (I think the round was later discovered lodged in the door of the Church across the road). Tragically, he then had a blockage on his SLR and by then they had escaped. Ralph stated he was in total shock and just sat down on the pavement with his rifle on the ground beside him. He could see that James was dead and everything around him became a blur until the other patrols came to assist – but by then it was too late. He always felt remorse for the stoppage which he encountered, but as we all know it happens to the best and was just a tragic circumstance. It is a tragic story and something Ralph has had to bear ever since.

I was a young 18-year-old in the same troop as James, who was a soldier who left a big impact on us during my first tour in Northern Ireland as part of City Centre Squadron. He was a well-respected lad and his death in the Rag Day shooting incident was a shock for us all. I will always remember that day. My troop was taken off patrol after the incident and we were all sitting in the canteen in deadly silence. Some were weeping and there was lots of internal reflection going on as

Civilian searchers, Belfast, 1979. (©Mark 'C')

to what had occurred. We all felt some shame! We had lost a comrade and a mother and child had lost a husband and father!

In those days there was no counselling for those affected by the trauma of losing someone whom you held as a family member in a troop. We were given 24 hours off and then it was back to what we had to do as professionals on the streets of Belfast. I recall after leaving Belfast – when our tour was over – that I spent the first weekend in London and I was passing St Paul's Cathedral and I went in to leave a prayer to him and his family. I remember signing the 'In Memory' book, which was located in the building for visitors to leave their remarks. I simply wrote the following words: "To James 'Nifty' Nowasad; murdered by the PIRA, 3 March 1978 Rag Day shooting, Belfast. Will never be forgotten."

(The author stood proudly on the steps of that hallowed building in September 2008 along with his partner Helen – alongside fellow writer and Royal Artilleryman Tim Francis – to commemorate the fallen of Op Banner.)

In 2004, I revisited Belfast and took time away from my friends to re-walk down the street where James was shot that day. The whole area has changed; gone are the shops on the left, which are now a public car park. I sat for 10 minutes, just staring at the area, reflecting back on that day. It left a strange feeling; the loss of two good people and yet there was nothing to signify them giving their lives to protect others. I wondered was it all worth it? Two people with families who never saw each other again, and what for? I must admit it left us angry and sad at the same time.

Today in the UK we have political correctness pushed in our face by those who don't understand; we have British businesses banning staff from wearing Poppies in our own communities and young children being told they can't wear their fathers' medals at community events because it may offend!

We are in sad times Ken!

In 2011, the Provisional IRA apologised for the killing of all *'non-combatants'* who died during its campaign of terror. In a statement, which bore all their usual piety and hand-wringing, the Republican terror group offered its ' *... .sincere apologies and condolences* ... .' to the families of victims during 30 years of violence. At the same time it said it acknowledged the grief and pain of the families of the combatants – police, soldiers and Loyalist paramilitaries – killed during the violence. It is estimated that they killed nearly 2,000 people during its terror campaign – close on 650 of them civilians. One wonders if this included Norma Spence; it certainly didn't include young Nowasad.

The day after the 'Rag Day murders' a foot patrol of 2 RGJ were in the town of Crossmaglen when they spotted an Irish tricolour atop a telegraph pole in the Town Centre close to the Parochial House. This was an illegal act and Rifleman Nicholas 'Nicky' Smith (20) was ordered to shin up the pole and remove it. Unknown to the soldiers, PIRA had booby-trapped the flag with a deadly explosive device and as the young Jacket tugged it, it exploded – killing him instantly and throwing his shattered body to the ground. Another soldier standing beneath his comrade was also badly injured in the blast. Immediately afterwards, gunmen with automatic weapons opened fire on the shocked survivors, who returned fire and the gunmen ran off. Rifleman Smith was from Battersea, London and his funeral was held at Putney Vale Crematorium in Wandsworth. He was the 19th Green Jacket to die in Northern Ireland.

NICKY SMITH
Bernie Parker, Royal Green Jackets
It was a brick from 7 Platoon, 'B' Company. The brick commander was called Foster, but I can't remember his first name. Also in the brick were Riflemen Kelly Herbert, Paul Thomas and – of course – Nick Smith. I was back at base when they were out on foot patrol. I remember being in the TV room at the time. We all heard the explosion followed by a long burst of gunfire. We heard almost immediately that we had lost a man from the contact report.

Once all had settled down and the patrol had returned to base, we found out that their Saracen had parked next to a telegraph pole which had a tricolour flying from it and Nicky climbed onto the 'Sarry' to pull it down for a souvenir, but it was booby-trapped. Rifleman Herbert, having just seen his best mate blown up, fired off a belt of 50 rounds in pure anger – although it was not aimed at anyone. I also pulled a tricolour from a telegraph pole a week or so before and have often felt that it could have easily been me. Also I have felt guilt as I may have helped set a pattern; that part still eats at me to this day.

Two days later, an RUC Land Rover driving along Boucher Road in West Belfast came under automatic fire from hidden PIRA gunmen. Over 20 shots were fired from gunmen in Rodney Parade, but although several of the rounds hit the police vehicle, none of the three officers were wounded. Just moments later, a joint army/RUC patrol in Woodstock Road, East Belfast came under fire also from PIRA gunmen. At around the same time, shots were fired at Mountpottinger RUC Station in Ballymacarrat, Belfast and there was a brief fire fight in Keady, South Armagh when a Green Jacket patrol came under fire. There were no injuries. The Jackets were again in action just 48 hours later when over 200 rounds were expounded in a gun battle with the Provisionals in the border area around Cooldeery, Crossmaglen. The soldiers were in a covert OP in a derelict house some 400 yards from the border when they came under fire. A later search on both sides of the border failed to catch any of the terrorists. A day of several actions ended when an IRA gunman opened fire on an army foot patrol at Glen Road, Andersonstown and a soldier was wounded. Schoolchildren in a nearby school had to dive for cover as some of the gunman's shots hit their playground.

The following day, a two-man IRA team tricked their way into a house in Gransha Park on the Turf Lodge and held the two female occupants as hostages whilst they set up a firing point in one of the bedrooms. As a foot patrol returned to Fort Monagh army base, one of the gunmen opened fire with an automatic weapon and one soldier was struck in the chest and badly wounded. At least 18 shots were fired. The two IRA men escaped through the back and melted away into the Nationalist estate. Shortly after this incident, over in Armoy, Co Antrim the Provisionals attempted to blow up a sub post office. Three armed men burst into Drumdollagh Post Office and fired three shots into the ceiling before planting an explosive device and escaping in a stolen car. An extremely brave member of staff carried the device into the street where it exploded just seconds later. The staff member was unhurt, but there was some damage to the exterior of the building.

SEXUAL COMFORTS IN 'BANDIT COUNTRY'
Ken Pettengale, 2nd Battalion, Royal Green Jackets

When I was sent out for my first tour of Northern Ireland in 1978, I was a gobby 19-year-old from the East End of London. My battalion had been allocated the bandit country of South Armagh, and 'C' Company were 'rewarded' with the wonderful area of Forkhill – a strategic location due to its proximity to the border. Of course, strategy and tactics weren't high on my priorities just then; my priority was getting through the tour intact. According to the old sweats in the company though, that wasn't a likely option because this was PIRA country. The boyos out here were professional, used exactly the same tactics as us and could choose the time and place of our demise.

My first foot patrol was in and around the town of Forkhill the same day we arrived. We drew ammo and went out. No standing on ceremony; no welcoming committee – just get on with it. I was a wiry thing in those days, but my 'weapon of choice' was the GPMG – although I had been told that if we did get a contact, one of the NCOs (my brick commander in fact) would take it off me so HE could cabby off. I was, in effect, his gun bearer – or so he thought! That first patrol was really nerve-wracking for me. If the truth be told, I was shitting myself. Every glance from a local; every car that drove by; every curtain that twitched was just seconds away from contact. Although we had studied the area intensely in the months leading up to the tour, I didn't have a clue where I was except that I was still in Forkhill! That patrol lasted for what seemed like hours, although it was in reality a very short familiarisation patrol. Back, in, unload, debrief, many cigarettes and bravado – what today would be termed as 'cool' and 'laid-back'.

The next few patrols consisted of being heli-dropped out for a few days at a time. It was proper soldiering, but we were always miserable – cold and wet. The monotony soon made me relax and be less jumpy as I settled into the tour. Monotony gave way to boredom, which needed an outlet. Mine was a sangar which overlooked part of a housing estate. One of these houses was a few metres away and was occupied by a woman known as 'Mrs X'. She had an unusual way of entertaining the troops and, despite the warnings that she was being used as a 'distraction' to stop us doing our jobs, I was a young bloke with raging hormones and a distinct lack of female company; I succumbed! Anyway, mutual appreciation soon blossomed into wanting to physically meet up – and I put a plan into action.

At first there would be just a few of us – men looking for female company – and we would arrange the odd, unconventional patrol in the direction of aforementioned lady's house. Each man would have his own task, and an all-round defence would be formed for our protection – and I don't mean condoms – and to ensure we weren't slotted by one of our own; the sangar sentries would be told where we were going. My only stipulation was that I was always to be the first for comfort!

As time went on, these 'patrols' got to be very big – the biggest was about 15 blokes – but this sort of illicit operation though can only lead to disaster. The start came when one of my patrols bumped into one of the company officers wearing combat trousers, a civvie jumper and running shoes and carrying a 9mm pistol! He looked shocked, we thought we had all been caught and then the penny dropped! This 'Rupert' was also availing himself of Mrs X's favours!

Anyway, this was my last patrol because the very next day I was dragged before the OC, Major Myers, and the C.S.M, 'Nobby' Winkworth, and was given a real bollocking. When Major Myers asked Nobby what should happen to me, I don't know who was more shocked at his answer – me or the O.C. Nobby said: "Send him on an NCO's cadre, Sir. He obviously has a knack for leading men and organisation!" And that was it – no further action was taken with me at all.

On the 8th the Loyalist UVF which had, by its bloody standards, been quiet for a while was involved in a double killing in Co Armagh. Both victims were Catholic, but only one of them was a paramilitary. Loyalist gunmen on a stolen motorbike had stalked INLA gunman Thomas Trainor (29), who was known to sign on at the Labour Exchange in Armagh City. He was walking along Armagh Road in the company of a fellow Catholic, Dennis Kelly (21), an acquaintance but someone who was not connected with either the INLA or any other Republican organisation. As the two men walked along the road, one of

Somewhere in South Armagh. The original caption wittily notes 'Result of underfunding of the N.I. education system!' (©Alan Simons)

the UVF gunmen dismounted the motorbike and opened fire with an automatic weapon on Trainor and Mr Kelly. Both men died at the scene.

On the 11th, IRA gunmen took over a house in Gleveagh Park, West Belfast and held a family hostage whilst they set up a firing point in order to ambush an army convoy in Glen Road, Andersonstown. Shots were fired but no soldiers were hit. The gunmen held a woman and her two terrified young children at gunpoint whilst they tried to kill soldiers. An RUC foot patrol in Moss Road, Lisburn was fired on by an IRA sniper the same day, but his shot narrowly missed a policewoman.

On the 13th, there was some cross-border co-operation between the RUC and the Gardaí Siochana after an IRA attack at Killea, close to the Londonderry to Letterkenny Road. An army foot patrol was on the Heater Road, just a few yards from the border, when a machine gun opened up on them from the Irish side. There were only slight injuries, but as the PIRA gunmen were attacking, Gardaí entered the area. Although there were no arrests, a search of a derelict farmhouse revealed 120 rounds of spent ammunition and 20 live rounds. A van used by the gunmen was found abandoned a short distance away.

Three days later, a brief exchange of fire between IRA gunmen and the army in Andersonstown left two men wounded – a civilian and a soldier. A foot patrol came under fire on the Glen Road and a soldier was hit and fell wounded to the ground. A gunman was seen and he was shot – and he too fell wounded. People in the area reported hearing about a dozen shots and then to seeing a soldier on the ground and one man – injured, but still standing and with his hands in the air. A large crowd gathered – as was often the case – but more troops were called in not only to ensure the evacuation of both men to the nearby MPH, but also to reinforce the original foot patrol. In instances such as these, it was not uncommon for PIRA sympathisers and active helpers to try and seize the wounded terrorist and spirit him across the border for treatment and to evade capture. Both men recovered in hospital and the IRA member was later sent to prison. In nearby Hannahstown, thanks to a tip-off, the RUC found a bomb in Hannahstown Hill Cemetery behind a wall where the army was known to regularly set up VCPs. The device was defused. The bomb was made up of 50lbs of explosives and was attached by wires to a firing point some 200 yards away behind the cover of gravestones.

On the 16th, a soldier from the Parachute Regiment was fatally wounded in a brief exchange of shots with a future hunger striker, Francis Hughes, at Glenshane Pass, Co Londonderry. Lance-Corporal David Jones (23) was among a small section of his unit's Close Observation Platoon and were hiding in bushes – keeping an eye on a house where a UDR soldier lived. They had received intelligence that a PIRA ASU was en route to kill the off-duty soldier. They observed two armed men in combat jackets walking towards them and, thinking that they were UDR, stood up to speak to them. The men immediately opened fire – hitting the para NCO and one of his comrades. Jones, though badly wounded, fired back and hit one of the men – PIRA member Francis Hughes – and wounded him. The IRA men then melted into the bush and the Close Observation Platoon radioed in for medical assistance. Lance-Corporal Jones died in hospital the following day. His funeral was held in his home area of Bromsgrove in the Midlands. Hughes was captured very close by, the next day – hiding, badly wounded in undergrowth where he had been left by the other Provisional.

Mick, 1 Glosters

We were deployed to the old RAF base at Ballykelly where they had previously flown Shackletons for coastal command. Situated about midway between Coleraine in the east and Londonderry in the west – and within a stone's throw of the Northern Ireland coast alongside the main Belfast Highway, which passed its front gate – it was ideally situated for a resident infantry unit base. Two Companies were out in the TAOR: one in County Londonderry centred on Kilrea and the other in South Tyrone and centred on Dungannon. There were also lots of smaller unit bases and it was a very busy time out there for your six weeks' rotation.

Operations went on in a similar fashion to other tours, with search ops–VCPs and reconnaissance a daily and routine affair. There were Eagle VCPs (airborne in a Wessex or Puma or Lynx or Scout – swooping down on a vehicle in a lonely area of moor or mountain) flying out of Kilrea. We spent a lot of time perfecting these techniques, and in this we much preferred the Navy flyers who would go almost anywhere and do almost anything asked, whilst the RAF stuck very much to the strict interpretation of the rules and the task was second best.

The wide open spaces of the hills and mountains around South County 'Derry were much used by the Provos for transit–weapons caches and training, but finding them was a needle in a haystack task in this type of country. However, sometimes we got lucky and after a team had bumped an ASU near Maghera (Glenshane Pass), we were called in to do the follow-up. One squaddie had died and another was hit seriously, but in the fire fight – at a range of just a few metres – they had hit one and the blood trail from the contact point was a foot wide and 25 metres long, until it suddenly stopped. After close examination you could clearly see where he had used grass and moss to stuff into the wound and stop the bleeding, but a faint trail was still visible and it led up the hill to a large thicket of trees and gorse. Two of the guys went in and after a shout and the clicking of cocked weapons and safety catches, there came another cry of "Ok, I give in." It was a known player, Frankie Hughes!

Frankie Hughes had been wanted for some time after the killing of several UDR soldiers by UVBT and other shootings. He was carrying a chromed .38 revolver, which was removed by the SB officer, and the large and bloody hole in his side – made by the SLR round – had been stuffed with a Jay Cloth as well as grass and moss. He was taken away and after interviews he went into the Kesh, but the saving of his life was a waste of time because he starved himself to death later as one of the hunger strikers.

At his trial he was sentenced to prison and he died during the 1981 hunger strike in HMP Maze. In February 1980 he was sentenced to a total of 83 years in prison. He was tried for, and found guilty of, the murder of one soldier (for which he received a life sentence) and wounding of another (for which he received 14 years) in the incident which led to his capture – as well as a series of gun and bomb attacks over a six-year period. Security sources described him as 'an absolute fanatic' and 'a ruthless killer'.

On the 20th, a bomb warning was telephoned through to the RUC in Strabane – stating that there was a bomb at Ballymagorry. A patrol car containing three officers were alerted to attend, but as they passed under a flyover on their way there, IRA gunmen opened fire on them with automatic weapons. Several shots hit their vehicle and two of the officers were wounded – albeit only slightly – and were later taken to hospital. On the same day, there was another attempt on the life of a PO – again in the North Belfast area. The off-duty officer was driving along Madrid Street, on the southern periphery of the Nationalist Short Strand, in the company of a friend. A car, hijacked earlier in the New Lodge, was waiting on the exact route which the man always took after leaving Crumlin Road Jail. As the PO's car passed, gunmen inside the hijacked vehicle opened fire and the shots shattered the windscreen of the PO's vehicle. Both he and his companion were injured by flying glass, but they were able to accelerate away. The IRA unit escaped into the nearby Short Strand and abandoned their stolen car. As was common in these cases, they went to safehouses where they were given fresh clothes and a quick bath in order to remove any forensic evidence. Lemon juice was generally on hand and was very useful for removing even the tiniest of powder residue from their bodies. Their original clothes were dumped elsewhere and their weapons dismantled and smuggled out of the area -generally underneath sleeping babies in prams.

On the 22nd, there were two major incidents – amongst several blast and incendiary explosions – in the Province. In the first incident, a foot patrol on the Turf Lodge came under fire from a lone PIRA gunman. As the soldiers reached the junction of Monagh Drive and Norglen Drive, they spotted three men armed with rifles. One of the gunmen opened fire before running off with the other two. Members of the foot patrol returned fire, but claimed no hits. Shortly afterwards a UDR soldier, Glen Espie, was ambushed and wounded by an IRA unit at Killygonland, Co Tyrone.

Glen Espie

The morning of 22 March 1978 was a normal March morning – not too cold with a cloudy overcast sky. I left for work about ten past eight, but before leaving my house I would look through the window to see that there were no suspicious vehicles parked near my home that could conceal an ambush team in waiting. Then I would check my car for undercar booby-traps before driving off. I was unable to vary my routes to and from work to any degree because of the location of my home and workplace. On arrival I would park in different locations in the car park – trying not to set a pattern. After clocking into work I would check my work's van for under-vehicle booby-trap bombs under the watchful eyes of some of my work colleagues, who were players or suspected PIRA members.

My first job that day was in Parkview Pomeroy – a Republican estate to the north of the village. At lunchtime the foreman called me over and said that he had just received a call that the copper cylinder had burst at 3 Killygonlan beside the Diamond in Ardboe. This was on the shores of Lough Neagh, about 11 miles from Cookstown, and a Republican area. This could be a 'come on' situation as there had been a lot of PIRA activity in this area. Soldiers had shot and killed a Terrorist loading a bomb into a car at a derelict house close to the village three weeks earlier. (Paul Duffy (23), an IRA member, was shot and killed by soldiers in Washing Bay, Co Tyrone on 26 February. He was a member of the Tyrone Brigade of the IRA.) In another incident, a UDR soldier was travelling through the Ardboe area on his way home when PIRA fired 23 rounds – striking his car but fortunately not hitting him – just two weeks earlier.

I worked in these areas daily, and my civilian job was a plumber with the Northern Ireland Housing Executive (NIHE). I was always wary when called out to emergency jobs as the house could have been taken over by PIRA and used to mount an assassination attack. On my way to 3 Killygonlan I called at home and put on my concealed body armour. I didn't always wear it at work because of the physical activity involved and you sweated like a pig wearing it.

The day had cleared up with some hazy spring sunshine as I drove a roundabout route to get to Killygonlan. The properties are pre-war, two storeys three-bedrooms with a downstairs bathroom at the bottom of the stairs. The properties are set in a square bounded by the main road – six terraced houses facing the main road with two semi-detached houses at either side of the terraced block. On arrival I drove up to the house and reversed my van up to the door and kept the wing mirror in line with the front door. I never took my eyes off the door – watching for signs of suspicious activity. I got out of the van and walked towards the door. My heart was pounding – expecting the door to be flung open, or a burst of gunfire from the house or entry on my left as I walked the short distant from my van.

I stood to the side of the door and knocked so that if someone fired through the door they would be unable to hit me. The door was opened slightly by a male person. I advised him that I was there to repair the burst cylinder from the Housing Executive. He said: "Ok son, go ahead. It's at the top of the stairs." I pushed the door open as the male in the house went through a door on my right into the living room and closed the door behind him. Having talked with the male at the door, that I assumed to be the tenant, I relaxed as it appeared to be just another burst cylinder … all in a day's work. On entering the hall of the house, I turned left and walked to the bottom of the stairs. I became aware that the curtains were pulled on the circular window at the bottom of the stairs and the hall – even though it was about 2.15pm. It was very dark.

The door into the downstairs bathroom was open. It was to the right of the hall at the bottom of the stairs. As I was taking all this in, a male of stocky build emerged from the downstairs bathroom in front of me. I saw that he was wearing a black balaclava mask and I could see his eyes and mouth perfectly. He had a pistol in a two-handed grip pointed at my chest literally inches away.

The initial shock to the system literally stopped me in my tracks as I stared at this frightening figure. My first thoughts were: "Fuck, this is it!" He fired and hit me on the left side of the chest – just below the nipple, in the heart area – and the force of the shot was like being kicked by a horse. It lifted me off my feet and propelled me backwards and I fell to the ground – lying against the open front door. As I looked up at the gunman, he had stepped forward and levelled the pistol at my head. In those milliseconds, my life really did pass in front of me like a cinema screen in fast-forward: my wife, children, mum and dad – all the people who really mattered in my life flashed across my brain in a fraction of a second.

As the gunman levelled the pistol at my head I ducked and rolled out of the open front door – and getting to my feet, I ran past my parked van to get away from the gunman, who fired again. I could feel rounds going past my head and had covered about 10 to 15 yards when I was hit again in the left shoulder. The impact of the bullet spun me round and down with the impact of a kicking horse. As I was running, I was trying to get the zip down on my boiler suit as I had a .22 Walther Pistol tucked into a holster on my left side. I was now lying on my back on the ground – looking over my head back towards the door. Two PIRA terrorists ran from the door of the house towards me to finish me off. They looked to be running in slow motion and it was only later I discovered that because of the adrenaline pumping in my system, my brain was thinking so fast that everything in real-time looked to be in slow motion.

As I lay on the ground I was able to pull my pistol from its holster, but because of the gunshot wound to my shoulder I couldn't pull back the slide to cock it in the normal manner. I pushed the pistol into my left hand, held the slide and pushed the pistol forward with the right hand – chambering a round – and as I did this I brought the pistol up and over my head and fired at the two men. I can still see them to this day – and by this time they were about halfway between me and the house. When I fired, both gunmen hit the deck and I rolled over onto my belly and went to fire again, but nothing happened. The pistol had jammed. I couldn't clear it as they were too close, so I jumped to my feet and ran around the side of the last two semi-detached houses at the end of the square. There was a five-foot high chain-link fence at the rear of the garden and I jumped clean over the fence. Adrenaline does work! I ran behind a filling station, over a wooden fence and across an open field for about 150 yards.

As I ran, my breath was coming in large gasps; my heart was pounding and my lungs were on fire – and the hedge at the far side of this open field seemed so far away. I was expecting to be shot again, but I jumped up into this large thorn hedge and tore through it. I was able to clear the jammed pistol and take stock of my situation. I looked back towards the rear of the filling station and could see men moving about and pointing towards the hedge where I was. I was aware that the front of my boiler suit was all bloody. It was coming from my mouth because the round hit my concealed body armour and impacted against my left lung. I had never been shot before and was alone and wounded in this Republican area with the nearest haven of safety the Unionist village of Coagh five miles away. To get there I was going to have to commandeer a car and either drive it or force the driver at gunpoint to drive me there.

I was very much aware that this being a Republican area, no-one would have reported the shooting to the police. Therefore the gunmen involved could still be looking for me in the area. I used the cover of hedgerows to make my way across country to a bungalow. To get to the bungalow I had to cross a secondary road about 350 metres from the house in which I was attacked, so I waited until there was no traffic and scrambled over the hedge and ran up the drive and to the rear of the bungalow to be out of view from the road. No vehicle was visible but I tried the rear door, which was unlocked. On entering I found the bungalow unoccupied. I remember checking out each room in turn and finding a very large map of the Ardboe Area fastened to the wall in a bedroom. I wondered had I stumbled into a PIRA ops room? This was long before mobile phones and luckily for me, the bungalow had a telephone. I dialled 999 and asked for the police. On speaking to them, they thought it was a 'come on' situation to get Security Forces into the area to ambush them. I told the police operator my name and that I was a part-time lance-corporal with 'G' Company 8 UDR based in Cookstown. I also told them that my civilian job was a plumber for the Housing Executive and I had been shot and wounded twice and needed help and medical attention.

There were no further deaths in the month of March, but there were several other major incidents. On the 28th, two men threw a primed grenade through the glass doors of the Queen's Bar in Thomas Street, Portadown. This was one of several incidents in the town, which involved attacks on the RUC and a major sectarian punch-up on the train in Portadown Railway Station. The grenade exploded almost immediately and one man standing near the door was very seriously wounded. Several other drinkers were hurt in the blast. The men who threw the grenade were spotted by a passing foot patrol and soldiers fired several shots at the men who escaped. In the City Cemetery just below the Creggan Estate in Londonderry, an Easter Commemoration at the Republican plot to remember the 1916 uprising degenerated into a riot. Several RUC officers were injured and 14 arrests were made. Seven of those arrested were from the Irish Republic. The author and a friend visited the plot in 2008 and stood by the graves of the people killed on Bloody Sunday in January 1972. It was a cold, November day and the windswept cemetery was deserted – deserted other than the souls of those who had died in the Troubles and for other more natural reasons. Amongst the graves was the poignant final resting place of Ranger William Best, a Creggan boy who was in the British Army, lured home by the promise of a safe passage and then cold-bloodedly murdered by the OIRA (see *The Bloodiest Year 1972* by the same author). As we walked out of that sad place in a sad area of a sad city, we passed by a statue of an INLA gunman. The author's companion remarked: "*Even their statues are masked!*"

On the 29th an RUC mobile patrol spotted a car – which had been hijacked earlier in Andersonstown as they drove along the Finaghy Road in South Belfast – and cautiously approached it, weapons drawn. It was as well they did, for three men jumped out carrying weapons. They were ordered to stop and one of the men turned and pointed his gun at the police and was promptly shot and wounded. The injured man, aged 21, was arrested but the other two disappeared into nearby streets. The car contained a primed bomb, which was later defused by EOD, and a follow-up search found a Walther revolver which had been thrown into a nearby garden.

That was the final chapter of an incident-packed month which had left seven people dead. Of these, four were soldiers and one of their civilian searchers – Norma Spence – all of whom were killed by the IRA. There was one other civilian death – that of a Catholic – killed by the UVF as they shot dead an INLA member. None of the deaths this month could be said to be overtly sectarian.

40

April

Deaths would remain low again this month ('acceptable' by the bloody standards of the last) and it was hoped by many Ulster men and women – wearied by almost nine years of murder, violence and bombings – that February and La Mon was just a blip. Six people died in April, but two of those were police officers and yet another UDR soldier was murdered off duty.

On 'All Fools' Day', two IRA members were stopped at a snap VCP on the Broadway between the Falls Road and Donegall Road in Belfast. Both men were arrested after a loaded pistol was found in the car. The weapon was later linked to several murders. Three days later, acting on information received, the RUC raided a house in Kansas Avenue, North Belfast and found an M60 machine gun (not the same one which killed Paul Sheppard of the Royal Artillery) as well as four revolvers, ammunition and bomb-making equipment. There was also a lucky escape for a heavily pregnant woman when an IRA bullet, which had been aimed at a foot patrol on Whiterock Avenue, West Belfast, went through her kitchen window. It missed her by inches and lodged in the kitchen wall, but she suffered shock and slight deafness as a consequence of the absolute irresponsibility of the Provisional IRA.

On the 7th, several IRA gunmen in a stolen car approached Charles Street, Lurgan and parked opposite Lurgan courthouse to wait for the normal RUC patrol which opened the security gates each morning. Three policemen, accompanied by a British 'Red Cap' (RMP), were in the process of unlocking the gate and several civilians were in the immediate location. Despite the proximity of the passers-by, the gunmen opened fire on the SF group. The RMP and one of the RUC officers received slight head wounds as the bullets grazed them and one officer was hit in the hand. The civilian was badly wounded in the back. After firing several shots, the gunmen jumped back into the car, which drove off at speed in the direction of a Nationalist area.

The 7th also saw major talks between the British Government and their Irish counterparts. Airey Neave, then Conservative Party spokesperson on Northern Ireland, said that power-sharing no longer represented practical politics. James Callaghan, then British Prime Minister, held a meeting with Jack Lynch, then Taoiseach, at the European Community summit at Copenhagen. The talks were designed to help ease relationships between the British and Irish Governments.

On the 8th, the first murder of the month occurred in the Twinbrook area of south-west Belfast. At least eight armed men entered the house of Brendan Megraw (22) and seized his wife, who was pregnant at the time. She was immediately grabbed and questioned by the men – all wearing surgical gowns and masks. One of them stabbed her with a syringe and she collapsed semi-conscious to the floor. When her husband walked into the house, he was interrogated by the men about 'guns' and then taken away. Before he was dragged away he managed to reassure her that he had done nothing wrong. That was the last time that she saw him again, dead or alive. That he was taken away and tortured and then killed by a PIRA 'Nutting Squad' (also known somewhat euphemistically as the 'Central Administrative

Team') is not in doubt. What happened to his body and why he was killed is a question which has only been partially answered. Brendan McGrew became one of the 'disappeared' – a sad group of people who were murdered by the IRA and their bodies hidden away from public view. The list includes Jean McConville, who was murdered on 7 December 1972 and two 'Freds" Seamus Wright (murdered 2 October 1972) and Kevin Mckee (murdered on the same day). Please see *The Bloodiest Year 1972* by the same author. In March 1999 – a staggering 21 years later – the Provisionals finally admitted to murdering Mr McGrew, but accused him of being an 'agent provocateur' and a member of a British Army undercover team.

The Provisionals like to portray themselves as freedom fighters and resister of the 'British war machine' – especially to their sycophantic Irish-American audience – and profess to be honest and open in their dealings with the Catholic community. They have been anything but and the scandal of the 'disappeared' lingers painfully on. Belfast journalist Malachi O'Doherty wrote: "It took another four years and an exhaustive search of a beach in County Louth before Jean McConville was found. The search for her body had closer media coverage – probably because it was easier for broadcasters to marshal their cameras on a beautiful beach in fine weather. Reporters watched a digger scoop and sift the sand – hour after hour, day after day – looking for clothing or a few bones. The searching seemed to unite the scattered McConville family and they erected a small shrine to their mother at the beach. The search itself proved fruitless. The body was found at a separate beach. It then became clear that Jean McConville had died of a single bullet wound to the head. There were two unsuccessful searches also for Danny McIlhone – in 1999 and 2000 – before his remains were found last year in the Wicklow Mountains. The story behind his death is that the IRA had been questioning him about the theft of some of their weapons and that he had been killed in a struggle to escape. The IRA admits to having killed four other missing people: Kevin McKee, Columba McVeigh, Brendan McGraw and Seamus Wright. The families of the disappeared still meet formally twice a year for a Mass on Palm Sunday and a small ceremony at Stormont on All Souls."

On the same day that Mr McGrew was taken away by a PIRA 'Nutting Squad', gunmen from the same organisation ambushed a military vehicle at the RVH. The vehicle had just pulled up outside the Casualty Department and as a soldier and a policeman got out, shots were fired by IRA members hidden behind some air conditioning units and hit both of the SF men. A nurse was right in the line of fire and desperately threw herself to the ground in order to escape the crossfire. Over 60 shots were exchanged whilst she lay terrified as rounds passed over her. The gunmen eventually ran off – leaving two policemen and a soldier wounded and the nurse very badly shocked.

THE RVH: CARE AND BIGOTRY
Raymond Clark, Royal Regiment of Fusiliers

In 1976, I was a SNCO serving with the Regimental Band of The Royal Regiment of Fusiliers in Cambridgeshire – and the regiment was to go on a tour of duty to Belfast. Three SNCs from the Band were to go and work alongside 1SNCO from the regiment and our 'patch' was to be 'The Royal' or, to give it it's full title, The Royal Victoria Hospital – one of the world's leading hospitals specialising in trauma

---

* 'Freds' was a term applied by army undercover groups to IRA members who had been 'turned' and who spied on their former comrades. The Republicans referred to this as 'touting'.

victims. Our role was to live and work in the hospital for six months; to interview and record their details in a register of all those injured (details were recorded in red and were used for injury claims); in the case of deaths, to record their details and sometimes attend operations; and to collect 'evidence'. Security was provided by armed Fusiliers for people deemed to require it (i.e. security personnel – civil and military – witnesses who may have been injured and, of course, suspected terrorists). The Royal is bordered by The Falls Road and The Grosvenor Road – both of which are in predominately Nationalist areas – and doors to the main corridors were accessible from these roads.

As we were working and living within the hospital our dress was 'barrack dress' and not 'combat' as worn on patrol. We were the public face of the army – both helping and advising. Because of the nature of the work we worked very closely with all the frontline staff: casualty; reception; ambulance; doctors; nurses; and ancillary staff, which included the mortuary staff; cleaners; security; catering and even bar staff in the Doctors' bar! At the time one of the questions that the powers-that-be had on their forms was: religion! We were often advised by staff that if this was not given you can try and work it out by getting their name, address and senior school attended (i.e. 'Sean from the Falls Road going to St Benedict's School' stood a fairly good chance of NOT being a Protestant).

One day we went to collect the meal trolley from Bostock main kitchen and we were greeted by the head kitchen worker (a strong Loyalist from the Shankill Road area) with the comment: "I hear two children have been brought in with severe petrol bomb burns?" I replied that was correct and she said: "Poor wee ones. Where were they from?" I gave an area and she simply replied: "Oh, Fenians. It's ok then as it might save them growing up into big Catholics!" I was stunned that a fellow human being that would do anything to help the troops could think and say something like that about two kids.

Another time we were given some homemade cakes etc by one of the bar staff, who was a Roman Catholic, and she told us that she would get into deep trouble from her husband (who worked on the security in the Royal and did not like the 'Brits') if he knew and asked us never to speak if we saw her in the corridor etc. I asked her why she was doing it and she replied that she would like to think that someone was keeping an eye on her son whilst he was at university in England. I remember a young lad who had been brought in because of a shooting incident. He had been 'kneecapped' and would be crippled for life because of an 'offence' he had committed. He was seen speaking to the police and army. I remember he was in his late teens and built like the proverbial, but was terrified. His father was present in the ward when I chatted to him but would make no comment because of the consequences that would await him by the 'local administers of justice' if he did. His father, obviously tired with all the Troubles, said: "You are worried about what 'they' will do to you if you talk! You should be worried what I will do to you if you do not play your part in stopping all this hatred."

This bigotry has not gone away – despite all the talk that politicians say and all the agreements that are signed. I recall two young gay men who lived in my local village in Northern Ireland talking about the 'Troubles'. One was Protestant and the other Catholic and they said: "Everyone from Northern Ireland should go and live abroad for a while. Once you have lived there you start to realise that people are not interested in your name, address etc which may indicate your religion. They accept you as being 'Paddy', 'Mick', 'Fred' etc." Bigotry is ignorance and will always provide a martyr for the cause, but bigotry is the enemy within.

On the 10th, Captain Michael James Kett (27) of the Royal Artillery, on attachment to the Army Air Corps, was killed in an 'aircraft accident' somewhere in the Province. The author has been, at the time of publication, unable to discover more details. He was from Norwich and his funeral was held at Horsford Parish Church in Norfolk.

The UVF were back in action on the 12th as a bombing team targeted the Republican drinking club – Kelly's Bar on the Whiterock Road – during the lunchtime drinking session. Armed men, guarded by an armed man and driver outside, stormed inside the pub and planted three explosive devices before escaping on the Ballygomartin Road towards the Loyalist Woodvale area. The drinkers very quickly evacuated the bar before the first of the bombs exploded – quickly followed by the second. The blasts brought the roof down and caused extensive damage – and children in the adjoining Catholic Primary School, St Aidan's, were evacuated for their own safety. On the same day, the *Belfast Newsletter* reported that a 27-year-old man would appear in court for the Gilford bombing on New Year's Eve in 1975 (see Chapter 12) and also for the murder of Thomas Rafferty in February 1976. This was covered in Chapter 14 of this book.

On the 13th, Irish Gardaí – acting on a tip-off from an informer – managed to intercept and seize a quantity of explosives in Dublin docks after a South African ship had docked. Over the border with the North, a PIRA landmine came close to wiping out a mobile patrol in Keady, South Armagh. A two-vehicle patrol group was on the Crossdall Road, just outside Keady, when the lead vehicle was hit by the blast from a 200lbs landmine. The vehicle was picked up and hurled into a bank and ended up in a ditch. It left a crater 10 feet deep, but miraculously the only injuries were to a soldier and two RUC officers. Troops from the second vehicle set up all-round defence, as it was an IRA tactic to open fire on the shocked survivors. On this occasion, the gunmen had fled across the border.

THE BORDER
Private 'B', Parachute Regiment
The border … the fucking border … that was a bastard. We suffered all kinds of shit thrown at us from the IRA, but we weren't allowed to fight them on a level playing field. They would shoot and scoot; explode their bombs and then run over the border and know that they would be protected by the Irish police and the army. Even when they got caught, the judges and all would just fine them a couple of punts for being a member of an illegal organisation and they'd do six months in a holiday camp or run away to America where the Yanks saw them as some sort of resistance movement to the Brits. The truth was that most of the people in Northern Ireland wanted to be part of the UK and they had no desires to be part of a country with its religious thinking rooted three centuries ago!

I seen a geezer once who had been hit by a shot from a terror Mick who had then run across some fields and into the Republic. The lad had been hit in his shoulder and survived, but he was white as a sheet and trying to speak – coughing up big gobs of blood. One of our lads fired a full burst from his GPMG at the twat as he ran away – somewhere into Co Monaghan. The lad firing was so fucking incensed about his mate being injured that he was firing wild. A full screw eventually stopped him, but later some Mick farmer put a complaint in about us scaring his sheep!

One of the lads from another platoon – who later did selection for the SAS – met up with me in Aldershot after one of the tours and over a pint told me about a covert op they did somewhere in Dundalk inside Ireland. They lifted an IRA geezer right out of his bed and took him in his bleeding pyjamas into Ulster and handed him over to an RUC patrol on the right side of the border. I would have paid a fortune to see the git's face when he saw them peelers! We should have been allowed to do that more often, because the cowardly bastards knew they could kill us and then nip over the border and sit in their local boozer and have a pint in the safety of Ireland. It wasn't right mate and I'll tell you this: I hated them Irish bleeders then and I still do.

On the 14th, another part-time soldier from the UDR was killed as Republican terrorists targeted him whilst he worked at his full-time job. Corporal William McKee (61) was a school bus driver and on the day of his death, was delivering school meals to schools in the area of Cookstown, Co Tyrone. He was on the main road from Omagh when he was ambushed by three armed PIRA volunteers – including two members of the *Cumann mBan* (Women's' IRA). The first fusillade of shots badly wounded him, but despite his injuries he continued driving for the safety of Cookstown. His killers were ruthless and pursued him until his vehicle slewed to a halt at Creggan Crossroads as he lost control. They entered the bus and shot him three more times in the head and stomach as he lay helpless. His cowardly assassins then drove off – leaving him lying half in, half out of the bus. Despite his mortal wounds, he tried to crawl away but sadly died on the cold tarmac of a British spring day. The local newspaper covered the murder and the school bus, with its registration number of DJI 6136, stands silent and a black body bag lies in front – another human being sacrificed on the IRA's altar to its insane demands for a British withdrawal from a part of the United Kingdom.

On the same day as this cowardly murder, the UVF showed that it too could stoop to such depraved and barbaric standards when it killed one of its former members. Robert McCullough (26), from Rathmore Drive on the Loyalist Rathcoole Estate, was a former UVF paramilitary who had left the UVF and turned to God – investing his energies into youth and community work. Loyalist gunmen got into his house and shot him dead as he lay asleep in his bed with his wife. She was uninjured and a spokesman for the group claimed that he had been executed for being an informer. With something of a supreme irony, one of his convicted killers also 'found' God. This author believes that God was never 'lost' and deprecates those who claim that they became 'born again' after committing a hideous murder.

On the 15th, another policeman was killed by the IRA when they planted a booby-trap on a farm in Armoy, Co Antrim. John Moore (57) was a part-time policeman and spent his days farming the land which had been in his family for many decades. He had never married and gave his spare time to working to keep his community safe – and the previous year had fought off two IRA gunmen who had burst into his house and tried to shoot him. On this occasion the IRA had left an explosive device on the lane which ran into his farm.

He drove to tend his sheep – which were kept a few miles away – and part of his route took him past the deadly booby-trap. In his car were his collie and a lamb which had been rejected by its mother. The device detonated as he was passing by and the car was utterly wrecked – parts of it being flung over 100 yards. The RUCR man and both animals were killed absolutely instantly.

The day after, a soldier suffered a broken arm when PIRA exploded a culvert bomb at Kinawley, Co Fermanagh as an army mobile control was checking for such devices. Gunmen opened fire from a nearby hillside, but when the troops returned fire the gunmen fled. On the 17th, army EOD was called to Flushtown Bridge between Strabane and Clady to investigate some suspect devices. They found several milk churns packed with explosives and intended for a passing army mobile patrol. Command wires were found which led across the border into the Republic. They were made safe but had they exploded, would have caused utter carnage. On the same day, there was a gun attack on an RUC mobile patrol on the Tullyhagnas Road near Dunloy in Co Antrim. A total of 12 shots were fired at the police vehicle and several hits were recorded, but no policemen were injured.

On the 19th, James Callaghan – British Prime Minister – announced that legislation would be brought forward to increase the number of Members of Parliament (MPs) who represented Northern Ireland at Westminster from 12 to between 16 and 18. A Bill was later passed on 28 November 1978 which increased the representation to 17 seats. Even whilst Callaghan was speaking, the Provisionals launched a gun attack on Portglenone RUC Station near to Ballymena in Co Antrim with the sole intention of killing police officers. A female RUCR officer was just closing the security gates after admitting a police Land Rover when the attack commenced. She was wounded in the head but recovered after treatment.

Three days later, an IRA gunman tricked his way into the house of an RUC officer as he relaxed off-duty at his home in Woodland Park in the HQNI town of Lisburn. Millar McAllister (36), father of two, was a police photographer and a keen pigeon fancier. Two men, both armed PIRA, turned up at his home and tricked their way in – claiming an interest in pigeons – but as the RUC man showed them around they shot him four times at almost point-blank range, mortally wounding him. They ran off – past the shocked teenaged son who had let them into the house – leaving Mr McAllister dying. He managed to summon up the final pieces of energy to crawl into his kitchen where he died moments later.

On the 24th, in an unusual display of diligence, the Gardaí signalled a car coming from Co Londonderry to stop at a VCP in St Mary's Road, Buncrana. The car, containing two IRA volunteers, failed to stop and accelerated away but Gardaí gave chase and eventually the car they were chasing crashed and the two occupants ran off. Inside the crashed car, the Irish police found an M60 machine gun – the second to be seized this month – and 500 rounds of ammunition. It was a major blow for the Provisionals to lose two of the deadly weapons in such a short space of time. There was a further blow to them the following day when soldiers saw two men acting suspiciously as they patrolled on Lower Road in Londonderry's Bogside area. The patrol from the Cheshire Regiment challenged the men, who ran off – leaving behind a sack in the road. The soldiers carefully searched the sack and found four of the lethal American Armalites, a pistol and over 200 rounds of ammunition. Also on that day, the Green Jackets lost another officer when Major Thomas Fowley (51) collapsed whilst on duty and sadly died. Other than the fact that he lived in Winchester and was buried at Magdeline Cemetery in the home of the Jackets, nothing further is known.

The Cheshires lost eight men during the Troubles, but strangely only one of their losses was in open action. This occurred on 4 July 1974 when Corporal David Smith died of his wounds after being fatally injured in a shooting on the Ballymurphy Estate. The regiment – whose motto is 'Ever Glorious' – has battle honours which date back to Martinique in 1762 and includes Gallipoli, El Alamein and the Italian campaign. It lost seven of its soldiers killed in the INLA bombing of the Droppin' Well disco in Ballykelly, Co Londonderry on 6 December 1982 when 17 people were killed. The atrocity was the work of Dominic McGlinchey.

The month ended with two major incidents involving the IRA's Newry Brigade as they struck twice in the Co Down town. On the 26th, gunmen hiding inside an old building at Canal Quay opposite the courthouse opened fire on a foot patrol as they passed by. A total of 20 shots were fired at the soldiers and some passed through the windows into the building where a case was being held. Staff and others were forced to take cover as the gunmen clearly didn't care just who they killed. In the second incident, a two-man team was waiting close to Newry courthouse in order to murder a member of the Judiciary – against whom they were conducting a campaign. However, they mistook a local Employment Exchange Manager for a Magistrate and shot the man as he left by the Bridge Street entrance of the Crown Building. He was shot and wounded four times in a hail of bullets and badly wounded. He was rushed to Daisy Hill Hospital where he later recovered. After the shooting, the two gunmen dashed to a waiting getaway car and sped off towards the border.

April ended with seven deaths: three were soldiers and two were policemen. Two civilians died – neither of whom were overtly sectarian; one killed by the IRA and one by the UVF.

41

May

There were only five killings this month – one of which was sectarian, but the IRA's 'Nutting Squad' had a busy month. The subject of the 'disappeared' raised its ugly head again. For only the second time in the period under review, there were no military deaths.

On the 2nd of the month, an incident in Co Fermanagh almost made the first paragraph to this chapter somewhat redundant as a UDR soldier came close to death. The part-time soldier – who worked at the Department of the Environment drainage works at Aghavea, Brookborough – had just started his bulldozer when a booby-trapped device exploded. He was badly injured but survived those injuries. The device was thought to have been planted by the Provisionals. On the same day another UDR soldier – who also worked for the Forestry Commission – came under fire as he worked on his own in Castlewellan Forest Park. He had just arrived by Land Rover at the section of the forest he was working when hidden gunmen opened fire on him. He was wounded in his stomach, arms and legs but fortunately – as he was close to his home – the shots were heard and he was found and rushed to hospital. That day finished with a sniper attack on the sangar at Springfield Road RUC Station with one of the most miraculous escapes of the Troubles. Sinn Féin had organised a protest rally outside the station, which sat strategically on the 'Peace Line' and close to the Falls Road and not far from the Shankill Road. The protest degenerated into a stoning match – and under cover of the riot a sniper fired several shots at the station. One soldier was struck on his steel helmet and the shot ricocheted away. Had he been wearing a beret as most of us did, that man's name would now be on the ROH and this chapter would have been so different.

Over the next two days, a series of concerted attacks on the railway infrastructure caused chaos throughout the entire rail network. The Provisionals chose the disruption of trains at one of their 'our targets for this week' meetings. First of all, bomb attacks on five railway bridges caused chaos on the Dublin-Belfast-Londonderry Line with explosions in South Armagh and then further north in the Ballykelly area of Co Londonderry. The first attack was a massive bomb at Kilnasaggart near Newry and three men were arrested shortly afterwards. The following day a rail security guard confronted several men at Waterside station in Londonderry who he saw acting suspiciously. However, they overcame him after a struggle and locked him in a cabin. They then planted four bombs around the station and in a diesel train and these exploded shortly afterwards.

On the 5th, the IRA attempted to kill a solicitor in Maghera, Co Londonderry whom they considered an enemy simply because he had prosecuted members of the paramilitary group. A UVBT was attached to his car, which was parked outside the courthouse. As he drove off the detonator fired, but due to being badly fitted it failed to ignite the 4lb bomb. The solicitor heard the initial bang, but it wasn't until he arrived home and saw the wires still attached to the bomb that he realised how close he had come to death. The device was later defused by EOD. The army disposal team were called out again the same evening when a foot patrol in Moybane Road, Crossmaglen discovered several milk churns packed with 100lbs of explosives. Command wires were traced to a firing point on hills just inside the Irish border.

The following day, an explosion on the Crumlin Road slightly injured a boy on a bike as he drove past a bomb hidden in a manhole cover. A bomb then exploded on the Upper Springfield Road after the IRA had hijacked a van on the Falls Road and then abandoned it on the known route of army mobile patrols. It exploded prematurely and there were no injuries. Shortly after, Belfast City Centre was thrown into chaos by a series of bomb hoaxes and deliberately abandoned stolen vehicles which the army and RUC were forced to examine. Suspect vehicles were left at Monagh Road Roundabout, Dunmurry Lane, Cromac Square, Corporation Street, the Short Strand, Suffolk Road and under the Sydenham Bypass.

On 7 May, the dangers inherent in joyriding in Northern Ireland during the Troubles became very apparent with the death of John Collins (17) near to Andersonstown RUC Station. The station stood on a triangle formed by the meeting of Glen Road and the Falls Road as they converge opposite Milltown Cemetery. It was dominated by a huge security tower with anti-rocket netting and tons of armour plating. Today the triangle lies empty – surrounded by huge rocks (presumably to keep squatters away) – and adorned by pro-Republican, anti-PSNI propaganda. The barber's shop from where IRA gunmen shot Blues and Royals' soldiers Thornley and Dykes in April 1979 (see Chapter 52) is still there; its red and white pole still beckoning in its male customers for a short-back-and-sides or something more modern if that is possible in this sad part of Belfast.

In the very early hours of that May morning back in 1978, a car containing four joyriders – including young Collins – attempted to bludgeon its way through an army VCP next to the RUC station. Troops were entitled to open fire under ROE and did so, with several shots striking the vehicle which was stolen. It ground to a halt several hundred yards up Glen Road and two youths were seen to run away. As soldiers cautiously approached the car they found two men inside; one was mortally wounded and the other was wounded in the back. He was rushed to hospital where he later recovered. He and the other two who had run off were later charged and convicted of the theft of the car from Gransha Park. John Collins died en route to hospital – a victim of the violent times in which he had lived and tried to flout the law. The troops manning the VCP were from the Parachute Regiment and were not the type of soldiers with whom to mess. There were echoes of this tragedy on 30 September 1990 when teenage joyriders failed to stop at a VCP – also on Glen Road – and by a tragic coincidence, also manned by the Parachute Regiment. On that day Private Lee Clegg shot and killed Karen Reilly – who was 18 – and fatally wounded Martin Peake, who was also 17 and who died shortly afterwards.

On the following day, a gunman – thought to have been either PIRA or INLA – fired shots into a house in Ballygawley, Co Tyrone and badly injured a young girl. As it was the home of a Protestant family, it is thought likely that the intended target was the male head of the house. The girl, aged 11, was in the hallway of the house and the gunman fired seven shots with an Armalite through the door – hitting her in the arm and badly wounding her. No organisation ever claimed responsibility. The most obvious explanation is that the Republicans were targeting a PO and had attacked the wrong house. PIRA planted another manhole bomb similar to the one on Crumlin Road a few days earlier – this time at the junction of Suffolk Road and Glenveagh Drive in the Nationalist suburb of Hannahstown, West Belfast. It was intended to hit an army foot patrol but could have easily claimed the lives of children playing nearby. The 10lb device – made up of homemade explosives – was packed into a gas cylinder and was later defused by EOD.

There was a rather controversial death on the 10th when the suspected killer of policeman Millar McAllister (see previous chapter) was found hanged in his prison cell at Castlereagh detention area. Brian Maguire (27) had been arrested the previous day at his home in Ardane Gardens, Lisburn and had been questioned about the murder which had taken place on 22 April. He had used a torn-off piece of sheet and tied it around his neck and then hung it on a ventilation grille. A senior UDA member, who had been held in the same area, made a claim that he had overheard RUC officers claim that they had killed Maguire because he was a 'cop killer'. The incident was subject to an internal investigation and the allegations were found to be unsubstantiated.

The following day, an unknown paramilitary group – thought to have been either PIRA or INLA – booby-trapped the car belonging to a security officer at a factory in Portadown. The man jumped into his car and began to reverse out of his parking space when the UVBT exploded – blowing the bonnet onto a nearby roof and wrecking the vehicle. Parts of the car were blown over 50 yards away. By a miracle, the 30-year-old was left without injuries.

On the 12th, mobs attacked the home of SDLP Leader, Gerry Fitt MP, for the second time and his wife was left badly shocked by the damage caused by rioters at their home in Antrim Road, Belfast. The Provisionals hijacked a lorry belonging to an English company as it was delivering products in the Markets area of Belfast. They held a passenger hostage before planting explosives on board and using the driver to deliver the proxy bomb. He was given instructions to drive the bomb to Belfast's law courts but he lost his way and abandoned the lorry on the Stranmillis Embankment. He raised the alarm and EOD carried out a controlled explosion which neutralised the bomb.

GUARDING THE IRA
Mel Price, 3rd Battalion, Royal Green Jackets
I cannot remember the exact date, but I think it was sometime in 1979 when the Northern Ireland prison officers went on strike. Any prisoners who had to go to court etc were not allowed back into the prisons during their trials and other hearings. As a consequence, the Royal Engineers were instructed to turn some old huts near the ranges at Magilligan into a camp – which, when finished, that looked like a stalag from the Second World War! There was barbed wire fencing, floodlights and sangars which looked like watch towers. It was like a scene from the German camp at Sagan from The Great Escape.

There were some really serious players involved at the time and it was our job to guard them. There at the time was the notorious Francis Hughes, or so we were told! (Francis Hughes: 28 February 1956 – 12 May 1981 – was a member of PIRA and at one time was the most wanted man in Northern Ireland until his arrest following a gun battle with the SAS – during which a soldier was killed. At his trial he was sentenced to a total of 83 years' imprisonment and he died during the 1981 hunger strike in HM Prison Maze.) It was a worthwhile job knowing we were helping to keep this lot off the streets.

What happened when the strike was over and the prisoners had gone left a really bad taste in my mouth. I was used to bullshit and leaving everything cleaner then you found it and I accepted that. But being told to clean up the huts after these bastards – who let's face it would love to have killed me and the rest of the lads given half a chance – was the last straw. As far as I know not one officer or senior NCO stood up for us and said my lads are not doing this; get in a civvie firm. We got the job done but it left a nasty taste in my mouth and I know I wasn't the only one. We got the job done but I was not happy and I know I wasn't the only one.

In March 1978 some PIRA and INLA prisoners refused to leave their cells to shower or use the lavatory because of alleged attacks by officers. Consequently they were provided with wash hand-basins in their cells. However, there were further demands from the inmates for showers inside the cells and this demand was refused. The outcome was that they then refused to use the hand-basins. At the end of April 1978 a fight occurred between a prisoner and a prison officer in one of the H-Blocks. The prisoner was taken away to solitary confinement and a false rumour spread across the wing that the prisoner had been badly beaten. The prisoners responded by smashing the furniture in their cells and the authorities responded by removing the remaining furniture from the cells – leaving the prisoners with just blankets and mattresses. The PIRA/INLA men then escalated their protest further by refusing to leave their cells and as a result, the prison officers were unable to clear them. This resulted in the 'blanket protest' where they refused to wear uniform and this degenerated into the so-called 'dirty protest'. The prisoners then resorted to smearing excrement on the walls of their cells. It is this to which Mel Price refers.

The 15th saw a nasty assault on a female soldier when a WRAC accompanying a patrol from the Parachute Regiment raided the Donegall Celtic Supporters' Club in the Turf Lodge. A mob separated her from the soldiers and forced her onto the ground where a Republican 'hero' thrust a broken glass into her face whilst his friends kicked the helpless woman. A para fired three rounds from his SLR into the ceiling and then dived in to rescue the woman soldier. A total of 21 arrests were made. The author visited the club in June of 2012 on a visit to the Turf Lodge, but wisely remained outside. Even after 15 years of 'peace' there was a feeling of menace in the air – and on every face of the residents of the Turf Lodge, Whiterock and the 'Murph there was a look of suspicion.

The day after, the oft-mentioned thin gossamer thread of fate again played a role in keeping three policemen alive in the Clogher area of Co Tyrone. An RUC patrol along the border drove past an IRA landmine at Ballywholan and was observed by a command wire team in nearby hills. The detonate command was sent but in the second-or-two delay in firing, the RUC vehicle had moved about 25 yards. The explosion tore a huge crater in the road, but all the officers suffered was shock at this incredible escape.

On the following day, the Provisionals planted a bomb in the post office in Dial House, Upper Queen's Street as the action returned to Belfast City Centre. Three IRA men – all armed – had carried devices into the building and then ran off. A double blast caused major damage and a huge fire, but fortunately the RUC had cleared the area and there were no casualties. Traffic in the area was disrupted and there was major chaos around Howard Street and Wellington Place. The author also visited the building on a return trip in June 2012 and shopped in the ground floor sales area where the bombs exploded.

On the 18th, a wedding party in the Falls Road area was caught up in the drama of the Troubles. The wedding was taking place at St Paul's Church, which sits on the junction of Cavendish Street with the Falls Road and opposite the RVH. A man was arrested at the party after a foot patrol found several boxes packed with ammunition and were forced to seal the area off and delay the wedding by 90 minutes. It was not the only time that a wedding was disrupted at St Paul's, as the following account testifies.

PIG AT A WEDDING
Lance-Corporal, Royal Corps of Transport

I was stationed at Springfield Road RUC Station and in those days the top part of Violet Street was sealed off, so we had to turn left at the side entrance of the station; drive down Violet Street and then we hit Cavendish Street, which was one-way only. We would then turn right and in order to get back onto Springfield Road would have to turn right up Crocus Street – a real ambush black spot – and then back onto Springfield Road itself. Anyway, on this day we had to get onto the Falls Road where there had been a shooting incident – and soldiers on foot patrol had radioed in a contact. My skipper told me to get there fucking fast and I really didn't want to fuck about. At the bottom of Violet Street I illegally turned my Pig left, thinking that if there was any traffic coming against me they would soon shift!

Fuck me, but as I get near the end of Cavendish Street there's only a wedding taking place and they're all blocking the road! No way did I have time to stop and reverse back up the road and do it legally, so I just ploughed through them. The guests just scattered and people just scrambled out of the way as I muttered my apologies and carried on towards the Falls and the contact. There were a few clumps and thumps as things were thrown against the side of the Pig, but we just continued and got to the contact point. I don't suppose we won many 'hearts and minds' that day!

Later that same day, an off-duty RUC officer came very close to death as a PIRA murder gang went to the fitness gym where the officer had gone for a workout. The policeman had just arrived at McShane's Studio in Arthur Street, Belfast when armed men burst in. The quick-thinking officer threw a case at them, but they fired several shots – hitting him in the chest and side – badly wounding him. There were six gym users close to the officer, but the gunmen fired anyway. They ran off – leaving the policeman seriously hurt and lying in a pool of his own blood. He later recovered after an emergency operation. McShane's was where Belfast Olympian Mary Peters trained in her early days

On the 22nd, an army foot patrol observed three men in a car behaving suspiciously in Beechmount Avenue close to the Falls Road. One member of the patrol stepped in front of the car and the driver suddenly accelerated away – knocking him to the ground and slightly injuring him. The other members of the patrol opened fire and several of their rounds struck the fleeing vehicle – hitting the driver – and the car crashed into a wall several hundred yards away. Two of the men ran off, but at least one of them was injured as bloodstains indicated. The wounded driver, aged 17, was arrested and taken to the nearby RVH.

This author has previously mentioned the 'disappeared' and sadly, two more were added to that tragic list. The Provisional IRA had no heart and no soul and was a professionally ruthless killing machine which had cornered the market on cant, hypocrisy and callousness. On at least 10 occasions (Jean McConville, Robert Nairac et al.) their 'Nutting Squad' – or CAT – killed its enemies real or imaginary; guilty or innocent; and dumped their bodies in inaccessible or secret places – their actions thus denying their grieving loved ones of the comfort of closure and the victims of the honour of a known grave. On the 25th, two local men from Andersonstown were abducted by PIRA gunmen, taken away to be interrogated and presumably tortured before being killed. John McLory (18) and his friend Brian McKinney (22) set off for the Mary Peters Track where one of them worked. Mary Peters OBE won Olympic Gold in München in 1972 and was a Belfast girl. The sports centre was named in her honour.

Little is known of their abduction and torture and eventual death, but PIRA alleged that they were robbers – and as 'anti-social' elements they were executed (although they did not admit this until March 1999). Their bodies were buried in, at the time, unknown locations and were not discovered until 29 June 1999 – over 21 years after their murders. After tip-offs from Sinn Féin, an extensive search of bogland at Colgagh, Iniskeen in the Irish Republic unearthed their skeletons in shallow graves. Two more of the 'disappeared' had been returned to their loved ones. Where is the body of Captain Robert Nairac, Mr Adams? His loved ones would dearly like to know.

On the 27th, Colette Brady (27) was walking along Cavehill Road in the northern suburbs of Belfast with a male friend as they returned from a disco. Miss Brady was a Catholic and was employed in a local brewery. She and her companion had been dancing in the city centre and were en route for a friend's house. She was from Andersonstown and as such, was a long way from home. Why two members of the UFF should suspect her of being a Catholic and single her out for murder is unknown. The Cavehill Road starts at a section of the Antrim Road and then winds its way in a north-westerly direction towards the mountain from which it takes its name. The two men demanded money from the pair and then asked her which religion she was. Being worldly-wise, she replied that she was a Protestant but they clearly did not believe and drew guns on the pair of them. Her companion had a revolver pointed at his head and the trigger was pulled twice, but failed to fire and they then drew knives and began stabbing at him. After a brief scuffle, he managed to run off but heard several shots being fired. These were the fatal head shots which killed Miss Brady and they ran off – leaving her mortally wounded in the street. She was rushed to the Mater Hospital in Crumlin Road where she died shortly after admittance. Her wounds – she was shot three times in the back of the head – proved untreatable.

On the 31st, an IRA murder squad went to the home of a PO from Crumlin Road Jail with the intention of killing him. Two armed men called at the house in Outram Street, Belfast and when the PO's wife answered, demanded to see her husband. Correctly, she refused and closed the door before starting to walk up the stairs. The men then fired several shots through the glass section of the door and rounds struck her several times. She was hit twice in her side and badly wounded. She later recovered in hospital. The final event of May took place in Co Armagh when a Green Jackets foot patrol at Cullaville near Crossmaglen uncovered two five-gallon milk churns packed with 300lbs of explosives concealed in a grass bank where soldiers were known to patrol. The devices were found at the side of a Concession Road which ran from Castleblaney to Dundalk in the Irish Republic. The explosives were taken to a safe place where they were detonated safely. A follow-up search found command wires leading across the border where they found a detonator, batteries and a pair of binoculars.

The month of May saw five deaths – all five of whom were civilians. Four were Catholics and one was a Protestant. There was one overtly sectarian death during the month. It was not for lack of effort on the part of PIRA that no soldiers or policemen died.

42

June

June saw four soldiers or former soldiers killed along with three police officers. It was also a month in which the Provisionals lost three of their men in a major shoot-out with the British Army. It was a month which saw the officially recognised death of a soldier from the SAS – an organisation whose very presence in Northern Ireland is still unacknowledged by the MOD.

On the 1st of the month, David Cook – then a member of the Alliance Party (APNI) – became the first non-Unionist Lord Mayor of Belfast. Cook secured this post because of a dispute between Unionist councillors. It was not until 1997 that a Catholic became Lord Mayor of Belfast. At the start of the month, in an attempt to postpone a major embarrassment for the British Government, Roy Mason – Secretary of State for Northern Ireland – asked Amnesty International to delay publication of a report it had written into alleged ill-treatment of detainees at Castlereagh detention centre. The report was eventually published on the 13th.

Earlier in the year, the Provisionals had launched a major mortar attack on the Green Jackets in South Armagh and they followed this up with another attempt to kill and maim British soldiers at Crossmaglen on the 2nd. On this occasion, the Gardaí were involved in helping foil an attack from their side of the border. A lorry – the launching pad for explosive rockets – had been reinforced with iron plates and was carrying five huge mortars towards the selected firing point in a remote rural area on the border. A Gardaí patrol vehicle intercepted the lorry in a very narrow lane at Drummackavall en route for Crossmaglen. The driver of the PIRA vehicle desperately tried to reverse back up the lane, but was forced to stop and eventually jumped from the cab and escaped across fields. Many lives were saved that day thanks to the well-organised Gardaí Siochana. Later that day, a PIRA sniper almost claimed the life of a soldier on sangar duty at Glassmullan Camp on the sprawling Andersonstown estates. The sniper had taken up a firing position in Glassmullan Gardens and fired a single shot which hit the soldier in the back. His comrades dragged the stricken man under cover before returning fire on the gunman. He later recovered in hospital.

On the 3rd, the obscene double standards of the IRA were aptly demonstrated by their statement that they had 'executed' an 'anti-social' element at Jonesboro, Co Armagh. Daniel McErlean (26) was abducted by an IRA 'Nutting Squad' and taken across the border into Co Louth where he was ruthlessly interrogated – which in Provisional-speak was a euphemism for tortured. He was later taken over the border to fields near Edenappa where he was bound and hooded before being shot dead. He was a known Republican but also had dabbled in robberies and as such, was considered a 'hood' and fell foul of an organisation which killed without mercy. He was also wanted by the RUC for questioning about serious crimes and it is thought likely that he would have been better treated by the police.

Two days later, Lance-Corporal Anthony Peter Bennett (29) of the Glosters was killed in an RTA in Belfast. His transport was in collision with another army vehicle whilst en route to Belfast Docks. The soldier was on his way to meet his wife and newborn twin daughters who were coming over on the ferry. Sadly he never was given the chance to see or hold his children.

On the 6th, a former Republican internee aged 25 was stalked by a Loyalist murder gang – thought to have been UVF – at his place of work in the Smithfield Market area of Belfast. The man was shaving behind the counter of the shop where he worked when two men walked into the store and straight to where he was standing and shot him twice. One of the rounds missed, but the other entered his head just below his eye and he fell to the floor badly wounded. He later recovered. His crime was that he had once been in the IRA.

The phenomena of the Road Traffic Accident (RTA) and the British soldier – especially the UDR – has been covered times passim by this author in all of his works on the Troubles. Literally hundreds died in the Province from this admittedly prosaic cause of death – certainly not prosaic to their loved ones, but sufficiently so that the Whitehall mandarins do not consider a worthy enough cause of death to ensure a listing in the ROH. Lost Lives concurs, but have reserved a place in their list of the dead for Staff Sergeant David Naden (31) of the Scots Guards – attached to the SAS – killed on the 7th. He was possibly on undercover ops when his car crashed, or was forced off the road by an IRA unit at Shanalongford Bridge near Limavady, Co Londonderry. Whatever caused the impact must have been considerable as his vehicle was split completely in two when it hit the stone bridge. This author understands that it is merely speculation on his part when the suggestion is made that the IRA were involved.

Michael Riley was a former member of the UDR who lived in Denmark Street just off the Shankill Road. Although he had not been part of the regiment for some time, his past association was enough to condemn him to death. On the night of the 8th, two armed men walked into his house and shot him at close range in the chest – badly wounding him. He was rushed to hospital where he was treated for his dreadful wounds. He died on 19 August. Shortly after he was shot, the IRA exploded three devices at a post office garage in Clifton Street, Belfast. Several vehicles were destroyed in the no-warning explosions. A major fire broke out and several fire engines – now no longer on strike – were called out to fight the blaze. Just five minutes after the third blast, an architect's office in nearby University Street also exploded – again without warning. To add to the utter chaos and confusion, another IRA bomb exploded at a Government office next door.

On 10 June another Republican terrorist and would-be car thief chose the wrong vehicle to steal following Colm McNutt's death in December 1977 (see Chapter 36). Just as McNutt (INLA) tried to steal a car in Londonderry in which two armed Det-14 operatives were sitting, so too did Dennis Heaney (21) remove himself from the gene pool with the same unfortunate choice of vehicle. Heaney and another IRA man attempted to hijack a car in the centre of Londonderry in which another two heavily armed undercover soldiers were sitting. The soldiers shot him dead. The other IRA man made good his escape and later the area was the scene of a major riot. His family later made a claim in court that he had been a victim of the 'shoot to kill' policy and tried to claim compensation. The case was thrown out as the judge ruled that Heaney was an armed terrorist who was prepared to murder. Their claim for damages was rejected – as was their demand that the two undercover soldiers appear in court.

Also on the 10th, the Provisionals proved again what a deadly and ruthlessly effective terrorist force they were – especially down in Crossmaglen; the heart of what Merlyn Rees MP had coined as 'bandit country'. Having killed a young paratrooper there two years earlier, James Borrucki (see Chapter 20), they planted a booby-trap in the derelict market house close to Crossmaglen Square and on the route which soldiers took in order to return to the RUC base. As a patrol hurried past, the device was detonated and two soldiers were caught in the blast and slightly injured. It is thought that the thickness of the walls prevented the full force of the bomb from causing further injury or death.

On the 12th, a blast in Co Fermanagh left a young 19-year-old soldier with severe injuries as an army mobile patrol was hit by a PIRA landmine. The military convoy was travelling along the road between Newtownbutler and Wattlebridge when the lead Land Rover was caught in the blast and blown onto its side. The soldier was seriously wounded and four others were slightly injured. There was another PIRA explosion in Crossmaglen and another paratrooper was badly injured by shrapnel. There was some embarrassment for the police on the 13th after a report from Amnesty International claimed that people held at Castlereagh RUC detention centre on the outskirts of Belfast had been ill-treated. Kenneth Newman, then Chief Constable of the RUC, rejected the claims. Later on Roy Mason, Secretary of State for Northern Ireland, promised an inquiry into the allegations.

The Provisionals planted a total of 10 bombs at the Ulsterbus depot in the Smithfield area of Belfast. The blasts left the depot with extensive damage and destroyed a total of 21 buses. The *Belfast Newsletter* led with '10 Bomb Blitz on Bus Depot'. Their reporter wrote: "Thousands of people in Belfast's suburbs and East Antrim will be walking to work today or depending on lifts from car-owning friends after an IRA 10 bomb blitz on the city's main Ulsterbus depot last night. And the bombers who struck at the Smithfield depot serving the northern suburbs forced residents of the Winetavern-Samuel Street area to take to the streets when many were preparing for bed. The bombs were planted at about 10.20pm by three armed men who held up staff at the depot. The bombs were placed in strategic positions underneath and alongside and at the back of the single-decker buses. A warning was telephoned through to the Samaritans about four minutes before the first device went off at 10.26pm. No-one was injured and 100 residents ... many still wearing pyjamas, were able to get clear."

A resident of the area told the author in 2012: "I lived through the German blitz on the city back during the war. I was only a wee girl, but I remember the air raids so well and the people me Ma knew who were killed. That night the IRA blew up the bus place brought those awful memories racing back to me, sure they did." (Her name will be withheld at her request.)

On Thursday the 15th, a young soldier on sangar duty outside Cookstown RUC Station had the sort of day which he will remember – even on his death bed. An IRA gunman in a concealed position fired a burst of fire from an automatic weapon at the man as he leaned out of the sangar. Two rounds struck him just below his neck and exited through the collar of his flak jacket – one of which continued onwards and gouged a huge strike mark in a metal plate behind him. This author has identified 1,306 names of soldiers killed in, or as a consequence of the Troubles; it could so easily have been 1,307.

LIKE WILD ANIMALS
Kevin Campbell, King's Own Scottish Borderers

Later I will tell you about my 'accidental' shooting of a BBC cameraman – and whilst this was the funny side of the tour for me, although not for the man concerned, something which happened in Grosvenor Park will stay with me for the rest of my life.

Even though I was shot at more than once; was involved in bombing incidents, riots etc one incident which stays with me and is still – all these years later – the cause of my nightmares, occurred later that month. We were called to a suspect car bomb outside the Sinn Féin office. We set up the usual cordon and were abused as usual by the locals. We set up in defensive positions in and around the bushes on the edge of the park. A woman, who would be around 40, was walking towards me and by this time I was no longer the green 17-year-old and was suspicious. Why, I thought, was she was heading straight for me? I challenged her and told her to get back and she replied: "It's alright son. I just want to tell you we're not all bad; we don't all want this here. I have kids too and I know that your mother, God bless her, will be worried sick about you."

By now she was really close to me and she bent forward and told me: "May God bless and protect you, son" before walking off back towards the crowd. I watched as she got close to them. I will never know what she said, but they set on her with such brutal force – kicking and punching her as she was dragged into the crowd. They were like a pack of wild animals as they laid into her with a terrible anger. I never saw her again and never found out what happened to her, but I never forgot her words and it made me see the rest of my tour through different eyes. I still think of her and she still inspires me. Even though she is the cause of some of my nightmares, she's also the reason that I never judge everyone just because of their circumstances.

This oft-repeated incident was a mere four years after the incident in which Queen's Lancashire Fusilier Gary Barlow was abducted by a mob from the same area prior to being shot by an IRA gunman. The women of that Falls/Divis/ Balkans and Springfield Road area were more violent than the men – or certainly as vicious as their menfolk. These were the people who would hurl excrement, urine – even soiled sanitary wear – at passing soldiers without a thought for their actions. They would scream and spit and hurl abuse as the soldiers passed by on foot patrol and participate with the other rioters who threw stones, broken paving slabs and broken glass – as well as petrol and nail bombs at members of the Security Forces. Ten years later these same people, or their Andersonstown and Turf Lodge counterparts, would almost tear to pieces two corporals from the Signals prior to them being cold-bloodedly 'executed' by IRA terrorists. This author was once asked by a BBC interviewer if he hated all the Irish. The author replied: "No, but I can give you a list of the ones I do." Numbered on that list are the aforementioned hags who were in evidence in Kevin Campbell's account of an incident in Grosvenor Road.

On the following day, another young police officer was added to the RUC ROH, which eventually topped the 300 mark. Constable Robert Struthers (19) was a member of the RUCR and worked full-time in an electronics factory in Lorne, Co Londonderry. He was an apprentice electrician and had just finished typing a letter to a member of the firm's clerical staff when two armed men – who had simply walked into the factory – found their way into the Admin section and shot the part-time policeman dead in front of his shocked colleagues. It is thought that one of the assassins had either been into the office previously by subterfuge or had been briefed by a sympathiser in the company. The young officer lived on Glen Bank in the west of the city and was rushed to Altnagelvin Hospital where he died shortly afterwards. It was later revealed that Republicans had threatened his life if he joined the RUC, but bravely chose to ignore the threats. Robert Struthers was the first of three policemen to be killed in the space of two days.

Two young Catholic boys had an extremely lucky escape when a Loyalist murder gang – likely to have been UVF – pulled their stolen car alongside them as they walked along the West Circular Road. A gunman aimed his weapon at the two boys from very close range and they were too shocked to react. The trigger was squeezed several times, but jammed on each occasion before the car raced off out of Belfast along the Upper Springfield Road. The Provisionals then surreptitiously left a bomb outside the front sangar of North Queen Street RUC Station and, without any warning, the device exploded. The soldier escaped serious injury, but the blast demolished the sangar and bent his SLR into a 'U' shape. Parts of the rifle were found several hundred feet away. North Queen Street runs along the south-eastern axis of the Nationalist New Lodge area and as such, was extremely vulnerable to attacks from the New Lodge Road, Spamount Street and several other residential areas of the 'Long Streets'.

An error of judgement and a chance encounter with a Loyalist murder gang led to the death of a young Catholic man – Kevin Dyer (26) – on the 17th. The young man, from Glenalina Road on the Republican Ballymurphy Estate, was enjoying an after-work drinking session in and around Belfast City Centre. He and a companion walked over to the Crumlin Road and found a pub in which to drink. He was aware of where he was and the dangers therein, but as he was in the presence of a Protestant workmate, perhaps thought that he was safe as long as nothing drew attention to the fact that he was a Catholic. However, a group of Loyalists from the UVF were suspicious and waited in a group in order to see which way he walked after he had left the pub. The fact that he walked over the Shankill Road in the direction of the Nationalist Springfield Road sealed his fate. The young man saw someone whom he recognised as they stopped close to the Lawnbrook Social Club and foolishly, or perhaps naively, mentioned the Ballymurphy Estate. The man shouted to the Loyalist gang that they were Catholics and the men ran towards them. His Protestant friend ran off when the UVF men came towards them, but young Dyer didn't. He was forcibly taken to waste ground in the Glencairn area where he was beaten and eventually a heavy piece of metal engine casing was dropped onto his head as he lay helpless on the ground. He died almost immediately – a victim of the savage hatred of animal-like Loyalist murderers. His wife was pregnant at the time and another child would grow up in the Province never having known their father.

On the following day, two policemen were attacked as they drove through the area of Sturgan's Bay close to Camlough in Co Armagh. Their vehicle was ambushed by a gang of Provisionals who opened fire from behind a hedge with automatic weapons. The RUC car was hit at least 20 times and Constable Hugh McConnell (32), father of two, was hit several times and died almost immediately. However, despite evidence that his colleague Constable William Turbitt (47), father of four, had been badly wounded there was no trace of his body. Although hit in the head and fatally injured, the gunmen revealed an utterly depraved opportunistic streak and abducted the dying policeman. Later evidence suggested that he would have died within minutes anyway but he was dragged into a stolen car and driven to a derelict farm – then after death, dumped into a marshy area before again being taken to a remote farmhouse in the area.

On 10 July 1978 the body of Constable Turbitt was discovered. It was evident that that the gang had considered using him as a bargaining chip, but all that came to nothing. The UVF kidnapped a Catholic priest to hold as a counter-threat, but he was later released unharmed. A spokesman for the Provisionals claimed that he had been interrogated and revealed some information, but an inquest was told that his death would have been " ... rapid ... " and in any case, after such a traumatic head wound, would have been highly unlikely to have said a word. Hugh Murphy, a Catholic priest, was kidnapped in retaliation for the abduction of Constable Turbitt the day before. The kidnappers issued a statement saying that they would return the priest in the same condition as the RUC officer was returned. A number of Protestant ministers appealed for the priest to be released and, as stated, he was subsequently returned unharmed.

The next death occurred in a Loyalist shebeen – an illegal drinking club – and there was some mystery surrounding the demise of Edward Ferguson (40), who was shot by an armed UVF member. Mr Ferguson was a former PO and worked for the docks police at the time of his death. Apparently he had been asked to leave the drinking den and was threatened by a UVF member with a revolver. The former PO was shot and fatally wounded – later dying in hospital. In court, his killer – who was convicted and jailed for life – claimed the gun had discharged accidentally. The UVF were again busy the following day when gunmen in a stolen car driving along the Ballygomartin Road close to New Barnsley RUC Station spotted eight youths whom they took to be Catholics. The gunmen opened fire and drove off before doing a U-turn and returning to open fire a second time. None of the youths were badly injured.

On the 21st, as the first day of the British summer dawned, a three-man PIRA ASU stole a white Mazda car and packed it with arms and explosives with the intention of blowing up a GPO depot in Belfast. The car drove from the Bone/Oldpark area in North Belfast towards the depot in Ballysillan Road only a mile or so away. Unknown to the Provisionals, the operation was already compromised thanks to a possible high-ranking informant – and a well-armed unit of undercover soldiers were already in waiting at the depot. The car parked at Wheatfield Drive a few hundred yards from the post depot. Here the various accounts differ: Sinn Féin state that the men were unarmed and were cut down in an indiscriminate hail of bullets – thus demonstrating a 'shoot to kill' policy. The soldiers on the ground state that they challenged the gunmen, who opened fire, and under ROE returned fire and killed the three Provisionals. Sadly a fourth man, an innocent Protestant bystander, was also hit and died at the scene. All of the three IRA men died at the scene. They were Denis Brown (28), Jackie Mailey (31) and James Mulvenna (28). The innocent Protestant who was caught in the crossfire as he walked across a nearby playing field was William Hanna (27).

There was more drama just a few days later as Loyalist paramilitaries attacked the funeral procession of the three PIRA bombers as it wound its way from North Belfast to Milltown Cemetery. As the cortege passed Lepper Street in the New Lodge, a small explosive device went off – causing disruption and shock – but three police officers and two soldiers were injured as a store was wrecked and dozens of windows in the area were shattered. Earlier there had been scuffles on the Antrim Road between mourners and the RUC as the officers tried to remove illegal tricolours from the coffins.

Patrick McEntee (53) was a married man with five children and five years before his death, had been the victim of an IRA 'punishment' shooting. He had been accused of being a former British soldier and an army sympathiser. Had he been so, he would have hardly continued to live in the black heart of 'bandit country', the town of Crossmaglen (or XMG as it was known to soldiers). On the 24th he was driving with his wife in the area of Drumuckavall, South Armagh when his car was stopped by an IRA IVCP. Mrs McEntee was ordered out of the car and gunmen got in and took her husband across the border after giving her one of their famous hollow 'assurances' that he would be released unharmed. He had been picked up by the Provisionals' local 'Nutting Squad' and was taken into the Republic where he was beaten and tortured before being shot in the head as a 'tout'. There is no substantial evidence to prove that he had been informing and it is thought that the pious Provisionals were trying to justify their latest barbarity.

MEMORIES OF A LONG TOUR
Marcus Townley, Welsh Guards

I was 19 at the time and some salient memories really stand out for me. I can remember stepping out of some dark shadows to P-Check a local walking home in the dark; I remember the sense of relief that it was SF (army) on the faces of the Catholic civvies – in the knowledge that they would be getting home to see their loved ones; patrolling past known players and nodding a 'hello', which would have surely pissed them off; like when one of our lads was killed – Guardsman Paul Fryer – an old woman crying and saying sorry about our sad loss – it was at night when she said all this; like patrolling through Camlough where the local 'Mr Big' had a pub which was called the 'Mickey Mouse Bar'. He was a former U.S. Marine in a town which was hostile to say the least.

I recall patrolling through another nameless village – the name escapes me now – and as we moved through, fires would be lit in the hearth of the houses and the chimney stacks would bellow out smoke … plotting our route no doubt. Once we couldn't be picked up by chopper, so we had to tab a few miles to be picked up by Sarras by our neighbouring company. We had to be taken back to Bessbrook via the Derrybeg in Newry, and hearing the side being hit constantly by bricks. There is a plaque on that estate to a 10-year-old boy who was shot and killed by SF. What the plaque didn't tell you was that during a firefight between SF and the IRA he was shining a torch to illuminate the troops. That was until a soldier put one or two rounds at the light source.

It was around this time the PIRA used a new tactic: a patrol by members of 2 Para was compromised at an old disused farm building. They bugged out and left the place, but later returned – only for the PIRA to install a baby monitor so that they knew when the soldiers returned. They triggered a bomb which killed or badly injured two I think. We were once tasked to take part in a 'lurk patrol' at the farmhouse of a UDR member as we knew that the 'freedom fighters' were going to pay the man a house call. We got into position and laid in wait, but it started to snow heavily. We waited for five hours, but the players never showed up. Another incident happened when we were sent down to the XMG area to do a few ops. We moved out after dark, but shortly afterwards we heard the tell-tale sound of an explosion. When we returned to XMG a few days later, we were told what had happened. The (XMG) company would always pick up the Sarra by the Borucki sangar and PIRA dickers clocked this.

A PIRA team placed a bomb in a water bottle carrier and left it at the base of the sangar. One guardsman noticed it and attempted to reach, but was stopped by a quick-thinking sergeant who used a length of cord and detonated the bomb – fortunately causing only minor damage. Red faces all around for our XMG Company.

On the 25th, a two-vehicle UDR mobile patrol was called to a suspected robbery at Belcoo Post Office in the small village of Scribbagh, Co Tyrone. As they debussed, a landmine exploded nearby causing some minor injuries. However, an IRA team using one of their American M60 machine guns, which they had set up over the border in Co Leitrim, opened fire. The firing point was in hills located near Gubmanus and the fusillade of 7.62mm rounds hit several soldiers in the patrol. The rounds, which have a muzzle velocity of 2,800 feet (853 metres) per second, broke one soldier's arm but Private Alan Ferguson (25), from Enniskillen, was mortally wounded and died at the scene.

The Loyalist 'window cleaners' were back in action after a lull of several months when they attacked and attempted to murder two Catholic women at their home in Richmond Square, North Belfast in the early hours of the 27th. Using a ladder propped against a bedroom wall, an armed man partially levered open the bedroom window and opened fire – wounding both women in their legs. The injured were a woman of 65 and her 35-year-old daughter. Their would-be assassins escaped in the direction of the Loyalist Ballysillan or Westland areas. The next morning, an unnamed paramilitary group went on to a building site in Lurgan and asked for a workman by name. The man was a Protestant and it is thought likely that his attackers were either INLA or PIRA. The man, who was in a workmen's' hut on Lough Road, was shot in the head and badly wounded. The gunmen then drove away in a stolen car and the man, who was thought to have no Army/RUC connections, recovered after a long time in hospital.

The month ended with two false alarms after a warning was telephoned through to the RUC that an explosive device had been left at the Stormont Hotel. Controlled explosions were carried out in the car park, but these turned out to be hoaxes. Finally, an RUC officer came out of his flat in the Belvoir area of South-East Belfast and upon inspecting underneath his car, found a cardboard box with wires leading from it. Army EOD were called in, but upon examination the box was found to be empty.

June had been a more violent month than of late, and 16 people were killed. The army lost three soldiers – and a former soldier was also killed. The RUC lost three officers. A total of six civilians were killed; four Catholics and two Protestants. The Provisionals lost four members, all killed by the army. Of the six civilian deaths, two were overtly sectarian.

43

July

The month of July saw a total of 10 deaths – with seven of the deaths being Security Forces (SF); four of who died in two separate RTAs. The new PIRA tactic of manhole bombs saw the death of a paratrooper and the death of a young boy allegedly at the hands of the SAS.

The month began with the loss of two more Light Infantry boys – this time as a result of a traffic accident. Lance-Corporal Terence Wilson (19) from Pontefract in West Yorkshire and Private Kevin McGovern (22) from Sunderland, Tyne and Wear died on the 1st and 3rd respectively. Given the nature of their deaths – RTA – and the fact that they were in the same battalion in Northern Ireland, leads one to speculate that they were involved in the same accident. They were buried in their respective areas of Heworth, Tyne and Wear and Pontefract (close to the author's home prior to emigration). The 1st also saw PIRA carry out one of their brutal punishment shootings and two brothers received gunshot wounds to their arms and legs in the Nationalist New Lodge area. There was a suggestion of an 'own goal' bomb explosion in what the IRA called the 'Planet of the Irps' – the Divis Street flats – when a blast caused some damage and two people were hurt – including a 22-year-old man who was very badly injured.

On the 2nd of the month, the Royal Artillery lost Gunner Roger Edwards (22) in a tragic, but accidental shooting. The circumstances are vague and what few eyewitnesses are available are reluctant to speak. It would appear that there was a negligent discharge of a weapon and Gunner Edwards was mortally wounded and died shortly afterwards. It must be stressed that the author is acting upon information received, but cannot vouch for the veracity of said information. Gunner Edwards was from Beaconsfield, Herts and is buried in Holtspur Cemetery in his hometown. On the morning of the 4th, the Provisionals killed another policeman – this time in Castlederg, Co Tyrone. RUCR Constable Jacob Rankin (37) had left the police station in order to visit a local shop and buy cigarettes and had wisely covered up his uniform. A car, hijacked earlier by IRA gunmen, drove past the part-time policeman and opened fire – hitting him several times and mortally wounding him. He was rushed to Tyrone County Hospital in Omagh where he died shortly afterwards. It is not known if he was recognised and then shot, or that he was observed coming out of an RUC base and his killers assumed that he was a policeman. Constable Rankin had three young children and lived in Castlederg close to the station. The town, whose name in Irish is 'Caslanadergy', was one of the most bombed towns in the Province during the Troubles. With the border with the Republic just a stone's throw away, it was a popular target to hit for the Provisionals as their sanctuary and bolthole was so close.

On the 7th an IRA gunman ambushed a patrol of the Parachute Regiment at Coolderry, close to Crossmaglen, as soldiers searched along the border area for signs of incursion. A lone gunman in a stolen car had driven just inside the border with the North and then had walked towards a chosen firing point before sniping at members of the foot patrol. As the paras came into view, he loosed off around six shots – several of which came close to finding targets – but as he tried to escape, at least one round fired by the paras hit him. There were blood stains at the firing point and also inside the car, which was abandoned inside the Republic. The following day, a customs post was attacked along the border at Rosslea, Co Fermanagh. A small bomb exploded just as an RUC patrol reached the building, but there were no injuries.

On the 11th, there was a killing near Dunloy, Co Antrim which left a sour taste in the mouths of many people in Northern Ireland – and one in which the army did not exactly cover itself in glory. A young boy – John Boyle (16) – had found an IRA arms cache in a cemetery close to his home and immediately told his father. As a consequence, his father – a Catholic – informed the RUC and the case was handed on to the army. A surveillance team dug in to watch the cache and apprehend IRA operatives who came to collect any arms. The four members of the SAS were briefed by RUC on the ground extensively before they dug in and warned that the family might approach the site because of the proximity of the farmland which they were working on.

Tragically for the young and naïve boy, he returned to the cemetery – unaware of the presence of undercover soldiers – in order to look at the weapons. A soldier opened fire, allegedly without warning, and shot the boy three times in the back. The teenager died at the scene. His brother and father, on hearing the shots, raced to the scene to find the dying boy and were promptly and insensitively arrested. They were later released without charge. There was naturally an inquest and the judge eventually accepted that the soldier had opened fire because he believed that his life was under threat. One of the men, however, was described as: " … .an unworthy witness, eager to make unmeritorious points … " and there were allegations that the SAS men, when giving evidence, were less than helpful. They were eventually acquitted, but this author believes that the killing was unnecessary and gratuitous. Their mission was to kill any IRA men attempting to recover the weapons and the boy stumbled in on the operation.

There was also a slightly more humorous side to surveillance, as the following contribution by a man for whom I have the greatest respect – Martin McGartland – attests. Marty, as he is known to his friends, infiltrated the IRA for RUC Special Branch and saved many lives by his brave, undercover work. This author recommends his highly readable *Fifty Dead Men Walking*, which describes his life as an informer deep inside the Provisional IRA.

SURVEILLANCE
Martin 'Marty' McGartland

When we were kids the British soldiers would often pull pranks on us and other kids. The solders would often use the Moyard flats as temporary observation posts whereby they would climb into the blocked-up drying rooms – through small holes in the block-work – where they would then carry out surveillance on properties and also individuals (including PIRA members – aka 'players') in the local Ballymurphy area. Those drying rooms were pitch-black inside and as young kids we would often climb in. Sometimes the soldiers would stay in the old drying rooms and stairwells for hours, if not days, just waiting and watching.

However this was not known to many unless they too were visiting someone who lived in the flats. One night about 10pm, a pal of mine and his girlfriend climbed into one of the old drying rooms in the block of flats which had been blocked up at some point, but which some blocks had been broken. Sam and

Fay climbed into the room and were doing things they should not have been doing when they both heard a laugh, then another coming from inside the pitch-black room. Sam ran with his jeans half-on, half-off and he jumped head-first through the small hole of the drying room and landed on his head on the other side. He left poor Fay in the pitch-black room, screaming at the top of her voice. Sam ran straight past me and the girl I had been standing with on the stairwell. He did not say a word as he rushed past us. We thought he had done something to her, but it turned out it was the soldiers in the drying room. The sounds coming from in there were like something you would hear in a very scary horror film!

Anyway, we ran up to investigate and it turned out that the soldiers inside were trying to calm poor Fay down, but that was having the opposite effect as she became even more hysterical and she was squealing at the top of her voice. She only began to calm down after some of the soldiers switched on their flashlamps, but poor Fay got the biggest fright of her life that night. One of the solders was so drunk that he virtually had to be carried down the stairwells to a waiting army vehicle, which had arrived soon after, along with RUC officers. Fay was taken home by the girl I had been with. We were surprised at the amount of equipment that was being taken out of the drying room by the RUC and army. There was all sorts of kit – cameras and surveillance equipment … all this despite one or two of the soldiers showing signs of being heavily intoxicated. We learned that the soldiers inside had been on a surveillance operation and poor Fay and Sam had unwittingly walked into the middle of it. They were both very lucky they were not shot due to being mistaken as PIRA terrorists.

The solders must have got so bored that most of them had been drinking while on the job. The next day we gained enough courage to climb in to the drying room – which was still pitch-black even during daylight – and with flashlights we could see that the army must have been in the drying room for some time. There was loads of food packaging lying around; lots of empty beer cans and even some full beer cans they had left behind unopened along with empty cigarette packets which they had left behind in their haste to get out of the flat. Poor Fay was badly traumatised by her experience and was reluctant to even go near the flats – let alone the drying rooms.

The drying rooms also had a more sinister reputation – as did the flats – because both the IRA and INLA would use them to carry out some of their most savage so-called 'punishment beatings' where their poor defenseless victims would be very badly beaten and even shot in the legs. Some of my close friends were on the receiving end of such beatings and shootings.

Martin 'Marty' McGartland is the author of *50 Dead Men Walking* and I am indebted to him for contributing to this book.

On the day after the killing of young John Boyle, a soldier from the Parachute Regiment was killed by the comparatively new PIRA tactic of the manhole bomb. Devices placed just underneath manhole covers were detonated by remote control at the optimum time for the firer. Private Jack Fisher (19), a 'monkey hanger' as the people of Hartlepool are known, was patrolling along Dundalk Road, Crossmaglen and had just reached St Joseph's Primary School. As the young private, who was due to leave Northern Ireland within the week,

Engineers demolishing a sangar, Victoria Street, Belfast, 1979. (©Mark 'C')

passed the manhole it exploded – killing him instantly. It also injured other members of the six-man patrol. Damage was also caused to the school building and nearby houses. On the same day, five RUC officers attempted to break up a crowd disturbance at Carlisle Circus where the Crumlin and Antrim Roads meet in North Belfast. They were then attacked by a 50-strong mob and all of the officers were badly beaten and hospitalised. Another soldier died on that day and became the first of two 13/18 Hussars to perish in RTAs in a period of a week-and-a-half. Trooper Paul Shepherdson (20) died on the 16th and a comrade, Philip Jonathan Ridgway Smith (19), died on the 27th. The latter received a full military funeral at Catterick Garrison in North Yorkshire.

On the 17th, a mini bombing blitz by the Provisionals saw severe damage caused in Belfast City Centre – including hundreds of thousands of pounds' worth of damages to stock at Watson's Car Showroom in Little Victoria Street. Several other premises were hit by a mixture of blast bombs and incendiaries. A paper company and picture-framing company were also destroyed. A photograph of destroyed buildings in Little Victoria Street, which appeared in the *Belfast Telegraph*, resembles a scene from the London blitz in 1940-41.

On the 19th, Private Mark Carnie (18) – on attachment to the Queen's' Own Highlanders – was killed by an IRA culvert bomb in Co Tyrone and became the first member of that superb Scottish regiment to be killed in over seven years. The regiment, whose motto is *Nemo Me Impune Lacessit* (*No-One Provokes Me With Impunity*), was founded in 1739. Its battle honours include Guadaloupe, 1759; South Africa 1846-7; Boer War, 1899-1902; Mons, 1914; Somme, 1916; Dunkirk, 1940 and Burma, 1944. Private Carnie was the middleman of a three-man patrol and was killed instantly by the culvert bomb as he patrolled along the Ballygawley Road near Dungannon. The other members of the patrol were also injured. His murder attracted a surprising response from a local Catholic priest who not only condemned the bombing, but was also most critical of the Provisionals.

On the 24th, a PIRA gunman opened fire on an RUC foot patrol as it walked through the Nationalist Ardoyne in Belfast. The policemen had just turned on to the Crumlin Road and as it did so, it passed a small group of children playing in the street. Several shots rang out and a little girl was hit twice in the back and a policeman was hit in his legs. One of the rounds passed straight through her whilst the other lodged near her spine. Both injured persons were taken to hospital and a follow-up search found three American Armalites in a derelict house in the area. The girl later made a full recovery in hospital. On the following day, a soldier was critically injured following an explosion in Clonard Gardens in the Falls Road area. As a foot patrol passed St Vincent's Monastery, a bomb concealed inside a lamppost exploded. The patrol from the Royal Anglians bore the full brunt of the explosion, but three civilians – including an elderly woman – were also injured. The platoon commander, a young lieutenant, received terrible injuries and was immediately rushed to the RVH for emergency treatment. The monastery received some structural damage as the Provisionals clearly demonstrated their utter contempt for their own supporters.

NEAR-MISS AT HASTINGS STREET
Kevin Campbell, 1 KOSB

It was 12 July 1978 – the glorious 12th if you were an Orange man! I am of Irish-Catholic descent, so the only thing I was celebrating was that we were stagging on at Hastings Street police station away from the rest of the company – and it meant no patrols in the blistering sun. I had just come off break and was taking over on the front gate from Jock Bow. There was a girl called Avril, with whom I was chatting, and she was really nice. Anyway at 3pm the RUC relief arrived and he was dropped at the gate on his way in from a mobile patrol. I noticed immediately that he stank of booze and he headed straight into the sangar and flaked out on the chair.

Around 3.30pm I had to open the gates to let in a Hotspur. The gates were at the end of a road about 75m long, if I remember right, and were constructed of corrugated sheets about 20 feet high. Just as I was closing the gate, a gunman opened up from the direction of the Divis flats. He couldn't see me through the sheeting as this ran the length of the road on both sides. What he was doing was taking a line onto the top edge of the gate as he looked down from the top of the flats, dropping his aim and firing through the sheeting on the road side.

As the first round hit the ground just in front of me I convinced myself that it had not happened, but a few seconds later there was another splash of tarmac thrown up in front of me – then another and another. I ran the length of the road onto a street. I can't remember its name, but it was the one that linked Divis Street with the Crumlin Road (Northumberland Street). I got out onto the road and scanned the Divis with my SLR as cars drove past me on both sides. I had the sudden realisation that I was on my own, with no cover and was at serious risk from both the gunman and the cars. I took cover behind one of the concrete bollards on the left side, but it was too late … the IRA had done their usual 'shoot and scoot'.

When I got back to the sangar the copper I had been on with had been ghosted away and Avril had been put back on stag. It transpired that he was nearing his pension and they wanted him out the way before the brass got there. I was dying for a smoke but had to wait till I had been debriefed on position and the brass had gone. I sat in the chair, pulled the Golden Virginia out of my map pocket took out a fag paper. It was only then, as the adrenaline rush had died, that I realised just how scared I was. I could not get the tobacco onto the fag paper as I was shaking so much. Avril gave me one of her 'straights'.

This was the most exciting thing that had ever happened to me and I was as high as a kite from the adrenaline rush. I have tried lots of things since trying to get that high again, but nothing has ever come close. Incidentally, I still have a scar on my leg where some of the tarmac thrown up from the impact of the round broke the skin. When I look back at it now, I only reacted the way I did through the level of training we had before the tour – that and more likely the fact that at 17 you think you're invincible and nothing, not even the IRA, could get me.

Although the Provisionals' England Department had been decimated by arrests before and after the Balcombe Street Siege (see Chapter 12), they had enough operatives or willing sleepers on the mainland to be a dangerous nuisance. On the 26th a parcel, posted in London and addressed to the Conservative Central Office in Westminster, was intercepted and examined. It was found to contain enough explosives to be fatal to the opener and it was defused by the army. Over 100 people were evacuated from the building and it is thought that the future Prime Minister and then Leader of the Conservative Party, Margaret Thatcher, was not in attendance at the time.

On the 26th – on a day of incendiary attacks, blast bombs, hoax warnings and a busy day for army EOD – an innocent Catholic was killed by Loyalists in what can only be described as a sectarian murder. Noel McKay (29) was an engineer who worked for the then GPO. He lived in the Finaghy area of South-East Belfast. In what was thought to have been a targeted Loyalist attack, a murder gang from either the UVF or UFF shot him as he arrived home from work and parked outside his house. Two armed men were waiting for him and as he got out of his van, they shot him 10 times – leaving him lying in a pool of blood to be found by his pregnant wife. There was speculation that the Provisionals might have been involved, as the car the gunmen hijacked had been taken from the Falls Road and the car which they used to escape in was later abandoned in the Nationalist Stewartstown Road. This could also have been a Loyalist ploy to confuse the authorities and lay the blame at the door of the Provisionals.

Mark 'C', UDR and Royal Artillery

Ref the shooting of Noel McKay at Finaghy Road North: Finaghy is South Belfast and I know that area of Ardmore well as I had school friends there up to and just after the beginning of the Troubles. Near there is Orchardville, which is built on the original field the Orangemen used to go to on 12 July. It is very close to Andytown and because of the start of the Troubles we moved away from there in the early seventies. Anyway that area had a few Prod families right up to 1973-4 but by 1978 would have been 100 per cent RC – and looking where the cars were hijacked and then abandoned I cannot see it being a Loyalist attack and in Lost Lives the RUC believed it was not sectarian.

The last action of July took place at the border crossing of Augher, Co Tyrone when PIRA gunmen ambushed an RUC mobile patrol with bullet and bomb. The terrorists had lain in wait and when the police approached the ambush point, exploded a small device which caused their Land Rover to stop. They then opened fire with automatic weapons as the officers jumped out from their damaged vehicle. Heavy gunfire poured in from the PIRA men, but none of the officers were hit. Fire was returned but the gunmen escaped across the border. On the 30th Tomás Ó Fiaich, Catholic Primate of Ireland, paid a visit to Republican prisoners in the Maze. The prisoners were taking part in the 'blanket protest' with over 300 Republicans refusing to wear prison clothes or follow normal regulations in an attempt to secure a return of special category status.

July had ended with 10 deaths. The army lost seven men and the RUC lost one officer. Two civilians, both Catholics, were killed – one of whom could be described as sectarian.

August

This month saw a total of eight soldiers, or former soldiers – killed as a consequence of their past military association – die in the Province. It included the death of a soldier on undercover ops and two other sneaky beakies were killed in an RTA which may have been security-related.

August could have so easily started with multi-fatalities as the irresponsibility of the IRA was again in evidence. Children playing in their play area in Newcastle, Co Down found a part of an explosive booby-trap device which was intended for an army foot patrol. Wisely they did not touch the device, but called the RUC and the army later defused the device. On the same day, a van was hijacked and the driver forced to drive to the City Cemetery on Whiterock Road. A bomb was loaded on board and he was instructed to drive to New Barnsley RUC on the northern tip of the Ballymurphy Estate. The driver drove the short distance up Whiterock Road and along Springfield Road and once he had reached the RUC base, managed to alert police officers. The van later exploded, but thanks to the brave and quick-thinking driver there were no injuries.

On the 2nd of the month, Tomás Ó Fiaich's comments were pounced upon by Sinn Féin/IRA and used for propaganda purposes in the USA. A new campaign painting the British Government as solely responsible for the filthy conditions, which the prisoners themselves have created, was very successful to an Irish-American audience desperate for some anti-British news – and NORAID's collection tins were filled to overflowing.

However even whilst naïve Irish-Americans were donating their money in order to swell PIRA's arms fund, their 'freedom fighters' were busy killing another policeman. John Lamont (21), an RUCR constable, was walking in the direction of Ballymena police station in the small Co Antrim town. He was in George Street – only a minute or two from his base – when a car, stolen earlier in Toomebridge, pulled past him and shots were fired from the rear window. He was hit several times and slumped to the street mortally wounded. Drinkers from a nearby pub rushed out to help him and he was then rushed to the nearby Waveney Hospital. He died shortly after arrival. During the Troubles, there were 11 deaths in or near Ballymena. Eight people were killed by various Loyalist groups and three by Republican groups – mainly PIRA. Two of the IRA's victims were members of the RUC. All other victims were civilians. Of the 11 victims, six were Protestant and five Catholic.

On the 7th, the IRA tried to blow up a Protestant-frequented supermarket on the Crumlin Road, but their attempts were foiled by the shop manager and the army were able to minimise the blast damage following a controlled explosion. The Mountainview Tavern on the Shankill Road was hit by the IRA for the third time in another gun and bomb attack. There was some damage, but no injuries. In Belfast City Centre there was a narrow escape for four policemen as they almost became victim to what the Belfast Telegraph called 'hanging bombs'. The devices were attached to a security grill and a metal fence at a business in Kent Street, Belfast close to Royal Avenue. The RUC was alerted and four officers were sent to investigate as dusk approached. Just after 1930 hours, the bombs all went off – causing some damage to the building and a nearby carpet store. Two of the police officers received injuries – including shock. More of the 'hanging bombs' were left by PIRA operatives outside Armagh House in Belfast City Centre and a team of cleaners were forced to run for their lives as the devices exploded.

Shortly afterwards and several miles away near Omagh, fate smiled on the crew of an RUC mobile patrol as it drove over a culvert at Beragh – a tiny hamlet in Co Tyrone. Packed into the culvert was a 300lb device which was designed to cause carnage to police or soldiers. As the patrol passed over the culvert, the detonator fired but failed to set off the explosives. The small explosion was heard and the vehicle stopped some distance away in order to investigate. The army was called out to defuse the device and were on-hand also to defuse a PIRA bomb left in creamery cans and packed into a hijacked car at a farm near Strabane. The vehicle's owners were forced to drive this proxy bomb to an army VCP. There were no injuries in either incident.

On the 8th of the month, the Provisional IRA tried to kill and maim soldiers and set up a bomb attack along a regular route. They chose a wall which bordered Mackie's Engineering and placed a large device behind it. Mackie's eventually closed in 1999. At its height James Mackie & Sons was one of the largest employers in Belfast. Mackie's, as they were known locally, were a major supplier of munitions during the Second World War. The bomb exploded prematurely however and three civilians – two of whom were pregnant – were chatting at their front doors in the time-honoured manner, were caught by the blast. One of them, 60-year-old widow Mary McCaffrey, was blown over and received a broken leg and other – at the time unknown – internal injuries. Her neighbours found her crying for help – covered in dust and blood – and she was later taken to hospital. Complications set in and she died on the 28th.

The home of outspoken SDLP Leader Gerry Fitt was attacked again – for the fourth time – as a Republican mob caused some damage to his house in Belfast's Antrim Road. Fitt was a keen critic of both the army and the RUC and his constant sniping criticism was bound to ruffle a few feathers. He was again critical of the RUC for taking a long time to respond to his 999 calls. Three simultaneous attacks by PIRA gunmen on soldiers returning to their base after patrols were made on the evening of the 9th. Several shots were fired at soldiers at McCrory Park RUC base, Moyard RUC base and New Barnsley RUC Station. There were no injuries. Less than an hour later the RUC were called into Glen Road, close to Andersonstown, to remove a barricade and came under small arms fire – as well as rocks and bottles thrown by rioters. A total of six police officers were taken to hospital and there was a similar story when the UDR started to remove another barricade in Agincourt Avenue near the Stranmillis Embankment in South Belfast. Reinforcements were required and there were several soldiers injured.

DON'T SHOOT THE BBC!
Kevin Campbell, King's Own Scottish Borderers
This is my account of the events of 9 August 1978 and just to give you the background I was serving with 4 Platoon, 'B' Company, and 1 KOSB. I was only a boy of 17-and-a-half – stationed at North Howard Street Mill – and this was my first time out of Scotland. Anyway to the point …

We were part of a multiple mobile patrol. We had just left the mill in Pigs and turned right up the Falls towards the edge of our area, which included the RVH.

As we came to Grosvenor Park we were met by about 2,000 locals all on a demo in and around the park, but centred on the Sinn Féin office only 20 feet or so away from us. Directly in front of us, blocking the road was a sky-blue Ford Transit, which was well alight and had thick black smoke billowing out from it. Needless to say, the locals were less than pleased that we had gatecrashed their demo and started to help us on our way by throwing the usual bottles, bricks, stones etc. There was a Sinn Féin man there with a camera and he was clearly interested in what we were up to.

Our platoon sergeant told the RCT driver to floor it and ram the van – instructing him to stop for nothing! We braced ourselves and then there was a loud crash as the Pig smashed into the van. No sooner had we hit it than we ground to a halt as the 'Paddie' bars on the front of the Pig had burst the soft skin of the van and we were now embedded and stuck firmly! Thick black smoke was now pouring into our vehicle and we were all gasping for air. The sergeant told us to secure the area whilst the driver got the Pig extricated from the burning van.

He shouted to me: "Right, 71 get that FRG (Federal Riot Gun) loaded. This is going to be brutal! When the doors open, you hit the cameraman square on, right?" I shouted: "Aye, Sarge!" and the doors swung open. This was it – my big moment of glory. I adopted the standing position and from a distance of 15 to 20 feet, fired my baton round – hitting the cameraman square in the chest; making him reel backwards; camera flying in the air. A split-second later he was lying flat on his back and I started to reload, but just as the sense of pride started to well up inside me, I felt a thud in my back as the sergeant punched me. He screamed: "You fucking idiot, 71! I meant the Sinn Féin cameraman, not the fucking BBC!" The Pig freed itself and as soon as we got out, it was straight back on board and we got out of there as fast as we could.

All of the lads thought it was hilarious and ripped the shit out of me rotten! Later that night, whilst still on QRF we were watching the TV when the news came on. They were showing this so-called peaceful protest from earlier in the day when the reporter from the BBC says: "Even our own crew were not immune to the violence shown by the army!" This was followed by pictures of me de-bussing from the Pig – a puff of smoke and then a beautiful shot of a brilliant Belfast summer sky. Fame at last!

On the 11th, an undercover soldier on covert ops in Letterkenny Road, Londonderry was killed by several PIRA gunmen. Lance-Corporal Alan Swift (25), a Lancashire lad, was with the Scots Guards whose origins lie in the personal bodyguard of King Charles I of England and Scotland. Its lineage can be traced as far back as 1642. However, at the time of his death he was attached to Det-14. During the early afternoon, as he sat in his 'Q' car in a layby, he was spotted by dickers and a PIRA ASU was dispatched to a weapons cache to collect rifles. In a stolen car they pulled up in front and opened fire on the soldier – who was wearing, naturally, civilian clothes. He was hit numerous times and died almost immediately.

Also on the 11th, armed men hijacked a bus in Andersonstown and forced the driver to drive it to the army base in the Ballymurphy Estate once they had ordered all of the passengers off at gunpoint. They then placed a bomb on board and the terrified driver was

Lance-Bombardier Chris Hunter, 23 Battery, 27 Field Regiment RA,
North Howard St Mill, Falls Road, 1979-80. (©Dave Malster)

told that his family would be harmed if he refused to follow their instructions. The driver drove to the heavily fortified base at the Henry Taggart Memorial Hall, where he managed to alert the soldiers, and he was dragged to safety. The bomb went off – wrecking the bus and damaging the front of the hall and surrounding houses.

On Monday 14 August the *Daily Mirror*, a leading British tabloid newspaper, announced its support for a British withdrawal from Northern Ireland. To many soldiers this was a betrayal as it appeared to be failing to support them in a difficult period. At the same time as the *Mirror*'s comments, Roy Mason – then Secretary of State for Northern Ireland – announced that a sports car factory would be built in West Belfast and would mean 2,000 new jobs. The new factory was seen as a breakthrough in securing American investment in Northern Ireland. However the DeLorean factory required a British investment of £56 million out of a total of £65 million. At the time a number of commentators expressed reservations about the potential success of the venture – and indeed the business did fail with the loss of substantial public funds.

On the 15th, there was more trouble on the extremely unpleasant Nationalist Kilwilkee Estate in Lurgan where RUC officers attempting to control a riot came under heavy attack from around 100 trouble-causers who threw bricks and bottles – and several officers were hospitalised. Incidentally, in order to bring readers up to date, the Kilwilkee Estate in Lurgan is the heartland of the dissident Republican movement and where the killing of PSNI Constable Carroll took place in 2008.

Just 48 hours later the Royal Marines lost one of their men – killed by a car bomb planted by PIRA in the centre of Forkhill, Co Armagh. As his four-man brick was returning to Forkhill RUC Station they passed by a Cortina which, unknown to them, had been hijacked in the Republic and Northern Ireland number plates fitted to reduce suspicion. The bomb detonated and the young marine from South Wales was killed absolutely instantly and the other three marines were all injured. The author spoke to a medical professional about these types of death and whilst nothing can be proven definitively, it is considered that when a human being is killed in this manner they probably feel no pain whatsoever – just hopefully a powerful flash of whiteness and then no more.

On the 16th, a soldier from the Gloucestershire Regiment – the Glosters – died in a tragic accident at an RUC base. The author has learned of the nature of the man's death and prefers not to publish any further details. He was Private David James McCahill (24) from Henbury, Bristol. On that same day the Light Infantry also lost a soldier – again the cause of death is listed as 'unknown'. Private Gary Stewart Hardy (18) was from Morden in Surrey. His funeral was held at North East Surrey Crematorium.

On the 17th, there was a close call for an RUC inspector who was driving to Omagh for a conference. Just after he had passed Cookstown, a white van which was in front of him began to slow down and on the narrow country roads – with few safe overtaking points – the policeman was unable to get past. Suddenly the rear doors opened and two gunmen using bales of straw for cover riddled the police car with bullets. The RUC managed to turn his car around but was hit in the back. He drove eight miles, though badly wounded, back to Cookstown RUC Station from where he was rushed to hospital. At the same time an IRA murder team had just arrived in a stolen car at the house of a UDR soldier in Coalisland, Co Tyrone prior to attacking. The part-time soldier chose that very moment to take his dustbin outside for the following morning's collection. Unprepared for this the gunmen prematurely opened fire and the UDR man, though wounded, managed to get back inside his house and the would-be killers drove away.

Throughout this author's works there has been utter condemnation of the both the Provisional IRA and the INLA for their intentional murders of former UDR, RUC or regular soldiers on the basis of their past associations. During the course of the Troubles, a total of 64 former UDR members and five former Regular Army men were killed by Republican terrorists. On the 19th, a Saturday night, Thomas Johnston (25) and his girlfriend had called into a shop in Victoria Street in Keady, Co Armagh. The couple had intended to buy a packet of crisps to eat as they walked through the town. As they stepped onto the pavement two IRA gunmen, armed with Armalites, opened fire without warning and Mr Johnston was hit in the head and died immediately – and his girlfriend was wounded in the arm. The Provisionals claimed responsibility and tried to justify their brutal murder by stating, erroneously, that the former UDR man was still involved with the army which he had left almost four years earlier.

Shortly after the killing of the former UDR soldier, another man who had left the regiment died from the injuries he had received in June – Michael Riley (31) (see Chapter 42). The Provisionals – having attacked economic targets – now turned their hands to destroying the culture of Ulster with an attack on the Bell Art Gallery on Malone Road, Belfast close to Queen's University. A warning was telephoned through and although damage was considerable – destroying many priceless works of art – there were no injuries. Two bombs inside the gallery exploded and a third bomb in a car outside was defused by the army EOD.

On the 18th, the IRA replicated their recent attack on the Ulsterbus depot in Belfast and made a similar attack on the firm's depot in Newry where they destroyed seven buses. Later in the day an officer from the Royal Anglians was badly injured in the Falls Road area. A 15-man patrol from the regiment's 3rd Battalion was in the Clonards area when the officer saw wires leading from a concrete lamp standard. He got his men under cover and went to investigate, but as he reached it, it exploded and he was hurled 30 feet through the air and badly injured. He suffered shrapnel wounds to his face, chest and legs.

On the 21st, a young soldier from an unnamed regiment was arrested by the RUC when he apparently had a mental breakdown whilst on duty in Belfast City Centre. The soldier opened fire with his SLR and fired several shots at the American Consulate in Queens Street. Some of his shots penetrated the building and consular staff had to dive for cover. Further south, a snap VCP by the army on the Banbridge-Newry Road netted two IRA volunteers and a staggering 1,700 rounds of ammunition – as well as four pistols and several magazines.

Before that day was over, the Provisionals – having received intelligence that a part-time UDR soldier regularly drove a works bus in the Enniskillen area – decided to ambush the bus and kill him. The ambush was set for Duffy's Cross between Belcoo and Garrison as the bus with fishery workers on board travelled towards Lough Melvin to prepare for an angling competition. As the UDR man drove through Duffy's Cross, he saw the masked gunmen leap out from behind a hedge and they opened fire with automatic weapons. The bus was riddled and everyone on board – including the UDR man – was wounded. He bravely accelerated away and manged to get the wounded – as well as himself – to safety and medical attention. However, one of the men – Patrick Fee (64) – who had been sitting in the front seat was terribly wounded and close to death. The wounded UDR man drove the bus for a further two miles to a small village and ran to a house where he begged for help, but the householder refused and he was forced to run to a country shop where the alarm was finally raised and police and ambulances called. The female proprietor of the shop said: "I went out to the van with my husband and saw a man lying across the front seat. There was nothing we could do. He was in a terrible condition and I think he was dying. We washed the injured men's wounds, gave them minerals and tried to make them as comfortable as possible until the ambulances arrived. There was blood all over the place. It was like a butcher's shop. I tried to bandage a bullet wound for one of the men with a homemade cloth, but he was so nervous he just wanted to be left alone." (*Belfast Newsletter* – 22 August 1978) The same newspaper shows the white, bullet-riddled works bus with the words 'Fermanagh District Council' emblazoned on the side; the interior photograph shows the detritus of the carnage.

Five days after the murder, sniffer dogs and alert soldiers discovered a bomb which had been planted inside a derelict pub and designed to kill Orange Order marchers. The Bridge Bar once stood at the junction of Madrid Street and Albert Bridge on the periphery of the Nationalist Short Strand and was on the Loyalist marching route. The parade would just touch on the Short Strand – close enough to wind up the Nationalists and provoke a reaction. The bomb was discovered behind a wall with command wires leading to the rear of the ruined club. This would have given the firer a safe point at which to detonate the bomb and then the ability in the confusion to melt way into the Nationalist enclave. He would have found a warm welcome in any of a dozen safehouses in Lisbon Street or the Arans or Andersons.

Later on the Provisionals hijacked a tipper truck and drove it to the Dundalk Road, Crossmaglen and used it as a mortar launch to attack the RUC station there. A total of 17 bombs were fired. Accuracy was not the IRA's strong point and two landed in a nearby garden – causing damage to a shed and a fence. The other 15 landed on a nearby sports field and of those, eight failed to explode. Houses nearby were evacuated as EOD were called in to defuse. Once again, the Provisional IRA 'defenders' of the Nationalist community had put their own supporters at risk. As stated their main weakness was accuracy, but they only needed to be accurate once in order to cause carnage. This became evident when they launched a mortar attack on Newry RUC Station in 1985 some years later. In the early evening of 28 February 1985, nine Mark 10 mortars were launched from the back of a lorry that had been hijacked in Crossmaglen. Eight overshot the RUC station in Corry Square, but one landed directly on a portacabin containing a temporary canteen. Nine police officers were killed and 37 people were injured – including 25 civilian police employees. The death toll was the highest inflicted on the RUC in its history.

On Sunday the 27th, approximately 10,000 people took part in a march from Coalisland to Dungannon, Co Tyrone to commemorate the first civil rights march 10 years earlier. Some observers feel that the original event was the main precursor for the Troubles.

On the 28th, Mary McCaffrey (60) – who had been badly injured in an IRA bomb almost three weeks earlier – died of her injuries after a brave fight for life in hospital. She was a widow and a Catholic. On the final day of the month, two soldiers from the Army Intelligence Corps were killed in an RTA in the Province. The author is not permitted to say if they were killed whilst working undercover or if it was simply a prosaic tragedy; that is, prosaic by the standards of the Troubles. Corporal John Peter Roeser (30) and Corporal Michael John Bloor (28) were killed at approximately the same time.

The month ended with more explosions in Belfast as the Provisionals continued with what history eventually saw as a flawed campaign to cause a British withdrawal from Ulster. In achieving the 'distinction' of causing more damage to Belfast than Hermann Wilhelm Göring's *Luftwaffe* they caused untold misery, suffering and hardship for thousands of Northern Irish people. Even by this stage the leaders of Sinn Féin and the Army Council of the Provisionals knew that they could never achieve what they termed a 'British withdrawal' from Northern Ireland. They were aware that they could not achieve this either politically or militarily. Therefore, the killing which continued for 20 more years can only be viewed as killing for killing's sake.

August ended with 11 deaths – amongst them eight British soldiers and a policeman. Two civilians died – a Catholic and a Protestant – both at the hands of the IRA. In fact, the Provisionals were responsible for at least seven – and possibly nine – of the deaths in August.

45

September

The month saw the Troubles-related deaths of 11 people – including two regular soldiers and one army cadet officer – as well as another policeman. It also saw PIRA attack an airfield and destroy planes in an escalation of its so-called 'economic war' and it saw the death of another civilian searcher following the death of Norma Spence in the 'Rag Day' shootings.

The Creggan Estate in Londonderry sits high on a hill above the city of Londonderry. It is 100 per cent Nationalist – as evidenced by the plethora of tricolours – and it was a very dangerous place to be an RUC officer or a soldier during the Troubles. It apparently still is, because when I returned to Northern Ireland in 2008 it was a place where I felt fear and menace. When I went back in 2012 I was warned unequivocally not to enter the estate known in Irish as *'An Creagán'* – meaning 'Stony Place'. It was the first housing estate built in Londonderry specifically to provide housing for the Catholic majority. The estate is very close to the border with Co Donegal and the Irish Republic. Ballymore Road and Glassagh Park on its far north-western extreme are only 7,500 feet – or a mile-and-a-bit – from the unmarked and porous Irish border. On the first day of the new month, a gunman – firing a high-velocity weapon thought to have been an Armalite from a bedroom window of a house where the family were being held at gunpoint downstairs – fired a round at a passing army Land Rover. The round missed and continued onwards – entering the lounge window of a family who were watching TV. They were forced to dive for cover and the lethal round embedded itself near the television set.

Later on that same day – over in the aforementioned Republic – a young British Army lieutenant was marrying his Irish sweetheart at a church in Navan, Co Meath. Dickers had alerted the Provisionals and two gunmen lay in wait for the couple to leave the church and as they did so, they callously opened fire. He was badly wounded in the chest and stomach and was airlifted to hospital where he later recovered. On the same day a soldier from the Royal Engineers died in circumstances unknown. Corporal James Andrews (27) was a native of Glasgow and his funeral was held in his hometown. No further details are known.

On the 2nd, Private Noel Patterson (27) of the UDR died in circumstances unknown. It was only five days since his 27th birthday and it is thought to have been an RTA.

On the 5th, an Army Cadet Officer (ACF) was shot and killed by the Provisionals – making him the fourth member of the Cadets to be killed during the Troubles. The others were: Cadet Leonard Cross (11 November 1974), Corporal Edward Wilson (26 January 1975) and Captain Paul Rodgers (19 April 1979). William McAlpine (45), father of four, held the rank of Major in the ACF and was also an engineer. He worked in Newry and was in the habit of driving home for lunch every day – a routine which PIRA dickers had noted. As he drove along Chapel Lane, close to St Mary's Church, a gunman who had been hiding behind a wall opened fire on the car – wounding the ACF man and causing him to lose control and crash. As he lay helpless in the damaged car, the gunman ran over to him and reached into the car and shot him in the head at point-blank range. He died instantly. The usual PIRA apologist was wheeled out to make a statement for their sycophantic supporters on the Nationalist housing estates and over in Irish bars down the Eastern seaboard of the United States. Their pathetic and incredible excuse: Mr McAlpine was a part of the 'British war machine'.

The day after – almost as though to rub salt into the wounds of Mr McAlpine's loved ones – Gerry Adams, then Vice-President of Sinn Féin, was cleared of a charge of membership of the Provisional IRA when the judge hearing the case ruled that there was insufficient evidence to prove that he was a member of the organisation. One recommends *Voices from The Grave* by IRA apologist Ed Moloney and that the reader should peruse Brendan Hughes' comments about his one-time comrade.

In December 1971 the UVF bombed McGurk's Bar in the New Lodge area and killed 15 innocent Catholics. For a more detailed account please see *The Bloodiest Year 1972* by the same author. In November 1975 the RUC received intelligence that a man called Robert Campbell, a high-ranking UVF member, was responsible. In March 1976 the RUC received further intelligence that linked Campbell and four others to the McGurk's bombing. Campbell was arrested on 27 July 1977 and held at Castlereagh RUC base. He was interviewed seven times during 27 and 28 July where he admitted his part in the bombing, but refused to name the others. On 29 July 1977 Campbell was charged with the 15 murders and 17 attempted murders. On 6 September 1978 he pleaded guilty to all charges and received life imprisonment with a recommendation to serve no less than 20 years. He is the only person to have been charged for the bombing. On the day of his conviction the *Belfast Newsletter* led with: 'Bar bomber gets life 16 times over'. The judge referred to the bombing as 'callous' and Campbell told him that he was glad that it was over and that the killings had bothered him ever since.

On the 8th, the notorious Lawnbrook Social Club (see references *passim* to the 'Shankill Butchers') was back in the news again when two UVF members who had grievances with several members of the club went in there seeking revenge. The men, who claimed that they had been assaulted and ejected, went back on the same evening and fired several high-velocity shots through the thin walls. Several people inside were wounded, but William Crawford (17) was fatally injured. He was rushed to hospital, but died of his wounds on 13 September.

Following the recent IRA mortar attack on the SF base at Crossmaglen, a live round which had lain undiscovered since the attack was found by children. The army was called in to defuse it and this was achieved safely. The live round lay undiscovered until the 8th. The following day, Republican gunmen fired shots at a Loyalist social club on the Shankill Road and two shots penetrated the building – leaving two young Protestants wounded.

On the 11th, an off-duty policeman was killed by IRA gunmen as he worked on a house which he had bought for himself and his bride-to-be. RUCR Constable Howard Donaghy (24), who also worked for the GPO, was renovating the house at Loughmacrory Road, Omagh, with his brother and another friend at the time of his death. Three men brandishing rifles made their way onto the land which was owned by Mr Donaghy, Senior and opened fire – hitting the young policeman. He slumped to the ground wounded and the three gunmen stood over his prostate body and fired into him from close range several times. He died at the scene – cradled in the arms of his distraught mother – leaving his brother and friend deeply shocked and a heartbroken fiancée who was due to marry the murdered policeman the following year. On that same day an army foot patrol in the

Canal Basin in Strabane came under fire from an IRA sniper. No soldiers were hit, but the gunman was hit as the foot patrol members returned fire. The wounded terrorist escaped and fled across the border – no doubt to receive medical attention from a friendly doctor.

There were more bombs planted in Belfast City Centre where the Provisionals continued to employ the 'hanging bomb' concept and devices were left on security grills outside a furniture store in Carlisle Circus. There was also a case of attempted murder when Republicans shot a 22-year-old man at the Sportsman's Bar in Coalisland, Co Tyrone. The motives were never established, but he later recovered in hospital. At the same time, acting on a tip-off, the RUC raided a house in Mayo Street in the Loyalist Shankill where amongst the finds was an SLR stolen from the UDR and a Steyr rifle thought to have belonged to the RUC. A 25-year-old fitter, thought to have been a member of the UDA, was arrested and charged with arms offences.

On the 18th, another hanging bomb was discovered outside the Busy Bee Shopping Centre in Belfast and the army was called in. A solider from EOD and also a marksman fired several rounds at the bomb until it fell to the ground (it was then safely defused). In Newry an IRA bomb was left in a van with the intention of transporting it to an army or RUC base. The explosives packed into gas cylinders were clearly volatile and the army were called in to investigate the van in the Mallin Park area. It was eventually made safe, but such was the potential threat that 150 houses were evacuated. On the 21st, two RUC officers were badly injured when they investigated a telephoned warning of a bomb at Ravensdene Manufacturing in University Street, Belfast. The building was badly damaged in the blasts and the two officers were rushed to hospital. There were also blasts within hours in the Boucher Road area of Belfast where two further factories were hit by the IRA. On the same day, the same organisation tried to kill a PO as he drove home from work at the Crumlin Road Jail. The man, who worked in the prison hospital, was riding home on his motorcycle and had reached the bottom of the Antrim Road when a car pulled alongside him. A gunman had already wound the window down and as the car was level, he fired two shots at the PO – wounding him and causing the bike to crash. The car sped off and the officer later recovered in hospital despite a chest wound. The day after witnessed the death in another RTA of a UDR soldier, Alister Samuel James Cooke (20). He is buried at Edenderry Presbyterian Churchyard in the Irish Republic.

On the 22nd, as a part of its escalating 'economic warfare', PIRA targeted a flying club at Eglington Airfield near Londonderry. The main business there was a charter flights company which flew Londonderry businessmen to meetings in England and Scotland – as well as Europe – and was a vital link for those who didn't wish to drive the 70 miles to Belfast to use the City Airport. In the dead of night several explosive devices were planted in the main terminal – in the hangar which belonged to Keysair – and underneath the two planes which were stored there. No warnings were given and the terminal, hangar and both planes were destroyed by the blasts. A 2012 search by the author revealed no details of a surviving company which traded under the name Keysair. Also on the 22nd, Roy Mason – Secretary of State for Northern Ireland – and Airey Neave, the Conservative Party spokesperson on Northern Ireland, issued statements rebuffing calls in Britain for a British withdrawal from Northern Ireland.

Several hours later a spate of bomb hoaxes had led to hundreds of families being evacuated – mainly in West Belfast – and then traffic chaos as abandoned lorries across the city had to be investigated for bombs. Once the Provisionals had paralysed the city, three real bombs exploded at business premises on the Antrim Road. The following companies were hit: Capital Cars, Calvert Electrical and the Swift Screw Company at Dunmore Industrial Estate. The nearby Dunmore Stadium, where a greyhound meeting was taking place, had to be abandoned and races cancelled. Further hoaxes led to evacuations in the south of the city and a device left outside the Northern Bank in Ormeau Road led to mass evacuations there also. Two newspapers were also targeted and separate hoax bombs led to the evacuation of staff at the *Irish News* and the *Belfast Telegraph*. Finally an oil tanker was hijacked from the Falls Road and abandoned across the entry to the M1 motorway, which led to its closure.

On the following day a proxy bomb was placed inside milk churns and gunmen forced the driver to drive the device to Castlederg RUC Station. He managed to alert the police and the van was abandoned. Part of the 200lb device later exploded, but there were no injuries. There was also another attempt on the life of a PO when a PIRA gang went to his house in Saintfield Road – south of Ormeau Road in Belfast. As he answered a knock on the door, a gunman fired a single shot at the outline in the glass and the officer was shot in the leg. The gunmen escaped on a stolen motorcycle.

On the 28th, an unarmed civilian searcher employed by the army/RUC to help with security checks was shot dead by the IRA. Brian Russell (31) was accompanying members of the RMP in a search in Waterloo Place in Londonderry City Centre. In the company of another civilian colleague he was chatting to passers-by when a single round from an IRA gunman rang out and he was hit in the head. He was mortally wounded and died a short time afterwards in Altnagelvin Hospital. That his murder was sanctioned by the Londonderry Brigade of the Provisional IRA – the leader at the time, allegedly was one Martin McGuiness – is in no doubt in this author's mind. That the killing was claimed by a hitherto unheard of splinter group, the 'Irish Freedom Fighters', is of no surprise. The killing was not a popular one amongst their supporters and it was clear that they quickly needed to distance themselves from the murder. Even a later statement from the splinter group which claimed that: " ... he was not the intended target ... " rang hollow somehow. Mr Russell's wife was pregnant with their second child at the time.

Two more deaths followed on the 29th, but there was an element of tragic farce and misunderstanding about them – so much so that this author considered not including them in the toll of the Troubles. The incident involved an undercover soldier from the Queen's Own Regiment who thought that his life was in danger and reacted naturally, but tragically. Samuel McHugh (20) and Tony Fisher (21) – both Catholics and both from the Ballymurphy/New Barnsley area – and another friend had been out drinking. The friends had just left the Terry McDermott Social Club on the Upper Glen Road, Andersonstown and apparently were trying to hail a taxi. They saw the 'Q' car driven by an undercover soldier and ran towards it. The soldier thought that he had been rumbled and that his life was in danger. Consequently he accelerated and hit all three men – two of whom were killed and the third man was seriously injured. The deaths were tragic and avoidable, but then this author has never before found himself in such a situation.

On the same day that the two innocent Catholics were killed, the Provisionals tried to kill a former RUCR man. The former policeman had left the service some years ago, but that mattered not to the men on the Provisional Army Council. The man and his father-in-law, Joseph Skelly (74), were driving along Quay Street in Newry from the Greenbank Industrial Estate where Mr Skelly helped out in order to supplement his pension. In Quay

Street, shots were fired from IRA gunmen and both men were hit. The younger man was attempting to drive to the nearest hospital and had reached Lower William Street, where a pursuing car fired more shots at them. The car finally ground to a halt near Daisyhill Hospital, where further shots were fired. Mr Skelly died shortly afterwards and his son-in-law was badly wounded in the back.

On the 28th, Joshua Eilberg – then a Democrat Congressman – and Hamilton Fish, then a Republican Congressman, paid a five-day visit to Northern Ireland. The two men later argued that the USA should play a part in finding a political settlement in the region. "Why not," were the thoughts of most British soldiers. "You lot are financing it and prolonging it."

A foot patrol of the Royal Marines on the border in South Armagh can thank a poorly-trained IRA bomb-maker for their lives. As they approached a culvert some 50 yards ahead of them, a bomb consisting of three gas cylinders and 50lbs of explosive was detonated by remote control. Fortunately the bomb was badly made and only one cylinder detonated. The marines were showered in debris, but all of the patrol were uninjured.

The final incident of the month resulted in yet another avoidable death and again involved an undercover soldier. Protestant James Taylor (23), father of two very young children, was a water surveyor and was on a hunting trip at Ballinderry River in Co Tyrone. He and some colleagues had returned to their parked car and found that all of the tyres had been let down. Not realising that he still had his shotgun cradled in his arms, he confronted some men who were nearby. The men, soldiers, claimed that they considered that their lives were in danger and shot Mr Taylor. He was hit twice in the back and died at the scene. At the inquest the soldiers' explanations were challenged by the other members of the hunting party, but they were acquitted.

The month had proven more violent than of late and a total of ten people died. The British Army lost three and the RUC lost one officer. Five civilians were killed – made up of three Protestants and two Catholics – and included the civilian searcher. None of the deaths could be said to be overtly sectarian. The Provisionals were responsible for four of the fatalities this month.

46

October

The month of October saw deaths at just four – amongst the lowest number of fatalities since the early days of the Troubles. One soldier was killed, as were three civilians – including a young teenage boy. It was, however, the month in which the Provisionals detonated four bombs on a packed train – and by some miracle only one person was killed.

On the second day of the month the IRA attempted to kill an off-duty UDR man whom they knew regularly attended a cattle market in Newry. The soldier, who doubled his life as a farmer, was just driving out of the Patrick Street Market when three gunmen stood in front of his lorry. Captain Charles Henning (52) jumped from the cab and attempted to run back into the market, but he was hit three times as the gunmen opened fire. He was hit in the back and received a fatal head wound. He was immediately rushed to Daisyhill Hospital in the town, but he died of his wounds on the 6th. At the same time, further north, an IRA bombing unit planted two devices in the world-famous Customs House in Belfast. Warnings were telephoned through to the Samaritans and the building was evacuated. The bombs went off within three minutes of each other and a major fire was started. Because of the fear that other bombs might be in the building, the firemen were only able to deal with superficial blazes in or around the ground floor.

On the 3rd, traffic in Belfast City Centre was again thrown into chaos after explosions in Corporation Street and the placing of a suspect car near Queen's Bridge. The first two bombs caused serious damage to a shipping office and came close to killing a passing cyclist who was blown off his bike in the first blast. The entire area was sealed off – causing both traffic and commercial disruption as people were unable to get to work. On the following day PIRA gunmen ambushed an RUC Land Rover at Derrymacesh close to Lurgan. A 999 call had lured them to a spot close to the M1 motorway to investigate youths stoning passing cars from a bridge. Gunmen had positioned themselves on high ground overlooking the spot where the RUC were expected to park. Almost 20 rounds were fired, but the police received no injuries. The gunmen escaped before the army were able to flood the area.

No bombs had exploded on the English mainland for some time, but on Saturday 7 November the Orange Hall in Everton Road, Liverpool was targeted by a Republican group possibly acting independently of both the England Team and the IRA Army Council. A 44-year-old member of the Orange Order was badly injured when the bomb – a UVBT – exploded underneath his car. On the same day a lone undercover soldier on covert duties in Ann Street, Dungannon was attacked by two IRA gunmen who had been watching him for some time. They approached the car (in a car park) from the rear and then opened fire – hitting the soldier in the head and also wounding him in his back. Six shots were fired before they ran off.

A number of groups in Londonderry – including Sinn Féin – held a march to commemorate the 10th anniversary of the 5 October 1968 Civil Rights March. It remembered the Loyalist ambush at Burntollet Bridge – the images of which were flashed around the world – and from then onwards it was downhill at a rapid speed. The Democratic

Unionist Party (DUP) staged a counter-demonstration attended by Loyalists and led by Ian Paisley. Trouble developed and 67 RUC officers were injured in clashes with Loyalists. Two RUC officers were also injured in confrontations with Republicans. Nine days later the DUP organised another march in Londonderry to protest against the march in the city on the previous Sunday (8 October). There were clashes between Loyalists and RUC officers – which resulted in 32 policemen being injured – and there was also damage to property in the city.

On the 9th, PIRA gunmen on a stolen motorcycle attempted to murder an off-duty RUC officer as he drove home. He was driving on the Balmoral flyover, en route for Lisburn, when the pillion passenger opened fire as they passed the officer's car. The officer received two wounds to his thigh and buttock, but was able to drive himself to hospital. Later in the day a motorbike – very likely the one from which the RUC officer was shot – was used in two shooting attacks on police VCPs in the West Circular Road and Springfield Road areas and later in the Clonards.

On the 10th, a Loyalist gang threw two petrol bombs into the home of a Catholic family in Bristol Road just off the Antrim Road. The attacks were made at the back of the house – one through a bedroom window and the other through a ground floor window. The householder tried to beat out the flames with his bare hands – sustaining bad burns – but he still managed to get his wife and four young children to safety. On the day after, the IRA needlessly put the lives of hundreds of Andersonstown residents at risk after they abandoned a hijacked double-decker bus packed with explosives outside the RUC station. The station, which would witness the deaths of four soldiers there the following year, was located close to Milltown Cemetery and sat strategically on the junction of the Falls Road and Glen Road. The bus had been hijacked near Glen Road when gunmen boarded and forced the passengers off. They then forced the driver take the bus, by this time loaded with explosives, to the RUC base. Hundreds of civilians were forced to leave their homes for over five hours whilst EOD made the bombs safe.

On the 12th, the Provisionals plumbed new depths of depravity just at a time when most observers thought that was impossible to do. Several bombs were planted on the Dublin-Belfast Enterprise train, which they knew would be packed at the time. The bombs – four in all – had been left in a compartment and the planters had exited the train. This service was known to be packed with shoppers from the Republic looking for bargains in Belfast and on a cheap day excursion – as well as commuters who lived in the south and worked in the north. The Provisionals phoned a warning through to the Samaritans, but insufficient time was left – and in any case the caller stated that the bombs were on the Belfast-Dublin line and not the Dublin-Belfast service. The train arrived at Belfast South at around 0800 and the first bomb exploded. Passengers – many said to have been carrying empty shopping bags – numbering about 100 began a major panic as they desperately sought to find a way off the train. Eyewitnesses stated that there was pandemonium and that just as the second bomb exploded, passengers were throwing themselves out of the doors and falling to the track and desperately stumbling away. The narrow doorways were jammed as four or five people tried to squeeze their way through spaces designed for one person.

In the confusion it was not known when injuries were caused, but there was a second and then a third blast. In total five passengers were injured – four of them seriously, suffering traumatic amputations – and Letitia McGrory (55), mother of five girls, was killed instantly. Mrs McGrory was from Dublin and had been looking for cheap bargains in Belfast, but she was killed by the bombers of the Provisional IRA. An apologist later had the brass neck to blame the RUC for not passing on the warnings. It wasn't however the first time – and nor would it be the last – that PIRA gave insufficient or misleading warnings. To further demonstrate their complete lack of humanity, the following day the IRA telephoned the RUC and warned that further bombs were on that day's train service. The train was halted and evacuated, but there were no bombs on board. To exacerbate things further two PIRA bombers blew up the main signal box on the line, which caused further delay and confusion. One wonders if the Irish drinkers on the United States' Eastern seaboard dug deeper into their pockets when the NORAID collecting tins came around once the train bomb news had filtered through.

Each dollar a bullet, each victim someone's son – and Americans kill Irishmen as surely as if they fired the gun.

The much-respected *Irish News* on the 13th stated: 'Wave of horror and revulsion at bombing of express from Dublin'. Their lead writer continued: "A wave of horror and revulsion swept Ireland yesterday in the wake of the bomb attack on the Dublin-Belfast Enterprise express when a middle-aged woman died and four people were seriously injured. The outrage brought a call for the reintroduction of the death penalty for murder from one political party and utter condemnations from all others." Alderman Seamus Lynch, a Republican, was also quick to condemn and he described the attack as an act of " ... fanatical hatred designed solely to kill and maim civilians..."

On the 14th, there was a tragic death in the Woodvale area of Belfast involving a friend of the son of a UVF member. The august tome *Lost Lives* deems it worthy of being listed as a Troubles-related death. Graham Lewis (13), from Leopold Street just off the Crumlin Road, was playing with friends in the Woodvale area – one of whom was the son of a known UVF member. The boys were inside the UVF man's house when they found a revolver – hidden inside a gas heater – and began messing around with it. The gun was accidentally discharged and Graham Lewis was hit in the head and died almost immediately. His sad death was of course tragic, but who other than his grieving loved ones would notice one more tragedy in a sea of tragedies?

On the 16th, the IRA then planted incendiary devices at printing works and two clothing factories in the Donegall Road area of Belfast – setting off five separate blasts in a 10-minute spell and causing entire streets to be evacuated. There was extensive damage to the area and several people were treated for shock. During the Second World War, the British Midlands city of Coventry was blitzed on the night of 1940 and people died – with large parts of the city laid waste. The British coined the term to 'Coventrate', which described the destruction which RAF and USAAF Bomber Command created in Germany. There was now a new word to describe the piecemeal destruction of Belfast by the Provisionals: to 'Belfastrate'. The following day, a spate of hoax bombs in the city centre caused further chaos and disruption to commercial and business life. At one particular hoax, in Donegall Square East, shots were fired by gunmen at RUC officers who were examining yet another suspect package; no officers were hit. Two days later an RUC officer attended a community meeting at Magee University and left his car under the observant eyes of the university watchman. However, an IRA unit abducted the man at gunpoint whilst they fitted a UVBT to the policeman's vehicle. Fortunately the watchman's absence aroused the RUC man's suspicions and when he checked under the car he saw the device; it was defused by EOD.

On the 19th, PIRA gunmen and soldiers on foot patrol on New Monagh Road, Turf Lodge exchanged around 20 shots but there were no casualties. On the following day and the day after, the IRA called in a number of sick bomb hoaxes – claiming that they had planted more bombs on the Dublin-Belfast and Bangor-Portadown lines. It resulted in a day of utter chaos on the line as services were cancelled or delayed so much that travel by rail became nigh-on impossible. More hoaxes on the next day led to many travellers abandoning the trains and took to the roads – again further adding to the transport chaos. Everyone naturally was reluctant to get on a train again after the murder of Letitia McGrory a week earlier. On the third day, more hoax bombs led to further cancellations as the IRA claimed that they were targeting the Londonderry-Bangor line. In just a week, the Provisionals had virtually paralysed the entire Northern rail network.

On the 24th, RUC officers were despatched from Mount Pottinger RUC Station after reports that their patrol vehicles were being regularly stoned by youths in the Short Strand area. When they arrived at Maria Street on the periphery of the Nationalist enclave, they came under fire from American Armalites. Several rounds impacted near their vehicle, but due to the proximity of civilians (it was a PIRA tactic to use civilians as cover as they knew that SF wouldn't fire back) they were unable to return fire. Shortly after this incident – and across Belfast at Springfield Road – PIRA bombers were busy causing more disruption. Several devices were planted at a company called SPD and exploded without warning – forcing over 100 workers to race for cover. The blasts started a massive fire – described by the *Belfast Newsletter* as 'spectacular'. Its front page the next day showed a photograph of a dense cloud of smoke drifting eastwards across Belfast.

The final killing of the month, though never claimed by them, was committed by the Loyalist UFF when they shot a Catholic in North Belfast. William Smyth (54) had been drinking in a CESA club in Ardilea Street in the Oldpark area. The club, run by the Catholic Ex-Servicemen's Association, included among its members former Irish soldiers – as well as former British soldiers – and it was there that Mr Smyth spent many happy hours drinking with former comrades. He had walked towards his home in Ballyclare Street, which is approximately 200 yards away and involves crossing the Oldpark Road. When he was just yards from his house, a gunman walked up behind him and fired a single shot into the back of his head – mortally wounding him. He was rushed to the nearby Mater Hospital, but the dash was in vain as he was found to be dead on arrival.

As the month ended, two of the 'Shankill Butchers' were in court and the *Belfast Telegraph* reported that William Moore and Robert 'Basher' Bates had pleaded guilty to the slaying of seven Catholics. The report went: "It took just 22 minutes for Moore and Bates to plead guilty to a total of 36 charges, which included 21 charges of murder; six attempted murders; three kidnappings; possession of guns and ammunition with intent and under suspicious circumstances; conspiracy to murder; assault and membership of the UVF. Moore pleaded guilty to 11 charges of murder and Bates to 10. Moore, in addition to admitting his membership of the UVF, pleaded guilty to the kidnapping charges and conspiracy to murder Catholics on the Falls Road in March 1977."

It was such a catalogue of crimes that it almost dwarfed those committed by Peter Sutcliffe – the 'Yorkshire Ripper' – whose heinous activities terrified thousands of women in the Leeds, Bradford, Huddersfield and Heavy Woollen Districts of Yorkshire around the same time as the 'Shankill Butchers'. The leader of the UVF murder gang – Lenny Murphy – was in prison on lesser charges and would escape 'Butcher' charges, but he had an appointment with PIRA killers just a few years later.

The month was over and although it included 'only' four killings, PIRA's intent was to kill many times that number – and it was only sheer good fortune that they failed. One soldier and three civilians died – two Catholics and a Protestant. Two people died at the hands of the Provisionals and one at the hands of Loyalists – the latter killing being overtly sectarian.

47

November

Six people died during the month of November (half of whom were soldiers) and another PO died – this time a very senior officer – and the Provisionals declared 'the long war'. This was after the second of two mini-blitzes across the Province.

On the 1st of the month the Provisionals' South Armagh Brigade ordered the abduction of a local Crossmaglen man suspected of being a possible informer. The man was dragged over the border and interrogated for several hours, but was then released unharmed and dumped at Ballsmills just three miles from home. When the 'Nutting Squad' was called into action there was generally only one outcome – and it involved a hood over the head, two rounds into the base of the skull and burial in a shallow grave. On the day after, at a VCP manned by the RUC in the centre of Lurgan, there was an attempt to kill officers as a van drove straight at them. The officers opened fire and an exchange of shots left one PIRA man wounded. An automatic weapon was seized and a large amount of blood found in the wrecked car suggested that another of the passengers had also been wounded.

In Belfast the IRA planted two bombs in College Gardens, close to Queen's University, on window ledges with the intention of causing injuries and/or death to the emergency services. Both bombs exploded within three minutes and extensive damage was caused to both properties and a policeman and a firefighter were both injured. Minutes later, bomb warnings led to the evacuation of both Marks & Spencer and Woolworths in Royal Avenue and more disruption to the commercial heart of Belfast. The next morning, Encore Music Supplies on Lower Donegall Street was damaged by a bomb and a stolen car packed with explosives was left outside Modern Office Supplies in the same street – which was made safe by EOD – as PIRA continued to attempt to bomb the British Government to the negotiating table. Also on the 2nd, a British Army intelligence document – 'Northern Ireland: Future Terrorist Trends' – was uncovered. The document contained an assessment of the capacity of the Provisional IRA. It noted that the calibre of members was high and that the new 'cell structure' that the Active Service Units (ASUs) had adopted made them less vulnerable to informers. The Social Democratic and Labour Party (SDLP) annual conference voted that British withdrawal was 'desirable and inevitable'. The party also called for fresh talks between the British and Irish Governments and representatives of the two communities in Northern Ireland.

In Newry a driver was stopped at gunpoint in the Nationalist Derrybeg by masked gunmen who placed explosives into his car and, having ascertained his name and address, warned that unless he drove to Edward Street his family would be harmed. The driver did as he was bid, but left the car and informed the RUC who called Army EOD who made the bomb safe. Two hours after the shoot-out in Lurgan, RUC officers arrested another IRA man and recovered a further automatic weapon as they followed up the initial incidents. At around the same time Newry was hit again by the Provisionals and the offices of the Department of the Environment were badly damaged by a car bomb which exploded just a few yards away. A further seven devices all exploded within minutes and extensive damage – but no loss of life – was caused to the city centre.

On Tuesday 7 November there was a development in the search for Thomas Niedermayer. Thomas Niedermayer was a German industrialist who ran the Grundig plant at Dunmurry in the western part of Belfast. He was abducted on 27 December 1973 by two men who lured him outside his house on the pretext that they had crashed into his car. The incident was witnessed by his 15-year-old daughter Renate, who had answered the door to the kidnappers, and by a neighbour who worked at the Grundig factory. Niedermayer was never seen alive again (see *Sir, They're Taking The Kids Indoors* by the same author). The search for the German industrialist took a new twist when the RUC – after some incredibly resourceful detective work – began digging up Antrim Road, Belfast. They believed that he was buried at Tavanagh near Cushendall. His body was eventually discovered and he was finally laid to rest on consecrated ground in March 1980.

Even as the police were searching for the body of the murdered industrialist, a three-man PIRA team was trying to kill their colleagues further north in Draperstown, Co Londonderry. After driving close to the RUC station in a stolen car, two gunmen opened fire with automatic weapons on the manned base. Almost 30 rounds hit the station, but officers inside were unable to return fire due to the proximity of civilians in the area. The gunmen fled and abandoned the stolen car close by and escaped in a second car which had been parked strategically. Draperstown was founded in 1798 and received its name in 1818 after the London Drapers' Company.

On the 9th, there was more violence in Crossmaglen and a young Royal Marine was mortally wounded in a PIRA bomb explosion. A foot patrol from 42 Commando was en route for the RUC base and had just reached the junction of Loughview Park and Castleblaney Drive opposite a derelict house. A massive blast ripped through the area – causing major damage and injuring three of the marines. Gareth Wheddon (19), from Sussex, was dreadfully injured and was rushed by helicopter to hospital. After a three-day fight for life, he died of his injuries in hospital on the 12th. 42 Commando had just two weeks left of their four-month tour. Their motto is: *Per Mare, Per Terram (By Sea, By Land)*.

MARINE WHEDDON
Tony Price, Grenadier Guards

I recall that the advance party from our company, 1 Grenadier Guards, had arrived at the base early November 1978. The particular patrol which Marine Wheddon was a part of was a joint patrol of marines and guards. I can't recall all the names, but I'll always remember that the company medic – Sergeant Keith Regan – was part of that patrol as well as another grenadier along with Marine Wheddon. As we learnt later, the patrol was crossing the road to avoid a derelict building – as was standard procedure back then. As a result of crossing the road they were contacted by the device, which was hidden behind the stone wall on that side of the road, in two gas canisters. They were remotely detonated by terrorists presumably sitting in a nearby car on the Castleblaney Road. We learnt that Marine Wheddon received most of the blast and that the other grenadier and the medic were also blown across the road by the shockwave and debris which followed.

The grenadier was injured, but not to any great extent. Sergeant Regan apparently picked himself up off the floor and was able to check himself over before going to the aid of Marine Wheddon. I believe every single field dressing that he had on him – plus those of the rest of the patrol – were used before the QRF arrived. Shortly afterwards, the casevac helicopter landed in order to take him to hospital. I don't think the grenadier and Regan went to hospital as their injuries were eventually dealt with back at XMG Base – lacerations and bruises mainly and shock.

I'll always remember the marine contingent back in base feeling like their world had been torn apart. I don't think they had suffered any fatalities up to that point during their whole tour. The joy of nearing the end of the tour for them was soon over.

The Royal Anglians lost one of their young soldiers on the 13th when Private Stephen Foster (22) was accidentally killed at Palace Barracks, Belfast. The exact circumstances of his accidental death are not known and this author has made representations to the MOD in order to have the causes of death of over 50 soldiers made public.

On Tuesday the 14th, the Provisionals carried out a number of bomb attacks in towns across Northern Ireland. Serious damage was caused in attacks in Armagh, Belfast, Castlederg, Cookstown, Londonderry and Enniskillen. Thirty-seven people were injured in the attacks. Another mini blitz followed this series of bomb attacks and represented part of a renewed bombing campaign as over 50 bombs were exploded during the next seven days. All of the targets were in streets in which the security barriers had been removed to aid the run-up to Christmas. It was intended to give some financial relief to hard-pressed retailers, but instead merely served to compound their misery.

On the 16th, a massive PIRA bomb exploded in the Ulster brewery in Glen Road, Andersonstown – causing massive damage and a huge fire. The bomb had been planted by a group of masked gunmen who had held the security guard in his office and drove in through the brewery gates. They burst into the warehouse and planted a large bomb and then left a smaller device – hidden behind stock – before accelerating away in their stolen car. The first device exploded moments later and firemen were called in to fight the flames. As they did so the second device exploded as Sub Officer Wesley Orr (53), father of three and a fireman for over 30 years, was hit and killed instantly. The veteran fireman caught the full blast and did not stand a chance. Several of his colleagues were also injured. Shortly afterwards, bombs planted nearby by a different PIRA ASU exploded – wrecking Finlay Packaging on Ballygomartin Road. On the following day, bomb hoaxes caused traffic chaos and panic amongst civilians as Belfast City Centre ground to a halt. The level of bombing and bomb hoaxes was the worst since the bloodiest year of 1972 and the IRA was demonstrating its strength and its ability to cause disruption and destruction over a long and sustained period of years. The day also saw the M1 motorway closed and the rail network almost emasculated by the Republican terror group. In Londonderry, a series of IRA bombs almost replicated the disruption which Belfast was suffering some 70 miles to the south.

From the 18th to the 23rd the destruction continued and Strabane Golf Club was hit. Although EOD managed to defuse one of the bombs, there was extensive damage caused to the club house at Ballycolman Road. During this period, the IRA hijacked a CIE freight train carrying 2,000 kegs of Harp lager and Guinness beer. Suspect devices were left on board and EOD were called out to examine them. Two bombs exploded under parked cars in the centre of Dublin, but as no group claimed responsibility it could well have been Loyalists attempting reprisals – albeit on a more truncated basis. Finally, on the 23rd the Belfast-Lisburn rail service was closed after the IRA detonated a large device near the embankment at Abingdon Street/Utility Street pedestrian bridge in South-West Belfast.

It is always interesting that the Provisional IRA/INLA and OIRA can kill so easily and without mercy – and yet when one of their members was killed in perhaps the same manner, could whinge and complain and call out 'not fair'. Patrick Duffy (54) was a member of PIRA's Londonderry Brigade and was killed – probably by undercover soldiers – at one of their arms caches in a house on the periphery of the Bogside. Acting upon information received, arms were discovered in the house and a four or five-man unit were inside the house. Duffy, a known player, went into the house – presumably with the intention of retrieving weapons. Exactly what happened inside the house has not been made public, but his daughter – who was outside – heard two bursts of fire from within. The PIRA man was hit at least 11 times and died more or less instantly. He was unarmed when he went into the house. Circa 1,800 people were killed by the Provisionals during the period 1970-97 – some by bomb and others by bullet. The research required to ascertain the exact number of people – military, police and civilian – shot dead by them without mercy and often whilst unarmed, is beyond the ability or timescale of this author. Further comment is superfluous.

On the same day that Duffy was killed, the IRA showed their scant regard for innocent civilians when it firebombed a music shop on Lisburn Road, Belfast. The fire spread to a Chinese restaurant next door where three children were sleeping in a flat above. The residents fled the building as flames and smoke made survival extremely precarious. At one stage there was a panic by the Chinese owners of the restaurant as they thought that their children were trapped by the flames and soldiers and police prepared to brave the fire in order to rescue them. However, it transpired that another family member had already rescued the three young children and led them to safety.

On Sunday the 26th, Albert Miles (50) – the Deputy Governor of Crumlin Road Prison – was shot dead by an IRA gunman at his home in Evelyn Gardens, North Belfast. Three IRA members smashed the front door open and rushed in – one of them grabbing the PO's wife and the other two found Mr Miles and shot him several times in the head, killing him instantly. The IRA gunman who held his hand over Mrs Miles' mouth was Charles McKiernan, who lived in the Unity flats in Belfast. He admitted under police questioning to taking part in the murder of the Deputy Governor. The trigger was pulled by fellow terrorist Kevin Artt – one of the 1983 Maze escapers. They then ran out and escaped in a waiting stolen car and drove off in the direction of the New Lodge. On the following day, Robert Batchelor (36) – a sergeant in the UDR – had just left work at the main GPO in Belfast and had just returned to his car in Institution Place near Hammill Street. He was in the habit of parking there and walking the short distance to the GPO sorting office where he worked full-time as a postman. The part-time soldier had established this habit and had clearly been dicked, as on this occasion IRA gunmen were waiting nearby in a stolen car. Institution Place is only 200-250 yards from the Divis Tower and the former Divis complex known to soldiers as the 'Zanussi'. As such, it was a relatively short run or drive for the gunmen to the safety of a hardline Republican area. As the part-time soldier got into his car, the waiting gunmen came up behind him and shot him eight times in the back of the head –

killing him instantly. His cowardly killers escaped and were never caught – although a taxi driver from the Falls Road area was later jailed for a year for conspiracy.

On the 28th, a Bill was passed in the House of Commons to increase the number of Northern Ireland Members of Parliament at Westminster. The number was increase from 12 to 17 seats. On the final day of the month, the Provisionals carried out a number of bomb and firebomb attacks in 14 towns and villages across Northern Ireland. They later issued a statement admitting the attacks and warning that it was preparing for a 'long war'. They further reiterated that there would be no Christmas truce again this year. 1978 was drawing to a close and the tragedies of Warrenpoint and Mountbatten were moving ever closer. Over 100 police officers had been killed during the four years of this study; another 14 would be killed in the final year of this book.

The month had ended with just six deaths – three of the dead were soldiers, two of whom were killed by the IRA. No civilians died this month, although the two non-military deaths were a fireman and a PO. One Republican paramilitary was killed this month. Of the total of six deaths, four were at the hands of the Provisional IRA.

48

December

ecember was a watershed with technically no civilians killed – with the exception of a member of HMP, a clerical assistant, shot by the IRA as they continued to target POs. However it was one of the worst months of the year for military deaths, with eight soldiers being killed in a variety of incidents including a mysterious helicopter crash which cost the lives of two squaddies. It was also a month in which the bombing terror returned to the English mainland.

The month began as the previous month had ended with a mini-blitz as PIRA bombs exploded in 11 cities and towns across the Province. Damage was immense, but there were no fatalities as a result of the blasts. On the second day of the month there was a helicopter crash, which killed the two pilots and one of the passengers. In situations such as this, it is difficult to elicit information from the MOD – especially if the mission involved covert operations and the secret insertion of troops. On that day, the crash claimed the lives of Captain Allan Johnston Stirling (41) – Army Air Corps (AAC) from Paisley near Glasgow – and Corporal Roger David Adcock (25), Parachute Regiment (attached to the AAC), from Aldershot. Both men were cremated in their respective hometowns. What the author has gleaned from unofficial sources is as follows: Because of the specialist nature of operations in Northern Ireland, a particularly important piece of role equipment was introduced in the form of the 'Nightsun' 3.5 million candle power searchlight. Operations at night were greatly enhanced with the introduction of Night Vision Goggles (NVGs) – although these missions could still be hazardous. This was evident on the night of 2 December 1978 when the pilot of XW614, 659 Squadron, became disorientated during a sortie and crashed into Lough Ross, Co Armagh close to Crossmaglen – killing both members of the crew. XW614 was the last of five Scouts written off during operations in the Province.

The *Daily Mirror* of the 4th reported that the Provisionals were threatening a renewed bombing campaign on the English mainland. They reported: "IRA terrorists are threatening to unleash a pre-Christmas firebomb blitz on English cities. Provo chiefs lit the fuse last month when four of their bombers slipped into the centres. Meanwhile other terror teams have been laying low in England awaiting orders to launch a wave of destruction. 'Clean' of Republican involvement, they are virtually undetectable by Scotland Yard anti-terror squads. The havoc bombs – which have turned Ulster's high streets into ruins – could be triggered off by a coded advert in an English newspaper." It was a commonly held view that the PIRA Army Council was dangling the threat over the heads of the British Government in an effort to force them into producing a timetable for withdrawal.

On the 4th, another member of the UDR was killed in an RTA in the Province whilst on duty. Private Trevor Herron (25) lost his life in a car crash in the southern part of Co Antrim. His funeral was held in his hometown of Comber. The following day, PIRA operatives launched a major car-bomb blitz on Belfast as they hijacked a dozen cars, packed them with explosives and forced their terrified owners to drive them to pre-determined points inside Belfast. A railway embankment, a bus depot and an office car park were blasted and hundreds of office workers and terrified Christmas shoppers were sent running for safety as the bombs brought chaos to the city. The Provisionals clearly had the financial ruin of the Province in their sights as they fought to escalate their economic warfare.

In the early evening of the 11th, three members of the administration team at Crumlin Road Jail were driving home and had used the eponymous Crumlin Road to travel in the direction of Carlisle Circus. John McTier (33), a colleague aged 54 and another friend had finished work for the day and had been – unknown to them – followed by a car which was parked on Crumlin Road. As the PO's car slowed down, the following car drew alongside them and a gunman opened fire with an automatic weapon and a burst of bullets hit their car. Two of the prison workers were hit in the head and the car slewed across the road and came to a halt against a wall – thanks to the other colleague's quick-thinking attitude in pulling on the handbrake. Both of the wounded were taken to hospital, but the younger man was fatally wounded and died in hospital on the 14th. His older colleague was in hospital for over two years.

On the same day as the attack on the POs, PIRA took their campaign against the officers to new lengths with a concerted letter-bomb campaign. Letters and parcels were addressed to prison officers' homes and before warnings could filter through, seven people had been injured. Three of the victims were wives of officers who opened mail addressed to them. The first indication of the campaign occurred at a sorting office in Lisburn when three postal workers were injured as several devices exploded as they were handling letters and parcels. A Province-wide warning was issued by the RUC for POs and their families to be on their guard. The warning came too late, however, for a postman who was badly injured in Dundonald, Co Down when a letter in his mail sack exploded. On the 13th, there were farcical scenes in a French court as the Government of West Germany applied to have a suspected PIRA bomber extradited to face trial on charges of bombing British Army bases. The man walked free when the man's defence team claimed that the suspected bomber, James McCann, was really Joseph Kennedy and that McCann had actually been killed in Belfast in 1978. Appeal Court judges at Aix-en-Provence ruled that the man wasn't McCann and ordered his immediate release to the chagrin of both the German and British Governments.

On Sunday the 17th, the IRA carried out a series of bomb attacks on cities in England and bombs exploded in Bristol, Coventry, Liverpool, Manchester and Southampton. The *Daily Mirror*'s front page headlines for the 18th screamed: *'Taste Of Terror To Come'*. The report continued:

> The IRA bomb blitz on England yesterday is feared to herald a Christmas terror campaign. Godfathers of the Provisionals ordered blasts in five cities as a taste of things to come. Security experts believe it could be London's turn next. At least one group of terrorists are already hauled up in London waiting for orders to plant much larger bombs. Yesterday's attacks on Manchester, Liverpool, Bristol, Coventry and Southampton were unleashed as a reprisal following the breakdown of informal talks between the Provos and The British Government two days ago ... When the word is given the 'sleepers' will set out to burn city centres using a new weapon – tiny bombs made from tape cassettes and packed with highly flammable material. Provo chiefs aim to avoid the human carnage that did them more harm than good in previous blitzes on Britain. Instead, they will produce the type of devastation that has turned

high streets all over Ulster into ruins without risking the revulsion of their own supporters ... . A senior spokesman at the Scotland Yard said: "We consider yesterday's bomb strikes were a possible prelude to a bigger campaign. For that reason, we urge everyone to be on their guard and take no chances."

In Bristol, six young men and a girl were hurt when a bomb blew out the front of a major store in Clifton. One of the men was wounded when a piece of plate-glass stabbed him in the back – and all of the group were deafened for a time. A senior policeman said: "The area is popular for clubs and restaurants and we should count ourselves lucky that people were not killed." In Southampton two 5lb bombs were planted 300 yards apart, but fortunately only one exploded. The blast in the early hours of the morning devastated shops in East Street. The other bomb was timed to go off shortly afterwards in nearby Bargate, but it did not explode. The police later made a statement believing that the terrorists were posing as courting couples – cuddling together to disguise the placing of bombs.

In Coventry hundreds of youngsters were packed into four nightclubs when a blast in a shopping precinct at 0130 caused major damage, but there would have been absolute carnage if the bomb had gone off 20 minutes later as the precinct was where the clubgoers would have exited. In Manchester, a huge blast at Barton Square at 0200 sent restaurant customers racing into the street. They had just been cleared to go back to their tables when another explosion ripped through Deansgate. A policeman said: "The first bomb may have been designed to attract people into the area. That has happened before, but it could have just gone off early." In Liverpool, a young couple were injured by flying glass when another early-morning blast blew in a wall at the city centre Taverna Club. Moments later another bomb went off under a children's roundabout in the St Johns (sic) Shopping Centre. An eyewitness said: "Everyone was eating when this tremendous bang came. It was bedlam afterwards."

The *Daily Express* led with 'London Blasted' as its main headline and inside with 'Inter City Horror' and warned that: "Bombers launch new wave of attacks throughout Britain" (Edition 18/12/1978). All of the nationals spoke of the size of the bombs being used and opined that the profligacy of the bombers demonstrated that PIRA had explosives to spare and was their way of telling the British Government that there was lots more where that came from!

A lorry driver was later praised for saving a city from major devastation. A massive bomb was taped to a tanker en route for a massive oil refinery. The driver however saw the explosives -19 sticks of gelignite – and steered the lorry away from other oil tankers. The driver very wisely asked the police not to name him. A witness however said: "He knew the terrible chance he took. He just put other peoples' lives before his own." The bombers planted the explosives at the Lex Tillotson Garage at Redbridge in the Midlands. The massive Fawley Refinery was the main target. Had the bombers been successful, the loss of life would have been simply appalling. The front page of the Daily Express (19/12/1978) under a headline of 'Bomb Hero' spoke of: "Two army men went in – their lives trembling on the spring of a cheap watch. They did a swift job in what must have seemed a lifetime."

On the same day, Provisional Sinn Féin issued the following statement: "We deliberately chose the time and the target. Your intelligence service has given us – and will continue to give us – logistical problems which, however, we can overcome. We now give due warning to you, the English people, that in future both the targets and the timing may be changed.

Continuing acts of brutality against prisoners would force the IRA to consider inflicting civilian casualties." Their statement dripped with hypocrisy and cant. Few were fooled by the double standards of the Republicans, but the overtly worded threat was taken seriously.

On the 19th, it was only the news of a tragic train crash between London and Brighton – which killed five passengers and injured over 40 – which kept the continuing bombing news from the main headline. The *Daily Mirror* reported that suspected IRA members had opened fire on a policeman near Farnham in Surrey when he attempted to flag down the car. He was forced to dive to the ground and once he had radioed his colleagues, a massive police hunt was launched in the Surrey/Hampshire area. As most readers will know, the British police – with the exception of Northern Ireland – are not routinely armed, but the Metropolitan police flooded the main shopping areas of London to protect the shoppers. The operation, which went under the imaginative title of 'Operation Santa', involved 2,000 officers – all of whom were armed.

Sean O'Callaghan names Kevin McKenna as the head of PIRA's Northern Command and, as such, effectively overseeing the England department or England Team – different terms for the same thing. Owen Coogan was the actual head of the team and was also charged with prosecuting their murder campaigns in Germany, Belgium and Holland – as well as on the English mainland. The former quartermaster-general of the Provisional IRA – a man responsible for co-ordinating the stockpiling of the Provos' massive arsenal – is said to have masterminded a number of high-profile IRA operations including the Brighton bomb in 1984. There are claims that he is now a member of the so-called 'Real IRA'.

McKenna was greatly influenced by the 1971 Internment campaign, when flawed intelligence – often based on information from the 1940s and 1950s – led to many unnecessary arrests. Not only was the information flawed, but virtually no Loyalist paramilitaries were picked up, which led to accusations of bias and ended any chances that the army was being even-handed in their treatment of the Catholics/Nationalists. McKenna joined the IRA in the mid-1960s before he emigrated to Canada. After internment was introduced in Northern Ireland he returned to Ireland and again became involved in IRA matters – forming a new ASU based in Aughnacloy. When McKenna returned from Canada – and following the departure of Brendan Hughes in 1972 – he became the commander of the Tyrone Brigade. Another major player in the England Team was Glaswegian – and former British soldier – Pat Murray. O'Callaghan describes him as a man with a long history of violence and a " ... .classic sociopath ... " Together with Pat Dingus Magee, the England Team contained a formidable gang of violent, committed terrorists.

The next day, attention was once again focused in Northern Ireland as the IRA killed a soldier in North Belfast. Corporal James Burney (26) of the King's Own Scottish Borderers had been part of a search team and was just leaving a house in Baltic Avenue close to the Antrim Road. A sniper – concealed in an upstairs window of a derelict house on the Antrim Road – fired a single shot from a Lee Enfield .303 fitted with a sniper scope. The round hit the NCO from Cumbria – the traditional recruiting ground for this regiment – and he died shortly afterwards. Another soldier was also wounded by the same round. The rest of the patrol raced to the house where they seized the weapon, but the killer had just melted away.

NEW LODGE, BELFAST: 1978
Stephen Griffiths, 1st Battalion, the Green Howards

I had started the long haul of walking the streets of Belfast in areas such as the New Lodge, Ardoyne, and – of course – the city centre. Like most units on active service, your day is split up into different times such as two hours on immediate and then 10 minute rest. Then comes all the rest camp duties; ops room; sangars; gate duty – the list is endless and tiring. Like many others I was only 18 when I landed in Ulster and raring to go.

The first couple of weeks were very quiet and not a lot was happening. That was all to change! We had riots, contacts, kneecappings, bombs and robberies – as I said before the list was endless! It seemed like a big game at first … going out to riots; giving protection to the RUC; checking people; VCPs; house searches and the like.

Later I was stood down at North Queen Street police station – having a drink and a burger in the choggy shop waiting for my next patrol. I was talking to Corporal Jim Burney – from the 1st Battalion of the King's Own Borderers – who was just going out on patrol. He said to me: "See you in a couple of hours! Get them pool balls set up."

It never happened! He had just two weeks to the end of his tour when he was hit in the chest by a sniper. That's when it hit me; the short time I had known him, I had found him a great bloke and morale booster. RIP, Jim.

The next day in Northern Ireland – the 21st – the army lost three of its soldiers in a PIRA ambush in Crossmaglen. It was one of the worst incidents for several years and it involved the Grenadier Guards. The guards, whose motto is Honi soit qui mal y pense (Evil be to he who thinks evil) can trace their lineage to 1656 and were originally the loyal bodyguard of King Charles II. A four-man patrol from the 1st Battalion was patrolling close to the centre of Crossmaglen. A green GPO van drove up and parked not far from the four soldiers. They moved towards it in order to investigate, although unknown to them the van had been hijacked just an hour or so earlier and was carrying heavily armed PIRA terrorists. As they closed on it, gunmen opened fire with an assortment of weapons – newspaper reports later claimed that it was the deadly M60 machine gun – spraying the soldiers with over 200 rounds. Civilians were forced to dive for cover as rounds flew everywhere – and after return fire from a grenadier the vehicle sped away. Three soldiers lay in pools of their own blood – all mortally wounded.

The three were immediately casevaced to hospital by a military helicopter – which landed in the square in order to try and save precious seconds – but the three wounded men were all dead on arrival at hospital. The soldiers were: Guardsman Kevin Johnson (20) from Blackpool; Guardsman Glen Ling (18) from Suffolk and Guardsman Graham Duggan (22) from Cheshire. The *Daily Express* on the following morning led with the simple words: 'Wiped Out!' The report continued:

They were soldiers three – like Kipling's famous friends – and they were shot to death under the lights of a village Christmas tree. The IRA admitted the cold-blooded murder on the Ulster border. And last night a grieving mother remembered the brave and prophetic last words her guardsman son spoke to her at her home. "When I said I was very worried that he was going back to Ireland, he told me: 'Don't worry mum, a bullet is quick; you don't feel anything'. Graham Duggan (22) from Cheshire always stuck close to Kevin Johnson and Glen Ling when on dangerous patrol for they were Frontline friends in the Grenadier Guards. Kevin (20), from Blackpool, and Glen (18), from Saxmundham, Suffolk covered Graham yesterday as he moved up to investigate a suspicious green van parked in the tinselled square of Crossmaglen village. The backdoor of the van swung open revealing a sandbag-mounted M60 machine gun – a terrible American weapon which fires 600 rounds a minute and outshoots anything a soldier on patrol can carry. In a shattering long burst – 'a bullet's quick' – it killed all three men instantly. Then the van drove off – presumably across the nearby border to Eire. Helicopters and foot patrols hunting them on both sides of the line found no trace. At Kevin Johnson's Blackpool home last night a Christmas tree was shining in a window. Glen Ling, the Suffolk country boy, completed his training at Pirbright, Surrey barely four months ago. "His mother was worried," a friend said, "but Glen shrugged it off."

Within minutes CVOs from the regiment were being given orders to report to homes in Lancashire, Cheshire and Suffolk to impart the tragic news to the guardsmen's families. Once there, each CVO would knock on the door of a neighbouring house and appraise the shocked woman or man of the news which he had to deliver to the mother of a soldier next door. The CVO would instruct her put the kettle on and then, whilst it boiled, walk to the house – usually in the company of a vicar or a priest – and pass on the news which would forever break the hearts of the recipients; an early Christmas present from the Provisional IRA. For one of the CVOs there would be another daunting task just 48 hours later when Guardsman Paul Weaver (21) died from violent or unnatural causes. The author has been informed that this may have been caused by the earlier tragic loss of one or more of his friends. Accordingly, this author will pass no further comment on the death of this young soldier from Oxford.

One dissenting voice was raised during the research for this book and the former soldier – who wishes to be described only as the Patrol Commander – told me the following:

On 21 December 1978 at 1145 hours I was a multiple commander operating in the South Armagh village of XMG. I had split my men into three four-man bricks. I was patrolling down the Castleblany Road when I heard a shot coming from the direction of the camp! We were running back towards the camp when I received a radio message that a sangar sentry had had a negligent discharge. So as not to create a pattern, I led my men towards and down the Newry Road – the only road that led directly away from the border. The road was deserted and, as I approached the Rio Bar, I noticed a van parked on the left with its nearside wheels on the pavement approximately 40 metres to my front. I had Guardsman Duggan behind me with the LMG, Guardsman Johnson, on the other side of the road with Guardsman Ling behind him. As I looked towards the van I noticed it was like a BR delivery van – tailboard with a roller shutter that pulls down. The strange thing was it was piled to the roof with what appeared to be parcels, which appeared to be flush to the tailboard. I raised my rifle to my shoulder to look through the SUIT site. As I did, I noticed four firing slits cut in the boxes! I fired a full mag at the back of this wagon at the same time that they opened fire! The weapons which were being fired at us were three Armalites and an AK47 – all on full auto. When my mag was expended I ducked behind a wall and gave a quick contact report. All my men were down, though Duggan was still able to talk. I ran back, took his LMG and let them have the whole mag, which quietened them down a bit. When the mag was expended I ran across the road and carried on with another SLR from one of my other fatally injured men. At that moment, the van drove off. It was a very professional, well-set-up ambush and my men – who were the best in the platoon – did not have a chance to fire a shot!

I recall that the back of the van behind the boxes was armour-plated; I know because every fourth round I fired was tracer and I could see them going straight up in the air as my rounds hit the van. The van was not parked in the square; it was about 200 yards down the Newry Road just past the Rio Bar on the left. We were not doing VCPs – we were hard patrolling towards it! We were all concentrating on our jobs. Christmas aside, it was just another serious foot patrol; no time for thoughts of anything apart from doing our jobs! Poor Duggan did not die until he was on the chopper. He was talking to me and in fact he said: "Fancy being shot outside a pub and it's closed!" He had been shot by an Armalite round which had split into three pieces and ripped into his liver. There were four automatic weapons being fired at us – and not an M60 as the cheap sensationalism of the newspapers stated – in order to sell their wares. My men were all professional soldiers and although fully alert to danger, were unsuspecting of the ambush because that is what it was! PIRA's plan was also very well thought out and should have killed us all. I opened fire a fraction of a second before they did, which is one of the things that saved my life. Another was the fact that I had converted my

View from a sangar over the Ardoyne. (©Brian Sheridan)

SLR back to the fully auto for which it was originally designed. They were shocked when they got a full mag in one burst, which put whoever was firing at me off their aim. I could still see rounds hitting the road all around me and the wall to my left. One round went through the right arm of my smock and for hours afterwards I was deaf due to the rounds passing close to my head!

I have given the author this information because I want it written as it was and not how the press made it out

The Province was quiet on the Boxing Day, but the Primate of Ireland – Archbishop O' Fiaich – chose the day to boost his standing amongst Nationalists by calling for a 'British withdrawal' from Northern Ireland. He described the option as: " ... the best hope of producing an acceptable long-term solution ... ." He called for a five-year plan in order to bring the troops 'home' – conveniently forgetting that Northern Ireland was a part of the UK and for the thousands of UDR troops, Northern Ireland was 'home'. He added that it would need a carefully phased exodus because of the threat of civil war. The churchman was clearly a man who lived in a utopian world and had no grasp of what it was like to be a soldier – trapped like 'piggy in the middle' between warring factions – nor the fears felt by both sides of the sectarian divide; deeply suspicious of the other fellow.

December was finally over and a total of nine people had been killed in Troubles-related incidents. Eight soldiers and a civilian prison officer, a Protestant, had died – of whom five were at the hands of the Provisional IRA.

1978 was over and 110 people had died in the Troubles:

British Army	49
RUC	11
Civilians	44*
Protestants	26
Catholics	18
Republican	6
Loyalists	-

*21 of these were overtly sectarian. Following the 259 sectarian murders in 1976-77, this was a welcome – though far from ideal – fall

Part Five

1979

This was to be the year when the British Army lost more soldiers in a single day than at any time since the Arab Police mutiny in Aden. The year would witness the deaths of 78 serving or former soldiers. It was the year of Warrenpoint and the year of the murder of Lord Louis Mountbatten (1st Earl, Mountbatten of Burma), the Queen's cousin. It was the year of the assassination of yet another British ambassador and it was the year that INLA murdered a future Secretary of State for Northern Ireland within the very precincts of the Houses of Parliament.

49

January

The New Year would open with just five Troubles-related deaths – two of which involved an IRA 'own goal' where two bombers would remove themselves, unintentionally, from the gene pool and two soldiers would die in circumstances unknown. Towards the end of the month there was some mystery as to the motive for the killing of a salesman from England.

On the 2nd of the month, as the snow began to fall throughout the Province, a special Gardaí Siochana task force was set up inside the Republic with one specific aim: to stop terrorist action. Their brief was to stop PIRA and INLA from operating in the South and crossing to the North and to stop the Loyalists from the opposite terror journey. Many RUC officers and soldiers – especially those who operated in the dangerous 'cuds' (border areas) – felt that the Gardaí were soft on the IRA. It was felt that they often 'did a Nelson' and turned a blind eye to their activities. The Irish SF had to be aware of PIRA activities on the Irish side – in particular when they (PIRA) set up firing positions to snipe at troops on the border.

On the 3rd, an RUC/army patrol in Londonderry's Shantallow area – soldiers from The Royal Welsh Fusiliers (RWF) acting on a tip-off – went to a house in Danesfort Crescent and found arms and ammunition. In the afternoon, another RWF platoon on the Creggan Estate also discovered arms and ammunition including two stolen British Army SLRs. The UDA also announced that their prisoners – UFF paramilitaries – in the Maze would begin a three-day fast. It was to protest against the 'lack of humanitarianism' shown by the Northern Ireland Office (NIO) in their 'unfair' treatment of UFF prisoners.

Two days later there was a further setback for the Provisionals as two of their members from the North Belfast Company killed themselves in a classic 'own goal' explosion. A two-man bombing team was tasked to plant a bomb in Belfast City Centre and were moving explosives from a safehouse in Northwick Drive in the Ardoyne. Francis Donnelly (24) and Lawrence Montgomery (24) were packing explosives into a stolen car when a detonator fired – resulting in a huge explosion. Both men were mortally wounded and died a short time after they arrived in to hospital. Donnelly was a known player, but Montgomery was unknown to the SF. A contemporary newspaper showed photographs of RUC officers collecting body parts and placing them into plastic bags. It was a scene reminiscent of 'Bloody Friday' and evoked memories of emergency services shovelling the shattered remains of PIRA's murderous attack on Belfast City Centre.

The two men belonged to the Belfast Brigade of the Provisional IRA and was the largest of the organisation's command areas. It was founded in 1969 along with the formation of the Provisional IRA. It was historically organised into three battalions: the 1st Battalion was based in the Andersonstown/Lenadoon/Twinbrook area of South-West Belfast; the 2nd Battalion was based in the Falls Road/Clonard/Ballymurphy district of West Belfast; and the 3rd Battalion organised in Nationalist enclaves in the north (Ardoyne, New Lodge,

South African-made 9mm LPD sub-machine gun, found by 25 Field Regiment Royal Artillery, Roy Street, Markets area of Belfast, October 1979. (©Mark 'C')

Ligoniel), south (the Markets, Lower Ormeau) and east (Short Strand) of the city. Next to the South Armagh Brigade, it was the most prolific killing machine of the organisation.

On the 6th, an undercover RUC Special Branch officer was spotted by Republican dickers in the RVH and an ASU was called in. The officer's duties that day have not been revealed, but it is likely that he was guarding wounded policemen. As he stood in a corridor near one of the wards, gunman opened fire and shot him several times in the chest. Although injured, he was not seriously wounded and eventually returned to duty. It sparked memories of the shooting of Royal Anglian 'Tiny' Rose in the hospital in May 1977 (see Chapter 20). On the 9th, UDR soldier Lance-Corporal Thomas Forde (56) died in unknown circumstances. The author regrets that he has no further information.

The whole of Britain had entered what the anti-Labour newspapers famously labelled the 'Winter of Discontent' in this early part of 1979. The Labour Government of James Callaghan had tried to staunch the 'bleeding' of the economy by imposing a blanket five per cent pay increase across the country and across all professions. The Ford workers went on a five-week stoppage and the petrol tanker drivers threatened the same. The Provisionals had come close to crippling the economy and now the militant unions would achieve in a few short weeks what the Republicans had spent almost 10 years trying to do.

The first blow to the Labour Government's attempt to impose a five per cent limit on pay rises that winter had come when the Ford motor company settled their strike by paying a 17 per cent increase. Callaghan was left powerless after he lost a key Commons vote to impose sanctions on the car maker. Then 8,500 Esso, Texaco, BP and Shell tanker drivers gave notice they would strike from 3 January 1979 in pursuit of their 25 per cent pay claim. As it happened, Tony Benn – who the cabinet papers show had earlier urged Callaghan to adopt a 'no confrontation' policy with the unions – was the Energy Secretary and so the cabinet minister responsible for the tanker drivers.

This settlement set off a chain reaction. The local authority manual workers and NHS ancillary staff prepared for a campaign of industrial action. As the ambulance drivers refused to answer 999 calls and the dead went unburied in municipal cemeteries, Mrs Thatcher's Conservatives prepared for their May 1979 General Election victory. The same applied in Northern Ireland and soldiers were flown in from England – along with other specialist tanker drivers – to assist in the maintenance of essential fuel supplies. There was a major oil refinery at Sydenham near Belfast and troops and strike-breaking drivers were used to ensure that all priority needs – hospitals, aged care, schools etc – were taken care of. The state of emergency ended on the 14th. The writing on the wall was evident – and for Callaghan, it was terminal. In a crucial vote of confidence in the House on 28 March, the votes were deadlocked at 310:310 with one vote to be cast – that of Gerry Fitt, SDLP MP. He voted against the Labour Government and it was forced to go to the country. Northern Ireland had brought the British Government down.

On 17 January 1979 the UVF carried out its only major attack in Scotland when its members bombed two pubs in Glasgow frequented by Catholics. Both pubs were wrecked and a number of people were wounded. It claimed the pubs were used for Republican fundraising. In June, nine UVF members were convicted of the attacks.

On the 18th, in a repeat of earlier attacks on the public transport infrastructure, Provisionals broke into the Falls Road bus depot close to Andersonstown RUC Station. Under cover of night, they set fire to several buses and the resultant blaze saw 25 buses destroyed at a cost of over £1 million.

THINGS HAD TO CHANGE
Mick 'Benny Hill', Royal Anglians

In early 1979 we were back in Belfast – Palace Barracks, Holywood to be precise. In the five years since we had first been deployed to Belfast, things had changed – but now we were back for a Resident Battalion tour. Things were different – better equipment for starters; the radios were smaller and better; no more A41s to lug around; urban patrol boots were much better for tabbing the streets than DMS boots; and the flak jackets had patches and ridges on the shoulder so that rifle butts didn't slip. Also, we had half-decent waterproofs. It has been said by someone much wiser than I am that you do not commence a conflict with the army trained and equipped for that conflict; you commence with the army and equipment you've got! How very true this has proved to be over the centuries.

Training had improved beyond all recognition. The 'Tin Cities' at Lydd and Hythe and in Sennelager gave young soldiers the training they needed for the 'job'. The 'Int' courses were superb too. Unfortunately, we weren't the only ones to have learned lessons. The IRA no longer conducted random shoot-outs. Their ambushes were usually well-planned 'shoot and scoots'. They learned the hard way that a drawn-out gun battle with well-trained soldiers has only one result: you lose! The battalion was organised for a long tour. A big Int Section; a Recce Platoon appropriately trained and equipped for COP (Close Observation Platoon) work; Heavy Weapons Company turned into a Rifle Company and a small Camp Security Section. The CONCOs were all experienced corporals or sergeants who were permanently detached – in pairs – to all the SF bases in West Belfast (the Aldergrove Battalion performed the same service for the North Belfast bases). Their long-term knowledge was invaluable to Roulemont Companies – especially during the first few weeks of a tour. Most of the companies valued their expertise and local knowledge and treated them very well. The CONCOs lived on the bases for weeks at a time with only the occasional weekend or couple of days off in Palace when the Roulemont Companies were settled in – and the two never both at once.

I can only remember of two cases of friction. One was a major personality clash where a platoon commander didn't appreciate the CONCO's wealth of local knowledge and didn't consult him at all. An 'interview without coffee' with his OC did a lot to clarify the situation and explain the error of his ways! (They still didn't like each other but managed to work together and appreciate each other's good points, which was far more important.) At another base, the incoming CSM decided that everyone in his base would do their share of gate guards and 'Dixie Land' (cookhouse fatigues). He was quite surprised when a scruffy, long-haired unshaven bloke in trainers, jeans, and a very dodgy anorak knocked on his door and produced an ID card showing him to be a colour sergeant in 3 Royal Anglian. After five minutes of very amicable conversation the duties roster was immediately changed and the two CONCOs reverted to their normal routine of loads of patrols and int cell duties.

Liaison is very important. Just because your units have fixed boundaries doesn't mean the 'other side' have the same restrictions, so knowing what is going on in other areas is vital. Just because a 'face' lives on your patch doesn't mean he drinks on your patch or sees his mates on your patch. Liaison and co-operation is easier face-to-face rather than a disembodied voice on the phone – and it is easier to build up trust with a person you actually know rather than a unit. My duties brought me into contact with all sorts and ranks. Luckily, I can make people laugh and I can remember jokes. It helps sometimes after a really shitty week having someone make you laugh and just be prepared to listen to you rather than talking 'at' you; it can be a big help. Luckily my accent was easy on the ear (to the Ulstermen at least) and my difficulty in pronouncing 'th' and aitches was often a source of amusement. 'Three' and 'free' may sound the same, but obviously mean different amounts!

Our COP had a very experienced colour sergeant – a veteran of nearly 20 years – with medals from Malaya, Cyprus, Aden, several Op Banner tours and possibly somewhere I've forgotten. Their task was cover OPs, which basically meant hiding in an attic, derelict building or somewhere with a bit of cover; eating cold food for days on end; crapping in poly bags and pissing in bottles; and observing and remaining undetected for days at a time – not very glamorous and most wearing on the nerves. Getting rid of all of the detritus bought out of an OP wasn't really a task to be relished either.

All in all, a long tiring tour with one of the section killed (Paul Wright) and one seriously injured. It may have only been one, but it was all the world to Paul's family. Nothing to make headlines or make 'wannabes' think: "This is exciting. I want to do that!" but we played our part in making Ulster a safer, better place.

No glory there then – just insults and incomprehension from civvies when it was all over. Plus la change, c'est la meme chose!

On the 23rd, the IRA carried out a plan whereby several of their gunmen dressed as road sweepers and carrying the stolen accoutrement of the trade (brushes, shovels etc), attacked the SF. An RUC sergeant, en route for Hastings Street police station, was walking along West Street close to the Markets area when the gunmen dropped their tools and opened fire. The officer was seriously wounded and fell to the ground – having been hit five times. The gunmen escaped in a waiting car. Within an hour of this incident a traffic policeman was on duty close to the M1 junction on Kennedy Way, Andersonstown. Two IRA gunmen had taken over a house in Stockman's Lane with one downstairs holding the family at gunpoint whilst the other set up a firing point in a bedroom overlooking the junction with the M1. He fired a single high-velocity shot which hit the policeman in the shoulder – hurling him to the ground. He was rushed to hospital and later recovered from the wound which, an inch or two further over, would have resulted in his death.

On the 25th, a member of the Royal Military Police (RMP) died in circumstances unknown. Corporal William Ian Snaith (22) is remembered on the wall at the National Memorial Arboretum at Alrewas, but the author has no further details. On the same day an army foot patrol approached a suspicious car to the south of the Bogside. As they did so, four PIRA men in the car jumped out and opened fire on the soldiers – wounding two of them – but their comrades returned fire immediately. One terrorist was hit and as he fell; was dragged away by his fellow Republicans. The troops gave chase, but the PIRA gang disappeared into a 'rabbit warren' of Nationalist housing. When the car was searched, it was found to contain arms and bomb-making equipment.

On the following day it was a case of PIRA shooting first – even if civilians were in the firing line. As an army mobile patrol drove along the Whiterock Road in West Belfast, gunmen opened fire from the walls of the city cemetery. Their high-velocity rounds missed the Land Rovers, but instead wounded two schoolboys as they walked home from their nearby school. The boys, aged 13 and 15, were rushed to hospital but thankfully survived their wounds. RUCR Constable Nigel Beattie had a lucky escape when shots were fired at him by a PIRA gunman – Michael James Ryan – in the Coagh, Co Tyrone area. Ryan was later tried for this and other attempted murders. Earlier in the day an IRA bombing team had placed a large device at the offices of the Housing Executive in Dungannon, Co Tyrone. It was a clear attempt to disrupt the Government infrastructure in their campaign to make Ulster ungovernable. One device exploded – causing some structural damage – but army EOD officers were able to defuse the others.

STORIES OF MY DEATH
Major Allan Harrhy, RRW

Whilst on foot patrol in Coalisland, it was brought to our attention by a civvie that there was a suspicious-looking package tied to the window sill of a nearby bank. We checked his story and it was correct, so true to our training we evacuated the area and threw a cordon around several surrounding streets – and I looked at the package through my binoculars and confirmed that it was very likely to be a bomb. I radioed for the ATO and also the RUC and received instructions that the former was on his way.

I got the message back that ATO was on his way and the route he would take and I needed to let the patrol know this – and then I made what was nearly a fatal mistake. Instead of going behind the shops to see the rest of the cordon, I decided to avoid all the mud and the puddles and instead walked past the bank – on the opposite side of the street of course – and the suspect package. As I got directly opposite and just 20 feet away, I heard the timing device go (just like an egg-timer sounding) and I dived into the doorway right next to me and it exploded! It shattered all the windows around me and set fire to the bank – and a huge chunk of metal whizzed past where my head would have been and straight through the window of the doorway. My ears were ringing and I was dazed and I couldn't believe that I was alive.

Despite this incredible ringing in my ears, I heard my radio burst into life – and I will never forget, to my dying day, what was being shouted. It was Lance-Corporal Murphy and he called: "The colour sergeant is dead; he's been killed!" I quickly got on the radio and explained that rumours of my death had been greatly exaggerated.

There was an air of mystery about the fourth death of the month – on the 28th -and could have resulted from a man many consider, with the obvious benefit of hindsight, to have possibly been a 'Walter Mitty' character. Arthur Lockett (29) was a salesman for several European countries and plied his trade through mainly Germany, France and Switzerland. He had occasion to find himself in Dublin and became involved with some INLA men to whom he may have foolishly boasted of his 'connections' in British Intelligence and/or the army. It is likely that he exaggerated his relationship with the army – confined to selling glassware to members of BAOR – and this was his 'death warrant'. On a cold winter's night, he was taken to a rural area just outside the Irish capital and beaten close to death with Hurley bats and left to die from a combination of serious head injuries and exposure to the cold night air. An INLA member – James McDaid – was later tried and convicted of the murder of Mr Lockett.

On the 29th, an almost completed hotel in Downpatrick was attacked by a Provisional bombing team less than a month before it was due to open. A three-man team planted several devices in the Abbey Lodge Hotel on the Belfast Road. The first device exploded – causing extensive damage to one wing of the hotel – but the other devices were made safe by EOD. The final two incidents of the month took place in Belfast City Centre. In Academy Street an RUCR officer was returning to his car when he was confronted by three gunmen who had been waiting close to where he had parked. He was shot several times at point-blank range – including a wound in his face; he made a full recovery. The gunmen ran off to a waiting car, but it crashed as they made good their escape. The gunmen – one of them limping – got away on foot.

The month ended with just five Troubles-related deaths – two soldiers and one civilian, a Protestant, died. His death was not sectarian. The IRA lost two of their volunteers in a premature detonation.

50

February

The month saw the deaths of nine people, including four soldiers – two of which were very controversial. It also witnessed the outrageous murder of a retired PO and his wife – killed by the IRA because of 'past associations'. It was also the month in which the infamous 'Shankill Butchers' were finally sent to prison.

On the 1st of the month, Provisional gunmen attempted to assassinate a leading Protestant businessman in the centre of Belfast. As the 56-year-old man walked along Upper Queen Street, gunmen in a stolen car parked on his route opened fire several times – hitting him in the chest and upper arm. He was taken to hospital where he recovered. Several thousand miles away, one of PIRA's European teams was caught attempting to smuggle arms into Greece. The team had collected the arms from a Middle Eastern terror group in the Lebanon and had smuggled them through Syria and into Turkey. Their plan was to cross into Greece where a friendly tanker would ship them to Ireland from one of the many Greek ports. The plan went awry as they crossed over the Turkish border and the men's car was directed to a search area by armed soldiers – tipped off by British Intelligence. Two men – one from Belfast and one from Newry – were arrested and a large cache of arms were also seized.

In 1970 a major arms trial (Irish: Géarchéim na nArm or Triail na nArm) was held in the Republic, which created a major political scandal. Two cabinet ministers — Charles Haughey and Neil Blaney — were removed from office for allegedly attempting to illegally import arms for the IRA. Thereafter, other sources were required. Irish-American groups – backed by NORAID – sent huge sums of money to the terror group and many arms were smuggled across the Atlantic. However, the bulk of their arms came from the crazed Libyan dictator Muammar al-Gaddafi – as well as from other Middle Eastern groups such as the PLO (Palestine Liberation Organisation) and also from the Comintern of the USSR. At around the same time that the PIRA smugglers were being arrested by Greek police, a Green Jacket soldier was shot and wounded in Strabane. Around 10 shots were fired at an RGJ VCP in the centre of the town at the 20-year-old, who was wounded in the thigh and was taken to hospital. The gunmen had crashed through the checkpoint in a stolen car before turning and firing a long burst at the soldiers. The border with the Republic is a quick one-mile dash down the A38 Lifford Road and over the Strabane Canal into Ireland.

On the 3rd, the peace of what had been a quiet – but cold – Saturday evening in Belfast was shattered by a double murder by the IRA. Patrick Mackin (60) was a retired PO and lived with his wife Violet (58) in the North Belfast area of the Oldpark Road. In the early evening a car hijacked in the Ardoyne area drove up to the retired couple's home and several gunmen forced their way in and found the couple relaxing in front of the television. Mr Mackin was shot several times – and it would appear from the wounds and position of her body that his wife bravely struggled to save him from being shot and threw herself across her mortally wounded husband. Both bodies lay undiscovered until the following morning when they were found by worried neighbours. A spokesman for Sinn Féin/IRA stated that the retired PO's wife had not been a target and had been shot in the confusion. Their apologist issued the following statement: "We also wish to inform all prison officers that if they resign and make their resignation known to the IRA, we will consider removing their names from our target list."

On the 5th, the Dungannon IRA executed a plan involving major disruption of public services – and in a well-co-ordinated attack planted bombs on several buses in the town's bus station. Bombs were also planted on buses at Benburb, Caledon and Aughnacloy. All of the devices exploded – causing hundreds of thousands of pounds' worth of damages and leading to a complete dislocation of all passenger services (including school buses). The team responsible for planting the bombs then attacked a local Protestant-owned transport company – Capper and Lamb, Tamnamore – and destroyed the bulk of their fleet of lorries. Further incendiary attacks were carried out through the Dungannon area, which resulted in major disruption of life. One former UDR soldier from the area told the author: "Looking around after a day of PIRA activity was like looking at photos and newsreels which I had seen growing up of the German air raids on Belfast. My parents were living near Harland & Wolff in the east of the city when it was bombed on the night of 15 April 1941 and they were bombed out of their home." (On that night, 900 people were killed and 1,500 people were injured. Outside of London, it was the worst night for deaths of the entire blitz.)

Lisnaskea sits in a salient of Co Fermanagh, which juts into Counties Monaghan, Cavan and Leitrim – and, as such, is of strategic importance to the IRA in the movement of arms and explosives into the North. During the Troubles the RUC station was a heavily fortified and permanently manned SF base. The main road south led directly to Co Monaghan through the rolling green hills and pleasant pastureland of Fermanagh down to the Irish border. It was a dangerous place for both soldier and policeman – and the ROH of SF dead for the Troubles reflects this danger. On the 5th, warnings had been received of an explosive device in the Bank Brae area of Lisnaskea and the RUC were deployed to divert traffic from around the immediate area. However, the device exploded earlier than the IRA warning had suggested and two RUCR officers were badly injured by flying shrapnel and debris. The explosion brought down power cables and part of the town was blacked out. A second device was defused by EOD.

There was a near-disaster on the 7th of the month when two undercover soldiers – possibly 14 Det – were operating in the Maghera area of Co Londonderry. PIRA dickers had spotted the two soldiers, who were wearing civvie clothes, near the corner of Station Road and Crew Road and quickly alerted a local ASU. The PIRA unit quickly got into place and found a firing position, but fortunately for the soldiers the terrorists opened fire prematurely and although both were hit, they remained sufficiently in control to return fire and hit at least two of the IRA men who escaped in a stolen car – leaving several bloodstains. A nearby unit of the 1st Glosters was immediately called into action and a massive manhunt was launched in tandem with RUC officers around the surrounding countryside. Although two of the terrorists were wounded, they attempted to escape across the border to the sanctuary of the Republic. On the following day, several men were arrested and weapons were found in the abandoned car.

On the 12th, the British Government finally recognised the bravery of Captain Robert Nairac and announced the award of a posthumous George Cross. The citation read: "For exceptional courage and acts of the greatest heroism in circumstances of extreme peril." The award was presented to members of Captain Nairac's family. The GC is the second highest decoration of the British honours system, which includes some countries of the Commonwealth. It is ranked second only to the Victoria Cross. It was famously awarded to the entire island of Malta for its collective gallantry in the face of overwhelming Nazi bombers and for being ' ... a thorn in Rommel's side ... .' More recently, the RUC also received a collective George Cross. The then GOC of Northern Ireland, Lieutenant-General Sir Timothy Creasey, commented: "I am delighted that Robert Nairac's devotion to duty has been so properly rewarded." On a fitting footnote, three days later six RUC officers were awarded George medals. Five won Queen's Gallantry Awards and five were awarded the Queen's Commendation for brave conduct.

On the same day on which Nairac's courage was being recognised, an internal fall-out amongst members of Co Donegall IRA led to the death of Patrick Sills (27). The IRA man was attacked whilst visiting a neighbour's house in Castlefin inside the Irish Republic. He was dragged to a field close by where he was beaten with Shinty sticks and shot in both legs. It is considered likely that he crawled or dragged himself towards the shelter of a nearby building on the border, but died either from exposure or – more likely – loss of blood. Later on his lifeless body was collected and taken over the border to Laghtfoggy near Castlederg, Co Tyrone. The IRA never acknowledged his murder, but most informed sources attribute the death to an internal dispute. Friends and family of the dead Republican claimed that he received drawings of coffins through his letterbox in the days before his murder and that one of the coffins contained Sills' name. Earlier in the day – also in Co Tyrone – PIRA had placed a landmine in a culvert underneath the Annaghmore to Coalisland Road designed to kill or maim a passing army mobile patrol. The device was triggered prematurely and a farmer and his 11-year-old son working on a nearby hayshed were caught in the blast and both were injured. The blast left a crater 20 feet wide and seven feet deep. The Provisionals killed over 600 members of their own community during the course of the Troubles and this author is unaware of any apologies to the farmer or his son by these doyens of Irish-American society.

On the 14th, a popular young officer from the Royal Welch Fusiliers (RWF) was killed by a PIRA gunman in Londonderry. The RWF, whose motto is *Ich Dien* (*I Serve*), was formed in 1713 and saw action in virtually every campaign from the War of the Spanish Succession through the American War of Independence and both World Wars. A patrol from the regiment had set up a VCP close to Craigavon Bridge at the junction of Wapping Lane and Abercorn Road. Lieutenant Steven Kirkby (22), from Erith in Kent, was supervising his men when a single round was fired by a PIRA sniper – reputed to be from the Creggan IRA – hitting him the chest. The lieutenant, who had just arrived by mobile patrol, slumped to the ground mortally wounded as his men attempted to locate the gunman and return fire. He was rushed to the Altnagelvin Hospital but he died shortly after admission. On the same day there was a meeting between Roy Mason, Secretary of State for Northern Ireland, and Michael O'Kennedy, Irish Minister for Foreign Affairs, in London to discuss cross-border security matters. One wonders if the news of the death of the young RWF lieutenant was passed on to the two high-ranking politicians.

On the 19th, there was a lucky escape for an RUC mobile patrol and for a family of four driving in a private car in the Andersonstown area of Belfast. Three masked PIRA gunmen burst into a house at Riverdale Park and held the family hostage. One of the gunmen set up a firing point – very professionally, with sandbags according to one soldier who spoke to the author – in a back bedroom and waited for the expected RUC vehicle. As the police car came into his sights he opened fire – loosing off over 20 rounds – but as he did so, a private saloon car crossed with the policemen. In all the two cars were hit a total of 18 times, but miraculously there were no injuries. There was a similar lucky escape for another police officer in Co Tyrone later on the same Monday. A 25-year-old policeman was driving along a narrow lane at Gorey, near Cabragh, when three IRA gunmen opened fire on his vehicle from behind a thick hedgerow. He was badly wounded and his car careered to a halt around about 100 yards from the scene of the ambush. Although badly wounded, he survived the attack.

The trial of the 'Shankill Butchers' came to an end on 20 February 1979. Eleven men were convicted of a total of 19 murders and the 42 life sentences handed out were the most ever in a single trial in British criminal history. The 11 found guilty were: William Moore, Robert 'Basher' Bates, Sam McAllister, John Townsley, Benny Edwards, Arthur McClay, Norman Waugh, Edward Leckey, Sam McIlwaine, James Watt and John Murphy. Moore pleaded guilty to 11 counts of murder and Bates to 10. The trial judge, Lord Justice O'Donnell, said that he did not wish to be cast as 'public avenger' but felt obliged to sentence the pair of them to life imprisonment with no chance of release. He stated that their crimes were " ... a catalogue of horror ... " and " ... a lasting monument to blind sectarian bigotry."

The *Daily Express* reserved their centre pages for the trial and headlined: 'The Butchers: And the weapons they used' with a photograph showing a terrifying array of metal knives which would not have looked out of place at the Co-op Butchers in Austhorpe Road, Leeds where the author's late parents sent him as a young boy to purchase meat. It featured photographs of grim-looking men who stared back at the police photographer with that sick look of knowing that their bloody reign of terror was almost at an end. The Express journalist wrote under a sub-heading of 'Victim who got away': "The 'Shankill Butchers' made one mistake in their campaign of mass murder – they only half-killed victim no 20. And when 24-year-old Gerard McLaverty left hospital he put the finger on his attackers. As the gang was sentenced yesterday, McLaverty – in fear – was planning a new identity and life abroad. He is certain to be top of the fanatical Protestants' death list and if he stayed in Ulster they would not be likely to make a mistake next time. McLaverty was left for dead ... .beaten up; his wrists gashed; a noose tight around his neck. But only a week later he left hospital, disguised, and was driven in an unmarked car along the Shankill Road where strikers were lining the pavements. And in the crowd, McLaverty spotted two of the gang."

And the rest, as they say, is history.

The group of 11 'butchers' were sentenced to life imprisonment for 112 offences (including 19 murders). The 11 men were given 42 life sentences and received 2,000 years imprisonment, in total, in the form of concurrent sentences. Other sentences included: Moore and Bates were sentenced to spend "the rest of their living lives in jail"; McAllister, Edwards and McClay received 20 years; Waugh 18 years; Townsley received an indefinite sentence; Bell received life; Watt received a 10th life sentence; Leckey 10 years and McIlwaine, eight.

Bates was freed two years after the paramilitary ceasefires of 1994 and Moore released under the Good Friday Agreement of 1998. Without a doubt, the best – and certainly most definitive – study of the murder gang is Martin Dillon's *The Shankill Butchers* (Arrow Books, 1990). Martin Dillon's own investigations suggest that a number of other individuals (whom he was unable to name for legal reasons) escaped prosecution for participation in the crimes of the 'Butchers' and that the gang were responsible for a total of at least 30 murders.

After the trial, leading RUC Detective Jimmy Nesbitt's comment was: "The big fish got away," which was believed to be a reference to Lenny Murphy's brother, John, and who was referred to in the book as 'Mr B'. In November 2004 the Serious Crime Review Team in Belfast said they were looking into the unsolved death of Rosaleen O'Kane – aged 33 at the time of her death – who was found dead in her home in September 1976. Her family and authorities believe the 'Shankill Butchers' may have been involved in her death.

The author Martin Dillon confirmed to me in a conversation in 2012 that he revealed the identity of 'Mr B' because the *Sunday World* newspaper contacted him after John Murphy, Lenny's older brother, died in a car accident. He was free legally to reveal that John Murphy was 'Mr B'. Ironically, John Murphy died in an accident in the Lower Falls close to the Grosvenor Road. Catholics went to his aid, but were unable to save him. They did not know his identity – the supreme irony that the butcher and psychopathic slayer of Catholics was being tended to by the hated 'Taigs' no doubt lost on him as he drifted in and out of consciousness. The *Sunday World* made the error of declaring that John was 'Mr A', which he was certainly not. 'Mr A' was a much more serious prime mover within the gang and is still alive. I have checked the veracity of my comments with the author – Martin Dillon – and he confirms that I am accurate in every way. 'Mr A' has never been unmasked for legal reasons.

Jimmy Nesbitt was quoted as saying that he regretted the fact that the two men were not brought to justice – though 'Mr B' was later unmasked by Martin Dillon as John Murphy. 'Mr A' is still alive and Mr Dillon cannot name him for legal reasons, but when he passes on – as will some of the others close to the gang – one expects this esteemed author and journalist to reveal to us the true horror and bizarre make-up of the 'Butchers' gang. As the last echoes of the 'Butchers'' court case were dying down – and the gang were being led below to begin their sentences – a PIRA ASU attacked an RUC patrol close to Albert Street Mill. The joint RUC/army patrol was on Cullingtree Road when shots were fired by gunmen in spite of the proximity of children. A 15-year-old schoolgirl frantically tried to escape the crossfire, but was hit in both her arm and legs. The author cannot substantiate what happened later as the girl's parents gathered at their shocked daughter's hospital bedside at the nearby RVH and discussed the incident. However, it is a safe bet to assume that the shepherding Sinn Féin councillor/PIRA apologist no doubt blamed the RUC for their irresponsibility in firing back at the IRA gunmen. One wonders if even their most sycophantic supporters actually swallowed Sinn Féin's/IRA's pious propaganda as another 'mini Joseph Goebbels' was wheeled out – yet again to milk the publicity.

On the 24th, there was further need for a Sinn Féin/IRA apologist to step up to the microphone and face the music as they yet again caused the blood of their community to stain the streets and fields of Northern Ireland. This time the innocent blood was spilled around the Newtownhamilton, Co Armagh area. A PIRA bombing team had primed explosives and planted them on and around a stolen trailer which they abandoned in a rural area along the road, which runs from what the troops called NTH and Keady near the village of Darkley. It is unclear if the plan was to lure troops or RUC to the area to investigate the stolen vehicle or if it was intended to blast a passing mobile patrol. However, sometime on the Saturday night a group of five young friends en route for the local bus to take them to a disco strayed too close to the trailer and activated the explosives. In a massive blast, which left a five-feet-deep crater, the five young men were hurled to the ground with one of them – James Keenan (16) – being killed absolutely instantly. His friend, Martin

McGuigan (also 16), was mortally wounded and died a few hours later despite the best efforts of surgeons to save his shattered body. One of the group lost a leg and another was left paralysed for life. The bombers were secreted some 500 yards away and immediately opened fire on the shattered bodies with automatic weapons before slinking over the border with the Republic less than two miles away.

Once the elated Provisionals had celebrated and revelled in the deaths of 'soldiers' – before being brought down to earth with the news that they had wrecked the lives of members of their own communities – a spokesman was conjured up in order to issue a grovelling apology. One wonders if they had ready-made template apologies prepared for each and every occasion. "Tragically, the youths and their position on the road were mistaken for the movements of soldiers and the bomb was set off." Presumably this was why they also fired on the bodies? The apology was somewhat delayed and it was not issued for a week – by which time the dead boys' bodies had been interred and their loved ones' grieving processes were just beginning; a process that would take a whole lifetime to complete

1979 was to be a tragic year for the Blues & Royals – the regiment in which Leeds United footballer Jack Charlton served his National Service – as they lost four of their men. There was some mystery – and not a little controversy – about two of the deaths which occurred on the 25th. For several years the events of an incident at an RUC station in South-West Belfast were hushed up by both the army and the MOD, but were brought back into the public domain by the Troops Out pressure group 'Oliver's Army'. A soldier – Trooper Eddie Maggs (20) – was alleged to have lost control in a drunken moment and killed another soldier before being killed himself by RUC officers and another soldier. *An Phoblacht* (*Republican News*) – the organ of Sinn Féin/IRA – also picked up on the story and made unproven allegations that another soldier had also 'gone berserk' in the Andersonstown area.

Trooper Edward 'Eddie' Maggs was on duty at Woodbourne RUC Station and had apparently been drinking – certainly more than the 'two cans a day' ration which we were allowed to consume whilst in Northern Ireland. The soldier was, according to some comrades, 'troubled' and this should have been picked up by his platoon or company commander and he should have been sent home to convalesce. A comrade has reported that pre-tour: "Trooper Eddie Maggs had always been a bit of a loner – often brooding and tucked up in himself. He'd suddenly launch into an aggressive outburst for little or no apparent reason ... He looked pissed off. I asked: 'What's the matter, Eddie?' Eddie looked up. 'Fuck off. When I get to Northern Ireland, I'm going to shoot me some Irish twats'. At the time, I didn't pay him much attention." (Source: 'Bullet Magnet' Mick Flynn)

According to some accounts, Maggs had been drinking inside the Woodbourne RUC Station when he had suddenly started firing at other soldiers. Staff Corporal John Tucker (32) from Bushey, Herts tried to reason with the deranged trooper and even attempted to approach him in order to calm him down and disarm him. For his troubles he was shot and fell to the ground – mortally wounded. Maggs then shot and seriously wounded Lance-Corporal David Mellor. According to a trusted source in the Army Dog Handler's Unit (ADU), the decision was taken to shoot the out-of-control soldier and the fatal rounds were fired by RUC officers and possibly another soldier. Maggs was then shot and killed instantly by the aforementioned combination of Security Forces.

His father, retired bank official Douglas Maggs, told the *Daily Mirror* the day after: "We don't know what went wrong yet. All we've been told is that Eddie cracked up, ran amok with a rifle and was shot dead by another soldier to prevent further bloodshed. This wouldn't have happened if he hadn't been sent to Northern Ireland for a second time. He was a victim of Northern Ireland just as surely as if he'd been shot in the back by a sniper's bullet. My son loved the army, but four months out there last year finished him. He was terrified of going back. He planned to get out before his 21st birthday this September and he'd applied for a job as a fireman in London. He was a good soldier and I only hope that some good will come out of this tragedy." His mother, Pamela Maggs, added: "We adopted Eddie when he was six. Before he came to us his life had been rotten. We gave him all the love we could. He was always crazy about being a soldier, but he was desperately scared of returning to Northern Ireland."

THAT DAY IN WOODBOURNE
Dougie Durrant, Army Dog Handlers' Unit

This life event story might stir up a bit of controversy from some who were there at Woodbourne Base on 25 February 1979. There are some who were there and don't like to discuss what happened on the night. I am not sorry for bringing it up as it has, over the years, had an impact on my life. Some say the system was to blame; some say the officer commanding was to blame; I say it was the individual who was to blame that started the tragic events of the night of 25 February 1979. It was a normal cold February night in Woodburn Base and I'd just walked my ADU dog, Bluce, after a hard day's work searching in and around the Blues & Royals TAOR. On the way back to the kennels I had a short chat with Corporal Major Tucker – the unit search team advisor for the Blues & Royals. We chatted about the day's operations and what his intentions were for the next few weeks. We also discussed the disco which was to take place in the base that night and I had admitted to him that it was the first time I had seen a unit in West Belfast plan such an event, but he seemed ok with it. He had a few reservations – mainly to do with women from the surrounding area coming onto the base.

I went back to my room and watched a bit of TV and then showered, changed and had a quick power-nap before taking Bluce for his late-evening walk. I could hear the disco in full swing, but on arrival at the kennel two high-velocity rounds went whizzing past my head. As normal I ran back to my room with Bluce in tow, grabbed my kit and went straight to the ops room. On arrival there, it was clear there was panic in the air with people not knowing what to do – and above all what was happening. It soon became clear that a solder was on the rampage around the camp and that he had discharged his weapon in the unloading bay. He had been loading or unloading his rifle and he had fired a number of rounds at the QRF who were returning to base. Two soldiers were sitting in the ops room suffering from shock. It appeared they were shot at during the prevailing incident. I gave them some warm blankets and told the Ops that they needed medical help soonest. All in the ops room were in blind panic mode – dealing with a 'blue on blue' incident.

I left them to it and went outside and walked towards the cookhouse, when suddenly more shots rang out. I hit the deck hard, thinking: "What the fuck is going on?" I turned a corner leading to the rear of the cookhouse and saw that there were two men down. One was Corporal Major Tucker and the other was the

QRF commander. Both had been shot several times by one of their own. Just then there was another shot which sounded different to the others. I later learnt that it was a member of the RUC who had shot the soldier who had been firing and that he was dead. Being a dog handler I carried more first field dressings than most so I gave them to the guys trying to keep both men alive and left as I could see they wanted to look after their own. I went back to the ops room and it was there I had found out that Corporal Major Tucker had been killed along with Trooper Eddie Maggs. The QRF commander was on his way to hospital and would later recover from his ordeal.

There are a few things that I still feel need answering. Was the fact that a disco was on the camp to blame? It was alleged that Trooper Maggs was drunk on duty. Why was he allowed to be if that was the case? Or was Eddie Maggs just another victim of the Troubles? John Tucker was a well-respected individual amongst his troops and his sheer presence commanded respect in my eyes. RIP, Sir.

Eddie Maggs' name is not on the MOD ROH and nor is his name engraved on the wall at the National Memorial Arboretum at Alrewas in Staffordshire. Whatever the rights and wrongs – and this author will not excuse the murder of Corporal Tucker – of Maggs' breakdown and death, he was killed in Northern Ireland as a consequence of the Troubles as much as if he had been shot by a PIRA sniper or blown up by an INLA bomb. On the same day as the tragedy at Woodbourne, Lance-Corporal Richard Davies (29) of the Royal Corps of Signals was killed in an RTA in the Province.

In the final action of the month, the Provisionals came close to claiming the life of another off-duty UDR soldier. A 38-year-old NCO was returning to his home in Donaghmore between Pomeroy and Dungannon in Co Tyrone. His rural property was accessible only via a narrow and lonely country lane. An armed gang – thought to have comprised three men – lay in wait on a blind bend in the road where the part-time soldier would have to slow down. As he did so they opened fire with automatic weapons and he was hit several times – sustaining a bad neck injury. He was, however, able to drive out of the ambush and reached the safety of home – from where an ambulance was sent for and he recovered later in hospital.

February had ended. The 'Butchers' were in prison and Lenny Murphy's days, although he didn't know it, were numbered. A total of nine people had died as a consequence – directly or indirectly of the Troubles. Four soldiers had been killed, as had four civilians – including the retired PO and his wife. Two Catholics and two Protestants were killed – all by the Provisionals. One Republican died in an internal dispute and the IRA was responsible for six of the deaths – none of which were overtly sectarian.

51

March

This month witnessed the deaths of 13 people – including eight soldiers – and the Conservative MP and Shadow Spokesman on Northern Ireland, Airey Neave. It saw another British ambassador assassinated by the IRA. It also brought forward the return of the Conservatives at the General Election in May – and the Provisionals were then on a collision course with Margaret Thatcher.

On the 1st of the month, the efforts to trace the killers of Lieutenant Steven Kirkby the previous month bore fruit and arrests were made amongst the Nationalist community on Londonderry's Creggan Estate. On the same day an IRA member on the Turf Lodge was jailed for membership of the organisation. He received a paltry two years, but at least it was one terrorist less on the streets of the Province. It was, however, but a pinprick against the Provisionals.

Between the 1st and the 30th, a total of six UDR soldiers died in circumstances for which the author has no information. The soldiers were: Private Joseph Hogg (54) on the 1st; Private James Hunter (19) on the 4th; Sergeant Patrick McMulkin (48) on the 9th; Sergeant Thomas Johnston Doak (51) on the 13th; Lance-Corporal William Crawford (50) on the 15th and Private Victor Wilson (32) on the 30th. The author has no further information.

On the following day PIRA bombers targeted Balmoral Furnishings in the South Belfast suburb of Dunmurry as part of their ongoing economic warfare. Three masked gunmen walked into the store and one of them held a gun to a female receptionist's head whilst his two colleagues planted holdalls packed with explosives. They ran out and warned the staff not to touch the holdalls or to call the RUC. However, a security guard took his life into his hands and bravely carried one of the bombs into the car park where the army later defused it. The other device failed to explode. This was not the first time that Balmorals had been bombed and the Provisionals had tried earlier in 1976. Amongst those arrested for the earlier raid in Dunmurry was Bobby Sands, who later became the first of the hunger strikers to die during the 1981 campaign. He was charged with involvement in the October 1976 bombing, although he was never convicted of this charge – the presiding judge stating that there was no evidence to support the assertion that Sands had taken part. However, after the bombing Sands and five others were alleged to have been involved in a gun battle with the RUC – although due to lack of evidence Sands was not convicted. In the firefight, the PIRA ASU left behind two of their wounded friends: Seamus Martin and Gabriel Corbett. Sands, Joe McDonnell, Seamus Finucane and Sean Lavery tried to make their escape in a car, but were apprehended. Later, one of the revolvers used in the attack was found in the car in which Sands had been travelling. His trial in September 1977 saw him being found guilty of possession of firearms as forensics linked the pistol found in the car to the one used after the Balmorals' bombing.

He was later sentenced to 14 years' imprisonment and ended his life in HMP Maze on 5 May 1981. The arrest, which led to his death on the hunger strike, was not his first brush with the law. In 1972, shortly after he joined the Provisionals, he was arrested when four handguns were found in the house where he was staying at the time. He was charged with possession of weaponry and was sent to Long Kesh – being released in 1976. Sands was born in Newtownabbey, but the family moved to the Loyalist Rathcoole area of North Belfast and he spent his formative years there. However, his Catholic family was intimidated off the estate at gunpoint and they moved to the Nationalist Twinbrook area of West Belfast where he joined PIRA.

Whilst the RUC and EOD were focusing their attention on the Dunmurry area, the Provisionals caused traffic chaos in the city centre by planting no less than 11 suspect devices at important road junctions. Ten of the devices were hoaxes and traffic was gridlocked for miles around as drivers were held up for hours and public transport, commercial traffic and school-run convoys simply ground to a halt. In one of the most major incidents, a hijacked lorry with wires strategically – and ominously – placed was abandoned at the junction of Wellington Place and Fountain Street close to City Hall. Other lorries were left at major traffic junctions such as York Street and Great George's Street and Tennent Street and the Shankill Road. Loyalists fumed in the long jams as even their own heartland was embroiled in traffic inertia at the behest of their hated Republican rivals. The Crumlin Road was at a standstill and devices near the airport led to massive delays and cancelled flights. The one device which was genuine – and indeed did explode – was left at the junction of Donegall Road and Roden Street. Devices were also left at York Road railway station and the rail network was severely disrupted.

On the following morning, just after the Sinn Féin/IRA apology for the Darkley deaths, their paramilitaries planted a series of bombs in Belfast City Centre which necessitated calling out EOD. One of the IRA's major targets was the Ulster Bank in Market Street, which EOD managed to safely detonate. A short while later, children playing on waste ground adjacent to Melvin Park in Strabane found a cocked and loaded Lee Enfield .303 rifle which appeared to have been abandoned. The parents of the children sensibly called in the police and army and the weapon was found to have been booby-trapped. An IRA bomb-maker had hollowed out the butt of the rifle and filled it with explosives. Although the children played with the weapon, it failed to explode. EOD were again in action.

That week's edition of the *Belfast Newsletter* led with: 'UVF behind many attacks on prison officers – allegation'. Their writer followed with: "The scale of alleged UVF attacks on officers in the Newtownabbey area from 1976 until last year was revealed yesterday. A police inspector told Belfast City Commission that there had been 18 attacks on prison officers in the area between October 1976 and October last year. 'These attacks were carried out with firearms, anti-personnel bombs or the setting off of devices at officers' houses. I was involved in all these allegations and believe that quite a number were carried out by the UVF.'" The report centred on the trial of William McGookin for the attempted murder of a prison officer's wife at Carmoney on 11 March 1977 (see Chapter 27).

Republicans were busy all over the Province on the 5th and there was a lucky escape for a soldier who was flying over the village of Crossmaglen in a helicopter. A PIRA sniper fired at him as he sat in the doorway – and from some distance – and against a moving target, succeeded in wounding the soldier in his lower leg. The pilot was also wounded by flying glass as three high-velocity rounds impacted the military aircraft. In Belfast the RUC came under attack from a mob – estimated at 1,000 strong – protesting against conditions in the 'H' blocks. The officers were trapped at the junction of Castle Street and

Bomb in Post Office van, Hightown Road, Belfast, 1979. (©Mark 'C')

King Street and there were some quite nasty injuries amongst the 10 injured officers. Finally, in Londonderry, PIRA bombing units attacked the Carraig Bar and the nearby Coles Bar and an unnamed bar in Strand Road. Damage was slight in all three attacks.

On the 6th, the IRA attempted to kill an off-duty UDR soldier in Portadown, Co Armagh. The part-time soldier had been dicked as he parked in a car park in West Street and whilst he was away from his vehicle, an INLA bombing team planted a UVBT beneath the car and awaited his return. As the soldier started the vehicle, the device exploded – wrecking the car and shattering his lower body. The dreadfully injured man, who suffered traumatic amputations, was dragged from the mangled wreckage by brave passers-by and rushed to hospital for emergency treatment. The dreadfully injured soldier – Private Robert McNally (20) – fought for his life, but a series of emergency operations were unable to save him and he died on the 15th. He left a very young widow.

The day after – following a major surveillance operation by the army/RUC in the Nationalist Short Strand area of Belfast – the largest find of ready-made bombs at that stage in the Troubles was made. Shortly before 0100, during what the Belfast folk call the 'wee hors', soldiers and police sealed off a large area around Kilmood Street. In a shed belonging to one of the houses, searchers found 42 gas cylinders each containing 10lbs of explosives and timing devices. There was enough explosives to devastate the whole of Belfast City Centre according to an RUC source of the author. An ATO officer said that had just one of the bombs had exploded, the chain reaction would have set off the others and the Short Strand might easily have been removed from the map of East Belfast. There is little doubt that the successful operation prevented mass damage, injury and death on a large scale in the Belfast area – as well as being a major blow against the Provisionals.

Illegal Vehicle Checkpoints – or IVCPs – were the IRA's way of controlling their areas and cocking a snook at Security Forces. They would often set up IVCPs at random times and in random areas in order to demonstrate their strength to their followers. Their South Londonderry Battalion made an unfortunate choice of time and venue on the 7th and they were caught napping by a chance army foot patrol. The soldiers confronted masked gunmen and, as they were entitled to do under ROE, opened fire on the gunmen. At least one gunman was hit and arrested and two weapons were recovered.

On the 9th, PIRA attacked the Co-op Supermarket in Omagh – planting four incendiary devices on window sills. The outlet on the Dromore Road was evacuated and the army managed to make them safe, but moments later further devices – for which no warnings were given – exploded nearby. The Housing Executive offices at Gortin Road were damaged by a mixture of explosives and petrol and nearby homes also suffered structurally.

There was further evidence of the Provisionals' absolute contempt for the safety of their own community on the 10th when a bomb was hidden in a drainpipe outside a pub on an army foot patrol route – despite nearby residences and the proximity of civilians in the immediate vicinity. The Rock Bar in Belfast's Whiterock area was targeted as a known route and a patrol had passed by only seconds earlier when the device exploded. The bombing unit must have seen a civilian car parked outside the bar containing three girls – presumably eating crisps whilst their parents enjoyed a quiet drink. The explosion caused a mass of flying glass and all three children were cut, necessitating hospital treatment. Two days later the safety of an innocent child was the last thing on their minds when they attempted to murder an off-duty police reservist in Stewartstown, Co Tyrone. A 35-year-old RUCR officer was taking his two children to school when his car was ambushed by PIRA gunmen close to his home. Several shots were fired at the car, which crashed, and the man's eight-year-old daughter was hit in the neck and shoulder and badly injured. The policeman and his son, aged 11, escaped unwounded and the gunmen raced off in a waiting stolen car which was found abandoned in a Nationalist area.

On the 16th, the RUC attempted to stop a car at a snap VCP near Abercorn Square, Belfast. The car contained at least one PIRA gunman and the driver panicked and sped through the checkpoint. The police gave chase and the PIRA man threw a Lee Enfield .303 rifle and ammunition out of the window. The car was later found abandoned and even more ammunition was discovered.

That same day was also to witness one of the largest bombs of the entire Troubles at that stage, when PIRA literally tried to remove the RUC base at Kinawley from the face of the Earth. Kinawley, from Irish 'Cill Náile' – meaning 'Náile's Church' – is a small village in Co Fermanagh. It sits astride the busy B108 and is only a few miles from the border with the Irish Republic. As such, it is of strategic importance to the British Government and it was an easy five-minute 'shoot and scoot' for the Provisionals. Trooper Gordon Scott of the 13/18 Hussars, from Hull in East Yorkshire, was manning a sangar at the base.

On that quiet Sunday evening in early spring, Trooper Scott observed a 4x4 car pull up to the security gates, quickly detach a horsebox and then roar away. There were two security ramps outside the base and the 4x4 towed the horsebox slowly over the first ramp, then detached itself and drove over the second ramp – leaving the horsebox sitting between the two ramps outside the main gate. At that stage, what Scott didn't know was that the box was packed with explosives. His training and instincts kicked in and he dived to the floor of the sangar and instantly pressed the bomb alarm button – thus warning everyone of the imminent danger and giving them that precious second or two to get clear of the front of the base. Just seconds later the explosives, one of the largest ever in the Troubles, exploded – completely removing the anti-blast wall of the border outpost and creating a crater six feet deep and over 15 feet wide. The blast also completely demolished several nearby houses and an entire farm building. Trooper Scott's quick thinking saved the lives of many soldiers and policemen that night. I am grateful to John Hunter for additional information relating to this attack.

Three days later the RUC base at Newtownhamilton came under mortar and rifle attack, which resulted in the death of a soldier and a further eight people were injured. Four soldiers from the Queen's Regiment, two RUC officers and two civilian workers were injured by the mortar explosions – some badly. Newtownhamilton takes its name from Alexander Hamilton – a descendant of Scotland who founded Hamiltonsbawn in 1619 and the parish was created in 1773 out of the neighbouring parish of Creggan. The modern Irish name of Newtownhamilton is 'an Baile Úr', or 'the new town' – although the Nationalists sometimes use 'Baile Úr Uí Urmoltaigh'.

On the afternoon of the 19th, a PIRA ASU penetrated to within 100 yards of the heavily fortified base and fired seven high-explosive devices at the base from the bed of a hijacked lorry. All seven hit their intended target, although there was also damage to surrounding properties. Several civilians were buried alive in the wreckage of a hotel and several shops and rescuers were forced to free them with their bare hands. Private Peter Woolmore (23), a London boy, was terribly injured and died very shortly afterwards. He had been off duty at the time and was in the washroom, which took a direct hit – giving him no chance of survival. Within minutes, in what was clearly a co-ordinated attack, another ASU attacked the RUC base at Kinawley with several mortars. There were no SF fatalities, but two civilians were badly injured. The PIRA unit parked suspicious vehicles across the route out of the town, which needed to be investigated by the army/RUC – thus giving the bombers time to flee towards the nearby border.

NEWTOWNHAMILTON AND THE DEATH OF PRIVATE PETER WOOLMORE
Private Martin Riley, 3 Queen's

I can only give my story from the view of a nig (new soldier) on my first tour of active duty. I was with our platoon at the aftermath of the Newtownhamilton mortar attack as part of the XMG response team. We were standby section – having just come off our town patrol in XMG. We were now beginning our four-hour standby and were still in full kit for any emergency response that might occur. Only 10 minutes into our standby, we got the call from the ops room to prep up and get ready. Newtownhamilton had just been mortared and a chopper was en route to airlift us out to provide support. A Puma arrived on the helipad within minutes and we boarded her for the bumpy flight to Newtownhamilton. It was 19 March 1979.

I remember the flight – hedge-hopping all the way near enough – and then the chopper dropping into the valley down to the town. The LZ was on the rough grassland in front of the camp and there was no time to think or look or take anything in – just a rapid debus from the chopper and we all went to ground. The chopper quickly took off again and we were commanded to immediately take up firing positions around the base, which we did.

Newtownhamilton is just another sleepy-looking village belying a hidden danger under its surface. You could smell the scent of burning wood and clearly see the RUC station had been damaged by a number of mortars. I think that three or four made direct impact on the building. There were roadblocks in position at each end of the road (Dundalk Street and Newry Road/Newry Street) and various people all over the place – RUC, troops and search teams.

The attack (from my memory now) was late in its delivery (fortunately). Most of the lads based there had already eaten and were out of their bunks on various duties. This most likely helped reduce the number of casualties. From what we understood at the time, the mortars were small in size (2-3 inches) and when launched had gone through the mortar netting, which was designed for much larger missiles – something the IRA normally used in their attacks. As for the timing of the attack, well it did cause major damage and injuries to a number of personnel and one fatality. However, had it been some half an hour earlier it may well have killed so many more people.

I remember this day well. Early 1979 had been regarded as the coldest spell in 10 years and it had been freezing cold – except for this particular day. It was a milder day with overcast sky, but bright and the air was still. It was around 1400. Not long after the first chopper left, another chopper came in to land and I was ordered to unload a tripod case for the GPMG SF (General Purpose Machine Gun: Sustained Fire) role. For the uninitiated, the GPMG was mounted onto a tripod – making it very stable and accurate over a long distance. However I am only very short and small in frame, and trying to unload this very heavy piece of kit in its bag was very difficult. I then had to cart the heavy load across the very rough grass and hand it over to the gunner. Needless to say I had to drag the bloody thing because it was too far and too heavy for just me on my own.

Immediately after this I was then tasked to carry out a search using a probe and headphones. This was something I had never done or been trained to do, but once shown the basics off I went along the undergrowth that ran parallel to the camp. I have to admit that I was constantly shaking because we were not sure if this may have been a 'come on' (a lure to expose troops to a sniper or another mortar attack).

There were numerous other teams carrying out their respective searches and one or two dog handlers further along the hedgerow. It was strange as everything was now eerily quiet apart from the sound of the odd voice giving out orders. I proceeded to carry out my search in the designated area. I then heard the pitch of frequency increase in my headset and it got me worried, as I suspected there was a device in the small hedge where I had inserted the probe. This was at least a false alarm as the device had detected a small screw, but I still had to get my hands into the scrub to find it. I have to say that searching was not my first choice of job. I knew only too well in training how easy it was to mistake what appeared to be an inert object absolutely lethal.

I did not know Private Peter Woolmore. Even though we were in different companies there is a respect and concern for all those in your regiment – and especially during times like these. Peter was two years older than me, but that loss has never been forgotten even to this day. I know of guys now who still mention his name on various regimental groups, but the impact of that day was very profound for us all. It heightened the alertness of everyone at XMG and it was clear that everyone was in deep thought about this tragedy. No-one really spoke about it at the time. We were all wrapped up in our own thoughts and then we had to move on. We were only in our second or third week of duty and I was hoping I would make my four-day R&R in early April.

To those of you who know or knew Peter Woolmore, I am sure that all those of us in 'A' Company felt for your loss. For us it was frustrating that all we could do was provide as much support as we could and continue in a professional way. All those men lost during these Troubles will not be forgotten during our lifetime. We carry the burden of our memories to the grave and the names and faces of those who died serving their country.

Three days after the death of Private Woolmore, a team of IRA assassins operating on the European mainland killed the British ambassador to the Netherlands and a civilian Embassy worker. It was only two years since the murder of Sir Christopher Ewart-Biggs – the British Ambassador to Ireland – and the Provisionals continued to make a mockery of the British Diplomatic Protection Services. The ambassador had declined the use of bodyguards and his fateful decision – combined with the Embassy's failure to put in place a covert watch – culminated in two unnecessary deaths. Sir Richard Sykes (58) lived in the official residence in the centre of Den Haag (The Hague) and had been observed over the course of several weeks by a PIRA hit team being collected by the Embassy chauffeur, Karel Straub (19). The car arrived on time as always, and the ambassador got into the back as Straub held the door open. The young Dutchman walked around to the driver's side and as he was about to enter, the assassins struck – firing several times – killing the ambassador and mortally wounding the driver. Mr Straub, despite the intense pain and loss of blood, managed to drive to the nearest hospital where he collapsed and died. Sir Richard was a wartime hero and was awarded the British Military Cross and the French Croix de Guerre in 1945. He had been ambassador to the Netherlands for less than two years. It would be another year before the Provisionals admitted the double murders.

On the following day the IRA turned its attentions back to the Province and its economic bombing campaign. A total of 23 banks were targeted across the country, with no less than nine branches of the Ulster Bank coming under attack. One of their branches – in Stewartstown – was completely destroyed. Other banks affected were the Bank of Ireland; Trustee Savings Bank (TSB) and the Allied Irish, whose branch in Dungannon was completely destroyed. Finally, the Waring Street, Belfast branch of the Northern Bank had its complete ground floor gutted by an incendiary blast. The bank's Donegall Square branch was famously robbed by the IRA – some seven years after the ending of armed hostilities – and a total of £26.5 million was stolen.

On the 27th, the growing list of the 'disappeared' increased by one as Gerald Evans (24) went missing from a roadside at Castleblaney in the Irish Republic – some 10 miles from his home in the North at Crossmaglen. He had apparently no paramilitary links and it is considered that he had somehow fallen foul of the Provisionals. He was picked up well inside the border and it is unlikely that Loyalist paramilitaries would have been operating that deep inside the border on the off-chance of killing a Catholic. Besides, the body would have been dumped in an area where it would have been easily discovered and serve as a warning to the Nationalist community. It seems more likely that he was abducted by a Provisional 'Nutting Squad' and tortured before being murdered. If PIRA had realised that they had made a mistake, it would have been in their own interests to remain silent and simply bury the body in remote farmland. Mr Evans remains – like several others – on that tragic list known simply as the 'disappeared'.

On the 29th, Republican thugs ambushed a lone RUC officer in the centre of Belfast and pushed him through a plate-glass window – seriously cutting him. As other officers raced to the scene in Donegall Square West, a hidden IRA gunman opened fire. His shots missed, but an innocent bystander was hit and seriously wounded. Several hours later and 70-plus miles further north, an RUC patrol in the Carnhill area of Londonderry was ambushed by PIRA gunmen armed with Armalites. As the patrol passed along the street, around 20 shots were fired at them from a concealed alleyway. No officers were hit and no shots were returned at the gunmen, who fled in the direction of the Nationalist Shantallow area.

On the 30th, in what was a stunning coup for the still-fledgling INLA, a major blow was struck at the very seat of power in Britain: the Houses of Parliament in the heart of Westminster. The killing of a man who not only represented the future hardline against Republican paramilitaries, but was one the country's quintessential war heroes sent shivers down the collective British spine. Airey Neave DSO, OBE, MC was a former British soldier, barrister and politician. He was one of the few servicemen to escape from Colditz. At the time of his death he was Shadow Spokesman for Northern Ireland and had already made enemies amongst the hardline Republicans. Neave served in France in 1940, was wounded and captured by the Germans in the heroic rearguard action at Calais on 23 May 1940.

Airey Neave was killed in mid-afternoon of the 30th after finishing his duties at the House of Commons for the day. A magnetic car bomb fitted with a ball bearing tilt switch exploded under his Vauxhall Cavalier as he drove out of the Palace of Westminster car park. Both of his legs were blown off and he was mortally wounded. He died in hospital an hour after being freed from the wreckage. The INLA admitted responsibility for the killing. Margaret Thatcher led tributes to Neave, saying: "He was one of freedom's warriors. No-one knew of the great man he was except those nearest to him. He was staunch, brave, true and strong – but he was very gentle and kind and loyal. It's a rare combination of qualities. There's no-one else who can quite fill them. I, and so many other people, owe so much to him and now we must carry on for the things he fought for and not let the people who got him triumph." Labour Prime Minister James Callaghan – soon to lose the General Election – said: "No effort will be spared to bring the murderers to justice and to rid the United Kingdom of the scourge of terrorism."

The INLA issued a statement regarding the killing in the August 1979 edition of The Starry Plough. "In March, retired terrorist and supporter of capital punishment, Airey Neave got a taste of his own medicine when an INLA unit pulled off the operation of the decade and blew him to bits inside the 'impregnable' Palace of Westminster. The nauseous Margaret Thatcher snivelled on television that he was an 'incalculable loss' — and so he was — to the British ruling class." To date, no terrorist has ever been brought to justice for the murder of Mr Neave.

The *Daily Express* on the morning of Saturday the 31st led with the banner headlines: 'Bloody Murder' and 'IRA kill top Tory in Commons bomb outrage'. Their front page on the morning after shows an overhead photograph of Neave's damaged car and, poignantly, a single shoe amongst the debris of the explosion. Alan Cochrane and Derrick Hill wrote:

> This is the horrifying wreck of a car in which an IRA (sic) bomb at the House of Commons yesterday killed Mr Airey Neave – war hero Tory MP and Shadow Ulster Secretary. A young man in a dark suit and white shirt was seen running from the scene and last night a vast hunt for the bomber was going on in London and at airports and seaports ... In Dublin the Provisional IRA said it did it, but a splinter called the Irish Liberation Army (sic) also claimed responsibility. Big Ben was chiming three o'clock when 63-year-old Mr Neave – one of Mrs Thatcher's closest advisors and probable Ulster Secretary in a Tory Government – started up his blue Vauxhall Cavalier in the Commons' underground car park and drove up the ramp. It is believed that the bomb, which twisted the car like a tin can, was a new limpet-type stuck underneath – perhaps activated by a row of ball bearings running into contact on the slope. Scotland Yard said it would be impossible for a bomber to break the car park's security system of police checks and TV cameras, so possibly the bomb was fitted earlier while the car was outside Mr Neave's flat near the House.

The newspaper continued with 'Maggie's Grief' and then a sub-headline of 'Against all odds they fought to save his life'. Graeme Bowd wrote:

> The battle to save Airey Neave's life began at 3.04pm on the blood-spattered ramp to the Commons' car park. Two minutes earlier the alarm bells rang at Westminster ambulance station at Causton Street, half a mile from the Mother of Parliaments. It signalled 'Echo Delta' – ambulance code for 'Explosive Device' – and sent crews racing to Mr Neave's tangled, shattered Vauxhall. In the first ambulance were 23-year-old Brian Craggs and 21-year-old Barry Davies. Said Mr Craggs: 'There was this Vauxhall on the ramp to the car park. It was a real mess. All the panels were twisted and the windows were shattered. In the driving seat was a man. I think he was wearing a greyish suit. I thought at the time that he was an MP ... I didn't recognise him. He was in a terrible mess. The whole of his front, including his face, was badly charred. We couldn't open the doors of the car so I climbed on the bonnet and through the hole where the windscreen had been. Then I crouched on the passenger seat. I saw then that the bottom of the car had blown out. Perhaps the bomb had been placed under the driver's seat, but I can't be sure about that. Anyway the poor chap had lost his right leg below the knee and his left leg was only held on by a flap of skin. Surprisingly there wasn't too much blood around, but I think a lot had gone through the bottom of the car. His pulse was very weak, but he was breathing and I put a plastic pipe down his throat to help him breathe more easily.

The interview went on to say that as firemen were sawing through the tangled metal, both the ambulance men desperately tried to apply dressings to Neave's shattered lower body and fit saline drips into his arm. The MP arrived at Westminster Hospital shortly after

3.30pm without regaining consciousness. Just eight minutes later as medical staff fought to save him, he died.

Over the years the conspiracy theories have abounded, with some claiming that the bomber was 'allowed' into the car park by a Republican sympathiser employed by the House of Commons – or even that said sympathiser planted the bomb himself; others that it was a British Secret Service plot to eliminate Mr Neave. Kevin Cahill, an Irish investigative journalist, claims Neave was on the verge of a massive overhaul of the security services – possibly involving a merger of MI5 and MI6 – and arising from his belief in corruption in the security services. Mr Cahill's most frequent claim was that 'everyone knew' the story behind Neave's death, but that no-one could talk about it in detail because it would have been too dangerous. Cahill claims that many did not believe that the INLA killed Neave, but that it was an 'inside job'. Cahill concluded that he was killed by the security services – in all probability MI6 agents working with the CIA because Neave sought to prosecute senior figures in the intelligence establishment for corruption. The final claim is that INLA claimed the murder purely as an opportunistic way to elevate their status as terrorists. This author prefers to believe the more prosaic explanation that the device was fitted outside the MP's house.

As an aside, a film was made of Thatcher's life – *The Iron lady* starring Meryl Streep – and the murder of her great friend is covered. There is one major historical inaccuracy in that a horrified Thatcher (Streep) is shown running up the car park ramp at the House of Commons to find Neave's shattered body. The scene shows that she had to be held back from the scene by security officers. In fact, she was not in Westminster at the time of his death and was informed of it while carrying out official duties elsewhere. On the same day that the INLA killed Airey Neave, Martin McConville (25) – a Catholic from Armagh who worked for the Inland Revenue – was murdered by the UFF. The murder was a purely sectarian killing – the first for some time – and his body lay undiscovered in the River Bann close to Portadown almost four weeks later. He was abducted whilst walking to his home in Craigavon from Portadown. He had been seriously assaulted and then thrown into the river, where he drowned. His death attracted considerably less column inches than the death on the same day over at Westminster of Colditz hero, Mr Neave.

On the final day of March an armed PIRA gang was involved in a shoot-out with Gardaí officers at a farmhouse on the Co Monaghan side of the border with the Republic. The armed gang was confronted by the Gardaí patrol at a derelict building and the gunmen shot and wounded two officers before escaping – firing over 100 shots in the process. In Andersonstown at around the same time, Republican troublemakers attacked an RUC Land Rover with petrol bombs. The attack was clearly premeditated owing to the supply of ready-prepared petrol-filled bottles. Several officers were injured and under precedents already laid down in 1970-71, the police opened fire on one of the bombers – aiming three rounds from his SMG as a youth was about to hurl a bomb. He was seen to fall to the ground and was dragged away by his friends – leaving blood streaks. He was never apprehended and it is likely that he smuggled over the border to be treated by a medical sympathiser.

The month of March was over. Deaths had not been high by the standards of the Troubles, but had – nonetheless – been momentous given the nature of the attack in the very heart of British Government. Thirteen people had died during this month. Eight were soldiers – two of whom killed by the IRA – and five were civilians. Two of the dead were

Catholics – the death of one of whom was overtly sectarian. Republicans were responsible for six of the deaths and Loyalists for one.

52

April

D eaths would increase in quite dramatic fashion this month with the loss of nine soldiers, four policemen and two prison officers. Additionally, a PIRA member would be assassinated by Loyalists. It would also witness the moral bankruptcy and degeneracy of Republicanism as they shot dead a PO as he attended his sister's wedding.

On the 1st of the month – always an unfortunate choice of date for a major announcement – two companies of the 2nd Battalion UDR from Co Armagh were merged into a new, stronger company as part of the regiment's streamlining. As part of their first operation they swapped their Land Rovers for helicopters and they swooped on Camlough in what were termed 'Eagle patrols' in order to set up searches, patrols and snap VCPs. The move, known as the 'Glennane merger', was the final part of an operation to combine some companies in the same centres – and so free soldiers engaged on duplicate administrative tasks for more active operations.

As this was being undertaken, the Provisionals demonstrated that they had yet more moral depths to plumb when they made an opportunistic attack on RUC officers. They had previously shot and killed an RUC officer as he cradled an injured woman following a car crash – and on the 1st of the month, armed men spotted the police attending an injured dog. A patrol car containing two male and one female officer had stopped on a road in Armagh City to treat a badly injured dog when a car containing armed PIRA drove past. As the officers tended to the animal, several shots were fired from the car – slightly wounding the three RUC personnel. It was a chance shooting, but it further demonstrated their gutter tactics. One wonders what the contributors to NORAID might have made of the terrorists' attempts to murder policemen on an errand of mercy.

On the following day the small town of Markethill, Co Armagh was targeted by the Provisionals. It was a predominantly Protestant town and the attacks were clearly meant to intimidate the Loyalist population – rather like the later, 1983 sectarian attack on the Protestant church in nearby Darkley – into realising that PIRA could hit any time of their choosing. A massive car bomb exploded that day – blowing up the local factory, two chemists' shops, the cattle mart and several residential homes. That there were no fatalities was little short of a miracle, but fate was reserving that for the future – and in the 1980s, two RUC officers were shot down in cowardly fashion by IRA gunmen as they guarded the town.

BEFORE NORTHERN IRELAND
Marcus Townley, Welsh Guards

I would like to begin my story, if I may, sometime before my battalion deployed to Ulster. My battalion was stationed in Berlin – and like all tours to the 'funny farm', ours started as merely a rumour. Sometime in 1979 I was posted down the American zone of Germany to take part in the SA80 trials with nine other Welsh Guardsmen. Our CO came and told us our future plans, and yes we were

Royal Artillery on patrol near Armagh, 1979. (©Walter Stirling)

Royal Artillery on patrol near Armagh, 1979. (©Walter Stirling)

going to Northern Ireland – and to South Armagh with the Battalion HQ based in Bessbrook; the dreaded 'bandit country' which we had heard so much about not only from other guardsmen who had served out there, but daily from the newspapers.

As we were in the American zone of Germany, we received daily newspapers a day late. One morning I glanced at a British paper and saw the headline: '4 Killed in Blast'. I read on and it reported that four RUC constables had been blown up by a 1,000lb bomb in the border town of Camlough, Co Down and all four were KIA. As I was reading this, I just thought to myself: "Fuck; we are as sure as hell going into the firing line!" Was I worried? The truth is, yes I was. It really made you sit up and think, but with the optimism of youth after a while I put this snippet of news to the back of my mind.

(This incident took place on 17 April 1979. The four RUC officers were constables Richard Baird, Paul Gray and Noel Webb and Reserve Constable Robert Lockhart. All four men were killed when their RUC Land Rover was caught in the blast of an IRA van bomb. This incident will be dealt with in further detail in this chapter.)

I just thought: "Well these bastards are killing British soldiers and policemen. Will I be able to cope and not let my mates down?" It was a feeling which remained with me until I had completed my Northern Ireland training and had actually set foot in that bloody Province. Anyway our battalion got back from Berlin in July 1979 and after embarkation leave, the CO spoke to us and told us our company locations. Prince of Wales got Crossmaglen; 2 Company got Forkhill, but for some reason they got sent to Newry instead. My own 3 Company were to be based in Bessbrook at Battalion HQ and our Drums & Support got Newtownhamilton.

We did our Northern Ireland training on Salisbury Plain – then onto Lydd and Hythe. There is one incident which still sticks in my mind whilst we were in Salisbury Plain. It was the Monday, also my 19th birthday, after the double tragedy of Warrenpoint and Mountbatten getting killed – and rumours soon spread through the unit. The number of dead kept rising, including the Jock battalion we were taking over from – the Queen's Own Highlanders – and also members of 2 Para (whom we served with in Berlin). Everyone was stunned at the huge loss of life, and a little later my platoon commander came over to give us a prep talk. Rather stupidly, in all our opinions, he started with a bit of an insensitive comment. He said: "What a shame about Lord Louis Mountbatten," and I burst out with: "Fuck him sir; what about the 18 dead soldiers?"

He just looked at me, rather shocked, but didn't respond! The one thing that I was really scared of was not getting killed or maimed; it was not letting my comrades down and I am sure that is uppermost in most squaddies' minds.

On the same day as the Markethill bombing, PIRA volunteers parked a van up in the centre of Omagh having primed 300lbs of explosives. A warning was telephoned through to the Samaritans and the RUC were called in to evacuate the area. As they were shepherding the frightened shoppers and retail staff away from the van bomb, it suddenly detonated. The bomb, which was planted outside the Allied Irish Bank, exploded and three RUC officers

– including a female – were badly injured by the blast, which also injured two civilians. The bank took the full force and the 115-year-old building was badly damaged – as were several other buildings and shops.

The Blues & Royals, having been hit by an earlier tragedy in February with the deaths of Eddie Maggs and John Tucker, suffered another double tragedy on the 5th of the month. The regiment, Royal Horse Guards and 1st Dragoons – whose motto is *Honi soit qui mal y pense* (*Evil be to him who evil thinks*) – can trace its lineage back to Tangier 1662, suffered badly in the Hyde Park outrage in 1982. On that day, 22 July, a car bomb planted by the Provisional IRA in the South Carriageway killed four soldiers and seven horses as they rode along towards Buckingham Palace. On 5 April, two of their soldiers died in a less salubrious place and their blood stained the grim concrete of Glen Road, Andersonstown. This author has previously written about dickers and the term 'dicking'. The Provisionals made good use of dickers and, given the nature of urban guerrilla warfare where everyone looks the same other than the soldiers, these low-lives could blend in so easily. Given also that – often through no fault of their own – many Catholics were jobless they had an excuse for hanging around on street corners; outside pubs; outside their own front doors etc – all precisely the very places where soldiers and police patrolled. The dickers could watch, observe and note down routines, habits, Standard Operating Procedures (SOP) etc and build up a useful intelligence dossier of SF behaviour. The dickers had long been observing the routines outside Andersonstown RUC Station – particularly in relation to exit and re-entry of mobile and foot patrols.

Today, in 2014, Mcaneny's pub stands on the corner of Divis Drive and Glen Road and the pub would have provided excellent observation points for dickers masquerading as innocent drinkers. Next door is the Imperial Palace Chinese Restaurant (the author has no knowledge of what stood there in 1979); next to that Archer, Heaney & McGee Solicitors where, had it been the same 30-plus years ago, would have had a steady stream of Catholic men seeking legal advice. Finally – and more saliently – there is M.D. Bradley & Sons, hairdressers. Of one thing the author is certain: on the day that two Blues & Royals were killed, it was a men's barbers. Armed with information from their army of dickers, several armed PIRA members had taken over the barbers' shop and with one gunman posing as a customer downstairs to keep an eye on the owner and his customers, the other two had gone to an upstairs room and set up a firing point. Their observations had illustrated the methods which soldiers employed when returning to the RUC station and, in particular, the way two men always held open the security gates until the vehicle was safely inside.

As a Saracen returned to the Glen Road entrance, two soldiers – troopers Anthony Dykes (25), father of two, and Anthony Thornett (20) – ran either side of the vehicle and shepherded it inside. As they did so, several shots rang out and both men fell – mortally wounded – to the street. Both soldiers died en route for hospital – their wounds being so severe. Trooper Dykes was from Doncaster in South Yorkshire and is buried in Harworth Parish Church. Trooper Thornett was from Coventry and is buried at London Road Cemetery in the city.

On the 6th, an RUC officer was badly injured when two bombs exploded at a factory in North Belfast. The devices had been left at the Lombard factory at Limestone Road and RUC officers were helping to evacuate surrounding residences. The officer was rushed to hospital and fire crews fought the blaze once it was established that no further devices were inside.

The King's Regiment recruited from the Greater Manchester and Merseyside districts of England's North-West – officially known as simply 'The Kings' – and was an infantry regiment of the British Army (part of The King's Division). It was formed on 1 September 1958 by the amalgamation of The King's Regiment (Liverpool) – which had been raised in 1685 – and The Manchester Regiment, which traced its history to 1758. Its motto is *Nec Aspera Terrent (Difficulties be Damned)*. During the Troubles, 'The Kings' toured Northern Ireland many times and lost a total of 18 men from 1972 to 1990. It returned for another tour in 1979 and parts of the regiment were located as follows: 'A', Coy-McCrory Park (Whiterock Road); 'B', Coy-Fort Monagh; 'C', Coy-Moyard; 'D', Coy-North Howard Street; and Tactical HQ, Springfield Road. Although not used on this tour, the regiment had also been based at Vere Foster School on the Ballymurphy Estate. The Vere Foster School is also famous for being the alma mater of Martin 'Marty' McGartland – former British agent who infiltrated the Provisionals.

One of the 'Kingo's' companies was based at Moyard and had its TAOR on the Whiterock Road side of the notorious 'Murph. One of its armoured vehicles was a Saracen, which was known to have had faulty doors which wouldn't close and which left a substantial gap – wide enough to be noticed. Concerns were raised, but the vehicle was sent out – driven by an RCT driver and with (the author understands) two soldiers in the back. The men were Kingsman Christopher Shanley (21), from Liverpool, and Lance-Corporal Stephen Rumble (19), also from Huyton, Liverpool. The armoured vehicle had driven towards the Bull Ring from Glenalina Road before driving down Ballymurphy Road and then turning into Glenalina Crescent – with the intention of driving up this street and returning to Glenalina Road. At the very bottom of the crescent, at least two PIRA gunmen had broken into a house whilst the owner was at work and set up a firing point in a bedroom. The author has been unable to ascertain if the route which the Saracen took that day was a regular route and the dickers had passed on this information, or if the vehicle was not the intended target and the gunmen were waiting for a passing foot patrol.

As the Saracen passed the house at the bottom of Glenalina Crescent, it started up the slight incline to continue its circuit. At least one shot was fired into the back of the vehicle through the slightly opened doors. The shot hit Kingsman Shanley before ricocheting around the armoured insides and fatally wounding Lance-Corporal Rumble. To the startled driver the sounds may have seemed like multiple strikes – and there is a suggestion that he naturally panicked and raced back to base. The shocked RCT man arrived back and was apparently too shaken to relate what had happened. What happened next was related to me by an army dog handler attached to the Kings, but I have decided for the sake of both decency and sensitivity not to divulge his information. Kingsman Shanley was already dead and Lance-Corporal Rumble, whose wife Karen was heavily pregnant with their daughter, was critically injured. He died on the 19th with his family at his side in hospital.

An impeccable source told the author: "I cannot say definitively as to whether on that occasion it was the door. Although a problem had been reported, I can't say. I initially heard that a foot patrol was the intended target, but that a moving vehicle with an open door created a better opportunity for the gun team."

Mrs Rumble had a daughter, whom she named Stevie, and this author has had both the honour and the pleasure of meeting both ladies on several occasions. This author understands that there is an ongoing investigation into the events which led to the double murder and hopes in a later publication to reveal the outcome of such. As a postscript, a

25-year-old PIRA member was later jailed for his part in the killings and for a later killing (see Chapter 57).

LANCE-CORPORAL STEPHEN RUMBLE
Dougie Durrant, Army Dog Handlers' Unit

On 11 April 1979 I found myself on a normal cold overcast day in Moyard Base in West Belfast. I had been there many times over the years being an arms explosive search dog handler with the Army Dog Unit (ADUNI). However, this day would change my life – along with a number of other traumatic incidents over the course of the next 30 years. Some things you put to the back of your mind as the only people who are able to understand them are the people who were there. It would re-live itself in my mind later in life in the finest detail – and although I have long forgotten the names of people involved, the incidents remain there.

I was walking my dog, Bluce, around the small base situated in the west of the city – overlooking the Ballymurphy. I had fed him and now it was time for my normal army breakfast. As I popped into the cookhouse I bumped into Lance-Corporal Stephen Rumble and his men, who were just about to depart on a mobile patrol around the 'Murph. Stephen wanted to be a dog handler so we would often talk over a hot brew about what he needed to do. Anyway, I wished him well and off they went in the six-wheeled Saracen armoured personnel carrier. I just remember the front gates slamming shut as they left. A bit later, shots rang out around the area.

At once solders started to run to their posts – and with that I ran to my bunk and grabbed my kit ready for the follow-up operation. I got Bluce ready and walked towards the Saracen, which had returned to the base. The Company Sergeant Major (CSM) was standing there – and the look on his face told me he had a man down. Bluce jumped in the back of the vehicle, like we had done on numerous occasions, but the CSM shouted: "Doug, call Bluce out of the vehicle!" With that, I looked into the Sarra and it was covered in blood and parts that only a high-velocity round can cause. Bluce jumped out, covered in blood. I was informed that one man was dead and one man – Stephen Rumble – was very seriously injured. They had come under contact from an IRA sniper and one round through the slightly open back door of the Saracen had caused this carnage. The third member of the patrol had returned fire and they had returned back to base as fast as possible. Lance-Corporal Rumble died from the terrible wound he had received.

THE 'MURPH
Gary Weeks, Royal Engineers

Anyone who has been in the Ballymurphy will relate to this – let alone us wearing the uniform of the British Army. We were on a house search. The cordon was set and in place, so we're as safe as we could be in the 'Murph. We searched the house, but found fuck all as usual because the weapon etc had already been moved. Then there was a major drama … We were out of ciggies, so it's off to the shop up on the waste ground. In we went, but the old fella behind the counter won't serve us. He told us that he was sorry, but he had no anger or hatred in

Royal Artillery, Armagh, 1979. (©Walter Stirling)

his voice. "I can't serve you 'cos the Provos will come and teach me a lesson for collaborating with the occupation forces!" He was scared shitless they'd kneecap him for selling us 20 Bensons, so we left saying goodbye and wishing him the best and he says the same. So they were all against us? I don't think so, but it wasn't a war or ethnic cleansing or anything nasty like that according to the politicians. Maybe they should have went to the 'Murph for a bit.

Two days later an off-duty UDR was driving home after finishing work for the day as a gamekeeper on the Caledon Estate in Co Armagh. Lance-Corporal Thomas 'Tommy' Armstrong (64) was driving along Corr Road in Tynan in his van when he reached a point some 400-500 yards from the Irish border. Fit for his age – the oldest UDR killed in the Troubles – he clearly represented a threat to the Provisionals and they must have feared for their lives judging by the amount of gunmen and firepower which they used to murder him. In the region of six terrorists ambushed him – unarmed as he was – and he was hit twice in the back as at least 15 rounds hit his van. It is likely that death was mercifully quick. His cowardly murderers may have scoured the bullet-riddled van for his service weapon, but he never carried it around with him despite the threats to his life. This author has been criticised for committing the 'cardinal sin' of attempting to interact with the reader. However, I ask Mr Gerry Adams, Mr Martin McGuiness, Mr Daniel Morrison,

Royal Artillery, Armagh, 1979. (©Walter Stirling)

Mr Martin Galvin of NORAID and any Republican sympathiser to publically explain to me – and I will meet them in Northern Ireland – how the death of this old soldier advanced their cause of a United Ireland? The following words of a former UDR man dwarf my own eloquence and I urge the reader to linger over his thoughts.

THE DEATH OF A UDR MAN: 1979
RSM Haydn Davies, 2 UDR

I was posted as RSM of the 2nd Battalion of the UDR in Armagh City. While I was there I befriended Lance-Corporal Tom Armstrong. He was the gamekeeper to the Earl of Caledon on his estate near to the Irish border at Middleton. Caledon Estate was a large and beautiful wooded country estate where deer and wildlife ran wild.

The present Earl was second in command of the battalion and the son of the late Earl Alexander of Tunis. Tom was 65 and overage to serve in the UDR, but a few white lies were told to allow him to serve and look after the security of the estate while guarding the battalion second in command. Tom was armed with a service rifle and a personal protection weapon – a small .22 pistol.

Tom was certainly out on a limb; he was often alone by day and night. Being right on the border, his life was positively under threat. We all feared for his safety. The estate had been attacked recently and UDR members had been killed locally. Tom actually lived on the Irish border – with the back door of his cottage virtually in the south. I visited his house several times and found it quite unnerving. We had his chimney fitted with night marker flares. In the event of attack he could pull a cord and the flares would shoot skywards. A British Army infantry company was situated at a border checkpoint about one mile away.

Some nights I spent some hours with Tom on the battlement roof of the estate house at Caledon. I once introduced him to the 'Starlight scope', which allowed vision at night. Tom thought it quite magic, but thought it would never replace his 'eyes and ears' for knowing what went on around and about the estate. As we packed up to leave on these evenings Tom would place his rifle in the Earl's arms room and lock it up with a chain lock. Several times I said to Tom: "Why don't you take your rifle home with you?" His answer was always the same: "When they come for me there will be too many of them."

They came for Tom on 13 April 1979. The estimation is that there were between three and six of them. Tom was ambushed in his little van on the way home after feeding stock at the estate during early morning. He died at the scene from multiple gunshot wounds. I attended Tom's funeral with a heavy heart. He was most certainly one of the world's nice fellows – gone! I recalled his stories of how he would heat the greenhouse each spring time and always produce new potatoes on St Patrick's Day for the Earl's lunch; also how he thought he knew who bombed the main Caledon house and that he would 'have a word with him one day'.

As I stood at the graveside I looked out over the countryside and saw three castles: One a medieval Mott and Bailey affair; the other a 17th century castle still occupied. A little distance away was the third – a British Army tinned and sandbagged fort! I looked at all three defensive sites dating over 10 centuries – all situated within a kilometre square. I realised then that dear old Tom was far from being the last to suffer a violent death hereabouts.

The Oxford English dictionary describes 'depravity' as 'moral corruptness; wickedness'. Synonyms include 'debasement', 'degeneration', 'perversion' and 'corruptness'. This author has often been accused of overusing the word 'depravity', but the aforementioned synonyms of the word can all be applied in equal measure to the following murder. Just three days after the cowardly slaying of Tommy Armstrong, a PIRA ASU dragged itself from its moral sewer and drove towards St MacCartan's Church in Clogher, Co Tyrone to the wedding of a PO's sister. Dickers in the local Catholic community had forewarned the IRA that Michael Cassidy (31), a PO from Dunlambert Avenue in the Fortwilliam Park area of North Belfast, would be visiting the village for his sister's wedding on Easter Monday. What transpired next was indeed sickening, but one must also remember the hands of those who informed the terrorists; those same hands are covered in an innocent man's blood. Those who informed and contributed to the wickedness of the day must question their roles.

With the ceremony over – confetti thrown and photographs taken – the newlyweds bade their farewells and Mr Cassidy walked towards the departing car clutching the hand of his three-year-old daughter. As he did so several gunmen shot him several times and, as he slumped to the ground, shot him twice more in the head as he lay defenceless. Brave guests tried to wrest the weapons from the killers' hands, but to no avail. One can only begin to comprehend the horror and confusion felt by the little girl as she saw her beloved daddy torn from her hands and be dragged away by concerned loved ones as his life ebbed away. The author has seen a photograph taken at the murder scene several hours after the slaying. It shows a body – covered by a plastic sheet – alone and left there awaiting the forensics team to do its job and then be taken to a mortuary in the Co Tyrone area. The shocked guests have long departed and somewhere in the area is a bewildered, distraught child – orphaned by depraved murders from a depraved terrorist organisation.

With the gunshots and emotional repercussions still echoing around Clogher the Provisionals struck again within 24 hours – this time at Camlough, Co Armagh. An armoured Land Rover of the RUC – on mobile patrol out of Bessbrook Mill – was driving along Millvale Road en route for Camlough Road. They spotted a van parked at the side of the road and pulled out in order to overtake it. Unknown to them the van, belonging to a company from the Irish Republic, had been hijacked whilst delivering cheese and a PIRA bombing team had planted 1,000 lbs of explosives inside the van. This was believed to be the largest bomb used by the IRA up to that date. As the police vehicle drove past a bombing team, hidden behind bushes on a nearby hillside, detonated the bomb by electronic means. The blast obliterated even the armour of the RUC vehicle – in fact the Land Rover was mangled and torn beyond all recognition.

The resultant explosion severely damaged several other civilian vehicles travelling behind and 11 people – including several children – were injured. The IRA bombing team must have seen civilian cars in the immediate proximity, but so great was their obsession to kill the police and so great was their hatred that they simply had no qualms in risking the lives of innocents. The hijacked van, which had been taken from a nearby village, was parked beside the road in a valley overlooked by houses. Another RUC car some 200 yards away had its windscreen blown in by the blast and both officers inside were cut by flying glass. Several houses nearby were also damaged and one of the first civilians on the scene described how he was confronted by body parts – seemingly everywhere. He described his shock at finding boots with mangled feet still inside them – such was the ferocity of the blast. The RUC's most senior officer, Sir Kenneth Newman, said: "This is the worst single tragedy we have had. It is the first time that we have had four men killed in one incident."

The four officers were killed absolutely instantly and all were so mutilated that they could only be identified by dental records and fingerprints. The officers were: Constable Noel Webb (30); Constable Richard Baird (28); Constable Paul Gray (25) and RUCR Constable Robert Lockhart (44). A total of five children were left fatherless. In January 1981 Patrick Joseph Traynor, from Crossmaglen, was found guilty of the four murders and a range of other charges. He was jailed for life on each of the four murder charges and was sentenced to 12 years for the other terrorist-related crimes.

The day after the Camlough explosion, a foot patrol of the Royal Anglian Regiment was sniped at by a PIRA gunman as they walked along Norglen Parade on the Turf Lodge. One young soldier, 22-year-old Private William Lewis, was hit in the back and terribly injured. He was immediately casevaced to hospital for emergency treatment. The young private recovered from his wound, but the author was – until recently – unable to discover the outcome of the incident or of his further career in the army. The author was told by a reliable source in the regiment: "He recovered from his injuries. He used to live in Luton and I used to bump into him in the town centre quite often. Since I've moved to the suburbs I don't go into town as often and don't see him. He was in hospital for some time, but as far as I know made a full recovery."

On the 19th, a combination of ill luck, poor planning and an unbelievable lapse in security contributed to the death of a visiting army cadet officer from England. Captain

Paul Rodgers (37), from Herts in England, was visiting his local county regiment – the Royal Anglians – on their current tour of the Province. He was a teacher at St Edmund's School in Ware. The officer – along with an RCT driver, an escort from the regiment and a young cadet from the same school – had been visiting a wounded Anglian in the RVH and were returning to base in a Land Rover. As it reached La Salle Drive off the Falls Road, some half a mile from Milltown Cemetery, PIRA gunmen opened fire from a house in which they had taken the family hostage. Captain Rodgers was hit and died shortly afterwards – and the young cadet was wounded in the arm. The Land Rover attempted to escape, but drove into a dead end and the Anglian soldier – himself wounded – and the RCT man got the wounded men under cover. The gunmen raced off along the Falls Road and disappeared into safehouses in the Beechmounts. An elderly lady walking along the Falls Road was also hit and was taken to the RVH for treatment of gunshot wounds.

CAPTAIN RODGERS
Private, Royal Anglian Regiment

During the early part of 1979 whilst being stationed at Palace Barracks, Hollywood with 3rd Royal Anglian Regiment I had become interested in the mug photos of known/active members of terrorist groups – and being new to the battalion set about trying to learn all I could to remember the names to the faces. After a while not only was I remembering the names but their addresses, date of births etc.

During patrols, certain section commanders started asking me if I recognised a certain person that was stood in front of them – and of course being a keen 18-year-old trying to impress I would more often than not give their name, address and date of birth. This practice went on for a while without any thought.

There came up a recognition competition within the battalion, which I entered with relish. Whoever won was to be given three days off and they could do what they liked. Anyway, yours truly won the competition and was given the next three days off. During the first day off I was asked if I would escort two persons around Belfast the next day. Naturally, I said yes – again trying to impress.

The Land Rover turned up outside my barrack block and inside were two persons who I didn't have any idea were at that time, but found out as the morning progressed. Before setting off I was asked to face the rear of the Land Rover as we were going round the city – something I couldn't understand. As we started off I found out the person sitting down without a weapon was a 19-year-old army cadet and the bloke facing the front was an army cadet officer armed with an unloaded SLR. Then, for the first time, I questioned: "What the bloody hell was I doing here when I could be relaxing in the NAAFI?"

After a while we started driving up the Falls Road before going onto North Howard Street Mill for a smoke break and a cuppa. When we arrived the Land Rover commander went and did something or other – and me, the other two and the driver had our cuppa and chat and I had a smoke or two. Just before leaving the mill it started spitting with rain – and as I had had the foresight to bring along my rain jacket, I quickly donned it. I said to the cadet officer that I would face the front as I had my jacket on and if he faced the rear he wouldn't get so wet.

We visited the Royal Victoria Hospital and then set off for Andersonstown RUC Station. As we proceeded onto the Falls Road – heading towards the police station – I became aware of a known face stood on a corner and then as we drove past, a car backfired … or so I thought. But then, as quick as that car backfired, the officer slumped against me and I realised that we had come under fire – and I shouted to the driver and commander that the officer had been hit.

Whilst this had been going on another two or three shots had been fired – and I had seen where I thought the shots had been fired from and quickly cocked my rifle. I returned fire with maybe eight or 10 rounds. We then turned a corner and I grabbed the army cadet. My next thought was: "Oh, shit!" as we had driven into a cul-de-sac. As I said, I grabbed the cadet and my next thought was get him safe – as we probably had driven into a trap – so I shoved him under a nearby car and knelt down beside the car to protect him.

Before I realised anything else we were surrounded by a big crowd shouting, spitting and throwing objects. They started getting nearer so I fired two rounds into the air. Then, before I knew it, there were squaddies everywhere. It was at this point that I felt my left arm burning and warm fluid trickling down my face. I had two cut-like injuries to my head and left arm caused by two rounds grazing my skin.

Sadly the officer had been killed, but one known gunman had been found dead in the grounds of the local hospital. I had two slight injuries; the cadet was safe, but what must have been going through his mind God only knows. Everything from then just moved so fast and I was questioned about how many rounds I had let off; why I had fired into the air and everything that had happened and said from leaving Palace Barracks. Naturally, I told them everything.

It wasn't until later in life that I started asking questions about that day: Why was I asked to escort the two persons when I was one of the least experienced in the battalion? Why was I asked to face the rear of the Land Rover before leaving Palace Barracks? Why did we drop into North Howard Street when our first stop was supposed to be Andersonstown Police Station? What the hell was an army cadet doing there along with the unarmed cadet officer?

On the same day as the death of the cadet captain, the Provisionals turned their attention to POs once more and struck outside Armagh Jail. A group of four female officers had just left the jail at lunchtime in order to go for refreshments at a nearby café known for serving prison staff. The women were all dressed in a mixture of civilian clothes and PO's uniforms. Waiting PIRA gunmen in a stolen car drove up to where the women were walking as a group and opened fire from the rear of the stolen car. Three of the POs were hit immediately and fell to the ground; one of whom – Agnes Wallace (40), mother of six children – was fatally wounded. As the wounded women lay in a bloodied heap, one of the gunmen cynically threw a hand grenade at his helpless victims. The resultant explosion further injured the women and Agnes Wallace died shortly afterwards. The attack was cold, calculated, cynical and cowardly. It was, after all, the Provisional IRA. A passing doctor gave first aid, but for Mrs Wallace – a PO for only three months – it was too late. Her funeral was held in the same church where two weeks earlier she had proudly posed for photographs at her eldest daughter's wedding.

On the 20th, the Director of Public Prosecutions (DPP) made a public announcement that the undercover soldiers who had killed James Taylor at the Ballinderry River on 30

September of the previous year would not face prosecution (see Chapter 45). The 23-year-old had died when he was fired on by undercover soldiers as he and friends returned from a duck-hunting trip. It had been alleged that the soldiers were undercover and that they had 'developed a policy of shooting first and asking questions afterwards'. An SDLP spokesman said that Mr Taylor had been: " ... illegally shot in an incident in which the Security Forces were in no danger ... " He further made an unsubstantiated claim that a further 10 deaths could be attributable to this 'policy' in the last 12 months.

It has long been a source of bemusement to this author that the Republicans and their apologists and sympathisers could scream about human rights and 'State terrorism' and 'shoot to kill' when their doyens – the Provisional IRA – could take life so quickly; so arbitrarily; so coldly and without mercy – thus denying their own victims any sense of justice or fair play. It was a case of 'we can shoot you in the most cowardly fashion, but you must treat us with fairness and offer us the opportunity to surrender'.

On the 21st, the RUC prevented a major bombing attack in the city of Londonderry when received information led it to raid a power station on a Nationalist estate. Acting upon information received from informants and clever surveillance work, the substation on the Waterside was raided and a cache of 16 gas cylinder bombs – ready and primed – were discovered. Several arrests were made in the area. Earlier that day an armed man and an accomplice had boarded a train as it slowed on the Irish border prior to entering the North. Holding the train staff at gunpoint they had forced them to drive two to three miles inside the border, where they made them halt again. Once there, waiting accomplices loaded two milk churns packed with explosives onto the train. They abandoned the train and warned staff to do the same. The bombs exploded shortly afterwards – causing major damage.

On the 22nd, the then Governor of New York – Hugh Carey, Irish-American prima donna and IRA apologist extraordinaire in the author's eyes – made an outrageous demand of the British Government and the United Nations. Hugh Leo Carey (11 April 1919 – 7 August 2011) was an American attorney; the 51st Governor of New York from 1975 to 1982. In some eyes Carey led the Irish-American support for the Provisionals' campaign of violence in Northern Ireland. He was also behind an ongoing plot to stop the U.S. arms industry from supplying the RUC and now demanded that the U.N. implement 'Rhodesia-like sanctions' against the British Government!

Carey called for sanctions to force the British Government to pull out of Ulster. Naturally, the British were extremely angry at the latest round of U.S. meddling. He accused both Labour and the Conservatives of pandering to the Ulster Loyalists with a General Election just weeks away. When criticised about the U.S. involving itself in other nations' affairs, he rejected the suggestion – stating that the: " ... Irish tragedy is but a moral affront to the entire world community." He made spurious claims of 'official brutality in Ulster interrogation centres' and urged the U.S. Government to call upon the British to announce a plan for political and physical withdrawal from Ireland. Having researched the statement, one is most surprised that Carey made no condemnation of the IRA's murders of 11 people at the La Mon House; no condemnation of the killers of 10 Protestant workers at Kingsmills; no words of support or sympathy for murdered PO Agnes Wallace's six children – nor of the murder of pensioners with no connections with the Security Forces. This arrogant Irish-American apologist died in 2011. He will not be mourned by this author.

GOVERNOR CAREY
Jeanne Griffin

This was a typical example of arrogant Irish-American meddling in affairs that were none of the United States' business, but rather that of its staunchest ally (which happens to be the United Kingdom). This pathetic excuse of a politician did what most IRA apologists do – namely cherry-pick Troubles events in which Catholics were the victims such as Bloody Sunday, McGurk's etc. However, they fail to study the entire history of the Northern Ireland conflict beginning in 1921 when Michael Collins signed the Anglo-Irish Treaty in London ratifying partition. Therefore, Hugh Carey – whose ancestors were likely pursuing the American dream inside the apparatus of the corrupt Irish political machine – had no part in events which occurred after this watershed event, such as the Irish Civil War (which he probably did not know involved Irish people only in the Free State and was not a British-Irish squabble). He also did not – or chose not – to comprehend that Ulster was part of the UK because the Protestant majority wished it to be so.

He closed his eyes to PIRA bombings of men, women and children. He also most likely closed his eyes to the PIRA's links with the PLO, Soviets and Libya. The fact that an American State Governor actively encouraged his national Government to support a proscribed terrorist organisation with documented ties to the enemies of the U.S. – and by doing so was undermining NATO – is nothing short of treason. Hugh Carey was a nasty, sneaky meddling traitor. If he hated the British so much, why in hell didn't his ancestors sail for a Catholic haven like Brazil or Mexico? My Irish uncle (my dad's brother), Leo Griffin, was murdered by the henchmen of Irish-American political boss Tom Pendergast of Kansas City. The Irish-American politicians are as corrupt and bloodstained as their cousins in the 'Ould Sod' – shed copious tears as they sing 'Danny Boy' in their plastic shamrock-adorned bars, yet casually mete out death and destruction across the ocean and at home; useless idiots. Carey's arse should have been impeached; then slung into a federal prison.

On the 25th, Carey's heroes tried to kill another PO and an off-duty UDR soldier; they were successful in the latter case. The off-duty PO, who lived in North Belfast, worked in Crumlin Road Jail. He answered an early-morning knock at his door and as he opened it, he was blasted with a shotgun and critically injured. The author understands that he made a full recovery. A few hours later Private John Graham (55), father of five and a part-time UDR soldier, was ambushed as he drove his Milk Marketing Board lorry collecting milk churns from dairies in the Co Tyrone area. A member of 'F' Company, 5 UDR, he had just reached Garvallagh Crossroads close to Seskinore when hidden PIRA gunmen opened fire from behind a roadside hedge. At least a dozen rounds were fired into the vehicle's cab and the part-time soldier was fatally wounded when he was hit in the face and chest. He died at the scene. In the space of just 20 days, the IRA had left 24 children without a parent. Significantly, Governor Carey made no mention of this fact.

That same day a UVF murder gang consisting of William John Mullan and Billy Dodds visited PIRA man William Carson's home on Rosevale Street in Belfast's Oldpark area with the intention to kill him. They were told by his young son and daughter that their parents were not home, and left. They returned an hour later and as Carson (32) was still not home the men sat with his 11-year-old daughter, watching television, until he returned at 11.30pm – at which point they shot him in front of his child. He died in hospital in the early morning hours.

On the 26th, a Republican gang entered a bus close to Andersonstown and forced the passengers and driver off at gunpoint. A suspect package was placed on the bus and the gang ran off. Before the RUC could arrive, a senior figure from the bus company – motivated by a combination of foolhardy bravery and frustration at the number of vehicles his bus company had lost to the Provisionals – stepped on board. Despite the fact that he thought that a detonation was imminent, he carried the device into the street – where it was later found to be a hoax.

On the 27th and 30th, two UDR men in separate parts of the Province had miraculous escapes. In the first incident – at Forthriver Road, North Belfast – PIRA bombers placed a thermos flask bomb in the boot of a part-time soldier's car and then let down one of his tyres. The following morning the man discovered the flat tyre and went to the car boot in order to get the spare wheel. However, as he opened it he saw the thermos flask and quickly slammed the boot shut. The device exploded and he was injured; however the bulk of the blast was contained inside the boot. Three days later – in Ballymena – a postman who was a part-time UDR man was driving through the town when he noticed smoke pouring from his boot. Realising that it was probably a bomb, he screeched to a halt and dived out of the car. Seconds later it exploded – causing a small fire outside a nearby market. He was uninjured and there were no civilian casualties.

On the 29th however, two members of the UDR were killed – the first as a consequence of one of the seemingly ubiquitous RTAs and the other a result of a cowardly attack by the Provisionals on an off-duty soldier. Private William 'Billy' Morton (47) met his death in a tragic car crash in the Province. In previous works by this author, countless UDR men have written of their utter exhaustion during the Troubles. These men were physically and mentally tired as a combination of working full-time and then returning home before donning their uniforms, grabbing their weapons and then going out until the early hours on patrols and VCPs. Often they would spot and confront known players who also lived in their own communities and, more sinisterly, who knew where they lived too. Combine those factors and suddenly the reasons for the high incidence of RTAs and RTA deaths becomes clear. The author has managed to identify a minimum of 71 UDR soldiers who died in RTAs – and with approaching that number killed in 'unknown circumstances', the figure could well be much higher.

Earlier that morning Private G. 'Sammy' Gibson (52), father of two and a part-time member of the UDR, was cycling to work in Co Tyrone. He regularly cycled along the same route, which took him through Edendork. As he rode along the Coalisland Road at least two armed PIRA men were waiting for him and as he passed them, they opened fire with automatic weapons and he was hit 10 times and mortally wounded. An ambulance was called but he died very quickly after it arrived. Poignantly, his wife and children were driving along shortly afterwards and came upon the scene where her dying husband was being treated by ambulance men and police officers – and she was stopped and given the tragic news.

April had ended, and with it the lives of 16 people – up on the tallies of previous months. A total of nine soldiers had been killed – all but one at the hands of the Provisionals – and the same terror group had also killed four policemen. Two POs had been murdered by the

IRA and one Republican paramilitary had been killed by the Loyalists. The Provisionals were responsible for 15 of the 16 deaths in April.

53

May

The General Election would sweep the Conservatives back into power and Margaret Thatcher would become Britain's first female Prime Minister. Five soldiers would die this month – as well as two more policemen. There were also two 'guilty by past association' deaths in this spring month.

May Day 1979 fell on a Tuesday and General Election fever was high. The opinion polls were predicting a Conservative return to power and the political 'first' of a female Prime Minister. James Callaghan's mortally wounded Labour Party – soon to tear itself inside out with internecine fighting – would lose the election and begin a period of 18 years as an almost 'perma-opposition'. In Northern Ireland, over 30,000 soldiers and RUC were on 'red alert' for trouble and the feared PIRA spectacular. On that first day of the month a former RUCR officer was murdered because of his past associations.

Frederick Lutton (40) worked for the National Trust at Moy, Co Tyrone and was the father of two children. He was a former RUCR member, but had been retired from the force for some time. In the late afternoon of that fateful Tuesday as he prepared to lock the gates of Argory House, masked PIRA gunmen drove up in a car and shot him several times. He slumped to the ground, mortally wounded. The shooting was witnessed and the terrorists scuttled back to their car and raced off. He was rushed to hospital in Dungannon but died en route.

Internment had been a public relations disaster the first time around and permanently soured the fragile support some Catholics still had for the army. 'Operation Demetrius' on 9–10 August 1971 involved the mass arrest and internment of 342 people suspected of being involved with Irish Republican paramilitaries, but neglected to target their Loyalist counterparts. The intelligence lists were supplied by the RUC and were hopelessly out of date – often relating to the 1940s campaign and the border campaign of 1956. As stated, no Loyalist paramilitaries were included in the sweep – and many of those who were arrested had no links with Republican paramilitaries. However, by 1979 there were many in the senior echelons of the army who felt that given the increased intelligence and surveillance techniques, the Provisionals and INLA – as well as the Loyalist terrorists – could be effectively emasculated by a fresh round of internments. The increased activities of PIRA and use of new tactics and organisation, it was felt, would push the new Ulster Secretary into more draconian measures – which by definition included internment. Certainly, some members of the SF felt that valuable short-term advantages could be gained if they were free to hold known terrorists without trial for an indefinite period. Both PIRA and INLA had by this time become so security-conscious that evidence to secure convictions had become next to impossible to obtain. In particular, the development of the 'cell' system meant that many members never even saw or knew those who were actually giving the orders. It also meant that the task of informers was more problematical because if an operation was compromised, there were only a finite number of men in the know and there were fewer people to blame.

On the following Thursday Margaret Thatcher ousted the incumbent Labour Government of James Callaghan with a parliamentary majority of 43 seats. The election was the first of four consecutive election victories for the Conservative Party and Thatcher became the United Kingdom's – and Europe's – first female head of Government. On the 5th, Humphrey Atkins succeeded Roy Mason as Secretary of State for Northern Ireland. The appointment prompted the *Belfast Telegraph* to ask: 'Humphrey Who?' No doubt the Provisional IRA's Army Council was asking the same question as they frantically sent out for a copy of *Who's Who?* This is what they would have learned: Atkins was educated at Wellington College, Berkshire and served in the Royal Navy from 1940–48. He worked for a linoleum manufacturer and then as a director of a financial advertising agency. He contested the Scottish constituency of West Lothian in 1951 and was elected as MP for Merton and Morden in 1955. He became MP for Spelthorne in 1970 and was Conservative Chief Whip from 1973–77.

On the morning of the election, George Colley – the Tánaiste (Deputy Taoiseach) of the Irish Republic – called on the UK to withdraw from Northern Ireland. His timing was impeccable as he demanded that Britain should set a timetable for departure and end the constitutional guarantee that Ulster should remain part of the UK should the majority so desire. He claimed that under British rule the 500,000 Catholics would remain as 'second-class citizens' and that such an event would result in peace. Few people thought that the Fianna Fail politician actually believed the nonsense which he was spouting.

On the 5th, the Provisionals launched a sniper attack on soldiers patrolling in Crossmaglen as South Armagh again lived up to its reputation as 'bandit country'. One soldier was wounded as a foot patrol of the Queen's came under fire. He later recovered from his wounds.

THE WOUNDING OF LANCE-CORPORAL AVERY IN CROSSMAGLEN
Private Martin Riley, 3 Queen's

There was similar weather on this day, 5 May, to when Newtownhamilton was mortared. Our patrol had not long been in from a town patrol and we were on standby again. About an hour after we had returned, the alarm was raised by the ops room informing us of a sniper attack in the Carran Road, Crossmaglen. One of our lads – Lance-Corporal Avery – had been shot and hit close to his groin, and we were told later the round had exited his buttock. Although injured, he was still able to radio through a contact report and we were called out.

I remember leaving the base camp gate and just seeing this large group of squaddies rapidly moving across the square in tight formation towards the Newry Road. I remember thinking to myself: "If this is another 'come on' they are a perfect target." I am not afraid to admit that this made me back off the main group by about 30 yards. Our gunner, Jap, was behind me trying to catch up. I remember one of the sergeants shouting: "Riley, get a fucking move on!" and as I did so, Jap overtook me – struggling with the GPMG and the ammo belt round his knees, making him trip up.

As I was moving past Jap I offered to help him, but he just told me to move on – which I did – and we both caught up with the main group, which were now heading down Newry Road. The aim was to get to an area in the Newry Road that overlooked the fields that were to the right of the Carran Road. We were then positioned along the hedgerow to take up firing positions in the event we spotted the sniper trying to get away. Needless to say, they did get away.

After all the turmoil of that day, it came to light that these snipers had been lying in wait for at least two days. They had taken up position on a small residential building site opposite the school at the end of the Carran Road. They laid in wait until a patrol had come out of the Ardross Estate. Young Avery had just led his brick out of the estate and they were heading back towards the square. The sniper waited until all the soldiers in that brick were facing away from his firing position so they would not see the flash of the rifle muzzle when fired. He then took aim on the lead man, who was – of course – Lance-Corporal Avery. Avery must have turned to look back just at the moment the sniper took his shot; the rest you now know. I am pleased that we did not lose a member of our regiment during our tour, but the RUC did unfortunately – but that is a story for another time. Avery fortunately recovered in hospital.

When a search was carried out, the position the sniper had actually laid was a small hollow on the building site near the hedgerow – well-camouflaged and apparently tactically done. This unit had used plastic bags to put their food waste and faeces so that they would not be detected. This stopped any animals from getting curious and coming close – giving their position away – and they had been there for around two days just watching and waiting for their opportunity to take the shot and bug out. This position was the exact same spot that both Corporal Graham Booker and I had been laying in during the polling day at the school.

Anyone who thought that the IRA were just thick Irish men were very wrong. In many respects some of them were very well-trained and well-equipped – and we had a very healthy respect for what we were dealing with whatever their motivations were.

For myself I did not have to experience this kind of situation again (as I left the army in 1981), but I do often wonder the impact for all those involved in the atrocities of this so-called campaign. As I sit and reflect now after so many years, it has become apparent that Northern Ireland is a forgotten war. It is never mentioned and rarely gets recognition for the impact it had on so many lives. The Falklands, Iraq One and Two and Afghanistan are now the new breeding grounds for this type of guerrilla warfare. Technology may change, but the basic principles remain the same and the terrorist mindset has no regard for life in general – only a distorted ideology with a fanatical psychopathic or sociopathic sense of the world.

Three days after the General Election – with Margaret Thatcher settling in to 10 Downing Street – two undercover SF members (one army and one RUC) were killed in Lisnaskea, Co Fermanagh. The small town's name is taken from Irish: Lios na Scéithe – meaning ring fort of the shield – and is the second-biggest settlement in the county. It is almost equidistant between Northern Ireland's southern and western borders with the Republic and was of strategic importance to both the army and the Provisionals. On the day in question, Sergeant Robert Maughan (30) and RUC Detective Constable Robert Prue (29) – a father of two – were on undercover duties in Lisnaskea. Sergeant Maughan,

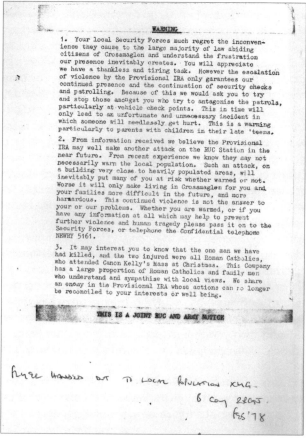

Flyer handed out to the local population by B Company 2 Royal
Green Jackets, Crossmaglen, 1978. (©Gary Cootes)

of the 9/12 Hussars, and DC Prue had been observed buying a Republican newspaper on
several preceding Sundays by PIRA dickers – and their regular pattern was to prove fatal.
As they pulled up outside Holy Cross Church the RUC man got out of the car and walked
towards a newspaper seller – leaving Sergeant Maughan in their unmarked car. As he did so,
masked gunmen ran from behind a wall and shot DC Prue – and seconds later the soldier.
Both men died instantly in a salvo of shots – some of which hit the outside of the church.
Lost Lives quote the local priest as saying: "I was called outside because I was told that two
men had been killed. One of the men was lying across the front seat of the car and partly
on the floor. The side window was smashed as if he had been shot at close range. The other
man was lying dead on the road and I saw that I could do nothing for him." (p.784) Robert
Maughan was from Newcastle-upon-Tyne and Robert Prue was a local man from the town.

On the day after the Provisionals sent an early warning to the incoming Conservative
Government and left a stolen car packed with explosives outside one of Dungannon's most
popular hotels – the Dunowen in Market Square. At around 2.15pm the bombers set the
device and then walked off in such a casual manner that no-one paid them much attention.
A warning was telephoned through and this gave the RUC and soldiers from the Royal

Regiment of Wales just enough time to evacuate the area. At 2.30pm the device exploded – obliterating the car and causing serious damage to the hotel and the next door branch of the Ulster Bank. There were no injuries, but some people were treated in hospital for shock.

Ardmonagh Gardens, on the Turf Lodge, is close to the Whiterock Road and the Whiterock Leisure Centre – and a stone's throw from the nearby cemetery. The Turf Lodge is the 'sister' estate to the 'Murph and is separated only by the length of the aforementioned Whiterock Road. It is a local authority housing estate built after the Second World War and the Black Mountain offers a stunning backdrop to the houses. The area was built in the late 1950s to house excess people from the overcrowded districts of the Lower Falls. The area had formerly been occupied by the Turf Lodge Farm and so the name was retained for the new estate. Much of the housing was of a low standard – consisting of blocks of flats and maisonettes – although following a campaign by local women in the 1970s some of the lowest-quality housing stock was demolished and redeveloped. The estate is encircled by ring roads – a state of affairs which has helped to encourage joyriding amongst local youth. This in turn engendered a culture of summary justice where the local PIRA handed out punishment beatings and kneecappings to those deemed guilty of what the Republican paramilitary hypocrites termed 'anti-social behaviour'.

Ardmonagh Gardens is also the place where a young lance-corporal from the King's Regiment lost his life to a callously-placed PIRA IED on the 9th of the month. A routine patrol from the Kingos was on the Turf Lodge and two men went into what they referred to as the 'Disco Block'. There were dance parties held there for the local children of the estate and a crèche-come-playgroup had been established in order to give the mothers a little respite. On the day of the patrol, the lower part of the block was full of young children – and a dance to raise funds for the Save the Children charity was under way. As the two soldiers climbed the steps in order to give cover from the roof, Lance-Corporal Andrew 'Andy' Webster (20), from the Merseyside area, was slightly ahead of his comrade. As he turned up the stairs a deadly IED was detonated and the blast killed him absolutely instantly. The blast was so severe that he would have mercifully known nothing at all. As the following contributor writes, it beggared belief that the Provisionals could put all those young children's lives at risk in order to kill and maim soldiers. Perhaps messers Kennedy, O'Neil, Carey et al would have seen their callous action as perfectly justifiable.

TURF LODGE
George Prosser, King's Regiment

I saw smoke coming from a large hole in the roof of the 'Disco Block' and I recall a great sense of disbelief where everything stopped and I didn't know what had hit me; this is shock. Confusion was overcome by an order from the patrol commander to follow him and we raced down four flights of steps – cocking our weapons as we ran. At the rear of the building as we ran through an alleyway, we were warned that we were in full view of the 'Murph and a secondary attack – used with great effect by the IRA – could occur. In Ardmonagh Gardens there was chaos and confusion as other patrols poured in and I got down on my belly in one of the gardens faced out towards Whiterock Road – making myself as small as possible. By now people were flooding out of their houses and there was another bang. I jumped as I knew it was a shot, but had no idea where it had come from. My heart was pounding. Things calmed a little as snap-searches were being made and we heard that someone had been killed and any door not opened immediately was kicked in. All the flats were empty apart from one in which a couple were sitting.

They were unwelcoming, but they knew from our mood that we weren't going anywhere until we had searched it. News began to filter through that one named guy had been killed, but we were not told that it was Andy Webster. A little later it was confirmed and I went into complete denial. It was such a hammer-blow, but I had to accept that there was nothing I could do about it. Back at Ardmonagh Gardens a Saracen ambulance was there and there were people milling about – including lots of children, which struck me as odd. Many of them were shocked and crying. Then we realised that the IRA had launched a bomb attack whilst a Save the Children playgroup was taking place – yes, the IRA had detonated a bomb as the children attended a nursery class! It beggars belief that the IRA, who claimed to have the interests of local people at heart, could carry out such a callous attack.

The contributor has, over the years, become a personal friend and a man I am honoured to know. Through him I have met Nell Webster, Lance-Corporal Webster's mother. She is a saddened, yet dignified lady, but to whom the loss of two sons – Andy's brother died after a severe asthma attack– the grief has taken its toll. One Kingo told the author that the IRA knew that the army used the roof for ad-hoc ops, and planting a bomb – with all the attendant risks in order to kill soldiers – was simply too good an opportunity for them to miss.

On the 10th – in the USA – a senior judge ruled that a group of men (all members of the IRA and also considered to be responsible for bombing Ripon Barracks in North Yorkshire) should not be extradited to Britain. This was situation normal for the U.S. courts

Turf Lodge, Belfast, c 1978. (©George Prosser)

at all levels – especially the Supreme Court, which for years did all that it could to delay and hinder trials and the extradition of wanted PIRA criminals (including those already convicted of murder, but who had escaped from UK jails). On one famous occasion, thanks to the lobbying of the all-powerful Irish-American lobby, the Supreme Court refused to allow an extradition hearing to take place on the incredibly spurious grounds that a form had been filled in wrongly! Defence used the argument that the crimes were political – the shooting of policemen, soldiers and prison officers and the blowing up of innocent people were adjudged to be political – and because of the U.S. Constitution, people could not be extradited for 'political crimes'. The constant lobbying from bleeding-heart Irish-American newspapers who saw the Provisional IRA as 'freedom fighters' meant that even when sympathetic, U.S. presidents from Nixon, Carter and Reagan onwards were unable to overrule these powerful institutions.

With absolutely exquisite timing – displaying no sensitivity whatsoever – Senator Edward Kennedy demanded that the British Government announce a new strategy on Northern Ireland. What he meant, echoing the Provisional IRA, was a fresh demand for a timetable of withdrawal. There should be no surprises there, as this unlamented politician once famously agreed to help with the 'repatriation of Scottish Protestants from Ulster back to Scotland'.

Back in October 1971 he said: " … Ulster is becoming Britain's Vietnam … " and demanded that British troops leave the northern counties. He called for a United Ireland and declared that Ulster Unionists who could not accept this 'should be given a decent opportunity to go back to Britain'.

On the same day that American politicians were once again involving themselves in another country's business, the British Army was forced to admit to the theft of a top-secret document written to the British Government. Further, it humiliatingly had to concede that the document had fallen into the hands of the Provisional IRA. In it, the army had analysed the last 10 years of its involvement in Northern Ireland and admitted that it could not defeat the IRA militarily – not playing by the ROE at least. With the death toll already topping 2,000 it stated that a British military presence would continue. The report stated that the army had to be prepared for PIRA to acquire within five years advanced weapon sights; anti-tank weapons; and anti-aircraft rockets such as the SAM-7, which had a range of around five miles. The report concluded that there was unlikely to be peace in the Province 'before 1983'. The compiler was only 14 years out in his predictions!

It went on to state that the report had been prepared for civil servants back in December 1978 and that the British Transport Police were investigating the theft of MOD documents after GPO mailbags had been stolen from a train travelling between Birmingham and London. It was indeed a worrying lapse in security and further demonstrated that the tentacles of Provisional IRA influence could stretch to places hitherto considered inviolate. It further brings to mind an unproven allegation – voiced by many soldiers who served – of the theft of letters home by IRA sympathisers working for the GPO. Soldiers – the author included – sent flimsy airmail envelopes home crammed with entreaties for money or sweets, or even comics or just declarations of love. These flimsies were known as 'blueys' and were a cheap and easy way to keep in touch with home.

There was a long-standing allegation that 'blueys' were being stolen at the sorting office and passed on to PIRA INT – thus providing the Provisionals with the soldiers' home addresses. There are far too many incidents involving PIRA writing to the families of dead or injured soldiers as part of the psychological warfare and mind games practised by the terror group. This author has previously written about the mental ordeals faced by loved ones – already numbed by shock at the loss of a son or a husband – when being taunted by Republicans who had learned their address. The information could have come, of course, from newspaper reports – particularly the regional press who might have written of the loss of 'such and such' from 'such and such street' in the town. Equally, the information might have been gleaned from 'blueys' falling into the wrong hands.

On the 19th, it was another 'guilt by association' death as the Provisionals killed a man who had retired from the UDR in 1975 – some four years previously. Jack McClenaghan (63) was a former part-time soldier who now worked as a delivery driver for a local bakery firm. His regular route took in Garrison, Co Fermanagh and he had been 'dicked' by a local PIRA sympathiser who knew full well that he was delivering an innocent man into the hands of his executioners. Garrison is a small village near Lough Melvin, through which runs the Roogagh River. As the former part-time soldier parked his delivery van, two masked gunmen on a stolen motorcycle pulled up alongside him and opened fire without warning. Mr McClenaghan was hit over half a dozen times and died instantly. His murderers raced down the rural B53 road and into the Irish Republic, which was less than .6 of a mile away – the amorality of their actions clearly defined by the fact that they could end an innocent man's life and then race down a road to what was, essentially, an artificial border in less than one minute and thus be immune from punishment for an act of evil. There can be no doubting the amorality of both sets of paramilitaries in the latest tranche of Troubles; none whatsoever.

On the following day – demonstrating a lack of contrition for the murder of the deliveryman and also further proof that their fanatical determination for the unachievable objective of Irish reunification blinded them to morality or decency – PIRA killed an off-duty RUCR man. It was their third attack in or close to a church in just two weeks. IRA INT had shown that David Wray (50) worshipped at Claremont Presbyterian near Pennyburn in the northern suburbs of Londonderry City. Constable Wray had just parked up outside the church and was walking towards the entrance in the company of his two children. Two armed PIRA men got out a car – which they had stolen earlier from outside a Catholic church – and walked up to the off-duty policeman and shot him several times in the back. He was mortally wounded and died very shortly afterwards as his shocked teenaged children looked on. His killers raced back to St Colman's in the Nationalist Bogside and left with its terrified owner. The killing outside a place of God and in front of shocked and innocent children horrified even the hardened ladies of the Creggan Estate – and they were moved enough to arrange flowers and letters of sympathy for Mr Wray's family deploring the murder. Did this make the killers and the men who sent them there any less unrepentant? Two weeks later and three more policemen dead – shot by Republicans – would tend to indicate no.

On the 25th – acting upon information received from a high-placed informer – a joint RUC/army operation in Lurgan, Co Armagh saved dozens of potential casualties and arrested three members of a PIRA bombing team. Lurgan is located south of Lough Neagh and some 20-plus miles from the border with the Republic. Its name is derived from the Irish an Lorgain – meaning the shin-shaped hill – and was once an important textile town. Close to midnight, three PIRA members in stolen cars drove into the centre of Lurgan and attempted to leave one of the cars – packed with explosives – close to the commercial heart of the town. Hidden SF forces pounced as the masked men ran towards the other car where a getaway driver was waiting. After a brief scuffle, all three bombers were arrested.

On the 26th, UDA leader Jim Craig was involved in what was thought to be an accidental shooting in the Royal Bar in the Shankill Road. However, other than the certainty that George Surgeoner (28) – a fellow UDA member – died, the circumstances surrounding his death are unknown. Given the air of secrecy and intimidation of witnesses with threats of death or maiming, all the circumstances of the death are unknown to all but a select few. Even Craig took the secret to his grave with him when he was shot by the UFF in the Bunch of Grapes pub in Beersbridge Road in Loyalist East Belfast in 1988. The facts of the Surgeoner shooting are somewhat hazy, but it would appear that Mr Surgeoner was in the poolroom of the Royal Bar when Craig fired a round at him – fatally wounding him. He died three days later. James 'Jim' Pratt Craig was born in Belfast and grew up in the Shankill Road. In the early 1970s, Craig – a former boxer – was sent to the Maze Prison for a criminal offence unrelated to paramilitary activities. Whilst serving his sentence at the Maze he joined the UDA and he was asked by the organisation's commander at the time, Charles Harding Smith, to take control of the UDA prisoners inside on account of his reputation as a hard man. Craig was asked by someone how he managed to maintain discipline amongst his fellow inmates. He replied: "I've got this big fucking hammer and I've told them if anybody gives me trouble, I'll break their fucking finger!"

On the 27th, the IRA returned to an earlier 'proven' tactic and attacked another bus depot. Thwarted in an attack on Andersonstown Bus Depot by the location of an army unit, they attacked the Ardoyne Depot again – planting nine bombs. Not all of the devices exploded, but damage was nonetheless substantial. All of the devices exploded late at night when the building was closed and unstaffed and there were no injuries. However, the bus company suffered financially and traffic throughout the city was disrupted and many services were curtailed. The following day, Trooper Gary Lines – (19)14/20 King's Hussars and 15/19 King's Royal Hussars – was killed in a tragic RTA thought to have involved a Saracen armoured vehicle. He was from the Newcastle-upon-Tyne area and his funeral was held in Birtley, Co Durham.

As the month drew to an end the Royal Hampshires – who were based in Londonderry – made a timely intervention of several PIRA bombers from the Creggan Estate and possibly saved lives. Three men had packed several milk churns with explosives weighing over 350lbs and had parked up in the city centre. They had placed one of the deadly devices on the pavement when they were disturbed when a patrol from 'Y' Company 1st Hampshire Regiment arrived on the scene. The bombers ran off and abandoned the four bombs – and eventually lost the pursuing soldiers in the maze of streets which made up the Nationalist Bogside. In these areas there were the 'ever open' doors of either safehouses or places of residence where the occupants had been warned not to lock up during operations. Once the PIRA volunteers were safely ensconced or had departed through the back, the doors would then be locked to searching soldiers or police.

On 3 March 1978 in the 'Rag Day murders', Trooper James Nowasad and civilian helper Norma Spence were shot dead in the centre of Belfast. On the 31st of this month, one of his killers was convicted of the cowardly murders and sentenced to a double life sentence. Close to midnight on the same day, three masked UVF gunmen attacked the family home of the jailed killer's parents on the Antrim Road. They fired several shots at random when they discovered the killer's father was not home. They caused substantial damage as anger at the cowardly killers spilled over.

Earlier in the day a staff officer – a captain – from 39 Brigade was driving into Belfast from nearby Lisburn when he had a narrow escape when he came under fire from a PIRA gunman. He was en route for the King's Base at Fort Monagh. As the officer's car, an unmarked 'Q' car, reached the junction of the Whiterock Road and the Falls Road, a gunman (who with four others had taken over a dental surgery) fired four rounds from an American Armalite – hitting the car and wounding him in the shoulder and cutting him with flying glass. Despite the injury he managed to radio the King's bases and drove into Fort Monagh where the regiment's 'B' Company was based. The King's made a fast follow-up – and following some enthusiastic and aggressive patrolling, managed to capture the gunman within 30 minutes of the murder attempt. They quickly established the firing point and discovered the getaway car used by the PIRA gang in the southern part of the Turf Lodge. Working with an ADU dog handler, the track was picked up by the highly-trained dog in the city cemetery and traced to the Bullring on the Ballymurphy Estate, where one of the gunmen was arrested.

The 2nd Battalion of the Royal Green Jackets were in action as May gave way to June with a major arrest in Strabane. A unit from the regiment – whose motto *Celer et Audux* underlies their speed of advance on the battlefield – set up a snap-VCP on the A38 Lifford Road, right on the border with the Republic. The men on the VCP were alerted by an undercover border watcher that a suspect van was coming towards them. The van approached the VCP and the driver was immediately forced to stop at the sight of armed troops cammed up and pointing SLRs at them. The business end of another SLR was aimed at them from the rear as the RGJ's cut-off man took up his well-practised position. Inside the van were two armed PIRA members, 400 rounds of ammunition and an Armalite rifle. The RUC were called and the Provisionals were two volunteers less!

The month ended with the death of an RCT officer and the circumstances of his death remain unknown. Lieutenant Nigel Brewer (22) was from the Beckenham, Kent area and the author has no further information.

In May, a total of nine people died. Five were soldiers – or former soldiers – and three were policemen or former officers. One UDA member died in what was possibly an accidental shooting. The Provisionals were responsible for six of the nine deaths during the month of May.

54

June

This month – the first of the British summer – would see the deaths of 12 more people and included four members of the UDR, four policemen and a shoot-out between what was thought to be SAS troops and PIRA (involving a future best-selling author). One of the major hypocrisies of the Northern Irish Republicans and their supporters who slammed Britain; deplored the presence of British troops on their streets; fought the lawful police organisation; and refused to fly the Union flag was/is their eagerness to grasp State handouts with open hands. Many were quick to deprecate and vilify the UK, but even quicker when it came to collecting unemployment and other social security payments. It would have come as an awful shock on the morning of the 1st when it was discovered that the previous day the Provisionals had stormed into Belfast's main DHSS building, held up staff and planted bombs which caused major damage. This author would have enjoyed being a 'fly on the wall' when it was announced to the claimants that payments were delayed courtesy of the Provisional IRA.

On the 2nd, a murder gang from INLA set out to kill a policeman at his home in Armagh City. RUCR Constable David Dunne (36) had just reversed out of his drive in Ballinahone Crescent – just on the eastern outskirts of the city – intending to drive to nearby Gough Barracks for his shift as a part-time policeman. As he was about to drive off he noticed one of his friends, David Stinson (31), a fellow darts player. Between them they had eight children. As Mr Stinson leaned into the RUCR man's car, a stolen car containing several INLA gunmen pulled close by and the men inside opened fire with automatic weapons – mortally wounding both men. Constable Dunne's son said later: "I ran to where my father was lying on the ground. When I saw the blood on his shoulder, I knew that he had been shot and I ran to get help." (*Lost Lives*, p.786) Both men died before an ambulance arrived. The Irish National Liberation Army – brainchild of Seamus Costello and home to psychopaths such as Gerard Steenson, Dominic McGlinchey and Seamus Grew – had left eight children fatherless in their pursuit of an impossible goal.

The town of Strabane has its name taken from the Irish an Srath Bán, which means the white Strath, or large river valley. It was historically spelt 'Straban' and is located in the western part of Co Tyrone. It has a population of around 20,000 and is the second-largest town in Tyrone after Omagh – lying on the east bank of the River Foyle. It is roughly equidistant from Omagh, Derry and Letterkenny. The Foyle marks the border between Northern Ireland and the Republic of Ireland. On the other side of the river and inside the Republic is the smaller town of Lifford, which is the county town of Co Donegal. The River Mourne flows through the centre of the town and meets the River Finn to form the Foyle. Strabane suffered huge economic damage in 1987 when much of the centre of the town was flooded and was a hotbed of Republican terrorism throughout the course of the Troubles.

Among the many seminal moments of the Troubles the murder of Gary Barlow, who was disarmed before being killed, is one which springs to mind. The following story by a

Patrol brief, Royal Artillery, Armagh, Christmas 1979. (©Walter Stirling)

Patrol brief, Royal Artillery, Armagh, Christmas 1979. (©Walter Stirling)

Green Jacket has ominous undertones of the Barlow murder – and whilst Mel Price was not abducted, the outcome might just have easily been the same.

STRABANE
Mel Price, 3rd Battalion, Royal Green Jackets

The following is my account of an incident which happened to me on a patrol in Strabane:

I was on a quick three-man patrol around the town centre – just to show a military presence – and we were only three because we were under strength. I think our platoon only had about 19 or 20 at the time instead of the standard 24-30. On the way to the town centre from the police station I noticed that the film playing at the cinema was Carry on England, but the word 'England' had a sticker over it which said 'Banging'. It was changed so as not to upset the locals. It was utterly pathetic in my opinion! I was 'tail-end Charlie' and as we came down

NOTICE OF ARRIVAL

Issued in solemn warning this _____ day of _____ 1978 is hereby given to the Friends/Neighbours/Wife/Girlfriend/Parents of

No _____ Rank _____ Name _____

Regt/Corps _____

Within the near future the above mentioned will enter once again into your midst to take up his place as a human being, in a free, safe and civilised society and to take up, once more, his delayed pursuit of happiness.

In preparation for his return you are advised to make considerable allowances for the crude environment, extreme poverty and lack of contact with the fair sex which has been his misery for the past four months. In all probability he will be suffering from a certain form of lunacy known as Op Banner Fever (official name for a tour in Northern Ireland). During the next few weeks (until he again becomes house broken) it would be advisable to be especially watchful when he is in the company of women, particularly young beautiful ones. Parents are advised to keep their daughters indoors during this period. It must be explained in all fairness, that his intentions are sincere even though they are of a dishonourable nature.

Treat him with kindness, tolerance and vast quantities of beer, wine, spirits, food, alka seltza, cigarettes, money, parties and holidays so that eventually the _____ you once knew will emerge from the hollow shell he is now.

Generally speaking, except for the odd grunt and a tendency to stare in wonder at carpets, settees, and other forms of comfortable furniture, he will be fairly calm and amiable. Your advised, however, to show no signs of alarm if he prefers to stand for hours, searching the odd passer-by or only allows visitors into the house after they have produced positive identifications. Be patient too if he climbs into the attic, removes a tile and scrutinises the surrounding area for two hours at a time. Just tell him when his two hours are up and he will probably be quite happy to keep you company for the next four hours. He will we hope, soon tire of this routine. Probably the three most important things to remember are:-

1. Make no complimentary comments about the Army.

2. Never suggest that he should help in the house chores, his reply will be most vile.

3. Try to keep him away from Irish neighbours and friends.

The following trends in behaviour and mannerisms are forwarded to you with suggested remedies which we hope will prove effective.

1. On seeing you read a paper or magazine he will shout 'was up? pass him the paper when you have finished. On no account pass it to a third person once he has shouted.

2. If you find him standing outside the kitchen door muttering two 'choggie burgers' make him two hamburgers and fill a plastic cup with tea or coffee. He will probably say 'book' make a list of what he has in a book until pay day.

3. If he keeps dodging in and out of doorways when he goes shopping just ignore him and keep walking. Only time will cure this peculiar habit.

4. If he can only sleep for four hours at a time, don't worry, there is no remedy for this, it can only be hoped that in time, his nightly slumbers will resume a normal pattern.

5. If you take him for a drink and he refuses to drink more than two pints tactfully explain to him that he may drink more if he wishes. He may be insistent that he cannot drink more, (which is very doubtful) if so do not attempt to force him.

6. He may insist on following any workmen around the house and staying with them while they carry out their task. This is a Forces Habit which is more common in case of acute Op Banner Fever. The only advice that can be offered is again to be patient and hope that time will cure the complaint.

7. It is possible that he will utter statements which could easily be misunderstood. Such as asking you to 'check his weapon' (meaning rifle) or ask for a 'P' Check. He is not being rude but has merely forgotten where he is. Re-assurance is the key in curing this complaint tell him his rifle is clear or in the case of a 'P' Check stand up, put your arms above your head and allow him to search you. If you do not he may become violent.

8. It is possible that he will work weekends and most evenings. Attempt to explain to him that there are such things as weekends in normal life. He may find this difficult to understand.

9. If he rushes outside at 0745hrs, empties dustbins and picks up cigarette ends tell him that there is not an inspection this morning. He will grin and answer " _____ good show".

10. He may prefer to eat all meals on a tray. Explain to him that a plate is and the different types available.

11. Do not wrap his gifts which you may intend to give him in brown paper as he will panic and immerse the parcels in a bucket of water.

12. Advise your younger children and those of neighbours not to point toy guns at him. He may put them some place where it would require major surgery to remove them.

13. If you are walking down a street and a car backfires, look for him in the nearest doorway or behind the nearest hedge or wall.

We sincerely trust the information given will be an aid to the rehabilitation of your son/husband/relative/boy friend/friend. Treat him with kindness and he will soon become the person you once knew. One of the most essential things to remember, is that if he should talk of volunteering or even accepting another Op Banner Tour he needs instant medical attention.

A final word of advice:-

Fill the refrigerator with beer, look all females in their rooms and get his civilian clothes out of moth balls.

Officer in charge of
Rehabilitation and Civilisation
(Army Section)

His Mark _____

Date _____

Letter given to all members of B Company 2 Royal Green Jackets, South Armagh, to send home to parents etc. (©Gary Cootes)

he scene of the helicopter crash at Jonesborough last Friday in hich Col Iain D Corden-Lloyd was killed and two others injured.

RGJ ARRIVE IN S ARMAGH

The Second Battalion The Royal Green Jackets have arrived in S Armagh, relieving the First Battalion The Queens Lancashire Regiment.

The Battalion, commanded by Lt Col I D Corden-Lloyd, OBE, MC, has returned from two years in sunny Gibraltar to spend Christmas in the Winter wonderland of Ulster's border area. 1 QLR are off home to a spell of well deserved leave followed by a tour in Cyprus. Lucky Devils!

the right: "All yours chum!!"
Noel Shepherd (1 QLR)
ts Cpl Joe Hider (2 RGJ).

FROM FRIENDS WHO LOVE
THE LORD AND CARE
ABOUT YOU — HE CARES ALSO.

ULSTER 1978
THANK YOU TO ALL OUR
SECURITY FORCES

Mosaic of newspaper clippings related to 2 Royal Green Jackets
in South Armagh, 1978. (©Gary Cootes)

a narrow street into the town square I noticed that there were the usual groups of unemployed men just hanging around – as well as people going about their daily business.

The other two in front of me had just gone around the corner and I saw about four men standing in the doorway of a bar. As back man, just for a second or two, I was out of view. As I got to the corner a man come past me and I immediately recognised him as a suspect who was on the watch list in the ops room. He was not a player, but was a bit of a 'gofer' and a trouble-maker trying to prove himself. As he drew level with me he pushed me sideways and instinctively I lashed out with the butt of my SLR, but it did not make good contact. At the same time a pair of hands grabbed the collar of my flak jacket and I went down. Immediately boots started to lay into me, but I did not feel them much as I was having a tug of war with the guy who pushed me. He had hold of the wrist sling, which he was trying to pull free – and although this was only a few seconds, believe me it felt a lot longer.

Fortunately the two soldiers in front of me saw what was happening and came running back towards me. I suppose they could have shot him as he was trying to get the SLR and I heard a weapon being cocked and saw the barrel of an SLR shoved in the face of my assailant. He then wisely let go of the sling and the ones doing the kicking disappeared into the crowd. I am glad nobody shot him because a large crowd had gathered and as I said earlier, it was a narrow street and the situation could have been made a lot worse. We had the guy under arrest but our QRF were busy elsewhere and the RUC took ages to come. The crowd became louder and aggressive with the standard foul-mouthed hags spitting and swearing. Anyway the three of us backed up the street with the prisoner towards the Hump VCP – but then the RUC arrived and we were able to leave the area. Yes it would have been easier to leave the toe-rag, but that would have lost us face – and the next time the mob would have been more adventurous. I did not think much about it at the time, but when I look at the other things that have happened – the two signals corporals for instance and Gary Barlow – I realise how it could have had a different ending if I hadn't hung on to my SLR for dear life.

The following day two more policemen were killed – this time by a PIRA bomb close to Silverbridge in Co Armagh. The Provisionals had been developing the black art of death by explosions for almost 10 years by this stage of the Troubles. By 1979 they were masters of killing and had developed a bomb expertise which was envied by other terror groups throughout the world. The PLO, Italian Red Army Faction, German Baader-Meinhof, Peru's Shining Path, Columbian FARC and Spain's ETA were all admirers of PIRA. Indeed, there was a programme of mutual co-operation between the Irish terror groups and their global compatriots. On this warm June day a joint RUC/army search operation was taking place in the area of Clonalig and Sheelagh close to Crossmaglen. The Queen's Own Highlanders were in the vicinity – soon to have their own tragedy in the coming weeks – and were aware of suspicious activity in the area. A QOH patrol had gone firm and observing two policemen – including a very senior officer walking towards the Sheelagh Youth Club – warned them not to proceed. There is much conjecture at this stage in relation to why the two RUC chose to keep on walking. One QOH saw them reach a wall and then saw and felt a huge explosion. When the smoke had cleared both officers lay dead – killed instantly and torn apart by the huge blast.

Knowing that the SF men would be certain to investigate reports of a suspect device in a nearby hall, the IRA had planted a huge device behind a wall and their bombing crew triggered it electronically as soon as the two men were in killing range. Superintendent Stanley Hanna (48) – father of three from South Belfast – and Constable Kevin Thompson (23) were the two dead policemen. The young constable, from Portrush, was due to be married in September and had been in the RUC for less than two years. The following day, south of the border, Gardaí Siochana officers arrested three PIRA men in Co Monaghan and they were held for questioning. A Crossmaglen OIRA member was later charged with the double killing and for the killing of a soldier the following month. He was cleared on the Silverbridge bomb deaths, but found guilty of killing a QOH soldier (see Chapter 55).

Three days later – as Normandy veterans throughout the world prepared to commemorate the 35th anniversary of the Allied landings in France on D-Day – the Provisionals attacked a full-time UDR barracks in a leafy Belfast suburb. 10 (City of Belfast) UDR were based at Malone Road approximately a mile south of Belfast City Centre. It was a typical 'hit and run' attack and a stolen lorry was reversed close to the camp late on the morning of the 6th. A salvo of at least 40 shots from automatic weapons was fired into the camp and four soldiers were hit. One of the PIRA men then threw a homemade hand grenade towards the wounded men, but it failed to cause any damage or further injury to them. All four collapsed to the ground, but one man – Private Alexander Gore (23) – was mortally wounded and died shortly afterwards. He had only been in the UDR for 16 months and he left a young, pregnant widow and a young son. The pair had only been married since February of this year. Colour Sergeant J.B. saw the mortally wounded soldier being dragged in by D.D., who was bravely trying to drag him to safety – ignoring his own head wound. J.B. ran across to help.

The gunmen raced off but opened fire on an off-duty RUC officer standing on Tate's Avenue. The policeman returned fire and the lorry drove off to be later abandoned near Milltown Cemetery. One former UDR soldier told the author: "Alex Gore, who was killed in the attack; his son used to come out with us on Remembrance Day to talk to people who knew his dad as he was only a baby when he got shot. He later joined the army himself and has done a couple of tours in Afghanistan. There is a postscript to Alex Gore's killing, as I found out from his widow when we met. There has only been one man convicted of the murder – the driver of the getaway car by the name of Brendan Patrick Mead. He also escaped from the Maze in the big breakout in 1983 and was released under the GFA. The HET has also completed the new investigation into the killing and found no new evidence, so the family still don't know who the shooters were and have probably walked past them in Belfast – or they indeed could be MLAs at Stormont ... who knows."

THE ATTACK ON 10 UDR AT THE MALONE COMPLEX
Corporal T.H., UDR

On 6 June 1979 I was a serving corporal at the Malone Complex – also known as Windsor Park Barracks – employed in the company office when the attack took place. A tipper lorry came down the Malone Road and stopped beside the fence of the complex opposite the garage. Everyone was doing their normal routine and no-one really noticed the lorry stopping. As a consequence, the attackers had the element of surprise.

I recall that the attackers threw an explosive device over the fence, which resulted in everyone diving to the ground when it exploded. The explosion was quickly followed by automatic fire from two gunmen at the back of the lorry. At the side of the fence was a portacabin running alongside and inside was sections of soldiers who were coming off or going out on patrols. The gunmen targeted this as they knew that there would be men inside – spraying it with automatic fire. Luckily enough, not one was hit or injured. They then fired at the company office where I was, but again there were no injuries. Sadly, the initial blast hit Private Alex Gore and Corporal D.D. (The author is aware of the identity of the wounded soldier, but has been requested to omit his name) as they were coming out of the main building and turning a corner towards the portacabins.

Private Gore was hit in the centre of the chest and Corporal D.D. was hit in the forehead. Just then the firing stopped and the terrorists drove off down the Malone Road in the direction of Belfast. I had a very good look at one of the gunmen and it looked as though he was out of his head on drugs. His eyes were wide and staring. Things started to settle down and soldiers began to emerge from cover and I was sent out to check on the injured. When I turned into the main entrance to the guardroom I saw Alex Gore just outside the main doors – being treated by two Greenfinches – and was clearly unconscious with blood pumping out of his chest. The Greenfinches were calling for more field dressings in order to stem the loss of blood. Shortly after this, civvie ambulances arrived at the scene – but I believe that it was too late for him and he was certified dead at the hospital.

The following information is taken from the Historical Enquires Team (HET) examination of the death of Alexander Gore. I am indebted to his son, Alex Jnr, and also to Mark 'C' for permission to use this.

About 9am a red, open-back tipper lorry was hijacked in Andersonstown Road, Belfast close to the junction with Finaghy Road North by two armed men who said they were from the Provisional IRA. At 11.18am the lorry drove along Malone Road in the direction of the city centre and stopped outside the headquarters of 10 UDR. About 40-50 high-velocity and low-velocity rounds were fired into the camp. Alexander (Gore), who had been standing near a flagpole talking to some colleagues, was struck in the chest and three of his colleagues were also injured in the attack. The lorry then sped off into Windsor Avenue. A motorist driving behind the lorry followed it for a short distance, but stopped when he was fired at by the gunmen. An off-duty policeman – who was re-fuelling his car at Malone Road – saw the lorry and fired two shots at it, but it is not known if either shot hit anyone. The lorry, with a man standing in the back, was next seen speeding along Tate's Avenue. The gunmen fired four or five shots at the patrol, but no-one was injured. The police did not return fire and the lorry was later found abandoned in Milltown Row, Andersonstown.

The report continues to describe how Private Gore was taken to Belfast City Hospital where he was pronounced dead at 11.50am – some 32 minutes after the attack was launched.

The report continues:

Later that day a statement was issued by the Republican Press Office, Falls Road, Belfast in which the Provisional IRA admitted they had carried out the attack on 7 June 1979. Police arrested five suspects – four of whom were interviewed and released without charge. One, Brendan James Mead, admitted his involvement in Alexander's murder. In 1980 Mead was convicted of Alexander's murder and sentenced to life imprisonment. He was also convicted of other crimes connected with the attack, for which he received prison sentences ranging from three to 15 years – all to run concurrently with the life sentence. He was released from custody on life licence on 15 August 1994 having served 15 years and two months' imprisonment.

He was also convicted of the attempted murder of two UDR privates; causing an explosion; possession of firearms; possession of explosives; hijacking of a lorry; and membership of PIRA. He was sentenced to a further 75 years in prison, to run concurrently.

(Mead) told officers that he had been a member of the IRA for about 11 months and that the attack on the UDR barracks was planned during the evening of Tuesday, 5 June 1979. His role was to hijack a lorry and drive it along during the attack. He described how early on the morning of Wednesday, 6 June he and others completed a 'dry run' of the route – during which he was told to stop precisely outside the UDR camp. He then hijacked a lorry from St Catherine's – an area close to his home – and took the (hijacked) driver to a house in the Whiterock area where he was to be held. Others with rifles then got onto the back of the lorry and he drove it to Malone Road. His instructions were to drive off when he heard shooting. He described the route back after the attack and remembered hearing shooting on the way. He drove back to St Catherine's and into the grounds of St Louise's School, where the gunmen got off. He then abandoned the lorry in Milltown Row.

Mead was one of the Maze 'Great Escapers' and his part in the Maze Prison escape of September 1983 is covered in the author's next book *(Northern Ireland 1980-83: An Agony Continued)*.

There was a further postscript to this sad story when it emerged that the soldier's grave had fallen into a state of disrepair and his widow was unable to pay for restoration work to be carried out. Duncan Elder in the *Newtownabbey News* wrote in August 2013:

Private Alexander Gore, a full-time soldier with the Ulster Defence Regiment's 10th Battalion, was killed in June 1979 in an IRA gun and grenade attack at a military base on the Malone Road in Belfast. He was 23 years old. Private Gore, from the Sandy Row area of Belfast, had only been married a few months. He was laid to rest beside his father in Carnmoney Cemetery. Over the years the granite headstone had become badly weathered and was in poor condition. Seeing that the stone could do with some attention, a group of big-hearted ex-servicemen and supporters of the Armed Forces from the Newtownabbey area chipped in for it to be professionally repaired. His widow said: 'The fellas paid the money themselves to have this done and I am extremely grateful to them. I can't thank them enough.' She added: 'They're not classed as war graves so the Commonwealth War Graves Commission don't bother with them, but whether they served here or abroad they were still British soldiers and their graves should be looked after – especially their headstones.'

Also on the 6th, the Irish Government – *Rialtas na hÉireann* – announced that it was adding an additional 1,000 new recruits to its army in order to 'reduce border terrorist activities'. A former officer, who didn't wish to be identified, told the author:

For those among us who enjoyed a good laugh, we thought that Eire's announcement of additional troops was just an April Fool's joke until we realised that it was June! But it had to be a joke because those of us who served in the border areas just knew that both the Gardaí and the Irish Army didn't have the will – nor inclination – and certainly not the ability to do anything. I have stood and watched in utter rage and frustration as cars or terrorists fleeing on foot have glided by Gardaí roadblocks with impunity – and then seeing the Free State Forces, stand-to to prevent us following. On one occasion, near Cullaville, we had an IRA man – still armed – run up a country road after shooting at my chaps and then throw his weapon into a bush in plain sight of an Irish Army mobile patrol and then just saunter past them. The Irish soldiers took no notice whatsoever and he just escaped, scot-free. We knew that his mates would recover the weapon under cover of darkness, but we were not permitted to cross over and wait for them. It was damned frustrating, but I am convinced that the Irish Government briefed their so-called border patrols to do a 'Nelson'.

As 'Ulsterisation' continued apace, the Northern Ireland Police Federation – the 'trade union' of the RUC – made an announcement on the 7th stating that British Army activity in the tough border areas was on the decline. An HQNI spokesman was quick to counter this – claiming that helicopter activity was in fact on the increase; that more troops were now stationed on the border; and that they were working longer hours. Moreover there were more undercover soldiers in the field, but the regular soldiers were only able to operate VCPs for a maximum of 15 minutes as terrorists were quickly alerted to their presence and that cross-border snipings were set up. The announcement by the Police Federation was yet more evidence of the new policy of 'RUC primacy' and the dissension between themselves and the military.

On the 8th, the UDR lost another soldier – this time to that ubiquitous of causes: an RTA. Corporal Ivan McCorkell (23) was killed in an on-duty traffic accident. No further details are known.

NEARLY FATAL
Kevin Campbell, King's Own Scottish Borderers

During our summer 1979 tour of West Belfast, we were on QRF at North Howard Street Mill with our Tactical HQ (Tac HQ) being at nearby Springfield Road RUC Station. This is around 2,000 feet – or less than half a mile – as the crow flies and has the Falls and Cupar Street sandwiched menacingly in between. I forget the exact time of day, but we received a report of a contact at Tac HQ and our company commander, Major 'H', called out the QRF with himself in attendance.

We raced to the scene – and given the short distance, were there within minutes. I have a photo of the incident and all these years later I don't need to look at it, as it is crystal-clear in my mind's eye. I remember seeing the RVH (Royal Victoria Hospital) on the Falls Road and in the middle distance, a soft-skinned Bedford four-tonne lorry. What had happened was that as it exited the rear of the RUC station onto Cavendish Street, it came under heavy fire from one of the houses close to the rear exit. The rounds were fired from about 15 or 20 feet, with a further volley of small-arms fire both sides.

The truck was manned by a driver and escort – and whilst I am unsure of the exact regiment, I am led to believe that it was the 'Duke of Boots' (Duke of Wellington's) and the escort was one of our company medics. The first burst caught both men and the driver was shot through the neck and in the face. The medic – although wounded – got out of the truck and in the face of continued heavy fire, ran round the front and dragged the driver into cover despite suffering further injuries himself.

When we arrived there were still gunshots coming from the rear of the house – and our officer shouted to us to go through the door and follow up. Something wasn't right and our section commander, Lance-Corporal Jim Black, shouted out that it was a 'come on' and to us to hold our positions – much to the officer's dismay. Anyway we set up a cordon whilst our neighbouring company followed up through the churchyard at the rear, but the IRA had done their usual 'shoot and scoot'.

It transpired that the house had been taken over the night before and the elderly residents – a couple – were taken hostage. Through the night, the PIRA ASU had constructed a massive and most deadly booby-trap. When the house was finally made safe, a gigantic nail-bomb was found on the stairs at chest-height facing the front door. Had that detonated, any human body within its deadly range would have been literally shredded! Thank God Jim had the sense to realise it was a 'come on' and stopped us following up. I've said it before, but that man saved my 17-year-old arse on more than one occasion. It was following this incident that they stopped using soft-skinned vehicles for deliveries; they had learned their lesson, but way too late. As for the aforementioned officer (name removed by the author), he clearly hadn't learned a lesson and took the whole company – including me – on a road run-out of the mill up the Falls and then into the Springfield Road, Cupar Street areas and finally down the Shankill and back to the mill. The lads did the run in denims, boots and military sweatshirts with only two vehicles and four weapons covering us. He even brought all the sections in from ops – leaving each OP dangerously undermanned. There were consequences to his career which I will not mention here, but the big thing was that he lost the respect of every single soldier serving under him.

Sorry for the rant, but all these memories seem to roll into each other and I'm shaking with anger and fear as I write this 33 years afterwards.

Three days after the killing of Private Gore, two Republican paramilitaries died in separate incidents. In the first the UFF targeted OIRA member Joseph McKee (34), who was also employed as a bouncer at an amusement arcade in Belfast City Centre. He had been targeted by UFF members from the Woodvale area and they had stolen a motorcycle to make a quick entry and exit to the scene of the intended killing. The Loyalists were aware of his movements – and of the fact that on a Saturday morning he always visited a butchers' shop close to where he worked in Castle Street (and not far from the Abercorn Restaurant which had been bombed by PIRA in March 1972). As the OIRA man stood outside the butchers', the stolen motorcycle approached him and the pillion passenger fired four times at very close range into the back of his head. McKee died instantly and his Loyalist killers sped off and later abandoned the motorcycle on the Ardoyne, but close to the safety – for them – of the Crumlin Road.

Later on the same day a PIRA ASU attempted to carry out a rocket attack from the back of a stolen lorry on a Royal Green Jackets patrol in Keady, Co Armagh. The ASU – which included Dessie O'Hare, the so-called 'Border Fox' – opened fire on soldiers. Their aim was bad however, and the Jackets – professional soldiers to a man – once alerted to the presence of gunmen returned fire – hitting three of the IRA men. Both O'Hare and Peadar McElvenna (24) were amongst the wounded and the driver of the lorry managed to drive off in the direction of the border. However it paused outside the home of a PO who lived nearby, but – alerted by the gunfire – he had already equipped himself with his shotgun and was prepared. When the men on the truck began shooting at his house, he opened fire and possibly inflicted more hits on the already-wounded men.

The lorry then raced down the B3 road, which is a short six-mile drive to Bree on the border – abandoning a getaway car in the process. From there the wounded were taken to Monaghan Hospital for treatment, but McElvenna was already dead; another PIRA

Crumlin Road area looking towards Holy Cross, Belfast. (©Brian Sheridan)

On patrol, Royal Artillery, Armagh, 1979. (©Walter Stirling)

martyr had been created. There was one exception, and that was O'Hare, who hijacked a car – and although wounded twice, managed to lead the Gardaí on a cross-country chase through Co Monaghan before he crashed and was arrested. The police on both sides of the border linked him to a series of killings and attacks – including the attempted murder of UUP member Jim Nicholson.

It is rumoured that best-selling military author Andy McNab – a former Green Jacket who later joined the SAS – was honoured for his part in the action with a MM. O'Hare later joined the INLA. O'Hare had previously joined the South Armagh Brigade of the Provisional IRA at the age of 16 and was part of a unit that targeted off-duty members of the RUC and UDR. His colleagues nicknamed him the 'Border Fox' following his escape from a number of shoot-outs with the Garda Síochána and the RUC. In 1975 he was convicted for the first time for possession of explosives and received a suspended sentence. In October 1977 O'Hare and his unit killed Margaret Ann Hearst – a part-time UDR member – in front of her three-year-old daughter (see Chapter 34). He was also linked to a series of killings and attacks – including the attempted murder of Ulster Unionist Party politician Jim Nicholson. He once famously told journalists that he was only interested in 'the bomb and the bullet' and did not believe in politics. He also confessed to murdering 26 people. At his trial in 1980 he was sentenced to nine years' imprisonment for possession of a firearm. He was released in 1986. The following year he was at it again – and after kidnapping a Dublin dentist in 1987 and cutting off two of his fingers, he was recaptured. He was imprisoned until 2006 when he was granted extended temporary release. To date, he is a free man.

On the 10th, PIRA again tried to plant a car bomb in Londonderry City Centre but were thwarted by the army. A stolen car containing two milk churns packed with 200lbs of explosives was left close to the city's commercial heart. ATO were called, and assisted by 'Y' Company of the Royal Hampshires, were able to defuse both devices and the car was removed – together with absolutely invaluable forensic evidence including the 'signature' of the bomb-maker.

Readers of the author's previous works which covers 1973-74 (*Sir, They're Taking the Kids Indoors*) will be aware of the Birmingham pub bombings of 21 November 1974 which killed 21 people and injured 182. Just 56 months later, the clearly 'sensitive' Provisionals again attacked Britain's 'Second City'. On the 12th, a package exploded in a Royal Mail sorting office in the city and seven employees were injured – some seriously. After the 1974 bombings there had been such a backlash in a city with a proud Irish heritage and culture that it was considered that Birmingham would not be targeted again. However, on that day 13 devices either exploded or were defused at post offices in the Birmingham area. Photographs from the time show the aftermath of the explosions with bags of mail littering the ground and security guards helping shocked workers away from the sorting office. A police spokesman said: "Only minor injuries were caused by those that exploded. The incidents necessitated protracted searches being undertaken at postal sorting offices – and the manner in which this dangerous work was carried out reflected highly upon the officers concerned."

On the 16th, 'B' Squadron of the Queen's Own Hussars (QOH) was patrolling the Andersonstown area in Saracen-armoured vehicles when they came under attack from the Provisionals. The QOH (motto: *Nec Aspera Terrent,* which translates as: *Nor do difficulties deter*) mobile patrol was passing by one of the regular markets in the area – and civilians were clearly in evidence when PIRA gunmen opened fire. With a clear disregard for the safety of the innocents, several shots were fired at the soldiers – with just two striking one of the vehicles, but also hitting two women and a small child who were close by. The three injured were immediately rushed to hospital with a military escort, but fortunately all three survived. The QOH would lose three soldiers the following month.

On the 19th, Private John Hannigan (33) became the first of two UDR soldiers to be killed by Republicans in the space of just five days when he was shot en route for work. A total of three SF members would die in this brief period and 12 children would be left fatherless. Private Hannigan also worked in the cemeteries department of Omagh City Council and as he walked to work on a bright, sunny morning he called into a sweet shop. When he emerged, gunmen – who had been waiting in a parked stolen car – walked over to him and shot him five times in the chest and a further twice in the head as he lay helpless and fatally wounded in the street. Two PIRA members were later convicted and jailed for their part in the cowardly murder of the father of three – one of whom was also convicted of the murder of John Graham in April of this same year at Seskinore, Co Tyrone (see Chapter 52).

SHOOT TO KILL
Lance-Corporal, Green Howards

Ok, I have read much on this subject – especially as we are now having all these bloody inquiries about how we didn't fight fair and how we shot first and asked questions later – and it is getting on my tits! Before you asked me to write for you, I had just read that there is going to be an inquiry into how the SAS didn't stick to the rules. What fucking rules? They weren't any as far as the IRA were concerned. They just shot without warning and the more helpless a target, the better for those cowardly twats!

Take for example the killing of that UDR lad in Omagh. He were just on his way to work. He was unarmed and popped into a spice shop (confectionery) to buy some spice to eat on his way in. He obviously had been dicked and the IRA knew his journey patterns. So up they pop and shoot him down like a dog outside the shop. What warning did they give him? Did they abide by the rules of engagement? Did they offer him a chance of surrender? Did they fuck! And yet, when one of their lot got shot down by us they were whining and whingeing and complaining about 'rules' and now we have all these investigations and inquiries. They make me sick. They'd kill us in cold blood without a second thought and drink in their slum pubs and cheer about 'killing a Brit' – and then when the same thing happened to them they'd be whining and crying to the Yanks and European Courts of Justice. I'm only sorry that we weren't allowed to take more of the bastards out! Martyrs? I would have loved the chance to create a few more of the bastards. I'd have given them more martyrs to sob into their pints over.

The previous comment from someone I know well might contain some most controversial views, but I can understand the bitterness and the frustration which he expresses. This author may not always agree with the views of the oral contributors, but on this occasion would be hard-pressed to argue with him.

On the same day of the murder of the off-duty UDR soldier, the IRA bombed five seaside resort hotels throughout the Province. In the most serious attack they bombed the Marine Hotel in Ballycastle, Co Antrim – terribly injuring one guest. William Whitten was rushed to hospital with serious burns and he spent just over six weeks in hospital fighting for his life. He died as a result of those bombing injuries on 3 August (see Chapter 56).

The day after, Francis Sullivan (34) – and the father of two toddlers – was killed by the UFF at his home in the Falls Road area in what was a blatant sectarian murder. Mr Sullivan – a Catholic – lived in Bombay Street, which today sits in the shadows of the permanent metal 'Peace Line' which separate Cupar Way and Loyalist territory from the Nationalist Falls area. Today, one can stand in the side garden of 2 Bombay Street and stare up at the hideous metal and mesh structure which has Berlinised this part of West Belfast. The very fact that it still stands – some 18 years after the end of hostilities – bears witness to the fact that there still needs to be sectarian separation for the safety of both sides of the divide. In June 1979 Bombay Street was different. The houses were blackened terracing and the 'Peace Line' not so permanent. Back then there was easier access for the Loyalist murder gangs – and on the 20th they knocked on the front door of Mr Sullivan's home and asked his wife if he was in. When he went to see who was there they produced a pistol and chased him towards the rear of the house – watched by his terrified family. As he reached the kitchen, one of the men fired one round into his back – mortally wounding him – before walking calmly out of the house. He died shortly after reaching the nearby RVH.

The first day of the British summer dawned and the longest day of the year saw the King's Regiment in action again as their tour neared its end. It had been eventful – with the loss of three popular soldiers – and the Merseyside-based unit was no doubt looking forward to a home posting and some relative peace. They were involved on both the 21st and the 22nd – with 1 Kings in Belfast's Ballymurphy Estate being particularly involved. A search of one garden discovered a well-hidden weapons' hide beneath paving stones of a house in Glenalina Park. The search team, led by CSM Wearing, discovered a milk churn – inside which were an Armalite rifle, a 9mm pistol, safety fuse and almost 500 rounds of ammunition. On the following night the Kingos were again involved in major disturbances after making arrests in drinking dens in the Whiterock and Ballymurphy districts. 'A' and 'C' Companies were forced to fire baton rounds before being evacuated from the area as the rioting rapidly escalated into an out-of-control and highly dangerous situation. Bottles and chairs, glasses and bar stools had been hurled with venom at the soldiers – and six members of 'A' Company were injured.

There was also a UFF attempt to kill Catholic drinkers at Murdoch's Bar at the corner of Springfield Road and Cupar Street – and very close to the sectarian murder of Francis Sullivan just 48 hours earlier. The bar – formerly known as The Orient – was 'suspected' by Loyalists to be a PIRA haunt, but the truth of the matter is that any Catholic bar was a legitimate target in their bigoted eyes. Today, a bar bearing the name stands on nearby Springfield Crescent – and on the night of the 22nd, a member of the UFF slipped an explosive device into the pocket of a jacket hanging up in the cloakroom of Murdoch's. Fortunately, it did not fully detonate and the smouldering clothing was thrown into the street (where it was later made safe).

Also on the 22nd, the Provisionals shot and killed a part-time policeman at Ardboe, Co Tyrone as he went about his normal work duties. Reserve Constable John Scott (49),

H Block riot, Durham Street/Grosvenor Road, Belfast 1979 – 25
Field Regiment, Royal Artillery. (©Mark 'C')

father of nine, drove milk tankers for a living and his rounds included the Lough Neagh area. He had clearly been observed by PIRA dickers – and his movements patiently monitored and noted – and his murder had been planned with equal patience. In mid-afternoon he reached Hill's Corner, close to Coagh and the battery, when a PIRA gunman armed with an American Armalite stepped into the road and shot him several times in the head. Mortally wounded, the RUCR man lost control and the tanker crashed into a hedge. Moments later another car arrived on the scene and the gunman ran off. However, as the driver reached Constable Scott, he could see that he was already dead. He was due to celebrate his silver wedding anniversary in July and a massive family celebration was planned. The same Armalite was later taken from the body of one of two PIRA men killed in a shoot-out with the SAS in late 1983.

THE UDR
Marcus Townley, Welsh Guards
There is absolutely no doubt in my mind that the bravest people I met during the Troubles has got to be the Ulster Defence Regiment. During my service in the Province we came into close contact on numerous occasions – be it joint patrols and/or VCPs. It's ironic really, but in my opinion they were much friendlier than the RUC. Often, before a town patrol, you would go to the INT cell for briefing and tasking to be met by the smiling, friendly faces of these gallant people. What I admired was the cheerful way they went about their task – which was to try and bring a peaceful solution to their native country – only to be attacked and killed by their fellow (sic) countrymen. They never gave their names, but beneath the joyful smiling faces their eyes gave away the huge amount of stress that had to endure – and after the patrol was over we offered our hands to them to thank them for their help that particular night, but they would simply say words along the lines of: "No, thank you and please stay safe." After over 30 years I am still humbled by these brave gentlemen and ladies of the Ulster Defence Regiment.

Sadly I had to attend the aftermath of one poor soul's murder. Sorry I can't remember the time or place, but it was just north of Bessbrook between 1979 and 1980. A UDR reservist was shot and killed at his remote cottage. I attended with my company commander, Major 'G', as his escort. The lad's car windscreen was shattered and there was a pool of blood where his life was swept away. The gable end of his house was pockmarked with the strikes of the rounds. What struck me was how peaceful and quiet the whole scene was. Another sad life snuffed out.

The UDR man was Private Joseph Porter (64) and one of the oldest members of the SF to be killed in the Troubles. He lived at Mountnorris in Co Armagh and was shot and killed at his home by an IRA murder squad on 24 June 1979. Private Porter lived alone at Creggan Road and at least two armed PIRA men burst into his house as he relaxed and dragged him into the road and shot him dead with automatic weapons. He was left lying in a pool of blood as they re-entered his house – stealing his service-issue weapon and leaving his lifeless body, lying like an animal, struck by a truck.

Targeting the RUC reservists and part-time UDR personnel became almost a 'pastime' for the Provisional IRA and INLA. As the last contributor has said, the hits were relatively easy to set up as their INT cells already knew names and addresses and regular patterns of movement. They knew the routes which the men took and knew the times of departure for work and times of arrival back from their places of employment. The ASU knew the lie of the land and were generally from the local community and familiar with the terrain. The army – in order to keep these men and their families safe – occasionally employed lurk patrols (meaning, quite literally, to lurk unnoticed) and on several occasions when they were able to surprise and confront PIRA murder squads, the end result was one or more dead terrorists. Sinn Féin, over the many years of the Troubles, bleated about a 'shoot to kill' policy – and events such as Loughall leave one in no doubt as to the efficacy of these tactics. However, one finds it somewhat rich for the IRA killers – who had only the intention of shooting dead the off-duty personnel – to actually complain, when allegedly the army used the same tactics on them!

On the 25th, U.S. General and NATO Chief of Staff Alexander Haig was targeted by terrorists in Belgium and it has long been considered that an explosion underneath his car – which injured several aides – was the work of the Provisionals. Belgian police blamed the IRA, but with so much Irish-American money at stake it is unlikely that the Republican terror group would have risked losing their U.S. 'cash cow' by attacking such a senior American. Four days later Princess Alexandra paid a surprise visit to Northern Ireland in order to pay tribute to the RUC fallen. By this stage of the Troubles – nine years gone and with a mammoth 19 years still to run – 204 RUC officers had been killed by terrorists. The Princess unveiled a Book of Remembrance to the 204 at RUC HQ in Belfast. Almost 100 more names would be added to that list before the Troubles ground to a halt in 1997. Today, there is sadly a growing list of the PSNI dead.

On the 30th, PIRA attacked the post office in Killeter, Co Tyrone – a little village a shade over two miles from the Irish border and north of the dense Carrickaholten Forest. Masked gunmen stormed into the post office and forced terrified staff to leave before planting several devices. The devices detonated shortly afterwards and the blast and resulting fires destroyed the building – as well as an adjoining house. There were no injuries and the terrorists disappeared over the border.

June ended with 12 Troubles-related deaths – of whom four were soldiers and four were policemen. Two civilians – a Catholic and a Protestant – were killed. One of the deaths was overtly sectarian. Additionally, two Republicans were killed – one in a shoot-out with the army and the other was by Loyalists. Of the 12 deaths, Republicans were responsible for eight.

55

July

This month would witness the deaths of five soldiers – all but one would be accidental or to 'unknown' reasons. It would be the 'lull' before the carnage of August and the disaster at Warrenpoint. Another policeman's name would be added to the RUC Book of Remembrance – unveiled only four weeks earlier by Princess Alexandra – and there would be another sectarian killing.

On the 1st day of the month, the Reverend Ian Paisley – then leader of the Democratic Unionist Party (DUP) – made a somewhat bizarre statement alleging that the army had arrested the entire Belfast PIRA Command and then released them without charge or investigation or the involvement of the RUC. A spokesman for the RUC vehemently denied this and stated that a number of people had been arrested by soldiers in a house in the Turf Lodge area and immediately handed over to the police. The men were all questioned and then released some hours later. Paisley, ever controversial, was in particularly fine form this month and was involved several times in different matters. On the 17th, he interrupted the opening proceedings of the European Parliament to protest that the Union flag was flying the wrong way up on the Parliament buildings. The following day he tried to interrupt Jack Lynch – then Taoiseach (Irish Prime Minister) and President of the European Council – but was shouted down by other Members of the European Parliament (MEPs). Finally, on the 21st, it was announced that Pope John Paul II would pay a visit to Ireland on 29 September 1979. Mr Paisley – to whom a Papal visit was a red rag to a bull – warned in most vociferous terms that he should not visit Northern Ireland.

On Monday, 2 July 1979 the INLA was declared illegal across the whole of the United Kingdom. This was the Thatcher Government's natural reaction to the murder of Airey Neave on 30 March 1979 (see Chapter 51). However, just 10 days later the British Prime Minister was forced to criticise the BBC after it had controversially broadcast an interview with a member of the INLA. This incident was to set a pattern of confrontation between the media – particularly the broadcast media – and Conservative Governments during the 1980s and 1990s. It culminated in a later order by the (1992-97) John Major Government which banned the broadcasting of Sinn Féin spokesmen's voices on TV or radio. This resulted in the ludicrous sight and sounds of actors speaking the words of messers Adams, McGuiness et al – albeit in Northern Irish accents. In the modern vernacular, it was lip-syncing gone mad!

On the 4th, Corporal Alan Bohan and Trooper Ronald Temperley – the two SAS soldiers who had shot and killed 16-year-old John Boyle at Dunloy, Co Antrim in July of the previous year (see Chapter 43) – were acquitted of his murder. The young boy – who discovered a PIRA arms cache on his father's farm and who had indirectly alerted the authorities – was shot dead as he innocently, but foolishly returned to look at the weapons. In a reserved judgement the Lord Chief Justice, Sir Robert Lowry, found the two men not guilty after he stated that the case could not be proved. After the verdict was announced, the senior British soldier in Northern Ireland – Lieutenant-General Sir Timothy Creasy,

GOC – said: "I have never doubted that the two NCOs (sic), who were on an operation – properly mounted by the RUC – acted in good faith."

The following day, Ranger Robert Quail (18) of the Royal Irish Rangers died in circumstances unknown. Unfortunately – although the MOD has confirmed his death – no further information has been forthcoming. On the 8th, the death of a soldier in Crossmaglen Village Square led to recriminations within the Queen's Own Highlanders (QOH) after earlier intelligence had been ignored. A QOH foot patrol on the 5th had reported seeing a suspicious wire protruding from the letterbox of a house which they had passed en route back to the RUC base. The patrol commander apparently reported this to INT but no follow-up search was made – and the next morning a foot patrol was again dispatched into Market Square. As the patrol reached the very same house, a PIRA unit remote-detonated a device and several soldiers were injured by the blast. Private Allan McMillan (19) was fatally wounded and was immediately evacuated by helicopter to hospital in Belfast. He was taken to the military wing at the Musgrave Park Hospital (MPH) where his parents were flown from Evanton, Ross-shire to be at his bedside. He died of his terrible wounds on the 8th. The eldest of five children, he was buried at Kilternan.

On the 10th, the 'European' department of the Provisional IRA attacked a British Army barracks in Dortmund, West Germany. With the collapse of the USSR, Eastern European Communism and the bringing down of *Der Berlinermauer* still over a decade away, British commitment to maintaining the peace in Europe was at its zenith. The British Army of the Rhine (BAOR) was attacked many times by the IRA during the course of the Troubles – and a perusal of the ROH demonstrates that for many, it was not a safe place to be (that included wives and children of service personnel also). On the 10th, two bombs planted by the IRA exploded at West Riding Barracks and Ubique Barracks in Dortmund in the North Rhine-Westphalia area. The 2nd and also the 26th Field Regiments of the Royal Artillery were based there at the time. The first of the two explosions took place at 0500 in the officers' mess of 26 Regiment and the second occurred a mere five minutes later in the sergeants' mess of 2nd Field Regiment. Neither explosion caused any casualties.

PROVOS IN GERMANY?
Mark 'C', Royal Artillery and UDR

Around about the time of the bombings in Dortmund I was in 25th RA then in Paderborn doing the last of our own Northern Ireland training prior to deployment. There had been heightened security at all the camps previous to this. Sandbags put round the guardroom; extra patrols; weapons issued (no rounds) etc. One night we went into Paderborn for a drink. In one of the bars a couple of guys approached us saying they were squaddies also, but we were suspicious from the off as one of them had a Belfast accent and maybe one of the others slightly foreign. They were asking questions about what unit we were and what barracks, so we told them to fuck off and went to Sennelager to the Monkeys Guardroom (RMP) to report it. A sergeant questioned us, but I quickly got the impression that he didn't trust or like me because of my accent. He was asking me stupid questions about what part of Belfast did one of the guy's accent sound like – and to be honest I never really realised the difference in accents in Belfast so he was getting really shitty with me instead of trying to find out who these guys were, but I suppose that went with the territory at times with some soldiers.

I don't think they ever found out who they were, but on orders it seems they had been seen around other squaddie bars in the district asking the same questions so maybe if the MP Sergeant hadn't been so obsessed with me, we might have caught them and found out what they were up to.

Three days after the death of Private McMillan in a cross-border chase involving a stolen cabin cruiser and a helicopter, a Crossmaglen man was arrested as he tried to swim across Lough Ross into the Irish Republic. The boat, which contained bomb-making equipment, was seized and a further two men were arrested – one of whom was wounded by soldiers He was also charged and convicted of the murder of RUC officer Stanley Hanna in June (see previous chapter). The incident started when Gardaí raced to investigate reports of a boat and a trailer which had been stolen in Dundalk. The stolen boat was traced to Lough Ross on the Irish side, but was stolen again under the noses of Gardaí who immediately and correctly informed the RUC on the other side of the Lough. An army helicopter containing RUC and QOH personnel began patrolling the eastern side of the Lough and found the boat anchored and with one man already ashore. The aircraft landed and a gunman on or near the boat opened fire. He was then seen running for the mouth of the feeder river (the other side of which was the Republic) and soldiers fired at him – hitting him – and although wounded, managed to wade across to the Irish side. The other men were quickly arrested as they tried to return to Ireland.

Troops had gone onto the streets of the Province in the very early days of the conflict – and if not exactly untrained, they were certainly naïve and so, tragically, were many of the tactics employed by the British Army. By the time of the eighth or ninth year of deployment soldiers were better-trained, more streetwise and more receptive to the dangers of an urban war. No longer did patrols either pause or merely saunter across the entrances to roads or alleyways or stand under streetlamps – and they learned to avoid the white-painted walls which would frame them in a sniper's sights. Soldiers had learned that whereas the IRA accepted the 'collateral damage' of shooting their own communities, they would often pause before opening fire. They knew that if they stood near civilians, they had a good chance of staying alive. The piece by Mick Hill serves to illustrate how tactics, equipment and common sense had improved greatly – and although PIRA/INLA still took a tragic toll of soldiers' lives, the numbers of both fatalities and wounding would continue to spiral downwards. The following is the incident to which the last contributor refers.

Mick 'Benny' Hill, Royal Anglians

An example of how the Security Forces were co-operating and collaborating happened well into our 1978-79 tour. Some senior RUC officers arrived in Palace Barracks one afternoon. The COP and (I think) another platoon were put on immediate standby. Big Jimmy, the provost sergeant and the provost staff went to the other ranks' dining hall and guarded all the doors – with Big Jimmy in the master cook's office. Sometime later, minibuses full of RUC arrived in barracks and were unloaded outside the dining hall and shown in. The RPs had orders that no-one was to leave and Big Jimmy stopped anyone using the phone. We found out later that in Belfast, neighbouring police stations had staggered shift change times and that at several stations finishing their shifts at the same time, the officers weren't allowed home and weren't allowed to phone anyone (no mobile phones in those days). They were loaded into minibuses and driven to Palace. They were forbidden to contact their families – hence Big Jimmy guarding the phone – and, at their duty stations, there was no apparent difference in the usual comings and goings; no sudden influx of staff at unusual times as comings and goings at RUC stations was often noted by the other side. The reason for all the secrecy was that there was very good intelligence of a bomb factory in the Short Stand area of the city, which was in a 'police primacy' area – in other words, the RUC was responsible for all policing and anti-terror activity and called on the army only when absolutely necessary. Tea and sandwiches were laid on for the police, they were briefed and the op went ahead with our two platoons as the outer cordon and on call if things got noisy. The op was a great success and a large bomb factory was put out of business; a successful op and a great example of how different parts of the Security Forces could co-operate to everyone's mutual benefit.

Also on the 11th, the Provisionals' Central Administration Team – or 'Nutting Squad' – was in action after one of their major bomb stores in the Nationalist Short Strand area of Belfast was discovered by the army after a tip-off. The discovery and seizure of such a massive amount of ordnance was a major blow to PIRA and an immediate investigation was launched. Given the amount and depth of penetration by both the army and the RUC/Gardaí Siochana Special Branch of the IRA, this type of SF coup is most unsurprising. Perusal of at least half a dozen informer books demonstrates that much is true. However, the 'Nutting Squad' needed an informant and despite the fact that they knew that they didn't

Foot patrol, Sandy Row, Belfast, 1979. (©Mark 'C')

always necessarily execute the correct person, the occasional – and public – execution served a purpose. It either deterred those thinking of becoming a tout or reminded the already in-place tout that it was a risky occupation. It further kept the rank-and-file volunteers in line. The unfortunate victim was Michael Kearney (20) from Glenveagh Drive in Lenadoon, West Belfast.

He had been arrested earlier by the RUC and taken to the Castlereagh Detention Centre, where after extensive interrogation he cracked and revealed the location of a bomb store. He also agreed to be a paid informer. However, on release he immediately went to his company command and admitted everything – stating that he had no intention of informing. The case was passed onto the 'Nutting Squad' and he was abducted from somewhere in the Andersonstown area. He was taken and shot – with his body left at the border near Newtownbutler, Co Fermanagh. At the time the Provisionals stated that he was one of their volunteers and was executed for '*breach of general army orders*'. Between 2001-03, at the insistence of the Kearney family, an investigation by the Provisionals finally cleared the dead man of charges that he was a paid informer at the time of his death – and it also admitted that he was not responsible for informing on one of the IRA's biggest-ever operations.

BELFAST DRUNK
Herb Jackson, Royal Artillery

On a funny note, this particular evening we came across this fellow moving about in the gutter trying to get comfortable. We pulled up and discovered he was as pissed as a fart and covered in blood. We dragged him from his comfortable drain griddle and lifted him into a sitting position on the tail of the Land Rover. He was mumbling away in 'drunkese', which usually involves the words 'fuck' and 'bastards'. They are used in abundance – often mixed as 'fuckstard' – and served with a growl or a drool … and that's just the polite conversation.

We followed the trail of blood all over him to a gaping great hole in his neck and we thought this guy had been glassed or stabbed in some pub brawl. It was only later that we discovered he was from one side of the sectarian divide and decided that he'd had the right amount of alcohol to qualify him for the invincibility passport, and chose then to go over to a pub on the other side of the divide and say hello! He was lucky he wasn't dead, as his hosts had given him a very severe welcome. Typical soldier humour dictates that we had to take the piss when checking him out – and comforting this drunk – by telling him: "Your face is a mess mate, but don't worry – I can see you're an ugly bloke anyway."

This kind of broke the ice and I am sure the drunk didn't really notice what was said as it was done in a 'caring' sort of first aid way. Then, as if looking for a fight after mumbling repeatedly the same thing for a while, he made the extra effort to lose his native 'fuckese' and use broken 'English drunkard' for a brief moment in time. "Have you a fucking cigarette?" We sniggered at this outburst and Jeff reached into his pocket to extract a pack of Regal King Size and offered one to the drunk – still swaying about all over the place. "Well, do you want one or not?" Jeff said. The drunk reached out a blood-soaked hand – waving it about in the air like he was trying to catch a pet budgie. Jeff, stepping back, said: "No, I will get it for you." Not wanting blood all over himself he lit a cigarette for the guy;

then reached out saying: "Where do you want this? I know … it will fit nicely in here." He promptly popped it in the gaping hole in his neck for a moment before retracting it and shoving it in the gob of the unaware drunk. We cracked up at this scene, though we continued to offer first aid through giggles galore. The humour was eventually broken by the attention of the CO who, as all this went on, had been busy chatting with the RSM and contacting the RUC and ambulance for this chap. "Let's go bombardier; the ambulance and RUC have arrived. Leave it to them," he ordered and off we went.

It's funny that I can remember this guy's neck more than I remember him – perhaps because for a moment it had a Regal King Size sticking out of it.

On the 15th, a PIRA murder gang drove a stolen Ford Cortina into the car park of Andersonstown's Fruithill Bowling Club and searched for the Toyota which belonged to an OAP, Patrick O'Hanlon (69). One man got out of the car and walked inside the club to inform the pensioner, whilst the driver and a gunman waited by the two cars. Once inside they located Mr O'Hanlon and persuaded him to come outside and inspect the damage. As the two men walked out of the club together, it is likely that they struck up a brief conversation centred on the PIRA man's sincere-sounding apologies. Lulled into a false sense of security, the older man walked calmly towards his executioners. He was shot several times as he reached his damaged car and mortally wounded. He died before reaching hospital. His crime – for which in the perverted eyes of the IRA meant his punishment was death – was to report to the RUC that his car had twice been hijacked. On the second occasion the IRA hijackers were caught – and for the Provisionals, this was tantamount to touting. He left three grown-up children.

Two days later another civilian died needlessly and three were injured – one very, very seriously – whilst standing at a bus stop, at the bloody hands of the Provisionals. The attack took place close to Rosslea, Co Fermanagh on the road to Lisnaskea. Quite how Sinn Féin spokesmen could stand straight-faced in front of a phalanx of pressmen and spout their usual nonsense about them being the protectors of the Nationalist community is beyond the comprehension of this author. The bombers had packed around 500lbs of explosives into several milk churns and left them on a trailer – only yards from a rural bus stop. Their objective was a two-vehicle mobile patrol from the 4th Battalion (Co Fermanagh) UDR, which was known to use the main Rosslea to Lisnaskea road.

The command wires ran back to the firing point where the bombing unit waited inside a residential caravan, where they had taken the family hostage. As ill luck would have it, a shoppers' special bus was due to stop there en route for Enniskillen. Four people – including a mother and adult daughter and a brother and sister – waited for the bus just as the UDR patrol drove towards them. What is extremely controversial and damning of the PIRA ASU is that they had a clear view of the bus stop and the passengers – as well as the UDR vehicles – when they detonated their bomb. There is no doubt of that and there is no excuse which the IRA apologists could use for what happened next. The explosion blasted the leading Land Rover off the road – injuring all four occupants – and caught the civilians who were standing only 10 yards away. Sylvia Crowe (32), who worked for a Christian organisation, was killed instantly and her mother was very badly injured – as were the brother and sister. The bus arrived just a minute or so later – the driver having heard the massive explosion as

EBRINGTON BARRACKS

**IF SUSPICIOUS PHONE LISBURN
GARRISON GUARD ROOM – Ext. 3133
AND TELL YOUR OPERATIONS CENTRE**

ISSUED BY THE SECURITY FORCES 015/76

A poster issued by the Security Forces after a bomb attack. (via author)

he drove along. Had the bus and the military vehicles arrived at the same time, then there could have been absolute carnage.

HEART AND MINDS
Graham 'Bernie' Briggs, Royal Artillery

Every now and then we would swamp entire areas with scores of troops as we wanted to put on a show of strength for the locals – just to let them know that we were there and to ensure that the IRA were kept on their toes and restrict their movement of arms and ammunition. This one night, in the New Lodge, was one of those occasions.

We had been patrolling for about two hours and the word was passed back that we were getting ready to head back to Girdwood Barracks – our base just off the Antrim Road. Just as we prepared to head back there, the troop sergeant told us that a suspect car had been spotted on Lepper Street and we had to put a cordon in as 'Felix' (Ammunition Technical Officer) was en route to investigate. The Republican New Lodge area is made up of back-to-back terraced housing with all the streets running parallel to each other. Haliday's Road ran across the top and North Queen Street along the bottom – with the aforementioned Lepper Street in the middle.

Anyway, the troop sergeant decided that we had enough men on the streets and could afford to put an inner – as well as an outer – cordon in to protect 'Felix'. I was tasked to start knocking on peoples' door to tell them of the situation – and as usual when you knocked on the doors, the occupants were not interested. I just thought: "Sod this!" and the next door I knocked on, I just shouted: "Suspect device; you know the score!" and walked on. I carried on doing this until I had done my side of Stratheden Street. I was then tasked to repeat the warnings over on Lepper Street.

I then noticed a bit of an altercation going on and there was this local woman – no idea where she came from – having a real go at one of the lads. Anyway, he walked away and she carried on verbally abusing him and then turned her attention to the next soldier who passed her and so on and so forth – abusing a different one in turn. This had been going on for about 15 minutes and then she made the mistake of turning her foul-mouthed attentions to me. As I was trying to patrol up the street, she deliberately stood in front of me – walking backwards so that she could keep me in sight and continue to abuse me. I told her to go away, but she took no notice and just carried on swearing. Eventually, I snapped and told her to: "Fuck off!" as diplomatically as I could. She just smirked and shouted back: "Why soldier boy; ye gunna shoot me?"

As she spat the words at me, I unclipped my SLR – transferred it into my left hand and brought my unloaded Federal Riot Gun (for firing baton rounds) and put it right in front of her mouth and said: "No, but this will shut you up!" The look on her boat race – talk about seeing the white of her eyes – and as she stood there, mouth open, all of the colour drained from her gobby face. It was good – just for once – to wipe the smirk off her ugly, foul-mouthed mug. Just then I heard my name being called and as I looked across the street, Sergeant 'X' was walking towards me, asking what was going on. I explained that she had been giving grief to all the lads all the time we had been doing the roving patrol. He sent me across the road and just ushered the shocked woman away. I thought that I was in for a major bollocking, but it was all dealt with the usual nod and a wink. Looking back, I don't suppose that I won many hearts and minds in the New Lodge that day!

On the 18th, Private Geoffrey Davis (19) of the Army Catering Corps died in circumstances unknown. He was to be the first of two soldiers to die with no reason being made public in the space of 24 hours. The Army Catering Corps (ACC), or – as it is known throughout the British Army, the Aldershot Cement Company – was originally formed in March 1941 as part of the Royal Army Service Corps and became a corps in its own right in 1965. Its cooks are known as 'Slop Jocks' and through its diligence – often in difficult circumstances – has helped to maintain the saying, as attributed to Napoleon Bonaparte, that *an army marches on its stomach*'. Just 24 hours later Major Rhodri Lloyd Howell (33) of the Royal Army Education Corps died – and this author has no further information. Despite his most Welsh name he was buried at Swindon, Wiltshire.

Three days after the two unexplained deaths, Private Ronald Stafford (20) of the Light Infantry was killed in a RTA whilst on duty in the Province. He was from the Sunderland area and his funeral was held at Bishopwearmouth. He was due to celebrate his 21st birthday less than three weeks later.

On the same day as Major Howell died, the IRA attempted to kill and maim members of an army foot patrol in the Andersonstown area. A 'footsie' from the King's Own Scottish Borderers (KOSB) was walking through the area when a medium-sized device exploded near to some houses. Three of the men were slightly injured, but all three recovered. There were no further injuries. The regiment was raised in 1689 to defend Edinburgh during the Jacobite Rebellion and its proud motto is *Nisi Dominus Frustra* (*Without the Lord, everything is in vain*). The regiment lost a total of nine soldiers in Northern Ireland – and one of their number would die in a tragic RTA later this year (see Chapter 58).

On the 23rd the Provisionals put into action a well-planned, well-co-ordinated operation of total disruption throughout the Province. It was aimed at demonstrating just how ungovernable they could make the country – and also at stretching the SF to breaking point. PIRA volunteers hijacked commercial vehicles in Belfast, Londonderry, Coalisland, Moy, Keady, Newtownbutler, Lisnaskea and Pomeroy. A further three lorries were hijacked south of the border and all the vehicles were used to carry a mixture of real and hoax devices – although in every case, ATO were called out to investigate. A total of 14 controlled explosions were made during the day of disruption. One of the most dangerous parts of the operation took place inside the Irish border. Armed men forced a goods train to halt and the crew were forced off at gunpoint. One of the IRA men forced the driver to set the train in motion before both men jumped off and the train began to pick up speed as it hurtled – totally unmanned – towards the North. The terror group had absolutely no regard for what or whom the runaway train might hit; it simply increased speed and disappeared over the border. It reached Goraghwood, Co Down some three to five miles due north of Newry before it hit a bend at an uncontrollable speed and derailed in a tangle of twisted metal with shattered rolling stock littering the line. ATO had to first declare the wreckage free of explosives before the workmen were allowed to begin the task of clearing the area.

The vehicles hijacked in the South were made safe by the Irish Army and several controlled explosions were made. In Londonderry City, a bus passing close to the Creggan Estate was stopped by armed IRA men and once the passengers had been forced off at gunpoint, a parcel was placed under one of the seats. Seconds after they had run off a passing foot patrol from the Duke of Edinburgh's Royal Regiment (DERR) came upon the scene and ATO were called in as the DERR soldiers formed a safety cordon and evacuated nearby houses. ATO found that the parcel contained a viable device and made it safe.

EAST BELFAST INCIDENT
'Skip' Hansford, Royal Horse Artillery

It was during the late 1970s and whilst on patrol in East Belfast – in the Ballymacarrat area – during the engineers' strikes. My battery of 1RHA were in the middle of a very big set of riots/marches just prior to the Orange (Loyalists) of 12 July, which always took place in Belfast City Centre.

We were en route to liaise with another section who were having trouble in the area of Mountpottinger Road/Arran Street. The section had been split and one half-brick was cut off. In the ensuing confusion, one of the lads got separated and was trapped in a doorway. He was having trouble with a lot of Catholic women who were trying to relieve him of his weapon. On seeing this, our sergeant came up to me and grabbed my baton round gun off me and asked for a 'special round'. I understood immediately and handed him an assortment of old pennies and batteries. As cool as you like he then walked over to the group of women and without as much as a pause, fired – and shot one in the face!

I have never seen a street clear so fast – ever! "Ok lads," he said, "back to camp quick as we can." There is a postscript to that story. In the early 1980s I was in the Province again when on the news came a headline that a woman – who had been shot whilst walking 'innocently' down a street in East Belfast – was awarded thousands of pounds for facial injuries received from overzealous soldiers in 1974! Bloody cheek, if you will pardon the pun.

On the 26th, the Provisionals continued to defy those who thought that they were unable to sink any lower when they bombed a hotel for the elderly and infirm. Six members of the Provisional IRA walked into the Belgravia Hotel on Ulsterville Avenue, close to the Lisburn Road in South Belfast – five of whom were carrying bombs. One member held the owner, Pearl Richardson, and some of her colleagues at gunpoint in the office and told the staff they had half an hour to evacuate the building. Meanwhile, the other five men placed bombs around the building. One bomb was left under the chair of a sleeping resident in the lounge. Miss Richardson told the *Belfast Telegraph*: "It was so frightening; we only just managed to get the feet of the last resident off the front doorstep before the first bomb went off. None of us had time to take a single thing. The building just went up in flames so quickly." The terrorists had promised that the first bomb would explode in 60 minutes. In fact, the first explosion occurred after just 23 minutes. Given the nature of the residents – infirm and elderly and aged between 70 and 97 – it seems clear that the intention was to kill. Quite why PIRA wished to terrorise the elderly was never made clear.

Despite the trauma of seeing her family home disappear she managed to get every resident out of the old building safely and into temporary accommodation that night.

Royal Artillery, Armagh, 1979. (©Walter Stirling)

Pearl Richardson's bravery and initiative was rewarded with an MBE. Most of the building was deemed structurally unsafe and had to be demolished. In 1987, on the site of the old Belgravia Hotel, Oaklee Belgravia was built as a supported housing scheme for the local community.

The following day a bombing unit from INLA targeted a former RUCR officer at his home in Portadown. Under cover of darkness, one of their units placed a UVBT beneath the car of Jim Wright (48) in Corcrain Drive in the small Co Armagh town. The following morning – the 27th – he set off to work accompanied by his 21-year-old daughter. As he began to drive, a mercury tilt device – identical to that which killed Airey Neave, MP at the House of Commons car park – detonated and he was killed instantly. His daughter received dreadful lower-body wounds and was lucky to recover after a long time in hospital. *Lost Lives* report that half of the population of the mainly Protestant town of Portadown attended Mr Wright's funeral. He had left the RUCR in 1977, but this did not deter the mad dogs of the INLA. Three days later the same Republican terror group killed a serving police officer in Armagh City.

Retaliation was expected – and was not long in coming – as gunmen from the Mid-Ulster Brigade of the UVF killed a Catholic in a blatantly sectarian murder and set off another tragic and violent tit-for-tat. A young Catholic, James McCann (20), was walking through the town some 24 hours after the murder of Mr Wright when a stolen car containing UVF gunmen pulled alongside and opened fire – hitting and mortally wounding Mr McCann. The incident took place in Obins Street and although dying, he dragged himself to the doorway of a nearby pub where drinkers called for an ambulance and tried to comfort him. He was rushed to the nearby Craigavon Hospital, but it was too late. A day later – in what was seen as an act of poignancy and mutual grief which bridged the sectarian divide – the son of murdered Jim Wright visited the McCann family.

On the final day of the month the INLA showed their ruthlessness and killed another police officer – this time in Armagh City. A stolen car containing armed INLA men drove up to the courthouse where they knew RUC men would be on duty. When they arrived they spotted Constable George Walsh (51) sitting in a car as he waited for colleagues. One gunman, armed with an American-supplied Armalite, opened fire on the officer's car – spraying it – hitting Constable Walsh multiple times and killing him instantly. The killers roared off in the car, which was later found burned-out close to the border.

July had ended, but very soon the name of Mountbatten and the small Co Down town of Warrenpoint – with its population of less than 7,000 – would be echoing simultaneously around the world. During the month of July, 11 people were killed in the Troubles. Of these, five were soldiers; two were RUC (or former RUC); and three civilians – two Catholics and a Protestant – died. One of the deaths was overtly sectarian. One Republican was killed at the hands of the IRA's 'Nutting Squad'. Of the 11 deaths, six were carried out by either PIRA or the INLA.

56

August

ugust was to prove an absolute tragedy for the Parachute Regiment in particular – and for the British Army in general – as 25 soldiers and one airman were killed in a variety of places and to a variety of causes. It was a month which witnessed the death of Lord Louis Mountbatten and one in which the toll exceeded 30 for the first time in many, many months.

The month began with the finding of the proceeds of a PIRA robbery in Portadown. Armed IRA men had threatened the staff of the main GPO in the city with handguns and had tied up staff whilst they rifled over £200,000 from the safe. After their getaway a substantial part was hidden outside the town, but on the 1st – thanks to a tip-off – the army and RUC were able to recover a substantial part of the money. Soldiers from 45 Field Regiment, Royal Artillery assisted in the finding of the money, which was hidden underneath straw in a derelict house. More money was found in an adjoining house and one man was arrested. Although money was still flooding in from NORAID, their war chest needed topping up from time to time – and that was achieved through a series of robberies – as the 'urban guerrillas' proved themselves to be cheap hoods underneath. On the same day the UDR lost Private Norman John Wysner (48) in circumstances unknown.

This author has never been slow to criticise the Irish-Americans for their obsessive support for their former 'homeland' – a homeland from which their ancestors had departed many generations back – and the influence the Irish-American lobby had on all aspects of the U.S. administration and judiciary. On the 2nd there was more controversy as a major row broke out and threatened the so-called 'special relationship' between Britain and the USA. President Jimmy Carter had been keen to continue to supply arms to the RUC – often at favourable rates – but he was overruled by the un-Godly alliance of Edward Kennedy, Moynihan, Carey and Tip O'Neil who effectively brought about a ban on the sale of arms. These 'denizens' of U.S. political life were seemingly less than enthusiastic when it came to helping a legally constituted and legitimate police force combat crime and terror.

On the same day that the real hypocrisy of the U.S. Government was being revealed – and with the 10th anniversary of deployment fast approaching – the Provisionals were back to killing soldiers, this time in Co Armagh. A three-vehicle mobile containing soldiers from the Royal Artillery, UDR and the Royal Signals was returning from investigating a burned-out car which had been used by the INLA killers of RUC Officer George Walsh two days earlier. As the convoy drove along Cathedral Road between Moy and Armagh City, a 400lb bomb concealed in a culvert was detonated by watching PIRA men. The second vehicle took the full brunt of the explosion and two soldiers were killed instantly – and at least three more were seriously injured. The third vehicle containing UDR soldiers crashed head-first into the massive crater left by the explosion and more injuries were caused.

As the injured UDR men began to scramble from their wrecked vehicle – and the first vehicle stopped and reversed back to the scene of utter devastation – the watching gunmen began spraying them with automatic weapons. The soldiers reacted professionally

Mobile patrol, Royal Artillery, Armagh, 1979. (©Walter Stirling)

and returned fire – causing the gunmen to run off across fields to waiting stolen cars and escape into the Republic. The two soldiers who were killed outright were Gunner Richard Furminger (19) – an Essex boy who had only been in Northern Ireland for nine days – and Signalman Paul Reece (also 19) from Crewe in Cheshire. Like his Royal Artillery comrade, he had also been in-Province for only nine days.

Michael Flannery, a NORAID fundraiser, was sickeningly quoted in the Montreal Gazette as saying: "The more British soldiers sent home from Ulster in coffins, the better." The same newspaper in its 15 August edition wrote: "The body of Gunner Richard Furminger came home last week – the 301st (sic) army victim of the war in Ulster. The husky young soldier had been planning a homecoming to celebrate his 20th birthday. Instead, he was blown to pieces by the IRA. At his funeral at St Mary's Roman Catholic Church in Crewe, his parish priest said this of Ulster: 'This world is haunted by the faces of sorrowing mothers.'" It went on to say, on the day after the 10th anniversary of deployment: "It began this haunting when the British Army's peacekeeping force arrived in Northern Ireland ' ... to help out the police for a few weeks ... ' Yesterday, it had been there for 10 years."

Later that day an RUC officer was killed in Belfast as he responded to a hoax call in what tragically turned out to be a classic IRA 'come on'. Even during those terror-ridden days the RUC still had to investigate burglaries, petty theft, stolen cars – of which between PIRA hijackings and joyriders there were many – vandalism and the like. Their stations still received 999 calls and these all had to be investigated – albeit dressed in body armour and their .38 Ruger Security Six Revolver or Ruger Mini-14 to hand (and possibly even cocked in the eventuality of a terrorist attack). On this day the police at Springfield Road received a call relating to a burglary at Clondara Street just under a mile from the station and south-westwards down the Falls Road (and very close to Milltown Cemetery). As the police Land Rover arrived, Constable Derek Davidson (26) – a Scotsman – jumped out. An IRA sniper – using a high-powered rifle – fired from the bedroom window of a house opposite, which they had taken over some hours previously. The officer was hit by a single round to the head and he died instantly. He was the father of a young child. The other officers dived to the ground and returned fire – one of whom was hit by a burst of automatic fire – but the bullets tore through his uniform without hurting him. The gunmen escaped through a back door and fled towards the nearby cemetery.

On 12 April 2000 the RUC was awarded the George Cross for Bravery in dealing with terrorist threat – a rare honour which had only been awarded collectively once before (as the author has previously mentioned) to the nation of Malta. The award stated: "For the past 30 years the Royal Ulster Constabulary has been the bulwark against, and the main target of, a sustained and brutal terrorism campaign. The force has suffered heavily in protecting both sides of the community from danger; 302 officers have been killed in the line of duty and thousands more injured – many seriously. Many officers have been ostracised by their own community and others have been forced to leave their homes in the face of threats to them and their families."

On the following day, Co Down pensioner William Whitten (65) died from the blast and burn injuries which he had received during an IRA explosion. He had been a guest at the Marine Hotel in Ballycastle on 19 June (see Chapter 54) on the day that the Provisionals bombed a total of five seaside hotels. In Portadown, the SF struck a massive blow against the UVF when a joint RUC/army search operation – in all likelihood alerted by undercover operatives – raided an arms workshop/store in the Mount Pleasant area. Gun-making equipment – including lathes – was seized as well as five homemade pistols. Many of the arms seized were in the one house, but more was found in a hut some 100 yards away from the premises. A number of Bren guns, rifles, shotguns and revolvers were also seized – as well as 10,000 rounds of ammunition. It was not only one of the biggest seizures of the Troubles, but it was the biggest blow ever struck against the UVF.

TEMPTATIONS AND WHAT IF AT LOYALIST CLUB
Kevin Campbell, King's Own Scottish Borderers

We were sent out from North Howard Street Mill (NHSM) on a mobile patrol to cover the 'Peace Line' at the junction of Cupar Way/Lawnbrook Avenue and we parked up the Pigs in Lawnbrook Avenue just opposite the Loyalist-controlled social club*. This was around 300 yards from our base at NHSM. We had been there for about an hour or so when their doorman came over and introduced himself. He asked the brick commander what we were doing, as it was scaring his customers. It was explained to him that we were there as a response – should anything happen in the area – rather than waiting in the mill for a shout. At this he seemed happy and went back inside the club.

About 10 to 15 minutes later he returned and asked if we wanted to come in for a drink, so a quick briefing was held and it was decided that two should stay

---

*   On 8 September the previous year, the UVF shot and fatally wounded a Protestant civilian in the same Lawnbrook Social Club. William Crawford, who was only 17, died in hospital five days later.

with the Pigs and the rest would go for a pint. I was 'volunteered' to stay along with one driver whilst the other lads went in, but no sooner had they entered they came straight back out. Apparently the weapons were scaring the customers. To my amazement, the lads had only come back out to put their rifles in the Pig and then they returned to the club! Me and the driver were left there to look after the rest of the weapons!

However, within a minute or so a group of gorgeous young women came out to talk to me and the driver. At first it all seemed totally innocent and they were just having a laugh, but soon they were coming on to us really strong – trying to get us to come into what was meant to be one of their houses just a couple of doors away. As much as we were tempted, we resisted as we would never have been able to secure and protect all the weapons and vehicles. The girls seemed very persistent. God alone knows why – and the boys seemed to be away for ages. Eventually they came out from the club – worse for wear – and we made our way back to the mill. Naturally the lads had to keep their heads down and stay out of the way, but in the maze and vast expanse of rooms which was the mill, this was easily done.

Looking back at the incident I have often wondered: Were we being set up? Being Loyalists, were they about to have two brick's worth of weapons and ammo added to their cache of weapons? But worst of all, what could have happened to me and the driver because after all, the club was where the 'Shankill Butchers' based their operation from. We all know the main man (Lenny Murphy) walked free from that – and being a Saturday night was probably in the club at the time.

NB. The 'Shankill Butchers' have been dealt with in other chapters in this book, but in terms of the previous contributor's speculation about the leader of the murder gang – the mad dog Lenny Murphy – he may be correct. Murphy may have occasionally used the Lawnbrook Social Club, but he was also known to use the upper floor of the Brown Bear pub – at the corner of Mountjoy Street and the Shankill Road near his home – as an occasional meeting place for his unit. Most of the gang were eventually caught and, in February 1979, received the longest combined prison sentences in United Kingdom legal history. However, gang leader Lenny Murphy and his two chief lieutenants – one of whom is known to have been one of his brothers – escaped prosecution. He was killed in November 1982 by PIRA who were, in all likelihood, acting upon a tip-off from Loyalist sources.

On the 7th, the Provisionals raided a bank at Tramore, Co Waterford inside its 'homeland' in order to top up its funds. Masked gunmen entered the bank and forced staff and customers lie on the floor whilst they rifled the safe. One of the customers – Eamon Ryan (32), father of two – was on holiday in Tramore at the time and was with his three-year-old child. He was shot and fatally wounded as he lay helpless – and the circumstances behind his shooting are somewhat hazy. Eyewitness accounts are unclear and whether he moved in order to calm down his toddler son – or if he saw the face of one of the robbers, or indeed was shot accidentally – is open to conjecture. However, he was shot and died later in hospital. It later emerged that three unarmed Gardaí had turned up but were overpowered by the armed robbers and also held hostage. Sometime later the money from the robbery – £5,500 – turned up and as a result of a Gardaí agent inside the local IRA, two men were arrested and convicted of the killing and robbery. On 1 September 1987 the alleged agent

– Eamonn Maguire – was tried by an IRA 'Kangaroo Court' and executed by the 'Nutting Squad'.

Interestingly enough, the weapon used to kill Mr Maguire was later used in the murder of the most senior RUC officers to die in the Troubles. On the afternoon of Monday, 20 March 1989 Chief Superintendent Harry Breen and Superintendent Bob Buchanan – both high-ranking officers in the RUC – were returning from an informal security conference with senior officers of equivalent ranks of the Gardaí Siochana in Dundalk, Co Louth. The two RUC officers were travelling without escort in Buchanan's personal unmarked car (a red Vauxhall Cavalier, which was not armoured-plated nor had bulletproof glass). They were stopped by armed PIRA men at an IVCP. The gunmen approached the car and immediately began shooting – mainly at the driver's side – hitting the two officers. Buchanan made two frantic attempts to reverse and escape, but his car stalled on each attempt and he was likely already dead before his car came to a rest. Examination of the car the following day found it still to be in reverse gear with Buchanan's foot fully pressed against the accelerator. Breen, despite his gunshot wounds, managed to stumble out of the car – waving a white handkerchief at the gunmen in a gesture of surrender. According to eyewitnesses one of the gunmen walked over to him, told him to lie on the ground and fired a shot into the back of his head – killing him instantly. Another gunman then approached Buchanan's already dead body in the car and shot him again in the side of the head at point-blank range.

On the same day as the robbery in Tramore, four young IRA members – in what was seen as an act of reckless bravado – opened fire on a foot patrol from 'D' Company, 1 KOSB walking through the Ballymurphy Estate with an RUC contingent. The PIRA men had driven up in a stolen white van and the soldiers formed a phalanx across the road and ordered them to stop. As the van screeched to a halt in Springhill Avenue, one of the men inside the van opened fire. Soldiers from the famous Scots regiment immediately returned fire and two would-be terrorists were hit and wounded. To add insult to injury, they were also arrested. Two other men in the car dashed out and escaped in the direction of Ballymurphy Road. Less than 48 hours later – to mark the anniversary of internment – PIRA snipers opened fire on soldiers at several locations throughout West Belfast. Several troops were wounded, but all recovered from their wounds. Following three gun battles in the Falls area, young Republican thugs looted and burned out several shops. They saw the wanton damaging of Catholic-owned businesses as their part in the 'liberation' of the North.

On the night of the 10th – acting upon their own flawed information – an IRA murder gang attacked a house close to the village of Garvagh in Co Londonderry. They had been led to believe that a family with UDR connections lived in the house, but they were wrong. Although their victim – William McGraw (29) – had three brothers in the regiment and a fourth brother was a PO, he was not a member in any capacity at all. Mr McGraw had been drinking that evening and several men befriended him – buying him drinks and offering him a lift home to his house in the remote Moneycarrey Road area. However, when they arrived and they saw that there were no UDR members there they shot him six times in the face and chest. He died just minutes later.

No further terrorist-related deaths followed in the Province for a period of 17 days, but when that happened over 20 people – including 18 soldiers – would die in the space of a few hours. Meanwhile, on the 16th, Lance-Corporal Kathryn Waterland (20) – Women's Royal Army Corps (WRAC) – died in a tragic RTA whilst on duty in the Province. She was one of eight WRACs who died during the Troubles – five of whom perished in traffic accidents. Four days later on the 20th, Private Douglas McKelvie (20) of the Argyll and Sutherland Highlanders was killed in a similar accident. He was the first Argyle killed in Northern Ireland in almost seven years. No other Argyle would be killed for 15 months – and then it would be 18 years before three more were killed in the same accident. On the 24th, two soldiers from QOH were killed in a helicopter accident. It was the prelude to a further tragedy for this relatively new Scottish regiment, which would unfold within the next 72 hours. Their motto is *Cuidich 'n Righ* (*Aid the King*) and they were based in Co Down for the 1979 posting. In the accident they lost Lance-Corporal David Lang (25) from Nairn, Scotland and Lance-Corporal David Alexander Wares (23). The author has no further information in relation to the accident in which they died.

THE DAY I WAS SHOT!
John Mozley, Royal Artillery

In August 1979 I was serving in the Maze Prison with my unit (45 Regiment, Royal Artillery) and I was the regimental medical assistant. One particular day we were tasked to go to Musgrave Park Hospital (MPH) to collect medical supplies. We had to use a loan Land Rover ambulance as ours had broken down that morning. The one we were given was brand new, but with no Makralon on it or radio fitted. We were also taking a REME lad with us as his mate had been admitted to MPH the previous day.

Because we had no radio we had to book out with the ops room and then ring them from MPH once we arrived. We set off on just a routine supply run – or so I thought! We were on the M1 motorway – approaching the slip-road for our turn-off – when I decided to move the little transistor radio we took with us from the dashboard as we were not meant to have it. At that precise moment I heard what I thought was us running over gravel or grit – then a bang on the passenger side door. I looked at the door to see a hole in it and the REME lad in the back shouted that we were being shot at and he dived down between the stretchers in the floor well. He probably saved his own life because just as he did so – as I found out later – a round whizzed over his head missing him by a few inches. I then folded my arms and tried to duck down below window-level. It was then that I felt the blood on my left arm. I looked and saw a lot of blood oozing from a hole so I grabbed the nearest thing to plug it, which just so happened to be my driver's beret. Well I wasn't using my own!

We then got to MPH as fast as we could and I got out of the ambulance. My mates had always told me that you shit yourself on your first contact – and I could feel something wet running down my left leg! It was then that my driver, Sid, told me that I had two holes in the back of my left leg. We went into reception and called our ops room at the Maze to tell them what had happened. At first they did not believe us, and it was only when a WO2 from MPH told them that they got a contact report out. I had two operations in about a week and spent two months in the hospital – and Sid was given three days off to recover. The IRA firing point was from a house in Andytown which they had taken over and held the family hostage. The window they used had a great view between two groups of trees overlooking the motorway. My CO came to the hospital to visit me later that day with a copy of what I think was some NORAID paper stating we were part of a heavily armoured convoy carrying military intelligence personnel and SAS – but, as he put it, we didn't have an ounce of intelligence between the three of us. You can imagine the bullshit the IRA told the Irish-Americans about how their 'brave' volunteers' had taken on the British war machine!

This incident took place three days before Mountbatten and Warrenpoint occurred, so we were very quickly forgotten news as the double tragedy eclipsed everything else. The following week the hospital was buzzing with everywhere being cleaned and dusted as the Secretary of State for Northern Ireland was visiting. I was made to get out of my bed and sit in a chair next to it; then the CO of MPH arrived with some bod in a suit and he introduced himself as Government Press Agency and said that Margaret Thatcher was coming to see me in 20 minutes or so and did I mind pictures being taken. I looked at the CO and he nodded ok; then this bod asked if I wanted to express my views on the Ulster situation to the PM. Again I looked at the CO and he had his hand in a fist and was shaking his head, so I said no. The Prime Minister arrived and sat on my bed and we spoke for about five minutes and had some pictures taken by the hordes of press and TV crews who accompanied her – and then she went on her way!

SQUALOR IN THE NEW LODGE
Graham Briggs, Royal Artillery

During my tour of Northern Ireland I was a member of one of the battery search teams – and this one particular day it was our turn to do the searching. On the morning in question we started early – up at 0400 – and had to be at the property at approximately 0500 for the early morning call by the RUC. We had to be there early so that the occupants were not expecting us. (The dawn raid, or the '4am knock', was perfected by the British in South Africa during the interminable Boer War. They quickly learned that at that time in the morning the human body is at its absolute emotional and physiological nadir.) The property we were tasked to search was a flat in one of the high-rise blocks in the New Lodge area of Belfast.

On arrival the RUC officer did his usual thing – banging like fuck on the door until he got a response. When the occupants finally opened the door there was this fusty, unclean smell coming out. The whole search team entered and went into the living room (I use this term loosely) except one lad, left to guard the door. The occupants were all woken and brought into the living room. They were the parents and two young children of about six or seven years of age. As we entered the living room I had a quick look around and thought I was back in a training house in 'Tin City'. ('Tin City' was a training ground in Sennelager, West Germany constructed to resemble a Belfast or Londonderry street.) This flat was minimalistic even before minimalistic had become fashionable. The décor was the same throughout the property – a nice colour of grime over paint. The living room consisted of two armchairs, one settee, a sideboard and a rug – the colour of which I cannot remember; just remember that it was incredibly filthy. There was a TV on a stand and that was it – no pictures, no ornaments.

We started to search the flat and my partner and me went into the main bedroom whilst the other two lads went into the smaller one. I got a shock when I entered the bedroom as it contained a double-bed with nylon sheets on and only two blankets. I should point out that it was winter and it was bloody freezing. In the bedroom there was a small dresser and a grotty-looking rug that I would not have put a dog on. On the walls were smears of human excrement as well as the grime colour on the paintwork – and that horrible stale smell of urine. The curtains? Well, I've used better hessian on vehicles for 'camming' up and they were so filthy I don't know when they had last seen the inside of a washing machine. In fact, I don't think I saw a washing machine in the flat whilst we were there. This was more like doing a rummage search instead of a property search as there was hardly anything in the property to hide anything in. I took off the wall vent for the heating duct as this was the size of a rifle – nothing.

We then moved into the kitchen and, like the rest of the flat, this was filthy. There was a cooker, which was white enamel, complete with decorative grease and food splashes over it. The table and chairs were the type you would have seen in a 1950s transport café (i.e. thin metal legs with a thin piece of wood covered in plastic – sticky-back, wood pattern). The chairs were of the same design except they had a thin piece of covered foam on the seat. There was simply nowhere to hide anything. I took off a wall panel and shone my torch inside – nothing.

The search came to an end and as we left the flat I thought to myself: "How can anyone live like this? They weren't living; they just existed on the very edge of poverty. I know that during the Troubles times were hard, but personal hygiene costs nothing – nor does keeping a flat clean. When I got back to Girdwood it was straight into the shower – and all my clothes went straight into the washing machine. I'm glad we only got one property like this to search during our tour.

People who are reading this account – and did not serve in Northern Ireland or the British Army – may think that this is just another ex-squaddie ripping an Irish family apart. I come from a family of seven; that's my mum and dad, three sisters, a brother and me. I have always lived on housing estates in a city – in the East Midlands – where we had some rough areas and rough families, which would have given parts of Belfast a run for their money. The author of this book wanted true accounts of what we went through whilst we were serving in Northern Ireland; that is what I have tried to do here.

For the author, the overwhelming memory of searches such as this was an overpowering smell of boiled cabbage and stale urine. One remembers soiled nappies littering the floor; unwashed dinner plates and squashed beer cans and old newspapers. Looking down upon these scenes of squalor was inevitably a stern-looking poster or mass-produced painting of Jesus or an angelic Virgin Mary.

The morning of Monday, 27 August dawned with the promise of late summer British sunshine. It would prove to be a black day in British history as 18 soldiers would die – the worst terrorist incident in relation to the army of the Troubles – and a member of the Royal Family would be killed as well as other innocents in his party to further the cause of the Provisional IRA. The army has suffered worse days since the end of the Korean War – the Arab Police mutiny at Khormaksar, Aden on 20 June 1967 when 22 British soldiers died in a single day for example, and on several days during the 1982 Falklands War – but this was an appalling day for both the Parachute Regiment and the QOH.

Lord Louis Mountbatten – Admiral of the Fleet, 1st Earl Mountbatten of Burma – was a British statesman and naval officer; an uncle of Prince Philip, Duke of Edinburgh, and second cousin once-removed to Elizabeth II. He was the last Viceroy of India (1947) and the first Governor-General of the independent Union of India (1947–48) – from which the modern Republic of India emerged in 1950. From 1954 until 1959 he was the First Sea Lord – a position that had been held by his father, Prince Louis of Battenberg, some 40 years earlier. Thereafter he served as Chief of the Defence Staff until 1965 – making him the longest-serving professional head of the British Armed Forces to date. During this period Mountbatten also served as Chairman of the NATO Military Committee for a year.

Mountbatten usually holidayed at his summer home in Mullaghmore, Co Sligo – a small seaside village between Bundoran, Co Donegal and Sligo Town on the North-West coast of Ireland. The village was only 12 miles away from the border with Northern Ireland and near an area known to be used as a cross-border refuge by the Provisionals. Despite security advice and warnings from the Gardaí he went lobster-potting and fishing in the Shadow V, which had been moored overnight in the harbour there. On the fateful morning, Mountbatten (79) set off for a yachting trip from Mullaghmore. On board were his grandsons (twins) Nicholas and Timothy Knatchbull; cabin boy Paul Maxwell; Lady Doreen Brabourne, who was the mother-in-law of Mountbatten's daughter; and Lord Brabourne, his son-in-law. PIRA member Thomas McMahon had slipped onto the unguarded boat that night and attached a radio-controlled 50lb bomb. Mountbatten was aboard and had set sail for Donegal Bay. Just a few hundred yards from the shore, the bomb was detonated. Who activated the radio-controlled bomb is not known, as one of the chief suspects – a known player by the name of Thomas McMahon – had been arrested earlier at a Gardaí checkpoint between Longford and Granard. However, in his 2014 book *What Price Truth?* Raymond Gilmour who infiltrated the IRA names Padraig Mullaine, Rory Stanley and Fred Davey as the men who killed Mountbatten. This will be dealt with in a later book by this author. Source: *What Price Truth?* Raymond Gilmour, pp 248, 249.

When the device exploded, the 30-foot yacht was torn to pieces and reduced instantly to matchwood. Mountbatten was fatally wounded, but was pulled alive from the water by nearby fishermen. He succumbed to those injuries en route to the shore. Nicholas Knatchbull (14) was killed outright – as was Paul Maxwell (15). Nicholas' twin brother – Timothy – was dreadfully injured, but recovered in hospital. The twin lost an eye in the explosion and was ill for some time. Lady Bradbourne (83) was fatally wounded and died in hospital the next day.

A day or so later, one of the survivors – Lord Brabourne – described the moment of impact and the immediate aftermath: "We had just got out of the harbour and I was sitting on the side of the boat when it happened. The boat was moving slowly to the lobster pot. We were just about to haul it up when the explosion happened. Everything went up like that. I must have lost consciousness because I remember coming to under the water and fighting to reach the surface." The Peer had lost one of his twin sons – as well as his mother – and was himself badly injured in the explosion.

Paul Maxwell's father had dropped off his young son at the boat and had just driven off. He heard the explosion and immediately drove back towards the harbour. His poignant words about the loss of a young Irishman, killed by fellow Irish, speak volumes: "I knew that my son was dead. I couldn't believe that anybody survived such an explosion. There was little left of the boat apart from debris floating on the surface. I knew he was gone. He was a better Irishman than those who did that foul deed." His emotional words can be contrasted with the nauseating mellifluence of Mr Gerry Adams (see below).

Later on that terrible day, an IRA/Sinn Féin apologist gloatingly issued the following statement: "The IRA claim responsibility for the execution of Lord Louis Mountbatten. This operation is one of the discriminate ways we can bring to the attention of the English people the continuing occupation of our country."

Adams added his comments in a sickeningly similar fashion: "The IRA gave clear reasons for the execution. I think it is unfortunate that anyone has to be killed, but the furore created by Mountbatten's death showed up the hypocritical attitude of the media establishment. As a member of the House of Lords, Mountbatten was an emotional figure in both British and Irish politics. What the IRA did to him is what Mountbatten had been doing all his life to other people – and with his war record I don't think he could have objected to dying in what was clearly a war situation. He knew the danger involved in coming to this country. In my opinion, the IRA has achieved its objective. People have started paying attention to what is happening in Ireland."

Sean O'Callaghan, in his excellent book *The Informer* (Bantam Press, 1998), was greatly affected by the Mountbatten murder and he wrote: "These murders had a profound impact on me. Not only had the IRA targeted a man who had been visiting that area for many years and was the softest of soft target, they had exploded the bomb knowing that other people who were not remotely associated with the Royal Family would also be killed. They carried out the operation in the Irish Republic in direct contravention of their own orders. This had to be a decision taken at Army Council level. For me though, it was the final straw."

In *The Informer*, the author (ex-PIRA member turned informer) Sean O'Callaghan stated that the PIRA were paid £2 million by the Syrian Government for Lord Mountbatten's murder. The idea to kill Mountbatten had been conceived by senior IRA leader Brian Keenan – son of a former RAF officer – who together with Ivor Bell was seeking to push the organisation in a Marxist direction. According to O'Callaghan, Keenan had close contacts with GRU (the Soviet Military Intelligence), East Germany and Libya. During his discussions with GRU and the East Germans he was asked to prove PIRA's sincerity in its move towards Marxism by 'striking at the heart of imperialism'. He and Bell received GRU's approval in their choice of Mountbatten and the IRA subsequently received their money from Syria via the GRU. O'Callaghan suggested that the IRA's links were mainly with GRU and the East Germans.

O'Callaghan also speaks of several plots to kill the Irish Taoiseach Charles Haughey over a period of years to revenge the death of Mountbatten. He was aware that the Taoiseach, like the murdered Lord, also had a passion for sailing. Haughey's boat – the *Celtic Mist* – was moored in Dingle. Like Mountbatten's it had little or no security and he planned to sneak on board and place an explosive charge designed to explode when it was in deep water. The plan was later abandoned.

One wonders just what the death toll would have been; how much more the grief would have been widespread; how many more millions of pounds of damages would have been caused had it not been for a brave and select band of agents and informants. We owe much to the bravery of Marty McGartland, Sean O'Callaghan, Kevin Fulton, Raymond Gilmour and dozens of other unsung heroes who dared to defy the Provisional IRA.

Thomas McMahon was a member of the South Armagh Brigade of PIRA. He was one of their most experienced bomb-makers. He was convicted of the murder of Admiral of the Fleet Lord Mountbatten of Burma and three others. As stated earlier, McMahon was arrested by the Gardai two hours before the bomb detonated – having been initially stopped on suspicion of driving a stolen vehicle. He was tried for the murders in the Republic of Ireland and convicted by forensic evidence supplied by Dr James O'Donovan that showed flecks of paint from the boat and traces of nitro-glycerine on his clothes. He was sentenced to life imprisonment for murder on 23 November 1979, but was released in 1998 under the terms of the Good Friday Agreement. He has twice refused to meet Paul Maxwell's father, John, who has sought him out to explain the reasons for his son's death. Mr Maxwell stated that he had: " ... made two approaches to McMahon; the first through a priest, who warned me in advance that he thought there wouldn't be any positive response, and there wasn't. I have some reservations about meeting him, obviously. It might work out in such a way that I would regret having made the contact. On the other hand, if we met and I could even begin to understand his motivation; if we could meet on some kind of a human level – a man-to-man level – it could help me come to terms with it, but that might be very optimistic. McMahon knows the door is open at this end."

He helped with Martin McGuiness's Presidential Campaign in 2011 – erecting posters for the former 'Butcher of the Creggan' around Carrickmacross. He has never apologised for the Sligo murders and has refused to meet any of the victim's relatives.

The world thought that it could not get any worse, but at a picturesque place called Warrenpoint in Co Down, events would prove them wrong. Warrenpoint, the guidebooks tell us, is: " .... ..a small town in Co Down. It lies on the northern shore of Carlingford Lough and is separated from the Republic of Ireland by a narrow strait. The town sprang up within the townland of Ringmackilroy (from the Irish Rinn Mhic Giolla Rua, meaning MacIlroy's Point) and is locally nicknamed 'The Point'. Warrenpoint is known for its scenic location; the Maiden of Mourne Festival; the Blues on the Bay Music Festival; the passenger ferry service between Warrenpoint and Omeath; and the nearby Narrow Water Castle which dates from the 1660s." In July 2013 the author visited the area for the first time and was impressed by its beauty – in particular the old Elizabethan castle which, although propped up by scaffolding, nevertheless still stands five-and-a-half centuries after its construction. By the side of the busy main road which runs through it is a place called Narrow Water and over a small stretch of water sits the green forests of the Irish Republic – a beautiful place which would be forever scarred by violent death.

Just after 1630 hours on that fateful Monday, an army mobile consisting of a Land Rover and two lorries was driving past Narrow Water Castle on the A2 road. As it passed by a trailer loaded with straw bales, a watching PIRA unit detonated a 500lb device. The explosion caught the last lorry in the convoy – hurling it on its side and instantly killing six soldiers of 2 Para, whose bodies were scattered across the road. The driver was sadly unrecognisable and identifiable only by forensic science. Of the eight men in the lorry, only two survived and both were appallingly injured. Immediately after the blast, the soldiers from the other vehicles mistook the sounds of 7.62mm ammunition 'cooking off' in the burning lorry for incoming gunfire. It was common for PIRA gunmen to pour fire into the groups of shocked survivors following an explosion – and although what happened next is extremely regrettable, it was a natural reaction for the paras to think that they were being fired on. They thought that the incoming was being received from woods on the other side of the border, which was less than 200 feet away, and they began firing across the water.

Although it was forbidden under International Law and under ROE to fire into the Republic, they reacted as per their training and instincts – and this author will not condemn them. Tragically their rounds found two innocent targets – and one man, Royal Coachman Michael Hudson (29), whose parents lived in the Royal Mews, was killed instantly. His cousin, Barry Hudson – who had been bird-watching with him – was also hit and badly wounded. He survived his wounds.

On hearing the explosion, a Royal Marine unit alerted the army and reinforcements from other units of the Parachute Regiment were dispatched to the scene by road. A rapid reaction unit consisting of medical staff and Lieutenant-Colonel David Blair, who was CO of the nearby unit of the Queen's Own Highlanders together with his signaller Lance-Corporal Victor MacLeod, was sent by Gazelle helicopter. A larger Wessex helicopter was also dispatched to collect the wounded. Upon landing, Lieutenant-Colonel Blair as senior officer took command and immediately set up an ICP (Incident Command Post) at the other side of the road behind a farm lodge wall. The wall, which belonged to a lodge, was approximately 120 yards and diagonally opposite the scene of the first blast. Over the years of the conflict PIRA INT, as well as their army of 'dickers', had carefully watched the army's standard responses to shootings and explosions – and copious amounts of handwritten scrawl in dog-eared notebooks, still photos and (later) camcorders had recorded how they would react. They were correct in this instance and it doubled the tragedy for the army.

As a consequence, a second device – weighing 800lbs – had been concealed behind the wall where the ICP had been set up. Satisfied that sufficient soldiers were now assembled there (some 30 minutes after the first blast), a watching PIRA unit detonated the second bomb – causing utter carnage. When the smoke cleared, 12 more soldiers had been killed absolutely instantly and others terribly injured. Lieutenant-Colonel Blair's body was never found as he had been vapourised by the blast – and indeed could only be identified by his bloody epaulette, which was found nearby. His signaller was also killed – as well as 10 more paratroopers. One of the soldiers, whom I will not name, had his entire face torn off by the blast and could only be identified when it was found almost intact in the nearby water. General Sir Mike Jackson – then Major Mike Jackson – was on the scene and in his various writings described how he saw body parts hanging from trees, scattered across the road and floating on the surface of the nearby water. Cameraman Peter Molloy, who arrived at the scene of what could only be described as utter carnage, came close to being shot by a distraught paratrooper. Molloy was seen taking photos of body parts and clearly more intent on that than helping. The para aimed his SLR at the photographer, but his comrades hustled him away. Molloy was told to "fuck off" and ordered away from the scene.

One soldier who had been due to travel in the first lorry was Private Peter Grundy. However, as there was insufficient room he travelled in another vehicle. He survived the first and second blasts, but his luck ran out on 16 December when he was killed by the IRA at Forkhill (see Chapter 60).

The soldiers who were killed were: Lance-Corporal Donald Blair (23); Corporal Nicholas Andrews (24); Private Gary Barnes (18); Private Raymond Dunne (20); Private Anthony Wood (19); Private Michael Woods (18); Private John Giles (22); Private Ian Rogers (31); Sergeant Walter Beard (33); Private Thomas Vance (23); Private Robert England (23); Private Jeffrey Jones (18); Corporal Leonard Jones (26); Private Robert Jones

(18); Lance-Corporal Chris Ireland (25); and Major Peter Fursman (35). All were members of the Parachute Regiment. The two Queen's Own Highlanders killed alongside their para comrades were: Lieutenant David Blair (40) and Lance-Corporal Victor McLeod (24). Both of the QOH soldiers were from Scotland and the paras were from English towns and cities – although Robert Jones was Welsh and David Blair, like his QOH namesake, was a Scot. Several children were left fatherless by the double blasts and the widow of Leonard Jones said: "I don't know why he had to die. I feel so numb and confused. It seems so wrong that a young man with everything to live for should be killed like this." The soldier, from Manchester, left a toddler daughter who would now be around 35. This author would be honoured if she or any of the other children of Northern Ireland veterans or the fallen would care to contact him at the email address at the rear of this book.

Alexandra Blair, daughter of the QOH CO who was killed by the second bomb, was interviewed by the *Irish Independent* on the 25th anniversary of the outrage.

> 'David's dead.' The words were barely audible, but moments later I heard my mother sobbing in the next room. Numb with shock and disbelief, I carried on watching *The Great Escape* with Andrew – my eight-year-old brother. Then my grandfather came to us. He, too, was in tears. That was exactly 25 years ago – the evening of 27 August 1979 – and I was 10 years old. My father – Lieutenant-Colonel David Blair, commanding officer of the 1st Battalion, The Queen's Own Highlanders – had been killed by the IRA at Warrenpoint along with Lance-Corporal Victor Macleod and 16 soldiers from the 2nd Battalion, the Parachute Regiment.
>
> My father had been my hero. Dark-haired, 6ft tall with green eyes, he was fit, strong and handsome and always with a ready smile. My father treated me as an adult – encouraged me to explore and learn. The last words I remember him telling me before he left our home in Redford Barracks in Edinburgh – where we lived with the rest of the regiment – were: "Look after mummy and Andrew." My father's death was quick – just a fraction of a second. All that remained of him were two epaulettes. He was 40 years old. Eleven other men also died – almost vapourised by the blast. News of Lord Mountbatten's death and the first bomb had just reached my mother in Edinburgh. Anxious to reach my father, she rang the headquarters late that afternoon. "The colonel is unavailable," a voice said. He was probably already dead.

Brendan Burns [considered to be one of the Warrenpoint bombers] died nine years later – accidentally blowing himself up. He is thought to have killed at least seven other people with large-scale bombs. My father's other killer still walks free. In a sense, the absence of justice never mattered to my family. We knew that neither justice nor revenge would bring our father back. Instead, we were looked after by the tight-knit community of the Queen's Own Highlanders. Nobody could have wished for a closer family and without them we would not have survived. There is no memorial at Warrenpoint for fear that it would be defaced. A harmony of a sort reigns in the area now – and with that lives the hope that one day both sides will talk openly and make a permanent peace."

(Source: *Irish Independent* 28 August 2004: htp://www.independent.ie/unsorted/features/the-day-my-dad-was-killed-by-the-provos-160814.html)

The following morning the world's press revealed the real horror of the event – many (unfairly in this author's opinion) concentrating on the murder of Mountbatten and his party rather than what had unfolded at Warrenpoint. The *Daily Express* referred to Mountbatten as 'Britain's favourite uncle'. Under a justifiably angry headline – it proclaimed: 'These Evil Bastards' – followed by 'Horror Killing of Mountbatten – then soldiers are massacred as IRA unleash day of death'. The front page continued: "As the world recoiled with horror at the murder of Lord Louis Mountbatten, IRA killers struck again in Northern Ireland. At least 15 British soldiers died. Lord Mountbatten – one of the greatest men of the century – was the first victim in Britain's blackest day in Ireland for a decade."

It quoted villagers from Mullaghmore as being in mourning, saying: "The whole place is shocked. We feel ashamed that such a thing could happen here." The reporter wrote that: "House blinds are drawn. A group of people prayed at the harbour-side and flowers were thrown into the water where pieces of wreckage are being washed in."

He quoted a local resident – a retired nurse – as saying: "If only those who planted the bomb could see the terrible injuries they inflicted or a boy calling out for his daddy."

The reporter also quoted other eyewitnesses: "As the boat went out, the Earl waved at us." Minutes later they heard the explosion. "We went to the edge of the cliff and there was nothing but matchsticks."

Denis Devlin said: "The boat just went up; there was nothing left."

John O'Sullivan: "I heard the injured survivors crying for help – I will never forget it."

Christina Curran: "As soon as the people ashore realised what had happened, all the boats took to sea to help."

The newspaper also wrongly reported that 15 soldiers had been killed – although in all the chaos and confusion of the double disasters, they perhaps can be forgiven for their error.

On pages 2-3, the headlines were: 'Blown up by Lurking Killers' and '15 Soldiers (sic) die in horror blasts'. It continued: "At least 15 soldiers were killed yesterday in an IRA massacre. Late last night it was feared the death toll might be as many as 23. It was the highest death toll for one outrage ever suffered by the army in Ulster. All the dead men were from the Parachute Regiment – blamed for the Bloody Sunday killings in Londonderry seven years ago – and the Queen's Own Highlanders. Two massive booby-trap bombs took most of the lives in an ambush near Warrenpoint, South Down only yards from the border with the Irish Republic ... As well as the dead, at least eight soldiers were seriously wounded."

The newspaper report went on to describe how a medical helicopter was just taking off when the second blast occurred. It described how: "Hundreds of police and troops were at the scene sifting through the debris and completing the grisly task of looking for human remains. Police and army officers said they were startled at the pinpoint accuracy of the attack. The terrorists not only hit the first lorry-load of troops, but accurately judged the reactions of the soldiers. Said a senior police officer: 'It was cool and calculated. You would have expected them to have retreated after the first attack for fear of the Irish police and army, yet they waited a full 25 minutes before detonating the second bomb where they expected the troops to de-bus.'"

Somewhat incredibly – and somewhat belatedly – President Jimmy Carter of the USA decided to act and the U.S. State Department condemned the men who were behind the murders. A White House spokesman urged Americans not to support any of the organisations in the violence which led to the explosions in Ireland. The *Daily Mirror* quoted the spokesman as saying: "I reiterate in the strongest terms the condemnation of the U.S. Government of all groups or organisations which seek goals in Northern Ireland through violence. We again urge all Americans to refrain from supporting all such organisations."

One of the gang of four hypocrites – Tip O'Neill, Speaker of the House of Representatives – reiterated his clamour for the British withdrawal from Northern Ireland and said with the sort of sincerity which only a mother could believe: "We Irish-Americans must reject those who seek to unite Ireland through the use of violence." This then was the same U.S. politician who put his influence behind the move to prevent the RUC from purchasing weapons to combat these same men of violence whom he was allegedly condemning. Senator Edward Kennedy was quoted as being 'shocked' – there were many soldiers and members of the British establishment who would have stifled a smile at this had they not been grieving at the day's tragedies.

Other Irish-American comments included a senior NORAID figure, who was quoted as saying: "All members of the enemy camp were legitimate targets." This presumably included the young Irish cabin boy and the Earl's twin 14-year-old grandsons?

On the following day the *Express* interviewed Lieutenant-Colonel Jim Burke from the Parachute Regiment – by which time the newspaper had revised the number of dead soldiers to 18. He said: "I am cold and numb and all I can say is that we are very angry. We feel a sense of monumental loss. One is left numbed by it. But what we are left with is a great resolve to get on with the job. We will not allow this to cause us to overreact because we pride ourselves in every respect on being professionals." In the same article, the father of one of the dead soldiers – Private Jeffrey Jones – said: "His mates were against serving in Ulster too. My son said that none of them could understand what they were supposed to be fighting for."

Finally, the *Express* was angry at the inertia of both the Gardaí Siochana and the Irish Army, who as usual were found to be wanting when it came to policing their side of the border. Their reporter wrote: "There was concern in Ulster last night that the IRA ambush gang was able to operate for almost half an hour from a position just inside the Irish border without interception by the Irish Security Forces. The time-lapse was revealed as an investigation into the massacre at Warrenpoint, Co Down got under way. Ulster police confirmed that immediately after the first bomb went off, a message was flashed to the Irish police – yet 20 minutes later the hidden terrorists detonated a second bomb. About 30 minutes elapsed before Irish troops and police reached the wooded hillside overlooking the ambush scene. By then the killers had melted away."

Where the first blast took place is a flimsy wooden fence – over which one can see the strip of water which delineates the Irish border. It is there that former paras and their loved ones have built a makeshift shrine to their fallen. It consists of a small wooden square – on which there is a plastic wreath-holder – and placed underneath, a dozen or more small wooden crosses. Although weather-faded, the names of individual soldiers can be just about read. On the day that the author visited the wreath had been removed, the plastic holder smashed and the crosses all kicked over – no doubt the work of PIRA or some other Republican grouping's pathetic supporters. During this author's visits to Northern Ireland, he has encountered several Republican shrines. At no time has it ever crossed my mind to desecrate these homages to their fallen. One can only imagine the outpourings of outrage if this were to happen. If former soldiers or Loyalists desecrated Republican shrines in the same manner that they have damaged those at Warrenpoint or Kingsmill etc, every Sinn Féin councillor or MLA would be screaming blue murder.

During the construction of this book – in July 2013 – there was a further poignant reminder of that appalling day when one of the survivors of the first blast died. The *Daily*

Telegraph reported the death of one of the survivors – Lance-Corporal Paul Burns – who had died in hospital in Reading where he had been recovering from an accident sustained while bicycling in a charity event. The newspaper wrote: "The four-tonne truck in which Burns was travelling took the brunt of the blast. Six of the eight men on board died. A second explosion killed a further 12 soldiers. Burns had no memory of the bombing or of the seven weeks that followed. He was taken to hospital in Northern Ireland and then flown to England where his left leg was amputated below the knee. His right leg was also severely injured (it too was eventually amputated in 2012). A year passed before he was well enough to leave hospital. 'I didn't wake up for weeks. I should have been dead,' he said. 'I went down to five stone. I couldn't eat and had drips on both arms. I had tremendous guilt about being alive.' Re-joining his battalion after a year's rehabilitation, he continued to serve with the army until 1991 – working as a rigger for the Joint Services Parachute Centre. He completed more than 1,000 parachute jumps – even joining the Red Devils display team. In the same period he joined the British Limbless Ex-Service Men's Association (BLESMA) and learnt how to sail – also qualifying as a ski instructor."

Two days after the attacks (with Irish Taoiseach Jack Lynch preferring to remain on holiday under the Portuguese sun) Britain's Prime Minister, Margaret Thatcher, flew directly to Warrenpoint to survey the scene of the carnage and also fired a 'broadside' of the Irish Government – accusing them of a feeble and apathetic response to the IRA's handiwork. The Irish responded with a reward of £100,000 for the capture of the killers – and whilst conceding that the killers were known, admitted that they might never be brought to justice. She also visited the military wing of the Musgrave Park Hospital in Belfast, but five of the more badly wounded paras were too ill to be seen. The Parachute Regiment went straight back out on patrol. Any suggestion their 18-month tour of duty would be curtailed was swiftly rejected. A memorial service was held for the dead at the Royal Garrison Church in Aldershot on 26 September.

Lost in all the attacks, carnage and outcry there was an attack on a bandstand in Brussels on the day after Warrenpoint. An army band from the Duke of Edinburgh's Royal Regiment (DERR) was playing at an open-air concert when a device – planted by the Provisionals' European Team – exploded and slightly injured seven of the DERR musicians. It was a chilling dress rehearsal for an event which would take place in Regents Park, London on 20 1982 when seven members of the Royal Green Jackets were killed by the same terror group.

Over the years there have been many calls to investigate collusion between the army/RUC and Loyalist paramilitaries. Indeed, this author concedes that there may well have been evidence of this as possibly the SF felt that the Loyalists were fighting a common enemy. However, one cannot condone this – and this author has been extremely careful not to reserve his opprobrium for just Republican terror groups and has never shirked an opportunity to decry the likes of the UVF, UFF and the Red Hand Commandos. However, one needs to demand answers from the Irish Government in relation to allegations of collusion between Gardaí and the Provisional IRA.

The Smithwick Tribunal was a judicial inquiry being held in Dublin into the events surrounding the killing of Chief Superintendent Harry Breen and Superintendent Robert Buchanan of the RUC. The men were killed in a Provisional IRA ambush near the Irish border at Jonesborough between Co Louth and South Armagh on 20 March 1989 as they returned in an unmarked car from a cross-border security conference in Dundalk with senior Gardaí officers (see earlier in this chapter). When the subject of 'lost' evidence relating to the Warrenpoint attack was raised, some very interesting facts were announced.

A leading forensic expert – Dr Alan Hall – told the tribunal he was 'furious' when he discovered that the scene of the Warrenpoint bomb attack in 1979 had not been preserved. Dr Hall first inspected the 'nest' where the IRA unit had waited and detonated their bombs – on the evening of Thursday, 30 August – four days after the attack. But when he returned with a forensic team the following morning, he found 'the complete area had been obliterated'. He told the tribunal: "I can't see what advantage you would gain by scything the vegetation to the ground. I was furious at the loss of potential evidence. I was furious that having gone to the effort of setting up a whole team to do a job that was no longer necessary." Further, he said that the clearance was either 'unbelievable incompetence or deliberate obstruction'.

Dr Hall said he had told the plain-clothes Gardaí in charge of the site the first time he visited it that he would return the following morning with a full forensic team. He said he did not know the name of the officer he had spoken to. A former RUC officer told the tribunal that the plain-clothes officer was Detective Sergeant Owen Corrigan. Mr Corrigan, who was represented at the tribunal, denied the allegations of collusion which the tribunal was investigating.

Dr Hall said his recall was that there were still items at the scene such as sandwich wrappers, from which fingerprints might be recovered when he first visited it. Mr Dermot McGuinness – on behalf of the Gardaí commissioner – said that the scene had already been forensically examined by Gardaí forensic officers before Dr Hall arrived at the scene.

Allegedly, RUC Special Branch (SB) officers and a uniformed Gardaí sergeant warned an RUC chief inspector assigned to the border in 1979 to be careful of what he said in the presence of Gardaí officers because of security leaks, the tribunal was told. The SB officer was one of the first investigators on the scene following the Warrenpoint ambush in which 18 British soldiers died in August 1979. The retired detective chief inspector said he was told by RUC Special Branch to be careful what he said in front of Gardaí Detective Sergeant Owen Corrigan. He said he was later told by a uniformed Gardaí sergeant to be careful what he said because of leaks, but the Gardaí sergeant did not name any particular officer. At the time of writing, the tribunal was still ongoing.

LIFT ON SIGHT
Graham Briggs, Royal Artillery

The troop was on night patrol in the New Lodge and included a couple of UDR lads who were attached to us. We had been out for about two hours and were starting to make our way back to Girdwood via Dawson Street. I remember that there was a big wall near the flats; someone had painted 'We got 18 and Mountbatten' - a sick reference to the murder of 18 soldiers at Warrenpoint along with Lord Mountbatten of Burma by PIRA.

As we were approaching the junction of Dawson Street and the Antrim Road, Andy called to us and told us that there was a bit of trouble and ordered me to load the FRG (Federal Riot Gun) and I did so – handing my SLR to another member of the brick. When we got onto the Antrim Road we turned right and we saw JC's brick with two people - one of whom was a known player (the PIRA Quarter Master (QM) for the New Lodge) and there seemed to be a rather heated argument going on. I stood right in front of the known player with the FRG aimed at his chest. It's amazing how these so-called hard men suddenly become co-operative when they are looking down the barrel of a weapon and there are 10 squaddies around them.

Andy started to speak to JC and found out that all they wanted to do was 'P' check them both. The checks were carried out and a quick body search was done; they then went on their way and we returned to camp. The following day we were back out on patrol, but during the briefing we were told that the PIRA QM was now a 'lift on site' as he was wanted for questioning. There was no siting of him at any time during the day, which was unusual as he was always around the area. In fact, there was no sign of him on the entire Lodge.

Later that evening – during the briefing for the night patrol – the INT officer announced that the troop was going to patrol around the flats on Dawson Street and then go firm to seal the flats off as a joint army/RUC team were going to the QM's house and arrest him. My section left the base in two bricks, and as usual we 'star-burst' out of the gates – fast as we could – for safety. We then formed up in patrol order and started our patrol. At the end of Kinnaird Street, we turned right and then headed into Dawson Street. We patrolled the area until all the troop was on the ground. Andy then told us that we were to go to the waste ground at the back of the flats. This area was dimly lit by the streetlights of the flats and had plenty of shadow to hide in. Once there we were put into our covering positions and told where to watch. Mine was at the end of an alleyway looking directly at the QM's living room window.

I remember that the backs of the house were ankle-deep in rubbish and the locals must have just tossed all their crap over thinking that it was an extension of their dustbins! A lot of the lads who served out there just wondered how they could live in all this filth! Anyway I got down in the prone position and took aim at the target's window – he had red curtains and the light was on – and started to observe my area. It was so quiet … it was eerie – and even though I knew that comrades were within six feet of me, it was unnerving as I felt so alone! After what seemed hours we were moved out as the main team had gone in the front door and done a search; no sign of the PIRA man. Later – at the debrief – we were told that although he was not at the address he was definitely to be lifted the next time he was seen.

Anyway, the next day we were back out on patrol in the New Lodge area. Andy suddenly informed us that there was going to be a 'Rat Trap' by our QRF. The QM had been spotted by one of our ops getting into a yellow car and we were going to have him! Andy had the one and only radio, and as we entered Lepper Street (where Gunner Rob Curtis was shot dead in March 1971) he told us to go firm as the target car was in North Queen Street. It was assumed that it would then turn into New Lodge Road. Once the trap was sprung, our job was to move onto the New Lodge Road and stop any vehicles going up towards the trap area.

We had been firm for a few minutes when we noticed a yellow car go by and collectively wondered if that was the one. We were then ordered to move and witnessed the execution of a well-sprung trap! We saw the known player being manhandled into the back of a Land Rover and he was on his way for interrogation at North Queen Street RUC Station. It took us three days, but we got him. It shows how much we had to be on our toes to catch the IRA.

With their perverted sense of justice and honour, the UVF decided that it would begin the process of retaliation over Mountbatten and Warrenpoint and set out to kill a known member of the Provisionals. They targeted a PIRA member who was known to live in Ashton Street in the Nationalist New Lodge. However, they were thwarted by their target being out and instead simply knocked at the first random house they found in the same street. An entirely innocent Catholic – John Hardy (43), father of 10 children – answered the door. As he did so, in front of his curious children, the masked UVF men shot him the head and chest – killing him immediately. When asked by the trial judge at their subsequent court case, one of the killers said that they had randomly shot Mr Hardy because they had been told not to come back without a result.

Also on the 28th, Private Peter Mcclelland from Bangor, Co Down was struck by a vehicle at a VCP near his hometown. He was badly injured and died on the 4th of the following month. Finally, on that same day, the RAF lost LAC Jack Hawkins (20) – killed in an accident near Carrickfergus, Co Antrim. He is buried at Victoria Cemetery in his hometown.

August ground to a bloody halt. It was the worst month of the year and the bloodiest for quite some time. In all, 36 people had lost their lives in the Troubles or Troubles-related incidents. A total of 26 military personnel had been killed – 20 of whom at the hands of PIRA. One policeman had died also. Nine civilians, six Protestants and three Catholics, had been killed – of which just one was an overtly sectarian killing by the UVF. Of the 34 deaths, a staggering 30 were at the hands of Republican terrorists.

57

September

The month of September – in comparison with the previous one – was a period of 'only' 13 deaths. Seven soldiers died in non-terrorist related deaths, but there were three overtly sectarian murders by the Loyalists and two POs were shot and killed by the Provisionals. It was almost as if the Republicans had been sickened by the gross bloodletting of the Warrenpoint/Mountbatten killings and had eased off. That, however, was not the case – as the next 18 years would prove. The RUC had lost 129 officers killed and over 1,000 injured during the 10 years of the Troubles and would shortly be recruiting an additional 1,000 officers. This month a quite staggering total of 31 children would be left fatherless by murder gangs from both sides.

On the very first day of the month, the Loyalist 'backlash' continued in the wake of the IRA attacks against the paras and the man whom the *Daily Express* had referred to as 'Britain's favourite uncle'. Gerry Lennon (35) was a Catholic who lived and worked on the Antrim Road at a fruit and veg store in a small parade of shops south of Glandore Avenue. Today the small parade of shops is still there, but the business where Mr Lennon was murdered is long gone. The space is now occupied by four shops including a hairdresser's, a newsagent, Cedar Cabs and the almost ubiquitous Chinese takeaway. At around 9.30am two armed UVF men – who had arrived and parked a stolen motorcycle in Cedar Avenue – casually walked into the shop and shot him in the back and head as he bent over arranging a display of fruit. He was killed instantly and the two men dashed across the Antrim Road – avoiding traffic – and down Cedar Avenue where the stolen motorcycle was parked. It was later abandoned in the Protestant Glencairn area. On the same day, ATO was called out to defuse several PIRA devices which had been left at Cliftonville Golf Club. Two masked men forced their way into the club, situated on Westland Road, and placed the devices (three in all) in various locations – warning the terrified staff and golfers that they would explode in 10 minutes. All those present – it is thought in excess of 60 – were evacuated and RUC and army personnel were called in to make the devices safe. Some damage was caused, but there were no deaths or injuries.

On the following day the UFF – the military wing of the UDA – 'declared war' on the Provisional IRA in direct retaliation for Warrenpoint. At a press conference, hooded men – flanked by armed minders – stated that they would target members of the Provisional IRA and their homes or places of work. They had never been backwards at coming forwards, but now warned that there would be no hiding places for PIRA men or women. This threat was put into action the next day, but their flawed intelligence led them to kill an innocent Catholic – and it could only be seen as another sectarian murder. Henry Corbett (27) was a local darts player who lived in the Shore Road area of North Belfast. In the very early hours of the 3rd, four masked UFF men burst into his home as he was preparing for bed and chased him through his house – relentlessly shooting him as he desperately tried to escape. He was hit in the back a staggering 19 times before he finally collapsed and died in front of his horrified wife. His house was located at Bawnmore Grove – not far from Belfast

Docks – and his killers had the relatively simple task of escaping up the Shore Road to the mainly Protestant Whiteabbey area or the Loyalist Rathfern or Rathcoole. Mr Corbett had extremely tenuous Republican connections and it is thought that the Loyalist murder gang was after 'bigger fish'. Not that the Loyalist paramilitaries needed excuses, but they felt that the killing was justified after the Joseph Cunningham /Sinn Féin Cumann's decision to place an obituary on behalf of the dead Catholic. The following morning, Private Peter Alan McClelland (21) – the UDR soldier badly injured at a VCP outside Bangor the previous month – died of his injuries.

The RUC was quick to respond to the Loyalist 'declaration of war' and a spokesman issued the following statement: "The public is assured that the RUC is determined to act against any organisation taking part or threatening to participate in violence." The response to the UVF's statement that they would no longer indulge in sectarian murders – false as posterity has recorded – and actively target Republicans showed that the RUC wished to allay suspicions from the Nationalist community. On the same day – on the English mainland – a soldier by the name of Stephen Shepherd committed suicide in Roman Barracks, Colchester. The author has no further details, including age or unit. He had apparently witnessed the death of three of his friends in Northern Ireland and shot himself with an SMG. His name does not appear on the NMA ROH.

ANOTHER DAY AT THE OFFICE, 1979
Dougie Durrant, ADU

In late 1979 the Royal Military Police (RMP) started a small unit called The Pointer Team – a small unit of only four men – whose task was to respond to any incident in their TAOR and act accordingly. This meant any incident such as bombings, shootings etc; anything that was terrorist or military-related.

They operated out of Glassmullan Base – situated on the Andersonstown Road – and it was our task to support them with tracker and search dog capability. We were called to a post office robbery just off the Andersonstown Road – during which a number of terrorists had entered the post office and held up the cashier and got away with £5,000 or more.

We arrived at the location of the robbery and looked around – always weary of a 'come on' situation; coast seemed clear. The RMP team entered the post office with the RUC in support. The woman explained what had happened: two armed men had entered the post office with pistols and took the money and ran off in 'that direction' – and she pointed to the north. I walked up the road a short distance and was asked if we needed a tracker. "Not at this point," I said. "Let's just follow the money," as the robbers had unknowingly dropped a number of £5 notes in the direction of the housing estate up towards the Glen Road. So we followed the trail of cash and after about 500 metres it disappeared into a house. During the follow-up operation two men were arrested for armed robbery.

On our way back we got a call informing us to make our way to the Stewartstown Road area of Belfast as workmen had found an unexploded shell, so I tagged along for the ride rather than go back and sit by myself in the ops room. On arrival at a building site I saw a few workmen gathered around a JCB and someone was banging what I thought at the time was a hammer on the bucket of the JCB. As I got closer it became apparent that it was not a hammer but a 105mm shell with the fuse in! I shouted for them to stop, which they did. I then asked them to place the shell on the floor and move away. Not taking any chances we called ATO, who arrived a few minutes later and blew up the shell in situ.

The young workman who was banging the shell off the JCB bucket walked over to me and said: "Sure, I was going to take that home and show the kids!" I then asked him how many kids he had. "Six" came the reply – and I told him that he would have needed seven coffins! He asked me why and I smiled: "Six kids and you!" He just muttered: "Fuck!" and wandered off; just another normal day at the office.

On the 5th, Prime Minister Thatcher attended the funeral of Lord Louis Mountbatten – murdered the previous month by the IRA in Co Sligo. The State funeral was held at Westminster Abbey and was attended by representatives from all over the world – especially heads of the Commonwealth nations. The President of Ireland, Patrick Hillery, was present at a memorial service for Mountbatten in St Patrick's Cathedral in Dublin. Mountbatten was buried in Romsey Abbey after a televised funeral in Westminster Abbey, which he himself had comprehensively planned. The procession from Wellington Barracks, near Buckingham Palace, to Westminster Abbey was accompanied by the sound of bells and the solemn brass of Royal Marine bands. The cocked hat of an admiral of the fleet – his sword of honour and his gold stick – were laid on top of the Earl's coffin. Lord Mountbatten's horse, Dolly, was led near the head of the parade with the admiral's boots reversed in the stirrups. Thousands lined the route of the procession and the memorial service at Westminster Abbey was attended by royalty, leaders and politicians from all over the world. The Archbishop of Canterbury praised the Earl for his 'lifelong devotion to the Royal Navy'. President Carter of the USA delivered a snub to the British and did not attend the funeral – instead sending his representative, William Averell Harriman, to attend. It was later revealed that Mountbatten had expressed a wish that no Japanese attend his funeral – stemming from his experiences of their brutality during the Second World War.

Sadly for the 18 soldiers killed at Warrenpoint there was no State occasion and their sand-filled coffins were interred or cremated at private family funerals or with a military send-off from their grieving comrades. There were 18 separate funerals up and down the UK – none as grand as that which occurred at Westminster Abbey, but each – nonetheless – containing the same grief and poignancy.

Jack Lynch, Gerry Fitt and leading Unionist James Molyneaux were among the Irish attendees from both sides of the border. Thatcher later met with senior Irish politicians in London in order to discuss security matters. Over in Ireland Lynch had finally cut short his holiday in Portugal in order to deal with the cross-border security crisis, which was partly the fault of the inertia and apathy of the Irish Government. He was also stung by Thatcher's justifiable anger and justifiable criticisms following Warrenpoint. If collusion between the Gardaí and the Provisionals was on the agenda, it is not a matter of public record. Three days before, Lynch had rubbed more salt into the wounds when he stated that he opposed all of Britain's demands for tougher action against the IRA. He further stated that he didn't wish British troops to cross the border in pursuit of terrorists; refused to allow the RUC to cross the border to question suspects and ruled out the possibility of security contacts between the Irish and British armies.

CAR BOMB: DUNGANNON
Dave Pomfrett, Royal Green Jackets

I can't remember the date of this incident, but I will always remember it for a couple of reasons: 'The Dungannon Jeweller' and the force of the blast that shook our barracks on top of Castle Hill. I was in my room with my brick – 31C – with our full screw (Randy, Hovis and Tibs). The radio was on because we were due to go into a briefing and we liked to listen to Down Town Radio because we used to get more intel from that radio station than we did in our briefings. We heard on the radio that a suspect vehicle had been found in the town centre of Dungannon. At that moment, we were getting our kit ready for mobile patrols and drinking a brew – and generally taking the piss – when we heard a massive boom.

Now I had heard that sort of boom before, but we all jumped – except Randy, who laughed (probably at us jumping). Hovis got under his bed and the whole place shook. I thought our window was going to come in; you could see it shaking. Randy told us to get ready and get out by the rovers and he left the room. Minutes later he joined us outside and he gave a quick briefing by the unloading bay. His briefing was: "Load and Cock." Now that was the first time we had left the barracks with authorised cocked weapons on this tour! We walked out of Castle Hill Camp and when we got into the first street we could still see the smoke and the dust on the far side of the square to the right side. We hard-targeted down the hill and across the square; by then everyone were there (fire, ambulance, RUC and UDR).

Irish Street was a very narrow street which came out into the square from the far-right corner as you looked at it from Castle Hill up to the corner of Scotch Street. Irish Street was a long, narrow retail street that went downhill to William Street. I think the bomb was in a Datsun or maybe a Toyota car, but its position was chosen for maximum devastation – and that part of the plan worked. It totally devastated the whole length of Irish Street. As you will all know, blast will go round corners – and this blast certainly did that. The engine block of the car flew up and over rooftops – landing close to Lance-Corporal Keating and Rifleman Ivor Lane, who both had lucky escapes.

Luckily – and due to the quick actions of the RUC and UDR – no-one was seriously injured. It was mostly just shock – and just a big hole in the tarmac in the street outside the jewellers' shop. This was at the top of Irish Street, which was close to the seat of the explosion, and we gave these premises probably more attention than all the others! Well, they had to start the investigation somewhere I suppose. But you would have thought many were injured or killed by the scum which had planted that bomb … The unbelievable sight of devastation that met my eyes is something I will never forget. What was even more unbelievable was that most were back trading within weeks. We stayed out on the town for the rest of the day and into the night as contractors worked to make the buildings safe. I seem to remember a Republican bar on the right side of the street as you walked down the hill from the barracks. Standing out in front was a couple of gobby PIRA wannabes that were lifted by the UDR/RUC that night, but no follow-up. That is my memory of just one busy day in Dungannon in 1979.

On the 6th, a Loyalist murder gang burst through the doors of a taxi company on the Falls Road, which they suspected of being PIRA-connected. The waiting room was full of waiting passengers and a gunman – armed with a Sub-Machine Gun (SMG) – tried to spray the passengers. However, the SMG jammed and the would-be murderers fled in a stolen car. The following day a known Republican on Springfield Road was targeted by Loyalists as they painted white target circles on his front door and front wall. When he came out to remove them they opened fire with automatic weapons and badly wounded him. He recovered later in hospital. On that same day the Nationalist New Lodge area of North Belfast was flooded by soldiers from two battalions of the Royal Anglians and by the 1st Battalion of the Green Howards. With well over 100 soldiers on the ground – backed by eight search teams and five ADU dogs – several houses were raided and searched. In Hillman Street, a massive cache of arms and explosives was uncovered. The ATO considered the explosives too dangerous to transport and he carried it to waste ground where it was destroyed in a controlled explosion. The callousness of the Provisionals in storing such volatile matter in a residential street was further illustration of their attitude towards their own community.

BOMBS?
Mark 'C', Royal Artillery and UDR
During my tour in Belfast City Centre with 25th Field Regiment RA in 1979-80, we had several bomb scares and one big real one during that time. One of the scares was frightening because at the time we did not know if the bombs were real or not. Our brick had been called to the Anderson and McCauley store at the corner of Castle Street as there was a report that a security guard had found VHS cassette-type incendiary bombs. We headed round to the rear doors in Fountain Street and we had nearly reached them when the glass door burst open and the end of a large spade appeared with a load of black cassettes on them. It was then swung in our direction and the cassettes landed all around us. Well, as you can imagine, there was then a scattering match back into Castle Street.

What happened was the guard – fearing they were real and about to go off – decided to get them out of the shop; so got them unto a spade and chucked them out the back doors without realising four soldiers were approaching outside. He couldn't apologise enough when he found out what happened and we had a laugh about it at the time, but now I still have a few nightmares about them being real and exploding at our feet.

The issue of setting up a border buffer zone was again urgently raised by the British Government – and in military circles the idea of a 317-mile, border-long concentration of towers and manned by a huge number of troops was mooted. The RUC was against this and wished to concentrate on their objective of isolating PIRA from the communities in which they operated. They maintained that their strategies were working and the recent Warrenpoint/Mountbatten incidents had occurred because of the lethargy and lack of political will in the South. However, a leading expert in counter-terrorism studies maintained that not only should the border wall be entertained, but at the very least a 15-mile-deep buffer zone straddling the border was the solution in order to counter terrorist activity. He maintained that there would not be issues of sovereignty or jurisdiction as the present border would remain, but the SF forces of both countries would be allowed to operate freely in the area. Whether or not the political will was there on the part of the British is not recorded, but the inert and vacillating Irish Government wanted no part of it.

There was more controversy however when a Euro MEP (Member of European Parliament) – John Taylor, a Loyalist – called upon UFF and UVF terror squads not to attack Catholics or Catholic targets in the North, but instead to attack the 'weak-kneed Government of the Republic'. He warned that Loyalists: " ... .would not remain dormant when all they are offered are the usual statements about undefined new security moves. If the leadership of the Loyalist paramilitaries find it impossible to refrain from renewed action, then it should be directed to targets within the Republic from which most of the more serious IRA targets now emanate." He went on to accuse the Republic of being 'a safe haven for the IRA'.

On the 7th, a heavy-handed OIRA punishment squad beat a man so badly that he died in hospital three days later. He had allegedly knocked down a girl in his car in Belfast's Twinbrook area. Hugh O'Halloran (28) – father of five – was targeted by the OIRA thugs as he walked up to his front door in Moyard Park, West Belfast after a night's drinking. Although he protested his innocence, the punishment squad from the 'Stickies' were in no mood to compromise and he was beaten with pickaxe handles and Hurley sticks to the point of unconsciousness; he died on the 10th from brain damage – drowning in his own blood. Two men were later jailed for 15 and 13 years respectively. On the same day, PIRA gunmen using automatic weapons opened fire on a low-flying army Gazelle helicopter in the South Armagh area. The aircraft was hit several times as it flew over the Cullaville Road close to Crossmaglen. None of the soldiers on board were injured.

Also on the 7th, the Provisionals – through the Republican Publicity Bureau in Dublin – issued a grim warning via a statement addressed to the 'British people'. "Now that you have buried your dead – and the understandable responses which followed the events of last week have begun to subside – we sincerely hope that you can now understand the problems which your Government's presence has created in our country." By 'British people', did they also include the vast majority of the population of the North who felt British and were prepared to fight tooth and nail for their 'Britishness'? It continued: "You must understand that while Britain continues to interfere in the internal affairs of the Irish nation, there will be many more deaths of both British and Irish people."

On the 11th, armed PIRA men hijacked a goods train just north of Newry in Co Down after flagging the driver down with a red warning flag. The cargo of mainly Harp lager and Guinness beer was strewn around the tracks and a call was made claiming that explosives had been planted. The lines closed and ATO and army search teams from the QOH and UDR had to ensure the safety of the product and the rolling stock before the line was re-opened. Despite exhaustive research by this author, it has not been established if the odd beer keg or two managed to find its way into the messes of the two units mentioned earlier.

Despite the earlier claims of the UVF that they had forsaken the sectarian murder path, an armed murder gang targeted a Catholic – Gabriel Wiggins (56), father of 14 children – who lived on the Springfield Road as it sweeps down towards New Barnsley. They knocked on the door late on the night of the 12th, but Mr Wiggins – a local gardener – wisely refused to answer. However, the gunmen fired several shots through the glass in the front door – mortally wounding him. One of his daughters heard the shots and dashed into the hallway in the darkness (her father had turned off the lights just before he was shot) and found him lying there. The UVF were sectarian murderers through and through and no amount of press conferences avowing the 'nobility' of taking the fight to PIRA would ever change that.

Less than 48 hours after the train hijack, the IRA's Co Down Brigade were again involved and several bombs were planted outside banks in Newry City. There was structural damage, but no injuries. Because of the increased threat of sectarian violence from the Loyalist paramilitaries, army/RUC patrols through Catholic areas were increased. Rather than allay the fears of Catholics, Sinn Féin complained that it was a cynical move by the SF to further infiltrate and control Nationalist communities.

On the 12th, Kevin McAteer – an IRA member from West Belfast who had given evidence against his former comrades – was publically sentenced to death by the local ISU (Internal Security Unit). He was forced to flee Northern Ireland and taken to England in order to begin a new life and new identity.

DEATH OF A PRISON OFFICER
Herb Jackson, Royal Artillery

One day we were sent out on an errand for the BQMS to Flax Street Mill and we took a couple of store lads with us for a ride. We drove up to the mill, did our errand and headed back to our base at the Grand Central Hotel (GCH) in the centre of Belfast. The CO was busy with the RUC at the time and on our way down the Crumlin Road we were debating which way we should go back to GCH – a normal thing for us to do as changing routes was expected and encouraged (this was vital as PIRA had a veritable 'army' of dickers whose job was to observe and report British Army routine and predict patrol and vehicle patterns. Armed with this information, ambushes on soldiers were easier to plan and vulnerable points

Soldier outside Grand Central Hotel base, Belfast, 1979. (©Mark 'C')

easier to predict. Interestingly enough on the 13th of this month, three West Belfast youths were charged with several offences all related to dicking). We also invited choice from the lads in the back who had joined us that day. We finally made up our minds to turn off and head across to the Shankill Road and head into the GCH on that route.

A mate of mine called Jeff was driving and we had just turned a corner when we heard two or three gunshots. He stopped immediately and we agreed with each other as to the direction of the shots. We were spot-on in our assessment and I immediately radioed in: "Hello, Zero; this is Zulu niner; Contact. Wait. Out." By now we had turned and reached the junction of the road and turned right in the direction of the shots. Literally 200 yards later we came across the RAOB (Royal Antediluvian Order of Buffaloes) Lodge – a charitable organisation; some might uncharitably say 'the poor man's Masons'.

A body lay in the doorway – a pool of blood beside him. A brick had also quickly arrived on scene, which freed us up to run back to the 'Landy' and follow a directed route where the gunmen had sped off in a car. We raced off quickly – sending a quick sit-rep (situation report) over the radio to inform of our action. The brick on the ground would take control and fill in details at the scene. We travelled at high speed looking for the guilty – sadly in vain as they had too much of a head-start and so many roads to choose their escape route.

On our return – after searching several streets for the gunmen – the RUC were now there and another brick had arrived. The man we saw in a pool of blood earlier was a prison officer from the nearby Crumlin Prison. He had been shot dead at point-blank range – shot more than once and more than necessary. He was off duty and going for a drink at his club. His life ended on a cold, wet pavement simply because he chose the wrong job. I could very often find myself understanding the arguments made by both sections of the Northern Irish community regarding the Troubles, but never understood their targeting choices or methods.

As we eventually headed back to the GCH it became clear to me that fate is a very real thing. Had we not turned off that day we would probably have arrived at the scene as the gunmen were about to carry out their deed. After all, we were only 2-300 yards away when the shots rang out after making our turn. We may even have stopped it happening or even caught those responsible. A lot of ifs I know, but it was perhaps that man's fate that we preferred the Shankill to the Crumlin that day. Had we done the opposite, we might have saved his life and the grief of his family.

The prison officer killed that day – 14 September – was George Foster (30), who was off duty. He was shot by IRA gunmen outside Buffs Social Club, Century Street off Crumlin Road, Belfast. On that day the Provisionals targeted a regular lunchtime venue for POs close to Crumlin Road Jail. These men, enjoying a respite from a difficult and dangerous job, would be what Mr Gerry Adams might have called a 'legitimate target'. George Foster had driven to the café with three other colleagues and, having eaten lunch, the four POs drove off back to Crumlin Road. Unaware that they were being trailed by PIRA gunmen in a stolen car, they turned into Century Street just before they were due to turn left onto

Crumlin Road (just 2-300 yards from the jail). The gunmen in the following car then opened fire with an automatic weapon – with several shots entering the car. One of the POs was wounded in both arms, but Mr Foster was hit in the head and died very shortly afterwards. The gunmen then raced off in their stolen car and it was abandoned close to a Nationalist area in the Antrim Road. Provisional IRA bombers also targeted a bank in Dungannon and other shops in Londonderry on the same day. There were no injuries during any of the subsequent explosions.

CROSSMAGLEN BOMB
Joe Paterson, Royal Marines

I had been in Northern Ireland for about four months. As per normal, all was going well; lots of observations, checking persons and vehicles. On the day of 30 September, nothing seemed out of the ordinary. There were four patrols out on the street, but to our disadvantage there was always one street unmanned – being watched from the ops room by CCTV – until we entered the street. Until we radioed into control that we were moving into the street, they would continue to monitor.

As we entered the street adjacent to Newry Road I was the left-front of the brick (four-man team). I first moved to the right of the road to observe the forward street from a good firing position until my colleague came up to me from behind and indicated for me to move on. I then sprinted back across to the left of the road and maintained my observations as the rest of the patrol re-joined us now on the Newry Road. Everything at this point seemed ok – nice and sunny and good observations all around. As I started patrolling on the left of the street (I was still front-left) I observed forward and right of myself. Two guys, who looked like they were weed-killing in the grounds of the church graveyard, were just up and to my right. Now these guys had green backpacks on of the type that you would normally see gardeners wearing, but to me that did not seem right for reasons that I still can't explain. So as I was patrolling down said street, I informed my other three colleagues that I was going to question this pair. I also said that I would move to where I would be parallel with the church steps to my right and go up them.

At that point it was safety first and I looked forward to my cover positions whilst moving forward – thinking about where I would take up a fire position. My training kicked in and I wanted to make sure that I could observe the ground to my front and left. As I walked, I saw to my left about 60 feet away two detached houses with front-walled gardens – both being separated with a driveway. As I approached the driveway – at this stage I was about 15 feet away – I was thinking about taking up a fire position. I was going to stop and intended to crouch down and make myself a hard target as I knew you could see right through the driveway from the rear.

Now I don't know where the thought that came into my head came from, but out of the blue I heard my own voice saying: "DONT STOP!, DONT STOP!" I could not work this out, and as I was trying to I was still walking forward but I was fighting myself to stop. But for some unknown reason, I decided to go with my thoughts (I'm now at the corner of this wall). So I went forward and stepped off the pavement and onto the driveway – looking to my left to make sure I was safe; all seemed ok. But as I was stepping back onto the pavement off the driveway there was a massive high-pitched whine and something hit me on the top of the head, which made me bend forward slightly. I felt my beret come off my head at this point, and also to my right I saw something come past me about the size of two footballs put together. It was travelling upwards from about waist-height (I think it was part of the wall). It bounced off the armoured personnel carrier, which was now on my right side. The said item hit the mesh, which was attached to its left side, and then it bounced off. At this same time I was being pushed forward – not knowing why (possible force from bomb). I saw another driveway to my left and dropped into it and lay there. It seemed like things were on a slow motion, but as I lay there face-down I realised that a bomb had gone off and I hoped I was still alive. I realised I was and a tear came to my eye.

I don't know how long I was there, but some time later someone grabbed my left arm and tried to turn me over. I pulled my left arm back to the ground – and again my arm was grabbed – and I was turned over only to see a strange face looking at me. My first words were: "Who the fuck are you?" At this point this guy tried to talk to me, but I could not hear a thing. All I could hear was ringing in my ears. Just after I was turned over I also started seeing my colleagues coming towards me as I was still lying down. I was being checked over by this guy (I later found out he was a doctor from one of the two houses involved).

I then saw the APC with a red cross on it and thought: "That's here for me; I'm safe." I eventually walked back to the APC, which was about 10 feet from me. I was taken back to the ops room and immediately asked what I thought had happened. I told them that I wasn't sure, but my head was all over the place and I do remember telling them I had heard the same wall creak the night before as I had patrolled past it. Was it some sort of premonition? Perhaps I will never know.

Between the 15th and the 26th the UDR lost four more soldiers in circumstances unknown. The men were: Sergeant Joseph Turner Agnew (50) from Markethill, Armagh on the 15th; Sergeant Major James Warnock (56), also on the 15th; Corporal Ernest Atkinson (54) on the 23rd; and Corporal Cecil Stewart Roleston (45) on the 26th. Private Roleston was buried at Cloveneden Presbyterian Church close to Loughall in Co Armagh.

On the 15th, Corporal Robert Moore (28) of REME was killed in an RTA somewhere in the Province. Sadly the author has no further details about this accident. His funeral was held at Goytre Cemetery near the South Wales town of Port Talbot. Some 48 hours after the death of Corporal Moore, the IRA attacked a Protestant business – Herbert & Son Carpets – on the Boucher Road close to Balmoral Cemetery. Armed men forced the staff to remain on the premises and then deliberately misled them about the timings of the explosions. The workers were told that they had a good 30 minutes before the devices were due to detonate. However, the plan was also to lull army personnel into thinking that more time was available – and in the event staff were barely able to evacuate before the bombs started to explode. That day continued with a major RUC raid on a house in the Nationalist New Lodge area searching for arms and ammunition. Thanks to the work of an informer an Armalite and some 700 rounds of ammunition were seized and an arrest made.

Scene of the murder of a prison officer, Crumlin Road, Belfast, 1979. (©Mark 'C')

Car in which a prison officer was murdered, Crumlin Road, Belfast. (©Mark 'C')

Another PO was murdered by the Provisionals just five days later – this time a mere 200 yards from where PO George Foster was killed. Edward Jones (60), father of ten children, was returning to Crumlin Road Jail on the 19th along with another colleague. They had just driven down Cliftonpark Avenue and had halted at traffic lights before turning left into Crumlin Road. The jail is less than 100 yards to the left and on the day that the author visited – at the traffic lights where the assistant governor stopped – the jail is easy to see over a patch of waste ground. Back on 19 September 1979, if the PO had looked left his view of the jail would have been partly obscured by the blackened stone houses of Landscape Terrace (now long since pulled down). As the two men waited for the lights to change, a car (stolen earlier) pulled alongside and the front-seat passenger pointed a revolver at Mr Jones and fired twice – hitting him in the head and mortally wounding him. The stolen car raced through the lights – still at red – and disappeared towards the Falls Road where it was abandoned. Mr Jones was rushed to the nearby Mater Hospital but he was already dead. During the Second World War he had served with distinction in the Irish Guards – holding the B.E.M. As previously mentioned he was the second PO to die in less than five days. Four more would be murdered by PIRA before 1979 had finished.

VCP MADNESS
Mark 'C', Royal Artillery and UDR
From September 1979 to January 1980 I did a tour in the GCH Belfast with 25th Field Regiment RA – and there is one incident that stands out for me and shows how surreal the situation was in Northern Ireland at the time. Our brick was doing a VCP in Smithfield Market when we stopped a car. The brick commander, Bombardier 'L', was suspicious of the driver and decided he wanted the car back to the GCH for a more thorough search. However, the problem was how to get it back to base as there were no other units available and there were only four of us and a Land Rover. So the NCO decided in his wisdom to put me in the back of the suspect's car and accompany him to the GCH. So in I jumped, cocked my weapon and told the guy to follow the rover round to the base after telling him in no uncertain terms that I was under orders to shoot him if he tried to drive away.

Now I was in a bit of a dilemma. I had to hope the driver would comply with orders and not attempt to drive to the nearby Republican Divis or Unity Flats areas. If he was hiding something and was a terrorist, surely he knew where to escape to – and if he did do that would I then have to shoot him (possibly injuring or killing myself in the certain crash that would follow)? With all this going on in my mind we set off – with the driver chatting to me as if he was on a shopping trip! Being from Belfast myself, my answers were of one syllable – trying not to give my accent away to a potential terrorist – but as we got to the GCH, he said: "You must be UDR then, working with the Brits!" I said no and was very glad to see the guard let us in and we drove into the garage where 'Felix' (EOD) kept their vehicles. The car was searched, but nothing was found and I don't think the driver was a threat. It was just another mad incident in a mad 1970s Belfast.

On the 20th, there were several major attempts to kill both civvies and SF as the Provisionals continued their relentless murder campaign. In the first incident an armed PIRA gang took over a house close to the Whiterock Road – and whilst the family were held at gunpoint, an automatic weapon was set up in an upstairs bedroom. A hoax call relating to a bogus break-in was called through on the 999 line – a tactic which had seen the deaths of several policemen over the years – and the gunmen waited for an RUC response. As the police vehicle arrived the gunmen panicked and fired off a round at the officers who, now alerted, were able to take up defensive positions. The gunmen fled – thwarted for at least the time being. Then in shades of previous attacks – both failed and deadly – the IRA bombed a train in Belfast. As the Belfast-bound service pulled out from Finaghy Road North Station, the guard spotted a brown bag in one of the toilets. The train then made an emergency stop at Balmoral and the passengers were evacuated. The bomb exploded, with a second device failing to detonate. No-one was injured, but the disruption had the desired effect and all services were delayed. An elaborate hoax was perpetrated just several days later when Republican youths placed several beer kegs near the line at Lurgan. Naturally, the SF could take no risks and the area was sealed off and train services suffered further disruption. The beer kegs were empty, but controlled explosions and further searches resulted in the line being closed for most of the business day. On the following day a PIRA 'come on' almost resulted in the deaths of policemen on Shore Road in North Belfast. An RUC patrol was called to a suspicious vehicle seemingly abandoned in Skegoneill Road – and as officers were examining the car they came under fire from a car which had lain in wait in a side street awaiting their arrival. For the second time in 24 hours the gunman's shots were hurried and no officers were injured.

'FELIX'

Eddie Atkinson, Green Howards

I remember calling 'Felix' out in the Ardoyne as we had found a carrier bag with wires etc. It looked highly suspicious – and a possible bomb – near to the Flax Street Mill. Up comes ATO and susses it. He walked up to it and after a quick glance, picks it up and shouts: "Hoax!" When he came back, I said: "I wouldn't have your job for all the tea in China." He just looked at me and replied: "You know what; I wouldn't have your job. You never know what's coming. At least I know what I'm dealing with!" I will never ever forget it. God bless all 'Felix' teams.

On the 22nd, a pub was bombed in Forkhill, South Armagh – in all likelihood by the Loyalists. The bar was Catholic-owned and Catholic-frequented and two devices wrapped in plastic bags were thrown inside. There were no serious injuries, but the building was almost demolished. No claims of responsibility were made, but most observers would point to the proximity to Warrenpoint and to the avowed intention of Loyalist revenge. Three days later the Provisionals planted several devices inside the main Lisburn shopping centre. As usual, inadequate warnings were given and the police and army were evacuating the centre when the devices began to explode. A total of eight shoppers were injured by the blasts. On the Shankill Road, a foot patrol of the UDR – providing protection to an RUC arrest team – was mobbed by several hundred Loyalist supporters. Amidst cries of "Fucking traitors" and the like, the UDR patrol leader was forced to fire his weapon over the heads of the threatening mob in order to extricate both police and soldiers out of the area.

ALMOST AN ND
Herb Jackson, Royal Artillery

The nearest any of us knowingly came to being shot was when we got the taxi job of taking the 2IC (2nd In Command) – a Major – to the Crumlin Road Jail. We knew not why he was visiting the jail. Maybe it was a requirement during the tour. Anyway, I assumed that the pressures out there and the responsibilities of officers weighed heavy on them sometimes; well that's what I put it down to. The 2IC seemed preoccupied that day and a little rushed judging by the way he urged us on from the start. My mate Jeff was driving on this occasion. We got the job and picked up the 2IC in the garages and went on the relatively short drive to the nick on Crumlin Road. When we got there, the 2IC would have to relinquish his weapon into our care as he would not be allowed to enter the prison whilst armed.

The 2IC carried a 9mm semi-automatic pistol – as did most senior officers. There is a procedure for handing a weapon to someone. First of all the magazine is removed and the weapon cleared by cocking the weapon – showing the open and clear chamber to whoever you are handing it to; then the working parts are released forward with your finger up the slot where the magazine goes; then you would pull the trigger to release the mechanism then hand it separately to whoever, followed by the magazine.

Now when we came to a halt we reminded the 2IC he needed to give us his weapon. He clearly had lots on his mind and took out his pistol, cocked it with the magazine still in it, pointed it towards Jeff's leg as he sat in the driver seat and was about to pull the trigger. Those of us watching jumped in, instinctively, to stop him shooting Jeff in his 'credentials' – as did Jeff himself. One pair of hands pushing the barrel downwards – with someone else's thumb on the cocking mechanism – and hushed voices pointing out the error. "Whoah, Sir!" I heard someone shout: "Stand fast!" and we quickly took the 9mm from him and let him go on his way – saying: "It's ok Sir; we will sort it," as casual as you like. He then seemed to calm down and walked into the jail. We looked at each other and there was a collective sigh of relief and a breathed: "Fookin' hell!"

There were the usual jokes about us allowing the officer to shoot us in the foot in order for us to grab some sick leave! We never reported this or even mentioned it to any other lads. We didn't feel it necessary to crap on someone under stress for something that could happen to any of us if the circumstances were against us. Besides, if we did say something he was the 2IC with a lot of clout and we might have ended up on sangar duty for two months!

Four days before the planned arrival of the Pope, PIRA gunmen took over a house in Monagh Road in the Nationalist Turf Lodge. The raid was carried out under cover of darkness and the family were held hostage overnight whilst the gang set up a sniper shot on the army base at Fort Monagh, which was almost directly opposite. At first light – as a foot patrol bomb-burst from the fortified base – a gunman opened fire with an automatic weapon (thought to be a U.S.-supplied Armalite) and five rounds were aimed at the soldiers. As a result of the IRA's customary lack of consideration for civilians, they took no notice of two passing women and the proximity of the shots caused both to faint. A dog was hit and wounded; no soldiers were hurt. The gunmen were spirited away into safehouses where prepared hot baths and clean clothes were awaiting in order to eradicate all forensic evidence. The weapon was carefully dismantled and moved around the Turf Lodge in several component parts to be delivered to the local armourer once the heat had died down.

On the 29th, Pope John Paul II visited Drogheda, Co Louth in the Republic. He spoke to an estimated crowd of 250,000 people and appealed for an end to violence in Northern Ireland. Before travelling to Drogheda he was flown to Phoenix Park in Dublin where he delivered an open-air sermon to more than 1.25 million people – nearly a third of Ireland's entire population. He was loudly applauded at Drogheda when he said (in a direct address to the consciences of both terrorists and politicians): "On my knees I beg of you to turn away from the paths of violence and to return to the ways of peace." He continued: "To Catholics; to Protestants; my message is peace and love. May no Irish Protestant think the Pope is an enemy, a danger or a threat?" It is not recorded if any of PIRA's Catholic members heeded his heartfelt pleas. Perhaps he should have looked more deeply into collusion between his own Catholic priests and the Provisionals. There was massive security by both the Gardaí Siochana and the Irish Army as it was feared that there might be a Loyalist outrage in the wake of the Warrenpoint and Mountbatten murders, which had occurred only four weeks earlier. The Pope later returned to Dublin where an estimated 750,000 people watched his motorcade drive through the Irish capital.

Whilst the Pope was preaching to the Catholic faithful – and being ignored by PIRA and their supporters – Driver John Dorrity (30) of the Royal Corps of Transport (RCT) was killed in an RTA. On the same day two POs had a lucky escape as they drove home after their shift at Crumlin Road Jail. The two men were about to enter the M1 motorway at the Sprucefield roundabout when they came under fire from concealed gunmen. Fortunately – although the car was hit several times – neither officer was injured and the gunmen escaped in a waiting stolen car.

September had ended with 13 deaths – seven were soldiers – and two POs were murdered by the Provisionals. Four civilians died – three Catholics and a Protestant – and three of the deaths were overtly sectarian.

58

October

A total of 16 people would die this month – of whom nine were military personnel (including one former soldier killed because of his past association). There were more sectarian murders by the Loyalists and there was some speculation that the Provisionals had showed their gangster side when a civilian was killed in doubtful circumstances.

A Catholic family from Andersonstown had just returned from the Republic where they had been – just a minute – part of the estimated 1.5 million people who had been to see the Pope. As they pulled off the motorway directly opposite their house, they found masked gunmen already in-situ. PIRA gunmen were setting up a shoot at a passing SF mobile patrol and the family were pushed at gunpoint into a downstairs room and warned to keep quiet. They had set up Armalites on tripods and opened fire as an army Land Rover slowed down to exit the Belfast-Dublin M1 with a salvo of rounds – hitting the driver's section. The vehicle turned over, but fortunately – although only lightly wounded – the three occupants were able to scramble clear and take up all-round defence. The gunmen quickly packed up and disappeared towards the Turf Lodge. The *Belfast Telegraph's* front page the following day was justifiably predictable: 'Provo guns answer the plea for peace!' One of the injured soldiers describes the incident:

GETTING SHOT FOR A LIVING!
Michael Dackombe, Royal Green Jackets/Army Catering Corps
The incident happened on Monday, 1 October 1979 at 10.45am. We were proceeding along the M1 motorway and had just passed Andersonstown Cemetery. What I can only describe as a series of cracks echoed around us through the open lorry window. My instant thought was somebody was shooting at a patrol within the housing estate that ran alongside the motorway. Then, in that split-second, I realised that somebody was shooting at us. I instantly ducked into the footwell within the cab of the lorry.

Suddenly, the windscreen of the lorry shattered and then I felt what can only be, described as being hit in the side of the head with a hammer. The next thing I was aware of was the blood running down the side of my face. Whilst this was happening, the driver of the lorry was desperately trying to manoeuvre the vehicle along the motorway and around other vehicles that were in his path. He was doing this from a crouched position in the footwell! In what seemed a long time – but was only a couple of minutes – we had overtaken a diesel tanker in front of us which had also been caught in the line of fire. From what I gather from sources after the incident, the driver of the tanker was so scared of being caught in the line of fire that he drove his vehicle off the motorway and left it abandoned on the housing estate in his panic.

A minute or two after the initial contact – because that's all it took – the driver of the lorry drove us into the back gate of Musgrave Park Hospital and we pulled up and I climbed out looking a right mess with blood pouring over the left half of my face and down my flak jacket. I was greeted by a couple of medics who took me into the hospital reception area to be assessed in triage. The press were already in the reception and I was asked if I could give my account of the incident, but declined until I had spoken to my CO first. I believe that my incident was reported in the major newspapers within Northern Ireland and the northern half of the UK.

Whilst in triage I was assessed as having superficial lacerations to the side of my head – with shards of windscreen glass embedded into the skin – but it wasn't until the doctor had received the results of the x-ray that they discovered it was not glass embedded in my skin, but shards of bullet fragments. The picture of my skull looked like a pepper pot. I was then told that some of the fragments were lying close to the skull itself and they would try and remove as many of them as possible. However, even today in 2014, I still have several fragments lying against my skull as they had deemed it too dangerous to remove them. As I later found out at a military briefing on the incident, my ops room were not told about the incident until several hours later. It also transpires that the two members of the IRA team had set up a firing point from the back bedroom of a bungalow overlooking the M1 after first having taken hostage the family that had just returned from Dublin after having seen Pope John Paul.

As a result of the shooting I now have partial nerve loss around the wound site and scar tissue – and will have for the rest of my life – and I have a war pension for the injury and the inevitable PTSD injury. This was my first of many tours in Northern Ireland and I arrived at Castle Dillon in July of 1979 and was there when Warrenpoint took place – and having been through such a traumatic experience, over the years I have felt for all the lads and lasses that we have lost. I hope this piece will contribute – and can be used in your publications or written history of Northern Ireland – to bring to light to other people some of the things that the British Army went through over there, as it is a piece of my life history .

On the following day Sir Maurice Oldfield was appointed Chief Security Co-ordinator and he took up the role amid speculation that he had been put in place in order to bring the army and the RUC closer. 'Ulsterisation' – or 'police primacy' – was here to stay, but there was disquiet in the top ranks of both institutions and it was felt that Oldfield could be the man to bring them together. The urgency of his appointment had been triggered, many people felt, by the recent explosion in PIRA activity – unintentional pun – and also by the fact that both the RUC and the army were often working at cross-purposes and that intelligence was not being shared. Oldfield's role was to ensure that there was no duplication of work and that rivalry should now cease and cease forthwith if they were to defeat the increase in Republican terror. Although he died just two years later, it is known that he put the emphasis on targeting top Provos and concentrating efforts on cutting off the many heads of the terror organisation.

On the 4th, in a move which even the UDA condemned, the 'blacknecks' of the UVF murdered a popular local Catholic woman in a blatant sectarian slaying. Sarah 'Sadie'

Larmour (44), mother of two, was well-known in the Rodneys – an area of terraced housing just off the Falls Road close to Donegall Road. In the early evening, two gunmen on a stolen motorbike parked close to the house and the pillion passenger calmly walked through the unlocked front door and found her sitting with her sister and elderly mother. Without speaking the gunman shot her in the chest and then as Mrs Larmour's sister tried to protect their mother, the gunman fired again but missed before running out of the house. She died very soon after reaching the RVH, which is less than a mile away from the Rodneys. It was a blatant sectarian murder and even the UDA condemned the killing.

The same Loyalist terror group struck again the following day when their Mid-Ulster Brigade shot a man in Camlough, Co Armagh. Camlough is deep inside Nationalist territory and is close to both Newry and the Irish border. Striking so deep, the UVF were clearly showing the Provisionals that they would come into the very heart of their territory. Martin Rowland (26), a Catholic with no known Republican links, was singled out for murder because he lived in a remote area. He was shot dead by a group calling itself the South Armagh Action Group – a cover name for the UVF. Mr Rowland had set off for a stroll and had only walked some 400 yards from his house when he was shot by members of a Loyalist murder gang. His lifeless body was left in the lane opposite a rubbish dump.

WELCOME TO BELFAST
Graham Briggs, Royal Artillery

It was already late when we de-bussed and I got settled in – stowed my kit then over to the cookhouse for some scoff. After we ate we then went to the BQMS stores to draw our flak jackets and ammo. As I took the 7.62mm rounds I began to realise that it was serious; it wasn't training any longer.

I had time for a quick phone call home to let my parents and fiancée know where I was – and they got bit of a surprise when I told them that I was in Belfast! It must have been about 2200 hours when our duty officer came in and told me I was to relieve the sentry at the top gate. I had been in Northern Ireland for about five hours and was stagging on. When things like this happen, your body and mind starts to kick in that you are really in a hotspot.

Next morning I got to see Girdwood properly and started to acquaint myself with everything. About midmorning I was informed that I was going out on a mobile patrol with the Anglians and that our transport was a Pig, which was a new experience for me. We were going to North Queen Street RUC Station and as we drove the route the Anglians were pointing out different things and trying to familiarise me with my new surroundings, which was not easy looking through the observation slit of a Humber Pig. We arrived at North Queen Street and what a shock this was – nothing like any police station I had ever seen before as it resembled a fortress!

Maybe I didn't know what to expect but the sight of armed police officers; sangars on the front gate with blast doors when you went inside. So after we had finished it was back to Girdwood. My first taste of life in Northern Ireland and all was well. After lunch I was told that I would be going out on patrol with The Green Howards (the residential battalion). So it was off to the briefing room and then up to the top gate where we loaded our weapons and received instructions. I was told to go to the end of the wall and take up a defensive position and look down Clifton Park Avenue. I did as ordered and then the rest of the brick came out and we formed up into our patrol and off we went down Clifton Park Avenue and turned left onto Crumlin Road where I got a better view of the courthouse and nick.

The Lower Shankill was pointed out to me and then on we went to the place I came to hate during my tour: Unity Flats. What a fucking hole this place was. During our patrol around the flats I did my first 'P' check – something which I'll never forget. I stopped this youth of about 18 and the brick took up all-round defensive positions. I asked him his name, date of birth, address, where he had come from and where he was going. About the only thing they cannot do in training is get you used to the Northern Ireland accent with a Belfast twang. His answer to my question about where he was going sounded like "Mibrrrrr." I asked what he meant and he repeated "Mibrrrrr." It transpired that he meant his brothers' and I asked him why the fuck he didn't say that in the first place.

I gave his details to the brick commander, who sent them back via radio. He came back 'clean' and off he went. We carried on into what I used to call the car park area of Unity and went up onto the first floor balcony and got a look over the area in front of me. I never liked it whilst I was up there. I thought if anything happens, the quickest way out is over the balcony as the ends of the flats could be shut off by locals easily and quickly. During the rest of my tour neither I nor any of the brick I was in went up onto the balconies again.

So I had done my first patrol and over the next two weeks the rest of the battery came out and we got full command of the New Lodge. The first time I went into the New Lodge Road area, all the known players came out. One of the things which really pissed me off was you could see the murdering bastards; you give them the eyeball, but they knew that we knew who they were and they also knew that we couldn't do a thing about it! If they crossed the line, all you could do then was harass them and 'P' check them.

My tour was fairly quiet in that we had no major incidents. We had hoax bomb calls and a little bit of trouble from a couple of known players, but when they're looking down the barrel of an FRG they piss off very quickly. The IRA attacked and killed several prison officers whilst we were out there, which meant the army brought in the 'POP' run (Prison Officer Protection) – which we never liked doing. Every shift change we had to put in a VCP on the Crumlin Road whilst the POs got out of the prison and we could be there for up to 30 minutes and exposed to IRA snipers. Eventually they built a sangar which did the job of covering the shift change.

What do I remember of my time in Belfast were the Unity Flats. They were a 1960s grey concrete jungle – a pigsty of a housing estate. The next housing estate to it was on the edge of equally Republican New Lodge. This was a 1970s design of high-rise flats and was not much better – and the rest of the Lodge was a Victorian back-to-back terraced shithole. Patrolling through all three was like going through a time-warp. The young kids of five or six years of age stood in gaggles outside the pubs waiting for their parents to come out.

I was out on patrol and we had made our way down Crumlin Road to Unity Flats. We stopped and had a word with the guys in the OP there overlooking that shithole as they were from our battery.

We then went around the back of Unity into what I used to call the car park area and as we were patrolling, a bloke came onto the first floor balcony and started to shout abuse at us. Nothing unusual about this except in his hand was a big chef's knife. I even remember what he was wearing. He had on a mucky vest, his hair looked like he had just got out of bed and he had a massive beer gut. He carried on giving us grief. He was shouting: "I'll come down there and kill you, you Brit bastards! Fuck off out of here!" All the time he was waving this knife about.

He had been going on for about five minutes with this verbal abuse. He carried on shouting: "I'll fucking kill you!" So I turned around and looked up to him. I was on the left-hand side of the car park area and right in front of where he stood on the balcony. As I did this the rest of the brick took up defensive positions near me. I then put my arms out at shoulder-height and shouted: "Come on down then; the first one is free." He shouted back: "Oh, you're a big man with your gun!"

At that point I handed my rifle to my mate, Pixie, and shouted to him that I didn't have my rifle anymore. This shut him up – then he shouted: "You're fucking crazy!" I was thinking: "Yup, I must be to work in this shithole!" I took my rifle back off Pixie and we carried on with our patrol. As we got out of the area the lads turned and looked at me with incredulous looks on their faces.

With hindsight I realise this had been a stupid thing to do as it could have been a 'come on' and I could have put my life and my mates' lives in danger. But it was funny at the time. I still have a little giggle to myself even now when I think of it

Girdwood – where we were based – was sandwiched between this lot and the Antrim Road. All the houses around it were derelict and bricked-up. None of the locals seemed to give a shit about themselves. Some of the houses we searched were absolutely filthy inside. In fact, the houses we trained in were in better condition. Quite a few times we had abuse shouted at us, but as the saying goes 'sticks and stones may break my bones, but names will never hurt me'. I gave as good as I got some of the time. Another thing which always amazed me was how did the milkmen deliver milk as the amount of bottles that were thrown at us must have meant a real glass shortage?

My tour came to an end on 12 January 1980, but Northern Ireland never leaves you; it is always in the back of your mind. It is approximately 33 years since I left and I can still see everything as clear as if I was still there. Does it trouble me? I don't know, but I have a stress-related skin complaint and I have been told that I suffer from dysfunctional behaviour. Were these caused by my time out in Ireland?

Built by the Unionist Government of Stormont in the 1960s, the Unity Flats were seen as a solution to Belfast's terrible housing crisis of that time. Many Catholics were living in terribly overcrowded slums and it was thought that rehousing them in brand new blocks – sold to them as some sort of 'brave new world' – would ease some of the problems of social deprivation. The new flats, however, were not without their own problems and by the late 1960s Unity was best known for anti-social behaviour and crime – and, of course, a breeding ground for Republican dissidents.

Robert Hawthorne (37), father of three, had joined the UDR in the early 1970s and in 1974 had been shot and wounded by the IRA in Co Down whilst driving a Land Rover. Despite being wounded, he managed to keep the vehicle under control and later received a bravery award for his cool handling of the situation. In late 1978 he resigned from the UDR and began working as a forklift driver at a timber firm in Newry. On the morning of the 5th he arrived at work as usual and parked up at the Soho car park in Newry. As he and a colleague stopped the car and prepared to get out, a stolen car pulled up alongside and a gunman immediately opened fire with an automatic weapon – hitting both men. Mr Hawthorne was hit in the head and died instantly and his work colleague received serious wounds. To the psychopaths in the Provisional IRA, it mattered absolutely nothing that he had resigned and had no connections with the military. He was unarmed and helpless and posed no threats to them – and yet he was shot down in cold blood. The Republican terror group and their apologists in Sinn Féin had the gall to complain that British soldiers shot to kill – and this breathtaking hypocrisy was simply lapped up by the Irish-Americans. A spokesman later claimed that Mr Hawthorne was 'a part of the British war machine' and had indulged in 'active undercover activities for the Crown Forces'. Their excuses were simply laughable – and were it not for the tragedy of the murder one might have loudly guffawed at their pathetic press conference.

HEARTENING INCIDENTS
Trooper Ernest Martin, 5th Royal Inniskilling Dragoon Guards
I recall a couple of incidents during those years. In the first we were out in the Cuds somewhere doing an early-morning farm search late. The farmer's reaction to us poking about was to whisper: "Silly buggers! It's the next one; over the hill … that's the one you want – and look closely 'under' the barn!" He was right; there was a built-in hide with all sorts of goodies. God bless him.

The other one which I remember was a priest handing me a piece of paper at a PVCP on the border and telling me: "The RA* have this information, but they don't know I have copied it." I can tell you that as a direct result of that information, lives were saved. I have already checked and I found out that the priest died some years ago. I hope he has gone to his heaven.

In what clearly was a snub to the Pope's recent pleas for peace, a Sinn Féin apologist made the following statement: " … the Irish Republican Army rejects Pope John Paul II's call for an end to the violence in Northern Ireland. The IRA has widespread support and will continue to grow. Only Britain's withdrawal from Northern Ireland will end this. Force is by far the only means of removing the evil of the British presence in Ireland. We know also that upon victory the Church would have no difficulty in recognising us." The author does not intend to comment upon their remarks.

Between the 6th and the 29th of this month, three members of HM Forces died in Northern Ireland. These were: RAF Flight Sergeant Eric John Bronte Simpson (44), from RAF, Benson on the 6th (he was from Hailsham, Sussex); UDR Private Melvyn Doherty (23) on the 14th (he was from Aghadowey – near Coleraine in Co Londonderry – and is

---

* RA – or Republican Army – was how members and their supporters in Ireland referred to the organisation.

buried at Aghadowey Parish Church); and Corporal William McCrossan (27) on the 29th (it is thought that he was from Dunamanagh, Co Tyrone and is buried at Mountcastle Cemetery).

HQNI LIFE
Michael Shepherd, RAOC

I was posted from HQ Berlin Infantry Brigade to HQNI in mid-1978 as a Staff Clerk in the RAOC. I was employed within 'Q' Branch, which in later military terminology became G4 to conform with the rest of NATO. For me it was not the harsh living and working conditions of those that patrolled regularly and faced the hordes that were intent on creating a cloud of fear and hatred; instead I went to work in a corner office shared with three military clerks and three civilians. My accommodation was a small two-man room in a portacabin – which was either too hot or too cold – and from where I could hear the buzz of conversations and the metallic sound of cheap transistor radios. No TV rooms and no shared sitting rooms; these facilities were still better than the majority in the Province, and yet there were still those who complained.

Each soldier is attached to a roulemont unit for a week. I was at Woodburn Camp – a semi-derelict hotel in Belfast which looked after Dunmurry, Twinbrook and Ladybrook. For me it was exciting and worthwhile – and the lads from the Royal Anglian Regiment treated me well and took the mickey as often as they could. For me there was no complaining and no moaning – after all, it was for a week whilst they were there for a lot longer. The differing patterns of exiting and entering the base were new to me and had not been taught on the course – nor was the fun they got up to in the Kevlar-coated Land Rovers. The interaction with the local population was an eye-opener as we patrolled areas of both persuasions. My biggest scare occurred on one of the only two-night patrols that I took part in. We were in an area of Twinbrook which had rows of houses with lanes behind them and chain-linked fencing with a concrete shed-type building against each fence next to a gate. In the half-light – as we went down one of the lanes – I saw the corporal give the sign to get down; one knee as was the norm. As he signalled to move I got up – and at that moment a dog hit the fence barking. I nearly shit myself whilst the corporal tried to gain order amongst a group of giggling infantry soldiers. I was grateful for the week spent with those lads, but also happy to be going back to Thiepval Barracks. Subsequently I would join a mixed patrol of clerks, signalmen, REME and drivers to wander (on average) twice a month around Lisburn.

The duty that I most hated was escorting the bus to and from the docks to meet the incoming ferry from Liverpool. The bus was never the same two days running and was always run-down and ready to break down. Surprisingly, this never happened when I was escort. The escort was a masterpiece of military planning: a driver, an escort, two 9mm pistols and a radio. The instructions included radio frequencies, unit TAORs that we went through and the instruction to contact HQ 39 Bde on the merest hint of trouble or any suspicions. The RSM's brief was slightly contrary to that as he said if we got windy and cried 'wolf' too often, it would draw attention to the bus. So the general consensus was to do everything that you could not to use the radio. However, even that was not really a problem as there were so many black spots that we were only in contact for about two thirds of the route. The fact was that for two years there was not an occurrence – and no-one that I knew shouted for assistance.

On one of my trips to the ferry I had arrived in time to get a coffee, so clad in my desert boots, jeans and sweatshirt I bounded up the stairs to the canteen. Almost at the top, my 9mm pistol fell on the floor with a massive clatter and my heart stopped – not through fear, but because of massive embarrassment. What a tit! Looking around, it seemed that not many had seen what had occurred apart from a very large gentleman dressed in green stood at the top of the stairs – carrying what I thought was a version of the American M1 Carbine. He stood there, leant forward and said: "If you can't show me your ID card, I shall have to shoot you!" I produced and he smiled. After that I used the almost useless plastic issue shoulder holster with the stay cut off.

Anyway for two years I worked 12 to 14-hour days; completed the documentation for the movement of SAPA (Site Assembled Portable Armouries), Portaloos, multi-gyms and portable accommodation whilst venturing out into the world populated by Protestants, Catholics and the British squaddie. I have never boasted of my exploits and prefer instead to talk of the shit accommodation and long hours.

Three days later – in what was clearly a sectarian tit-for-tat – the UDA/UFF shot dead a young Catholic man in what could be seen as a purely sectarian act. Despite their criticisms of the UVF at the murder of 'Sadie' Larmour, the UDA had no qualms about indulging in the same sordid activities themselves. Mark McGrann (24) was walking across the Albert Bridge in East Belfast with his girlfriend and his younger brother in the very early hours of the 8th – en route for Carlisle Square having walked from the Nationalist Short Strand. A UFF gunman riding a bicycle saw the pair and cycled towards them – pulling a handgun as he did. Seeing the danger Mr McGrann's girlfriend warned him to run, but he bravely placed himself between his brother and his girlfriend – and the gunman who fired hit him in the chest. He collapsed to the ground and the gunman stood over the helpless man – and in cowardly fashion fired two more shots into him. He died very quickly afterwards. It is known that the murdered man had no paramilitary connections whatsoever.

Private Paul Wright (21) from Leicester (and a member of the Royal Anglians) was driving an unmarked 'Q' car – and along with a colleague from an unnamed regiment, was dressed in plain clothes on the afternoon of 8 October. As his car turned into Whiterock Road near St James Crescent, an IRA gang (who had taken over a hardware shop close to the Falls Road) opened fire – causing the car to crash. As the young soldier lay dying and with his badly wounded comrade helpless, the IRA gunmen fired further shots into the car – killing Private Wright. A weapon or weapons were seized and the gang fled. The wounded soldier died shortly afterwards. A spokesman for the British Army stated that the pair were on routine courier work, but it is a widely held view that the pair were working undercover.

On the 10th, Private Paul Brown Scott (19) of the KOSB was killed in an RTA in Northern Ireland. The author has no further information other than he came from the Edinburgh area and his funeral took place at Warriston Crematorium close to his

On guard, Belfast, 1979. (©Mark 'C')

hometown. He was the first member of this famous Scottish regiment to die in Northern Ireland for almost three years.

On the 12th, a young solicitor – John Donaldson (23), who worked for the Crown Prosecution Service – was shot dead as he rode out of Andersonstown RUC Station. The young man had been sent to the RUC base in order to deliver a witness summons to an officer based there – and his entry had been noted as gunmen were waiting for him to leave. A stolen van had been seen in the area and it had been circling the area around the base (Milltown Cemetery and Glen Road). As the young man drove off down Andersonstown Road, a gunman opened fire from the cut-out windows with an automatic weapon. Mr Donaldson was hit several times in the face and chest and died very quickly afterwards. The usual Sinn Féin apologist was wheeled out to explain their 'shoot to kill' policy and he claimed that they thought that he had been an RUC spy and 'apologised' for the mistake. It is not recorded how the loved ones of the murdered man received this 'apology'.

On the same day a number of terrorist court cases reached their conclusions – with heavy sentences being handed out to a number of PIRA men. Amongst those beginning a long term of imprisonment was the killer of Gunner Paul Sheppard in March 1978 (see Chapter 39) and the killer of Corporal Gerard Bristow of the Royal Welch Fusiliers in April 1972 (see *The Bloodiest Year* by the same author). Two PIRA men were jailed for throwing blast bombs at army patrols on the Garvaghy Road, Portadown on 24 August 1977. Both received 10 years. Another PIRA man – who was caught in possession of an American Armalite – was also sent to jail for 10 years.

On the 15th, a cold-blooded and cowardly murder was carried out by the IRA at a school in Roslea, Co Fermanagh. What was worse was that children were first held hostage and then forced to witness the murder of a part-time UDR soldier. Corporal Herbert 'Herbie' Kernaghan (36), father of two, was also a full-time delivery driver – and amongst his regular jobs was to deliver to St Tierney's Junior School in Roslea. Shortly before school started for the day, masked gunmen – knowing of the UDR man's regular patterns – arrived and immediately took the head and other teaching staff (together with many of the children) hostage. They intentionally left a number of children in the playground in order to give the illusion of normality. Just after 9am, Corporal Kernaghan drove into the school – pausing to smile at one of the young children who witnessed what happened next. As he slowed down an IRA gunman walked across to the cab and fired several rounds (eyewitnesses said six or seven) and he was mortally wounded – dying just minutes later. The cold-blooded, callous nature of the murder – using children as a distraction – was their clear message to the world that they had no emotions, no morals and had simply evolved into a ruthless killing machine. This was hardly the image of daring-do, heroic liberators which NORAID and their Democrat Party apologists liked to portray. Herbie Kernaghan's wife gave birth to their third child a fortnight after his death.

THE CAR CHASE
Herb Jackson, Royal Artillery

We were out and about this one particular day when over the radio came the familiar: "Rat trap! Rat trap! Rat trap!" call which alerted us to a stolen car and a possible chase – and our need to blockade off one of the rat-runs we were situated on. Quickly we pulled over and blocked the road – making a narrow chicane with our two Land Rovers – but the details were vague; just a few car details and a failure to stop action, but little more information. Just as we had dismounted, around a distant corner and coming towards us was a car fitting the description. It was as though the script of a new adventure had been written for us. It slowed as it got near and we became more alert as the adrenaline began to pump. The car was now slowly weaving so we took covering positions in readiness. Then it shot round us on the pavement and grass – narrowly missing a lamppost – and he raced off.

We quickly remounted and blasted off in pursuit – with everyone clinging on for dear life – as we chased this car round what seemed to be most of the streets in Belfast. We kept up with this large Vauxhall as it sped up and down streets until we found ourselves heading into the city centre. The car was screeching round every corner trying to get away – yet there we were in our heavy old 'Landy' – with four on board – still keeping up with him as we pitched and rolled around every turn. The guy in the car was losing ground on every corner as he skidded or spun his wheels frantically – perhaps in panic or because he was useless.

Finally as he rounded a corner near the City Hall, halfway down the street he saw an RUC roadblock and promptly lost control before crashing into concrete bollards and then bouncing over them and hitting a rather large office building window. When we dragged this guy out – with the help of RUC officers now on-scene – we found the driver expectedly drunk. We dragged him from the car and took control of him momentarily. He admitted to us that he thought he would test us out as he believed he could outrun us easily. He was wrong of course. It turned out that he was a member of the UDR and didn't want to get stopped for drinking and driving. He always thought he would get away from us if he ever had to. The tithead found out differently that day! He was close to being shot – let alone smashing his car up and done for drink-driving. Half the stuff out there was in no way linked to the Troubles; it was just the everyday crap of any big city that cops deal with on a daily basis. It used to hamper the more important stuff on many occasions. If you removed the general crime and pointless outrage of the community spirit, we would have had our feet up most of the tour.

The American singer Cindy Lauper once famously sang about 'True Colours' – and on the 16th the people of the Irish Republic demonstrated their true colours when the Dublin-based Economic and Social Institute revealed the results of an Ireland-wide survey into people's opinions. Despite the recent murder of a UDR man in front of shocked under-11s and the murders at Warrenpoint and that of Mountbatten, 21 per cent of Irish people supported the activities of the Provisional IRA and a staggering 41 per cent supported their motives. These findings however were rejected by the Taoiseach, Jack Lynch, who claimed that a BBC survey in 1978 put the figure of support at only two per cent. "That figure must be recognised as being more correct," he claimed. His tenure as Taoiseach was coming to an end. He resigned on 11 December this year and died in October 1999.

On the 16th, the ranks of the INLA were reduced by one when a volunteer from their Armagh Brigade – Tony McClelland (25) – was killed when the car he was riding in was involved in an accident in Co Monaghan during a pursuit by Gardaí officers. The car, which also contained the infamous 'Border Fox' Dessie O'Hare, refused to stop at a Gardaí VCP near Castleblaney, Co Monaghan. They were transporting weapons and were chased by officers in a marked car. After a chase of 10 miles they collided with an oncoming car at a crossroads – seriously injuring several innocent people. McClelland died at the scene and O'Hare was arrested and later jailed for nine years. Both men were armed with rifles. Somewhat incredulously, the priest at his funeral in Co Armagh said of the dead terrorist: "We know Tony was such a good man and nice person – and Christ will reward him for all his goodness." One trusts that was the case! As a postscript, O'Hare demanded bail at the Dublin Special Court as he was 'due to get married'. Quite naturally, this was refused.

The following day – in a series of moves against the leadership of the UDA – the RUC raided several homes in hardline Loyalist areas centred on the Shankill Road. Five senior members of the biggest Loyalist group were arrested and questioned about sectarian killings and other illegal paramilitary activities. On the same day a foot patrol of the KOSB was fired upon by several PIRA gunmen in the Falls Road area of West Belfast. Two soldiers were hit, but one was very seriously wounded and although he later recovered the author understands that he was eventually discharged on medical grounds.

KEEPING THE PLAYERS ON THEIR TOES
Graham Briggs, Royal Artillery

Whilst we were out there some of the houses at the bottom end of Spamount Street were being refurbished or updated by a firm, if my memory serves me correct, called 'Felons'. This firm seemed to employ a few of the local players, which was good for us as we saw them every time we were on patrol and basically knew where they were during the working hours. The firm had a storage area on Spamount Street and the compound was not that big – maybe the size of a normal terraced house. I have no idea who came up with this, but whilst out on patrol in the New Lodge we went into the compound for a quick look around whilst another brick gave cover outside.

As the patrol continued around the New Lodge streets, every time a brick went up or down Spamount a brick would go into the compound and have a look around. Also – during this time of patrolling – a well-known player was seen walking around so he got 'P' checked. To walk one of the streets in the New Lodge should take approximately 10 minutes, but this player took 30 to 45 minutes to get along the street as each brick would stop and 'P' check him. This was done by the brick commanders talking to each other over the radios and letting each other know which way the player was going and in which direction. If he changed direction, the OP overlooking the Lodge could give information as to where they were going.

We had done our patrol and had got back to Girdwood Park. The troop was in the briefing room awaiting debrief and the Battery Commander (BC) came in with the RUC officer who was attached to us. This had never happened before, so we all looked at each other in surprise. The BC started to tell us that the police had received a complaint that certain British soldiers had been harassing the building workers on Spamount Street. He told us that it had to stop. He was not shouting or using a raised voice – so it was not a bullocking – and the RUC officer was standing with a smile on his face, so we knew there would be no further action from him. So we had harassed them and they complained, but when the locals harassed us – throwing bricks and bottles at mobiles; spitting; verbal abuse; dogs trying to bite us – we never complained … we just got on with our job.

The streets of Belfast were all different, but one that sticks in my memory was just off North Queen Street. You turn right opposite the police station and you were facing an old mill-type building – I think it was Gallaghers cigarette factory. A short way up there was a place which was straight out of Victorian times. The houses were of the Victorian 'two-up, two-down' type. The front door opened straight onto the street. There were approximately 12 houses, but what amazed me was the street lighting. It was still gas and there was a bloke going along lighting the lights. The other thing was even though we were only just off North Queen Street, it was so quiet and the Troubles seemed so far away. Maybe this was Belfast's place to go to forget the Troubles – I will never know. I have said before that when you leave Northern Ireland or any other war zone, the war zone never leaves you.

On the 19th – following another incident in which a UDR soldier was shot and wounded – PIRA then targeted UDR Private James Robinson (20), who also worked as a milkman in Co Fermanagh. The part-time soldier had a regular delivery round and PIRA INT knew that he drove his milk float along Blackfort Road in the Omagh area. It is a remote and lonely rural road and PIRA gunmen were waiting for him – in all likelihood hiding in bushes. As the slow-moving milk float passed by, they leapt out and opened fire – his lifeless body was found slumped over the steering wheel after the vehicle had crashed off the road. The Provisionals described the murder as 'the execution of a member of the British imperialist war machine'. He was a member of 'C' Company, 6 UDR and was buried in his home village of Fintona surrounded by his family of 10 brothers and sisters.

On the same day OIRA man John McGuiness (31) died from injuries which he had received in early February 1971 after a PIRA-OIRA internal feud. He had been shot during a dispute with the then fledgling Provisionals and had been paralysed and confined to a wheelchair ever since. The coroner stated that although it was almost nine years since he was wounded, his death was a direct result of the shooting.

The day after, around 500 supporters of the Provisional IRA staged a demonstration through the centre of the ancient university town of Oxford. Contemporary newspaper reports state that it was well-policed and that there was no trouble. One is stunned by the brass neck of the supporters – and the ineptitude of the police for allowing it to go ahead – who had the audacity to parade through a town showing support for a terrorist organisation. Given that Oxford is close enough to Birmingham for memories of the 1974 bombings still to be fresh, one is simply amazed that this was allowed to happen. For example, would the New York City authorities have allowed a pro-Al Qaeda demonstration to take place in Manhattan after the 9/11 bombings? Please forgive the author's rhetoric.

On that same day – in West Belfast – there was a lucky escape for an RUC officer and then a mixture of luck for three men following the officer. As the officer drove along Ballygomartin Road, a UVBT – which had been attached to his car in South Belfast and

Ballygomartin Road, Belfast, October 1979 – a bomb had fallen off another
vehicle and three men were injured when their van ran over it, detonating it.
Incident dealt with by 25 Field Regiment, Royal Artillery. (©Mark 'C')

which had failed to explode – worked its way loose and fell into the road. However, a van carrying three innocent workmen immediately behind the RUC man's vehicle ran over the device, which then exploded. The front of the van was wrecked and the three men were badly injured. All recovered after hospital treatment. Had the following vehicle contained children on the school run, the results might well have been more catastrophic.

On the 24th, Walter Moore (50) – the owner of a restaurant on the Shankill Road – was murdered by PIRA gunmen outside his home in Ballygomartin, West Belfast. He had been involved in an argument – possibly with PIRA members at his restaurant – and there is some speculation (but it is just that, speculation) that he refused to pay the gangsters – *apologies* to NORAID supporters – protection money. He was followed to his home in Lyndhurst Parade – just under a mile away from his business. Just as Mr Moore and his wife settled down for the night, armed men smashed their way into the house and opened fire on the couple. Mr Moore bravely threw himself in front of his wife and all the shots hit him. He was hit five times and died at the scene. Whilst there is some doubt about the nature of the dispute, the RUC maintained that it was the IRA who killed Mr Moore; the idea of 'protection money' can be dismissed out of hand. In that part of Belfast, this particular aspect of gangsterism would have been handled by the UVF or UFF. It is more likely that it was a straightforward sectarian killing by the *non-sectarian* Provisionals.

The next day, Humphrey Atkins – then Secretary of State for Northern Ireland – announced that he was going to invite the four main parties (Ulster Unionist Party, UUP; Democratic Unionist Party, DUP; Social Democratic and Labour Party, SDLP; and Alliance Party, APNI) to a conference held at Stormont to discuss potential political settlements. The UUP rejected the invitation and called on the Government to introduce a system of two-tier Local Government. At the time of the Atkins initiative there was little support for another round of talks and some commentators believed the initiative was a response to try to ease growing American pressure for action.

On the 27th, there was another murder attempt at the RVH in Belfast (please refer to the shooting of Royal Anglian soldier 'Tiny' Rose in Chapter 20 in May 1977). Private Phillip Peet of the Duke of Wellington's Regiment was on duty at the hospital guarding a wounded soldier from KOSB. The IRA wanted to 'finish the job' and a gunman was sent to the hospital – and it is thought likely that he was guided to the wounded soldier's ward by a sympathiser amongst the hospital staff (both nurses and porters have in the past 'dicked' for the Provisionals). The Intensive Care Unit (ICU) was located in Ward 32 and just after 7.15pm a gunman – posing as a member of the hospital staff – knocked to gain admission to where the wounded KOSB soldier was being treated. Private Peet – thought to be from the Leeds area – went to respond, but as he looked through the glass panel he noticed that the man was holding a pistol. He reacted immediately and stepped back to draw his own handgun (a Browning 9mm), but as he did so the gunman fired – the bullet smashing through the soldier's wrist and making it almost impossible to fire back. The gunman then fired four or five more shots – one of which wounded Private Peet in his other arm. Another sentry alerted by the gunshots then appeared on the scene and fired several rounds at the fleeing terrorist, but unfortunately his shots missed and he escaped from the building; the alertness and courage of the 'Duke of Boots' soldier clearly saved the life of the already seriously wounded KOSB lad.

CAR THIEVES IN BELFAST
Herb Jackson, Royal Artillery

One time we were out – I think we were just off the Shankill Road – and had just received a report (as so often we would) of a freshly stolen vehicle. We turned onto a side street and, as luck would have it – about 50 yards in front of us – was this small, red Ford van. The RSM's crew shot round us to block it; we remained at the rear. One young lad had just got out of the van and another was leaning over talking to the driver. We thought we had 'em bang to rights only to see the lad in the van drive off over the pavement and round the RSM's rover – scraping it a little as it passed. The soldiers jumped back in and made chase with 'Bobby Rickshaw' standing up in the back leaning over the two seats in the front by resting against the canopy frame – looking like a sailor ready with a harpoon gun chasing Moby Dick.

We remained with the two other lads and began to talk to them whilst the CO discreetly called for a Pig – knowing at least one of these lads would be arrested. This kind of thing is always done carefully so as not to stir up trouble with the, er, law-abiding locals. Something both sides of the fence were guilty of on many occasions would be interference. As we waited, a few people emerged from their houses at the noise from these swearing and shouting teens. Before long there were at least 20 people out there huddling together and all of them aggressively asking us: "What was going on?" Some made up their own minds that these lads were innocent and the army were the ones causing trouble – yet focused as I was, I could only hear aggressive tones; the rest was just a noise to me.

Some began swearing at us (as was usual) but just as the Pig came round the corner one of the kid's parents arrived – loudly trying to take over the show. The orchestra of the crowd reached a crescendo of noise so I quickly put my hand on one of the lad's shoulders and said: "As a member of Her Majesty's Forces, I arrest you!" Well that was it; the pushing, shoving and gobbiness increased ten-fold – and as a four-man brick came round the corner, more people came from their houses. It was a comedy of errors in waiting. To calm things a little we encouraged the father to travel with his kid in the Pig. As arresting soldier I too had to travel with them.

The distance to Tennant Street RUC Station was not far, but really unpleasant with critical comments from the father – as well as his son's abuse – and an assortment of rehearsed glares learned at mammy's knee. All the time I was dying to say: "Your son was observed climbing out of a stolen vehicle; he was arrested – now shut the fuck up!" However, we had to be very careful what we said or did out there as so many simple little things could turn into a riot – or worse – in the blink of an eye. It could be a very volatile place some days. Personally, I found that it really didn't matter what you said or did because the trouble-causers would always find a cause for more aggro.

On the 28th, a mobile patrol set off from Springfield Road RUC Station intending to make a right-turn into the main road. Because Violet Street had been closed off for security and because Cavendish Street was one-way, it necessitated a right-turn across traffic in order to enter the Springfield Road. Unknown to the joint army/RUC patrol, PIRA gunmen had taken over a house on Crocus Street. The two RUC officers got out to halt traffic and WOII David Bellamy (31), father of two, moved into position to give covering fire to them. As he stood ready, the concealed gunmen opened fire from Crocus Street and hit three of the men. Constable John Davidson was hit several times in the neck and head and fatally wounded. He died on 18 November. A sergeant in the Duke of Wellington's was hit seven times in various parts of his body – including a near-fatal chest wound – and was very badly injured. He recovered after a long time in hospital. However, Sergeant Major Bellamy of the Army Physical Training Corps (APTC) was mortally wounded following a head shot. He died before reaching the RVH, which is only 4-500 feet from the ambush scene. The gunmen escaped in a stolen car towards the Ballymurphy/Whiterock area. The dead soldier was attached to the Duke of Wellington's. The APTC (motto: *mens sana in corpore sano – a healthy mind in a healthy body*) are the scourge of new recruits and are the men responsible for turning unfit civvies into lean, well-honed military men. David Bellamy was the only member of the corps to be killed during the Troubles.

WITH THE DUKE OF BOOTS ON THE 'MURPH
Dougie Durrant, ADU

I could so easily have called this: 'The Ballymurphy Social Club Saturday Night'.

A cool chill rushed through the air – another typical Saturday night in Moyard Base in West Belfast. The Duke of Wellington's Regiment had now taken over from the Kings – and as normal, most regiments or units come up with some sort of strategy on how they wish to stamp their authority on the TAOR. So we, as dog handlers, just went with the flow and continued the same as the last unit; in some cases, maintaining the difficult harmony with the locals. Some units found innovative ways of upsetting the locals – and thus setting an example for the rest of their tour. Some units were good at what they did and some are bad. I found that during my years in the west, there was no in-between.

I had not been out for some time – as it takes a few weeks for the unit to plan and conduct its search operation – so what I did was keep pestering the ops room into letting me tag along with a patrol so I could do a bit of rummage-searching around the area (most finds are done this way). One day, in the ops room, I was asked if I fancied tagging on to a patrol without my dog. I was told that the dog would be in one of the APCs and that they had a little task for me.

I went back to my room, grabbed my kit and walked to the briefing room. On arrival there was about a platoon's worth of men sat tooled up ready to move. The ops officer came in and said: "Right guys, this will be our first operation of the tour – and as you know we have a few teams on the ground around the area of the Ballymurphy Social Club. They have noticed that one of our top players is sitting in the in the bar. INT would like us to lift this man and get him off to Andersonstown RUC Station for a chat." He explained the details of the op and then looked in my direction and said: "As the dog handler has all the kit and is a big fucker, he will grab the subject and pass him down the chain to the QRF APC waiting outside, ok?"

With the briefing over, I put Bluce in the APC with one of the guys from the QRF and joined one section – and off we went on foot towards the Ballymurphy Social

Club. It was a Saturday night and it would be packed. I thought to myself: "Am I really agreeing to do this? Well I'm in it now!" We arrived at the club and saw that there were two guys at the door – one of whom demanded: "What the fuck do you bastards want?" We informed him that we were just going to check the bar and I walked in and it kicked off straight away. Bottles and chairs were flying past my head and I thanked fuck I had my visor down.

I managed to get to the far side of the bar – where the subject was sitting with friends – and he looked at me as if he already knew his fate. I grabbed him by the jacket and forced him in front of me, but as I did so a male jumped on my back so he came as well! Thud … a bottle had smacked off my helmet, but I managed to pass the subject onto the boys by the door – and in turn they bundled him into the APC waiting outside, which drove off. All hell had now let loose and then I realised that with the APC gone we would have to patrol back through the 'Murph on a Saturday night. This was going to be interesting.

It was a shit-storm, with bottles and chairs – and anything else they could throw at us – following me out the door! We made our way back across the notorious Nationalist estate – a real hotbed of Provisionals' supporters – followed by the crowd from the club. In fact, more seemed to join them as the residents came out of their houses to see what the fuck was going on. Then a brick had hit me in the back, which hurt like hell; then a stone hit me on the knee. Despite that, we finally managed to get back to base. However, cars were now burning all over the Springfield Road and in the 'Murph. Petrol bombs were being thrown and the odd shot rang through the air. The arrest of a leading player had really stirred the natives up. Later, when the QRF returned, they asked me to jump in with Bluce as we might be needed.

This went on for most of the night – with the place looking like hell on earth in the morning. I thought to myself that this was going to be an interesting and difficult tour for the Duke of Boots!

In two cases which have chilling echoes of the tragic death of QLR soldier Gary Barlow, Private Marc Brown and an unnamed RHA soldier found themselves alone in the middle of enemy country. Previously – on Monday, 5 March 1973 – a routine foot patrol of the QLR was passing through an area of the Lower Falls and reached Albert Street and McDonnell Street. Mysteriously – and for a reason which only Private Gary Barlow (19) knew and took to his premature grave – he lost contact with his comrades and found himself separated from them. His absence was only noted once the remainder of the patrol had returned to their base at either North Howard Street Mill or to Springfield Road Police Station after being collected by an armoured vehicle. He was held hostage by a gaggle of the Falls' hags and an IRA gunman shot him dead as they herded him into an isolated garage.

CROSSMAGLEN INCIDENT
Marc Brown, Royal Pioneer Corps
I had just come back from an R&R in 1979 and I was put straight on escort duties as they were doing a replenishment of the RUC base at Crossmaglen. I got dumped in the back of a 10-tonner, open-top truck in the middle of bloody winter and sent on our way into the heart of 'bandit country'.

Upon arriving in the village – but some way short of the base – a full screw (corporal) ordered a de-bus in the middle of the square because he thought there was a tailback of traffic. He clearly had forgotten about the danger there – and just as I got down, the vehicles started moving again and I was left stranded! Now, if any of you know Crossmaglen, you will know the fish and chips shop on the corner of said square. Well, me being a 'red arse' and not too bright, thought it would be a good idea to stand where I could see and be seen. This clearly was not a good idea and the crowd in the chippy decided to come out all at once – and some rather big men started to cross the road in order to 'introduce' themselves to me. At this time I was just turned 18, stood a huge 5ft 6" tall and weighed eight stone dripping wet.

I have to admit – not to put too mildly – that I started to get a bit worried as it seemed that I was being offered a lot of free chips and drink. Incredibly, one of them offered to hold my weapon whilst I ate them – even offering to place it somewhere handy. All I can recollect was me muttering something about wanting my mummy, when suddenly I heard a deep Yorkshire voice shouting: "Standoff!" Ever since then I have loved the Grenadier Guards – and if I see one to this day, I'll buy him a drink!

As the month ended there was still another death; still another reason for a CVO to be dispatched to an English, Scottish, Northern Irish or Welsh town or city; still one more family to grieve. On the 30th, Corporal Fred Irwin (43) – father of five and part-time soldier in the UDR – was murdered by the IRA. Corporal Irwin worked full-time 'on the dust' (as Britain's invaluable army of dustbin men and council cleansing department employees have referred to themselves). He lived in Moy, Co Tyrone and was known to drive to his place of employment in Dungannon every morning at around 8am. Like all good security-minded UDR men he did vary his route, but it was impossible to do so on the last leg of his journey. On this particular morning, a PIRA murder gang was lying in wait for him. As he reached Oaks Road and close to his place of work, masked gunmen opened fire from behind a wall with U.S.-supplied Armalites. His car was hit 30 times and he died almost immediately. In addition to his own five children, the dead soldier and his wife also fostered three other children following the death of his brother. One of the Armalites used in the murder was later taken off the body of PIRA gunman Brian Campbell on 4 December 1983. He was killed in a firefight with the SAS in Coalisland, Co Tyrone.

October ended with 17 deaths; 10 were soldiers/RAF or former soldiers – of whom six were killed by the IRA. Five civilians died (three Catholics and two Protestants) – of whom three of the deaths were overtly sectarian. Two Republican paramilitaries also died. Ten of the deaths were at the hands of the IRA and three at the hands of the Loyalists.

59

November

This month would witness the deaths of nine people – including two soldiers – but it would also see a tragic toll of prison officers as no less than three would be murdered by the Provisionals. Another policeman would die from wounds received the previous month and sectarian murders would continue.

On the 1st of the month – in what was a landmark court case in Belfast – three-year-old Catherine Gilmore was awarded damages for an incident which happened during her mother's pregnancy. In 1976 – in an incident not covered by this book – Mary Gilmore, who was heavily pregnant, was shot in the womb by a Loyalist murder gang. The round lodged itself in the spine of the unborn baby, who was born less than two hours afterwards. She was awarded £4,000. Just 48 hours later, Gardaí Special Branch detectives flew to Philadelphia in the USA to take part in a deportation hearing against a convicted PIRA bomb-maker. He had been on the run since 1976 when explosives were smuggled into the holding cells underneath Dublin Crown Court and he blasted his way to freedom. The known terrorist was also wanted for the murder of British Ambassador Christopher Ewart-Biggs on 21 July 1976 (see Chapter 19). The man – Michael O'Rourke – was eventually extradited to the Irish Republic in 1984 where he was sent to Portlaoise Jail (see also Chapter 19).

On the 2nd, Irish Security Forces seized a quantity of arms at Dublin Docks – which were believed to have originated in the U.S. – naturally bound for the IRA. The shipment numbered 156 weapons – and included M-60 machine guns – and was worth an estimated £500,000. For once the Irish had been proactive, but this was tempered when Taoiseach Jack Lynch stated that he believed that the conflict in Northern Ireland continued to be 'as intractable as at any stage in the last 10 years'.

At around this stage of the conflict, sources in the USA were linking a vicious organised crime organisation called the Winter Hill Gang to arms shipments to the Provisionals. The gang – led by Irish-Americans with a deep hatred of Britain and the English – were instrumental in supplying arms to PIRA. It was only the mass arrests of the gang leaders and its members for other crimes which led to the closing of this one particular conduit. It did little for the cosy image of PIRA as modern-day Robin Hoods and 'freedom fighters' that it was seen that they were being supplied by vicious thugs and gangsters. To the average blue or white-collar Irish-American who gave willingly to NORAID, the notion of the Irish Mafia being involved must have appeared unbelievable. It might or might not have dented their enthusiasm for the 'folks back home' somewhat, but in the end their naivety won through and the NORAID collection tins remained as full as ever.

The Social Democratic and Labour Party (SDLP) held its annual conference and the Troubles was a subject of much debate. In the end the party rejected calls for talks with the IRA. They also called for a joint approach by the British and Irish Governments to finding a solution to the problems in Northern Ireland.

On the same day as the SDLP 'great and good' expatiated on such weighty matters as the Troubles, the IRA planted four large devices at the HM Customs post south of

Newry. The post was situated on the main Dublin-Belfast border crossing and was partly demolished by the blasts. No personnel were injured.

On the 5th, an IRA murder gang hijacked a car in the Falls Road area and drove towards Crumlin Road Jail. They were aware that many POs from the jail parked up in and around Landscape Terrace – and whilst the getaway driver remained with the car, a gunman got out and walked to the junction of the aforementioned street where it meets the Crumlin Road. Thomas Gilhooley (25), a father of two who had served in the Province with the army, drove up to the T-junction and waited for a gap in the busy Crumlin Road traffic. As he did so the gunman shot him in the head and then fired two more shots into him as he slumped over the steering wheel. The PO died almost immediately. Another officer was nearby and he pulled out his Personal Protection Weapon (PPW) and fired several shots at the fleeing gunman and the stolen car into which he jumped. None of the shots were successful and the murder gang raced off towards the Falls Road. In a later statement the Provisionals named four POs whom they intended to 'execute' and described the POA as 'part of the British war machine'.

POP PATROLS, BELFAST
Graham Briggs, Royal Artillery

My battery was responsible for the New Lodge area of Belfast, which included the Crumlin Road – situated on which was the prison on one side and the courthouse on the other. My tour started on 7 September 1979 and we had been operational for approximately six to seven weeks when we were informed that PIRA had killed a couple of prison officers near the Crumlin Road Prison.* I cannot remember if they were killed or wounded. The prison service asked the army for protection for the prison officers during shift change as this is when the attacks had taken place.

The Prison Officer Protection (or POP) run – as it became known – was introduced and entailed the two bricks of the section to go out onto the Crumlin Road in Pigs and set up two VCPs: one outside the prison and the other outside the courthouse. Both VCPs had to be in place before shift change (0600, 1400 and 2200) seven days a week. This system went against everything that we had been taught during our training. We were setting a pattern and each one was roughly in the same area every time we set them up. We could see that and so could PIRA – even if our 'brass' couldn't!

The Crumlin Road is a straight road and there are not many places you can take up defensive cover, so the Pig driver was used as cover as well. His place was by the driver's door looking towards the city centre or up to the junction of Crumlin Road and Clifton Park Avenue depending which way the Pig was facing. The remainder of the brick – excluding the person doing the searching – took up positions on the pavement with one person covering the searcher. We tried to vary as much as we could, but there are only so many variations and combinations you can try. As the Crumlin is so straight it's a wonder we never came under sniper fire or a drive-by shooting.

---

* Two members of the Northern Ireland Prison Officers Association (NIPOA) were killed within the timeframe which Graham specifies. The aforementioned officer, Thomas Gilhooley, was the first. It is a moot point whether or not the terrorists were waiting for a 'target of opportunity' or whether they had deliberately targeted the officer.

After a while, PIRA then changed their tactics. They must have been watching what we were doing because the attacks stopped near the prison and they started following the prison officers home and attacking them away from our patch. One was shot and murdered outside his own house and in total I think eight prison officers were attacked – six of whom were killed.

The other part of the POP was the nightly patrol by two soldiers of the POA married quarters, which were next to Girdwood Park (where we were based). To get into the quarters' area you had to go to the ops room and draw the gate key and a patrol radio. Once you had these you went and let yourselves in. The quarters patch had around 20 bungalows with a gatehouse manned by two prison officers. The problem I saw with the quarters patch was at the bottom was a wall – and beyond that waste ground (maybe 100-150 metres across). I could see the Antrim Road and the top end of the New Lodge. It was a perfect sniper shoot straight into the quarters patch.

After the POP run had been in operation for a few weeks, the powers that be decided to build a sangar on the waste ground at the end of Clifton Park Avenue next to the petrol station. Whilst this was being built, it had to be guarded day and night. This was a difficult and trying time and we were constantly on alert. I think the Gods were on our side during this period – and once it was complete the prison officers took control of it and they could then turn all the traffic lights to red on the crossroad, which then allowed all the prison officers to leave at once in their cars. When the prison took control of the sangar I think a huge sigh of relief went up and we would no longer be doing the POP run – just normal patrols and mobiles along the Crumlin Road.

The other was David Teeney (25), who had joined the Northern Ireland Prison Service in July 1976 and served for over three years until his murder on 7 November. He worked as a wages clerk in Belfast Prison prior to his death and was waiting for a bus in Clifton Street in North Belfast to take him to work when he was shot by an INLA gunman. The murderer escaped in the direction of the Unity Flats. Mr Teeney was en route for work and at around 0800 hours a man – who had been waiting in the same bus queue – suddenly pulled out a gun and shot the PO at point-blank range. He was rushed to the nearby Mater Hospital but died 30 minutes after admission. He had almost certainly been dicked by the INLA, who knew his routine of catching the same bus every morning. Three men were later jailed for his murder.

The 8th witnessed three sectarian murders, as first of all the UFF shot four Catholics and then the Provisionals killed a Protestant in retaliation. The day began with controversy as the media were accused of encouraging Republican paramilitary activity – or at the very least of condoning it. The BBC was forced to make a public statement denying criticisms by the Government of a 'stunt' in Carrickmore. The BBC *Panorama* news programme had filmed masked gunmen in the village setting up roadblocks, questioning motorists and demanding identification and parading around with weapons openly displayed. It was a major embarrassment for the BBC, which was seen to be both glorifying and condoning Provisional activity. Two days later the *Guardian* newspaper would be accused of the same thing. Before the *Panorama* programme could be aired the police raided the BBC offices in Wood Lane, London and seized the film under the Prevention of Terrorism Act. The BBC had no choice but to comply, but it resisted Government accusations that they had contrived with the IRA over the 'show of strength'. At one stage, up to 140 armed terrorists were shown in total control of the village of Carrickmore.

Jack Lynch – clearly stung by criticisms from the British in general and from Margaret Thatcher in particular (especially the accusations of him being feeble and weak-kneed) – was eager to show that he could be decisive. He spoke to the U.S. President, Jimmy Carter, and demanded that the American Government stifle the flow of arms to the IRA from the USA. In a surprising move, he also denounced NORAID – whom at the time was sending almost £500,000 per annum to the Provisionals.

The day ended in tragedy as UFF gunmen targeted Kelly's Bar in Thompson Street, Belfast. Four Catholic friends from the Nationalist Short Strand in East Belfast had enjoyed a night's drinking and had just left the pub. Several masked UFF men in a stolen Mini drove alongside them and opened fire with automatic weapons. Two of the friends were cut down and the other two were unscathed by the hail of bullets. Marius O'Neill (23) was hit four times and mortally wounded. He died shortly afterwards. His best friend, Paul McCrory (23), was hit in the heart and died instantly. Mr McCrory had survived the bombing of the same bar in 1978, but fate caught up with him on this evening. His friend Marius had left Belfast to escape the violence some years before to live in America and he was due to return there after a trip to see his family in Belfast. The stolen vehicle was found abandoned in the Loyalist Newtownards Road very close to the heavily guarded UDA HQ.

Within the hour the bloody game of 'tit-for-tat' had commenced and a PIRA murder squad drove to the Mountpottinger Road – which is on the outskirts of the Short Strand – to the Sirocco engineering works. They knew that the security guard – Edward McMaster (57), father of eight – was a Protestant and after the killing of two Catholic boys, any Protestant would do. Mr McMaster was in a security hut watching late-night television when the armed men burst in on him. They shot him twice in the chest – mortally wounding him. He died very shortly after reaching hospital. His wife is quoted in Lost Lives poignantly saying: "The doctor at the hospital said he never saw anyone suffer as much. I don't know anyone who would do him harm, so the reason for his death must have been retaliation." (p.807)

On the 9th, a man and a woman believed to have been members of the Provisionals unwisely tried to escape from an RUC VCP at Strabane. The driver turned the car around and sped away – chased by a marked RUC vehicle. One of the occupants opened fire at the pursuing car and the officers naturally returned fire. Both the man and the woman were hit and wounded and the car overturned as the driver lost control. The two wounded Republicans were pulled from the car and taken under armed escort to hospital. Several weapons were recovered from the damaged vehicle. On the 12th, the British media – in the form of the *Guardian* – were again in trouble for the possible contriving of paramilitary activities. A reporter from the newspaper described how he had seen seven masked PIRA gunmen set up an IVCP on a remote border road in South Armagh.

He stated that neither he nor the other journalists there had invited the terrorists to put on a show of strength and that they had stumbled on the illegal VCP quite by chance. He was accompanied by three other journalists and they claimed that the first time they were aware of armed men was when two people dressed in anoraks and masked emerged from bushes brandishing automatic weapons.

The journalist stated that the show of strength – which included men posing in fields with Armalites and one lying in the prone position with a deadly M60 machine gun – was not of their making. The IVCP was just one mile from the heavily fortified RUC base at Crossmaglen. In the subsequent news report, the IRA claimed that they were not afraid of helicopters or the SAS and that they were able to openly mount five or more patrols in the area every day.

BLOODY JOURNALISTS
Soldier, Royal Artillery

As you know Ken, I did several tours of Northern Ireland and was based up on the 'Murph on a couple of occasions. As a consequence I saw my fair share of riots and shootings – and I had to use my FRG quite a few times and could never get used to that suffocating stink of CS gas, which we also used. Do you know what bothered me the most? Not getting killed – I was prepared for that – or even getting disfigured because I was ugly enough anyway. It was the fact that the BBC or ITV or some foreign TV crew were always there when the shit happened. When a couple of our lads were injured, there was a Swiss or German camera crew right on the spot to record them being dragged into a medical Pig. Coincidence or what? Then, on a lovely clear day, no rioters in sight and we were on a footsie around the Bullring. All of a sudden there's about 20 kids throwing rocks at us and then petrol bombs started flying in. I was taking cover behind a Pig and I looked to my left and there were three or four men with cameras and those big furry mikes and I'm thinking: "Where the fuck did these bleeders spring from?"

Another time we had the local yobs throwing bricks at us and one of our snatch squads grabbed a couple of the older ones – aged 16 or 17 – and we brought them back behind the shields for a kicking. Anyway, one of our full screws gets one of the lads by the throat and asked him what he was playing at. The kid went white and he blurted out that a couple of American men had given them £10 to throw some rocks at us so that they could bleeding film it! The next time I saw a cameraman filming us I kicked him the backside and 'accidentally' trod on his camera. He put a complaint in, but he couldn't identify me as we all looked the same with our steel helmets and visors! Nice one, son.

On the same day – the 13th – an army Beaver reconnaissance aircraft was hit six times by an IRA unit as it flew over Glassdrummond, South Armagh. The gunmen had mounted another IVCP in the area and the slow-moving Beaver was seen as 'a target of opportunity'. No soldiers or flying crew were injured and the aircraft landed safely. Shortly before – around 1300 hours – a four-man foot patrol from the Welsh Guards entered a field at Ford's Cross close to Crossmaglen. Earlier a PIRA bombing unit had concealed a large device behind a telegraph pole close to a gate where they had observed soldiers entering before. As Guardsman Paul Fryer (18) went through as back marker, the watching terrorist crew detonated the device. The young Welshman, from Gwent, took the full force of the blast and he was killed instantly. Another of his comrades was badly injured. His funeral was held at Danycraig Cemetery at Caerphilly.

FIRST CONTACT
Marcus Townley, Welsh Guards

We soon settled in and got to know our TAOR. We got to know the ground and, more importantly, we got to know who the local players were. We soon settled into a routine of three days' rural patrols – mostly along the border – and sometimes we were tasked to other companies' TAOR. Then it was three days of static sangar duty and acting as QRF (Quick Reaction Force – on permanent standby ready to be crashed out at a moment's notice to any security incident). That was followed by three sangars at Bessbrook (BBK), which included roof, gate and the helipad – the latter one used to rock whenever helicopters took off. We also manned the Permanent VCP there (PVCP), which was the site of the last official British fatality during the Troubles. But, as the author has shown, the last 'official' casualty was far from being the last soldier to be killed in Northern Ireland.

Our first contact was not long in coming! It was Tuesday, 13 November 1979 and it was my task that day to act as company runner. I was in the ops room and an officer came in and called out: "Did anyone hear a shotgun going off?" His question was met by blank stares, so he buzzed the rooftop sangar and received the response that it sounded like a car backfiring. Just then, the airways burst into life and we heard the dreaded: "Hello, Zero; this is 'one'. Contact; wait; out." The whole net went quiet – in line with SOPs – but professionalism kicked in and I was handed several padlocks and instructed to lock up all the phone booths in the base. (It was SOP to ban all communication with home in order to stop a soldier informing his family that a comrade had been shot and possibly killed. It was the sad duty of the Casualty Visiting Officer (CVO) to make the announcements official and it was not the remit of another soldier to innocently cause any unnecessary suffering back home through careless comments.)

The QRF was immediately crashed out and they departed the base at a rate of knots in order to provide instant back-up and support for any wounded. It transpired that an incident had taken place at Crossmaglen where a Welsh Guardsman had been badly injured. Rumour and counter-rumour swept the place – and it was just as well that none of us could add to the misery which was shortly to be visited upon a soldier's family back on the mainland. Tragically, it later emerged that one of our lads – Guardsman Paul Fryer – had been blown up by a PIRA IED as he stepped through a gap in a hedge.

Although I never knew the boy, we still all felt the loss as we were such a close-knit Welsh battalion. On that very same day the IRA tried to bring down an army spotter plane in the nearby area. Later that evening we were patrolling through BBK and it was dark as an old woman came up to us in tears at the sad loss of one of our boys. I somehow doubt if she would have spoken to us if it had been in broad daylight.

After Paul's death they recovered his GPMG (General Purpose Machine Gun) – and what shocked me was that it was almost bent double. We knew the weapon affectionately as the 'Jimpy' – and although not my weapon of choice, I found myself as the brick's 'Jimpy' man. About a week after Paul's death we were out on Cud patrol (rural areas) and every time we came across gates and telegraph

In the front seat of a scout flying fast and low back to Bessbrook, Armagh. (©Brian Sheridan)

poles I was literally sweating with fear. It was 'squeaky-bum' time – and we coined that phrase long before the Manchester United manager Sir Alex Ferguson did!

Another time, we had a tip-off that a UDR reservist was going to get a visit from the 'boys' (PIRA) – so we put in a lurk patrol to counter the threat. However, just as we got into position it started to snow – and in our waterproof greens we stuck out like sore thumbs! For obvious reasons we couldn't brew up or make any noise whatsoever – and after five fruitless hours the platoon commander ordered us back to base. The terrorists often targeted the off-duty UDR and RUC lads because they were 'easy' kills and soft targets for their cowardly killers. Fruitless lurks were par for the course over there!

On the 15th, a female UDR soldier died in unknown circumstances. The Greenfinch was Woman Private Hilary Graham (27) and it is thought that she may have been accidentally shot. Just three days later, RUC Constable John Davidson (26) – who had been fatally injured the previous month in the incident at Crocus Street which killed Sergeant Major Bellamy – died from his terrible wounds.

On the 23rd, Republicans killed another PO – the third this month – when they targeted an off-duty officer at his home in North Belfast. Gerald 'Gerry' Melville (45) worked at HMP Maze and was separated from his wife. He lived alone in Glengormley in the northern outskirts of Belfast. Officer Melville joined the Northern Ireland Prison Service in February 1964 and served for over 15 years. Mr Melville was shot at his home by PIRA gunmen and was found dead the following morning when colleagues reported he had failed to report for duty. He was survived by his wife and young daughter.

COMING CLOSE TO SHOOTING A 'GOOD' GUY
Peter Jojic, Royal Artillery

I was a brick commander on our 1979-80 tour and, as such, was in charge of any VCPs which we had set. The battery commander had told me that any car which, in my opinion, was attempting to run me – or any member of my brick – down was to be classed as an offensive weapon and that 'appropriate measures' were to be taken.

On one particular day we were doing a VCP outside Crumlin Road Prison in order to deter Republicans from attacking prison officers (see below). It took place at about 1730 hours on a cold and wet late December afternoon. Carl, a member of my brick, was standing at the front end of our Pig – using his torch to pull cars over. However, one car was refusing to stop and it was going straight for him. I was about five metres behind and shouted at him to jump out of the way, which fortunately he did. I brought my SLR up to fire at the driver, but was unable to do as Carl was in my line of sight. As the car pulled level with me I swung my rifle to hit the windscreen, but to my surprise I bloody missed it! The car then pulled over and I ran up to it and tried pulling the driver's door open, but it was locked. I shouted to the driver: "Get out of the fucking car!" – to which he responded with a two-word expletive!

By this stage, blood was already up and I was set to explode when he opened his window. I told him to get out of the car and he refused – and I was really pissed off then – so I poked my barrel into his face and said: "Get out of the car or I'll fucking shoot you!" He got out of the car and so did his passenger, who had been sitting quietly. Carl checked the passenger over while I asked the driver for his identification. It was then that I found out that he was a prison officer. I said to him: "Didn't you see my mate flag you down?" and he said: "Yes, but I thought that you didn't mean us!" I was furious and I said that he should know that we did this twice a day to protect him and his fellow officers. A couple of prison officers had been murdered by the INLA only recently in the Crumlin Road.

It was then that I noticed something different about his accent and I asked him where he came from and he told me: "Scarborough." "Fuck me," I thought. Not only the IRA and every other organisation are trying to kill us, but now even Englishmen. I pulled him to one side and said to him again that if he ever pulled that stunt again I'd kill him. He said that he would report me as he knew where I was based and he told his mate what I had threatened to do to him. Later I had to fill out a report when I finished our VCP and that was the last I heard of it. That was until the battery commander had a chat with us all and said that we have to be more careful. He said that he had just recently had an ND at the GCH unloading bay and now: "Lance-Bombardier Jojic has just threatened to kill a prison officer!"

If I've run on too much Ken, I do apologise – but as I was writing this to you, it brought it all back. Even now I'm shaking with rage after 30 years!

In November 2011 Northern Ireland's Justice Minister, David Ford, paid a poignant tribute to the 29 prison officers killed by terrorists – mainly the IRA and INLA – during the Troubles. He laid the first wreath at the Northern Ireland Prison Service annual memorial service at the organisation's training college in Millisle, Co Down. *The Belfast*

Telegraph quoted Ford's speech: "Throughout some very difficult years, prison service staff have served the whole community and performed their duties against a backdrop of murder, threats and intimidation. Today's service provides an opportunity not only to remember those who have lost their lives, but also acknowledge the suffering and pain of their families, friends and colleagues left behind. My thoughts are with them all."

29 prison officers – including two females – were murdered by Republicans between 1974 and 1993. The murdered officers included Agnes Wallace, mother of six, killed in Armagh 19 April 1979 (see Chapter 52) and Elizabeth Chambers, killed by INLA in Armagh, 7 October 1982. William McCully was the first to be killed.

DUNGANNON 1979
Sergeant Dave Judge, 2 RGJ

I was a sergeant in 9 Platoon and was based in Dungannon, North Armagh. My very new, but already very good, platoon commander was Second-Lieutenant David St John Homer. I can't remember the date, but I was on duty in the ops room doing my turn – manning the radios for a few hours. Part of my platoon was resting and part of it was out on the ground patrolling with the platoon commander. We had a report of a possible car bomb in the market square, and as per SOPs all of the usual things were done and cordons put in place etc – and the long wait for ATO began …

The ops room was a hive of activity: radios to Battalion HQ and the men on the ground were buzzing with hundreds of snippets of information coming in and going out – and lines were ringing … secure scrambled phones were all giving it max! My lads were out on the ground with the platoon commander and I stuck in the ops room. We were simply passing radio messages back and forth. I was a little beside myself with the fear that curiosity would get the better of my lads on the ground. Someone might just get too close or not be behind cover. Was this a 'come on'? Were there other devices positioned in areas likely to be occupied by my lads? There was always the very likely possibility of gunmen watching and waiting for an opportunity to shoot.

Anyway, to cut a long story short, 500lbs of explosives suddenly detonated, but thankfully all my lads were positioned away from the blast and were safe. ATO had not yet arrived. All I could think of was: "Thank God it went off!" Because every one of the troops involved in this incident now knew the impact involved in a blast of this kind. I knew at that moment that it would put them all in good stead for the next time – and having seen the devastation that this one device caused, I knew that they would give each and every one of the lads an example of what they would come across in the future. They were now aware of the respect and undivided attention which they would have to give in the future.

As a postscript, a jeweller's shop was extensively damaged by this blast – and a soldier was later to be given the name 'the Dungannon Jeweller'. You know who you are; so do I.

On the 23rd, Thomas McMahon was found guilty of the murder of Mountbatten – as well as the murders of Paul Maxwell, Nicholas Knatchbull and Lady Brabourne. One of the other men charged, Francis McGirl, was found not guilty by the no-jury Special Court (based on the Northern Irish Diplock system). McGirl walked free and McMahon was jailed for life. McMahon was the only Republican terrorist to be jailed for the murders. He has never publicly discussed his role in the bombing. However, in the year before his release from jail, his wife said: "Tommy never talks about Mountbatten – only the boys who died. He does have genuine remorse." Mrs McMahon has been politically active. She is a former Sinn Féin councillor and a former Mayor of Carrickmacross. McMahon had served the first 13 years of his life sentence in the IRA wing of Portlaoise. He and 10 others – armed with guns and explosives – failed in an attempt to escape in 1985. Three years later he fired a shot from a Browning pistol smuggled into a holding cell of Dublin's Four Courts. But, in 1992, he claimed to have turned his back on the IRA (source: UK Daily Telegraph).

GEORDIE'S BRUSH WITH DEATH, LONDONDERRY
Ian Cooper, Royal Regiment of Fusiliers

I had reached the dizzy heights of lance-corporal and, as such, was included in the battalion's advance party along with the officers and other NCOs. This was basically to liaise with the in-situ battalion; get the feel of the place; be briefed on the trouble spots and – more importantly – to be briefed (and sometimes introduced) to the known players.

The outgoing lot were the Sherwood Foresters – although with the passage of time I am not 100 per cent certain. What I am sure was that it was their first tour for quite some time and most of their NCOs were on their first tour – full stop. Anyway we tagged onto some of their patrols in our respective TAORs, which in our case took in the city centre, the docks and out to the Buncranna PVCP which was right on the border with the Irish Republic. It also included the Shantallow and Carnhill estates – a particularly troublesome area not just for the people living there, but for its patrolling problems. Two estates separated by a large piece of open ground and restricted approaches.

After we took command and the rest of the troops arrived, we set about business for real. The first few weeks on patrol duty were full-on – four to five-hour patrols, mainly showing a constant presence on the ground; letting the bad guys know we were in town and that we were not about to stay home for four months. Most of the patrols consisted of at least four call signs and a double mobile unit to satellite them (and also to act as the QRF on the ground). Things were going well – and for a brief moment I was feeling that it may be another quiet one until Lord Mountbatten was assassinated whilst on a fishing holiday. It was obviously the handiwork of some 'brave Republican'!

The natives were in buoyant mood from then on and started to become more restless as if there was more to come. One day I was on camp guard duty as guard commander when I heard a distinctive crack from the area of the Carnhill Estate. I reported to the ops room: "Single high-velocity shot from the Carnhill." "Roger that," was the expected reply. Thinking no more of it, we all carried on that day without any further incident. As evening fell, the night patrol exited for a look around the estate – and for the most part went without incident until the walk back, which was funnelled at one point along Racecourse Road. I can't be sure of all the facts as I was not on the ground, but that's not the important bit. What I do know from that night was that whilst patrolling south on Racecourse Road, two call signs crossed each other. One was led by the multiple commander and the other by an NCO whom I will call 'Geordie'.

Geordie told me later that the patrol was on the way back out of the Carnhill Estate and was crossing the road from east to west when he felt an enormous pain in his neck and promptly collapsed. Others from the patrol filled in the rest and I was shocked to hear that Geordie had been hit by a 5.56 Armalite round to the right side of his neck close to his collarbone. But he had another sobering discovery to make... After an extensive and very quick follow-up, the weapon – an Armalite with a telescopic sight – was recovered from the rear of an abandoned vehicle (with its engine still running) not too far away. This means, presumably, to the conclusion that they were very close to catching the shooter.

The weapon was taken away for early forensic examination and then test-fired on a Warminster bench. Results showed it was firing four inches low and two inches left. If it had been zeroed properly, Geordie may have been in a worse place than he was. What shook the rest of us was that the shooter had taken the shot from over a wall a mere 75 metres away. The guy had big balls in any language – either that or he was just plain stupid.

He recovered quickly in Altnagelvin Hospital and was soon back with us; still sore, but keen to carry on. He was told that he could carry on once he felt up to it and no pressure was put on him to get back on the streets. I think that he was quite rightly feeling that he had had a close call the last time and was given the choice of foot or mobile on his next multiple patrol. On his first patrol back (in the town around the area of Strand Road RUC Station, the docks and Waterloo Place), the IRA struck again! When his mobile approached the Strand Road from Asylum or Clarendon Street, a burst of gunfire hit the Land Rover he was in – luckily taking no casualties.

Later on, INT told us it was the work of the local M60 gun team. Geordie came back from that patrol and had words with the CSM and OC – and was allowed to see the rest of the tour out staying within the confines of Fort George.

On the 24th, a PIRA ASU were thwarted in their efforts to kill a soldier and found themselves confronted by a foot patrol from the Royal Regiment of Fusiliers (RRF). The murder attempt took place in Londonderry and the initial shots wounded a soldier. As the terrorists tried to escape, the RRF opened fire at them – causing their getaway car to crash. The men fled into a Nationalist area – leaving behind a high-powered Armalite rifle. Two days later the Provisionals launched a 10-city bombing blitz throughout the Province and the RUC/army found themselves stretched trying to contain the damage. In one of the incidents – in Newry, Co Down – a PIRA bombing crew had to abandon the car in which they were transporting a bomb when it broke down in the town centre. ATO were forced to enter the car and neutralise the device by controlled explosion. Soldiers tackled bombs and fires in shops, transport depots, cars and in at least two train stations. Two devices were planted at Belfast's Central Train Station – one of which was defused by ATO, but the second device caused considerable damage. As was common, on most days throughout Northern Ireland, a pall of black smoke hung in the air.

M16 AND A BIT OF PORNOGRAPHY
Graham Briggs, Royal Artillery

Bit of background … We were doing a lot of searches during our tour – and about two to three weeks into the tour INT had been received that an American sniper rifle – which had a killing range of two miles – had been smuggled into Belfast and was being moved about and had been taken into the New Lodge. Search team members were: Ronnie, who was Team IC; Andy, 2IC; Jock, Janner, Bugsy, Pixie, me and another lad whose name I've forgotten.

As usual it was a 'daft o'clock' time – about 0400 hours – and all we had time to do was get up, go to the loo, quick swill and shave, over to the cookhouse, make an egg banjo and brew and then into the briefing room for about 0500 hours. The battery INT officer started to brief us. I remember almost verbatim what he said to us all those years ago: "This morning we are going to an address in one of the tower blocks of North Queen Street to carry out a search. The patrols will go out after this briefing and make their way to the area; put in the cordon by 0545. Search team: you are to be ready to move by Pig as soon as the cordon is in place. On arrival at the address, the RUC sergeant will gain entry and then the search team will enter." It really is amazing – even after all these 30-odd years – that I can remember his words as well as if it had been yesterday.

We got all our gear ready and got into the Pig and, as was SOP, the search team did not carry weapons whilst on search other than the two members who guarded us. Anyway, we got the word and left Girdwood Park. About 10 minutes later we arrived at the tower block, debussed and made our way up to the address by the stairs as this was the safest way. There were lifts of course, but it would have been fatal if we were in there and a PIRA ambush took place – and they dropped grenades down the lift shaft! The flat was about midway up the block of flats and when we arrived, the RUC man knocked on the door until he got a response. He then shouted out exactly who we were and that we had come to search the property. The front door opened and we went in. Immediately, the two team commanders and the policeman went into the front room and started to question the head of the family. The rest of the team waited in the hallway.

Pixie stayed by the front door – as he was one of our armed guards – and the other armed guard positioned himself at the entrance to the front room. Jock whispered to us that we would not find anything here. I asked why not, and he said quietly: "Look around this place; it is too smart and clean." He was right. The property was well-presented, clean and tidy – not at all like some of the houses we had searched previously. Ronnie was asking the head of the house certain questions which had to be asked before we carried out the search. One question was: "Are you under duress to keep any weapons or ammunition at this property?" To my absolute surprise, the head of the house answered: "Yes." Ronnie asked where they were and the man replied that they were in the cupboard in the hall.

Andy, the 2IC, sprang into action and told us to search it and then changed his mind and did it himself. Clearly he remembered that there was a £10 reward put up by the BSM for the person who got the find. Andy's job was to make a report out during the search and not get involved in the searching. Whist all this commotion was going on, the rest of us were told to carry on doing the search. Janner and Bugsy were one pair; Jock and me the other.

We started in the bedrooms and went through all the wardrobes and drawers. We looked under the bed – lifting the carpet. We even looked at the photo albums for anything unusual. Just then, Janner told us in a quiet voice to follow him into another room. When we entered, Bugsy showed us this photo album which he had found. Well, there weren't the usual snaps of the family on a weekend to Blackpool or Margate, but were photos of the lady of the house in certain poses and various states of undress – proving some jobs do have their perks.

Nothing further was found at the address – and strangely, whilst we were searching, the head of the house was sitting in the front room playing some musical instrument and did not seem at all phased by what was going on around him. What was found at the address was an M16 Armalite rifle; a Smith and Wesson revolver; 360 rounds of M16 ammunition and spare parts for the M16. It was ready for use with a round up the spout. We were later told that the M16 had been used in previous attacks on the Security Forces.

There was a postscript; Andy got his £10, but would not split it with the rest of the team – and we weren't allowed to take the porn with us!

Although the find was a great success and there was a humorous interlude, it was not always so. Many weapons were smuggled into Northern Ireland for the Provisional IRA and INLA – as well as for the Loyalist paramilitaries – not just across the whole length of the porous border with the Republic, but also on isolated stretches of the coastline and through the various docks. Weapons were not only smuggled in (in packing cases and containers purporting to contain other, more innocent goods), but also in the hand luggage of Republican sympathisers and supporters who worked for lines such as Cunard or as crewmen on Merchant ships. All it needed was a nod and a wink from sympathetic or corrupt customs staff – or the revelation of a back-way out of the docks from an IRA-supporting docker – and another death-dealing instrument was on its way onto the streets of Belfast or Londonderry.

On the 29th, a massive landmine was detonated in the path of a Royal Marines mobile patrol in Co Fermanagh. The device – estimated at 1,000lbs – was detonated a fraction of a second too early and instead of three dead marines there were three serious injuries, but all survived after hospital treatment. The author has not been able to find out further details, but there is some mystery as the regiment was not officially in Northern Ireland during 1979.

RELIGIOUS DIFFERENCES?
Derek O'Loughlin, Royal Artillery
Another time we were patrolling in the Loyalist Waterside area. There had been some shots in from the Bogside and it was pitch-black as the streetlights had been turned off. These two old ladies invited us in for tea, but I had to laugh. They were staunch Protestants and five of the six-man patrol were Catholics – 'Taigs', they would have called us! I was mentally thinking about religious bigotry when she got some photos out of her son, who had died in the army in Hong Kong. To

my surprise, it turned out that he was our patrol leader's best friend when he was stationed out there. That was a revelation which I hadn't expected.

During the month, nine people had been killed – including two soldiers, a policeman and three prison officers. Three civilians died – two Catholics and a Protestant – all as a result of sectarianism. The Republicans killed six people and the Loyalists killed two.

60

December

The death toll in this season of goodwill and joy to all men would reach 16 – with 11 of the dead being soldiers or former soldiers. Two more POs would die and yet another policeman was killed. There would be a pre-Christmas bombing blitz by the Provisionals and bombs would explode in England again.

On the 2nd, the IRA exploded several bombs in three Co Down towns. These were Castlewellan, Rathriland and Newcastle. They mainly targeted shops, but in Rathriland they destroyed a bus depot – damaging or destroying several buses.

Over the course of the next two days the UFF carried out the sectarian slaying of a Catholic in West Belfast and the Provisionals killed a senior PO at his home in Belfast. David White (35) was a market man who operated several stalls in the Co Antrim area. Masked gunmen from a Loyalist murder gang – UFF – had traced him to his home in Brooke Crescent. The Brookes are a small estate sandwiched between Andersonstown and Ladybrook Park. The Loyalist murder gang entered by a back window and located Mr White's bedroom. As he lay in bed they shot him at least six times and mortally wounded him. In his dying moments he attempted to crawl to his door, but was unable to make it and his lifeless body was found on the floor. Although he was not connected with any paramilitary group, a UDA spokesman said that he had been 'executed' for being a 'storeman' in the IRA.

Just 24 hours later, William Wright (58) – father of three and a senior PO at Crumlin Road Jail – was murdered at his home in Lyndhurst Drive off the Ballygomartin Road in West Belfast. William Moore was murdered the previous month at Lyndhurst Parade, which was the next street to where the PO lived. He had finished work for the day at the jail and had driven the mile or so to the smart detached home in which he lived in a newish and upmarket area. He stopped his car and went to open his garage door when a gunman standing at the next house opened fire – hitting him six times in the back. He was mortally wounded and died minutes later as the gunman escaped in a stolen car. It was the second time that the IRA had tried to kill him following a gun attack on him in October 1978. He varied his route home, but it was too late as he had been dicked and followed home by PIRA INT (it is thought, on a number of occasions). He was a former soldier who had reached senior NCO rank in the Royal Marines.

JUNIOR DICKER
Graham Briggs, Royal Artillery
One night we were sent out to do a patrol around our TAOR of North Belfast. We gathered in the briefing room and we discussed the routine sort of stuff: 'P' checks, car checks and told to gather any INT that we could. We were then joined by the battery INT officer, who proceeded to tell us that the word was that something was expected to happen and that we should go out with our SLRS cocked – i.e. 'one up the spout'. He also informed us that a COP (Close Observation Platoon

292

- i.e. Covert OP) was already up around Haliday's Road. This was a dead-end street – in every sense of the word – between Duncairn Gardens and Limestone Road.

After the briefing – and a warning to be alert – we went up to the Cliftonville Avenue gate of Girdwood Park, made our weapons ready and star-burst out into the New Lodge. Outside the base there is a gate – and if you turn left for about 50 or 60 metres, on the left is a lamppost with bullet marks. This was where a gunner from another regiment had been fatally wounded. When you look at the lamppost, you could see where the gunman had fired from. In front there was a large builders' yard and then a set of factory windows – from where the gunman had had a perfect view of the foot patrol which he fired at. It was an unpleasant reminder to be on your toes at all times.

We carried on through various streets of the fiercely Republican New Lodge area and the names of the streets are etched into my memory: Cliftonpark Avenue, Cliftonville Road, Antrim Road, Hillman Street et al. We were patrolling along the top end of the Lodge and we reached Haliday's Road – and then the nerves and the apprehension became apparent. We had noticed the same group of lads standing on the waste ground and we had passed them a couple of times. One of the patrol, Pixie, came up to me and said: "Every time we pass this group, the lad in the blue anorak starts whistling," so I told Andy what was going on. I suggested that we should go around again and that I would grab him as he might well be a dicker. So we retraced our steps and as we came up to the youths, I noticed the lad that I wanted was in the middle.

I just grabbed him by his jacket and pulled him clear of the group – taking him to one side – and I stood with my back to the wall and him in front of me as a shield just in case we were be in targeted. I started to question him – asking him why he kept whistling when patrols were going by. All he did was shrug his shoulders and smile. I suggested that he was being a 'clever c***', but received no response. Next, I 'P' checked him and discovered his address was given as the lower end of Upper Meadow Street. He was told in no uncertain terms to go back down his end of the area and if he was seen up here again he would be lifted. Off he went and we carried on with our patrol. We went along Haliday's Road and onto Lepper Street. Guess who was hanging around there? Yes, the same lad I had just 'P' checked! This lad was very clearly a dicker and we couldn't do a damn thing about him.

On the 5th, Jack Lynch resigned as Taoiseach. His days were numbered after his ineffectual response to the Mountbatten and Warrenpoint murders the previous August. Seen by many as a 'lame duck', he was on borrowed time from shortly after the *Shadow V* was reduced to match stalks in the water off Mullaghmore. He was replaced by Charles Haughey on 7 December 1979 when the Fianna Fáil parliamentary party voted by 44 votes to 38 in favour of Haughey.

In a number of cities across Britain, 24 people were arrested on suspicion of being members of the IRA. This was an attempt to disrupt an anticipated Christmas bombing campaign and was carried out by armed police and the Anti-Terrorist Squad.

On the same day that Lynch was announcing his resignation, there was a shock for a Catholic family who lived in Old Strabane Road in Londonderry when they were held at gunpoint by masked PIRA men. They were put in a room and forced to keep quiet whilst the terrorists who had invaded their house executed their plan, which was intended to kill or maim SF members. Leaving the family under armed guard, two of the IRA men went out and hijacked a commercial van, packed it with explosives and parked it outside the post office at Spencer Road in the Waterside area. On returning to the hostages, the husband of the family was forced to telephone a bomb warning through to the RUC – giving the aforementioned post office as the location. The 1st Battalion of the Staffords were in the area and linked up with the RUC to form a protective cordon around the van and assist in evacuating the surrounding residences. All traffic in the Spencer Road/Craigavon Bridge area was diverted and ATO were tasked to make the device – later discovered to be 300lbs – safe. It did explode some time later and although there was substantial damage to houses and businesses, no-one was injured.

MERRY CHRISTMAS
Mark 'C', Royal Artillery and UDR

I did my first tour of Northern Ireland as part of the City Centre Battery 25 Field Regiment RA in 1979 – stationed in the GCH Belfast. For most of us, the tour was quiet apart from a few bomb scares and Republican marchers trying to get into the city centre. It was the start of what became the hunger strikes, which quickly turned into serious rioting. That was all to change on Christmas Eve and just as we were starting to wind down at the end of our four months. PIRA terrorists hijacked a red GPO van, packed it with explosives and left it in a small lane called Patterson's Place beside Belfast City Hall. It was close to one of the main segment gates into the city (X24 at Donegal Place), which happened to be the city centre's main shopping street.

The terrorists did not give a warning, but apparently the police received an anonymous tip-off that it was there. So we had to clear the whole area. Luckily it was Christmas and freezing cold so there was not many people about – and anyway, Belfast City Centre in those days was a ghost town after 7pm because of the Troubles. At the start of clearing the area etc we were not too concerned because I remember being given the impression that it wasn't a real bomb. At times we got very close to the van and from my final position on Donegal Square North I could also see it – probably about 120 yards away. Anyway 'Felix' arrived and it went from what we thought would be an hour at most on the cordon to an all-night job. Extra soldiers had to be brought in to help us and to relieve us so we could get a cup of tea and a warm-up because of the biting cold.

If memory served it took over six hours during the night to defuse it, so all praise to the ATO who had to work in those freezing conditions to keep us soldiers and civvies safe. However, looking back now it makes me shiver thinking how close we were at times to a massive bomb. Incidentally, a mucker in my brick says we had a bit of a fight with a BBC crew who tried to get too close and kept getting in the way, but I can't remember that; funny how different soldiers remember different things at incidents.

Foot patrol, Ormeau Road, Belfast, 1979. (©Mark 'C')

Foot patrol, Ormeau Road, Belfast, 1979. (©Mark 'C')

On the 5th, the UDR lost Private Arthur Langley (37). The author has no further details as to his death. On the 6th, PIRA launched their threatened pre-Christmas blitz and chose Lisburn, Co Antrim – the HQNI town. In an area packed with soldiers, it was the IRA's way of informing the SF that there was nowhere that they wouldn't or couldn't bomb! The day started with a spate of hoax warnings which the army and RUC were forced to take seriously and investigate. The first warning took the SF out to the very outskirts – during which a genuine bomb was planted in a shop in the town centre. ATO was then tasked back to the real bomb, but following a warning which was phoned in to the Samaritans too late for the SF to react, four bombs exploded – causing substantial damage. Whilst the SF were running around like '*blue-arsed flies*' the Loyalists attempted to murder Catholics at a betting shop in Belfast. It was a dress-rehearsal for an incident which happened just over 12 years later. On 5 February 1992 a mass shooting was carried out at the Sean Graham bookmaker's shop on the Lower Ormeau Road in Belfast, Northern Ireland. Five Catholics were killed and nine were wounded in the attack. On this occasion – on 6 December 1979 – UVF gunmen in a stolen car arrived at a betting shop in North Queen Street at the lower end of the New Lodge and opened fire on the gamblers inside. There were several wounded, but no-one was killed. Before that eventful day was over, the UDA/UFF had been dealt a severe blow when the RUC raided a major arms cache in the Loyalist Tullycarnet Estate in East Belfast. Amongst the items seized were machine guns and 5,000 rounds of ammunition.

CRUMLIN ROAD RTA
Herb Jackson, Royal Artillery

I remember once driving along – heading out of the centre of Belfast towards the Crumlin Road – and as we were about to cross a crossroads, my mate Jeff (in a voice like that of a child watching a fireworks display) shouted: "Oooh! Look at that; a motorcycle in the air!" Then, instantaneously, another voice added:"'Oh; and a rider too!" Sure enough, as we quickly turned and looked in the indicated direction, we were just in time to see the biker hit the ground in a crumpled heap. I brought the vehicle to a halt and we just stared for a moment. There had been a nasty crash at another junction up the road from us. We quickly diverted to the scene and leapt out to offer assistance. Two of us began checking things out whilst the CO got on the radio and others from the RSM's crew began covering the area.

It was obvious the injured rider was drunk as he had a broken leg and grazed arm – or was it the other way round? Anyway it was one or the other. A lot of effing and blinding was going on from the seemingly equally drunk car driver, but by the time the RUC and ambulance arrived the two guys were both admitting to each other that it was their fault. They were both patting each other on the back like old pals would and both wanting to get on their way home – even with broken bones with no bother.

They were not too pleased when the RUC made it clear that they were not about to let that happen – and the biker was positively irate at being taken to hospital. It was hilarious – and the emotions after the crash were so different to ones I had witnessed in the past. The car driver was irate at having to wait for an ambulance. It was as if we were splitting up a family or something. We hadn't done anything except help them. It was the RUC who were detaining them, but it was us who got all the aggro.

On the 7th, the newly-crowned Taoiseach – Charles Haughey – announced his arrival on the leadership stage with a warning for the British. At a press conference in Dublin, he announced that it would be his Government's intention to achieve a peaceful reunification of Ireland. The emphasis was on the word 'reunification' and he reiterated the 1975 Irish demand that the British announce immediately their intention to withdraw from the island of Ireland. In what was viewed by most sensible thinkers as simply rhetoric, he insisted that the British stop 'meddling in the affairs of the Irish' and further exclaimed that the Northern Ireland Secretary's plans for a future constitution for Ulster was 'wholly inadequate'. He stated that the Irish police and army were perfectly capable of protecting the territorial integrity of the Republic and dismissed criticism of his arms-smuggling past as 'just history'. [NB. The 'Arms Crisis' was a political scandal in the Republic of Ireland in 1970 when two cabinet ministers — Charles Haughey and Neil Blaney — were removed from office for allegedly attempting to illegally import arms for the IRA in Northern Ireland.]

Haughey's remarks were belligerent and ill-thought out as it sent a message to the British Government suggesting that Jack Lynch's latterly conceived plans for seeking agreement amongst the warring factions in the North would disappear without a trace. It further sent a mixed message to the Provisionals – effectively legitimising its actions to the extent that they could claim to be representing the wishes of the Irish State. If that were to occur, support from the Irish-Americans – which had waned slightly in the wake of the Mountbatten murder – would now pick up again.

Meanwhile in London, anti-terrorist police raided a number of houses in the capital's fashionable Holland Park area and arrested five men – including a man they believed was the head of the England Team under the Prevention of Terrorism Act. Although no explosives were seized, a number of weapons were and they believed that they had foiled a blitz on innocent shoppers in the lead-up to Christmas.

On the 12th, Sir Kenneth Newman – in what was one of his final speeches before retiring as Chief Constable of the RUC – spoke of community responsibilities. In remarks which were clearly aimed at the Nationalist communities and supportive of Republican terrorists, he said: "The community should ask itself how much longer it would allow small groups of self-appointed dictators to kill; to hold back economic development; to terrorise; to corrupt and destroy ... to exceed even the worst excesses of Mafia gangsterism; to hold us up to international curiosity and disdain."

On 12 December, Private Carl Alexander Rowe (20) of the UDR was killed in an RTA whilst on duty. Unfortunately, the author has no further details.

On the 16th, there were no less than six deaths as the Provisional IRA sought to 'celebrate' their 10th anniversary as a terrorist organisation. Five serving soldiers were killed in two separate incidents and a former UDR man was murdered in a third. In the first incident, a PIRA bombing team had planted 1,000lbs of explosives into containers and hidden them in a culvert underneath the road at Glenadush, Co Tyrone. There is no 'good' time for a parent to lose their child – and it is the same for any mother or father even if their son or daughter is a soldier. Christmas is an even more cruel time for such a tragedy. As Christmas 1979 approached, every parent's nightmare came true for four families of Royal Artillerymen serving in the Province. The 16th dawned – cold and crisp as a two-vehicle Royal Artillery mobile patrol passed Glenadush a few miles from Dungannon in Co Tyrone. It was en route for Dungannon and the patrol commander had chosen the Ballygawley Road. As the second vehicle passed over a culvert, a PIRA landmine was detonated and the explosives detonated – throwing the shattered vehicle high into the air, landing some 30 yards away in a field. All four soldiers were killed absolutely instantly. The only consolation to their loved ones was that there would have been no pain, no sensation – just a white flash.

A crater over 30 feet deep and as wide was left in the road – and the shocked occupants of the lead vehicle, which had stopped, jumped out to take up defensive positions. As they did so, they came under rifle attack from PIRA gunmen in concealed positions. The soldiers returned fire, but claimed no hits. One can only imagine the shock as they surveyed the shattered wreckage of the second Land Rover – knowing with certainty that their mates were dead. They would have looked at the rolling Irish countryside, located midway between Lough Neagh and the border, knowing that the terrorists were preparing to slip over there to be feted as heroes amongst the Republicans. The four dead soldiers were: Gunner Keith Richards (22), from Bromsgrove in the British Midlands; Gunner Simon Evans (19), from Chippenham, Wiltshire; Gunner William Beck (23), from Knocknagoney, Belfast; and Gunner Alan Ayrton (21), from Accrington, Lancashire. Their unit had only been in Northern Ireland for a fortnight when the tragedy occurred.

Gunner Beck was from the Province and, as such, he could not be compelled to serve there. He was not prepared however to leave his comrades – and though he was shortly to be married, told his family: "If I don't go, someone else will have to go instead."

The Daily Express front page the next day cried out poignantly: 'Last Words Of A Soldier: Provos' bloody 'No' to truce for Christmas'. John Ley and William Hunter wrote: "Two women wept for the young soldier they loved last night, with nothing but his words to comfort them. Gunner Alan Ayrton – 21 – and three colleagues were blasted to death by an IRA landmine ambush yesterday. Just two days earlier the 21-year-old soldier had written in his last letter home: 'To tell the truth this is a very quiet area. The only incident we have had was a bank robbery this morning. It is a nice area really. Most of the population speak to you. I have had an easy time so far. If it continues like this until April, I shall be pleased.' Those words had given hope to his mother, Mrs Daphne Ayrton, at home in Accrington, Lancs. She said: 'I worried all the time Alan was in Belfast, but this time he said he was in a quiet area.' On Saturday he phoned his fiancée, hairdresser Linda Brown, at her home in Salisbury, Wiltshire. Linda said: 'He did not say anything about what he was doing; we just talked about the wedding.'"

Later, the East Tyrone Brigade of PIRA claimed responsibility and warned civilians not to travel close to military vehicles as they ran the risk of being caught in explosions. It was the case that in urban situations, if a civilian car was approaching a red traffic light and a military vehicle was stopped ahead of it, the driver would hang back until the lights had gone green as traffic lights and jams were favourite spots for PIRA to mount ambushes. Similarly military drivers would often run a red light as fast as possible or, if heavy cross-traffic didn't permit this, they would ease between the crossing vehicles rather than run the risk of ambush.

TRAFFIC SAFETY
Mark 'C', Royal Artillery and UDR

I was driving home up the Antrim Road with my wife and my then newborn son, who will be 30 next Tuesday. As we turned into the road at Carlisle Circus we got stuck behind three Pigs moving up the Antrim Road. I stayed well back with my lights dipped (as you did in them days). As the Pigs got to the junction with Kinnaird Street, about six petrol bombs rained down from the New Lodge side. I immediately stopped, but the army vehicles drove through it. I was then in a dilemma: whether to reverse, drive on or (it even crossed my mind) to drive into Girdwood where my mates would have been on duty. I was concerned about the possibility of a follow-up gun attack – which was very likely – and I didn't want the soldiers to think my car may be part of that. So I took the decision to put the boot down and drive through the still-burning fires. The Pigs had pulled in further up the Antrim Road and the soldiers had taken up all-round defence, but made no attempt to stop me – thankfully. It shows the dangers UDR soldiers and their families faced on and off duty. Luckily no-one was injured – and it makes a good war story for my son.

E Troop, 16th Air Defence Regiment, Royal Artillery. 1979. (©Walter Stirling)

GLENADUSH POSTSCRIPT
Walter Stirling, Royal Artillery
I was on ARF that day and as we flew over the scene. All we could see was a mass of tangled metal and a great big crater. When we landed I went forward to the edge of the crater with the medical officer – and when she saw the carnage in front of her she burst into tears. If I'm not wrong I think they were lads from 22 Locating Battery who were killed. They were attached to 14 Battery, so the lads in the leading Land Rover would have belonged to the same unit.

Trevor Bennett, Royal Artillery
We were in Cookstown and heard the explosion so we knew something major had happened, but we didn't know what it was. As the rumours started that a patrol had been hit we were sent out straight away to patrol the town – so we were all wondering what and who was involved. The first I knew that soldiers were killed was when an old man of about 80 called me into an alleyway as I passed and started crying. He apologised and told me that four had been killed. Then he dug out a bottle of Scotch from his coat pocket and gave it to me – and strangely, the fact that I didn't like Scotch was the first thought in my head!

We only found out who they were when we got back into camp – and having only arrived in the Province about 10 days or so earlier, it really was a terrifying time and a real wake-up call.

Keith Richards is only buried in Bromsgrove – a few miles from where I live – but I did not personally know him. I went to his grave a few years ago but can't go back to it now; too upsetting. Stupid I know, but that's how I feel.

RIP lads and I'll leave it at that because for the first time in years I'm crying about it. Soft gits really, ain't we?

CASTLE HILL ND
Dave Judge, 2nd Battalion, Royal Green Jackets

In 1979 I was based in Castle Hill Camp in Dungannon. It was a police station – and as the name indicates, it was situated on high ground above the market town of Dungannon. The town actually boasted a market square. I had been out of the camp for a couple of hours and when I returned, there had obviously been an incident of some sort! It transpired that there had been a 'blue on blue' shooting in the base. Using all of my sleuthing abilities, I soon discovered what had transpired during my short absence.

At the guard room, Rifleman 'M' had been on sentry at the gate – armed with a pistol. Herein lies the danger in giving a rifleman a pistol! At the end of his stag the aforementioned rifleman went to the unloading bay and unloaded the pistol – or so he thought. Instead of removing the magazine and then cocking the action to ensure the breech was empty, he had firstly cocked the pistol (thereby putting a live round into the chamber). He then inserted the mag back into the weapon and entered the guard room. As he entered the building he pressed the trigger to release the hammer. The round that was in the breech now fired! Unfortunately the other chap waiting to go out and relieve him was sleeping in a chair with his legs up on a table – legs slightly crossed! I should add that the sleeping soldier was Rifleman Heslop – the only black soldier in 'C' Company at the time. The now-discharged pistol had sent the 9mm round into the knee of the sleeping Rifleman Heslop!

The poor lad woke up the very instant that the round entered his knee. The round exited at the top of his thigh – in the area of his buttock to be more accurate. That was the extent of the 'blue on blue' incident. I can't recall but I think he was eventually invalided out of the army due to his wound, which as you can imagine was no flesh wound! It was, all in all, a very sad way to end your military service – and your time on stag! There is, however, a slightly funny postscript to this in that all of the other black troops in our other companies joked amongst each other that: "You don't want to be posted to 'C' Company because they shot all the black guys in it!" All joking aside, this was an example of poor weapon-handling with the worst possible outcome. We had a wounded – but thankfully not dead – soldier. Obviously, Rifleman 'M' was charged for this offence.

The 16th was far from over – and the next death was that of Private Peter Grundy (21), whom fate had spared at Warrenpoint some three months earlier when he had been moved from the first lorry to be blasted. He was on patrol with 2 Para in rural country at Tullydonnel at Forkhill, Co Armagh. He was part of a search team inspecting a derelict building in the area and he – or another soldier – pushed open a door, which (unknown to them) had been booby-trapped by the IRA. He was killed instantly by the blast and another comrade very badly injured. Private Grundy was from the Isle of Wight and had escaped the first blast at Warrenpoint by good fortune – and he had been close enough to the second blast to witness the horror of losing more comrades (less than 30 minutes after the first murders). He is buried at Ryde Old Cemetery and his inscription reads: '24509366 Private Peter Stephen Grundy, The Parachute Regiment, 16 December 1979, age 21: God Giveth Life and He Also Taketh Away'.

CLOSE OBSERVATION PLATOON
Corporal Ian Missenden, Duke of Edinburgh's Royal Regiment

The battalion had deployed to Bessbrook Mill and four teams were summoned to a briefing by the platoon commander. (Censored) post office was going to be robbed by two gunmen; this was sourced information. The post office had taken delivery of a large amount of money to pay out the giros the following day. The local PIRA were planning to rob the place shortly after it had opened – around 0800 hours. The village of (censored) centred on a crossroad – with the roads going to the north; south; east; and west. Each team was assigned a road to cover. I was not too chuffed at being given the road heading north. If I was a terrorist and robbed the place, I would head south and straight over the border. My team was to be the trigger for the op. We needed 'eyes-on' the post office and alert the other call signs, who would then move onto their roads and set up VCPs. The gunmen would be on a motorbike and would have to pass through one of the checkpoints. The plan seemed simple enough; not much room for a fuck-up.

It was nearly 1900 hours when the boss had finished his orders and we were due to leave at 2200 hours. Team commanders had to plan and select their positions from air photography (which was several years out of date) and maps. A hedgerow about 100 metres to the north-east of the post office, which stood on the south-west corner of the crossroads, appeared to be the best location for my team. It was about 50 metres from the Newry Road, which headed north, and allowed us time to trigger the op and then move onto the road. The teams were flown in by two Lynx helicopters. We were dropped off a couple of miles from the target. At the FRV I left two men and went forward with Mick Cunningham to recce for a position. The out-of-date air photography turned out to be more than useless. The hedgerow wasn't very thick and not possible for four men to hide in. We spent about an hour mooching around for a better location – not possible – so I settled for two positions: the one I'd selected off the air photography; and the second, the other side of the Newry Road. We had two radios, so it was workable.

Time was passing quickly and we had about an hour of darkness left – and we didn't need to be seen by the locals; compromising the job before it had even started! Mick and 'Taff' Newman left the FRV first; myself and Mick Loveridge followed shortly afterwards. Mick entered the hedgerow first, I checked that we'd left no ground-sign, and then followed him. Space was really tight – with just enough room to crouch. With any luck the job would be all done and dusted by 0830 hours. We settled in for the long wait. 0800 hours came and went. The post office was busy for a one-horse town. I smiled to myself: they hated the Brits, but they didn't mind cashing in the Government giros. By 12noon there was still no sign of the robbery and the post office had to be running out of cash (judging by the amount of customers they'd had). The boss had been on the net several times during this time – each time with a change of vehicles that were going to be used by the robbers. The big change to the plan came at about 1400 hours: when the robbery was in progress, my team was to patrol towards the post office and catch them in the act. The hours ticked by – and still nothing.

Just after 3pm a motorbike appeared on the pavement directly outside the door of the post office. Where it had come from – or if he was alone – I didn't know. I'd not heard from any of the other call signs. Mick informed the other call signs of the robbery in progress and we rushed out of the back of the hedgerow and onto the road. I kept my eyes on the motorbike as we moved. The guy on the bike was too busy looking into the post office to see us coming. As we approached and got within 20 metres of the post office, I could see the guy on the bike had a pair of socks on his hands. He still hadn't seen us – and didn't until we were a few paces away. In true PIRA tradition he took flight – revved up the bike and took off to the west. "Stop or I'll shoot!" I yelled. He must have taken my warning serious, as he stopped! 'Taff' Newman dragged him off the bike and flung him against the wall. As we were dealing with him, a guy in a bomber jacket came out of the post office – hands in pockets, head down and moving fast towards the south. "Where are you going, c***?" asked Mick Loveridge as he grabbed him by the collar and put him against the wall next to his mate. He began screaming: "It's not real; it's not real!" He too had socks on his hands. We found out what he meant. I found a replica handgun in his pocket along with a wad-load of banknotes. It looked real enough – especially if it was stuck in your face.

We passed the information to the boss and the other call signs. The RUC and ARF were dispatched to our location. The owner of the post office started to give us grief – shouting at me: "Brit bastard". He obviously thought we were being too rough with the two robbers. I reminded him that they had just held a gun in his face and he should show a bit of gratitude. He continued with a big mouth and was only saved by the two armoured Cortinas full of RUC men that arrived. The RUC took over the scene; the ARF was minutes away – and we were leaving. I was told that we couldn't leave; he needed statements. After an argument and a telephone call from the boss to the SB – and then a message on his radio – he reluctantly said we could go.

There is a follow-up to this incident, which can be found later in this chapter.

Before that day was over, another former UDR man would be dead – shot down in front of one of his children. Mr James Fowler (40), father of three, from Newtownstewart, Co Tyrone had resigned from the UDR in 1978 and now made a living working for social services and also operating a mobile fish and chips van. As he parked up in the Lammy Housing Estate in Omagh on the evening of the 16th, he would no doubt have been aware of the deaths of five of his former comrades earlier that day. He was accompanied by his 13-year-old son when they were flagged down by a man on Lammy Crescent, who indicated that he wished to purchase food. Mr Fowler prepared the food – and his son added salt and vinegar – but as the food was handed to the man, he produced a handgun and fired repeatedly at the former part-time soldier. Lost Lives (p.810) recounts the statement made by Mr Fowler's son: "The man, who was waiting on the order, then brought a gun up above the bottom of the hatch and started shooting. At first I thought he was bluffing with a cap-gun, but when I realised that they were real shots I threw a box at the gunman. It hit him and fell into the van again – and he continued to shoot at daddy. Daddy fell and the man ran away. I opened daddy's shirt to see if his heart was beating, but I don't think it was. The people came out from the houses and one of them took me into their house."

PLAYERS
Herb Jackson, Royal Artillery

Often during the tour the CO would be off doing briefings or PR work. When this happened we would find ourselves on a boring and cold sangar duty. On other occasions we might find ourselves doing a foot patrol around the inner city. Often we would go on patrol in the vehicles – sometimes paired up with the RSM's crew or sometimes just to take lads from different departments out on the streets. The BQMS staff loved to do a bit of active duty since they spent a fair bit of the time doing other boring stuff in the stores or regular duty on the segment gates or sangars. They loved a day out in Belfast in the back of our Land Rover Cabriolet with the wind in their hair; the sun on their cheeks – and all in -5 wind chill.

On foot we would get the chance to stop and check suspects from our gallery of pictures in the 'wanted/known or suspected' category. This was a booklet of photos of people we would stop and check on-site – or even arrest on-site. It was a strange feeling checking a known player – unless it was an 'arrest on-site' situation; you just went through the motions. We knew that they wouldn't have anything on them that would allow you to nab 'em – and they would always be co-operative, if a little silent. The less well-known – or the 'wannabe' types – would be the gobby ones. Every now and then you might see a 'top of the list' player with their steely-cold eyes – empty of feeling or emotion. Some would even be chatty; others would say little or nothing, then go quietly on their way after being checked – and all we could do was add to the endless intelligence data list reporting our encounter.

Each morning (or before most foot patrols) the men would be briefed as to who to look for and observe – and there was also a 'lift on sight' list for wanted PIRA/INLA 'players'. These were terrorist suspects whose arrest was highly desired and whose absence from the streets – even for a matter of hours – made the country a little safer both for soldiers and civilians alike. There was also the much-vaunted – though oft-denied – 'slot on sight' list, which the MOD and the British Army will deny with great alacrity. Discussion of this list – mythical or otherwise – will not please the mandarins of the Ministry of Defence and discussion will, therefore, be strangled voluntarily.

As Christmas approached, a Sinn Féin apologist announced that the Provisionals would not be holding a ceasefire – as was often the practice – and that the 'war' would continue throughout the festivities. The spokesman stated that 180 PIRA had been killed and over 1,000 arrested. On the 17th, the UK *Daily Telegraph* – a much-respected, right-wing broadsheet – announced that the police had uncovered a plan by PIRA's England Team to hijack a helicopter and fly over a London jail and help a convicted terrorist to escape. The plan was to have been put into operation just before Christmas – when staffing levels would have been reduced – and involved seven male and one female PIRA members of the London cell. The plan never went ahead.

In the early afternoon of the same day the IRA shot and killed another PO – the 18th to be murdered during the Troubles and the 10th this year alone – close to where George Foster had been killed on 14 September (see Chapter 57). William Wilson (58) had set off to have lunch at the RAOB Club in Century Street – close to where George Foster's car had been ambushed. The location is a little over 330 yards from Crumlin Road Jail and involved

Belfast, 1979. (©Mark 'C')

a brisk walk of only a couple of minutes. PO Wilson, father of two, had been in the habit of walking there and back most lunchtimes – and PIRA dickers were aware of this. As he arrived at the club and began walking up the steps to the entrance, a car pulled alongside him and a gunman leaned out of the window and shot Mr Wilson several times and he slumped to the ground – mortally wounded. The car raced off into Crumlin Road and disappeared into the lunchtime traffic. The PO died at the scene. He had been in the service since 1949 and held a senior position at the jail. He had turned down early retirement three years earlier. The murder weapon had been used in six previous murders of soldiers and policemen.

On the same day – on the English mainland – a letter-bomb containing a deadly amount of explosives was delivered to the home of Sir William Mather, Chairman of the Institute of Directors. He was at his Cheshire home when the letter arrived. As he started to open it he noticed wires and immediately took the device into his front garden and called the police. ATO were called in order to defuse what was a viable device. This was the third PIRA booby-trap to explode in a 24-hour period – one of which was in a Royal Mail sorting office at Gerrard's Cross in Bucks. All of the devices had been posted by PIRA operatives in mainland Europe. On the following day PIRA gunmen attempted to murder an off-duty PO in Belfast, but were foiled as the officer was armed with his PPW and they ran off.

During the period 21-29 December three UDR soldiers died in unknown circumstances or as a result of accidents – and the author has only basic information. On the 21st, Staff Sergeant Thomas James McCulloch (56) died; no further details are available. On the 27th, in what was thought to be an RTA, Private George Brown (25) died; he was from Irvinestown, Co Fermanagh and is buried at Dedrryvullan North Cemetery. Finally, on the 29th, Private Robert James Davison (44) also died in unknown circumstances. The author would welcome further details in order to fully honour these men.

BORDER FOLLOW-UP
Corporal Ian Missenden, Duke of Edinburgh's Royal Regiment

We left on the chopper that brought the QRF and were flown directly to Gough Barracks, Armagh. The boss met us there and we were debriefed by the SB. They, like us, were chuffed with the result. One of robbers had already done time for terrorist offences; the guy on the bike was an unknown – or, at least, he was until we grabbed him! The robbery had been planned to take place as soon as the post office had opened, and for some reason (which we didn't need to know) had been put on hold at the last minute – and then, for reasons unknown, it was back on. The two handguns that were to be used in the job – and were en route when the robbery was put on hold – were dumped in a ditch opposite a derelict building about 500 metres from the border. They were going to be picked up later that evening and we were tasked to recover them. It was only when they pointed the derelict out on a map I realised why we had to wait until after dark to pick them up. It was 500 metres south of the border! If we were caught in the south by the Gardaí or Irish Army, we had to bluff it out as a map-reading error.

The team loaded into the back of a covert van – the boss and a driver in the front – and off we went. It was still light when we left Bessbrook, but would be dark by the time we reached the drop-off. We had to beat the opposition to the weapons – and I hoped they'd still be there! We were dropped off not far from the border, and after a radio check we made our way across country – and within minutes we were in the south. It took us about 20 minutes to reach the FRV. The derelict stood about 100 metres away on the far side of the road.

We watched over the area for a while to make sure we were on our own. I went forward with Mick Loveridge and stopped at the blackthorn hedge that separated us from the road. There had been no vehicles on the road since we'd been in the area. It took us several minutes to find a place to crawl through the hedge. I left Mick and crawled through and into a ditch the other side. The derelict covered about 15 metres, so anywhere in that space could be called opposite! I worked slowly along the ditch. I'd reached the far end of the derelict and had decided to go as far as a telegraph pole a further 10 metres up the road. I was almost there when Mick hissed: "Headlights coming from the south." I stopped and tried to bury myself in the ditch. I soon heard the car getting closer. I could hear it slowing, and then it stopped level with me. The passenger door opened and a guy got out. I was sure he'd see me. I could have touched him if I wanted! He knew exactly where to go: the base of the telegraph pole. I saw the plastic bag he collected and heard the metallic clank of the weapons inside. Lucky for me, he wanted to waste no time; pick up the weapons and get the hell out of there. I sighed with relief when the vehicle sped off. I made a mental note of the vehicle registration as the white Mini raced north. Mick was already calling the boss on the radio by the time I'd scurried back to the hole in the hedge. 'Murphy's Law' – no comms! We returned to the FRV; then, as a team, we made our way north.

The boss had been driving a circuit, as we hadn't planned to be on the ground long. We finally got the boss on the radio as we crossed into the north. He passed the vehicle details to our ops room and we were picked up within minutes. The SB called it a result – although it didn't feel like one to me. I'd made the right decision by not interfering with the guys in the Mini and the weapons. The SB was happy with the vehicle details and the description of the two guys in it.

On the 23rd, the Provisionals murdered another policeman as he crossed over the border – whilst off-duty – from Co Tyrone to Co Monaghan in the Republic. Stanley Hazelton (48) was a part-time policeman who also ran a garage/repair service in Dungannon. The RUCR man lived at Moy and he crossed over the border two days before Christmas in order to buy a turkey from a farm in Co Monaghan. As he approached Glasslough on the Irish side, several masked gunmen leapt out from behind a hedge and opened fire on Constable Hazelton and fired over 20 shots into his car. He died at the scene. Although a Protestant, he was described by a Catholic priest as 'a good neighbour'. As he made the trip only rarely, it is unlikely that he had been dicked or that the Provisionals had set a one-a-year ambush. It seems more likely that someone with intimate knowledge of the planned trip to the Co Monaghan farm had tipped off the IRA – possibly the day before.

On Christmas Eve, the PM – Margaret Thatcher – paid a surprise visit to the Province in order to visit army units. She expressed her gratitude for the men's sacrifices and regrets at them not being able to spend Christmas with their loved ones. The trip was conducted in strict and heavy security and was an operation which was planned and executed in top-secret fashion.

In what may be seen as an unusual step in a book which is written from the perspective of the British soldier, I invited and have included the words of a Nationalist. The lady concerned is a well-respected journalist who works for the *Irish News* – and, might I add, an excellent writer. I have only known her for a little over a year and she recently told me a story from her past, which included a childhood spent during the Troubles. I cannot agree with every word she writes, but many soldiers and their loved ones will be moved by her sentiments. As an author and a former soldier, I am honoured that she agreed to write a piece for this book.

A CHILD IN THE TROUBLES
Allison Morris, *Irish News*

I grew up in the Andersonstown Estate facing the famous Casement Park Gaelic Athletic Ground, which is named after Roger Casement – a former British consul who was stripped of a knighthood and executed for treason against Britain in 1916. As a child, negotiating my way through armed soldiers crouched at the end of our garden path en route to school in the morning was normal. We didn't talk about it or think about it or even take the people in uniform under our notice. Unless they spoke directly to us, we ignored them – pretended they weren't there.

Living in those conditions is far removed from how my own children have grown up with Northern Ireland – now in relative peacetime.

With eight children, Christmas in our house was always a big event. Money was scarce, but festive spirit was in abundance. My mother was an obsessive cleaner. She worked as a cleaner in a local school all her life and said she did it so no daughter of hers would mop floors for a living. One Christmas Eve my mum opened the front door to clean the doorstep. I don't know what it was about cleaning doorsteps in the 1970s. In all my adult life I can't ever recall doing such a thing, but cleaning the front step was a weekly occurrence back then. When she opened the door, a soldier – a man in his early 20s – was sitting on our doorstep looking at pictures of his family.

In true Belfast fashion my mum said nothing and closed the front door. A few minutes later she opened the door again to find the 'Brit' gone, but his photographs and a brown envelope stuffed with cash had been left where he once sat. She lifted his belongings and ran up the street in her slippers after the foot patrol. When she finally stopped him and gave him back his personal possessions, she said he looked as though he was about to burst into tears and thanked her.

This story has always stuck in my head for a number of reasons. My mother had eight children and my father rarely managed to find work. Money was scarce on the ground, but the thought of keeping money that wasn't hers would have been an alien concept. My family had suffered greatly at the hands of the British; family members shot and jailed. But my mother just saw a young man far away from his family on Christmas Eve looking at pictures of happier times – wishing he was back home in the warmth of his family.

The humanity in what went on – mainly unspoken – between my mum and that unnamed soldier showed that even in those dark days of the 1970s there was decency and hope that we would eventually have peace despite the horrendous circumstances we all found ourselves in.

Finally, on the 29th, the Secretary of State for Northern Ireland – Humphrey Atkins – claimed that terrorism had decreased from the early 1970s. But he also warned against complacency as the Troubles were about to enter its third decade (it would be well into its fourth decade before it 'ended'). He stated that he hoped new initiatives would result from planned cross-party talks. As David Barzilay commented: "He was to be mistaken."

The following piece puts one in mind of that superb film *Butch Cassidy and the Sundance Kid* (Director George Roy Hill, 1969) in the scene where Paul Newman has to fight a new gang leader to the death. He promises that there will be no interference from Robert Redford's character, but then whispers to him words to the effect of: "If it looks like I'm losing, shoot him!"

EAST TYRONE 1979
Ken Pettengale, 2nd Battalion, Royal Green Jackets
I had been made up to lance-corporal, so this was my first tour as an NCO and I felt quite proud to be commanding blokes in a difficult location. I had passed out best recruit on my NCO's cadre the previous year so I was more than confident

that I would do a good job. As members of 11 Platoon, 'C' Company we were detached from the rest of the company and were based in Coalisland RUC Station. It was hard for us as we had to carry out all of the usual duties required: stagging on; manning the ops room; mobile patrols; foot patrols; fatigues; everything – and all with just a rifle platoon!

As you can imagine this wore us down pretty quickly, but I felt we had been put there for a reason. We were good and the OC felt comfortable with us being there. When we did town patrols there was always a group of boyos loitering around outside of the local hotspot, McGlinchey's Café. You know the sort: gobby individuals who were itching to become fully paid-up members of PIRA. Every time we patrolled near or past them we always got shitloads of abuse. There was one bloke who was always to the fore. We reckoned he was their un-elected leader; the one they looked up to and all stood behind – waiting for his lead.

One night I had had a bit too much of their spitting and abuse. I told them in no uncertain terms that if they ever wanted to look me up in London I would be more than happy to give them a real man-to-man kicking – one at a time or all-together. I wasn't bothered and I wasn't afraid of fuckheads like them! Their boss man said he was ok with that, and he felt the same. He said if we didn't have guns he would have a try there and then. At that point I flipped. I said that was fine and we should go at it there and then. He said he didn't think so as if he beat me, we would either shoot him or arrest him. I told him that wasn't the way I played. I turned to the guys in the brick and said that under no circumstances were they to join in, batter the twats or anything else. They weren't happy, but said they agreed not to butt in.

I took off my beret, handed over my belt order and rifle and we immediately set to. No pre-amble, no handshake, no rules. I went into that fight like my life depended on it. Even today, going over it in my mind, I can feel the sheer and utter animal that I was that night. I wanted to kill him with my bare hands – and I feel sure he felt the same. I wanted a victory for us! A little while in, and I realised that I should have taken off my flak jacket! It was one of those that had the thick collar and plastic shoulder-pads with a lip on to stop your rifle sliding off – not designed for bare-knuckle fighting!

Anyway I was starting to lose and I didn't know what was happening, but the fight was broken up. Gren Wilson and Steve Mears always carried batons with them shoved in their flak jackets – and I know they pulled them to stop the other boyos joining in! I then realised that, at that very moment, the platoon commander – Lieutenant Rigby – came into the square. Not good; it wasn't as if I could hide what had happened – and judging by my later bruising, wouldn't be able to for a few days!

I know for a fact though that we didn't get any crap from the locals after that. I don't know whether it was a grudging respect or the fact that they knew we weren't going to be governed by the 'rules' anymore. Either way, things got a little bit quieter in town. I lost the prize for the fight and I lost £500 in fines; lucky to have kept my stripe, I reckon!

The final death of the month – indeed of the year of 1979 and the decade – was Sean Cairns (19). He was a Catholic living only 400 yards from a Loyalist area and was murdered by Loyalist paramilitaries. He lived in Tralee Street in the Clonards area. The author remembers the street and the area, but the street is no longer there as Kashmir Road and the surrounding area have been redeveloped. Mr Cairns lived in the imposing shadow of Clonard Monastery, but only a stone's throw from the 'Peace Line' at Cupar Way and a short journey from the Shankill Road. It was nearing midnight and the Cairns family prepared to celebrate the New Year. As they were watching television they heard a noise from the front of the house and as they entered the hallway to investigate, they found a man there whom they thought was a family friend. However, as he entered their lounge, he pulled out a handgun and began firing at both Mr Cairns senior and his son, Sean. The younger man was hit in the head and died instantly and his father was hit in the temple and face and collapsed – seriously wounded. The man walked calmly out of the house. The last killing of the decade had just occurred. The older Cairns recovered in hospital, but was unfit to face an inquest for over 12 months.

The following piece from a soldier – who was based in the very heart of what the former Secretary of State for Northern Ireland (Merlyn Rees, MP) termed 'bandit country' – is outside of the parameter dates of this book. It is, however, deemed worthy of inclusion as it would be most churlish to omit it – and its omission would be to the detraction of the reader's interest. On a side note, the author had the pleasure of meeting Mr Rees at a constituency surgery in Beeston, Leeds in 1974. The MP was flanked by two burly Special Branch officers – each with an ominous bulge under their armpits. The author congratulated Mr Rees on his appointment and he replied laconically: "Well, thank you; I certainly have a difficult task." He could not have been more prophetic.

Marcus Townley, Welsh Guards

On one particular day our ration truck was doing a re-supply run down in the border area around Newry, Co Down. As the vehicle – a Bedford – drove past what turned out to be a hijacked van, the explosives inside were detonated. There was a massive explosion, but no-one was injured – although one of the NCOs in charge began spraying the hedgerow with automatic fire. The IRA firing team were long gone by this time. Somewhat incredibly, a guardsman in an earlier patrol had passed the van and ran his finger across the dirty exterior. He was well away when it exploded, but on returning he must have been just a little white-faced!

Another lucky escape involved one of the lads who was based at Borrucki Sangar at Crossmaglen. Out on a foot patrol, he noticed a water bottle just lying there – and the idiot's mind must have just gone blank and he reached out for it! Luckily for him an NCO saw it and made him step back. It was a booby-trap and it went off – causing minimal damage. The sound of the explosion was heard some distance away, as I was part of a team setting up a VCP. At the time I remember thinking that some poor bastard had copped it!

There are two events which remain with me today and still cause a shiver down my spine. Several times whilst patrolling around the town – and generally as 'tail-end Charlie' – I would be surrounded by kids who would try and open my ammo pouches or grab at equipment. I thought nothing of it until one day, when

I was being debriefed, I happened to mention to the INT boys that the kids always pounced whilst I was crossing a gap. Their ears pricked up because at that time PIRA was using 'through shoots' in the gaps between houses – and they were clearly hoping that myself or another soldier would stand there correcting and readjusting equipment after the kids had ran off. That set up a perfect target with either me or another soldier silhouetted perfectly in the gap! Even today when I see a group of kids, I go into a bit of a panic.

The other incident took place on New Year's Eve (on the last day of 1979). I was on QRF, but we were still allowed our customary two cans of beer and we celebrated with handshakes all-round. Perhaps 1980 would be the year when it all ended and we all went home? I was due on stag at 0100 so I went to grab an hour's kip. I was wakened by the sounds of the helicopters starting up and I knew that the QRF was going to be crashed out. I got my kit and went outside with rumours flying around about a shooting. But, as soon as it started, it stopped and we were stood down. It turned out that there had been a 'blue on blue' involving two paras who had accidentally fired at each other. Since that night I have never celebrated another New Year's Eve. As far as I am concerned, it is merely another day.

The two soldiers were Lieutenant Simon Bates (23), from Dorset, and Private Gerald Hardy (18), from Southampton, who had turned 18 only two days previously. Both soldiers were from the Parachute Regiment and were killed at Forkhill, Co Armagh by other paratroopers as they returned from a patrol. The incident took place in the very early minutes of 1 January 1980 and in the dark, the two men were mistaken for IRA gunmen and both tragically died at the scene.

Did I hate my time in Ireland? The answer is no; I enjoyed my time over there. Yes, it has left some mental scars, but reading your books has given me the chance to try and slay some of my demons and for that I thank you.

December had ended – and so had 1979. Sixteen people had died – of whom 11 were soldiers or former soldiers. One policeman had died – as had two POs. Two civilians had died – both Catholics and both were overtly sectarian in nature. The IRA was responsible for nine deaths; Loyalists for two.

1979 was over and 169* people had died in the Troubles:

British Army	96**
RUC	16
Prison Officers	10
Civilians	37*
Protestants	17
Catholics	20
Republican	9
Loyalists	1

* 14 of these were overtly sectarian
** two of whom were RAF personnel

In the five years under review in both volumes of the book the figures were:

British Army	292**
RUC	80
Prison Officers	18
Civilians	512*
Republican	76
Loyalists	47

*365 of these were overtly sectarian; 1,025 people had died as a consequence of the Troubles in a mere 60 months

** two of whom were RAF personnel

Postscript

Many of us have been back, this author included, but I have deliberately chosen just two reports of two men's return to Ulster.

Mike Donohue, King's Regiment

I went back about five years ago and never had any problems that weren't brought about by my own bravado – some might call it stupidity. I drove down the Falls and parked up outside the Andytown RUC Station; drove through the Rodney, the 'Murph and out to Black Mountain. Back down Springfield Road and had a few pints on the Shankill Road to finish. Next day, I drove over to Ballykelly to pay my respects at the 'Droppin' Well'. Then I drove on to Londonderry, over the new bridge into the Creggan and Bogside then back over the river for a few pints in Molly's Bar, Spencer Road. A day's driving took me to Letterkenny VCP, Buncrana, Strabane and Clady.

The day after I drove to Forkhill and made the decision to stop at the Spar garage/supermarket on the Forkhill Road, where I filled up with fuel and went into the shop to pay. I tried to buy a hot pie – only to be told the microwave wasn't working. I told him that I would have it cold, to be told: "We're closed; pay for your fuel and fuck off." I did a smart about-turn and fucked off rather smartly! I then drove over the border and went to Drogheda to a well-known players' bar and had a few pints – and a very deep conversation – with a terrorist who lost both his hands to an own goal! Before you ask, he drank his through a straw!

The purpose of my mission during that two weeks was to lay to rest the demons. I also laid a flower at all the unmarked locations where members of the regiment gave their lives to Op Banner. I came away with a better understanding of my feelings and I am much more comfortable with myself and my anger. I am not saying it's for everyone, but it worked for me. Would I do it again? Probably, but this time I'll not run low on fuel in Forkhill!

Marcus Townley, Welsh Guards

It's now almost 34 years since I was in Northern Ireland – and has it affected my life? In some ways yes, I suppose it has. I am always aware of my surroundings. I will always look around when walking the street. Even when it's pissing down with rain, I still refuse to wear the hood of my jacket (work-issued). A workmate once laughed when I said that I didn't wear hoods. I walked away and let him assume his own opinions. When I am out walking and if I hear footsteps behind me I often spin round – often startling the poor person. I once picked my son up from the school and his teacher asked to see me. Dreading the worst, I approached his teacher. She asked, as I was a postman, would I be so kind to talk to her class about being a postman? I refused – nonplussed. She asked why, so I told her about young children stopping me by gaps in houses in Northern Ireland (through shoots). She was almost shocked when I told the story. I still fly into a panic at the sight of young children in the street.

I have never celebrated New Year's Eve – now for 34 years – after two members of 2 Para were killed ('blue on blue') at two minutes past midnight. 1980 was two minutes old. I recently had a beer with two ex-para lads who were in the same company as them at Forkhill. I told them my tale and they were amazed, as they were on the follow-up. So come midnight on New Year's Eve I steal away, shed a tear and a silent toast to fallen warriors.

I was brought up a Roman Catholic. Since my tour I have no time for religion whatsoever. Whenever I am approached by religious groups, at first I am polite and say I am not interested. Woe betides them if they persist; then they get both barrels and the air gets blue. My wife goes apeshit when she hears me. To her my Northern Ireland tour is represented by my campaign medal(s), which I wear every Remembrance Day, and regimental reunions – not the bigotry every Op Banner vet has witnessed. Had I undertaken further tours, I may well have become agnostic. Often I will meet up with ex-servicemen for a beer or two. We call ourselves 'The Brotherhood' and chat about this and that. We will seldom recall our banner tour, but more often than not we take the piss out of each other. Civvies can't contemplate what we are saying, but fuck them. They wouldn't take the 'King's Shilling', which is their tough luck.

Afterthought … Once, during our tour, someone put the question: when you step off (leave the army), what occupation would I like to do. I replied that I would like to do a job which doesn't mean me getting up at 'stupid o clock' and walking the streets. I have now been a postman for 24 years now – albeit not walking backwards! My zap number in Northern Ireland was 3073. I joined Royal Mail, was issued with uniform and badge – and my badge number was 3073!

Watching Tony Blair; giving his excuse for going to war; against terror; and the cause of terror … The Good Friday Agreement stinks of hypocrisy somehow. Blair is another wanker who knows fucks all.

Poetry of the Troubles

I did my duty
I did my best
I hid behind my bulletproof vest
I walked the streets with gun in hand
I held the peace in a foreign land
People didn't want me there
They would often stand and stare
But my duty was to keep the peace
I tried to save a life, at least
I saw men die
I saw men suffer
Life couldn't get too much tougher
Bombs and bullets played their tune
And forced me deep into the gloom
My duty there was never done
I worked until the passing sun
Then one day the years have passed
My memories would last and last
No corner of my mind is safe
I am haunted by that foreign place
I try to run
I try to hide
My demons always by my side
Did I serve my country true
Would I really die for you

Did I do my very best
Did I need my bomb-proof vest
Did I see my colleagues die
Or is it just a wicked lie
All I know is this you see
I can never be set free
The Troubles – they have left their mark
They keep me trembling in the dark
So enjoy your freedom that I won
For this soldier's work is done

Steve Carr

Appendix II

Northern Ireland Roll of Honour 1969–98

1,336 Military Names

NB: Where the soldier was a member of the TA, they are included in the roll for their parent regiment with the TA initials annotated next to them (where known).

RTA: Road Traffic accident
DoW: Died of Wounds

9/12 Lancers

LT JOHN GARNER-RICHARDS	4/04/75:	RTA in Co Armagh in suspicious circumstances
TPR SEAN PRENDERGAST	5/04/77:	IRA landmine in Belleek, Co Fermanagh
SGT ROBERT MAUGHAN	8/05/79:	Shot on undercover duties by IRA, Lisnaskea
SGT PAUL ORAM, MM	21/02/84:	Shot dead on undercover duties by IRA, Co Antrim

13/18 Hussars

TPR ROBERT BARRACLOUGH	28/09/75:	RTA
TPR PAUL SHEPHERDSON	16/07/78:	RTA
TPR PHILIP SMITH	27/07/78:	RTA

14/20 King's Hussars and 15/19 King's Royal Hussars

SGT JOHN PLATT	3/02/71:	Killed in RTA following IRA ambush at Aldergrove
CPL IAN ARMSTRONG	29/08/71:	Ambushed at Crossmaglen by IRA
2ND LT ROBERT WILLIAMS-WYNN	13/07/72:	Shot by IRA sniper in West Belfast
TPR JOHN TYSON	28/02/74:	RTA
CPL MICHAEL COTTON	20/03/74:	Killed in friendly fire Co Armagh
CPL MICHAEL HERBERT	20/03/74:	Killed in same incident
TPR GARY LINES	28/05/79:	RTA

15/19 Hussars

TPR DAVID JOHNSON	18/10/71:	Accidental shooting
TPR JOHN MAJOR	29/11/74:	Death by violent or unnatural causes
SGT WILLIAM ROBSON	7/02/75:	DoW after being shot by IRA at Mullan, Fermanagh

17/ 21st Lancers

TPR JAMES DOYLE	24/11/70:	Cause of death unknown; died in Omagh
TPR ROBERT GADIE	17/02/71:	RTA at Ballygawley

CPL TERENCE WILLIAMS	5/05/73:	Booby-trap bomb, Crossmaglen
TPR JOHN GIBBONS	5/05/73:	Killed in same incident
TPR KENEALY	14/09/73:	Killed in helicopter accident, Gosford Castle

16/5th Lancers

| CPL DAVID POWELL | 28/10/71: | Bomb attack, Kinawley, Co Fermanagh |
| 2/LT ANDREW SOMERVILLE | 27/03/73: | IRA landmine, near Omagh |

5 Regiment Army Air Corps

SGT I C REID	24/06/72:	IRA landmine, Glenshane Pass, Co Antrim
L/CPL D MOON	24/06/72:	Killed in same incident
C/SGT ARTHUR PLACE	18/05/73:	Booby-trap bomb, Knock-na-Moe Hotel, Omagh
C.O.FH BR COX	18/05/73:	Killed in the same incident
SGT DB READ	18/05/73:	Killed in the same incident
WO D C ROWAT	12/04/74:	Killed in helicopter crash, Co Armagh
MAJ J D HICKS	18/12/75:	Aircraft accident
WO B A JACKSON	7/01/76:	Aircraft accident
CAPT MJ KETT	10/04/78:	Killed in helicopter accident
CAPT A J STIRLING	2/12/78:	Killed in helicopter accident
CPL RAYMOND JACKSON	5/07/80:	RTA
CPL BERNARD McKENNA	6/04/82:	Died of natural causes on duty
L/CPL SIMON J ROBERTS	28/11/83:	RTA
L/CPL TONY ORANGE	20/10/87:	RTA
S/SGT JEREMY CROFT	14/08/89:	Violent or unnatural causes

5th Royal Inniskilling Dragoon Guards

| SGT FREDERICK WILLIAM DRAKE | 3/06/73: | Died of wounds (bomb), Knock-na-Moe Hotel Omagh |

Adjutant General's Corps

| CPL GLEN A. SLAINE | 3/11/95: | RTA |
| L/CPL PAUL MELLING | 3/09/97: | Died whilst on duty |

Air Cadet Force

CDT LEONARD CROSS	11/11/74:	Murdered by the IRA near Creggan Estate, Londonderry
CPL EDWARD WILSON	26/01/75:	IRA booby-trap, Cavehill Road, Belfast
MAJ WILLIAM MCALPINE	05/09/78:	Shot by IRA in Newry, Co Down

Argyll and Sutherland Highlanders

L/CPL DUNCAN MCPHEE	10/09/72:	IRA landmine, Dungannon
PTE DOUGLAS RICHMOND	10/09/72:	Killed in same incident
L/CPL WILLIAM MCINTYRE	11/09/72:	DOW from same incident
2nd LT STEWART GARDINER	22/09/72:	Shot by IRA sniper, Drumuckavall, Armagh
PTE DAVID HARPER	12/11/72:	Killed by passing train whilst on patrol
CAPT WILLIAM WATSON	20/11/72:	IRA booby-trap, Cullyhanna

C/SGT JAMES STRUTHERS	20/11/72:	Killed in the same incident
PTE JOHN McGARRY	28/11/72:	Friendly fire
PTE DOUGLAS MCKELVIE	20/08/79:	RTA
CPL OWEN MCQUADE	11/11/80:	Shot outside Altnagelvin Hospital, Londonderry
CPL STEWART MARSHALL	20/08/98:	RTA
PTE WILLIAM BROWN	20/08/98:	RTA
PTE STEVEN CRAW	20/08/98:	RTA

Army Catering Corps

PTE LEONARD THOMPSON	31/12/71:	RTA
PTE RODGER KEALEY	18/06/72:	Killed in Londonderry; death by violent or unnatural causes
SGT PETER GIRVAN	12/02/77:	RTA
L/CPL BARRY HYLTON	17/11/77:	Cause of death unknown
PTE GEOFFREY DAVIS	18/07/79:	Cause of death unknown
PTE TERENCE M. ADAM	6/12/82:	INLA bomb attack, Droppin' Well pub, Ballykelly
PTE PAUL JOSEPH DELANEY	6/12/82:	Killed in same incident
PTE JOHN MAYER	19/03/83:	RTA
PTE RICHARD R. BIDDLE	9/04/83:	IRA booby-trapped car, Omagh

Army Cadet Force

CAPT PAUL ROGERS	19/04/79:	Shot by IRA sniper near the Falls Road, Belfast

Army Intelligence Corps

CPL PAUL HARMAN ***	14/12/77:	Killed on covert op by IRA, Monagh Road, Belfast
CPL JOHN ROESER	31/08/78:	RTA
CPL MICHAEL BLOOR	31/08/78:	Killed in same RTA
CPL MARCUS CHARLES-WILLIAMS	8/11/86:	Cause of death unknown
L/CPL BARRY JACKSON	16/02/88:	Cause of death unknown

Army Physical Training Corps

WO2 DAVID BELLAMY	28/10/79:	IRA ambush, Springfield Road, Belfast

Army Staff

COL Charles Eaton	30/06/76:	Thought to have been shot whilst off-duty by the IRA

Black Watch

PTE DAVID STEIN	4/03/71:	Accidental death
L/CPL EDWIN CHARNLEY	18/11/71:	Shot by sniper in East Belfast
PTE MARK D. CARNIE	19/07/78:	IRA bomb, Dungannon
PTE GEORGE IRELAND	21/06/95:	Cause of death unknown

Blues & Royals

TPR EDWARD MAGGS	25/02/79:	Death by violent or unnatural causes
STAFF CPL JOHN TUCKER	25/02/79:	Death by violent or unnatural causes
TPR ANTHONY DYKES	5/04/79:	Shot by IRA snipers, Andersonstown RUC Station

TPR ANTHONY THORNETT	5/04/79:	Killed in same incident
LT DENIS DALY	20/07/82:	Killed in Hyde Park bomb outrage
TPR SIMON TIPPER	20/07/82:	Killed in same incident
L/CPL JEFFERY YOUNG	20/07/82:	Killed in same incident
SQMC R BRIGHT	23/07/82:	DoW from same incident

Cheshire Regiment

CPL DAVID SMITH	4/07/74:	DoW after being shot, Ballymurphy Estate, Belfast
PTE NEIL WILLIAMS	6/12/82:	IRA bomb, Droppin' Well pub, Ballykelly
PTE ANTHONY WILLIAMSON	6/12/82:	Killed in same incident
L/CPL DAVID WILSON-STITT	6/12/82:	Killed in same incident
L/CPL STEVEN BAGSHAW	6/12/82:	Killed in same incident
L/CPL CLINTON COLLINS	6/12/82:	Killed in same incident
L/CPL PHILIP MCDONOUGH	6/12/82:	Killed in same incident
PTE DAVID MURREY	6/12/82:	Killed in same incident
PTE STEPHEN SMITH	6/12/82:	Killed in same incident

Coldstream Guards

SGT ANTHONY METCALF	27/08/72:	IRA sniper, Creggan Heights, Londonderry
GUARDSMAN ROBERT PEARSON	20/02/73:	Killed by IRA snipers, Lower Falls, Belfast
GUARDSMAN MICHAEL SHAW	20/02/73:	Killed in same incident
GUARDSMAN MICHAEL DOYLE	21/02/73:	Killed by sniper, Fort Whiterock, Belfast
GUARDSMAN ANTON BROWN	6/03/73:	Killed by sniper, Ballymurphy Estate, Belfast
CAPT ANTHONY POLLEN***	14/04/74:	Shot on undercover mission, Bogside, Londonderry
GUARDSMAN PAUL SIMMONDS	12/01/76:	Cause of death unknown
CPL JOHN SPENSLEY	25/12/81:	RTA
CORPORAL RICHARD DREWETT*	15/06/84:	Death by violent or unnatural causes
GUARDSMAN STEVEN SHAW	21/01/89:	Cause of death unknown
L/CPL SIMON WARE	17/08/91:	IRA landmine explosion, Cullyhanna, Armagh

Devon & Dorset Regiment

PTE CHARLES STENTIFORD	21/01/72:	IRA landmine, Keady, Co Armagh
PTE DAVID CHAMP	10/02/72:	IRA landmine, Cullyhanna, Co Armagh
SGT IAN HARRIS	10/02/72:	Killed in same incident
CPL STEVEN WINDSOR	6/11/74:	Killed by sniper, Crossmaglen
CPL GERALD JEFFERY	7/04/83:	DoW, IRA bomb, Falls Road, Belfast
L/CPL STEPHEN TAVERNER	5/11/83:	DoW, IRA bomb, Crossmaglen

Duke of Edinburgh's Royal Regiment

CPL JOSEPH LEAHY	8/03/73:	DoW, booby-trap, Forkhill, Co Armagh
S/SGT BARRINGTON FOSTER	23/03/73:	Murdered off-duty by the IRA
CAPT NIGEL SUTTON	14/08/73:	Died in vehicle accident, Ballykinler
PTE MICHAEL SWANICK	28/10/74:	IRA van bomb attack, Ballykinler
PTE BRIAN ALLEN	6/11/74:	Killed by sniper, Crossmaglen
PTE JOHN RANDALL	26/06/93:	Killed by sniper, Newtownhamilton, Co Armagh
L/CPL KEVIN PULLIN	17/07/93:	Killed by sniper, Crossmaglen

Duke of Wellington's Regiment

PTE GEORGE LEE	6/06/72:	IRA sniper, Ballymurphy Estate, Belfast
CPL TERRENCE GRAHAM	16/07/72:	Landmine attack, Crossmaglen
PTE JAMES LEE	16/07/72:	Killed in same incident
PTE BRIAN ORAM	7/04/73:	RTA
CPL DAVID TIMSON	7/04/73:	Killed in same incident
PTE JOSEPH MCGREGOR	24/05/73:	RTA
WOII PETER LINDSAY	28/08/73:	Unknown
2ND LT HOWARD FAWLEY	25/01/74:	Landmine attack, Ballyronan, Co Londonderry
CPL MICHAEL RYAN	17/03/74:	IRA sniper at Brandywell, Londonderry
PTE LOUIS CARROLL	7/04/74:	Cause of death unknown
CPL ERROL PRYCE	26/01/80:	IRA sniper, Ballymurphy Estate, Belfast
PTE JOHN CONNOR	24/02/88:	Cause of death unknown
PTE JAMES RIGG	25/11/88:	RTA
PTE JASON COST	25/05/95:	Cause of death unknown

General Staff

LT GEN VF ERKSINE-CRUM	18/03/71:	Died on duty

Gloucestershire Regiment

PTE ANTHONY ASPINWALL	17/12/71:	DoW after gun battle in Lower Falls area, Belfast
PTE KEITH BRYAN	5/01/72:	IRA sniper, Lower Falls area, Belfast
CPL IAN BRAMLEY	2/02/72:	IRA sniper, Hastings Street RUC Station, Belfast
PTE GEOFFREY BREAKWELL	17/07/73:	IRA booby-trap, Divis Street Flats, Belfast
PTE CHRISTOPHER BRADY	17/07/73:	Killed in same incident
L/CPL ANTHONY BENNETT	4/06/78:	Cause of death unknown
PTE D.J. McCAHILL	17/08/78:	Died during the tour - not as a result of terrorist actions
L/CPL A P. BENNETT	4/06/80:	Killed in vehicle accident, Limavady

Gordon Highlanders

WO2 ARTHUR MCMILLAN	18/06/72:	Booby-trapped house in Lurgan, Co Down
SGT IAN MARK MUTCH	18/06/72:	Killed in same incident
L/CPL COLIN LESLIE	18/06/72:	Killed in same incident
L/CPL A.C. HARPER	8/08/72:	RTA
PTE MICHAEL GEORGE MARR	29/03/73:	Shot by sniper, Andersonstown, Belfast
CAPT RICHARD LAMB	17/05/77:	RTA
CPL ALEXANDER CRUICKSHANK	26/06/77:	Accidental drowning
L/CPL JACK MARSHALL	28/08/77:	Shot in gun battle, Ardoyne, Belfast

Green Howards

PTE MALCOLM HATTON	9/08/71:	Shot by sniper, Brompton Park, Ardoyne
PTE JOHN ROBINSON	14/08/71:	Shot by sniper in Ardoyne, Belfast
PTE GEORGE CROZIER	23/08/71:	Shot by sniper, Flax Street Mill, Ardoyne
L/CPL PETER HERRINGTON	17/09/71:	Shot by sniper, Brompton Park, Ardoyne
PTE PETER SHARP	1/10/71:	Shot on Kerrara Street, Ardoyne

PTE RAYMOND HALL	5/03/73:	DoW, sniper attack, Belfast
PTE FREDERICK DICKS	5/06/74:	IRA sniper, Dungannon
MAJ PETER WILLIS	17/07/75:	IRA bomb, Ford's Cross, Armagh
CPL IAN METCALF	15/06/88:	IRA booby-trapped lorry, Lisburn

Grenadier Guards

CAPT ROBERT NAIRAC G.C.	14/05/77:	Murdered by IRA, undercover mission, Irish Republic
GUARDSMAN GRAHAM DUGGAN	21/12/78:	Killed in attack on army patrol, Crossmaglen
GUARDSMAN KEVIN JOHNSON	21/12/78:	Killed in same incident
GUARDSMAN GLEN LING	21/12/78:	Killed in same incident
GUARDSMAN PAUL WEAVER	23/12/78:	Death by violent or unnatural causes
CAPT HERBERT WESTMACOTT MC**	2/05/80:	Killed on SAS undercover mission in west Belfast
COL SGT JOHN WIGG	17/01/86:	Death by violent or unnatural causes
GUARDSMAN PAUL MACDONALD	5/03/86:	RTA on duty at Ballykelly
GUARDSMAN BRIAN HUGHES	11/03/86:	Killed in same RTA
L/CPL GARY KITELEY	28/12/86:	Death by violent or unnatural causes
GUARDSMAN DANIEL BLINCO	30/12/93:	IRA sniper in South Armagh

Intelligence Corps

| CAPT HENRIETTA STEEL-MORTIMER | 11/06/98: | RTA |

Irish Guards

| GUARDSMAN SAMUEL MURPHY | 14/11/77: | Murdered in front of his mother whilst on leave, Andersonstown, Belfast |

King's Own Royal Border Regiment

PTE GEORGE P RIDDING	10/05/72:	Died of natural causes after being taken ill
C/SGT WILLIAM BOARDLEY	1/02/73:	Shot in Strabane by IRA gunman
CPL JAMES BURNEY	20/12/78:	IRA sniper, Newington, Belfast
PTE OWEN PAVEY	11/03/80:	Accidental shooting, Crossmaglen
PTE JOHN B. BATEMAN	15/03/80:	IRA sniper, Crossmaglen
PTE SEAN G. WALKER	21/03/80:	DoW, car bomb, Crossmaglen
L/CPL ANTHONY DACRE	27/03/85:	Bomb attack, Divis Street Flats, Belfast
PTE DAVID HATFIELD	24/02/92:	Vehicle accident, Londonderry
PTE MARTIN THOMAS	17/01/95:	Vehicle accident, Belfast
PTE DARREN MILRAY	21/02/95:	Road accident

King's Own Scottish Borderers

S/SGT PETER SINTON	28/07/70:	Violent or unnatural causes
L/CPL PETER DEACONSIME	7/04/72:	IRA sniper, Ballymurphy Estate, Belfast
L/CPL BARRY GOLD	24/04/72:	DoW after gun battle at VCP in Belfast
C/SGT HENRY S. MIDDLEMASS	10/12/72:	IRA booby-trap, Turf Lodge, Belfast
PTE JOHN GILLIES	6/10/76:	Cause of death unknown
S/SGT H. SHINGLESTON,MM	25/11/76:	Accidentally shot
PTE PAUL B. SCOTT	10/10/79:	RTA
PTE JAMES HOUSTON	13/12/89:	Killed at VCP in gun and grenade attack, Fermanagh

L/CPL MICHAEL JOHN PATERSON.   13/12/89: Killed in same incident

King's Regiment

CPL ALAN BUCKLEY	13/05/72:	Shot on Turf Lodge, Belfast
PTE EUSTACE HANLEY	23/05/72:	IRA sniper, Ballymurphy Estate
PTE MARCEL DOGLAY	30/05/72:	IRA bomb, Springfield Road, Belfast
PTE JAMES JONES	18/07/72:	IRA sniper, New Barnsley, Belfast
PTE BRIAN THOMAS	24/07/72:	IRA sniper, New Barnsley, Belfast
PTE RENNIE LAYFIELD	18/08/72:	IRA sniper, Falls Road, Belfast
PTE ROY CHRISTOPHER	30/08/72:	DoW after bomb attack, Cupar St, Belfast
SGT DENNIS DOOLEY	15/03/75:	RTA outside of Londonderry; died in hospital
PTE DAVID OWEN	14/10/75:	Died of natural causes
PTE PETER KAVANAGH	14/11/75:	Death by violent or unnatural causes
PTE CHRISTOPHER SHANLEY	11/04/79:	Ambushed and shot, Ballymurphy Estate, Belfast
L/CPL STEPHEN RUMBLE	19/04/79:	DoW from same incident
L/CPL ANDREW WEBSTER	9/05/79:	Bomb attack, Turf Lodge, Belfast
PTE STEPHEN BEACHAM	24/10/90:	Killed by IRA 'proxy bomb', Coshquin, near Londonderry - five soldiers killed
L/CPL STEPHEN BURROWS	24/10/90:	Killed in same incident
PTE VINCENT SCOTT	24/10/90:	Killed in same incident
PTE DAVID SWEENEY	24/10/90:	Killed in same incident
PTE PAUL WORRALL	24/10/90:	Killed in same incident

Life Guards

CPL of HORSE LEONARD DURBER   21/02/73: DoW after riot in Belfast

Light Infantry:
1st Battalion

PTE RICHARD JONES	18/08/72:	Shot by sniper in West Belfast
PTE R ROWE	28/08/72:	Shot accidentally in Ardoyne, Belfast
PTE TA STOKER	19/09/72:	DoW after accidental shooting in Berwick Road, Ardoyne
PTE T RUDMAN	30/09/72:	Shot in Ardoyne, Belfast (brother killed in 1971 Northern Ireland)
PTE STEPHEN HALL	28/10/73:	Shot in Crossmaglen
PTE G M CURTIS	10/06/83:	IRA bomb, Ballymurphy Estate, Belfast
PTE NICHOLAS BLYTHE	12/11/87:	Killed in accident
PTE J J WILLBY	6/02/88:	Violent or unnatural causes
PTE B BISHOP	20/08/88:	Killed in Ballygawley coach bombing - one of eight soldiers killed
PTE P L BULLOCK	20/08/88:	Killed in same incident
PTE J BURFITT	20/08/88:	Killed in same incident
PTE R GREENER	20/08/88:	Killed in same incident
PTE A S LEWIS	20/08/88:	Killed in same incident
PTE M A NORWORTHY	20/08/88	Killed in same incident
PTE S J WILKINSON	20/08/88:	Killed in same incident

PTE J WINTER	20/08/88:	Killed in same incident
PTE GRAHAM SMITH	3/12/88:	Violent or unnatural causes
PTE A J RICHARDSON	12/03/97:	Killed in attempted ambush by IRA after ceasefire

2nd Battalion

PTE J R RUDMAN	14/10/71:	Shot in Coalisland area
SGT ARTHUR WHITELOCK	24/08/72:	IRA sniper in Londonderry
CPL T P TAYLOR	13/05/73:	Killed in bomb attack, Donegall Road
PTE J GASKELL	14/05/73:	DoW from same incident
PTE R B ROBERTS	1/07/73:	Shot by sniper in Ballymurphy Estate, Belfast
L/CPL TERENCE WILSON	1/07/78:	RTA
PTE KEVIN MCGOVERN	3/07/78:	RTA
PTE R STAFFORD	20/07/79:	Killed in car accident
PTE PAUL TURNER	28/08/92:	IRA sniper, Crossmaglen

3rd Battalion

PTE P K EASTAUGH	23/03/71:	Shot accidentally in the Ardoyne area of Belfast
LCPL A KENNINGTON	28/02/73:	IRA sniper, Ardoyne area of Belfast
LCPL C R MILLER	18/09/73:	Shot in West Belfast
PTE R D TURNBULL	29/06/77:	Ambushed and shot, West Belfast
PTE MICHAEL E HARRISON	29/06/77:	Killed in same incident
PTE LEWIS J HARRISON	9/08/77:	IRA sniper, New Barnsley, Belfast
CPL D P SALTHOUSE	7/12/82:	IRA bomb, Droppin' Well pub, Ballykelly

Light Infantry (Battalion unknown)

PTE GARY HARDY	16/08/78:	Cause of death unknown

North Irish Militia

RANGER SAMUEL M. GIBSON.	21/10/74:	Abducted and murdered off duty (TA)

Parachute Regiment

PTE PETER DOCHERTY	21/05/70:	Accidental death
PTE VICTOR CHAPMAN	24/06/70	Drowned
SGT M WILLETTS GC.	25/05/71:	Killed saving civilians in IRA bomb blast, Springfield Road, Belfast
PTE R A BARTON	14/07/71:	Shot protecting comrades, Andersonstown, Belfast
SGT GRAHAM COX	17/10/71:	Died of wounds after being shot by IRA in Oldpark area
FATHER GERRY WESTON, MBE	22/02/72:	Killed in IRA bomb outrage, Aldershot
PTE ANTHONY KELLY	18/03/72:	Killed in accident, Holywood, Co Down
PTE CHRISTOPHER STEPHENSON	24/06/72:	IRA landmine, Glenshane Pass, Londonderry
PTE FRANK T BELL	20/09/72:	DoW after being shot on Ballymurphy Estate, Belfast
CPL S N HARRISON	7/04/73:	IRA landmine, Tullyogallaghan
L/CPL T D BROWN	7/04/73:	Killed in same incident
L/CPL D A FORMAN	16/04/73:	Accidentally shot, Flax Street Mill, Ardoyne
WO2 W R VINES	5/05/73:	IRA landmine, Crossmaglen

A/SGT J WALLACE	24/05/73:	IRA booby-trap, Crossmaglen
PTE R BEDFORD	16/03/74:	Shot in IRA ambush, Crossmaglen
PTE P JAMES	16/03/74:	Killed in same incident
WO2 HERBERT COVEY	22/03/74:	Cause of death unknown
PTE WILLIAM SNOWDON	28/06/76:	IRA bomb, Crossmaglen
PTE J BORUCKI	8/08/76:	IRA booby-trap, Crossmaglen
L/CPL D A JONES	17/03/78:	Shot in gun battle, Glenshane Pass, Londonderry
PTE J FISHER	12/07/78:	IRA booby-trap, Crossmaglen
CPL R D ADCOCK	2/12/78:	Killed in helicopter accident
MAJ P J FURSMAN	27/08/79:	Killed in IRA double-bomb blast, Warrenpoint - one of 16 paras and two other soldiers killed
WO2 W BEARD	27/08/79:	Killed in same incident
SGT I A ROGERS	27/08/79:	Killed in same incident
CPL N J ANDREWS	27/08/79:	Killed in same incident
CPL J C GILES	27/08/79:	Killed in same incident
CPL L JONES	27/08/79:	Killed in same incident
L/CPL CG IRELAND	27/08/79:	Killed in same incident
PTE G I BARNES	27/08/79:	Killed in same incident
PTE D F BLAIR	27/08/79:	Killed in same incident
PTE R DUNN	27/08/79:	Killed in same incident
PTE R N ENGLAND	27/08/79:	Killed in same incident
PTE R D U JONES	27/08/79:	Killed in same incident
PTE T R VANCE	27/08/79:	Killed in same incident
PTE J A VAUGHAN-JONES	27/08/79:	Killed in same incident
PTE A G WOOD	27/08/79:	Killed in same incident
PTE M WOODS	27/08/79:	Killed in same incident
PTE P S GRUNDY	16/12/79:	IRA booby-trap, Forkhill
LT S G BATES	1/01/80:	Shot accidentally at covert op at Forkhill
PTE G M R HARDY	1/01/80:	Killed in same incident
A/SGT B M BROWN	9/08/80:	IRA booby-trap, Forkhill
L/CPL PETER HAMPSON	25/12/81:	Violent or unnatural causes
L/CPL MICHAEL C MAY	26/07/82:	RTA
SGT A I SLATER MM**	2/12/84:	Killed in anti-IRA operation, Fermanagh
SGT MICHAEL MATTHEWS	29/07/88:	DoW, IRA landmine, Cullyhanna
PTE ROBERT SPIKINS	25/03/89:	RTA, Belfast
L/CPL STEPHEN WILSON	18/11/89:	IRA landmine, Mayobridge (three soldiers killed)
PTE DONALD MACAULAY	18/11/89:	Killed in same incident
PTE MATTHEW MARSHALL	18/11/89:	Killed in same incident
PTE ANTHONY HARRISON	19/06/91:	Murdered by IRA in fiancée's home, East Belfast
L/CPL RICHARD COULSON	27/06/92:	Drowned crossing a river
L/CPL PETER H SULLIVAN	27/06/92:	Drowned trying to rescue his friend
PTE MICHAEL B LEE	20/08/92:	Violent or unnatural causes
PTE P F J GROSS	13/05/93:	Accidental death at Holywood
PTE CHRISTIAN D KING.	4/12/94:	Violent or unnatural causes
PTE MARC RAMSEY	21/08/97:	Accidental death

Prince Of Wales' Own Regiment of Yorkshire

PTE JAMES LEADBEATER	11/02/73:	Cause of death unknown
PTE DAVID WRAY	10/10/75:	DoW after being shot Creggan area, Londonderry
L/CPL GRAHAM BIRDSALL	23/08/86:	Cause of death unknown
PTE WILLIAM CARNE	20/07/96:	Cause of death unknown

Princess Of Wales' Royal Regiment

MAJ JOHN BARR	26/11/92:	Helicopter crash, Bessbrook Mill
L/CPL PAUL PARKIN	8/10/95:	Cause of death unknown

Queen Alexandra's Royal Army Nursing Corps

CAPT LYNDA SMITH	22/04/81:	Cause of death unknown

Queen's Lancashire Regiment

SGT JAMES SINGLETON	23/06/70:	Died on duty
PTE STEPHEN KEATING	3/03/72:	IRA sniper, Manor Street, West Belfast
PTE MICHAEL MURTAGH	6/02/73:	Killed in rocket attack, Lower Falls area, Belfast
PTE EDWIN WESTON	14/02/73:	IRA sniper, Divis Street area, Belfast
PTE GARY BARLOW	4/03/73:	Disarmed and murdered by IRA, Lower Falls area, Belfast
PTE JOHN GREEN	8/03/73:	Shot whilst guarding school in Lower Falls area, Belfast
L/CPL WILLIAM RIDDELL	6/01/76:	RTA
PTE IAN O'CONNER	3/03/87:	Grenade attack, Divis Street Flats, Belfast
PTE JOSEPH LEACH	4/06/87:	IRA sniper, Andersonstown, Belfast

Queen's Own Highlanders

PTE JAMES HESKETH	10/12/73:	Shot dead on Lower Falls, Belfast
PTE ALAN JOHN MCMILLAN	8/07/79:	Remote-controlled bomb in Crossmaglen
L/CPL D. LANG	24/08/79:	Killed in helicopter crash with another soldier
L/CPL D.A. WARES	24/08/79:	Killed in same accident
LT/COL DAVID BLAIR	27/08/79:	Killed in IRA double-bomb blast, Warrenpoint - one of 18 soldiers killed in same incident
L/CPL VICTOR MACLEOD	27/08/79:	Killed in same incident
CPL RICHARD TURNER	27/02/90:	Accidentally shot

Queen's Regiment

PTE DAVID PITCHFORD	27/06/70:	RTA
PTE PAUL CARTER	15/09/71:	DoW after being shot at Royal Victoria Hospital, Belfast
PTE ROBERT BENNER	29/11/71:	Abducted and murdered by IRA, off-duty at Crossmaglen
PTE RICHARD SINCLAIR	31/10/72:	IRA sniper, New Lodge, Belfast
PTE STANLEY EVANS	14/11/72:	IRA sniper, Unity Flats complex, West Belfast
PTE PETER WOOLMORE	19/03/79:	Mortar bomb attack, Newtownhamilton, Co Armagh
PTE ALAN STOCK	15/10/83:	Remote-controlled bomb, Creggan, Londonderry

PTE NEIL CLARKE	24/04/84:	IRA sniper, Bishop Street, Londonderry
PTE STEPHEN RANDALL	23/05/84:	Cause of death unknown
WOI JEFFERY BUDGEN	31/10/84:	Cause of death unknown
CPL ALEC BANNISTER	8/08/88:	IRA sniper, New Barnsley, Belfast
SGT CHARLES CHAPMAN	16/07/90:	IRA booby-trap, Army Recruiting Office, Wembley, London

Queen's Royal Irish Hussars

TPR HUGH MCCABE	15/08/69:	Killed by friendly fire, Divis Street, Belfast

Royal Air Force

FLT SGT JOHN WILLOUGHBY	7/12/69:	Natural causes
LAC ROBERT CALDERBANK	10/07/71:	RTA
LAC JACK HAWKINS	28/08/79:	Cause of death unknown
SGT ERIC SIMPSON	6/10/79:	Cause of death unknown
SAC STEPHEN HENSELER	12/03/80:	RTA
JNR TECH DAVID GILFILLAN	13/10/81:	RTA
SGT DAVID RIGBY	25/10/85:	Killed in helicopter crash at Forkhill
CPL ISLANIA MAHESHKUMAR	26/10/89:	Shot by IRA in Wildenrath, West Germany and killed alongside baby daughter Nivruti (six months old)
SQN LDR MICHAEL HAVERSON	26/10/92:	Helicopter crash, Bessbrook Mill Base, Armagh
FLT LT SIMON S.M.J. ROBERTS	26/10/92:	Killed in same accident
FLT SGT JAN PEWTRESS	26/10/92:	Killed in same accident

RAF Regiment

AIRMAN JOHN BAXTER	1/05/88:	IRA booby-trap, Nieuw-Bergan, Holland
AIRMAN JOHN MILLER	1/05/88:	Killed with his friend in the same incident
AIRMAN IAN SHINNER	1/05/88:	Killed by IRA sniper, Roermond, Holland
CPL IAN LEARMOUTH	30/08/89:	Unlawfully killed at VCP

Royal Anglian Regiment

MAJ PETER TAUNTON	26/10/70:	Death by violent or unnatural causes
PTE BRIAN SHERIDAN	20/11/70:	RTA
PTE ROGER WILKINS	11/10/71:	DoW after being shot on Letterkenny Road, Londonderry
L/CPL IAN CURTIS	9/11/71:	IRA sniper, Foyle Road, Londonderry
2/LT NICHOLAS HULL	16/04/72:	IRA sniper Divis Street Flats, Belfast
PTE JOHN BALLARD	11/05/72:	IRA sniper, Sultan Street, Lower Falls, Belfast
L/CPL MARTIN ROONEY	12/07/72:	IRA sniper, Clonnard Street, Lower Falls, Belfast
CPL KENNETH MOGG	13/07/72:	IRA sniper, Dunville Park, Belfast
L/CPL JOHN BODDY	17/08/72:	IRA sniper, Grosvenor Road area of Belfast
CPL JOHN BARRY	25/09/72:	DoW after gun battle, Lower Falls, Belfast
PTE IAN BURT	29/09/72:	IRA sniper, Albert Street, Lower Falls, Belfast
PTE ROBERT MASON	24/10/72:	IRA sniper, Naples Street, Grosvenor Road area, Belfast

PTE ANTHONY GOODFELLOW	27/04/73:	Shot manning VCP, Creggan Estate, Londonderry
PTE N MARWICK	12/09/73:	Shot accidentally, Creggan, Londonderry
L/CPL ROY GRANT	2/11/73:	Death by violent or unnatural causes
PTE PARRY HOLLIS	13/11/74:	Died of natural causes during his tour
PTE STEPHEN FOSTER	13/11/78:	Accidental death
PTE PAUL WRIGHT	8/10/79:	Killed on covert op, Falls Road area
PTE KEVIN BREWER	29/08/81:	RTA
PTE ANTHONY ANDERSON	24/05/82:	Killed by vehicle in confusion after petrol bomb attack, Butcher Street, Londonderry
PTE MARTIN PATTEN	22/09/85:	Murdered off-duty, Limavady Road, Waterside, Londonderry
MAJ ANDREW FRENCH	22/05/86:	Killed by remote-controlled bomb, Crossmaglen
PTE MITCHELL BERTRAM	9/07/86:	Remote-controlled bomb, Glassdrumman, Crossmaglen
PTE CARL DAVIES	9/07/86:	Killed in the same incident
PTE DAVID J. KNIGHT	26/07/86:	RTA
PTE NICHOLAS PEACOCK	31/01/89:	Remote-controlled bomb, Falls Road area, Belfast

Royal Army Dental Corps

| SGT RICHARD MULDOON | 23/03/73: | Murdered by the IRA whilst off duty |

Royal Army Education Corps

| MAJ RHODRI HOWELL | 19/07/79: | Cause of death unknown |

Royal Army Medical Corps

PTE DENNIS 'TAFFY' PORTER	24/04/72:	Violent or unnatural causes
CAPT HARRY MURPHY	15/03/73:	Violent or unnatural causes
CAPT JANIS CANT	8/11/84:	Cause of death unknown
PTE BRIAN ARMSTRONG (TA)	25/08/85:	RTA
WOII PHILLIP CROSS	2/11/91:	IRA bomb planted at Musgrave Park Hospital (killed with one other soldier)
CPL JOHN NEILL	13/04/92:	Death by violent or unnatural causes

Royal Army Pay Corps

PTE MICHAEL PRIME	16/02/72:	Shot in ambush at Moira roundabout near Lisburn
WOII GEORGE JOHNSON	16/03/76:	Cause of death unknown
L/CPL ANDREW SNELL	19/03/80:	Shot accidentally, McCrory Park, Belfast
PTE M A MCLEOD	15/12/93:	Cause of death unknown
L/CPL HENRY M. MCGIVERN		RTA

Royal Army Ordnance Corps

CAPT D A STEWARDSON	9/09/71:	Defusing IRA bomb, Castlerobin, Antrim
WO2 C J L DAVIES	24/11/71:	Killed by IRA bomb in Lurgan
PTE T F McCANN	14/02/72:	Abducted and murdered by the IRA, Newtownbutler
SSGT C R CRACKNELL	15/03/72:	IRA booby-trap, Grosvenor Road, Belfast
SSGT A S BUTCHER	15/03/72:	Killed in same incident

MAJ B C CALLADENE	29/03/72:	IRA car bomb outside Belfast City Hall
CAPT J H YOUNG	15/07/72:	Defusing IRA bomb, Silverbridge, near Forkhill
WO2 WJ CLARK	3/08/72:	Defusing IRA bomb at Strabane
SGT R E HILLS	5/12/72:	Attempting to make live shell safe, Kitchen Hill
CAPT B S GRITTEN	21/06/73:	Killed inspecting explosives, Lecky Road, Londonderry
SSGT R F BECKETT	30/08/73:	Killed pulling bomb out of a post office, Tullyhommon
CAPT RONALD WILKINSON:	23/09/73:	Defusing IRA bomb, Edgbaston, Birmingham
2ND LT L. HAMILTON DOBBIE	3/10/73:	IRA bomb, Bligh's Lane post, Londonderry
SSGT A N BRAMMAH	18/02/74:	Examining IRA roadside bomb, Crossmaglen
CPL GEOFFREY HALL	20/09/74:	Cause of death unknown
SSGT V I ROSE	7/11/74:	IRA landmine, Stewartstown, Tyrone
WO2 J A MADDOCKS	2/12/74:	Examining milk churn bomb, Gortmullen
WO2 E GARSIDE	17/07/75:	Killed with three other soldiers - IRA bomb near Forkhill
CPL C W BROWN	17/07/75:	Killed in same incident
CAPT ROGER GOAD	29/08/75:	Killed defusing IRA bomb, Kensington, London
CPL DOUGLAS WHITFIELD	13/03/76:	RTA
SGT MICHAEL G. PEACOCK	13/03/76:	Killed in same incident
SGT M E WALSH	9/01/77:	Killed dismantling IRA bomb, Newtownbutler
L/CPL MICHAEL DEARNEY	31/05/77:	RTA
SIG P J REECE	2/08/79:	IRA landmine near Armagh
WO2 M O'NEIL	31/05/81:	Examining IRA bomb near Newry
L/CPL ROBERT PRINGLE	24/08/81:	Death by violent or unnatural causes
PTE IAN ARCHIBALD	15/02/83:	RTA
L/CPL DEREK W GREEN	15/06/88:	One of six soldiers killed by IRA booby-trap, Lisburn
WO2 JOHN HOWARD	8/08/88:	IRA booby-trap, Falls Road, Belfast
L/CPL ANDREW DOWELL	17/08/92:	Cause of death unknown

Royal Army Veterinary Corps

| CPL BRIAN CRIDDLE, BEM | 22/07/73: | DoW; was wounded whilst defusing IRA bomb |
| CPL TERENCE O'NEIL | 25/05/91: | Killed by hand-grenade, North Howard Street, Belfast |

Royal Artillery

GNR ROBERT CURTIS	6/02/71:	Shot by IRA gunmen, New Lodge area, Belfast
L/BOMB JOHN LAURIE	15/02/71:	DoW after being shot on Crumlin Road, Belfast
GNR CLIFFORD LORING	31/08/71:	DoW after being shot at VCP, Belfast
SGT MARTIN CARROLL	14/09/71:	IRA sniper, Creggan, Londonderry
GNR ANGUS STEVENS	27/10/71:	IRA bomb attack, Rosemount RUC Station, Belfast
L/BOMB DAVID TILBURY	27/10/71:	Killed in same incident
GNR IAN DOCHERTY	31/10/71:	DoW after being shot in Stockmans Lane, Belfast
GNR RICHARD HAM	29/12/71:	Shot dead in the Brandywell area of Londonderry
L/BOMB ERIC BLACKBURN	10/04/72:	Killed in bomb attack, Rosemount Avenue
L/BOMB BRIAN THOMASSON	10/04/72:	Killed in same incident

GNR VICTOR HUSBAND	2/06/72:	IRA landmine, Rosslea, Co Fermanagh
GNR BRIAN ROBERTSON	2/06/72:	Killed in the same incident
SGT CHARLES COLEMAN	7/06/72:	IRA sniper, Andersonstown, Belfast
GNR WILLIAM RAISTRICK	11/06/72:	IRA sniper, Brooke Park, Londonderry
BDR TERRENCE JONES	11/07/72	Shot in the back by IRA, Londonderry
GNR LEROY GORDON	7/08/72:	IRA landmine, Lisnaskea, Co Fermanagh
L/BOMB DAVID WYNNE	7/08/72:	Killed in same incident
MAJ DAVID STORRY	14/08/72:	Booby-trap, Casement Park Base, Andersonstown
GNR ROBERT CUTTING	03/09/72:	Friendly fire incident, New Lodge (att: Royal Marines)
S/SGT JOHN GARDNER CRAIG	15/09/72:	RTA
GNR PAUL JACKSON	28/11/72:	Hit by bomb shrapnel, Strand Road, Londonderry
GNR IVOR SWAIN	23/03/73:	RTA, North Belfast (att: Royal Marines)
GNR IDWAL EVANS	11/04/73:	IRA sniper, Bogside area of Londonderry
GNR KERRY VENN	28/04/73:	IRA sniper, Shantallow Estate, Londonderry
SGT THOMAS CRUMP	3/05/73:	DoW after being shot in Londonderry
GNR JOSEPH BROOKES	25/11/73:	Shot in IRA ambush in Bogside area of Londonderry
BDR HEINZ PISAREK	25/11/73:	Killed in same incident
SGT JOHN HAUGHEY	21/01/74:	Remote-controlled bomb, Bogside, Londonderry
GNR LEONARD GODDEN	4/02/74:	Killed by IRA bomb on M62 in Yorkshire
BDR TERRENCE GRIFFIN	4/02.74:	Killed in same incident
LT/COL JOHN STEVENSON	8/04/74:	Murdered by IRA gunmen at his home in Northumberland
GNR KIM MACCUNN	22/06/74:	IRA sniper, New Lodge, Belfast
SGT BERNARD FEARNS	30/07/74:	IRA sniper, New Lodge area of Belfast
GNR KEITH BATES	4/11/74:	RTA, Central Belfast
GNR RICHARD DUNNE	8/11/74:	IRA bomb in Woolwich, London (pub bombings)
GNR GEOFFREY B. JONES	9/06/75:	RTA
GNR ANTHONY JEAL	11/07/75:	Cause of death unknown
GNR CYRIL MACDONALD	18/12/75:	IRA bomb attack at Guildhall Square, Londonderry
GNR MARK ASHFORD	17/01/76:	Shot at checkpoint, Great James Street, Londonderry
GNR JAMES REYNOLDS	13/03/76:	RTA
GNR WILLIAM MILLER (TA)	3/07/76:	IRA sniper at checkpoint Butcher Street, Londonderry
SGT DAVID EVANS	21/07/76:	Cause of death unknown
GNR ANTHONY ABBOT	24/10/76:	Ambushed and killed by IRA, Ardoyne, Belfast
GNR STEPHEN NICHOLSON	5/11/76:	Cause of death unknown
GNR MAURICE MURPHY	22/11/76:	DoW from same incident as Gunner Abbot
GNR EDMUND MULLER	11/01/77:	IRA sniper at VCP in Old Park area of Belfast
GNR GEORGE MUNCASTER	23/01/77:	IRA sniper, Markets area, Belfast
GNR PAUL SHEPPARD	1/03/78:	Shot in gun battle, Clifton Park Avenue, Belfast
MAJ GEORGE MILBURN	16/03/78:	Cause of death unknown
GNR ROGER EDWARDS	2/07/78:	Accidentally shot at Musgrave Park Hospital
GNR RICHARD FURMINGER	02/08/79:	Killed in IRA landmine attack with RAOC comrade, Cathedral Road, Armagh

GNR ALAN AYRTON	16/12/79:	Killed with three others in landmine explosion, Dungannon
GNR WILLIAM BECK	16/12/79:	Killed in same incident
GNR SIMON EVANS	16/12/79:	Killed in same incident
GNR KEITH RICHARDS	16/12/79:	Killed in same incident
GNR PETER A. CLARK	9/08/80	Killed accidentally whilst clearing barricades, Ligoniel
SGT SAMUEL MCCLEAN	30/05/81:	Cause of death unknown
L/BOMB KEVIN WALLER	20/09/82:	Remote-controlled INLA bomb, Divis Street Flats, Belfast
BDR PAUL CREE	5/02/88:	Cause of death unknown
GNR LYNDON MORGAN	26/04/88:	IRA booby-trap, Carrickmore
GNR MILES AMOS	8/03/89:	IRA landmine, Buncrana Road, Londonderry
L/BOMB STEPHEN CUMMINS	8/03/89:	Killed in same incident
L/BOMB DAVID SHEPPARD	18/03/89:	Death by violent or unnatural causes
MAJ MICHAEL DILLON-LEE	2/06/90:	Murdered outside his quarters in Dortmund, Germany
GNR DARREN OLDFIELD	1/06/92:	Death by violent or unnatural causes
CAPT NIGEL FRENCH	12/03/92:	Cause of death unknown
L/BOMB PAUL GARRETT	2/12/93:	IRA sniper, Keady, Co Armagh
2 LT JAMES C. FOX	21/01/95:	Violent or unnatural causes
GNR JON COOPER	22/02/97:	Violent or unnatural causes

Royal Horse Artillery

BDR PAUL CHALLENOR	10/08/71:	IRA sniper, Bligh's Lane post, Londonderry
GNR DAVID FARRINGTON	13/03/74:	Shot by IRA gunmen at Chapel Lane, Belfast City Centre
GNR TIMOTHY UTTERIDGE	19/10/84:	Shot by IRA, Turf Lodge, Belfast
L/BOMB STEPHEN RESTORICK	12/02/97:	IRA sniper at VCP at Bessbrook Mill Army Base

Royal Corps Signals

L/CPL MICHAEL SPURWAY	13/09/69:	Accidentally shot, Gosford Castle
SIG PAUL GENGE	7/11/71:	Shot by IRA whilst off-duty in Lurgan
SGT DAVID MCELVIE	13/03/73:	Unknown
CPL JOHN AIKMAN	6/11/73:	Shot by IRA gunmen, Newtownhamilton
SIGNALMAN MICHAEL E. WAUGH	4/02/74:	Killed by IRA bomb, M62, Yorkshire
SIGNALMAN LESLIE DAVID WALSH	4/02/74:	Killed in same incident
SIGNALMAN PAUL ANTHONY REID	4/02/74:	Killed in same incident
SGT DEREK BASSFORD	24/10/75:	Cause of death unknown
SIGNALMAN DAVID ROBERTS	13/03/76:	RTA
CPL ARTHUR FORD	7/01/76:	Aircraft accident
L/CPL RICHARD DAVIES	25/02/79:	RTA
SIGNALMAN PAUL J REECE	2/08/79:	IRA landmine, Armagh
L/CPL ROBIN LISTER	18/02/80:	Helicopter crash near Lisburn
L/CPL PAUL HOLT	3/11/80:	Cause of death unknown
SIGNALMAN BRIAN RICHARD CROSS	4/07/81:	Killed in road traffic accident, Lisburn, en route to Castlereagh

CPL MICHAEL WARD	1/04/82:	Shot with REME soldier by IRA in Bogside, Londonderry
SGT LESLIE MCKENZIE	24/05/83:	RTA
SIGNALMAN KENNETH ROYAL	28/03/85:	RTA
CPL DEREK T WOOD	19/03/88:	Beaten by mob, shot by IRA, Penny Lane, Belfast
CPL DAVID HOWES	19/03/88:	Killed in same incident
L/CPL GRAHAM P LAMBIE	15/06/88:	Killed by IRA bomb, Lisburn (one of six soldiers killed)
SGT MICHAEL JAMES WINKLER	15/06/88:	Killed in same incident
SIGNALMAN MARK CLAVEY	15/06/88:	Killed in same incident
CPL WILLIAM J PATERSON	15/06/88:	Killed in same incident
S/SGT KEVIN A FROGGETT	16/09/89:	Shot by IRA repairing radio mast, Coalisland RUC Station
SIGNALMAN WILLIAM DRYDEN	7/08/91:	Cause of death unknown
SGT MICHAEL NEWMAN	14/04/92:	Shot by INLA at Army Recruiting Office, Derby, England
SIGNALMAN JONATHAN EDMONDS	27/05/92:	Cause of death unknown
CPL PAUL SMITH	22/09/94:	RTA
SGT JOHN LIVINGSTONE	21/04/98:	Cause of death unknown

Royal Corps of Transport

MAJ PHILIP COWLEY	13/01/70:	Died on duty
CPL CHRISTOPHER YOUNG (TA)	29/07/71:	RTA
DRIVER STEPHEN BEEDIE	26/03/72:	RTA
DRIVER LAURENCE JUBB	26/04/72:	Killed in vehicle crash after mob attack, Armagh
L/CPL MICHAEL BRUCE	31/05/72:	IRA sniper, Andersonstown, Belfast
S/SGT JOSEPH FLEMING (TA)	9/07/72:	Shot dead by IRA in Grosvenor Road area of Belfast
DRIVER PETER HEPPENSTALL	14/07/72:	IRA sniper, Ardoyne area of Belfast
DRIVER STEPHEN COOPER	21/07/72:	IRA car bomb on 'Bloody Friday', Belfast Bus Depot
DRIVER RONALD KITCHEN	10/11/72:	IRA sniper at VCP in Old Park Road, Belfast
DRIVER MICHAEL GAY	17/03/73:	IRA landmine, Dungannon
SGT THOMAS PENROSE	24/03/73:	Murdered off-duty with two others, Antrim Road, Belfast
CPL ANDREW GILMOUR	29/08/73:	RTA
L/CPL EDMOND CROSBIE	23/11/73:	RTA
DRIVER NORMAN MCKENZIE	11/04/74:	IRA landmine, Lisnaskea, Co Fermanagh
DRIVER HAROLD J. KING	19/04/75:	RTA
DRIVER WILLIAM KNIGHT	17/05/76:	RTA
DRIVER VICTOR DORMER	1/10/76:	Cause of death unknown
SGT WILLIAM EDGAR	15/04/77:	Abducted and murdered by IRA whilst on leave in Londonderry
LT NIGEL BREWER	31/05/79:	Cause of death unknown
DRIVER JOHN DORRITY	30/09/79:	Cause of death unknown
DRIVER STEVEN ATKINS	29/11/80:	RTA
DRIVER IAN MACDONALD	8/03/81:	Cause of death unknown

DRIVER PAUL BULMAN	19/05/81:	Killed in IRA landmine attack along with four RGJs at Altnaveigh, South Armagh
DRIVER PAUL JOHNS	25/10/81:	Cause of death unknown
CAPT JOHN MEADOWS	8/08/84:	Cause of death unknown
L/CPL NORMAN DUNCAN	22/02/89:	Shot by IRA waterside area of Londonderry
THOMAS GIBSON (TA)	20/10/89:	Murdered by IRA as he waited for lift in Kilrea
DVR C PANTRY	2/11/91:	Killed by IRA bomb at Musgrave Park Hospital, Belfast
PTE MAURICE CARSON (TA)	13/06/81:	RTA

Royal Dragoon Guards

TPR GEOFFREY KNIPE	7/08/72:	Armoured vehicle crashed after mob attack, Armagh

Royal Electrical & Mechanical Engineers

CFN CHRISTOPHER EDGAR	13/09/69:	Violent or unnatural causes
CFN ANDREW PATON	26/05/71:	
SGT STUART C REID	24/06/72:	IRA milk churn bombs at Glenshane Pass, Londonderry
L/CPL D MOON	24/06/72:	Killed in same incident
CFN BRIAN HOPE	14/08/72:	IRA booby-trap Casement Park, Andersonstown, Belfast
L/CPL COLIN HARKER	24/12/72:	DoW after was shot by IRA sniper Lecky Road, Londonderry
CPL DAVID BROWN	14/03/73:	Unknown
SGT MALCOLM SELDON	30/06/74:	Shot in an incident inside his base (manslaughter by a comrade)
L/CPL ALISTER STEWART	9/10/74:	RTA
L/CPL DEREK NORWOOD	5/03/75:	Cause of death unknown
CFN COLIN MCINNES	18/12/75:	IRA bomb attack on army base in Londonderry
CPL ROBERT MOORE	15/09/79:	RTA
CPL PETER BAILEY	5/04/80:	RTA
CFN ALAN COOMBE	16/02/81:	RTA
L/CPL PHILIP HARDING	30/03/82:	Cause of death unknown
SGT MICHAEL BURBRIDGE	1/04/82:	IRA sniper, Rosemount Barracks, Londonderry
SGT RICHARD GREGORY	22/10/82:	Died of natural causes on duty
CFN WILLIAM PARR	6/07/90:	Cause of death unknown
L/CPL CM MONTEITH	5/08/91:	RTA
CPL MD IONNOU	15/04/95:	RTA
S/SGT SJ THOMPSON	30/06/95:	Died of natural causes whilst on duty
WO1 (ASM) JAMES BRADWELL	11/10/96:	DoW after car bomb attack by IRA on army base, Lisburn

Royal Engineers

SAPPER JOHN CONNACHAN	27/06/71:	Cause of death unknown
SAPPER DEREK AMOS	28/12/71:	RTA
SAPPER RONALD HURST	17/05/72:	IRA sniper whilst working on base in Crossmaglen

S/SGT MALCOLM BANKS	28/06/72:	Shot by IRA Short Strand area of Belfast
SAPPER EDWARD STUART	2/10/72:	Shot whilst working undercover, Dunmurry, Belfast
WO2 IAN DONALD	24/05/73:	IRA bomb, Cullaville, Co Armagh
MAJOR RICHARD JARMAN	20/07/73:	IRA booby-trap, Middletown, Co Armagh
SAPPER MALCOLM ORTON	17/09/73:	Cause of death unknown
S/SGT JAMES LUND	19/01/74:	Cause of death unknown
L/CPL IAN NICHOLL	15/05/74:	RTA
SAPPER JOHN WALTON	2/07/74:	IRA booby-trap, Newtownhamilton
WO1 JOHN NEWTON	24/06/75:	
SGT ROBERT MCCARTER	17/07/75:	IRA bomb, Forkhill
SGT DAVID EVANS	21/07/76:	IRA booby-trap, army base, Waterside, Londonderry
SAPPER GARETH GRIFFITHS	6/11/76:	Cause of death unknown
SAPPER HOWARD EDWARDS	11/12/76:	IRA sniper, Bogside area of Londonderry
SAPPER DAVIS THOMPSON	13/01/77:	Cause of death unknown
SAPPER MICHAEL LARKIN	10/02/77:	Cause of death unknown
CPL JOHN HAYNES	28/07/77:	Cause of death unknown
SAPPER STEPHEN WORTH	1/08/77:	Cause of death unknown
SAPPER JAMES VANCE	14/11/77:	RTA
CPL JAMES ANDREWS	4/09/78:	Cause of death unknown
SAPPER FRASER JONES	3/02/80:	Accidental death whilst on duty
COL MARK COE	16/02/80:	Murdered by IRA gunmen at army home in Bielefeld, Germany
SGT KENNETH ROBSON	18/02/80:	Helicopter crash near Lisburn
WOII EMANUEL MARIOTTI	22/08/81:	Cause of death unknown
SAPPER CHRISTOPHER BEATTIE	6/04/82:	Cause of death unknown
CPL THOMAS PALMER QGM **	8/02/83:	RTA
L/CPL DAVID HURST	6/10/86:	RTA
L/CPL MICHAEL ROBBINS	1/08/88:	Killed by IRA bomb at Mill Hill Army Camp, London
L/CPL PAUL CASSIDY	15/03/88:	RTA
S/SGT DAVID HULL	22/08/89:	RTA
S/SGT JAMES H. HARDY	12/06/90:	RTA
SGT MICHAEL CASHMORE	1/07/90:	Cause of death unknown
SPR DEAN PITTS	3/08/91:	Cause of death unknown
SAPPER JOHN ROBINSON	21/04/96:	Cause of death unknown

Royal Green Jackets

L/CPL MICHAEL PEARCE	24/09/69:	Violent or unnatural causes
RFN MICHAEL BOSWELL	25/10/69:	RTA near Omagh
RFN JOHN KEENEY	25/10/69:	Died in same incident
CPL ROBERT BANKIER	22/05/71:	IRA sniper, Markets area of Belfast
RFN DAVID WALKER	12/07/71:	IRA sniper, Northumberland Street, Lower Falls, Belfast
RFN JOSEPH HILL	16/10/71:	Shot by gunman during riots in Bogside, Londonderry
MAJ ROBIN ALERS-HANKEY	30/01/72:	DoW after being shot in Bogside area of Londonderry

RFN JOHN TAYLOR	20/03/72:	IRA sniper, William Street, Londonderry
RFN JAMES MEREDITH	26/06/72:	Shot in Abercorn Road, Londonderry
L/CPL DAVID CARD	4/08/72:	Killed by IRA gunman in Andersonstown, Belfast
CPL IAN MORRILL	28/08/72:	IRA sniper in Beechmount Avenue, Belfast
RFN DAVID GRIFFITHS	30/08/72:	IRA sniper, Clonnard Street, Lower Falls, Belfast
L/CPL IAN GEORGE	10/09/72:	Thought to have been shot by an IRA sniper, Belfast
RFN RAYMOND JOESBURY	8/12/72:	DoW after being shot whilst in Whiterock area of Belfast
RFN NICOLAS ALLEN	26/11/73:	Death by violent or unnatural causes
RFN MICHAEL GIBSON	29/12/74:	Shot along with RUC constable at Forkhill on joint patrol
CPL WILLIAM SMITH	31/08/77:	IRA sniper, Girdwood Park Army Base, Belfast
LT/COL IAN CORDEN-LLOYD	17/02/78:	Helicopter crash near Bessbrook
RFN NICHOLAS SMITH	4/03/78:	IRA booby-trap, Crossmaglen
MAJ THOMAS FOWLEY	24/04/78:	Died of natural causes whilst on duty
RFN CHRISTOPHER WATSON	19/07/80:	Shot and killed off-duty in Rosemount, Londonderry
RFN MICHAEL BAGSHAW	19/05/81:	Killed along with four others, IRA landmine at Altnaveigh
RFN ANDREW GAVIN	19/05/81:	Killed in same incident
RFN JOHN KING	19/05/81:	Killed in same incident
L/CPL GRENVILLE WINSTONE	19/05/81:	Killed in same incident
L/CPL GAVIN DEAN	16/07/81:	IRA sniper near Crossmaglen
RFN DANIEL HOLLAND	25/03/82:	Killed with two others in gun attack on Springfield Road
RFN NICHOLAS MALAKOS	25/03/82:	Killed in same incident
RFN ANTHONY RAPLEY	25/03/82:	Killed in same incident
WO2 GRAHAM BARKER	20/07/82:	Killed in IRA bomb outrage, Regents Park, London
BANDSMAN JOHN HERITAGE	20/07/82:	Killed in same incident
CPL ROBERT LIVINGSTONE	20/07/82:	Killed in same incident
CPL JOHN MCKNIGHT	20/07/82:	Killed in same incident
BANDSMAN GEORGE MEASURE	20/07/82:	Killed in same incident
BANDSMAN KEITH POWELL	20/07/82:	Killed in same incident
BANDSMAN LAURENCE SMITH	20/07/82:	Killed in same incident
RFN DAVID GRAINGER	10/04/83:	Thought to have been shot by IRA in Belleek
RFN DAVID MULLEY	18/03/86:	IRA bomb, Castlewellan, Co Down
L/CPL THOMAS HEWITT	19/07/87:	IRA sniper, Belleek, Co Fermanagh
CPL EDWARD JEDRUCH	31/07/87:	Killed in helicopter accident in South Armagh
SGT THOMAS ROSS	18/09/91:	RTA
L/CPL WAYNE HARRIS	8/11/91:	RTA, hit a bridge in Armagh
RFN CHRISTOPHER WILLIAMS	8/11/91:	Killed in same incident
CPL MATTHEW MADDOCKS	14/11/91:	Helicopter crash, Gortin Glen, Omagh
CPL LARRY WALL	12/12/91:	Death by violent or unnatural causes
RFN JAMIE SMITH	10/08/92:	RTA
RFN RICHARD DAVEY	29/10/92:	Death by violent or unnatural causes
RFN DAVID FENLEY	17/02/93:	Death by violent or unnatural causes
WO2 KEITH THEOBOLD	2/10/95:	Death by violent or unnatural causes

Royal Hampshire Regiment

PTE JOHN KING	13/03/73:	IRA booby-trap, Crossmaglen
PTE ALAN WATKINS	3/08/76:	INLA sniper, Dungiven, Co Londonderry
DRUMMER FRANK FALLOWS	10/11/76:	Died in accidental shooting, Magaheralin, Co Armagh
SGT MICHAEL P. UNSWORTH	2/01/77:	Drowned after helicopter accident, River Bann
PTE COLIN CLIFFORD	30/04/82:	IRA landmine, Belleek, Co Fermanagh
PTE ANDREW COCKWILL	17/05/89:	Cause of death unknown

Royal Highland Fusiliers

FUS JOHN B. MCCAIG	10/03/71:	Abducted and murdered by the IRA at Ligoniel, Belfast
FUS JOSEPH MCCAIG	10/03/71:	Murdered in the same incident
FUS DOUGALD P. MCCAUGHE	10/03/71:	Murdered in the same incident
L/CPL DAVID HIND	2/01/77:	Shot by IRA, Crossmaglen
CPL ROBERT M THOMPSON	20/07/80:	IRA car bomb, Moy Bridge, Aughnacloy

Royal Hussars

S/SGT CHARLES SIMPSON	7/11/74:	IRA booby-trap, Stewartstown, Co Tyrone
LT ROBERT GLAZEBROOK	14/11/76:	RTA

Royal Horse Guards

L/COH KEITH CHILLINGWORTH	14/06/72:	RTA

Royal Irish Rangers

SGT THOMAS MCGAHON	19/01/71:	RTA
CPL JAMES SINGLETON	19/01/71:	Killed in same incident
RANGER WILLIAM J. BEST	21/05/72:	Abducted and murdered when on home leave
RANGER THOMAS MCGANN	26/05/72:	RTA
L/CPL MICHAEL NORRIS	27/07/74:	Cause of death unknown
RANGER H THOMPSON	6/12/77:	RTA
RANGER ROBERT QUAIL	5/07/79:	Cause of death unknown
RANGER SEAN REILLY	4/09/81:	Cause of death unknown
RANGER DAVID LANHAM	10/01/83:	RTA
RANGER LAWRENCE PITMAN	5/07/84:	Cause of death unknown
RANGER WALTER LLEWELLYN	22/05/86:	Accidentally shot
SGT JOHN PEDEN	7/10/86:	Cause of death unknown
RANGER CYRIL J. SMITH QGM	24/10/90:	Killed saving colleagues during bomb attack at Newry

Royal Irish Regiment

L/CPL MICHAEL W.A. PATTERSON	6/09/92:	RTA (HOME SERVICE FORCE)
SGT ROBERT IRVINE	20/10/92:	Shot by IRA in his sister's home, Rasharkin
PTE BRIAN MARTIN	20/10/92:	RTA (HOME SERVICE FORCE)
L/CPL IAN WARNOCK	19/11/92:	Shot by IRA as he met his wife in Portadown
PTE STEPHEN WALLER	30/12/92:	Shot by IRA when on home leave, Belfast
L/CPL MERVYN JOHNSTON	15/02/93:	Shot by IRA at his in-laws' house, West Belfast

PTE WILLIAM HARKNESS	27/03/93:	RTA
PTE ROBERT GARDNER	28/03/93:	RTA
CPL ROBERT NEWELL	5/03/93:	Cause of death unknown
PTE CHRIS WREN	31/05/93:	Killed by IRA bomb under his car in Moneymore
CPL ROBERT ARMSTRONG	21/11/93:	RTA
PTE SEAN MAIR	17/04/94:	RTA
PTE WILLIAM SALTERS	30/04/94:	Died in a fire at RUC station
PTE WILLIAM TOSH	30/04/94:	Killed in same incident
PTE ADRIAN ROGERS	15/05/94:	Cause of death unknown
PTE REGGIE MCCOLLUM	21/05/94:	Abducted and murdered by the IRA whilst off duty
CPL WILLIAM WOLFF	25/05/94:	Death by violent or unnatural causes
PTE SIMON LECKY	31/07/94:	RTA
CPL TRELFORD T. WITHERS	8/08/94:	Shot in his shop, Downpatrick Street, Crossgar
CPL RONALD JACKSON	10/10/95:	RTA
PTE WILLIAM MCCREA	10/10/95:	RTA
PTE PAUL KILPATRICK	13/12/95:	Death by violent or unnatural causes
CPL ROBERT ANDERSON	19/05/96:	Cause of death unknown
PTE ALAN MCCORMICK	1/06/96	RTA
L/CPL STEVE RANKIN	23/09/96:	Death by violent or unnatural causes
PTE JAMIE CATER	25/10/96:	Death by violent or unnatural causes
PTE WILLIAM WOODS	3/09/97:	Violent or unnatural causes
WOII ROBERT BELL	9/01/98:	Died on duty
PTE MATTHEW FRANCE	1/05/98:	Violent or unnatural causes
PTE RONALD MCCONVILLE	30/06/98:	Died on duty
CPL JACKY IRELAND	13/07/98:	RTA
PTE JOHN MURRAY	28/08/98:	RTA
L/CPL STUART ANDREWS	16/09/98:	Died on duty
CPL GERALD BLAIR	21/10/98:	Died on duty

Royal Irish Regiment (V)

WO2 HUGH MCGINN	28/12/80:	Killed by INLA in his own home in Armagh
SGT TREVOR A. ELLIOT	13/04/83:	Killed by IRA at his shop in Keady
CPL TREVOR MAY	9/04/84:	IRA bomb under his car in Newry outside his work

Royal Logistic Corps

CPL TERENCE HEFFY	7/12/93:	Cause of death unknown
PTE MATTHEW EDWARDS	29/12/93:	Cause of death unknown
L/CPL DAVID WILSON	14/05/94:	Killed by bomb attack at VCP at Keady, Co Armagh
L/CPL MARK TREHERNE	29/07/94:	Cause of death unknown
PTE PAUL SHEPHERD	25/12/95:	Cause of death unknown
L/CPL RICHARD FORD	30/10/98:	Died whilst on duty

Royal Marines

BAND CPL DEAN PAVEY	22/09/89:	Killed in IRA bomb outrage, Marine Barracks, Deal
BAND CPL TREVOR DAVIS	22/09/89:	Killed in same incident
BAND CPL DAVE McMILLAN	22/09/89:	Killed in same incident

MUSICIAN RICHARD FICE	22/09/89:	Killed in same incident
MUSICIAN BOB SIMMONDS	22/09/89:	Killed in same incident
MUSICIAN MICK BALL	22/09/89:	Killed in same incident
MUSICIAN RICHARD JONES	22/09/89:	Killed in same incident
MUSICIAN TIM REEVES	22/09/89:	Killed in same incident
MUSICIAN MARK PETCH	22/09/89:	Killed in same incident
MUSICIAN ANDY CLEATHEROE	22/09/89:	Killed in same incident
MUSICIAN CHRIS NOLAN	18/10/89:	DoW from same incident

Royal Marine Commandos:
40 Cdo

MARINE LEONARD ALLEN	26/07/72:	Shot by IRA, Unity Flats, Belfast
MARINE ANTHONY DAVID	17/10/72:	DoW after being shot by IRA on Falls Road
MARINE JOHN SHAW	26/07/73:	RTA in highly controversial circumstances *
MARINE ANDREW GIBBONS	28/05/83:	Died at Camlough Lake, Co Armagh from gunshot wounds

* Marine John Shaw's death is recorded by the Royal Marines as 'killed in action'

42 Cdo

MARINE GRAHAM COX	29/04/73:	IRA sniper, New Lodge, Belfast
MARINE JOHN MACKLIN	28/03/74:	DoW after being shot in the Antrim Road, Belfast
CPL ROBERT MILLER	17/08/78:	IRA bomb attack, Forkhill
MARINE GARY WHEDDON	12/11/78:	DoW after bomb attack, Crossmaglen
MARINE ADAM GILBERT	15/06/89:	Shot in friendly fire incident, New Lodge Road

45 Cdo

CPL DENNIS LEACH	13/08/74:	IRA bomb, Crossmaglen
MARINE MICHAEL SOUTHERN	13/08/74:	Killed in same incident
MARINE NEIL BEWLEY	21/08/77:	IRA sniper, Turf Lodge, Belfast
SGT WILLIAM CORBETT	23/08/81:	Accidentally shot, Musgrave Park Hospital, Belfast

Royal Marines (HQNI)

| MAJ JOHN RICHARD COOPER | 16/02/82: | RTA |
| CPL MARK HARRY LAZENBY | 21/02/95: | RTA |

Royal Military Police

L/CPL WILLIAM G. JOLLIFFE	1/03/71:	Killed in crash in Londonderry after petrol bombing
CPL ALAN HOLMAN	11/02/73:	Cause of death unknown
CPL RODERICK LANE	20/05/73:	RTA
SGT SHERIDAN YOUNG	18/05/73:	Killed in IRA atrocity at Knock-na-Moe Hotel
CPL RICHARD ROBERTS	30/05/73:	RTA
CPL STUART MILNE	20/02/74:	RTA
L/CPL PAUL MUNDY	20/02/74:	Killed in same incident
CPL THOMAS F. LEA	21/01/75:	DoW eight months after IRA bomb attack, Belfast
CPL JOHN BOOTH	29/01/75:	Shot accidentally at Aldergrove Base
CPL MICHAEL HARDS	17/04/76:	Cause of death unknown

CPL WILLIAM SNAITH	25/01/79:	Cause of death unknown
CPL GEORGE MIDDLEMAS	8/11/77:	RTA
SGT DAVID ROSS	27/03/84:	Killed in Londonderry after explosion
L/CPL DUNCAN CHAPPELL	19/09/91:	Shot accidentally in friendly fire incident
CPL MICHAEL HEIGHTON	9/10/91:	Cause of death unknown

Royal Navy

NA (AH) DAVID SHIPLEY	11/01/87:	RTA
AB MARK CARTWRIGHT	11/01/87:	Killed in same incident
LT A. R. SHIELDS	22/08/88:	IRA bomb in Belfast (was naval recruiter)
LT CDR JOHN MCMASTER	18/07/91:	Shot off-duty by IRA, Church Lane, Belfast
CK1 THOMAS GILLEN		RTA
L/SMN GAVIN STEWART		RTA
STWD ROBERT STEWART		RTA
L/WREN ANNIE BYRNE		RTA
MEM ALAN BALMER		RTA

Royal Pioneer Corps

PTE IRWIN BOWEN	2/08/72:	RTA
SGT JAMES ROBINSON	8/02/73:	Died of natural causes whilst on duty
PTE PHILIP DRAKE	26/08/74:	IRA sniper, Craigavon, Co Armagh
PTE GRAHAM HAYES	2/05/75:	Cause of death unknown
PTE DAVID P. BONSALL	29/03/75:	RTA
PTE L. ROTHWELL	25/10/76:	Cause of death unknown
L/CPL GRAHAM LEE	22/08/80:	RTA
PTE SOHAN VIRDEE	5/09/81:	Murdered by the IRA whilst off-duty, Antrim Road, Belfast
PTE S HUMBLE	26/08/81:	Killed in shooting accident - negligent discharge
CPL DEREK HAYES	21/06/88:	IRA booby-trap, Crossmaglen

Royal Regiment Fusiliers:
1st Battalion

FUS ANTHONY SIMMONS	15/11/74:	Shot by IRA at Strabane
CPL PHILLIP BARKER	25/01/81:	Shot at VCP in Belfast
CPL T H AGAR	18/05/84:	Killed by IRA bomb under car at Enniskillen
L/CPL R V HUGGINS	18/05/84:	Killed in same incident
L/CPL P W GALLIMORE	18/10/84:	Died of heart attack after bomb attack, Enniskillen

2nd Battalion

MAJ J J E SNOW	8/12/71:	DoW after being shot by IRA in New Lodge area
L/CPL JAMES J MCSHANE	4/02/74:	Killed in IRA bomb outrage, M62, Yorkshire
FUS JACK HYNES	4/02/74:	Killed in same outrage
CPL CLIFFORD HAUGHTON	4/02/74:	Killed in same outrage
FUS STEPHEN WHALLEY	7/02/74:	DoW from same outrage
FUS K CANHAM	14/07/72:	IRA sniper in Lenadoon
FUS ALAN P TINGEY	23/08/72:	IRA sniper, West Belfast

CPL D NAPIER	9/03/73:	RTA
FUS GEORGE FOXALL	16/06/80:	Violent or unnatural causes
FUS THOMAS FOXALL	19/06/80:	As above - both were related. Based at Palace Barracks
FUS ANDREW GRUNDY	1/05/92:	IRA bomb at VCP at Killeen
L/CPL MICHAEL J BESWICK	9/02/93:	DoW after IRA bomb in Armagh

3rd Battalion

CPL JOHN L DAVIS	15/09/72:	Shot by IRA in Bogside, Londonderry
FUS CHARLES J MARCHANT	9/04/73:	DoW after being shot in ambush at Lurgan
CPL DAVID LLEWELLYN	28/09/75:	RTA
CPL E GLEESON	9/10/75:	IRA landmine, Lurgancullenboy
SGT S J FRANCIS	21/11/75:	IRA booby-trap, Forkhill
FUS M J SAMPSON	22/11/75:	Killed in major gun battle with IRA at Drumuckaval
FUS J D DUNCAN	22/11/75:	Killed in same incident
FUS P L McDONALD	22/11/75:	Killed in same incident
CPL DONALD TRAYNOR	30/03/76:	IRA booby-trap, Ballygallan
L/CPL WAYNE MAKIN	3/01/83:	Violent or unnatural causes

Battalion unknown

| FUS TERRY THOMAS | 25/01/72: | Death by violent or unnatural causes |

Royal Regiment of Wales

PTE ALAN ROY ROGERS	13/03/71:	RTA at VCP
L/CPL JOHN HILLMAN	18/05/72:	IRA sniper, Flex Street Mill, Ardoyne, Belfast
L/CPL ALAN GILES	12/06/72:	Shot in gun battle with IRA, Ardoyne, Belfast
PTE BRIAN SODEN	19/06/72:	IRA sniper in Ardoyne, Belfast
PTE DAVID MEEK	13/07/72:	IRA sniper, Hooker Street, Ardoyne, Belfast
PTE JOHN WILLIAMS	14/07/72:	Killed in gun battle with IRA, Hooker Street, Ardoyne
PTE GARY CHANNING	21/11/86:	Accidental death at VCP in Omagh
PTE GEOFFREY JONES	5/01/87:	Death by violent or unnatural causes
WO1 (RSM) MIKE HEAKIN	12/08/88:	Murdered at traffic lights by IRA, Ostende, Belgium
PTE WILLIAM DAVIS	1/06/90:	Murdered in Litchfield Railway Station by IRA

Royal Scots

PTE RODERICK D W C. BANNON	31/03/76:	IRA landmine explosion, Co Armagh
PTE DAVID FERGUSON	31/03/76:	Killed in same incident
PTE JOHN PEARSON	31/03/76:	Killed in same incident
COL SGT NORMAN REDPATH	2/02/81:	Died of heart attack whilst on duty
PTE PATRICK J MCKENNA	15/03/81:	Accidentally shot
PTE ALAN BRUCE	17/09/82:	RTA
L/CPL LAWRENCE DICKSON	17/03/93:	IRA sniper at Forkhill

Royal Scots Dragoon Guards

| TPR IAN CAIE | 24/08/72: | IRA landmine attack at Crossmaglen |

TPR DONALD ROY DAVIES   18/11/74:   Cause of death unknown

Royal Tank Regiment

L/CPL JOHN WARNOCK   4/09/71:   IRA landmine attack, Derrybeg Park, Newry
TPR JAMES NOWOSAD   3/03/78:   Shot by gunmen in 'Rag Day' killing, Belfast City
                                               Centre - also killed was a civilian searcher
TPR JULIAN MILLS   18/09/77: Drowned whilst on duty
L/CPL NICHOLAS BUSHWELL   2/10/80:   RTA
CPL STEVEN SMITH   2/07/89:   IRA bomb under his car, Hanover, Germany

Royal Welsh Fusiliers

CPL GERALD BRISTOW   16/04/72: IRA sniper, Bishops Street, Londonderry
FUS KERRY MCCARTHY   21/06/72: IRA sniper, Victoria RUC Station, Londonderry
CPL DAVID SMITH   21/06/73: IRA booby-trap, Strabane
CPL ALAN COUGHLAN   28/10/74: Van bomb attack at Ballykinler Army Camp
FUS ANDREW CROCKER   24/11/76: Killed by IRA at post office robbery, Turf Lodge
LT STEVEN KIRBY   14/02/79: IRA sniper Abercorn Road, Londonderry
CPL DAVID WRIGHT   16/12/93: RTA whilst on duty

Scots Dragoon Guards

TPR ANTHONY SUTTON   6/12/77:   Accidental death whilst on top cover in armoured
                                               vehicle
TPR DONALD DAVIES   17/11/74: Cause of death unknown

Scots Guards

GUARDSMAN JOHN EDMUNDS   16/03/70: Drowned
GUARDSMAN BRIAN HALL   4/10/71:   IRA sniper, Cupar Street, Falls area of Belfast
GUARDSMAN GEORGE HAMILTON   17/10/71: Ambushed and killed by IRA, Cupar Street, Lower
                                               Falls
GUARDSMAN NORMAN BOOTH   30/10/71: Killed in same incident
GUARDSMAN STEPHEN MCGUIRE   4/11/71:   IRA sniper, Henry Taggart Base, West Belfast
GUARDSMAN PAUL NICHOLS   27/11/71: IRA sniper, St James Crescent, Falls Road, Belfast
GUARDSMAN JOHN VAN-BECK   18/09/72: DoW after being shot by IRA, Lecky Road,
                                               Londonderry
GUARDSMAN GEORGE LOCKHART   26/09/72: DoW after being shot by IRA, Bogside, Londonderry
L/SGT THOMAS MCKAY   28/10/72: IRA sniper, Bishop Street, Londonderry
GUARDSMAN ALAN DAUGHTERY   31/12/73: IRA sniper, Beechmount Avenue, Falls Road, Belfast
GUARDSMAN WILLIAM FORSYTH   5/10/74:   Killed in IRA bomb outrage, Guildford (with four
                                               others)
GUARDSMAN JOHN HUNTER   5/10/74:   Killed in same outrage
COL/SGT DAVID NADEN **   7/06/78:   RTA
L/CPL ALAN SWIFT***   11/08/78: Killed on covert ops, Letterkenny Road, Londonderry
COL/SGT EDWIN MURRISON   9/04/80:   Killed on covert ops in a car chase
GUARDSMAN GARY CONNELL   12/10/80: Death by drowning at end of tour
L/SGT IAIN HANNA   20/10/80: Death by violent or unnatural causes
MAJ DONALD NICOL/ ARDMONACH   21/10/86: Died of natural causes whilst on duty

L/SGT GRAHAM STEWART	5/05/90:	Killed on covert ops, Cullyhanna, Co Armagh
GUARDSMAN PAUL BROWN	2/08/90:	RTA
GUARDSMAN ALEX IRELAND	11/09/90:	Death by violent or unnatural causes
GUARDSMAN DAMIAN SHACKLETON	3/08/92:	IRA sniper, New Lodge, Belfast
GUARDSMAN ANDREW WASON	3/09/92:	Death by violent or unnatural causes

Staffordshire Regiment

S/SGT JOHN MORRELL	24/10/72:	DoW after IRA booby-trap, Drumargh, Armagh
2ND LT MICHAEL SIMPSON	23/10/74:	DoW after being shot by IRA sniper, Londonderry
PTE CHRISTOPHER SHENTON	20/01/81:	IRA sniper whilst in OP, Bogside, Londonderry
L/CPL STEPHEN ANDERSON	29/05/84:	IRA landmine, Crossmaglen
PTE MARK MASON	15/08/89:	Death by violent or unnatural causes
SGT DEAN OLIVER	9/05/92:	Death by violent or unnatural causes
PTE WAYNE G. SMITH	1/07/95:	RTA

The Highlanders

| HIGHLANDER SCOTT HARRINGTON | 9/07/95: | Death by violent or unnatural causes |

The Royal Gloucestershire, Berkshire and Wiltshire Regiment

| CPL GARY LLEWELLYN FENTON | 22/06/98: | Run down and killed by lorry at VCP, Crossmaglen (Posthumous mention in Dispatches) |

Ulster Defence Regiment:
2nd Battalion

SGT HARRY D. DICKSON	27/02/72:	Murdered by the IRA at his home
PTE SIDNEY W. WATT	20/07/73:	Ambushed by the IRA at a friend's house
PTE KENNETH HILL	28/08/73:	Shot in Armagh City whilst attending an incident
CPL JAMES A. FRAZER	30/08/75:	Killed by IRA at a friend's farm
L/CPL JOE REID	31/08/75:	Murdered at home by IRA
L/CPL D. JOHN BELL	6/11/75:	Killed by IRA as he returned from work
C/SGT JOE NESBITT	10/11/75:	Shot by the IRA on his way to work
PTE JOSEPH A McCULLOUGH	25/02/76:	Shot by IRA
CPL ROBERT McCONNELLI	5/04/76:	Murdered at his home in Tullyvallen, Newtownhamilton
L/CPL JEAN LEGGETT	6/04/76:	Ambushed and shot by IRA on patrol in Armagh
LT JOE WILSON	26/10/76:	Killed at work by the IRA
PTE MARGARET A. HEARST	8/10/77:	Murdered at home by IRA near Middletown
CAPT CHARLIE HENNING	6/10/78:	Shot by IRA whilst at work
L/CPL THOMAS ARMSTRONG	13/04/79:	Ambushed and killed by IRA on his way home
PTE JAMES PORTER	24/06/79:	Murdered at home by IRA
PTE JAMES H. HEWITT	10/10/80:	Killed by bomb under his car
L/CPL FREDDIE A. WILLIAMSON	7/10/82:	Killed with a woman prison officer in INLA-caused crash
SGT THOMAS G. COCHRANE	22/10/82:	Abducted and murdered by IRA
CPL CHARLIE H. SPENCE	10/11/82:	Shot by IRA as he left work in Armagh
CPL AUSTIN SMITH	19/12/82:	Shot by IRA after parking his car near home

MAJ CHARLIE ARMSTRONG	14/11/83:	Killed by IRA bomb in Armagh City
PTE STEPHEN MCKINNEY	25/09/88:	Murdered by IRA as he arrived home after quitting UDR
L/CPL DAVY HALLIGAN	17/11/89:	Shot by IRA as he drove home
PTE PAUL D SUTCLIFFE	1/03/91:	DoW after IRA mortar attack in Armagh
PTE ROGER J. LOVE	1/03/91:	DoW from same incident
PTE PAUL R. BLAKELY	31/05/91:	Killed in IRA bomb at the Glenane Base with two others
PTE SIDNEY HAMILTON	31/05/91:	Killed in same incident
L/CPL ROBERT W. CROZIER	31/05/91:	Killed in same incident

3rd Battalion

L/CPL JOE JARDINE	8/03/72:	Shot by IRA whilst working
CPL JIM D. ELLIOTT	19/04/72:	Abducted and murdered by IRA - body then booby-trapped by his killers
C/SGT JOHN RUDDY	10/10/72:	Shot by IRA on his way to work
PTE THOMAS MCCREADY	17/11/74:	Shot by the IRA in Newry
CPL CECIL GRILLS	12/01/78:	Shot by IRA as he drove home from work
PTE JIM COCHRANE	6/01/80:	Killed by IRA bomb at Castlewellen - one of three killed
PTE RICHARD SMITH	6/01/80:	Killed in same incident
PTE RICKY WILSON	6/01/80:	Killed in same incident
PTE COLIN H. QUINN	10/12/80:	Shot by INLA as he left work
MAJ W.E. IVAN TOOMBS	16/01/81:	Shot by IRA in Warrenpoint where he worked
L/CPL RICHARD W.J. MCKEE	24/04/81:	Shot by IRA at Kilcoo whilst on duty
CAPT GORDON HANNA	29/11/85:	Killed when IRA bomb exploded under his car at home
CPL D. BRIAN BROWN	28/05/86:	Killed by IRA bomb when searching after a warning
PTE ROBERT W. HILL	1/07/86:	Killed when IRA bomb exploded under his car at home
CPL ALAN T. JOHNSTON	15/02/88:	Shot by the IRA as he arrived for work
PTE W. JOHN MORELAND	16/12/88:	Shot in his coal lorry at Downpatrick
PTE MICHAEL D. ADAMS	9/04/90:	Killed by IRA landmine with three others at Downpatrick
L/CPL J (BRAD) BRADLEY	9/04/90:	Killed in same incident
PTE JOHN BIRCH	9/04/90:	Killed in same incident
PTE STEVEN SMART	9/04/90:	Killed in same incident

4th Battalion

PTE FRANK VEITCH	3/09/71:	Shot by IRA at Kinawley RUC Station
PTE JOHNNY FLETCHER	1/03/72:	Abducted and murdered by IRA in front of his wife
L/CPL W. HARRY CREIGHTON	7/08/72:	Murdered by IRA at his house near Monaghan
PTE JIMMY E. EAMES	25/08/72:	IRA booby-trapped car at Enniskillen
L/CPL ALFIE JOHNSTON	25/08/72:	Killed in same incident
PTE TOMMY R. BULLOCK	21/09/72:	Murdered along with his wife at their home
PTE J. ROBIN BELL	22/10/72:	Shot by IRA whilst with his father

PTE MATT LILLY	7/09/73:	Shot by the IRA on his milk round
PTE ALAN R. FERGUSON	25/06/78:	Killed in IRA landmine and gun attack
CPL HERBIE G. KERNAGHAN	15/10/79:	Shot by the IRA as he delivered to his school - witnessed by dozens of children
CPL AUBREY ABERCROMBIE	5/02/80:	Murdered by the IRA on his farm
PTE W. RITCHIE LATIMER	7/06/80:	Shot by the IRA at his hardware store
PTE NORMAN H. DONALDSON	25/11/80:	Shot by IRA as he collected charity money at RUC station whilst off duty
L/CPL RONNIE GRAHAM	5/06/81:	Shot by IRA as he delivered coal - one of three brothers murdered by IRA
PTE CECIL GRAHAM	11/11/81:	DoW after being shot by IRA at his wife's house
CPL ALBERT BEACOM	17/11/81:	Murdered by IRA at his home
PTE JIMMY GRAHAM BEM	1/02/85:	Shot in front of schoolchildren by IRA
PTE JOHN. F. EARLY	3/02/86:	IRA landmine
CPL JIMMY OLDHAM	3/04/86:	Shot by IRA gunmen as he arrived where he worked
CPL WILLIE BURLEIGH	6/04/88:	Killed by IRA bomb under his car

5th Battalion

CAPT MARCUS MCCAUSLAND	4/03/71:	Abducted and murdered by the IRA
PTE THOMAS CALLAGHAN	16/02/72:	Abducted and murdered in the Creggan, Londonderry
PTE SAMUEL PORTER	22/11/72:	Shot and killed by the IRA as he walked home
PTE GEORGE E. HAMILTON	20/12/72:	Shot by the IRA as he worked on repairs at a reservoir
CAPT JAMES HOOD	4/01/73:	Murdered by the IRA at home
SGT DAVID C.DEACON	3/03/73:	Abducted and murdered by the IRA
CPL JOHN CONLEY	23/07/74:	IRA car bomb in Bridge Street, Garvagh
PTE ROBERT STOTT	25/11/75:	Shot by the IRA on the way home from work
PTE JOHN ARRELL	22/01/76:	Shot on board his firm's minibus by IRA
PTE JACK MCCUTCHEON	1/04/76:	Shot at work by the IRA
S/SGT BOBBY H.LENNOX	2/04/76:	Postman - lured to an isolated farm and shot
CAPT W. RONNIE BOND	7/11/76:	Shot outside his home in Londonderry as he got home
L/CPL JIMMY SPEERS	9/11/76:	Shot by the IRA at his garage in Desertmartin
L/CPL WINSTON C. MCCAUGHEY	11/11/76:	Shot by the IRA as he stood outside his house in Kilrea
MAJ J. PETER HILL	23/02/77:	Shot by IRA as he got home from work, Londonderry
PTE DAVID MCQUILLAN	15/03/77:	Shot by IRA as he waited for a lift to work, Bellaghy
L/CPL GERALD C. CLOETE	6/04/77:	Shot by the IRA as he drove to work in Londonderry
LT WALTER KERR	2/11/77:	DoW after IRA bomb under his car
CPL WILLIAM J. GORDON	8/02/78:	Killed along with daughter (10) after IRA bomb exploded under their car
L/CPL SAMUEL D. MONTGOMERY	10/02/81:	Shot by the IRA as he left work
PTE T. ALAN RITCHIE	25/05/81:	Killed in IRA ambush at Gulladuff near Bellaghy
PTE ALLEN CLARKE	12/09/81:	Shot by IRA as he walked through Maghera
L/CPL BERNIE V. MCKEOWN	17/12/83:	Murdered by the IRA in front of his 13-year-old son in their car
PTE JAMES MCSHANE	22/01/84:	Death by violent or unnatural causes

SGT BOBBY F. BOYD	18/11/85:	Murdered by the IRA at his front door
SGT TOMMY A. JAMISON	8/03/90:	Ambushed and killed by the IRA at work
PTE MICKEY BOXALL	6/11/91:	Killed in IRA mortar attack at Bellaghy

6th Battalion

PTE WINSTON DONNELL	9/08/71:	First UDR man killed by the IRA - manning VCP at Clady, Tyrone
SGT KENNETH SMYTH	10/12/71:	Shot whilst off duty by the IRA
PTE TED MEGAHEY	9/06/72:	DoW after IRA shooting
PTE WILLIAM J. BOGLE	5/12/72:	Murdered in his car as he sat with his children
PTE ROBERT N. JAMESON	17/01/74:	Shot by IRA as he got off a bus at Trillick
PTE EVA MARTIN	3/05/74:	Killed by IRA in rocket and gun attack at Clogher
CPL W. DEREK KIDD	18/11/76:	Shot and killed at work
CPL WILLIAM J. MCKEE	14/04/78:	Shot and killed by gunmen as he drove a school bus
PTE JOHN GRAHAM	25/04/79:	Shot by the IRA as he collected milk from farms
PTE JOHN A. HANNIGAN	19/06/79:	Shot by IRA as he came out of a shop in Omagh
PTE JAMES A. ROBINSON	19/10/79:	Shot and killed on his milk round
PTE WILLIE J. CLARKE	3/08/80:	Shot in the Republic visiting relatives
L/CPL JOHNNY MCKEEGAN	19/11/81:	Lured to a house in Strabane and shot by IRA
LT J. LESLIE HAMILTON	27/04/82:	Shot whilst delivering to a Londonderry supermarket
PTE H. A. (LEXI) CUMMINGS	15/06/82:	Shot by IRA as he prepared to drive home from work
PTE RONNIE ALEXANDER	13/07/83:	One of four men killed by IRA landmine at Drumquin
PTE OSSIE NEELY	13/07/83:	Killed in same incident
PTE JOHN ROXBOROUGH	13/07/83:	Killed in same incident
CPL THOMAS HARRON	13/07/83:	Killed in same incident
CPL RONNIE D. FINDLAY	23/08/83:	Shot by IRA as he left work
PTE GREG ELLIOTT	2/01/84:	Shot as he got into his van at Castlederg
L/CPL THOMAS A. LOUGHLIN	2/03/84:	Killed by IRA bomb planted underneath his work's van
C/SGT IVAN E. HILLEN	12/05/84:	Shot and killed at his farm in Augher by IRA
CPL HEATHER.C. J. KERRIGAN	14/07/84:	One of two UDR killed in IRA landmine, Castlederg
PTE NORMAN J. MCKINLEY	14/07/84:	Killed in same incident
PTE W. VICTOR FOSTER	15/01/86	IRA bomb planted under his car at Castlederg
PTE THOMAS J. IRWIN	26/03/86:	Shot and killed by IRA at his work in Omagh
PTE WILLIAM C. POLLOCK	8/04/86:	Killed by IRA booby-trap at home in Castlederg
CAPT IVAN R.K. ANDERSON	21/05/87:	Shot by IRA as he drove home from his school
L/CPL MICHAEL DARCY	4/06/88:	Murdered at home by IRA in Castlederg
PTE OLVEN L. KILPATRICK	9/01/90:	Shot by IRA at his shoe shop in Castlederg

7th Battalion

PTE JOHN B. HOUSTON	29/11/75:	Shot at work by the IRA
PTE PETER MCLELLAND	04/09/79:	Killed at VCP
PTE JOHN D. SMITH	27/03/81:	Shot by IRA as he walked to work in Belfast
L/CPL DAVID WHEELER	11/08/91:	Death by violent or unnatural causes

8th Battalion

PTE W. DENNIS WILSON	7/12/71:	Murdered at home in Curlough
L/CPL HENRY GILLESPIE	20/05/72:	Shot by IRA patrolling near Dungannon
PTE FRED D. GREEVES	15/12/72:	Shot by IRA as he left work in Armagh
CPL FRANK CADDOO	10/05/73:	Shot by IRA at his farm in Rehagey
CAPT CORMAC MCCABE	19/01/74:	Abducted and murdered by IRA in Irish Republic
CPL ROY T. MOFFETT	3/03/74:	IRA landmine on Cookstown to Omagh Road
WO2 DAVID SINNAMON	11/04/74:	IRA bomb in house in Dungannon
PTE EDMUND R. L. STEWART	29/04/76:	Lured to relatives house and shot by IRA
L/CPL STANLEY D. ADAMS	28/10/76:	Lured to remote farmhouse as mailman and shot by IRA
PTE JOHN REID	9/03/77:	Ambushed and shot by IRA as he fed his cattle
CPL DAVY GRAHAM	25/03/77:	DoW after being shot at work by IRA, Gortonis
CAPT W. ERIC SHIELDS	29/04/77:	Shot by IRA outside his home in Dungannon
2ND/LT ROBIN SMYRL	13/09/77:	Shot by IRA as he drove to work at Plumbridge
PTE BOB J. BLOOMER	24/09/77:	DoW after being shot at home by IRA in Eglish
SGT JOCK B EAGLESHAM (MID)	7/02/78:	A postman, he was shot by IRA on his rounds
PTE G. SAMMY GIBSON	29/04/79:	Shot by IRA as he cycled to work in Tyrone
CPL FRED H. IRWIN	30/10/79:	Shot by IRA driving to work in Dungannon
PTE W. JACK DONNELLY	16/04/81:	Shot by INLA at his local pub in Moy
L/CPL CECIL W. MCNEILL	25/02/83:	Shot by IRA at his work in Tullyvannon
PTE ANDY F. STINSON	4/06/83:	Killed by INLA booby-trap on his digger at work
PTE CYRUS CAMPBELL	24/10/83:	Shot by IRA at Carnteel as he drove to farm
PTE N. JIMMY JOHNSTON	8/05/84:	Shot by IRA disguised as ambulance men at his hospital
PTE ROBERT BENNETT	7/09/84:	Shot by IRA at his work in Pomeroy
PTE TREVOR W. HARKNESS	28/02/85:	Killed by IRA bomb at Pomeroy on foot patrol
PTE MARTIN A. J. BLANEY	6/10/86:	Shot by IRA as he drove home in Eglish
MAJ GEORGE SHAW	26/01/87:	Murdered by IRA at his home in Dungannon
PTE WILLIE T. GRAHAM	25/04/87:	Shot by IRA at his farm in Pomeroy
CAPT TIM D ARRMSTRONG	16/01/88:	Murdered by unknown gunmen (Falklands veteran)
PTE JOHN STEWART	16/01/88:	DoW after being shot by IRA at his home in Coalisland
PTE NED GIBSON	26/04/88:	Shot by IRA as he worked on dustbins in Ardboe
PTE RAYMOND A. MCNICOL	3/08/88:	Shot by IRA as he drove to work in Desertcreat
PTE JOHN HARDY	14/03/89:	Shot by IRA as he drove his lorry to Granville
WO2 ALBERT D COOPER	2/11/90:	IRA bomb planted in car left at his garage in Cookstown

9th Battalion

SGT MAYNARD CRAWFORD	13/01/72:	Shot as he waited in a car at Newtownabbey
CPL ROY STANTON	9/06/72:	Shot by IRA as he drove home
PTE HENRY J. RUSSELL	13/07/72:	Abducted, tortured and shot by the IRA, Carrickfergus
CPL DAVID W. BINGHAM	16/01/73:	Abducted and killed by the IRA
PTE THOMAS J FORSYTHE	16/10/73:	Killed in a shooting accident

PTE STEVEN CARLETON	8/01/82:	Shot by the IRA at petrol station in Belfast
PTE LINDENCOLIN HOUSTON	20/01/84:	Murdered by the IRA at his home in Dunmurry

10th Battalion

PTE SEAN RUSSELL	8/12/71:	Murdered by IRA at his home, New Barnsley, Belfast
PTE SAMUEL TRAINOR	20/03/72:	IRA bomb, Belfast City Centre
PTE ROBERT MCCOMB	23/07/72:	Abducted and murdered by IRA in Belfast
PTE TERENCE MAGUIRE	14/10/72:	Abducted and murdered in Belfast
PTE WILLIAM L. KENNY	16/03/73:	Abducted and murdered on way to UDR barracks
CPL JOHN GEDDIS	10/05/77:	Killed by UVF in explosion in Crumlin Road, Belfast
L/CPL GERALD W. D. TUCKER	8/06/77:	Shot by IRA as he left work at Royal Victoria Hospital
CPL JAMES MCFALL	27/07/77:	Murdered by IRA at his home in Belfast
CPL HUGH A. ROGERS	8/09/77:	Shot by IRA as he left for work in Dunmurry
SGT ROBERT L. BATCHELOR	27/11/78:	Shot by IRA as he left work in Belfast
PTE ALEXANDER GORE	6/06/79:	Shot by IRA at UDR base, Malone Road, Belfast
PTE MARK A. STOCKMAN	29/09/81:	Shot by INLA at work in Belfast
SGT RICKY CONNELLY	21/10/81:	Murdered at his home by IRA, Belfast
PTE BILLY ACHESON	4/09/82:	Death by violent or unnatural causes
PTE ALEX YOUNG	1/10/84:	Death by violent or unnatural causes
PTE FRED GALLAGHER	3/10/84:	Death by violent or unnatural causes
LT DUNCAN CARSON	6/04/85:	Death by violent or unnatural causes

11th Battalion

L/CPL VICTOR SMYTH	6/09/72:	IRA bomb underneath his car in Portadown
2ND/LT R. IRWIN LONG	8/11/72:	Shot by IRA in Lurgan driving to collect his daughter
SGT ALFIE DOYLE	3/06/75:	He and two friends shot dead by IRA as they returned from a meeting in Irish Republic
PTE GEORGE LUTTON	15/11/76:	Shot by IRA on duty in Edward Street, Lurgan
PTE ROBERT J. MCNALLY	13/03/79:	Killed by INLA bomb under his car, Portadown
PTE S. DAVID MONTGOMERY	8/03/84:	Shot by IRA at his works, Moira on the Airport Road
PTE DAVID CHAMBERS	4/06/84:	Shot by IRA as he arrived for work, Dollingstown
PTE WILLIE R. MEGRATH	23/07/87:	Killed by IRA as he drove home to Lisburn
PTE COLIN J. MCCULLOUGH	23/09/90:	Shot by IRA as he sat in his car with fiancée, Lurgan

4-6th Battalion

L/CPL KENNY A. NEWELL	27/11/91:	Abducted and murdered by IRA at Crossmaglen

7-10th Battalion

SGT DENIS TAGGART	4/08/86:	Shot dead outside his home by IRA in Belfast
PTE JOE MCILLWAINE	12/06/87:	Shot by IRA at his work in Dunmurry
PTE G. JOHN TRACEY	26/06/87:	Shot by IRA at his work in Belfast
PTE STEVEN W MEGRATH	17/09/87:	Shot by IRA at his relatives' house
PTE JAMES CUMMINGS	24/02/88:	Killed by IRA bomb in Belfast City Centre
PTE FREDERICK STARRETT	24/02/88:	Killed in same incident
L/CPL ROY W BUTLER	2/08/88:	Shot dead by IRA in front of his family in West Belfast shopping centre

PTE BRIAN M LAWRENCE | 17/06/91: | Shot by IRA as he arrived for work, Belfast

UDR (Battalion Unknown)

PTE THOMAS WILTON	22/10/70:	Died on duty
PTE JOHN PROCTOR	24/10/70:	RTA
S/SGT GEORGE GILKESON	11/10/71:	RTA
CPL THOMAS ADDIS	4/12/71:	Unknown
PTE EDWARD BROWN	13/12/71:	Unknown
L/CPL PHILIP THOMPSON	31/12/71:	RTA
PTE THOMAS MOFFETT	26/02/72:	Cause of death unknown
PTE GEORGE CURRAN	12/03/72:	Cause of death unknown
PTE DONALD KANE	4/04/72:	Cause of death unknown
CPL BRIAN HERON	18/05/72:	Death by violent or unnatural causes
CPL SIDNEY HUSSEY	20/05/72:	Cause of death unknown
SGT WILLIAM REID	28/05/72:	Death by violent or unnatural causes
PTE WILLIAM WILKINSON	12/07/72:	Cause of death unknown
MAJ ERIC BEAUMONT	25/07/72:	Cause of death unknown
CPL ALBERT JOHNSTON	1/08/72:	Cause of death unknown
PTE ANDREW SIMPSON	18/09/72:	RTA
PTE THOMAS OLPHERT	6/10/72:	Cause of death unknown
PTE EDMUND SIMPSON	10/10/72:	Cause of death unknown
PTE ROBERT MCKEOWN	13/10/72:	RTA
SGT WILLIAM CALDERWOOD	15/10/72:	Cause of death unknown
MAJ JOHN MUNNIS	16/10/72:	RTA
PTE THOMAS BOYD	28/12/72:	Cause of death unknown
PTE JOHNSTONE BRADLEY	23/01/73:	Unknown
CPL PATRICK DAVIDSON	17/03/73:	Unknown
PTE ALEXANDER MCCONAGHY	10/04/73:	Unknown
PTE SAMUEL BEATTIE	14/04/73:	Unknown
L/CPL HUGH WATTON	24/05/73:	Unknown
PTE COLIN MCKEOWN	17/10/73:	RTA
PTE WILLIAM MAGILL	19/10/73:	Unknown
L/CPL THOMAS BEATTY	4/11/73:	Unknown
CPL WILLIAM MARTIN	20/11/73:	RTA
PTE DAVID SPENCE	20/11/73:	RTA
PTE EDWARD GIBSON	30/05/74:	Unknown
PTE NOEL SEELEY	26/06/74:	Unknown
PTE ROBERT RAINEY	27/07/74:	RTA
PTE SAMUEL WORKMAN	25/08/74:	RTA
PTE WILLIAM BELL	21/10/74:	Unknown
PTE ROBERT ALLEN	25/10/74:	Unknown
PTE JOHN S. MARTIN	18/11/74:	RTA
PTE JOHN TAYLOR	30/11/74:	RTA
PTE DAVID ARMSTRONG	28/01/75:	Unknown
PTE DAVID WEIR MCDOWELL	26/01/75:	Shot accidentally by a soldier in Co Armagh
S/SGT IVAN NIXON	31/03/75:	RTA

SGT WILLIAM MILLAR	19/09/75:	RTA
PTE WILLIAM KEITH DONNELL	13/11/75:	RTA
PTE DAVID MOSGROVE	21/11/75:	RTA
L/CPL JOHN NIBLOCK	20/12/75:	RTA
PTE WILLIAM OVENS	27/03/76:	RTA
CAPTAIN GEORGE CHAMBERS	14/04/76:	Cause of death unknown
L/CPL ROBERT MCCREEDY	24/04/76:	RTA
PTE ISAAC STEWART	6/05/76:	RTA
PTE JOHN SCOTT	30/07/76:	Killed by PIRA bomb, Druminard, Co Londonderry
LT JOHN HIGGINS	8/08/76:	RTA
W/PTE ANN GAYNOR	9/08/76:	RTA
CAPT ERIC SCOTT	28/08/76:	RTA
CPL WILLIAM DUNN	27/11/76:	RTA
SGT FREDERICK PULFORD	18/02/77:	RTA
PTE ROBERT PURDY	29/05/77:	RTA
PTE SAMUEL GREER	30/07/77:	Cause of death unknown
PTE RAYMOND MCFARLAND	31/08/77:	RTA
PTE ALAN MCFARLAND	31/08/77:	RTA
PTE WILSON PENNEY	21/09/77:	RTA
S/SGT ROBERT GALLOWAY	9/01/78:	Cause of death unknown
CPL JOHN HILLIS	13/02/78:	Cause of death unknown
PTE ROBERT REID	14/02/78:	Cause of death unknown
PTE GEORGE FLEMING	23/02/78:	Cause of death unknown
PTE NOEL PATTERSON	2/09/78:	Cause of death unknown
CPL ALISTAIR COOKE	19/09/78:	RTA
PTE TREVOR HERRON	4/12/78:	RTA
L/CPL THOMAS FORDE	9/01/79:	Cause of death unknown
PTE JOSEPH HOGG	1/03/79:	Cause of death unknown
PTE JAMES HUNTER	4/03/79:	Cause of death unknown
SGT PATRICK MCMULKIN	9/03/79:	Cause of death unknown
SGT THOMAS DOAK	13/03/79:	Cause of death unknown
L/CPL WILLIAM CRAWFORD	15/03/79:	Cause of death unknown
PTE VICTOR WILSON	30/03/79:	Cause of death unknown
PTE WILLIAM MORTON	29/04/79:	RTA
L/CPL IVAN MCCORKELL	8/06/79:	RTA
PTE NORMAN WYSNER	01/08/79:	Cause of death unknown
PTE ALAN MCCELLAND	4/09/79:	RTA
SGT JOSEPH AGNEW	15/09/79:	Cause of death unknown
WO2 JAMES WARNOCK	15/09/79:	Cause of death unknown
CPL ERNEST ATKINSON	23/09/79:	Cause of death unknown
CPL CECIL ROLESTON	26/09/79:	Cause of death unknown
CPL WILLIAM MCCROSSAN	29/10/79:	Cause of death unknown
PTE MERVYN DOHERTY	14/10/79:	Cause of death unknown
PTE HILARY GRAHAM	15/11/79:	RTA
PTE ARTHUR LANGLEY	5/12/79:	Cause of death unknown
PTE ALEXANDER ROWE	12/12/79:	RTA

SGT THOMAS MCCULLOCH	21/12/79:	Cause of death unknown
PTE GEORGE BROWN	27/12/79:	RTA
PTE ROBERT DAVISON	29/12/79:	Cause of death unknown
L/CPL SAMUEL KELLY	5/02/80:	Death by violent or unnatural causes
W/PTE MARY COCHRANE	28/02/80:	RTA
PTE CONSTANCE BEATTIE	25/09/80:	Cause of death unknown
LT DAVID PATTERSON	24/04/81:	RTA
PTE SAMUEL WHITESIDE	20/08/81:	RTA
L/CPL BRENDEN MCKEOWN	26/03/82:	RTA
PTE JONATHAN MOORHEAD	22/02/82:	Shot accidentally with own pistol
PTE BRIAN WALMSLEY	1/05/82:	RTA
PTE ALAN D MAULE	2/01/83:	Death by violent or unnatural causes
PTE KENNETH KELLY	14/04/83:	Died accidentally whilst boarding a helicopter
PTE LEONARD GREER	16/04/83:	RTA
PTE BRIAN KIRKPATRICK	1/10/83:	RTA
PTE ROBERT ALEXANDER IRWIN	21/12/83:	RTA
PTE FRAZER BROWN	22/01/84:	RTA
PTE SAMUEL JOSEPH BRADFORD	21/12/84:	RTA
PTE ALBERT BROWN	21/04/85:	RTA
PTE MERVYN SALMON	28/01/86:	RTA
PTE BRIAN NICHOLL	28/03/86:	RTA
PTE ROY ALLEN	26/06/86:	RTA
PTE ANDREW MONTGOMERY	30/06/86:	RTA
W/CPL CIARA OUSBY	20/07/86:	RTA
LT PAUL MAXWELL	4/08/86:	RTA
PTE JOHN MCKERAGHAN	14/03/87:	RTA
CPL JAMES ANDERSON	25/04/87:	RTA
PTE THOMAS AICKEN	11/08/87:	RTA
PTE CARL PEARCE	11/08/87:	RTA
PTE WILLIAM REILLY	8/11/87:	RTA
PTE FRANCIS GIBSON	26/04/88:	RTA
L/CPL THOMAS BAILIE	9/01/89:	Cause of death unknown
COL SGT WILLIAM PAGE	13/02/89:	Cause of death unknown
PTE THOMAS JONSTON	8/05/89:	RTA
STAFF SGT RIBERT MCKIMM	22/07/89:	Cause of death unknown
PTE JOHN GUNNING	5/09/89:	Cause of death unknown
PTE MATTHEW CHRISTIE	11/09/89:	RTA
PTE JOHN JENNINGS	25/09/89:	Cause of death unknown
PTE ALEXANDER PHOENIX	16/03/90:	Killed at a VCP, Summerisland Road, Loughall
PTE BRIAN CORDNER	4/11/90:	RTA
PTE DAVID WILLIAMSON	15/11/90:	RTA
PTE ALAN C. MCCONNELL	9/09/91:	RTA
SGT GEORGE ROLLINS	27/09/91:	RTA
W/PTE ELIZABETH SLOAN	13/04/92:	RTA in Ballymena area
PTE STEPHEN SCANLON	11/05/92:	RTA
L/CPL THOMAS MCDONNELL	8/06/97:	Violent or unnatural causes

The following UDR Soldiers were killed in accidents - places unknown

WO2 BERNARD ADAMSON	31/05/72
PTE GEORGE ELLIOTT	26/06/72
PTE WILLIAM HAMILTON	4/08/72
PTE KENNETH TWADDELL	5/08/72
PTE THOMAS I. MCCLELLAND	26/04/87
L/CPL DAVID GASS	16/06/88
PTE KEVIN HUTCHINGS	12/07/89

Ex Ulster Defence Regiment Soldiers Killed in Northern Ireland

MR D.J. MCCORMICK	10/12/71:	Shot by IRA on way to work
MR ISAAC SCOTT	10/07/73:	Shot by IRA in Belleek, Co Armagh
MR IVAN VENNARD	3/10/73:	Shot dead by IRA on his postal round, Lurgan
MR GEORGE SAUNDERSON	10/04/74:	Shot by IRA at his school in Co Fermanagh
MR WILLIAM HUTCHINSON	24/08/74:	Shot by IRA at work
MR GEORGE MCCALL	2/08/75:	Shot by IRA in Moy, Co Tyrone
MR KENNETH WORTON	5/01/76:	One of 10 men murdered in Kingsmill Massacre
MR NICOLAS WHITE	13/03/76:	Shot at youth club, Ardoyne, Belfast
MR SIDNEY MCAVOY	12/06/76:	Shot at his shop in Dunmurry
MR JOHN FREEBURN	28/06/76:	Shot in Lurgan
MR NORMAN CAMPBELL	15/12/76:	Joined RUC and shot in Portadown
MR ROBERT HARRISON	5/02/77:	RUCR: shot by IRA Gilford, Co Down
MR JOHN LEE	27/02/77:	Shot by IRA in club in Ardoyne, Belfast
MR JAMES GREEN	5/05/77:	Shot by IRA whilst working as a taxi driver, Belfast
MR GILBERT JOHNSTON	19/08/78:	Shot by IRA at his shop in Keady, Co Armagh
MR MICHAEL RILEY	19/08/78:	Shot at his home by IRA in Shankhill Road, Belfast
MR ROBERT LOCKHART	17/04/79:	RUCR: killed by IRA bomb at Camlough
MR JACK MCCLENAGHAN	19/05/79:	Shot by the IRA whilst delivering bread in Fermanagh
MR DAVID STANLEY WRAY	20/05/79:	Shot by IRA on his way to church in Claremont
MR DAVID ALAN DUNNE	2/06/79:	RUCR: shot by INLA in Armagh
MR GEORGE HAWTHORNE	5/10/79:	Shot by IRA in Newry
MR JAMES FOWLER	16/12/79:	Shot by IRA as he drove his fish van in Omagh
MR CLIFFORD LUNDY	2/01/80:	Shot at work by IRA near Bessbrook, Co Armagh
MR HENRY LIVINGSTONE	6/03/80:	Shot by IRA at his farm at Tynan, Co Armagh
MR VICTOR MORROW	17/04/80:	Shot by IRA at Newtownbutler, Co Fermanagh
MR WILLIAM ELLIOT	28/06/80:	Shot by IRA at cattle market in Ballybay, Co Monaghan
MR JOHN ROBINSON	23/04/81:	Shot by IRA driving works van in Armagh
MR PTE JOHN PROCTOR	14/09/81:	Shot by IRA at hospital after visiting his wife and newborn baby at Magherafelt
MR HECTOR HALL	5/10/81:	Shot by IRA outside Altnagelvin Hospital
MR CHARLES NEVILLE	10/11/81:	Shot by IRA at work in Co Armagh
MR JAMES MCCLINTOCK	18/11/81:	Shot by IRA on his way home from work, Londonderry
MR NORMAN HANNA	11/03/82:	Shot by IRA at his works in Newry

MR THOMAS CUNNINGHAM	12/05/82:	Shot by IRA whilst working in Strabane
MR WILFRED MCILVEEN	27/08/82:	IRA bomb underneath his car in Armagh
MR CHARLES CROTHERS	5/10/82:	Shot by IRA at Altnagelvin
MR JAMES GIBSON	2/12/82:	Shot by IRA driving school bus at Coalisland
MR JOHN TRUCKLE	20/09/83:	IRA bomb underneath his car in Portadown
MR RONALD FUNSTON	13/03/84:	Shot by IRA on his farm at Pettigoe, Co Fermanagh
MR HUGH GALLAGHER	3/06/84:	Taxi driver - he was lured by IRA to Omagh and shot
MR MELVIN SIMPSON	8/10/84:	Shot by IRA at work in Dungannon
MR DOUGLAS MCELHINNEY	24/02/85:	Shot by INLA at friend's house in Londonderry
MR GEOFFREY CAMPBELL	25/02/85:	RUCR: one of nine killed by IRA mortar attack, Newry
MR HERBET MCCONVILLE	15/05/86:	Shot dead by IRA whilst delivering in Newry
MR HARRY HENRY	21/04/87:	Murdered by IRA at his home in Magherafelt
MR CHARLES WATSON	22/05/87:	Murdered by the IRA at his home, Clough, Co Down
MR NATHANIEL CUSH	15/06/87:	IRA bomb underneath his car in Belfast
MR WINSTON G FINLAY	30/08/87:	Shot by IRA at his home in Ballyronan
MR JOHN GRIFFITHS	4/05/89:	IRA bomb underneath his car
MR ROBERT J GLOVER	15/11/89:	IRA bomb underneath his car near Dungannon
Mr DAVID STERRITT	24/07/90:	RUCR: killed with four others by IRA landmine, Armagh
MR DAVID POLLOCK	20/10/90:	Shot by an IRA sniper in Strabane
MR NORMAN KENDALL	10/11/90:	Murdered with three others by IRA, Castor Bay, Lurgan
MR HUBERT GILMORE	1/12/90:	Shot by IRA, Kilrea, Co Londonderry
MR ERIC BOYD	5/08/91:	Shot by IRA as he left work Cappagh, Co Tyrone
MR RONALD FINLAY	15/08/91:	Shot at work by the IRA, Co Tyrone
MR DAVID MARTIN	25/04/93:	IRA bomb underneath his car, Kildress, Co Tyrone
MR JOHN LYNESS	24/06/93:	Shot by IRA at his home in Lurgan
MR JOHN ALEXANDER BURNS	30/10/93:	Shot by UFF at Eglington
MR ALAN SMYTH	25/04/94:	Shot by IRA in Garvagh
MR ERIC SMYTH	28/04/94:	Shot by IRA at his home in Co Armagh
MR DAVID CALDWELL	1/08/02:	Working on army camp in Londonderry - killed by 'Real' IRA booby-trap

(David Cadwell's name - although outside the dates parameter - is included because it is believed that he was targeted by the 'Real' IRA because of his former UDR involvement)

Welsh Guards

SGT PHILIP PRICE	21/07/72:	IRA car bomb on 'Bloody Friday', Belfast Bus Depot
GUARDSMAN DAVID ROBERTS	24/11/73	Killed by IRA bomb, South Armagh
GUARDSMAN PAUL FRYER	13/11/79:	IRA bomb, Fords Cross, South Armagh
L/CPL MARK HOWELLS	12/07/92	RTA

Worcester & Sherwood Foresters

PTE MARTIN ROBINSON	16/04/72:	Killed in gun battle at Brandywell Base, Londonderry
PTE MARTIN JESSOP	20/09/82:	Killed in rocket attack, Springfield Road RUC Station

CPL LEON BUSH	27/09/82:	IRA booby-trap, West Circular Road, Belfast
CPL STEPHEN MCGONIGLE	4/05/89:	IRA landmine, Crossmaglen
L/CPL STEPHEN KENT	2/02/90:	RTA
CPL GARY KIRBY	2/02/90:	Killed in same accident
PTE DAVID PEAT	24/07/94:	Cause of death unknown

Women's Royal Army Corps

W/PTE ANN HAMILTON	5/10/74:	Killed with four others in IRA bomb outrage, Guildford
W/PTE CAROLINE SLATER	5/10/74:	Killed in same outrage
L/CPL ROBERTA THAIN	25/03/75:	Accidentally shot dead in Shipquay Street, Londonderry
W/SGT ALISON STRYKER	4/06/76:	RTA
W/PTE KATHRYN WATERLAND	16/08/79:	RTA
W/CPL ELAINE NEEDHAM	14/02/83:	RTA
W/PTE MARIA HORNSBY	11/12/84:	RTA
W/PTE KAREN R. COWAN	10/11/85:	RTA

* Att Intelligence Corps

** Members of the SAS

*** Members of 14 Int.

Security Services (date and cause of death withheld by MOD)

GE JOHN ROBERT DEVERELL-ANNE CATHERINE MACDONALD

CHARLES APCAR	12/08/74:	Death by violent or unnatural causes
MARTIN GEORGE DALTO		
ROBERT DEVERELL		
ANN CATHERINE MACDONALD		

Although on the ROH, the following people are not included in the total number of Military Deaths

Civilian Searchers

NORMA SPENCE	3/03/78:	Shot by IRA in Belfast City Centre by IRA
BRIAN RUSSELL	28/09/78:	Shot by IRA, Waterloo Place, Londonderry
JOHN STUART HAYNES		
STEPHEN LEWIS RICKARD		

The following Army Women and Children were also killed as a result of terrorism:

MRS EMILY BULLOCK	21/09/72:	Murdered by IRA, Aghalane
MRS LINDA HAUGHTON	4/02/74:	M62 Coach Bomb outrage
MASTER LEE HAUGHTON	4/02/74:	Killed in same outrage
MASTER ROBERT HAUGHTON	4/02/74:	Killed in same outrage
MR GORDON CATHERWOOD	30/10/74:	Killed by IRA sniper aiming at his UDR son and wife, North Belfast
MR KIERAN MCCANN	22/01/75:	Shot by IRA gunmen in Eglish, Co Tyrone
TREVOR FOSTER	8/11/81:	Killed by IRA bomb meant for his UDR father

MISS LESLEY GORDON	8/02/78:	Murdered with her daddy by IRA, Maghera
MRS IRIS FARLEY	7/02/87:	UDR mother - killed by INLA, Markethill, Armagh
HEIDI HAZELL	7/09/89:	Murdered by IRA, Unna-Messen, Germany
NIVRUTI MAHESKKUMAR	26/10/89:	Murdered with her daddy, Wildenrath, Germany

Army Civilian Personnel Killed in Aldershot IRA Bomb Outrage (22/02/72)

THELMA BOSLEY

JOAN LUNN

MARGARET GRANT

JILL MANSFIELD

JOHN HASLAR

CHERIE MUNTON

Army Civilian Workers Murdered in Terrorist Incidents

Noor Baz Khan	26/06/73:	Murdered by the IRA in Londonderry
John Dunn	11/01/74:	Murdered by the IRA, Waterside, Londonderry
Cecilia Byrne	11/01/74:	Murdered in the same incident
Donald Farrell	23/03/74:	Army careers officer - shot by IRA
Mohammed Abdul Khalid	22/04/74:	Murdered by the IRA at Crossmaglen
Hugh Slater	11/11/74:	Murdered by the IRA, Londonderry
Leonard Cross	11/11/74:	Murdered in same incident****
Patsie Gillespie:	24/10/91:	Killed by IRA at Coshquin in 'Proxy' Bomb
Brendan McWilliams	18/04/92:	Killed at home by IRA

**** Leonard Cross was a member of the Army Cadet Force and is also commemorated as such.

Former Army Personnel Killed as a Direct Consequence of the Troubles

Brian Shaw (ex-RGJ): Murdered by IRA in Lower Falls area   21/07/74

Nicholas White (ex-Queen's): Murdered by IRA in Ardoyne   13/03/76

John Lee (ex-Parachute Regiment): Murdered by IRA in Ardoyne 27/02/77

James Green (ex-Royal Irish Regiment): Shot by IRA whilst working as a taxi driver 5/05/77

Nigel Smyth (ex-Royal Artilery): Shot by IRA, Central Belfast 23/05/94

Petty Officer Frederick MacLaughlin: George Medal. He was severely wounded during the vicious rioting in the Crumlin/Ardoyne in June 1970. A gunshot wound injured his spine. Died as a direct result of a gunshot wound he received whilst driving an ambulance during severe rioting in North Belfast on 27 June 1970. He refused medical treatment until he had completed the evacuation of another gunshot victim. He was awarded the George Medal for his bravery that day. Frederick died on 27 June 1993 aged 61 - exactly 23 years to the day he was shot.

Other soldiers, military families and civilian workers were killed or died during their time in Northern Ireland and the author invites anyone with further knowledge of these people with regiments, dates or causes of death to contact him on: ken_wharton@hotmail.co.uk I apologise for any erroneous information, for missing names or for misspelled names.

I gratefully and wholeheartedly acknowledge the incredible services of Emma Beaumont, without whom the compiling of this comprehensive Roll of Honour could never have happened.

Great assistance by individual regimental associations was also given and I would like to mention Mike Sangster, Royal Artillery; Norman Brown of the Royal Pioneer Corps; Kevin Gorman of the Scots Guards; Kevin Stevens, Royal Green Jackets; the late Pete Whittall, Staffords; Richard Nettleton, Grenadier Guards; and Robert Osborne, QLR. I gratefully acknowledge the Armed Forces Memorial Roll of Honour and the Northern Ireland Veterans' Association for the ability to cross-reference between these two excellent sites.

RUC Roll of Honour 1969–98

Surname	Forename	Rank	Killed	By	How Killed
Arbuckle	Victor	Constable	11-Oct-1969	Loyalists	Shot dead during riot on Shankill Road
Donaldson	Sam	Constable	12-Aug-1970	IRA	Killed by booby-trap car bomb in Culloville, Crossmaglen
Millar	Robert	Constable	12-Aug-1970	IRA	Killed by booby-trap car bomb in Culloville, Crossmaglen
Buckley	Robert	Constable	28-Feb-1971	IRA	Shot dead during riots at Alliance Avenue, North Belfast
Patterson	Cecil	D/Inspector	28-Feb-1971	IRA	Shot dead during riots at Alliance Avenue, North Belfast
Leslie	Robert	Constable	18-Sep-1971	IRA	Shot and fatally wounded in Castle Place, Strabane
Cunningham	Cecil	Constable	15-Oct-1971	IRA	Shot dead in Ardoyne, Belfast
Haslett	John	Constable	15-Oct-1971	IRA	Shot dead in Ardoyne, Belfast
Dodd	Ronald	Sergeant	27-Oct-1971	IRA	Shot and fatally wounded at Gallagh, Toomebridge
Devlin	Alfred	Inspector	29-Oct-1971	IRA	Killed in bomb at Chichester Road RUC Station, Belfast
Corry	Stanley	D/Constable	1-Nov-1971	IRA	Shot dead in Andersonstown, Belfast
Russell	William	D/Constable	1-Nov-1971	IRA	Shot dead in Andersonstown, Belfast
Hurley	Dermot	Sergeant	11-Nov-1971	IRA	Fatally injured in gun attack on Oldpark Road, Belfast
Moore	Walter	Constable	11-Nov-1971	IRA	Fatally injured in gun attack on Oldpark Road, Belfast
Denham	Raymond	R/Constable	12-Jan-1972	IRA	Shot dead at his civilian employment in factory at Waterford Street, Belfast
Gilgunn	Peter	Sergeant	27-Jan-1972	IRA	Fatally wounded in gun attack at junction of Creggan Hill/Helen Street, Londonderry
Montgomery	David	Constable	27-Jan-1972	IRA	Fatally wounded in gun attack at junction of Creggan Hill/Helen Street, Londonderry
Carroll	Raymond	Constable	28-Jan-1972	IRA	Shot dead as he repaired his car in a garage on Oldpark Road, Belfast
Morrow	Thomas	Sergeant	2-Mar-1972	IRA	Died from gunshot wounds following gun attack in Newry Road, Camlough, County Armagh

Surname	Forename	Rank	Killed	By	How Killed
Logan	William	Constable	15-Mar-1972	IRA	Died from gunshot wounds following attack in Coalisland, Co Tyrone
McAllister	Ernest	Constable	20-Mar-1972	IRA	Killed by car bomb as they helped clear civilians from Donegal Street, Belfast
O'Neill	Bernard	Constable	20-Mar-1972	IRA	Killed by car bomb as they helped clear civilians from Donegal Street, Belfast
Houston	David	Constable	26-Jun-1972	IRA	Shot and fatally wounded in Newry. He was posthumously awarded the Queen's Police Medal
Laverty	Robert	Constable	16-Jul-1972	IRA	Fatally wounded during gun attack on Antrim Road, Belfast
Gibson	Robert	R/Constable	21-Jul-1972	IRA	Killed by car bomb at Oxford Street Bus Station
Harron	Gordon	Constable	21-Oct-1972	Loyalists	Died from gunshot wounds in attack at Shore Road Belfast. He was posthumously awarded the Queen's Police Medal
Calvin	Joseph	R/Constable	16-Nov-1972	IRA	Killed by booby-trap car bomb in Enniskillen
Keys	Robert	Constable	28-Nov-1972	IRA	Killed during rocket attack on Belleek RUC Station
Nixon	James	Constable	13-Dec-1972	IRA	Shot dead off duty as he left Antrim Road
Chambers	George	Constable	15-Dec-1972	Official IRA	Fatally injured in gun attack in Kilwilkie Estate, Lurgan, Co Armagh
Dorset	David	Sergeant	14-Jan-1973	IRA	Killed in booby-trap car bomb in Harbour Square, Londonderry
Sandford	Henry	R/Constable	14-Jan-1973	IRA	Fatally injured in a landmine explosion on Ballygawley/ Cappagh Road, Co Tyrone
Wilson	Mervyn	Constable	14-Jan-1973	IRA	Killed in booby-trap car bomb in Harbour Square, Londonderry
Morrison	Charles	Constable	8-Feb-1973	IRA	Shot dead in gun attack, Donaghmore, Dungannon, Co Tyrone
Wylie	Raymond	Constable	27-Feb-1973	IRA	Fatally wounded in gun attack at Aghagallon, Aghalee, Co Antrim. He was posthumously awarded Queen's Police Medal
McCauley	Robert	Constable	25-Mar-1973	IRA	Fatally wounded in gun attack at Aghagallon, Aghalee, Co Antrim. He was posthumously awarded Queen's Police Medal
Purvis	David	Constable	5-Jun-1973	IRA	Fatally wounded in gun attack in Enniskillen

Surname	Forename	Rank	Killed	By	How Killed
McElveen	William	R/Constable	13-Aug-1973	IRA	Fatally wounded in gun attack in Cathedral Road, Armagh
Campbell	William	R/Constable	16-Oct-1973	IRA	Fatally wounded in gun attack on Antrim Road, Belfast
Doherty	John	D/Constable	28-Oct-1973	IRA	Shot dead in gun ambush as he visited his mother's home at Ballindrait, Lifford, Co Donegal
Megaw	Robert	Constable	1-Dec-1973	IRA	Shot dead in gun attack at junction of Sloan Street/Edward Street, Lurgan
Rolston	Maurice	Constable	11-Dec-1973	IRA	Killed in booby-trap car bomb outside his home in Newcastle Co Down
Logue	Michael	Constable	29-Dec-1973	UDA	Fatally wounded in gun attack Forthriver Road, Belfast
Rogers	John	R/Constable	26-Jan-1974	IRA	Fatally wounded in gun attack in Glengormley, Co Antrim
Baggley	William	R/Constable	29-Jan-1974		Fatally wounded in gun attack in Dungiven Road, Londonderry
McClinton	Thomas	Constable	2-Mar-1974	IRA	Shot dead at point-blank range in Upper Donegal Street, Belfast
Wilson	Cyril	Constable	17-Mar-1974	Loyalists	Fatally wounded in gun attack at junction of Tullygally Road, Ardowne Roundabout, Craigavon, Co Armagh
Robinson	Frederick	Sergeant	19-Mar-1974		Killed by booby-trap car bomb at his home in Greenisland, Co Antrim
McCall	Thomas	Constable	16-Apr-1974	IRA	Fatally wounded in gun attack in Newtownhamilton, Co Armagh
Bell	Brian	Constable	10-May-1974	IRA	Fatally wounded in gun attack at Finaghy Cross Roads
Ross	John	Constable	10-May-1974	IRA	Fatally wounded in gun attack at Finaghy Cross Roads
Forsythe	John	Constable	18-Jun-1974	IRA	Killed by bomb in car of Market Street, Lurgan
O'Connor	Daniel	Sergeant	22-Jun-1974	IRA	Fatally wounded in gun attack in Crumlin Road, Belfast
Flanagan	Peter	D/Inspector	23-Aug-1974	IRA	Fatally wounded by gunmen who singled him out in premises in George's Street, Omagh
Elliott	William	Inspector	6-Sep-1974	IRA	Fatally wounded as he challenged armed raiders at bank in Rathcoole, Newtownabbey, Co Antrim. He was posthumously awarded the Queen's Police Medal
Henderson	Arthur	R/Constable	8-Oct-1974	IRA	Killed by booby-trap car bomb in Stewartstown, Co. Tyrone
Forde	Robert	Constable	20-Nov-1974	IRA	Killed by booby-trap car bomb in Rathmore, Craigavon, Co. Armagh

Surname	Forename	Rank	Killed	By	How Killed
McNeice	David	Constable	14-Dec-1974	IRA	Shot dead in gun attack at Killeavey, Co.Armagh
Coulter	George	Sergeant	31-Jan-1975	IRA	Shot dead in gun attacked at junction of Dungannon/Donaghmore Road, Co Tyrone
Harrison	Mildred	R/Constable	16-Mar-1975	UVF	Killed by bomb as she and a colleague performed beat duty in Bangor, Co Down
Gray	Paul	Constable	10-May-1975	IRA	Fatally wounded in gun attack on Derry's Wall, Londonderry
Davis	Noel	Constable	24-May-1975	INLA	Killed by booby-trap bomb in stolen vehicle at Ballinahone Road, Maghera, Co Londonderry
Johnston	Andrew	D/Constable	7-Jul-1975	IRA	Killed by booby-trap bomb as he examined the scene of a burglary at a school in Sloan Street, Lurgan
McPherson	Robert	Constable	26-Jul-1975	INLA	Fatally wounded in gun attack in Dungiven, Co Londonderry. He was posthumously awarded a Queen's Commendation for Bravery
Love	David	D/Constable	6-Oct-1975	IRA	Killed by booby-trap bomb at Terrydromond, Limavady, Co Londonderry
Baird	Andrew	R/Constable	14-Oct-1975	IRA	Fatally wounded by bomb placed at security hut at Church Street, Portadown
Clements	Joseph	R/Constable	16-Nov-1975	IRA	Fatally wounded in landmine explosion near Cloghfin, Sixmilecross, Co Tyrone
Clarke	Samuel	R/Constable	25-Nov-1975	IRA	Fatally wounded in gun attack at Clonavaddy, Dungannon, Co Tyrone
Maxwell	Patrick	Sergeant	25-Nov-1975	IRA	Fatally wounded in gun attack at Clonavaddy, Dungannon, Co Tyrone
Evans	Clifford	R/Constable	5-Jan-1976	IRA	Fatally wounded in gun attack between Toomebridge/Castledawson, Co Londonderry
Bell	George	Inspector	22-Jan-1976	Unknown	Killed by a booby-trap bomb at Donegal Pass RUC Station, Belfast
Cummings	Neville	Constable	22-Jan-1976	Unknown	Killed by a booby-trap bomb at Donegal Pass RUC Station, Belfast
Blakely	James	Sergeant	6-Feb-1976	IRA	Fatally injured in gun attack near Cliftonville Circus, Belfast
Murtagh	William	Inspector	7-Feb-1976	IRA	Fatally injured in gun attack near Cliftonville Circus, Belfast
Hamer	William	R/Constable	12-Feb-1976	IRA	Fatally wounded in gun attack in Claudy, Co Londonderry

Surname	Forename	Rank	Killed	By	How Killed
Crooks	William	R/Constable	23-Apr-1976	IRA	Fatally wounded in gun attack at Dernagh Crossroads, Coalisland, Co Tyrone
Evans	Thomas	R/Constable	15-May-1976	IRA	Fatally wounded when a booby-trap bomb exploded near Belcoo RUC Station, Co Fermanagh
Hunter	James	Sergeant	15-May-1976	IRA	Fatally wounded in gun attack near Warrenpoint, Co Down
Kettles	Francis	R/Constable	15-May-1976	IRA	Fatally wounded when a booby-trap bomb exploded near Belcoo RUC Station, Co Fermanagh
Keys	Harry	Sergeant	15-May-1976	IRA	Fatally wounded when a booby-trap bomb exploded near Belcoo RUC Station, Co Fermanagh
Nelson	Kenneth	R/Constable	16-May-1976	IRA	Shot dead as he let his dog out at his home at Dungannon, Co Tyrone
McCambridge	John	Constable	22-May-1976	IRA	Off duty, he was ambushed and shot dead as he stepped out of his car at Corrainey, Dungannon
Baggley	Linda	R/Constable	2-Jun-1976	IRA	Fatally injured in a gun attack in Chapel Road, Londonderry. Her father, who was also in the RUC, was killed in 1974
McAdam	Ronald	D/Constable	2-Jun-1976	IRA	Off duty, he was shot dead as he collected friends outside the Royal Victoria Hospital, Belfast
Cush	Thomas	Constable	31-Jul-1976	IRA	Shot dead at security barrier at Church Place, Lurgan
Heaney	James	Constable	26-Aug-1976		Off duty, he was working at his car at his mother's house in Andersonstown when he was fatally wounded in gun attack
Craig	Albert	Sergeant	18-Sep-1976	IRA	Fatally wounded in gun attack at Shamrock Park, Portadown
McKay	Arthur	R/Constable	8-Oct-1976	IRA	Killed in booby-trap bomb at Drumsaragh Road, Kilrea, Co Londonderry
McCabe	Noel	D/Constable	2-Nov-1976	IRA	Fatally wounded in gun attack at junction of Clonard Street/Falls Road, Belfast
Scott	Joseph	R/Constable	3-Dec-1976	IRA	Engaged in his civilian employment as traffic warden, he was shot dead at the junction of Circular Road/ Killyman Road, Dungannon, Co Tyrone
Campbell	Norman	Constable	15-Dec-1976	IRA	Fatally wounded in gun attack at High Street, Portadown
Armour	Samuel	R/Constable	22-Dec-1976	IRA	Killed when booby-trap bomb exploded underneath his car at Maghera, Co Londonderry

Surname	Forename	Rank	Killed	By	How Killed
Greer	James	R/Constable	14-Jan-1977	IRA	Killed by booby-trap car bomb at his home at Portglenone, Co Antrim
McNulty	Patrick	D/Constable	27-Jan-1977	IRA	Shot dead as he left his car for service at garage in Strand Road, Londonderry
Harrison	Robert	R/Constable	5-Feb-1977	IRA	Fatally wounded in gun attack in Gilford, Co Down
McKane	Samuel	R/Constable	17-Feb-1977	IRA	Fatally wounded in gun attack at his home at Cloughmills, Co Antrim
Cobb	Harold	Inspector	24-Feb-1977	IRA	Fatally wounded in gun attack at Church Place, Lurgan, Co Armagh
Campbell	Joseph	Sergeant	25-Feb-1977	Unknown	Shot dead as he closed the gates to Cushendall RUC Station, Co Antrim
Brown	William	Constable	13-Mar-1977	IRA	Fatally wounded in gun attack between Ballagh Crossroads and Lisnaskea, Co Fermanagh
McCracken	John	Constable	8-Apr-1977	IRA	Fatally wounded in gun attack on the Moneymore Road, Magherafelt, Co Londonderry
Sheehan	Kenneth	Constable	8-Apr-1977	IRA	Fatally wounded in gun attack on the Moneymore Road, Magherafelt, Co Londonderry
North	Robert	R/Constable	20-May-1977	IRA	Was engaged in his civilian employment as bus driver when he was fatally injured in gun attack at Drumderg, Benburb, Co Tyrone
Davison	Samuel	Constable	2-Jun-1977	IRA	Fatally wounded in gun attack at Ardboe, Co Tyrone
Lynch	Norman	Constable	2-Jun-1977	IRA	Fatally wounded in gun attack at Ardboe, Co Tyrone
Martin	Hugh	R/Constable	2-Jun-1977	IRA	Fatally wounded in gun attack at Ardboe, Co Tyrone
Morrow	David	R/Constable	6-Jul-1977	IRA	Fatally wounded in gun attack at Aughnacloy, Co Tyrone
Crothers	Gordon	R/Constable	17-Feb-1978	IRA	One of 12 people killed in blaze which followed a bomb explosion at the La Mon House, Castlereagh, Co Down
Simpson	Charles	Constable	28-Feb-1978	IRA	Fatally wounded in gun attack at Clarendon Street, Londonderry
Moore	John	R/Constable	15-Apr-1978	IRA	Killed by landmine under his car at his home near Armoy, Co Antrim
McAllister	Millar	Constable	22-Apr-1978	IRA	Shot dead at his home in Lisburn, Co Antrim
Struthers	Robert	R/Constable	16-Jun-1978	IRA	Shot dead at his civilian employment in shop at Lorne Street, Londonderry
McConnell	Hugh	Constable	17-Jun-1978	IRA	Fatally wounded during gun attack on Camlough/Crossmaglen Road

Surname	Forename	Rank	Killed	By	How Killed
Turbitt	William	A/Constable	17-Jun-1978	IRA	Abducted after gun attack on Camlough/Crossmaglen Road. His body was recovered three weeks later at Cullyhanna
Rankin	Jacob	R/Constable	4-Jul-1978	IRA	Fatally wounded in gun attack outside Castlederg RUC Station
Lamont	John	R/Constable	2-Aug-1978	IRA	Fatally wounded in gun attack in George Street, Ballymena
Donaghy	Howard	R/Constable	11-Sep-1978	IRA	Off duty, he was fatally wounded as he worked at his house at Loughmacroary, Omagh
Baird	Richard	Constable	17-Apr-1979	IRA	Killed in a booby-trap van bomb at Millvale Road, between Bessbrook and Newry
Gray	Paul	Constable	17-Apr-1979	IRA	Killed in a booby-trap van bomb at Millvale Road, between Bessbrook and Newry
Lockhart	Robert	R/Constable	17-Apr-1979	IRA	Killed in a booby-trap van bomb at Millvale Road, between Bessbrook and Newry
Webb	Noel	Constable	17-Apr-1979	IRA	Killed in a booby-trap van bomb at Millvale Road, between Bessbrook and Newry
Prue	Norman	D/Constable	6-May-1979	IRA	Shot dead outside Holy Cross Chapel, Chapel Brae, Lisnaskea
Wray	Stanley	R/Constable	20-May-1979	IRA	Fatally wounded in gun attack as he and his family arrived to attend morning service at Claremont Presbyterian Church, Londonderry
Dunne	Alan	R/Constable	2-Jun-1979	INLA	Fatally wounded in gun attack outside his home in Armagh
Hanna	Stanley	Superintendent	3-Jun-1979	IRA	Killed by bomb near community centre, Clonalig, Crossmaglen
Thompson	Keith	Constable	3-Jun-1979	IRA	Killed by bomb near community centre, Clonalig, Crossmaglen
Scott	John	R/Constable	22-Jun-1979	IRA	Engaged in his civilian employment, he was fatally wounded in gun attack at Ardboe, Coagh
Walsh	George	Constable	31-Jul-1979	INLA	Fatally wounded in gun attack outside Armagh Courthouse
Davidson	Derek	Constable	2-Aug-1979	IRA	Fatally wounded in gun attack at Clondara Street, Falls Road, Belfast
Davidson	Gerry	Constable	18-Nov-1979	IRA	Fatally wounded in gun attack at Springfield Road RUC Station, Belfast
Hazelton	Stanley	R/Constable	22-Dec-1979	IRA	Off duty, he was fatally wounded in gun ambush at Glasslough, Co Monaghan
Crilly	Robert	R/Constable	3-Jan-1980	IRA	Fatally wounded in gun attack in Newtownbutler, Co Fermanagh

Surname	Forename	Rank	Killed	By	How Killed
Purse	David	R/Constable	12-Jan-1980	IRA	Fatally wounded in gun attack at Seaview Football Club, Shore Road, Belfast
Howe	Winston	Constable	11-Feb-1980	IRA	Killed in landmine explosion, Lisnaskea
Rose	Joseph	Constable	11-Feb-1980	IRA	Killed in landmine explosion, Lisnaskea
Montgomery	Bernard	R/Constable	4-Apr-1980	IRA	Fatally wounded in gun attack at Ligoniel, Belfast
Magill	Stephen	Constable	9-Apr-1980	IRA	Fatally wounded in gun attack at Stewartstown Road, Belfast
Wilson	Fred	R/Constable	11-Apr-1980	IRA	Shot dead as he arrived at his civilian employment in Franklyn Street, Belfast
Allen	Wallace	R/Constable	1-Sep-1980	IRA	Ambushed and abducted as he drove his milk lorry in Newtownhamilton area. His body was recovered 12 days later
Johnston	Ernest	R/Constable	22-Sep-1980	IRA	Fatally wounded in gun attack outside his home at Lisrace, Magheraveely, Co Fermanagh
McDougall	Lindsay	R/Constable	14-Jan-1981	INLA	Fatally wounded in gun attack in Great Victoria Street, Belfast
Stronge	James	R/Constable	21-Jan-1981	IRA	Fatally wounded in gun attack at his home, Tynan Abbey, Co Armagh
Lewis	Charles	R/Constable	6-Feb-1981	IRA	Fatally wounded in gun attack at Balmoral Avenue, Belfast
Scott	Alexander	R/Constable	8-Feb-1981	IRA	Fatally wounded in gun attack outside his wife's shop at My Lady's Road, Belfast
Acheson	Kenneth	Constable	2-Apr-1981	IRA	Fatally wounded in booby-trap car bomb at Berrywilligan Road, Bessbrook
Martin	Gary	Constable	27-Apr-1981	INLA	Killed in booby-trap bomb at Shaw's Road, Belfast
Ellis	Philip	Constable	6-May-1981	IRA	Fatally wounded in gun attack at Edlingham Street/Duncairn Gardens, Belfast
Vallely	Samuel	Constable	14-May-1981	IRA	Fatally wounded in rocket grenade attack at Upper Springfield Road, Belfast
Robinson	Mervyn	Constable	28-May-1981	IRA	Off duty, he was shot dead at Whitecross, Co Armagh
Dunlop	Colin	R/Constable	31-May-1981	IRA	Shot dead while he was on security duty at intensive care unit, Royal Victoria Hospital
Kyle	Christopher	R/Constable	17-Jun-1981	IRA	Off duty, he was fatally wounded in gun attack at his home near Omagh
Quinn	Neal	Constable	20-Jun-1981	IRA	Off duty, he was fatally wounded in gun attack in North Street, Newry

Surname	Forename	Rank	Killed	By	How Killed
Smyth	John	Constable	2-Aug-1981	IRA	Killed when a landmine exploded near Loughmacrory, Omagh
Woods	Andrew	Constable	2-Aug-1981	IRA	Killed when a landmine exploded near Loughmacrory, Omagh
Evans	Mark	Constable	7-Sep-1981	IRA	Killed in landmine explosion near Pomeroy
Montgomery	John	Constable	7-Sep-1981	IRA	Killed in landmine explosion near Pomeroy
Proctor	John	R/Constable	14-Sep-1981	IRA	Off duty, he was visiting his wife who had just given birth in the Mid Ulster Hospital, Magherafelt when he was shot dead
Stewart	George	Constable	26-Sep-1981	IRA	Off duty, he was fatally wounded in a gun attack at Main Street, Killough, Co Down
Beck	Alexander	Constable	28-Sep-1981	IRA	Fatally wounded when his Land Rover was hit by a rocket at Suffolk Road, Belfast
Lyttle	Silas	R/Constable	17-Nov-1981	IRA	Off duty, he was fatally wounded in gun attack outside his home at Grange, Ballygawley
Coulter	William	Constable	28-Nov-1981	IRA	Fatally wounded by booby-trap bomb at Unity Flats, Belfast
Duddy	Norman	Inspector	28-Mar-1982	IRA	Fatally wounded in gun attack as he and his sons left Strand Road Presbyterian Church, Londonderry
Brown	David	Sergeant	16-Apr-1982	IRA	Fatally wounded in gun attack at Springfield Crescent, Belfast
Caskey	Samuel	Constable	4-May-1982	IRA	Fatally wounded in gun attack at the Diamond, Londonderry
Reeves	David	D/Constable	11-Jun-1982	IRA	Killed by booby-trap bomb at Shantallow, Londonderry
Eagleson	John	R/Constable	1-Oct-1982	IRA	Fatally wounded in gun attack on way to his civilian employment in Upper Kildress Road, Cookstown
Crothers	Charles	R/Constable	5-Oct-1982	IRA	Fatally wounded in gun attack at his civilian employment at Altnagelvin, Londonderry
Hamilton	Paul	Constable	27-Oct-1982	IRA	Killed by bomb at Kinnego Embankment, Lurgan
McCloy	Allan	Constable	27-Oct-1982	IRA	Killed by bomb at Kinnego Embankment, Lurgan
Quinn	John	Sergeant	27-Oct-1982	IRA	Killed by bomb at Kinnego Embankment, Lurgan
Ewing	Gary	Constable	9-Nov-1982	IRA	Off duty, he was fatally wounded when a booby-trap bomb exploded under his car near the Lakeland Forum, Enniskillen
Corkey	Snowdon	R/Constable	16-Nov-1982	INLA	Fatally wounded in gun attack in Newry Street, Markethill

Surname	Forename	Rank	Killed	By	How Killed
Irwin	Ronald	R/Constable	16-Nov-1982	INLA	Fatally wounded in gun attack in Newry Street, Markethill
Brown	Eric	Sergeant	6-Jan-1983	IRA	Fatally wounded in gun attack at the Square, Rostrevor
Quinn	Brian	R/Constable	6-Jan-1983	IRA	Fatally wounded in gun attack at the Square, Rostrevor
Olphert	John	R/Constable	18-Jan-1983	IRA	Was serving customers in his shop at Sperrin Park, Londonderry when he was shot dead by gunmen
Magill	Edward	R/Constable	20-Feb-1983	IRA	Fatally wounded in gun attack at Warrenpoint RUC Station
Wilson	Gordon	Sergeant	21-Feb-1983	IRA	Fatally injured by booby-trap bomb at Lower English Street, Armagh
McCormack	Lindsay	Constable	2-Mar-1983	IRA	Fatally wounded in gun attack at Serpentine Road, Belfast
Morton	Frederick	R/Constable	15-Mar-1983	IRA	Was driving his bread van at Portadown Road, Newry when he was fatally wounded in gun attack
Cathcart	Gerald	Constable	16-May-1983	IRA	Fatally wounded in gun attack at Linkview Park, Belfast
Carson	Colin	R/Constable	26-May-1983	INLA	Fatally wounded in gun attack at Molesworth Estate, Cookstown
Wasson	John	Constable	7-Sep-1983	INLA	Fatally wounded in gun attack outside his home at Cathedral Road, Armagh
Ferguson	James	R/Constable	6-Oct-1983	IRA	Fatally wounded in gun attack at Meadowlands Estate, Downpatrick
Finlay	William	R/Constable	6-Oct-1983	IRA	Fatally wounded in gun attack at Meadowlands Estate, Downpatrick
Hallawell	John	Constable	28-Oct-1983	IRA	Fatally wounded in gun attack at Sheelin Park, Shantallow, Londonderry
Clarke	Paul	Constable	1-Nov-1983	IRA	Fatally injured in mortar attack at Carrickmore RUC Station
Fyfe	Stephen	Sergeant	4-Nov-1983	IRA	Fatally wounded by a bomb as he attended a lecture at the Ulster Polytechnic, Jordonstown
Martin	John	Inspector	4-Nov-1983	IRA	Fatally wounded by a bomb as he attended a lecture at the Ulster Polytechnic, Jordonstown
McFadden	John	R/Constable	5-Nov-1983	IRA	Fatally wounded in gun attack outside his home in Rasharkin
Fitzpatrick	William	R/Constable	10-Nov-1983	IRA	Fatally wounded in gun attack at his home near Kilkeel
Fullerton	William	R/Constable	10-Jan-1984	IRA	Fatally wounded in gun attack at Greenbank Roundabout outside Newry
Bingham	Thomas	Constable	31-Jan-1984	IRA	Killed by a landmine on the Newry/Forkhill Road

Surname	Forename	Rank	Killed	By	How Killed
Savage	William	Sergeant	31-Jan-1984	IRA	Killed by a landmine on the Newry/Forkhill Road
Dawson	Michael	Constable	12-Apr-1984	Loyalists	Killed by booby-trap bomb at University Street, Belfast
Elliott	Trevor	R/Constable	18-May-1984	IRA	Fatally injured in landmine explosion on the Camlough/Crossmaglen Road
Gray	Neville	Constable	18-May-1984	IRA	Fatally injured in landmine explosion on the Camlough/Crossmaglen Road
Todd	Michael	Constable	15-Jun-1984	INLA	Fatally wounded in gun attack at Lenadoon Avenue, Belfast
White	Malcolm	Sergeant	12-Aug-1984	IRA	Fatally injured by landmine on Gortin/Greencastle Road
McDonald	William	Sergeant	4-Nov-1984	IRA	Died as a result of injuries sustained in bomb attack at the Ulster Polytechnic, 1983
Campbell	Geoffrey	R/Constable	28-Feb-1985	IRA	Fatally wounded in mortar attack on Newry RUC Station
Donaldson	Alexander	C/Inspector	28-Feb-1985	IRA	Fatally wounded in mortar attack on Newry RUC Station
Dowd	John	Sergeant	28-Feb-1985	IRA	Fatally wounded in mortar attack on Newry RUC Station
Kelly	Ivy	Constable	28-Feb-1985	IRA	Fatally wounded in mortar attack on Newry RUC Station
McFerran	Paul	R/Constable	28-Feb-1985	IRA	Fatally wounded in mortar attack on Newry RUC Station
McGookin	Rosemary	Constable	28-Feb-1985	IRA	Fatally wounded in mortar attack on Newry RUC Station
McHenry	Sean	R/Constable	28-Feb-1985	IRA	Fatally wounded in mortar attack on Newry RUC Station
Price	Denis	R/Constable	28-Feb-1985	IRA	Fatally wounded in mortar attack on Newry RUC Station
Topping	David	Constable	28-Feb-1985	IRA	Fatally wounded in mortar attack on Newry RUC Station
McCormac	Hugh	Sergeant	3-Mar-1985	IRA	Fatally wounded in gun attack as he and his family attended Mass in Enniskillen
Bell	John	R/Constable	29-Mar-1985	IRA	Fatally wounded in gun attack at Rathfriland
Kay	Michael	R/Constable	3-Apr-1985	IRA	Killed by booby-trap outside Newry Courthouse
Baird	David	Constable	20-May-1985	IRA	Killed by bomb at Killeen Customs post
Doak	Tracey	Constable	20-May-1985	IRA	Killed by bomb at Killeen Customs post
Rodgers	Steven	R/Constable	20-May-1985	IRA	Killed by bomb at Killeen Customs post

Surname	Forename	Rank	Killed	By	How Killed
Wilson	William	Inspector	20-May-1985	IRA	Killed by bomb at Killeen Customs post
Murphy	Francis	Sergeant	21-May-1985	IRA	Fatally wounded in gun attack as he dropped schoolchildren at Drumsallon Primary School
Agnew	William	R/Constable	16-Jun-1985	IRA	Off duty, he was fatally wounded in gun attack as he sat in his car with his fiancée in Kilrea, Co Londonderry
Gilliland	William	Constable	18-Jun-1985	IRA	Fatally wounded by bomb at Kinawley Road, Co Fermanagh
Vance	Martin	Inspector	31-Aug-1985	IRA	Off duty, he was fatally wounded in gun attack at Crossgar, Co Down
Hanson	David	Constable	15-Nov-1985	IRA	Killed by landmine explosion at Castleblaney Road, Crossmaglen
Clements	William	R/Constable	7-Dec-1985	IRA	Fatally wounded in gun attack on Ballygawley RUC Station
Gilliland	George	Constable	7-Dec-1985	IRA	Fatally wounded in gun attack on Ballygawley RUC Station
McCandless	James	Constable	1-Jan-1986	IRA	Killed by bomb at Ogle Street, Armagh
Williams	Michael	R/Constable	1-Jan-1986	IRA	Killed by bomb at Ogle Street, Armagh
Breen	Derek	D/Constable	11-Feb-1986	IRA	Fatally wounded in gun attack in Maguirebridge, Co Fermanagh
Hazlett	James	Inspector	23-Apr-1986	IRA	Fatally wounded in gun attack outside his home in Newcastle, Co Down
McBride	David	Constable	22-May-1986	IRA	Killed by a bomb at Larkin's Road, Crossmaglen
Smyth	William	Constable	22-May-1986	IRA	Killed by a bomb at Larkin's Road, Crossmaglen
McVitty	John	A/Constable	8-Jul-1986	IRA	Fatally injured in gun attack as he cut rushes on his farm at Drumady, Rosslea, Co Fermanagh
Allen	Charles	Constable	26-Jul-1986	IRA	Fatally injured in gun attack in Market Square, Newry
Blackbourne	Karl	Constable	26-Jul-1986	IRA	Fatally injured in gun attack in Market Square, Newry
Kilpatrick	Peter	Sergeant	26-Jul-1986	IRA	Fatally injured in gun attack in Market Square, Newry
Dobbin	Desmond	R/Constable	12-Oct-1986	IRA	Fatally injured in mortar attack on New Barnsley RUC Station
Patterson	Derek	Constable	10-Nov-1986	IPLO	Fatally wounded in gun attack at Fitzroy Avenue, Belfast
Crawford	Ivan	R/Constable	9-Jan-1987	IRA	Fatally wounded in bomb explosion in centre of Enniskillen
Nesbitt	Peter	R/Constable	10-Mar-1987	IRA	Fatally wounded in bomb explosion at Ardoyne, Belfast

Surname	Forename	Rank	Killed	By	How Killed
Bennison	John	D/Sergeant	23-Mar-1987	IRA	Killed in booby-trap explosion at Magee College, Londonderry
Wilson	Austin	D/Inspector	23-Mar-1987	IRA	Killed in booby-trap explosion at Magee College, Londonderry
Shaw	George	R/Constable	3-Apr-1987	IRA	Fatally wounded in gun attack on Ballynahinch RUC Station
Armstrong	Frederick	R/Constable	11-Apr-1987	IRA	Fatally wounded in gun attack at Portrush
McLean	Robert	R/Constable	11-Apr-1987	IRA	Fatally wounded in gun attack at Portrush
Ead	David	Inspector	20-Apr-1987	IRA	Fatally injured in gun attack outside Newcastle RUC Station
Cooke	Thomas	Sergeant	23-Apr-1987	IRA	Fatally wounded in gun attack as he left his golf club in Londonderry
McClean	Sam	Constable	2-Jun-1987	IRA	Fatally wounded in gun attack as he worked on the farm of his elderly parents at Drumbreen, Co Donegal
Guthrie	Robert	Sergeant	23-Jun-1987	IRA	Fatally wounded in gun attack outside Antrim Road RUC Station
Kennedy	Norman	Constable	26-Jul-1987	IRA	Shot dead in his Ballymena home as he watched television with his wife
Carson	Ernest	D/Constable	26-Aug-1987	IRA	Fatally wounded in gun attack in docks area of Belfast
Malone	Michael	D/Constable	26-Aug-1987	IRA	Fatally wounded in gun attack in docks area of Belfast
Finlay	Winston	R/Constable	30-Aug-1987	IRA	Was getting out of his car - driven by his wife - outside his home near Magherafelt when he was shot dead by gunmen
Armstrong	Edward	R/Constable	8-Nov-1987	IRA	Killed in the Enniskillen Poppy Day bomb
Gilmore	Colin	R/Constable	25-Jan-1988	IRA	Fatally wounded in drogue bomb attack at Falls Road, Belfast
Graham	Clive	Constable	21-Mar-1988	IRA	Fatally wounded in gun attack in Creggan, Londonderry
Warnock	John	D/Constable	2-Aug-1988	IRA	Killed by booby-trap bomb near Lisburn RUC Station
Larmour	John	Constable	11-Oct-1988	IRA	Shot dead as he worked in his brother's ice cream shop on the Lisburn Road, Belfast
McCrone	Hugh	R/Constable	26-Oct-1988	IRA	Fatally wounded in gun attack near Kinawley, Co Fermanagh
Monteith	William	R/Constable	21-Nov-1988	IRA	Fatally wounded in gun attack at town barrier in Castlederg
Montgomery	Stephen	Constable	28-Jan-1989	IRA	Fatally wounded in drogue bomb attack at Melmont Road, Sion Mills
Breen	Harry	C/Superintendent	20-Mar-1989	IRA	Fatally wounded in gun attack at Jonesborough as he returned from Dundalk Garda Station

Surname	Forename	Rank	Killed	By	How Killed
Buchanan	Robert	Superintendent	20-Mar-1989	IRA	Fatally wounded in gun attack at Jonesborough as he returned from Dundalk Garda Station
Black	David	R/Constable	27-Jun-1989	IRA	Fatally wounded by booby-trap bomb under his car in Londonderry
Annett	Norman	Constable	1-Jul-1989	IRA	Fatally injured in gun attack on his mother's home in Garvagh
Bell	Alexander	R/Constable	24-Jul-1989	IRA	Fatally injured in bomb attack between Waterfoot and Cushendall
Harris	Alwyn	Superintendent	8-Oct-1989	IRA	Fatally injured by booby-trap bomb under his car as he and his wife travelled to church
Marshall	Michael	Constable	20-Oct-1989	IRA	Fatally wounded in gun attack in Belleek
Monteith	Derek	Inspector	22-Jan-1990	IRA	Fatally wounded in gun attack on his home in Armagh
Starrett	George	R/Constable	28-Mar-1990	IRA	Fatally wounded in gun attack on his home in Armagh
Beckett	Harry	Constable	30-Jun-1990	IRA	Fatally wounded in gun attack in Queen Street/ Castle Street, Belfast
Meyer	Gary	Constable	30-Jun-1990	IRA	Fatally wounded in gun attack in Queen Street/ Castle Street, Belfast
Hanson	William	Constable	24-Jul-1990	IRA	Killed in landmine explosion between Armagh and Caledon, Co Armagh
Sterritt	David	R/Constable	24-Jul-1990	IRA	Killed in landmine explosion between Armagh and Caledon, Co Armagh
Willis	Cyril	R/Constable	24-Jul-1990	IRA	Killed in landmine explosion between Armagh and Caledon, Co Armagh
Robinson	Louis	D/Constable	16-Sep-1990	IRA	Abducted as he travelled back across the border after a fishing trip to the south. His body was found two days later near Killeen, Co Armagh
Todd	Samuel	Constable	15-Oct-1990	IRA	Fatally wounded in gun attack in High Street, Belfast
Murphy	David	D/Inspector	10-Nov-1990	IRA	Fatally wounded in a gun attack on the shore of Lough Neagh
Taylor	Thomas	R/Constable	10-Nov-1990	IRA	Fatally wounded in a gun attack on the shore of Lough Neagh
Wethers	Wilfred	R/Constable	20-Dec-1990	IRA	Fatally wounded in gun attack at Banbridge Road, Lurgan
Mcgarry	Spence	D/Constable	6-Apr-1991	IRA	Killed by booby-trap bomb under his car in Ballycastle, Co Antrim
McCrum	Samuel	Sergeant	13-Apr-1991	IRA	Fatally wounded in gun attack in Lisburn, Co Antrim
Gillespie	Stephen	Sergeant	2-May-1991	IRA	Fatally wounded in gun and rocket attack in West Belfast

Surname	Forename	Rank	Killed	By	How Killed
Carrothers	Douglas	R/Constable	17-May-1991	IRA	Killed by booby-trap bomb under his car at driveway of his home in Lisbellaw, Co Fermanagh
Spence	Edward	Constable	26-May-1991	IRA	Fatally wounded in gun attack at Lower Crescent, Belfast
Clarke	Erik	Constable	17-Sep-1991	IRA	Fatally wounded in rocket attack in Swatragh, Co Londonderry
McMurray	Colleen	Constable	28-Mar-1992	IRA	Fatally wounded in mortar attack on Newry
Douglas	James	Constable	10-Oct-1992	IRA	Off duty, he was shot dead in gun attack in Belfast City Centre
Corbett	Alan	R/Constable	15-Nov-1992	IRA	Fatally wounded in gun attack in Main Street, Belcoo
Ferguson	Michael	Constable	23-Jan-1993	IRA	Fatally wounded in gun attack at Richmond Centre, Londonderry
Williamson	Reginald	Constable	24-Feb-1993	IRA	Killed by booby-trap bomb under his car near Moy, Co Tyrone
Reid	Jonathan	Constable	25-Mar-1993	IRA	Shot dead by sniper in Crossmaglen, Co Armagh
Woods	Brian	R/Constable	2-Nov-1993	IRA	Shot dead by sniper near Newry RUC Station
Beacom	William	Constable	12-Dec-1993	IRA	Fatally wounded in gun attack in Fivemiletown, Co Fermanagh
Smyth	Ernest	R/Constable	12-Dec-1993	IRA	Fatally wounded in gun attack in Fivemiletown, Co Fermanagh
Beacom	Johnston	Constable	17-Feb-1994	IRA	Killed in rocket attack in Markets area of Belfast
Haggan	Jackie	Constable	12-Mar-1994	IRA	Shot dead while having a drink with his wife at Dunmore Greyhound Stadium
Pollock	Gregory	Constable	20-Apr-1994	IRA	Killed in mortar attack in Spencer Road, Londonderry
Seymour	Jim	Constable	2-Mar-1995	IRA	Died having been in a coma for 22 years following a gun attack on Coalisland RUC Station on 4 May 1973
Bradshaw	Darren	Constable	9-May-1997	IRA	Off duty, he was shot dead in a city centre bar in Belfast
Taylor	Greg	Constable	1-Jun-1997	Loyalists	Beaten to death outside bar in Ballymoney
Graham	John	Constable	16-Jun-1997	IRA	Shot dead while on patrol in Lurgan Town Centre
Johnston	David	R/Constable	16-Jun-1997	IRA	Shot dead while on patrol in Lurgan Town Centre
O'Reilly	Frank	Constable	6-Oct-1998	Loyalists	Fatally injured in blast bomb attack in Corcrain Estate, Portadown

Select Bibliography

Barzilay, David, *The British Army in Ulster* Volume 1 (Belfast: Century Books, 1973)

Clarke, A.F.N., *Contact* (London: Secker & Warburg, 1983)

Clarke, George, *Border Crossing: true stories of the RUC Special Branch, the Garda Special Branch and IRA moles* (Dublin: Gill & Macmillan, 2009)

Collins, Eamon, *Klling Rage* (London: Granta Books, 1997)

Cusack, Jim and McDonald, Henry, *UVF: The Endgame* (Dublin: Poolberg Press, 2008)

Dillon, Martin, *Political Murder in Northern Ireland* (Harmondsworth: Penguin, 1973)

Dillon, Martin, *The Shankill Butchers: a case study of mass murder* (London: Hutchinson, 1989)

Dillon, Martin, *The Dirty War* (London: Arrow Books, 1990)

Dillon, Martin, *Killer in Clowntown: Joe Doherty, the IRA and the Special Relationship* (London: Arrow Books, 1992)

Dillon, Martin, *Stone Cold: The True Story of Michael Stone and the Milltown Massacre* (London: Hutchinson, 1992)

Dillon, Martin, *God and the Gun: The Church and Irish Terrorism* (London: Routledge, 1999)

Dillon, Martin, *The Trigger Men: Assassins and Terror Bosses in the Ireland Conflict* (London: Mainstream, 2003)

Doherty, Richard, *The Thin Green Line: The History of the Royal Ulster Constabulary GC 1922-2001* (Pen & Sword, 2004)

Feeney. Brian & Gerry Bradley, *Insider: Gerry Bradley's Life in the IRA* (O'Brien, 2009)

Gilmour, Raymond, *Dead Ground: Infiltrating the IRA* (London: Little, Brown & Co, 1998)

Gilmour, Raymond, *What Price truth?* 2014 (Self-published)

Hamill, Desmond, *Pig In The Middle: the Army in Northern Ireland, 1969-1984* (London: Methuen Books, 1985)

Harnden, Toby, *Bandit Country: the IRA and South Armagh* (London: Hodder & Stoughton 1999)

Holland & Phoenix, *Phoenix: Policing the Shadows* (London: Hodder & Stoughton, 1996)

Jordan, Hugh, *Milestones in Murder* (London: Mainstream Publishing, 2002)

Latham, Richard, *Deadly Beat: Inside the Royal Ulster* Constabulary (Edinburgh: Mainstream, 2001)

Lister, David & Hugh Jordan, *Mad Dog: The Rise and Fall of Johnny Adair and 'C Company'* (London: Mainstream Publishing, 2004)

Maloney, Ed, *Voices From The Grave: two men's war in Ireland* (London: Faber & Faber, 2010)

McDonald & Holland, *INLA: Deadly Divisions* (Dublin: Poolberg Press, 2010)

McGartland, Martin, *Fifty Dead Men Walking* (London: John Blake, 2009)

McKitterick, David et al, *Lost Lives: The stories of the men, women and children who died as a result of the Northern Ireland Troubles* (Edinburgh: Mainstream, 2000)

Myers, Kevin, *Watching the Door: Cheating Death in 1970s Belfast* (London: Atlantic Books, 2008)

O'Callaghan, Sean, *The Informer* (London: Bantam, 1999)

Parker, John, *Secret Hero: The Life and Mysterious Death of Captain Robert Nairac* (London: Metro Books, 2004)

Potter, John, *A Testimony To Courage: the Regimental History of the Ulster Defence Regiment* (London: Leo Cooper: 2001)

Simpson, Alan, *Murder Madness: True Crimes of the Troubles* (London: GM Books, 1997)

Stone, Michael, *None Shall Divide Us* (London: John Blake, 2003)

Urban, Mark, *Big Boys' Rules: the secret struggle against the IRA* (London: Faber & Faber, 1992)

Van der Bilj, Nicholas, *Operation Banner: the British Army in Northern Ireland, 1969-2007* (Barnsley: Pen & Sword, 2009)

Wharton, Ken, *A Long Long War; Voices From the British Army in Northern Ireland, 1969-98* (Solihull: Helion, 2008)

Wharton, Ken, *Bloody Belfast; An Oral History of the British Army's War against the IRA* (Stroud: Spellmount, 2010)

Wharton, Ken, *Bullets, Bombs and Cups of Tea; Further Voices of the British Army in Northern Ireland* (Solihull: Helion, 2009)

Wharton, Ken, *The Bloodiest Year: Northern Ireland 1972* (Stroud: History Press, 2011)

Wharton, Ken, *'Sir, They're Taking the Kids Indoors: The British Army in Northern Ireland 1973-74* (Solihull: Helion, 2012)

Internet Sources:

http://www.belfasttelegraph.co.uk/lifestyle/day-two-the-victims-13413325.html#ixzz20dRSTW4g

http://www.telegraph.co.uk/news/obituaries/10203064/Lance-Corporal-Paul-Burns.html

http://www.parachuteregiment-hsf.org/

Index

372

Related titles published by Helion & Company

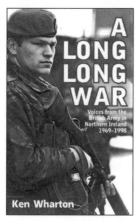

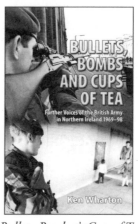

A Long Long War: Voices from the British
Army in Northern Ireland 1969-98
Ken Wharton
544pp Paperback ISBN 978-1-906033-79-8
eBook ISBN 978-1-907677-60-1

Bullets, Bombs & Cups of Tea:
Further Voices from the British Army
in Northern Ireland 1969-98
Ken Wharton
536pp Paperback ISBN 978-1-907677-06-9
eBook ISBN 978-1-907677-89-2

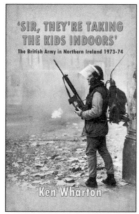

'Sir, They're Taking the Kids Indoors' – The
Bitish Army in Northern Ireland 1973-74
Ken Wharton
360pp Hardback ISBN 978-1-907677-67-0
eBook ISBN 978-1-908916-77-8

Wasted Years Wasted Lives Volume 1 -
British Army in Northern Ireland 1975-77
Ken Wharton
428pp Hardback ISBN 978-1-909384-55-2
eBook ISBN 978-1-910294-21-5

HELION & COMPANY

26 Willow Road, Solihull, West Midlands B91 1UE, England
Telephone 0121 705 3393   Fax 0121 711 4075
Website: http://www.helion.co.uk
Twitter: @helionbooks | Visit our blog http://blog.helion.co.uk